W9-DFC-627

Leslie Miller dedicates this book to her husband, Robert Miller,
and children, Zachary Kenneth Miller and Kia Anne Miller.
Robert Lovler dedicates this book to his wife, Patsy Lovler, his daughter,
Lauren Lovler, and his mentor at Hofstra University, Dr. William Metlay.

FOUNDATIONS OF PSYCHOLOGICAL TESTING

A Practical Approach

Sixth Edition

Leslie A. Miller

LanneM TM, LLC

Robert L. Lovler

Wilson Learning Corporation

Los Angeles | London | New Delhi
Singapore | Washington DC | Melbourne

FOR INFORMATION:

SAGE Publications, Inc.
2455 Teller Road
Thousand Oaks, California 91320
E-mail: order@sagepub.com

SAGE Publications Ltd.
1 Oliver's Yard
55 City Road
London EC1Y 1SP
United Kingdom

SAGE Publications India Pvt. Ltd.
B 1/I 1 Mohan Cooperative Industrial Area
Mathura Road, New Delhi 110 044
India

SAGE Publications Asia-Pacific Pte. Ltd.
18 Cross Street #10-10/11/12
China Square Central
Singapore 048423

Acquisitions Editor: Abbie Rickard
Content Development Editor: Emma Newsom
Editorial Assistant: Elizabeth Cruz
Production Editor: Jane Martinez
Copy Editor: Renee Willers
Typesetter: C&M Digitals (P) Ltd.
Proofreader: Alison Syring
Indexer: May Hasso
Cover Designer: Scott Van Atta
Marketing Manager: Jenna Retana

Printed in the United States of America

ISBN: 978-1-5063-9640-8

This book is printed on acid-free paper.

19 20 21 22 23 10 9 8 7 6 5 4 3 2 1

BRIEF CONTENTS

DETAILED CONTENTS

SECTION IV • USING TESTS IN DIFFERENT SETTINGS 347

Chapter 12 • How Are Tests Used in Educational Settings? 349

PREFACE

Psychological testing is big business. Not only are the numbers of individuals and organizations using psychological tests continuing to increase, but also the magnitude and consequences of the decisions being made using tests are increasing. For example, educators are using test results not only to make decisions about students (determine who will receive high school diplomas, who will be admitted to college, who will participate in special school programs, and who will earn high and low grades), but also to make decisions about teachers and schools, such as teacher performance, teacher pay, and school funding. Clinicians are using tests to help diagnose psychological disorders and plan treatment programs. Industrial and organizational psychology consultants are using tests to select people for jobs, measure individual job performance, and evaluate the effectiveness of training programs. Students are using tests to gain greater insight into their personal interests, decide which college majors to pursue, and determine the graduate or professional schools to which they might apply. Professional organizations and governmental agencies are using licensing and certification tests to be sure that individuals engaged in certain occupations have the necessary qualifications to ensure that the safety of the public is protected.

In spite of widespread use, psychological tests continue to be misunderstood and used improperly. At one extreme, these misunderstandings and misuses have led many people to believe that psychological tests are useless or even extremely harmful. At the other extreme, many other people believe that psychological tests serve as ideal and extremely precise instruments of measurement. More commonly, these misunderstandings and misuses have led to the misconceptions that psychological testing is synonymous with diagnosing mental disorders, that psychological tests can and should be used as a sole means for making decisions, and that anyone can create, administer, or interpret a psychological test.

OUR MISSION

We originally wrote the first edition of *Foundations of Psychological Testing* in response to the growing need for a scholarly, yet pragmatic and easy-to-understand, introductory textbook for students new to the field of psychological testing and to the concepts of statistics and psychometrics that support its practice. As with the five previous editions of this textbook, we had two primary objectives in writing the sixth edition. Our first objective was to prepare students to be informed consumers of psychological tests—as test users or test takers—rather than to teach students to administer or interpret individual psychological tests. To meet our objective, in each edition we have focused the first two thirds of the textbook primarily on the basic concepts, issues, and tools used in psychological testing and their relevance to daily life. We have focused the last third of the book on how tests are used in educational, clinical/counseling, and organizational settings.

Our second objective for each edition has been to present information in a way that is maximally conducive to student learning. Over the years, many of our students have lamented that textbooks do not always explain material as clearly as a professor would during a class lecture. Students have also said that textbooks lack practical application of the material covered. We have designed this textbook, and each edition, with those students' comments in mind. Not only does *Foundations of Psychological Testing* provide a fresh look at the field of psychological testing, but also we continue to write in a style that we believe will encourage and promote student learning and enthusiasm.

We focus on communicating the basics of psychological testing clearly and concisely, and we relate these basics to practical situations that students can recognize and understand. We also present information at a comfortable reading level and in a conversational format. Although current textbooks on psychological testing continue to move in this direction, we believe that some books are too complex and contain more detailed discussion of certain technical issues than is necessary for students' first introduction to testing.

NEW IN THIS EDITION

For the current edition, almost 19 years since the first edition was published, our primary objective was to again address the valuable feedback from our reviewers. At a global level, we made the following changes in the 6th edition:

- Added more detailed concept maps at the beginning of each section to graphically organize the relationship between concepts and ideas presented in each chapter within each section

- Integrated critical thinking questions at the end of each chapter, linked to the chapter learning objectives, to provide students more opportunity to engage in their own thinking

- Eliminated the computerized testing chapter, moving critical content to other chapters

- Renamed Chapter 3 to more accurately reflect the focus on the ethical responsibilities of test publishers, test users, and test takers

- Moved more important and more complex information into *In Greater Depth Boxes* within the chapters so that more advanced content could be either included or skipped at an instructor's discretion without loss of instructional continuity.

- Added a brief introduction to the first of three validity chapters to explain the reason for and organization of the three chapters on validity

- Added new content to the reliability and validity chapters to explain via concrete numerical demonstrations the impact that random error in measurement has on reliability

- Added a numerical demonstration of how to conduct a cross-validation of a test via regression

- Added additional content that explains and demonstrates how to correct for attenuation in validity due to unreliability, and links it to the newly included concept of operational validity

- Added a brief introduction to the survey chapter to explain why we've included a chapter on surveys in a psychological testing textbook

- Reviewed all content, terms, symbols, equations, and calculations to ensure content flowed smoothly, terms were defined clearly to eliminate existing vagueness in definitions, and symbols, equations, and calculations were accurate

- Ensured all links to online resources were functional and updated featured content in our *In the News Boxes* and *On the Web Boxes* to ensure currency

- Updated the Test Spotlights in Appendix A to reflect new editions of tests and additional available information on reliability and validity, as well as sample test reports.

Also new to the sixth edition is a new workbook with more practical utility for faculty and students: *Student Workbook to Accompany Miller and Lovler's Foundations of Psychological Testing: Practical and Critical Thinking Exercises.* Although we know that students can learn by reading chapter material, attending class, and engaging in discussion with faculty members, we also know that more actively engaging in the learning process can help students better learn and retain chapter information. The workbook provides students the opportunity to demonstrate their understanding of material presented in the textbook and apply their learning by completing critical thinking and practical exercises linked to specific learning objectives from the textbook. Also included are chapter-level projects for students to demonstrate their understanding of multiple topics within the chapter, as well as a progressive course project that instructors may assign. The text and workbook can be purchased together, for a bundled, discounted price. Or the workbook can be purchased through sagepub.com.

LEARNING STRATEGIES

As with the previous edition, to further promote student learning, our textbook includes multiple learning strategies. We preview, discuss, review, and reinforce important information in multiple ways at the text, section, and chapter levels. These learning strategies include the following:

- *Section Preview:* Each section of this textbook opens with a detailed concept map that pictorially displays the chapters covered in that section and a preview of those chapters. We intend these previews to provide two tools that appeal to two very different learning styles—visual and verbal—and to prepare students to receive the material to be covered.

- *Chapter-Opening Narratives:* Each chapter opens with narratives that pertain to the chapter topic. These narratives provide students with means to identify with the material by relating them to their own experiences.

- *Learning Objectives:* The introduction to each chapter includes clearly defined learning objectives that set expectations for what students should know and be able to do after studying the chapter.

- *Instruction Through Conversation:* In response to our students' cries of "Why couldn't the text have said it that way?" we have written each chapter the way our students best understand the information—at as simple a reading level as possible and, in most cases, in conversational style.

- *True to Life:* The concepts in each chapter are illustrated by real-life examples drawn from the testing literature and from our experiences.

- *For Your Information, In the News, and On the Web:* Each chapter contains these boxes.

- *Key Words and Concepts:* In each chapter, we have taken care to alert students to key words and concepts that are important for them to master. We introduce and define each term and concept within a logical structure to promote ease of comprehension. These appear at the end of each chapter and are provided in the Glossary located at the back of the book.

ORGANIZATION OF MATERIAL

Foundations of Psychological Testing: A Practical Approach is divided into four sections. The first section consists of three chapters that provide an overview of the basics of psychological testing. It includes discussions of what a psychological test is, where to find information about psychological tests, who uses psychological tests and for what reasons, the history of psychological testing, some concerns our society has about the use of psychological tests, and the ethical and proper use of psychological tests.

The second section consists of five chapters that cover psychometric principles. These chapters discuss the procedures we use to interpret test scores, the concepts of reliability and validity, and the methods for estimating reliability and gathering evidence of validity.

The third section consists of three chapters. The second and third chapters describe how to develop, pilot-test, and validate psychological tests. Because there are many overlapping design principles between psychological tests and surveys and because many of our adopters use this text as part of a course on measurements, we have also included a chapter on how to construct and administer surveys, as well as how to use survey data.

The final section of the textbook consists of three chapters that discuss how tests are used in three important settings: education, clinical and counseling practice, and organizations.

ANCILLARIES

SAGE Publishing offers an array of instructor resources on the cutting edge of teaching and learning. Go to **http://study.sagepub.com/miller6e** to access the companion site.

SAGE FOR INSTRUCTORS

The SAGE Instructor Companion Site, a password-protected resource, supports teaching by making the classroom a learning-rich environment for students. The following chapter-specific assets are available on the teaching site:

Test banks for each chapter provide a diverse range of questions as well as the opportunity to edit any question and/or insert personalized questions to effectively assess students' progress and understanding.

Sample course syllabi for semester and quarter courses provide suggested models for structuring a course.

Editable, chapter-specific **PowerPoint slides** offer complete flexibility for creating a multimedia presentation for the course.

Lively and stimulating **ideas for critical thinking** can be used in class to reinforce active learning. The creative assignments apply to individual or group projects.

ACKNOWLEDGMENTS

We could not have written the sixth edition of our textbook without the assistance of various individuals. First, we would like to thank the reviewers who provided helpful suggestions and recommendations that resulted in improvements to the organization and contents of the book. The reviewers include Gordon G. Cappelletty, PhD, Lenoir-Rhyne University; Darrin F. Coe, Peru State College; Lori A. Doan, University of Manitoba; Roseanne L. Flores, Hunter College of the City University of New York; Julia M. Fullick, PhD, Quinnipiac University; Michael Hein, PhD, Middle Tennessee State University; Louis H. Janda, Old Dominion University; Dr. Pauline Mercado, California State University, Los Angeles; Tara Stevens, Texas Tech University; and Holly Tatum, Randolph College. For the sixth edition, we'd like to thank the following reviewers: Elizabeth K. Gray, North Park University; Amy Martin, Rockford University; Jane L. Swanson, Southern Illinois University Carbondale; Holly E. Tatum, Randolph College; and Jessica S. Waesche, University of Central Florida. In addition, we wish to acknowledge those test authors who shared their photos and test information.

We would also like to recognize and thank Dr. Aimee Rhoads, who took responsibility for reviewing and updating the Test Spotlights in Appendix A.

Finally, we would like to express our sincere thanks to Abbie Rickard (our editor), Elizabeth Cruz (editorial assistant), Emma Newsom (content development editor), Jane Martinez (our production editor), and Renee Willers (our copy editor) at SAGE Publications, who have been particularly helpful during the editing and production of the textbook.

FINAL THOUGHTS

We hope our audience will find the sixth edition of the textbook to be a scholarly, informative, applicable, and appropriate introduction to the field of psychological testing. Because we strongly believe that assessment and feedback are vital to development and improvement, we encourage professors and students to send their feedback to us.

Leslie A. Miller, PhD, SHRM-CP, PHR (DrLeslieMiller@hotmail.com)

Robert Lovler, PhD (boblovler@gmail.com)

ABOUT THE AUTHORS

Leslie A. Miller, PhD, SHRM-CP, PHR, has broad experience in consulting, teaching, and researching in the area of organizational and educational assessment, measurement, and development. Currently the owner of her own consulting business, LanneM TM, LLC, she provides her clients with pragmatic and affordable talent management solutions to help them acquire, develop, and retain the talent they need to achieve desired business results. Her expertise includes designing performance improvement and management tools and knowledge tests, customizing and facilitating leadership training programs, providing assessment-based executive coaching, and designing and implementing business impact evaluation and return-on-value studies. She also spends her time as an adjunct faculty member teaching organizational behavior and psychology, research, and human resources courses at Rollins College, the University of Oklahoma, and for the School of Advanced Studies at the University of Phoenix. In addition, she chairs doctoral dissertations. Previously the vice president of leadership development and human resources at the Central Florida YMCA, she was responsible for contributing to the strategic plans of the organization by leading the association's talent management initiatives— recruiting, developing, and retaining the association's talent. Prior to joining the YMCA, she was employed by Wilson Learning Corporation (WLC), a performance improvement company, where she served as the director of business solutions, a senior project manager, and a business solutions consultant. In these roles, she was responsible for conceptualizing, designing, managing, and implementing traditional and technology-based assessment, measurement, and training performance improvement solutions for client organizations.

Prior to joining WLC, Dr. Miller served as the assistant dean of admissions at Rollins College, where she was also a faculty member of the psychology, organizational behavior, and human resources programs. Before joining Rollins College, she was a senior research psychologist for the U.S. Department of Labor, Bureau of Labor Statistics, in Washington, D.C. At the bureau, she designed, researched, and analyzed the results of some of our nation's most important surveys. In her current and previous roles, she has worked with various leading organizations in the high-tech, financial, pharmaceutical, and transportation industries. The holder of a doctorate in educational psychology from the University of Maryland, she has an extensive list of publications and presentations. She is a member of the APA, the Society for Industrial and Organizational Psychology, and the Society for Human Resource Management.

Robert L. Lovler, PhD, has over 30 years of experience working as both an internal and an external consultant to Fortune 500 companies in the areas of employee assessment and selection, organizational development, strategic human resource consulting, and training design and delivery. His career began at CBS Inc., where he served in several roles, including director of training for the retail consumer electronics unit, then moving up to vice president of two different units within the CBS Publishing Group. He is currently senior vice president of global human resources at Wilson Learning Corporation, an international consulting firm that focuses on human performance improvement. During his career, he has had the opportunity to design and implement a wide range of organizational interventions both domestically and internationally, working in Japan, China, South Korea, Hong Kong, England, and Italy. In the United States, he supervised the development and implementation of the assessment center used to select candidates for entry into the Environmental Protection Agency's (EPA) Senior Executive Service Development Program, presenting the results in Washington, D.C., to Christine Todd Whitman, the EPA administrator. He also developed the system used to help select commercial airline pilots for a major U.S. airline and worked with former senator Warren Rudman to develop and implement a nationwide survey of sales practices in the rent-to-own industry. He has served as a testing consultant to the California Bar Association and the state of Pennsylvania, and he oversaw the development of the licensure examinations for medical physicists in the state of Texas. He has been on the faculty of the State University of New York at Farmingdale and the adjunct faculty of Hofstra University and the University of Central Florida. Dr. Lovler received his BA degree in psychology from the University of California, Los Angeles, and holds master's and doctoral degrees from Hofstra University. He is a member of the APA and the Society for Industrial and Organizational Psychology.

OVERVIEW OF PSYCHOLOGICAL TESTING

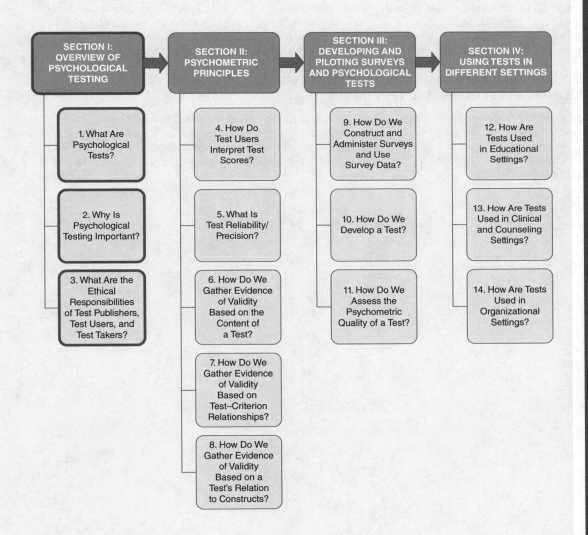

SECTION I: OVERVIEW OF PSYCHOLOGICAL TESTING → **SECTION II: PSYCHOMETRIC PRINCIPLES** → **SECTION III: DEVELOPING AND PILOTING SURVEYS AND PSYCHOLOGICAL TESTS** → **SECTION IV: USING TESTS IN DIFFERENT SETTINGS**

1. What Are Psychological Tests?

2. Why Is Psychological Testing Important?

3. What Are the Ethical Responsibilities of Test Publishers, Test Users, and Test Takers?

4. How Do Test Users Interpret Test Scores?

5. What Is Test Reliability/Precision?

6. How Do We Gather Evidence of Validity Based on the Content of a Test?

7. How Do We Gather Evidence of Validity Based on Test–Criterion Relationships?

8. How Do We Gather Evidence of Validity Based on a Test's Relation to Constructs?

9. How Do We Construct and Administer Surveys and Use Survey Data?

10. How Do We Develop a Test?

11. How Do We Assess the Psychometric Quality of a Test?

12. How Are Tests Used in Educational Settings?

13. How Are Tests Used in Clinical and Counseling Settings?

14. How Are Tests Used in Organizational Settings?

CHAPTER 1: WHAT ARE PSYCHOLOGICAL TESTS?

In Chapter 1, we discuss what a psychological test is and introduce you to some instruments you might never have considered to be psychological tests. After briefly exploring the history of psychological testing, we discuss the three defining characteristics of psychological tests and the assumptions we must make when using psychological tests. We then discuss how tests are classified and distinguish four commonly confused concepts: assessment, tests, measurement, and surveys. We conclude by sharing print and online resources for locating information about psychological testing and specific tests.

CHAPTER 2: WHY IS PSYCHOLOGICAL TESTING IMPORTANT?

In Chapter 2, we discuss why psychological testing is important, including how individuals and institutions use test results to make comparative and absolute decisions. We explore who uses psychological tests in educational, clinical, and organizational settings and for what reasons. We also discuss some of the concerns society has about using psychological tests, including controversies about intelligence tests, aptitude tests, and integrity tests. Covered is one of the most current controversies—the use of high-stakes testing in education.

CHAPTER 3: WHAT ARE THE ETHICAL RESPONSIBILITIES OF TEST PUBLISHERS, TEST USERS, AND TEST TAKERS?

In Chapter 3, we introduce you to ethical standards in psychological testing. We discuss the concept of acting ethically and what we mean by *ethics* and *professional standards*. We summarize some of the most commonly referenced and discussed professional practice standards relevant to the field of psychological testing. Following a discussion of the responsibilities of test publishers, test users, and test takers, we discuss issues related to testing special populations.

WHAT ARE PSYCHOLOGICAL TESTS?

"When I was in the second grade, my teacher recommended that I be placed in the school's gifted program. As a result, the school psychologist interviewed me and had me take an intelligence test."

"Last semester I took a class in abnormal psychology. The professor had all of us take several personality tests, including the MMPI [Minnesota Multiphasic Personality Inventory]. It was

awesome! We learned about different types of psychological disorders that the MMPI can help diagnose."

"This year I applied for a summer job with a local bank. As a part of the selection process, I had to participate in a structured interview and take a test that measured my math and verbal skills."

"Yesterday I took my driving test—both the written and the road test. I couldn't believe everything they made me do when taking the road test. I had to parallel park, switch lanes, and make a three-point turn."

If your instructor asked whether you have ever taken a psychological test, you would probably talk about the intelligence test you took as an elementary school student or the personality test you took in your abnormal psychology class. If your instructor asked what the purpose of psychological testing is, you would probably say that it is to determine whether someone is gifted or has a psychological disorder. Intelligence tests and personality tests are indeed psychological tests—and they are indeed used to identify giftedness and diagnose psychological disorders. However, intelligence and personality tests are only two of many available tests. There are many more types of psychological tests, and they have many different purposes.

In this chapter, we introduce you to the concept of psychological testing. We discuss what a psychological test is and introduce some tests you might never have considered to be psychological tests. Then, after providing an overview of the history of psychological testing, we discuss the three defining characteristics of psychological tests and the assumptions we must make when using tests. We then turn our attention to the many ways of classifying tests. We also distinguish four concepts that students often confuse: psychological assessment, psychological tests, psychological measurement, and surveys. We conclude this chapter by sharing with you some of the resources (print and online) that are available for locating information about psychological testing and specific psychological tests.

WHY SHOULD YOU CARE ABOUT PSYCHOLOGICAL TESTING?

Before discussing what a psychological test is, we would like to increase your understanding of the importance of psychological testing and why you should care about it. Psychological testing is not just another subject that you may study in college; rather, it is a topic that personally affects many individuals, including yourself. Each day, different types of professionals administer psychological tests to many different individuals, and the results of these tests are used in ways that significantly affect you and those around you. For example, test scores are used to diagnose mental disorders, to determine whether medicines should be prescribed (and, if so, which ones), to treat mental and emotional illnesses, to certify or license individuals for professional practice, to select individuals for jobs, to make acceptance decisions for undergraduate and professional schools (e.g., medical school, law school), and to determine grades. Psychological tests may even be used in the future to combat terrorism (see In the News Box 1.1). Good tests facilitate high-quality decisions, and bad tests facilitate low-quality decisions.

IN THE NEWS BOX 1.1
COMBATING TERRORISM

Imagine if psychological tests could be used to help combat terrorism, one of the most malicious threats to our society.

In May 2017, BBC News highlighted a research study Baez conducted with 132 individuals (66 incarcerated individuals thought to be members of a terrorist organization and 66 demographically similar nonincarcerated individuals).

In May 2017, BBC News issued the following news release:

> A project aiming to "scientifically understand the mindset of terrorists" has published insights that the scientists say could have implications for terror prevention.

Researchers worked with a group of 66 incarcerated ex-combatants from a paramilitary terrorist group in Colombia, a country with one of the greatest insurgency rates in the world.

This unique experiment revealed what the team described as an "abnormal pattern of moral judgment" in terrorists.

The scientists say a psychological score based on this could be an accurate way to discriminate between the mindset of a terrorist and that of a noncriminal.

The researchers, based in Argentina, the United States, Colombia, and Chile, published their findings in the journal *Nature Human Behaviour*.

Agustín Ibanez and Adolfo García, from Favaloro University in Buenos Aires, who were part of the international research team, told BBC News they had spent 4 years working with Colombian law enforcers to secure permission to work with this large group of dangerous, incarcerated terrorists.

The study participants were former members of right-wing paramilitary groups, all of whom had been convicted of murder.

Many had been involved in massacres with hundreds of victims.

They took part in a series of psychological tests, including an assessment of moral cognition.

This involved presenting the subjects with a series of scenarios in which characters either deliberately or accidentally caused harm to others.

Each subject was then asked to rate the scenario on a scale from totally forbidden (1) to totally permissible (7).

Dr. Ibanez said, "The typical response is that attempted harm should be more objected to than accidental harm. [But] the pattern in terrorists was the opposite."

The pattern this research revealed was that "extreme terrorists judge other people's actions by focusing on the outcomes of an action rather than its underlying intentions.

"This is the first study to demonstrate this psychological trait, [and it suggests that] a terrorist's moral code actually approves of any action if it contributes to achieving a given aim."

Brutal cognition

The researchers hope the conclusions could help build a psychological profile for use in forensics and law enforcement.

But they say further research will need specifically to examine how predictive this measure of moral cognition is when it comes to "identifying dangerous insurgent individuals."

They also pointed out that there were likely to be differences in the "origins and psychological traits of different forms of terrorism."

"For example, in the population we studied, religion does not seem to be a relevant factor. [In fact], most ex-combatants in Colombia joined paramilitary groups for economic reasons—because they were paid a salary.

"But I would envisage forensic psychologists ultimately using a moral score like this to help assess how much of a threat a particular individual poses—in addition to other measures of aggression and emotions, as well as other cognitive and social tasks," Dr. Ibanez told BBC News.

Prof Seena Fazel, from the University of Oxford, a psychiatrist focusing on the relationship between mental illness and violent crime, told BBC News that the study was "a step forward."

He said there was value in the study's comparison of terrorists and noncriminals—the team carried out the same battery of tests on 66 healthy individuals from the same geographical region who had no terrorist background.

"I'd be interested in identifiable and modifiable factors that can either stop people repeating [a violent act] or stop them committing it in the first place. That would be where research could be very useful.

"These type of assessments rely on detailed interviews, so we're not at a point where we could scale up and implement this."

Source: BBC News Services (2017).

The consequences of low-quality decisions can be significant. For example, a poor hiring decision can dramatically affect both the person being hired and the hiring organization. From the organization's perspective, a poor hiring decision can result in increased absenteeism, reduced morale of other staff members, and lost productivity and revenue. From the employee's perspective, a poor hiring decision may result in a loss of motivation, increased stress leading to depression and anxiety, and perhaps loss of opportunity to make progress in his or her career. Although you might never administer, score, or interpret a test, it is very likely that you or someone you know may have a life-altering decision made about him or her based on test scores. Therefore, it is important that you understand the foundations of psychological testing, specifically how to tell whether a decision is a good or bad one. Being able to do this requires that you understand the foundations of psychological testing.

WHAT IS A PSYCHOLOGICAL TEST?

Each anecdote at the beginning of this chapter involves the use of a psychological test. Intelligence tests, personality tests, interest and vocational inventories, college entrance exams, classroom tests, structured interviews, workplace simulations (e.g., assessment centers), and driving tests all are examples of psychological tests. Even the self-scored tests that you find in magazines such as *Glamour* and *Seventeen* (tests that supposedly tell you how you feel about your friends, stress, love, and more) can be considered psychological tests. Although some are more typical, all meet the definition of a psychological test. Together, they convey the very different purposes of psychological tests. For a continuum of some of the most and least commonly recognized types of psychological tests, see Figure 1.1.

Similarities Among Psychological Tests

A review of professional association publications and psychological testing textbooks indicates that no one distinct definition of a psychological test exists. For example, the most recent version of the *Standards for Educational and Psychological Testing* (American Educational Research Association, American Psychological Association [APA], and the National Council on Measurement in Education, 2014) defines a psychological test as "a device or procedure in which a sample of an examinee's behavior in a specified domain is obtained and subsequently evaluated and scored using a standardized process" (p. 2). In its *Report of the Task Force on Test User Qualifications*, the APA (2000) defines a psychological test similarly as "a measurement procedure for assessing psychological characteristics in which a sample of an examinee's behavior is obtained and subsequently evaluated and scored using a standardized process" (p. 7).

FIGURE 1.1 ■ A Continuum of Psychological Tests			
More Typical	←————————————————→		**Less Typical**
Personality tests Intelligence tests	Vocational tests Interest inventories Achievement tests Ability tests	Self-scored magazine tests Classroom quizzes and exams	Road portion of driving test Structured employment interviews Assessment centers

The Association of Test Publishers (2017) refers to tests as "professionally developed instruments . . . [that are] constructed responsibly and are responsive to existing professional standards . . . begin[ning with] a set of questions . . . to assess or measure a specific ability or characteristic" (para. 8-9). On the other hand, textbook author Robert J. Gregory (2010) defined a test as "a standardized procedure for sampling behavior and describing it with categories or scores" (p. 16), while Kaplan and Saccuzzo (2013) defined a psychological test as "a measurement device or technique used to quantify behavior or aid in the understanding and prediction of behavior" (p. 7). Salkind (2013) provided an even broader definition of a test as "a tool, procedure, device, examination, investigation, assessment, or measure of an outcome (which is usually some kind of behavior)" (p. 9).

Although associations and testing professionals might have slight differences of opinion about what constitutes a psychological test, most definitions reference a procedure, an instrument, or a device and behaviors. In a broad sense, a psychological test is a procedure, an instrument, or a device that measures samples of behaviors in order to make inferences. To increase your understanding of what a psychological test is, let's consider what all psychological tests have in common.

First, all psychological tests require a person to perform some **behavior**—an observable and measurable action. For example, when students take multiple-choice midterm exams, they must read the various answers for each item and identify the best one. When individuals take intelligence tests, they may be asked to define words or solve math problems. When participating in structured job interviews, individuals must respond to questions from interviewers—questions such as, "Tell me about a time when you had to deal with an upset customer. What was the situation, what did you do, and what was the outcome?" In each of these cases, individuals are performing some observable and measurable behavior.

Second, the behavior an individual performs is used to make inferences about some **psychological construct**—an underlying, unobservable personal attribute, trait, or characteristic of an individual that is thought to be important in describing or understanding human behavior. Because we cannot directly measure psychological constructs, we must instead make inferences about constructs from the behaviors we observe. For example, how you answer questions on a multiple-choice exam might be used to make inferences about your knowledge of a particular subject area, such as psychological testing. The words you define or the math problems you solve might be used to make inferences about your verbal ability or quantitative reasoning. Likewise, the questions you answer during a structured job interview or on a cognitive ability test may be used make inferences about how successful you might be in a management position.

Given the discussion above, we define a **psychological test** as a measurement tool or technique that requires a person to perform one or more behaviors in order to make inferences about human attributes, traits, or characteristics or predict future outcomes. By **inference**, we mean using evidence to reach a conclusion. For example, you might take a test designed to measure your knowledge of the material presented in one of the chapters of this textbook. You answer multiple-choice questions (the behavior), and based on your test score, your instructor might reach a conclusion (the inference) about the knowledge you have of the material. For example, you might take the Hogan Personality Inventory when applying for a job. You answer questions (the behavior), and an employer may use your test results to draw a conclusion (the inference) about how likely it is that you will succeed in the job.

Differences Among Psychological Tests

Although all psychological tests require that you perform some behavior to make inferences about human attributes, traits, or characteristics or predict future outcomes, these tests can differ in various ways. For example, they can differ in terms of the behavior they require you to perform, what they measure, their content, how they are administered and formatted, how they are scored and interpreted, and their psychometric quality (**psychometrics** is the quantitative and technical aspects of testing).

Behavior Performed

The one or more behaviors a test taker must perform vary by test. For example, a popular intelligence test, the Wechsler Adult Intelligence Scale–Fourth Edition (WAIS-IV), a general test of adult cognitive ability, requires test takers to (among other things) define words, repeat lists of digits, explain what is missing from pictures, and arrange blocks to duplicate geometric card designs (Pearson Education, 2018d). The Thematic Apperception Test (TAT), a widely used and researched projective personality test designed at Harvard University in the 1930s, requires test takers to look at ambiguous pictures showing a variety of social and interpersonal situations and to tell stories about each picture (Pearson Education, 2018c). The 2011 revised Graduate Record Examination (GRE) General Test, a graduate school admissions test that measures the verbal reasoning, quantitative reasoning, critical thinking, and analytical writing skills individuals have developed over time, requires test takers to do things such as answer multiple-choice questions, perform calculations, and respond to analytical writing tasks (Educational Testing Service, 2018). The road portion of an automobile driving test typically requires test takers to do things such as change lanes, make right and left turns, use turn signals properly, and parallel park. Assessment centers require job applicants to participate in simulated job-related activities (which mimic the activities they would perform on the job), such as engaging in confrontational meetings with disgruntled employees, processing email and paperwork, and conducting manager briefings.

Construct Measured and Outcome Predicted

What a test measures or predicts can vary. For example, the WAIS-IV requires individuals to explain what is missing from pictures to measure the construct of verbal intelligence. The TAT requires individuals to tell stories about pictures to identify conscious and unconscious drives, emotions, conflicts, and so on in order to ultimately measure the construct of personality. The road portion of a driving test requires individuals to perform various driving behaviors to measure the construct of driving ability. The GRE requires students to answer different types of questions to determine if they are ready for graduate-level work and predict success in graduate school.

More detail about the WAIS-IV can be found in **Test Spotlight 1.1** in Appendix A.

Some of the constructs psychological tests may measure include personality, intelligence, cognitive ability, motivation, mechanical ability, vocational preference, achievement in a school subject, and anxiety—to name just a few. Some of the outcomes that tests typically predict include worker productivity, success in college, and who will benefit from specialized services such as clinical treatment programs.

Content

Two tests that measure the same construct can require individuals to perform significantly different behaviors or to answer significantly different questions. Sometimes, how the test developers define the particular construct affects how the test is structured. For example, the questions on two intelligence tests may differ because one author may define intelligence as the ability to reason and another author may define intelligence in terms of **emotional intelligence**—"the abilities to perceive, appraise, and express emotions accurately and appropriately, to use emotions to facilitate thinking, to understand and analyze emotions, to use emotional knowledge effectively, and to regulate one's emotions to promote both emotional and intellectual growth" (American Psychological Association, 2018b, para. 10).

The difference in content may also be due to the theoretical orientation of the test. (We talk more about theoretical orientation and its relation to test content in the validity chapters of this textbook.)

Administration and Format

Psychological tests can differ in terms of how they are administered and their format. A test can be administered in paper-and-pencil format (individually or in a group setting), on a computer, or verbally. Similarly, a psychological test may consist of multiple-choice items, agree/disagree items, true/false items, open-ended questions, or some mix of these. There are also tests that ask respondents to perform some behavior, such as sorting cards, playing a role, or writing an essay.

Scoring and Interpretation

Psychological tests can differ in terms of how they are scored and interpreted. Some tests require test takers to document answers on scannable sheets that are then computer-scored. Some tests are hand-scored by the person administering the test. Other tests are scored by the test takers themselves. In terms of interpretation, some tests generate results that can be interpreted easily by the test taker, and others require a knowledgeable professional to explain the results to the test taker.

Psychometric Quality

Last, but extremely important, psychological tests can differ in terms of their psychometric quality. For now, let us just say that there are a lot of really good tests out there that measure what they say they measure and do so consistently, but there are also a lot of really poor tests out there that do not measure what they say they measure. Good tests measure what they claim to measure, and any conclusions that are drawn from the test scores about the person taking the test are appropriate (they have evidence of validity). Good tests also measure whatever they measure consistently (they have evidence of reliability). The concepts of reliability and validity are central to determining whether a test is "good" or "bad" and are covered in detail later in this textbook. These concepts are so important that four chapters are devoted to them.

Because tests can differ in so many ways, to make informed decisions about tests, you must know how to properly critique a test. A critique of a test is an analysis of the test. A good critique answers many of the questions in Table 1.1. (These questions also appear in Appendix B.) Not all questions can be answered for all tests, as some questions are not relevant to all tests. Your instructor may have additional ideas about what constitutes a good critique.

THE HISTORY OF PSYCHOLOGICAL TESTING

Scholars report that the use of psychological tests can be traced back to 2200 BCE during ancient China's Xia Dynasty. The Xia Dynasty was the first government in traditional Chinese history, and this government instituted royal examinations. A summary of ancient China's royal examinations, leading to 20th-century uses of psychological tests, can be found in For Your Information Box 1.1.

TABLE 1.1   ■   Guidelines for Critiquing a Psychological Test

General descriptive information

- What is the title of the test?
- Who is the author of the test?
- Who publishes the test, and when was it published?
- How long does it take to administer the test?
- How much does it cost to purchase the test?
- Is the test proprietary or nonproprietary?

Purpose and nature of the test

- What does the test measure or predict?
- What behavior does the test require the test taker to perform?
- What population was the test designed for?
- What is the nature of the test (e.g., maximal performance, behavior observation, self-report, standardized or nonstandardized, objective or subjective)?
- What is the format of the test (e.g., paper and pencil or computerized, multiple choice or true/false)?

Practical evaluation

- Is there a test manual, and is it comprehensive? (Does it include information on how the test was constructed, its reliability and validity, and the composition of norm groups, and is it easy to read?)
- Is the test easy or difficult to administer?
- How clear are the administration directions?
- How clear are the scoring procedures?
- What qualifications and training does a test administrator need to have?
- Does the test have face validity?

Technical evaluation

- Is there a norm group?
- If there is a norm group, who constitutes the norm group?
- If there is a norm group, what types of norms are there (e.g., percentiles, standard scores)?
- If there is a norm group, how was the norm group selected?
- If there is a norm group, are there subgroup norms (e.g., by age, gender, region, occupation, and so on)?
- What evidence exists of test reliability?
- What evidence exists for the validity of the test?
- Is there a reported standard error of measurement, and if so, what is it?
- Are confidence intervals presented, and if so, what are they?

Test reviews

- What do reviewers say are the strengths and weaknesses of the test?
- What studies that used the test as a measurement instrument have been published in peer-reviewed journals?
- How did the test perform when researchers or test users, other than the test developer or publisher, used it?

Summary

- Overall, what are the strengths and weaknesses of the test?

FOR YOUR INFORMATION BOX 1.1
PSYCHOLOGICAL TESTS: FROM ANCIENT CHINA TO THE 20TH CENTURY

2200 BCE: Xia Dynasty

The use of psychological tests is thought to date back approximately 4,000 years to 2200 BCE, when the Chinese emperor Yushun administered examinations to officials every 3rd year to determine whether they were suitable to remain in office. However, modern scholars of ancient China say that little archaeological evidence supports the existence of such an examination process.

618–907 CE: T'ang Dynasty

The use of examinations in imperial China appeared to increase significantly during the T'ang dynasty. Individuals applying for the state bureaucracy had to take a civil service exam assessing their knowledge of classics and literary style (vs. technical expertise). However, some evidence exists that the examination results were not entirely used; rather, aristocrats occupied most positions throughout the T'ang dynasty.

1368–1644 CE: Ming Dynasty

During the Ming dynasty, examinations appear to have become a more formal part of the government official application process, as the emperor needed large numbers of government officials to help govern China. Government positions were widely sought because the positions were considered privileged and the salary enough for men (the only ones allowed to take the exam) to support their families for many years. Examination results were associated with the granting of formal titles, similar to today's university degrees. Upon passing different levels of the examination, people received more titles and increasingly more power in the civil service. Although the examinations were reportedly distressful, they appeared to keep talented men in the national government and kept members of the national government from becoming nobility because of their descent. Seeing the value of the examinations for making important decisions, European governments, and eventually the governments of the United Kingdom, the United States, Canada, and other countries, adopted such examination systems.

© Wang Sanjun/iStockphoto

1791: France and Britain

France initially began using the same kind of examination system around 1791. However, soon after, Napoleon temporarily abolished the exams. The system adopted by France served as a model for a British system begun in 1833 to select trainees for the Indian civil service—the beginning of the British civil service.

1800s: The United States

Because of the success of the British system, Senator Charles Sumner and Representative Thomas Jenckes proposed to Congress in 1860 that the United States use a similar system. Jenckes's report, *Civil Service in the United States*, described the British and Chinese systems in detail. This report laid the foundation for the Civil Service Act of 1883, a federal law Senator George H. Pendleton sponsored, intended to improve the U.S. civil service. Among other things, the act required that individuals be awarded government jobs not on political affiliation but rather based on merit, which was to be determined by the results of competitive exams.

Just prior, in 1859, Charles Darwin published his book *On the Origin of Species*. Although it had long been recognized that no two human beings are the same, Darwin provided additional insight about individual differences and survival of the fittest—specifically how species with the most adaptive characteristics survive and then pass these characteristics on to their offspring. Applying Darwin's theory to humans, Sir Francis Galton (Darwin's cousin) published his own

(Continued)

(Continued)

book, *Hereditary Genius*, in which he shared his theory that some people are more fit than others because of their characteristics. He conducted subsequent experiments to test his theory of individual differences, focusing on motor and sensory functioning. Over time, Galton published extensively on individual differences and reaction time and first introduced the term *mental tests* to refer to a set of tests he had developed to measure various constructs, such as reaction time and human memory.

In 1879, Wilhelm Wundt introduced the first psychological laboratory, in Leipzig, Germany. At this time, psychology was still primarily the study of the similarities among people. For example, physiological psychologists studied how the brain and the nervous system functioned, and experimental psychologists conducted research to discover how people learn and remember. However, in the 1880s, James McKeen Cattell began

conducting additional research extending Galton's work, studying individual differences and mental processes. Strongly influenced by Cattell, psychologists began focusing more attention on exploring individual differences. Cattell and others realized that learning about the differences among people was just as important as learning about the similarities among people. They believed that developing formal psychological tests to measure individual differences could help solve many social problems, such as who should be placed in remedial programs, who should be sent to battlefields, and who should be hired for particular jobs.

Although Darwin's, Galton's, and Cattell's work on individual differences contributed to the development of the field of psychological testing, the experimental research of German researchers Ernst Weber, Gustav Fechner, and Wilhelm Wundt helped us understand the need for rigor with testing.

Source: Darwin (1859/1936), DuBois (1970), Eberhard (1977), Franke (1960), Galton (1869/2000), Ho (1962), Hucker (1978), Jenckes (1868), Kracke (1963), Miyazaki (1981), Pirazzoli-t'Serstevens (1982), Rodzinski (1979), Thorne and Henley (2001), and W. Martin (1870).

Most scholars agree that serious research efforts on psychological tests, particularly in the United States, did not begin until late in the 19th century, with the advent of intelligence testing. At this time, serious research efforts began on the use and usefulness of various testing procedures. One of the most important breakthroughs in modern-day testing was the work of Théodore Simon and Alfred Binet's research on intelligence in children.

Intelligence Tests

Alfred Binet and the Binet–Simon Scale

Late in the 19th century, Alfred Binet, whom many refer to as a self-educated psychologist, abandoned his law career to pursue his interests in psychology. Over the years, Binet became a major figure in the development of experimental psychology in France. He founded the first French psychology journal, and in his lab, he developed experimental techniques to measure intelligence and reasoning ability. He believed that intelligence was a complex characteristic that could be determined by evaluating a person's reasoning, judgment, and problem-solving abilities. Binet tried a variety of tasks to measure reasoning, judgment, and problem solving on his own children as well as on other children in the French school system. Binet was fascinated by the differences he observed among the children.

After accepting an invitation to become a member of the Free Society for the Psychological Study of the Child in 1899, and being appointed to the Commission for the Retarded in 1904, Binet and other society members began studying children more scientifically to address the problem of retardation among schoolchildren in Paris schools. Their hope was to be able to differentiate between normal children who could benefit from regular school programs and those with intellectual disabilities who, no matter how hard they tried, could not benefit from regular school programs. They wanted to help school administrators determine how to best help slow learners.

Binet was successful in measuring intelligence, and in 1905, he and Théodore Simon published the first test of mental ability: the Binet–Simon Scale (Binet & Simon, 1905). The purpose of the scale was to identify intellectually subnormal individuals, and it consisted of 30 items. To determine if a person was intellectually subnormal, Binet and Simon compared individual test scores with the scores of 50 children who were administered the test with exactly the same instructions and format, or what we call standardized conditions. The scores of these 50 children served as a frame of reference (standardization sample) for interpreting the test scores of other children. When a child took the test, his or her test score could be compared with the average of the group of 50 children to provide meaning to the child's score.

Over the years, significant improvements were made to the Binet–Simon Scale. The standardization sample was significantly increased, the number of test items increased, and the indicator mental age was added to indicate the level at which a child performed on the test. To help interpret test results, a child's mental age, based on his or her test score, was compared with the actual, or chronological, age. For example, a 10-year-old child's test score might have indicated a mental age of 8, 10, or perhaps 12. A tested mental age of 8 would indicate that the child was behind others in intellectual development, whereas a mental age of 12 would indicate that the child was more intellectually advanced.

Lewis Terman and the Stanford–Binet Intelligence Scales

Binet's work influenced psychologists across the globe. Psychological testing became a popular method of evaluation, and the Binet–Simon Scale was adapted for use in many countries. In 1916, Lewis Terman, an American psychologist and Stanford University faculty member, produced the Stanford–Binet Intelligence Scales (Terman, 1916), an adaptation of Binet's original test. The standardization sample was increased, and test items were revised and added. Added was an intelligence quotient (IQ) index. Developed for use with Americans ages 3 years to adulthood, the test was used for many years. A revised edition of the Stanford–Binet Intelligence Scale remains one of the most widely used intelligence tests today.

More detail about the Stanford–Binet Intelligence Scales can be found in **Test Spotlight 1.2** in Appendix A.

The Wechsler–Bellevue Intelligence Scale and the Wechsler Adult Intelligence Scale

By the 1930s, thousands of psychological tests were available, and psychologists and others were debating the nature of intelligence (what intelligence was all about). This dispute over defining intelligence prompted the development in 1939 of the original Wechsler–Bellevue Intelligence Scale (WBIS) for adults, which provided an index of general mental ability (as did the Binet–Simon Scale) and revealed patterns of a person's intellectual strengths and weaknesses. David Wechsler, the chief psychologist at Bellevue Hospital in New York City, constructed the WBIS, believing that intelligence is demonstrated based on an individual's ability to act purposefully, think logically, and interact and cope successfully with the environment (Hess, 2001; Rogers, 2001; Thorne & Henley, 2001). Wechsler published the second edition, the WBIS-II, in 1946.

In 1955, Wechsler revised the WBIS-II and renamed it the Wechsler Adult Intelligence Scale (WAIS). In 1981 and 1991, the WAIS was updated and published as the WAIS-Revised and the WAIS–Third Edition, respectively. In a continuing effort to improve the measurement of intelligence, as well as the clinical utility and user-friendliness of the test, the fourth edition was published in 2008 (Pearson Education, 2018d).

Personality Tests

In addition to intelligence testing, the early 1900s brought about an interest in measuring personality.

The Personal Data Sheet

During World War I, the U.S. military wanted a test to help detect soldiers who would not be able to handle the stress associated with combat. To meet this need, the APA commissioned an American psychologist and Columbia University faculty member, Robert Woodworth (1920), to design such a test, which came to be known as the Personal Data Sheet (PDS). The PDS was a paper-and-pencil test that required military recruits to respond "yes" or "no" to a series of 200 questions (eventually reduced to 116 questions) asked during a psychiatric interview that searched for emotional instability. The questions covered topics such as excessive anxiety, depression, abnormal fears, impulse problems, sleepwalking, nightmares, and memory problems (Segal & Coolidge, 2004). One question asked, "Are you troubled with the idea that people are watching you on the street?" During a pilot study of the test, new recruits on average showed 10 positive psychoneurotic symptoms; recruits who were deemed unfit for service generally showed 30 to 40 positive psychoneurotic symptoms (Segal & Coolidge, 2004). Unfortunately, because Woodworth did not complete the final design of this test until too late in the war, the PDS was never implemented or used to screen new recruits.

After World War I, Woodworth developed the Woodworth Psychoneurotic Inventory, a version of the PDS. Unlike the PDS, the Woodworth Psychoneurotic Inventory was designed for use with civilians and was the first self-report test. It was also the first widely used personality inventory.

Immediately following Woodworth's development of the PDS and the Woodworth Psychoneurotic Inventory, researchers continued development of structured personality tests. However, interest declined in structured personality testing, while interest increased in less structured measures of personality.

The Rorschach Inkblot Test and the TAT

During the 1930s, interest also grew in measuring personality by exploring the unconscious. With this interest came the development of two important projective tests based on the personality theories of Carl Jung: the Rorschach inkblot test and the TAT. The Rorschach, a projective personality test (described further in the "How Are Tests Used in Clinical and Counseling Settings?" chapter), was developed initially in 1921 by Swiss psychiatrist Hermann Rorschach and introduced in the United States in 1932. The Rorschach inkblot test was designed to identify personality disorders and assess mental functioning. Individuals look at inkblots and report their perceptions, which are then analyzed.

Two American psychologists at Harvard University, Henry A. Murray and C. D. Morgan, developed the TAT in the 1930s. The test was developed to measure an individual's patterns of thought, attitudes, observational capacity, and emotional responses to ambiguous test material. Individuals are shown ambiguous pictures and asked to tell a story for each picture, including such things as what led up to the event that is shown, what is happening, what the individuals in the picture are feeling and thinking, and what the outcome of the event is. As with the Rorschach test, individuals' responses are then analyzed.

Vocational Tests

During the 1940s, a need developed for **vocational tests** to help predict how successful an applicant would be in specific occupations. Such a test was needed because thousands of people had lost their jobs during the Great Depression, and thousands more were coming out of school and seeking work. Because there were not enough jobs, people were forced to look for new lines of work. As a result, psychologists developed large-scale programs to design vocational aptitude tests that would predict how successful a person would be at an occupation before entering it. In 1947, the U.S. Employment Service developed the General Aptitude Test Battery (GATB) to meet this need (Dvorak, 1956). The GATB was used for a variety of purposes, including vocational counseling and occupational selection.

By the mid-20th century, numerous tests were available, and they were used by many to make important decisions about individuals. Because of the increased use of psychological tests, to help protect the rights of the test taker, the APA (1953) established the eight-member Committee on Ethical Standards for Psychology, which collaborated with more than 2,000 psychologists to publish the 170-page *Ethical Standards of Psychologists*. (We discuss these ethical standards in more detail in the "What Are the Ethical Responsibilities of Test Publishers, Test Users, and Test Takers?" chapter).

Testing in the 21st Century

Psychological testing is a big, multibillion-dollar business. There are thousands of published, commercially available tests, as well as thousands of unpublished tests. Tests are developed and published by hundreds of test publishing companies that market their tests very proactively—on the web and in catalogs. Over the years, test publishers' revenue has increased significantly, as the desire to use test scores to make important decisions has increased. For example, whereas in 1955, test sales by publishers totaled approximately $7 million, by 2001 sales had increased to approximately $250 million (Association of American Publishers, 2002). In 2002, the standardized testing market was valued somewhere between $400 million and $700 million per year. According to the Society for Human Resource Management, in 2015, workplace assessments alone were estimated to be a $500 million a year industry growing at about 10% per year.

Furthermore, following passage of the No Child Left Behind Act of 2001 (NCLB), the Pew Center on the States reported that spending on standardized tests went from $423 million in 2001 to $1.1 billion in 2008. In 2012, U.S. schools nationwide spent approximately $1.7 million per year on assessments for kindergarten through 12th grade (Chingos, 2012). According to the *2014 Global Assessment Trends Report*, 73% of employers used skills or knowledge tests as a part of their hiring processes (Kantrowitz, 2014). Other tests included personality tests (62%), cognitive ability and general problem-solving tests (59%), job fit tests (47%), situational judgment tests, (43%), culture fit tests (33%), and job simulations (32%).

With such significant spending on psychological tests and the numbers of schools and employers using psychological tests, the number of people who take psychological tests is not surprising. For example, in the early 1990s, 20 million Americans per year were taking psychological tests (Hunt, 1993), of whom 1 million were taking the SAT, a college admission test you may have taken as you prepared to apply to colleges. By 2013, the number of college-bound students taking the SAT had increased to 1.6 million (College Board, 2013). 2017 was a record year for the SAT, with other 1.8 million students taking the SAT (College Board, 2018). During the 2012–2013 academic year, over 238,000 individuals took the Graduate Management Admission Test, a graduate admission test most business schools require as a part of the application process (Graduate Management Admission Council, 2014). Furthermore, each year, as many as 1.5 million people take the Myers–Briggs Type Indicator (MBTI), a personality inventory. Testing is indeed a big business.

Although there are many unpublished tests, many psychological tests are commercially available, published by test publishers. For the names and web addresses of some of the most well-known test publishers, as well as some of the tests they publish, see On the Web Box 1.1.

Today, psychological testing is a part of American culture. Psychological tests are in use everywhere. For example, let us take a look at the Society for Human Resource Management (SHRM). As the world's largest association devoted to human resources management, SHRM provides human resources professionals with essential information and resources (Society for Human Resource Management, 2018). One of the resources SHRM provides, in partnership with the Performance Assessment Network, is access to the SHRM Talent Assessment Center, which includes more than 400 tests and surveys, from over 50 test publishers. SHRM members who are qualified testing professionals can identify one or more tests or surveys to help make selection and development decisions about current and potential employees. Tests and surveys can be identified based on assessment type (e.g., personality, cognitive ability, skills and knowledge, 360° feedback), purpose (e.g., selection, development), level (e.g., individual contributor, leader or manager), industry (e.g., education, construction), occupation (e.g., legal, computer and mathematical), or competency. The testing center allows qualified testing professionals to purchase individual tests, administer the tests online, and receive electronic reports.

Let's also take a look at the NCLB, which in 2002 raised significant awareness about testing in the United States. President George W. Bush signed the NCLB into law on January 8, 2002, intending to improve the performance of America's primary and secondary schools. The objective was to make all children proficient in reading and math by 2014. The act contained the four basic strategies for improving the performance of schools—strategies that were intended to change the culture of America's schools by defining a school's success in terms of the achievement of its students (U.S. Department of Education, 2004):

1. Increase the accountability that states, school districts, and schools have for educating America's children by requiring that all states implement statewide systems that (a) set challenging standards for what children in Grades 3 to 8 should know and learn in reading and math, (b) test students in Grades 3 to 8 on a yearly basis to determine the extent to which they know and have learned what they should have according to state standards, and (c) include annual statewide progress objectives to ensure that all students are proficient by 12th grade.

2. Ensure that all children have access to a quality education by allowing parents to send their children to better schools if their schools do not meet state standards.

3. Increase the amount of flexibility that high-performing states and school districts have for spending federal education dollars.

4. Place more emphasis on developing children's reading skills by making grants available to states to administer screening and diagnostic assessments to identify children who may be at risk for reading failure and by providing teachers with professional development and resources to help young children attain the knowledge and skills they need to be readers.

Requiring more accountability of U.S. schools, NCLB required mandatory testing of all students in Grades 3 to 12, as well as public access to overall aggregate results and subgroup results (e.g., for major racial and ethnic groups, low-income students, students with disabilities). The NCLB was replaced in 2015 by the Every Student Succeeds Act, retaining the most important parts of the NCLB (such as required testing), but providing states more control over accountability, teacher evaluation, and correcting issues with achievement gaps and failing schools (U.S. Department of Education, 2018).

Similarly focused on improving student achievement in the United States, in 2009 our nation's governors and education commissioners, with input from experts, school

ON THE WEB BOX 1.1
NAMES AND WEB ADDRESSES OF TEST PUBLISHERS

Open your web browser, go to your favorite search engine, and conduct a search for "test publishers" or "psychological test publishers." You will find pages and pages of websites dedicated to psychological testing and publishing. You will also find the websites of hundreds of test publishers. Although there are many different publishers, some of the most well known, including some of the widely known tests they publish, are listed here:

Publisher	Website	Popular Published Tests
Educational Testing Service	www.ets.org	• Graduate Record Examination General Test and Subject Tests • SAT Reasoning Test and SAT Subject Tests • Test of English as a Foreign Language • Graduate Management Admission Test
Pearson	www.pearsonassessments.com	• Bar-On Emotional Quotient Inventory • Bayley Scales of Infant and Toddler Development, Third Edition • Behavior Assessment System for Children, Second Edition, Behavioral and Emotional Screening System • Bender Visual-Motor Gestalt Test, Second Edition • Watson–Glaser Critical Thinking Appraisal
Hogan Assessment Systems	www.hoganassessments.com	• Hogan Personality Inventory • Hogan Development Survey • Hogan Business Reasoning Inventory • Motives, Values, Preferences Inventory
PAR	www.parinc.com	• Self-Directed Search • NEO Personality Inventory • Personality Assessment Inventory
Psytech International	www.psytech.com	• Occupational Interest Profile • Clerical Test Battery • Values & Motives Inventory
PSI	www.psionline.com	• Customer Service Battery • Firefighter Selection Test • Police Selection Test
Hogrefe	www.hogrefe.co.uk	• Rorschach Test • Trauma Symptom Inventory • Work Profile Questionnaire Emotional Intelligence Questionnaire
University of Minnesota Press Test Division	www.upress.umn.edu	• Minnesota Multiphasic Personality Inventory–2
Wonderlic	www.wonderlic.com	• Wonderlic Personnel Test

administrators, teachers, and parents, introduced the Common Core State Standards (Common Core State Standards Initiative, 2014). Led at the state and local levels, the Common Core includes high-quality academic expectations created to ensure that all students, regardless of where they live, graduate from high school with the knowledge and skills they need to succeed. As with NCLB, testing plays a critical role in measuring achievement.

THE THREE DEFINING CHARACTERISTICS OF PSYCHOLOGICAL TESTS

As we have already discussed, a psychological test is a measurement tool or technique that requires a person to perform one or more behaviors to make inferences about human attributes, traits, or characteristics or predict future outcomes. All good psychological tests have three characteristics in common:

1. **All good tests representatively sample the behaviors thought to measure an attribute or thought to predict an outcome.** For example, suppose we are interested in developing a test to measure your physical ability. One option would be to evaluate your performance in every sport you have ever played. Another option would be to have you run the 50-meter dash. Both of these options have drawbacks. The first option would be very precise, but not very practical. Can you imagine how much time and energy it would take to review how you performed in every sport you have ever played? The second option is too narrow and unrepresentative. How fast you run the 50-meter dash does not tell us much about your physical ability in general. A better method would be to take a representative sample of performance in sports. For example, we might require you to participate in some individual sports (e.g., running, tennis, gymnastics) and team sports (e.g., soccer, basketball) that involve different types of physical abilities (e.g., strength, endurance, precision). This option would include a more representative sample.

2. **All good tests include behavior samples that are obtained under standardized conditions.** That is, a test must be administered the same way to all people. When you take a test, various factors can affect your score besides the characteristic, attribute, or trait that is being measured. Factors related to the environment (e.g., room temperature, lighting), the examiner (e.g., examiner attitude, how the instructions are read), the examinee (e.g., illness, fatigue), and the test (e.g., understandability of questions) all can affect your score. If everyone is tested under the same conditions (e.g., in the same environment), we can be more confident that these factors will affect all test takers similarly. If all of these factors affect test takers similarly, we can be more certain that a person's test score accurately reflects the attribute being measured. Although it is possible for test developers to standardize factors related to the environment, the examiner, and the test, it is difficult to standardize examinee factors. For example, test developers have little control over what test takers do the night before they take a test.

3. **All good tests have rules for scoring.** These rules ensure that all examiners will score the same set of responses in the same way. For example, teachers might award 1 point for each multiple-choice question you answer correctly, and they might award or deduct points based on what you include in your response to an essay question. Teachers might then report your overall exam score either as the number correct or as a percentage of the number correct (the number of correct answers divided by the total number of questions on the test).

Although all psychological tests have these characteristics, not all exhibit these characteristics to the same degree. For example, some tests may include a more representative sample of behaviors than do others. Some tests, such as group-administered tests, may be more conducive to administration under standardized conditions than are individually administered tests. Some tests have well-defined rules for scoring, and other tests have general guidelines. Some tests have very explicit scoring rules, for example, "If Question 1 is marked true, then deduct 2 points." Other tests, such as those that include short answers, may have less explicit rules for scoring, for example, "Award 1 point for each concept noted and defined."

ASSUMPTIONS OF PSYCHOLOGICAL TESTS

There are many assumptions that must be made when using psychological tests. The following are what we consider the most important assumptions:

1. **Psychological tests measure what they purport to measure or predict what they are intended to predict.** In addition, any conclusions or inferences that are drawn about the test takers based on their test scores must be appropriate. This is also called test validity. If a test is designed to measure mechanical ability, we must assume that it does indeed measure mechanical ability. If a test is designed to predict performance on the job, then we must assume that it does indeed predict performance. This assumption must come from a personal review of the test's validity data.

2. **An individual's behavior, and therefore test scores, will typically remain stable over time.** This is also called test–retest reliability. If a test is administered at a specific point in time and then we administer it again at a different point in time (e.g., 2 weeks later), we must assume, depending on what we are measuring, that an individual will receive a similar score at both points in time. If we are measuring a relatively stable trait, we should be much more concerned about this assumption. However, there are some traits, such as mood, that are not expected to show high test–retest reliability.

3. **Individuals understand test items the same way.** For example, when asked to respond "true" or "false" to a test item such as "I am almost always healthy," we must assume that all test takers interpret "almost always" similarly.

4. **Individuals will report accurately about themselves** (e.g., about their personalities, about their likes and dislikes). When we ask people to remember something or to tell us how they feel about something, we must assume that they will remember accurately and that they have the ability to assess and report accurately on their thoughts and feelings. For example, if we ask you to tell us whether you agree or disagree with the statement "I have always liked cats," you must remember not only how you feel about cats now but also how you felt about cats previously.

5. **Individuals will report honestly their thoughts and feelings.** Even if people are able to report correctly about themselves, they may choose not to do so. Sometimes people respond how they think the tester wants them to respond, or they lie so that the outcome benefits them. For example, if we ask test takers whether they have ever taken a vacation, they may tell us that they have even if they really have not. Why? Because we expect most individuals to occasionally take vacations, and therefore the test takers think we would expect most individuals to answer "yes" to this question. Criminals may respond to test questions in a way that makes them appear neurotic or psychotic so that they can claim that they were insane when they committed crimes. When people report about

themselves, we must assume that they will report their thoughts and feelings honestly, or we must build validity checks into the test. We discuss some the practical implications of this assumption in the "How Are Tests Used in Organizational Settings?" chapter.

6. **The test score an individual receives is equal to his or her true score plus some error, and this error may be attributable to the test itself, the examiner, the examinee, or the environment.** That is, a test taker's score may reflect not only the attribute being measured but also things such as awkward question wording, errors in administration of the test, examinee fatigue, and the temperature of the room in which the test was taken. When evaluating an individual's score, we must assume that it will include some error.

Although we must accept some of these assumptions at face value, we can increase our confidence in others by following certain steps during test development. For example, in Section III of this textbook, where we cover developing and piloting psychological tests, we talk about how to design test questions that are more likely to be understood universally. We also talk about the techniques that are available to promote honest answering. In Section II, which covers psychometric principles, we discuss how to gather evidence of test reliability/precision and validity for intended use.

TEST CLASSIFICATION METHODS

As we have already discussed, there are tens of thousands of commercially available psychological tests, and professionals refer to these tests in various ways. Sometimes professionals refer to them as tests of maximal performance, behavior observation tests, or self-report tests. Sometimes professionals refer to tests as being standardized or nonstandardized, objective or projective. Other times professionals refer to tests based on what the tests measure. In this section, we discuss the most common ways that professionals classify and refer to psychological tests.

Maximal Performance, Behavior Observation, or Self-Report

Most psychological tests can be defined as being tests of maximal performance, behavioral observation tests, or self-report tests.

- **Tests of maximal performance** require test takers to perform a particular well-defined task, such as making a right-hand turn, arranging blocks from smallest to largest, tracing a pattern, or completing mathematical problems. Test takers try to do their best because their scores are determined by their success in completing the task. Intelligence tests, tests of specific abilities (e.g., mechanical ability), driving tests (road and written), and classroom tests all are good examples of tests of maximal performance.

- **Behavior observation tests** involve observing people's behavior and how people typically respond in a particular context. Unlike with tests of maximal performance, many times people do not know that their behavior is being observed, and there is no single defined task for them to perform. Many restaurants use this technique to assess food servers' competence in dealing with customers. Sometimes managers hire trained observers to visit their restaurants disguised as typical customers. In exchange for a free meal or some predetermined compensation, observers agree to record specific behaviors performed by food servers. For example, observers may document whether food servers greeted them in a friendly manner. Other examples of behavior observations include documenting job performance for performance appraisals or clinical interviews.

- **Self-report tests** require test takers to report or describe their feelings, beliefs, opinions, or mental states. Many personality inventories, such as the Hogan Personality Inventory (HPI), are self-report tests. The HPI, a test used primarily for personnel selection and individualized assessment, asks test takers to indicate whether each of more than 200 statements about themselves is true or false.

Most psychological tests fit one of the above categories, and some tests contain features of more than one category. For example, a structured job interview (which involves asking all job applicants a standard set of interview questions) could include both technical questions and questions about one's beliefs or opinions. Technical questions, which are well defined for the interviewee, qualify the interview as a test of maximal performance. Questions about beliefs and opinions qualify it as a self-report test. An interviewer may also observe interviewees' behaviors, such as their greetings, which would qualify the interview as a behavioral observation.

Standardized or Nonstandardized

Standardized tests are those designed to measure a specific construct, and after development, are administered to a large group of individuals who are similar to the group for whom the test has been designed. To interpret test scores, an individual's test score is compared to others similar to the individual. For example, if a test is designed to measure the construct of writing ability for high school students, after development, the test would be administered to a large group of high school students. This group is called the **standardization sample**—people who are tested to obtain data to establish a frame of reference for interpreting individual test scores. These data, called **norms**, indicate the average performance of a group and the distribution of scores above and below this average.

For example, if you took the SAT, the interpretation of your score included comparing it with the SAT standardization sample to determine whether your score was high or low in comparison with others and whether you scored above average, average, or below average. In addition, standardized tests always have specific directions for administration and scoring.

Nonstandardized tests do not have standardization samples and are more common than standardized tests. Nonstandardized tests are usually constructed by a teacher or trainer in a less formal manner for a single administration. For example, in many cases, the exams you take in your college courses are nonstandardized tests.

Objective or Projective

Sometimes people make a distinction between objective and projective tests. **Objective tests** are tests where test takers choose a response or provide a response and there are predetermined correct answers, requiring little subjective judgment of the person scoring the test. Objective tests require test takers to respond to structured true/false questions, multiple-choice questions, or rating scales. What the test taker must do is clear, for example, answer "true" or "false," circle the correct multiple-choice answer, or circle the correct item on the rating scale. The GRE, Stanford-Binet Intelligence Scales, GATB, and most classroom tests are examples of objective tests.

Another example of an objective test is the NEO Personality Inventory–3, an objective self-report instrument designed to identify what makes individuals unique in their thinking, feeling, and interaction with others. Although there are two forms of the inventory, both measure five broad personality dimensions: neuroticism, extroversion, openness, agreeableness, and conscientiousness (PAR, 2018a). Test takers are asked to indicate whether they strongly disagree, disagree, are neutral, agree, or strongly agree with each of 240 statements. These statements are about their thoughts, feelings, and goals. For sample questions from the NEO Personality Inventory, see For Your Information Box 1.2.

On the other hand, **projective tests** are those on which test takers view and are asked to respond to unstructured or ambiguous stimuli such as images or incomplete sentences. The role of the test taker is less clear than with an objective test, and more subjectivity is involved in interpreting the test taker's answer. People who use projective tests believe that test takers project themselves into the tasks they are asked to perform and that their responses are based on what they believe the stimuli mean and on the feelings they experience while responding. These tests tend to elicit highly personal concerns. They are often used to detect unconscious thoughts or personality characteristics, and they may be used to identify the need for psychological counseling. The TAT is an example of a projective test. (The "How Are Tests Used in Clinical and Counseling Settings?" chapter contains more information on the TAT and other projective tests.)

> More detail about the NEO Personality Inventory can be found in **Test Spotlight 1.3** in Appendix A.

Dimension Measured

Psychological tests are often discussed in terms of the dimensions they measure. For example, sometimes we distinguish among achievement tests, aptitude tests, intelligence tests, personality tests, and interest inventories. We refer to these as dimensions because they are broader than a single attribute or trait level. Often these types of tests measure various personal attributes or traits.

FOR YOUR INFORMATION BOX 1.2
SAMPLE ITEMS FROM THE NEO PERSONALITY INVENTORY

The NEO Personality Inventory, developed by Costa and McCrae (1992), is an objective, self-report instrument designed to identify what makes individuals unique in their thinking, feeling, and interaction with others. The inventory measures five broad personality dimensions: neuroticism, extroversion, openness, agreeableness, and conscientiousness. Test takers are asked to indicate whether they strongly disagree (SD), disagree (D), are neutral (N), agree (A), or strongly agree (SA) with each of 240 statements. These statements are about their thoughts, feelings, and goals. In the following, we list a sample item from three of the five scales:

Neuroticism

Frightening thoughts
sometimes come into my head.   SD   D   N   A   SA

Extroversion

I don't get much pleasure
from chatting with people.   SD   D   N   A   SA

Openness

I have a very active imagination.   SD   D   N   A   SA

Achievement Tests

Achievement tests measure a person's previous learning in a specific academic area (e.g., computer programming, German, trigonometry, psychology). A test that requires you to list the three characteristics of psychological tests would be considered an achievement test. Achievement tests are also referred to as tests of knowledge.

Achievement tests are used primarily in educational settings to determine how much students have learned or what they can do at a particular point in time. Many elementary schools and high schools rely on achievement tests to compare what students know at the beginning of the year with what they know at the end of the year, to assign grades, to identify students with special educational needs, and to measure students' progress.

Aptitude Tests

Achievement tests measure a test taker's knowledge in a specific area at a specific point in time. **Aptitude tests** assess a test taker's potential for learning or ability to perform in a new job or situation. Aptitude tests measure the product of cumulative life experiences—or what one has acquired over time. They help determine what "maximum" can be expected from a person.

Schools, businesses, and government agencies often use aptitude tests to predict how well someone will perform or to estimate the extent to which an individual will profit from a specified course of training. Vocational guidance counseling may involve aptitude testing to help clarify the test taker's career goals. If a person's score is similar to scores of others already working in a given occupation, the test will predict success in that field.

Intelligence Tests

Intelligence tests, like aptitude tests, assess a test taker's ability to cope with the environment, but at a broader level. Intelligence tests are often used to screen individuals for specific programs (e.g., gifted programs, honors programs) or programs for the mentally challenged. Intelligence tests are typically used in educational and clinical settings.

Interest Inventories

Interest inventories assess a person's interests in educational programs for job settings and provide information for making career decisions. Because these tests are often used to predict satisfaction in a particular academic area or employment setting, they are administered primarily to students by counselors in high schools and colleges. Interest inventories are not intended to predict success; rather, they are intended only to offer a framework for narrowing career possibilities.

Personality Tests

Personality tests measure human character or disposition. The first personality tests were designed to assess and predict clinical disorders. These tests remain useful today for determining who needs counseling and who will benefit from treatment programs. Newer personality tests measure "normal" personality traits. For example, the MBTI is often used by industrial and organizational psychologists to increase employees' understanding of individual differences and to promote better communication among members of work teams. Career counselors also use the MBTI to help students select majors and careers consistent with their personalities.

Personality tests can be either objective or projective. The MBTI is an example of an objective personality test. Projective personality tests, such as the TAT, serve the same purpose as some objective personality tests, but they require test takers to respond to unstructured or ambiguous stimuli.

More detail about the MBTI can be found in **Test Spotlight 1.4** in Appendix A.

Subject Tests

Many popular psychological testing reference books also classify psychological tests by subject. For example, the *Twentieth Mental Measurements Yearbook* (*MMY*; Carlson, Geisinger, & Jonson, 2017) classifies thousands of tests into 18 major subject categories:

- Achievement
- Behavior assessment
- Developmental
- Education
- English and language
- Fine arts
- Foreign languages
- Intelligence and general aptitude
- Mathematics
- Neuropsychological
- Personality
- Reading
- Science
- Sensorimotor
- Social studies
- Speech and hearing
- Vocations

Reference books such as the *MMY* often indicate whether a test is (a) a test of maximal performance, a behavior observation test, or a self-report test; (b) standardized or nonstandardized; and (c) objective or projective. We discuss the *MMY*, as well as other reference books, later in this chapter.

PSYCHOLOGICAL ASSESSMENT, PSYCHOLOGICAL TESTS, MEASUREMENTS, AND SURVEYS

Before discussing much more, we should spend some time discussing some terms that students often confuse—*psychological assessment*, *psychological test*, *measurement*, and *survey*. Students often think of psychological assessment and psychological testing as one and the same. Similarly, students often do not understand the difference between a psychological test and a survey. This section is designed to help you distinguish among these terms that are commonly used in psychological testing.

Psychological Assessment and Psychological Test

A psychological assessment and a psychological test are both evaluative methods of collecting important information about people. Both are used to help understand and predict behavior. While the terms are often used interchangeably, they are different. Many experts view psychological assessment as a broader concept than a psychological test (see Figure 1.2). With a **psychological assessment**, we use multiple methods, such as personal history interviews, behavioral observations, and psychological tests, for gathering information about an individual. A psychological test is only one tool in the psychological assessment process. For example, a clinical psychologist may conduct a psychological assessment of a patient by interviewing the patient, interviewing the patient's family members, observing the patient's behavior, and administering a psychological test such as the Minnesota Multiphasic Personality Inventory–2.

Psychological Test and Measurement

Although their meanings overlap, *psychological test* and *measurement* are not synonyms. Measurement, like assessment, is a broader concept than psychological test (see Figure 1.2). **Measurement** is the process of assessing the size, the amount, or the degree of an attribute using specific rules for transforming the attribute into numbers (Nunnally & Bernstein, 1994). For example, we measure a woman's dress size following specific rules—using a tape measure to measure the bust, waist, hips, and inseam. Or we might measure or quantify the size of an earthquake using the Richter or moment magnitude scale, focusing on the magnitude and intensity of ground movement. A **measurement instrument** is a tool or technique for assessing the size, amount, or degree of an attribute. So a psychological test can be considered a measurement or measurement instrument when the results of the test are expressed in terms of a derived score.

Even though some differences exist, you may find people who use the terms *psychological assessment*, *psychological test*, and *psychological measurement* interchangeably. Although we do not use the terms *assessment* and *psychological test* interchangeably throughout the remainder of this text, we do follow the common practice of referring to all psychological tests as measurements.

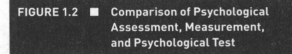

FIGURE 1.2 ■ Comparison of Psychological Assessment, Measurement, and Psychological Test

Psychological Tests and Surveys

Surveys, like psychological tests (and psychological assessments), are used to collect important information from individuals. Surveys differ from psychological tests in two important ways. First, psychological tests focus on individual outcomes, and surveys focus on group outcomes. Psychological tests provide important information about individual differences and help individuals and institutions make important decisions about individuals. For example, a psychological test may suggest that a child is unusually intelligent and therefore should be placed in a gifted or honors program. Surveys, on the other hand, provide important information about groups and help us make important decisions about groups. For example, an organizational

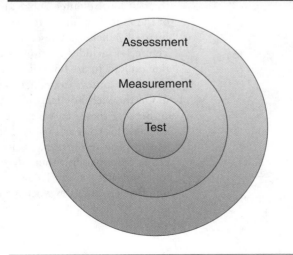

survey may suggest that employees are displeased with a company benefits program and that a new benefits program is needed.

Second, the results of a psychological test are often reported in terms of an overall derived score or scaled scores. Results of surveys, on the other hand, are often reported at the question level by providing the percentage of respondents who selected each answer alternative. Of course, in some cases, surveys focus on individual outcomes and are constructed using scales. In such a case, a survey approximates a psychological test. (The "How Do We Construct and Administer Surveys and Use Survey Data?" chapter is devoted to an in-depth discussion of surveys.)

LOCATING INFORMATION ABOUT TESTS

With so many psychological tests available, we are sure you can imagine that finding the most appropriate one for your specific purpose can be a difficult task. To choose an appropriate test for a particular circumstance, you must know the types of tests that are available and their merits and limitations. Prior to the 1950s, test users had few resources for obtaining such information. Today, however, numerous resources are available. Although all have the same general purpose—to help test users make informed decisions—the information such resources contain varies. Some resources provide only general descriptive information about psychological tests, such as the test's name, author, and publisher, and others contain detailed information, including test reviews and detailed bibliographies. Some resources focus on commercially available, standardized published tests, and others focus on unpublished tests. Some references include information about tests for particular groups (e.g., children), and others include a broad range of tests for various populations.

Some of the most commonly used resource books, including brief synopses of their contents, are described in For Your Information Box 1.3. The first four resource books, *Tests in Print* (*TIP*), the *MMY*, *Tests*, and *Test Critiques*, are often viewed as the most useful and popular.

Whether you are trying to locate tests that measure intelligence, self-esteem, or some other attribute, trait, or characteristic, we suggest that you begin your search with one of the first four books in For Your Information Box 1.3. *TIP* and the *MMY* are two of the most helpful references, and students often find it most helpful to begin with *TIP*. Figure 1.3 includes a descriptive guide of the type of information you will find in the *MMY*. Figure 1.4 includes a summary of how to use *TIP* to find tests. You can find more information on how to use both of these resources, as well as how to use the information contained in these resources to evaluate a test, on the Buros Center for Testing home page, discussed in On the Web Box 1.2.

Because there is a wealth of psychological tests available, there is a wealth of resources available for you to use in gathering information about psychological tests. You are not limited to print resources; advances in technology now allow you to access the Internet and gather information about psychological tests on demand. On the Web Box 1.2 discusses some websites you can access to locate information on psychological tests. For Your Information Box 1.4 discusses where you can locate unpublished psychological tests.

FOR YOUR INFORMATION BOX 1.3

COMMONLY USED RESOURCE BOOKS

Book Title	Contents
Tests in Print (multiple volumes)	*Tests in Print* (*TIP*) is published in multiple volumes. Each volume contains descriptive listings of commercially published tests that are available for purchase. *TIP* also serves as a comprehensive index to the contents of previously published editions of the *Mental Measurements Yearbook* (*MMY*). Each descriptive listing, or test entry, contains extensive information, including but not limited to the title of the test, the purpose of the test, the intended population, publication dates, the acronym used to identify the test, scores the test provides, whether the test is an individual test or group test, whether the test has a manual, the author(s), the publisher, the cost of the test, and available foreign adaptations. Each entry also contains brief comments about the test as well as cross-references to reviews in the *MMY*.
Mental Measurements Yearbook (multiple volumes)	The *MMY* is published in multiple volumes. Each volume contains descriptive information and test reviews of newly developed tests that are in English, commercially published tests, and tests that have been revised since the publication of the previous *MMY* edition. The *MMY* is cumulative, meaning that later volumes build on earlier ones rather than replacing them. Each descriptive listing, or test entry, contains extensive information about a particular test. If the test is a revision of a previous test, the entry also includes the volume of the *MMY* in which the test was originally described. Each entry also typically includes information about the test's reliability and validity, one or two professional reviews, and a list of references to pertinent literature.
Tests	*Tests* contains descriptions of a broad range of tests for use by psychologists, educators, and human resource professionals. Each entry includes the test's title, author, publisher, intended population, purpose, major features, administration time, cost, and availability.
Test Critiques (multiple volumes)	*Test Critiques* is published in multiple volumes. Each volume contains reviews of frequently used psychological, business, and educational tests. Each review includes descriptive information about the test (e.g., author, attribute measured, norms) and information on practical applications and uses. *Test Critiques* also contains in-depth information on reliability, validity, and test construction.
Personality Test and Reviews (multiple volumes)	*Personality Test and Reviews* is published in multiple volumes. Each volume contains a bibliography of personality tests that are contained in the *MMY*. Each entry contains descriptive information about the test as well as test reviews.
Tests in Education	*Tests in Education* contains descriptive and detailed information about educational tests for use by teachers, administrators, and educational advisers.
Testing Children	*Testing Children* contains descriptions of tests available for children. These descriptions include the knowledge, skills, and abilities measured by each test; the content and structure of the test; the time required to administer the test; the scores that are produced; the cost; and the publisher.
Tests and Measurements in Child Development: A Handbook	*Tests and Measurements in Child Development* contains a listing of unpublished measures for use with children as well as detailed information about each measure.
Measures for Psychological Assessment: A Guide to 3,000 Original Sources and Their Applications	*Measures for Psychological Assessment* is a guide that contains annotated references to thousands of less recognized assessment devices developed and described in journal articles.

FIGURE 1.3 ■ A Guide to Descriptive Entries in the Mental Measurements Yearbook

BUROS CENTER FOR TESTING

Mental Measurements Yearbook and *Tests in Print*

A Guide to the Descriptive Entries

Entry Number: The number cited in all indexes when referring to this test.

Title: Test titles are printed in boldface type; secondary or series titles are set off from main titles by colon.

Population: A description of the groups for which the test is intended.

Administration: Individual or group administration is indicated.

Distribution: This is noted only for tests that are put on a special market by the publisher.

Special Editions: Various types of special editions are listed here.

Author: All test authors' names are reported, exactly as printed on the test materials.

Cross References: For tests that have been previously listed in a Buros publication, cross references to the reviews, excerpts, and references will be noted here. "9:1410," for example, refers to test 1410 in the *Ninth Mental Measurements Yearbook*; "T4:3010" refers to test 3010 in *Tests in Print IV*.

[420]
The Hypothetical Test: Reading.
Purpose: Designed to "measure achievement in reading."
Population: Grades 9-12.
Publication Dates: 1989—1994.
Acronym: HYPE.
Scores, 3: Vocabulary, Comprehension, and Total.
Administration: Individual or group.
Forms, 3: Survey, Abbreviated, Complete Battery.
Restricted Distribution: Distribution of Survey Form restricted to school principals.
Price Data, 1995: $70 per complete kit including 100 tests, scoring key, and manual ('94, 120 pages); $9 per scoring key; $32 per manual.
Special Editions: Braille edition available.
Time: 50(60) minutes.
Comments: May be self-scored.
Author: Jane J. Doe.
Publisher: Hypothetical Tests, Inc.
Cross References: See T4:3010 (2 references); for reviews by John Roe and Robert Smith of an earlier edition, see 9:1410 (6 references).

Purpose: A brief, clear statement describing the purpose of the test; often these are quotations from the test manual.

Publication Date: The inclusive range of publication dates.

Acronym: Acronym by which the test may be commonly known.

Scores: The number and names of explicit scores are presented.

Forms: All available forms, parts, and levels are listed.

Price Data: Price information is reported for test packages, answer sheets, accessories, and specimen sets.

Time: This is the amount of time to take, and administer, the test. The first number is the actual working time examinees are allowed, and the second (parenthesized) number is the total time needed to administer the test.

Comments: Special notations and comments.

Publisher: The publisher's full address can be found in the Publishers Directory and Index.

Source: Buros Center for Testing, University of Nebraska–Lincoln (buros.org).

FIGURE 1.4 ■ How to Use Tests in Print

BUROS CENTER FOR TESTING

How to Use ***Tests in Print***

Tests in Print (TIP) *consists of descriptive listings, without reviews, of commercially published tests in print.* TIP *is also a comprehensive index to the contents of previously published* Mental Measurements Yearbooks.

1. If you know the TEST TITLE:

Use the "**Index of Titles**." The index lists all tests in that volume plus all tests out of print since last being listed. "2458," for example, refers to test 2458 in that volume; "9:1128" refers to now out-of-print test 1128 in the *Ninth Mental Measurements Yearbook*. *Citation numbers refer to entry numbers, not to page numbers.*

Example from "Index of Titles":

Short Tests of Clerical Ability, 2458
Shortened Edinburgh Reading Test, 2459
Shortened Aptitude Test, T4:2195
Signals Learning Test, 2461
Silver Burdett Music Competency Tests, 9:1128
Silver Drawing Test of Cognitive Skills and Adjustment, 2462
Simile Interpretations, T4:2198
Similes, T4:2199

2. If you know the TYPE OF TEST:

Use the "**Classified Subject Index**" to locate various categories of tests, such as achievement, intelligence, personality, etc. This index organizes all tests into 18 major categories; tests appear alphabetically within each category. *Citation numbers refer to entry numbers, not to page numbers.*

Example from "Classified Subject Index, Education":

Gifted Program Evaluation Survey, Gifted and talented programs, see 1040
Graduate Records Examinations Education Test, Graduate School candidates, see 1063
High School Characteristics Index, Grades 9-13, 4-13, see 1157
How a Child Learns, Classroom teachers, see 1175
Hudson Educational Skills Inventory, Grades K-12, see 1184

3. If you know the NAME OF THE TEST AUTHOR OR REVIEWER:

Use the "**Index of Names**." This index includes test authors (for example, "test, 1460"), review authors ("rev, 2589"), and authors of referenced articles ("ref, 2222"). (Parenthesized numbers indicate the reference number.) *Citation numbers refer to entry numbers, not to page numbers.*

Example from "Index of Names":

Caeglio, G.: test, 1460
Caffey, C. A.: ref, 2222(1)
Caggiula, A. A.: ref, 2563(449)
Cahalane, J.: ref, 268(395), 1043(39)
Cahen, L. S.: rev, 2589
Cahill, C.: ref, 1705(65), 2937(935)
Cahir, N.: ref, 1135(14), 2674(188)
Cahn, T. S.: ref, 268(90)
Cain, J.: ref, 93(84), 1690(84)
Cain, L. F.: test, 2844

Source: Buros Center for Testing, University of Nebraska–Lincoln (buros.org).

ON THE WEB BOX 1.2
LOCATING INFORMATION ABOUT TESTS ON THE WEB

Computer technology lets us connect to the Internet and locate websites containing valuable information about psychological tests. These websites include information such as the following:

- Frequently asked questions about psychological testing

- How to find a particular type of psychological test

- How to locate reviews of psychological tests

- How to select an appropriate test

- What qualifications are necessary to purchase psychological tests

- How to contact test publishers

- How to obtain copies of specific psychological tests

Although there are many available websites, here are four that we have found to be extremely valuable:

Website	Description
American Psychological Association www.apa.org/science/programs/testing/find-tests.aspx#findinfo	Although the APA does not sell or endorse specific testing instruments, it does provide guidance on testing resources and how to find psychological tests. This website contains answers to the most frequently asked questions about psychological testing. One section focuses on questions about published psychological tests (those that can be purchased from a test publisher); here you will find advice on how to find information about a particular test and about the proper use of tests, how to contact test publishers and purchase tests, and available software and scoring services. Another section focuses on unpublished psychological tests and measures (those that are not commercially available); here you will find advice on how to find unpublished tests in your area of interest and important information regarding your responsibilities as a user of unpublished tests.
Buros Center for Testing buros.org	The Buros Center for Testing promotes the appropriate use of tests and provides professional assistance, expertise, and information to those who use commercially published tests. This website contains a number of instructional resources, tools, and links. For example, it contains detailed instructions on what information can be found in two popular Buros publications that we have already discussed: the *Mental Measurements Yearbook* (*MMY*) and *Tests in Print* (*TIP*). This site also contains some great "how-to" resources, such as how to use *TIP* and the *MMY* and how to use the information in these resources to evaluate a test. In addition, it contains a link to Test Reviews Online, a service that provides access to more than 2,000 test reviews, beginning with those that were published in the *Ninth MMY*. Likewise, there are links to the Code of Fair Testing Practices (discussed further in the "What Are the Ethical Responsibilities of Test Publishers, Test Users, and Test Takers?" chapter) and the APA's frequently asked questions website mentioned previously.

(Continued)

(Continued)

Website	Description
Test Collection at ETS www.ets.org/test_link/about	The Test Collection at ETS is the world's largest database of tests and measurement instruments that have been available since the early 1900s. This online database contains descriptions of more than 20,000 tests (published and unpublished) and research instruments, collected from test publishers and test authors from around the world. Each description includes the title of the test or instrument, the author, the publication date, availability (how to obtain the test or measurement), the intended population, and specific uses of the test or instrument. In addition to providing information about specific tests, this database contains valuable information on how to order tests.
O*NET Resource Center www.onetcenter.org/guides.html	O*NET is sponsored by the U.S. Department of Labor and is a primary source for occupational information. Consisting of a comprehensive database of worker attributes and job characteristics, O*NET also provides valuable resources on testing and assessment—resources intended to support public and private sector efforts to identify and develop the skills of the American workforce. This website provides access to three extremely valuable testing and assessment guides: • *Testing and Assessment: A Guide to Good Practices for Workforce Investment Professionals* includes information on how assessment instruments can be used to promote talent development in career counseling, training, and other talent development activities. It discusses how to evaluate and select assessment instruments, administer and score assessments to meet business and individual client needs, and accurately and effectively interpret assessment results. It also lists the professional and legal standards related to assessment use in talent development. • *Tests and Other Assessments: Helping You Make Better Career Decisions* includes an explanation of how assessment instruments are used in employment selection and career counseling and provides tips and strategies for taking tests and other assessments. • *Testing and Assessment: An Employer's Guide to Good Practices* helps managers and workforce development professionals understand and use employment testing and assessment practices to meet their organizations' human resources goals.

FOR YOUR INFORMATION BOX 1.4
LOCATING UNPUBLISHED PSYCHOLOGICAL TESTS

Although there are thousands of commercially available tests, there are just as many, if not more, unpublished tests designed and used by researchers. A number of print and nonprint resources are available for locating information on unpublished tests.

Two of the most popular print resources are the *Directory of Unpublished Experimental Mental Measures* (Goldman & Mitchell, 2007) and *Measures for Psychological Assessment: A Guide to 3,000 Original Sources and Their Applications* (Chun, Cobb, & French, 1975).

Three of the most popular nonprint resources for locating information about unpublished or noncommercial tests are Tests in Microfiche, the PsycINFO database, and the Health and Psychosocial Instruments (HaPI) database.

PsycTESTS

This subscription-based database contains thousands of psychological measures, scales, surveys, and other instruments that were originally developed, but are not available commercially. The psychometric properties are reported for many of the instruments, and the instruments are updated monthly. All of the research instruments are available for download.

Directory of Unpublished Experimental Mental Measures

This directory provides easy access to more than 5,000 experimental mental measures, tests, and surveys that have been used by other researchers but are not commercially available. Topics range from educational adjustment and motivation to personality and perception. The measures, tests, and surveys are arranged in a 24-category system and grouped according to function and content, noting purpose, format, psychometric information (where available), and related research. First published in 1974 and currently in its ninth edition, this resource is updated periodically by the publisher.

Measures for Psychological Assessment: A Guide to 3,000 Original Sources and Their Applications

This guide includes annotated references to psychological measures that have appeared in journal articles and other publications. Although a bit outdated, it can be a useful resource. It has two sections: primary references and applications. The primary references section includes the name of each measure, the reference in which the measure originally appeared, and one or more other researchers who have used the measure in experimental research. The applications section includes other research studies that have used the original measures and references other experimental tests.

Tests in Microfiche

This resource can be accessed through the Test Collection at ETS. It contains a variety of educational and psychological instruments that are cited in the literature but are either out of date or unpublished. It contains more than 800 tests, and new tests are added each year. For more information, go to www.ets.org/test_link/about or check with your college's library.

PsycINFO Database

This bibliographic database indexes published studies in psychology. By using the Form/Content field "Tests & Measures" to search the PsycINFO database, you can find tests that have been used in research and written about in the literature. For more information, go to www.apa.org/pubs/databases/psycinfo/index.aspx.

HaPI Database

This computerized database includes citations to unpublished health and psychosocial evaluation and measurement tools (e.g., questionnaires, interviews, tests, checklists, rating scales) that have appeared in journals and technical reports since 1985. HaPI is updated quarterly and contains more than 15,000 measurement instruments. HaPI is provided online by Ovid Technologies, which typically must be accessed through BRS Information Technologies at your college's library. Some libraries maintain the database on CD-ROM. For more information, see www.ovid.com/site/catalog/DataBase/866.jsp.

Chapter Summary

By now, we hope you understand that psychological testing extends well beyond the use of intelligence and personality tests. Any measurement tool or technique that requires a person to perform one or more behaviors to make inferences about human attributes, traits, or characteristics or predict future outcomes can be considered a psychological test. The quizzes and exams you take in class are psychological tests. The written and road portions of driving exams are psychological tests. Even the structured job interviews you have participated

(Continued)

(Continued)

in, or will participate in as you conduct your job search, qualify as psychological tests.

Psychological tests have various similarities and many differences. All psychological tests require an individual to perform one or more behaviors, and these behaviors are used to measure some personal attribute, trait, or characteristic thought to be important in describing or understanding behavior or to predict an outcome. However, psychological tests can and do differ in terms of the behaviors they require individuals to perform, the attributes they measure, their content, how they are administered and formatted, how they are scored and interpreted, and their psychometric quality.

Although the use of psychological tests can be traced to ancient China, most scholars agree that the advent of formal psychological testing did not begin until Binet published the first test of intelligence in 1905. Today, psychological testing is a big business, with tens of thousands of commercially available, standardized psychological tests as well as thousands of unpublished tests.

All good tests have three defining characteristics in common. First, they include a representative sample of behaviors. Second, they collect the sample under standardized conditions. Third, they have rules for scoring. When using psychological tests, we must make some assumptions. We must assume that a test measures what it says it measures, that any inferences that are drawn about test takers from their scores on the test are appropriate, that an individual's behavior (and therefore test scores) will remain stable over

time, that individuals understand test items similarly, that individuals can and will report accurately about their thoughts and feelings, and that the test score an individual receives is equal to his or her true behavior or ability in the real world plus some error.

Testing professionals refer to psychological tests in various ways. Sometimes they refer to them as tests of maximal performance, behavior observations, or self-reports. Sometimes they refer to them as standardized or nonstandardized. Other times they refer to them as objective or projective. Professionals also refer to tests based on the dimensions they measure.

It is important to remember the distinctions among four commonly misunderstood terms: *psychological assessment*, *psychological test*, *measurement*, and *survey*. First, although both psychological assessments and psychological tests are used to gather information, a psychological test is only one of many tools in the psychological assessment process. Second, a psychological test can be considered to be a measurement when the sampled behavior can be expressed in a derived score. Third, psychological tests are different from surveys in that psychological tests focus on individual differences and often report one overall derived score (or scaled scores), and surveys focus on group similarities and typically report results at the question or item level.

Last, but not least, a number of resources are available, in print and online, to locate information about published and unpublished psychological tests and measures. The *MMY* and *TIP* are two of the most popular references for learning more about available tests.

Engaging in the Learning Process

Learning is the process of gaining knowledge and skills through schooling or studying. Although you can learn by reading the chapter material, attending class, and engaging in discussion with your instructor, more actively engaging in the learning process may help you better learn and retain chapter information. To help you actively engage in the learning

process, we encourage you to access our new supplementary student workbook. The workbook contains critical thinking activities to help you understand and apply information and help you make progress toward learning and retaining material. If you do not have a copy of the workbook, you can purchase a copy through sagepub.com.

Key Concepts

After completing your study of this chapter, you should be able to define each of the following terms. These terms are bolded in the text of this chapter and defined in the Glossary.

achievement tests	measurement instrument	psychometrics
aptitude tests	nonstandardized tests	self-report tests
behavior	norms	standardization sample
behavior observation tests	objective tests	standardized tests
emotional intelligence	personality tests	surveys
inference	projective tests	tests of maximal performance
intelligence tests	psychological assessments	vocational tests
interest inventories	psychological construct	
measurement	psychological test	

Critical Thinking Questions

The following are some critical thinking questions to support the learning objectives for this chapter.

Learning Objectives	Critical Thinking Questions
Explain why you should care about psychological testing	• What are three specific reasons you should personally care about psychological testing?
Define what a psychological test is, and understand that psychological tests extend beyond personality and intelligence tests.	• Locate and read about two psychological tests that measure the same construct. How would you classify each test and why? How would you describe the similarities and differences between the two tests?
Trace the history of psychological testing from Alfred Binet and intelligence testing to the tests of today.	• What is the value of understanding the history of psychological testing? • What approach could you use to visually explain the history of psychological testing?
Describe the three characteristics that are common to all psychological tests, and understand that psychological tests can demonstrate these characteristics to various degrees.	• Imagine you were making a presentation to other students on the WAIS-IV. What opinion would you share about the degree to which the test meets the three defining characteristics of a good psychological test? • What are the implications of a psychological test not exhibiting all the three defining characteristics of a good psychological test?

(Continued)

(Continued)

Learning Objectives	Critical Thinking Questions
Describe the assumptions that must be made when using psychological tests.	• What might be the implications of using a psychological test without understanding the fundamental assumptions of psychological tests?
Describe the different ways that psychological tests can be classified.	• What are all the different ways you could classify the NEO Personality Inventory? What is the value of classifying tests? • What might some consequences be if a test publisher or user incorrectly classified a psychological test?
Distinguish the differences among four commonly used terms that students often get confused: *psychological assessment*, *psychological test*, *psychological measurement*, and *survey*.	• How are psychological assessments, psychological tests, psychological measurements, and surveys similar and different?
Locate print and online resources to obtain information about psychological tests.	• Which online resource would you find most helpful for locating information about commercially available tests an organization might use as part of a selection process? • What are some of the reasons that knowing about these resources are important to users of psychological tests?

2

WHY IS PSYCHOLOGICAL TESTING IMPORTANT?

"I have a 4.0 grade point average, but I didn't do so well on the Law School Admission Test. I'm going to apply to some top-rated law schools and, to be safe, to some law schools where the test scores aren't as important."

"The college I'll be attending didn't award me the scholarship I wanted. Because all the applicants had similar grade point averages and great letters of recommendation, the scholarship review committee decided to give the scholarship to the applicant who had the highest SAT score."

"I told my academic counselor that I didn't know what I wanted to do with my life. She sent me to the college career services office. A career counselor talked with me for a long time, asking me about my likes and dislikes and my hobbies. She had me take several interest and vocational tests, and she used the test scores to help me find major that aligned with my interests."

You have probably had to make some important decisions in your life, such as where to apply to college and what college major to pursue. Likewise, others have probably made important decisions about you. For example, a college admissions dean may have decided to admit you, a scholarship committee may have decided not to offer you a scholarship, an organizational manager may have decided to hire you, or a school psychologist may have decided to place you in a gifted program. There is a good chance you or others used your score on one or more psychological tests to make many of these decisions.

In this chapter, we discuss why psychological testing is important. We look at who uses psychological tests and for what reasons. We also discuss some of the concerns society has about the use of psychological tests.

TYPES OF DECISIONS MADE USING PSYCHOLOGICAL TEST RESULTS

As you learned in the prior chapter, psychological testing is important because people use test results to make important decisions such as the decisions just mentioned. These decisions affect every one of us. Consider some of the decisions we (the textbook authors) have made in our roles as college faculty, industrial and organizational psychology practitioners, and organizational leaders using test scores:

- What grade to award a student
- Whether to hire a job candidate
- Whether an employee will receive a merit increase (and if so, how much)
- What coaching advice to offer a business leader

Likewise, consider some of the decisions others have made about us or our families based on psychological test scores:

- Whether to admit us or our children to specific colleges
- Whether to invite our children to participate in elementary school gifted programs
- What grades to award our children
- Whether our children will receive college scholarships
- Whether to certify us a Society for Human Resource Management (SHRM) certified professional

We and others make many types of decisions using the results of psychological tests. These decisions are often classified as individual versus institutional and comparative versus absolute.

Individual and Institutional Decisions

Both individuals and institutions use the results of psychological tests to make decisions. If test takers use their test scores to make decisions about themselves, these are referred to as **individual decisions**. For example, you may take the Law School Admission Test (LSAT), a half-day standardized test required for admission to most law schools. Because you know that some law schools are more competitive than others, the score you receive on this test might influence the law schools to which you apply. If you do very well on the test, you may apply to more competitive law schools. Or perhaps you are having a difficult time deciding what career you would like to pursue. You might seek assistance from a career counselor to explore and discuss various career options. As part of the process, the career counselor may ask you to complete an interest inventory. Based on the results of this inventory (as well as other information), you may decide to pursue a career in, for example, teaching or computer science. In this case, you (the individual who took the test) used the test results to make a decision about your career.

Institutional decisions, on the other hand, are those made by another entity (e.g., a human resource manager, a clinical psychologist, a teacher) about an individual based on his or her test results. For example, let us say that because you did well on your LSAT, you have decided to apply to a highly competitive law school (which is an individual decision). Administrators at the law school to which you apply may use your LSAT score, among other things, to help them make a decision about whether you will be offered admission to their law school. Likewise, let us say that an acquaintance of yours is attending counseling sessions with a mental health professional. As part of these counseling sessions, the mental health professional may administer a number of psychological tests and use the results to develop a treatment program for your acquaintance. In each of these cases, someone else—usually representing an institution—has used the results of a psychological test to make a decision about another individual.

Comparative and Absolute Decisions

When institutions use test scores to make decisions about those who took a test, they do so using either a comparative method or an absolute method. **Comparative decisions** are made by comparing the test scores of a number of people to see who has the best score. For example, imagine you applied to and were accepted into the law school of your choice. Now imagine that the law school is going to offer an academic scholarship to only one individual who was offered admission. Based on interviews and letters of recommendation, you advance as one of four finalists for the scholarship. Who will get the scholarship now depends on LSAT scores. Because you scored higher than the other three finalists, you receive the scholarship. This decision is a comparative decision because all of the finalists' LSAT scores were compared, and the individual with the highest score was selected. Or perhaps you applied for a job at an organization where psychological tests were used as part of the selection process. If after you took these tests, the organization decided to continue to consider your application because you scored better than 75% of the other applicants, the organization would be using the test results to make decisions using a comparative method.

Absolute decisions, on the other hand, are decisions made by others (institutions) by looking at who has the minimum score needed to qualify. For example, let us consider the same scholarship example, with you advancing as one of four finalists for the scholarship. However, this time the school offers the scholarship to any finalist who has a score of at least 160 (where the minimum score is 120 and the maximum score is 180). Or suppose the organization to which you applied for a job called and informed you that the managers would like you to come in for an interview because you scored at least 50 on one of the tests that were administered. In each of these cases, the institution made a decision about you not by comparing your score with the scores of other test takers but rather by basing its decision on some minimum score. This minimum score is also sometimes called a cut score. We will have much more to say about cut scores in the chapter, "How Do We Assess the Psychometric Quality of a Test?"

WHICH PROFESSIONALS USE PSYCHOLOGICAL TESTS AND FOR WHAT REASONS?

A variety of professionals use psychological tests for many different purposes in a number of different settings. Psychiatrists, psychologists, social workers, mental health counselors, career counselors, human resources directors, administrators, and many other professionals all use psychological tests. As you can see in Table 2.1, professionals use psychological tests in three primary settings: educational, clinical, and organizational. While we have devoted Section IV of this text ("Using Tests in Different Settings") to an in-depth discussion of how tests are used in these settings, here we provide an overview to help you understand the widespread use of tests.

TABLE 2.1 ■ Who Uses Psychological Tests and for What Purposes

Educational Settings		
Who	**Where**	**Why**
Administrators	Primary schools	To select students into schools
Teachers	Secondary schools	To award scholarships
School psychologists	Colleges and universities	To place students in programs
Career counselors		To measure student learning
		To identify problems
		To identify career interests

Clinical Settings		
Who	**Where**	**Why**
Clinical psychologists	Mental health clinics	To diagnose disorders
Psychiatrists	Residential programs	To plan treatment programs
Social workers	Private practices	To assess treatment outcomes
Counseling psychologists		To counsel and advise
Licensed professional counselors		
Marriage and family counselors		

Organizational Settings		
Who	**Where**	**Why**
Human resources professionals	Organizations	To make hiring decisions
Industrial/organizational practitioners	Consulting companies	To determine training needs
	Consulting practices	To evaluate employee performance

Educational Settings

Administrators, teachers, school psychologists, and career counselors in primary schools (elementary school), secondary schools (middle school and high school), and colleges and universities all use psychological tests. For example, in colleges and universities, administrators (e.g., admissions officers, deans of admissions) use the results of tests such as the SAT to help make admissions decisions and award scholarships. Originally developed in 1926 by Carl Campbell Brigham for the College Examination Board, today the SAT is the most widely used standardized college admission test. Used by most U.S. colleges and universities and taken by over 2 million students in 2017, the SAT measures student reasoning in three areas (critical reading, math, and writing) based on knowledge and skills gained during educational coursework and believed critical for academic success in college (College Board, 2018).

More detail about the SAT can be found in **Test Spotlight 2.1** in Appendix A.

In primary and secondary schools, teachers administer tests to measure student learning and assign course grades. The same is true for faculty at colleges and universities. In primary and secondary schools, school psychologists use the results of tests to determine eligibility for gifted programs and to identify developmental, visual, and auditory problems for which children might need special assistance. In colleges and universities, career counselors use the results of tests to help students identify career interests and select major areas of concentration and careers that are consistent with students' skills and interests. These are only some of the ways in which professionals use tests in educational settings. A more detailed discussion of how tests are used in educational settings is in Section IV of this text.

Clinical Settings

Various clinicians and consultants administer psychological tests in clinical and counseling settings. Psychotherapists and others responsible for providing treatment to clients administer tests. Psychologists who serve as consultants to psychotherapists, physicians (and other medical providers), attorneys, school personnel, and hospital treatment teams administer tests. Mental health professionals, including psychologists, counselors, social workers, psychiatrists, and psychiatric nurses, administer tests to assist in diagnosis and treatment planning. A more detailed discussion of how tests are used in clinical and counseling settings is in Section IV of this text.

Psychological tests are invaluable in clinical and counseling settings before, during, and after treatment. At the beginning of treatment, tests are used to assess the kinds of problems a client is struggling with and to assess the severity of a problem. Tests are used during treatment, to monitor progress, and at the end of treatment, to assess treatment outcomes. Tests are also used to clarify diagnoses and to assess obstacles to progress when treatment is not as effective as expected. Finally, psychological tests are an important component of a therapeutic assessment, a form of assessment that provides insight to clients and promotes change.

Organizational Settings

Human resources professionals and industrial and organizational psychology practitioners use psychological tests in organizations. For example, they administer tests to job applicants to measure whether applicants have the knowledge, skills, abilities, and other characteristics (e.g., cognitive ability, personality) necessary to effectively perform a job and/or to predict the likelihood of success on the job. They use the test results, along with other information,

ON THE WEB BOX 2.1
THE LEADERSHIP PRACTICES INVENTORY
www.lpionline.com

Developed by Jim Kouzes and Barry Posner, the Leadership Practices Inventory (LPI) is a 360°, or multirater, leadership assessment tool that measures the extent to which individuals demonstrate the Five Practices of Exemplary Leadership (published by John Wiley & Sons, 2000–2018).

1. Model the way
2. Inspire a shared vision
3. Challenge the process
4. Enable others to act
5. Encourage the heart

In a 360° process, surveys are sent to those people an individual works closely with, including managers, peers, subordinates, and customers. These individuals are asked to provide feedback on the extent to which the individual demonstrates key behaviors.

Because Kouzes and Posner believed that leadership is a measurable, learnable, and teachable set of behaviors, the LPI 360 provides leaders with the opportunity to gather feedback from those they work with on a day-to-day basis on the extent to which they engage in 30 leadership behaviors associated with the Five Practices of Exemplary Leadership. Using a rating scale ranging from 1 (*almost never*) to 10 (*almost always*), peers, direct reports (subordinates), others the individual works with, and the leader's manager rate the extent to which the individual leader demonstrates each of the 30 leadership behaviors. Individuals also rate themselves.

Available for electronic implementation through a web-based application, LPI Online offers easy-to-use administrator and leader websites as well as a just-in-time, streamlined, and easy-to-interpret personalized report. This report presents 360° results in a number of ways, including the following:

- Five practices data summary, with self, manager, and individual observer ratings (coworkers, direct reports, others in the workplace), and overall average scores for each of the five practices in table and bar chart format

- Ranking of all leadership behaviors from most frequently demonstrated to least frequently demonstrated

- For each practice, how the self, manager, direct report, coworkers, and others rated the individual on each of the six leadership behaviors—both numerically and graphically

- A comparison of how self-scores, manager scores, direct report scores, and coworker scores compare with the scores of thousands of individuals who have taken the same version of the LPI

- All responses to any open-ended questions that were included in the survey

If you want to learn more about the LPI, go to www.lpionline.com/demo/demo.html and view the online demonstration.

to make hiring decisions. Even the National Football League (NFL) uses psychological tests to make player selection decisions (see In the News Box 2.1 for more information). Human resources professionals and industrial and organizational psychology practitioners use psychological tests to identify employees' strengths and opportunities for development and ultimately to determine employees' training and development needs (for an example of such a test, the Leadership Practices Inventory, see On the Web Box 2.1). These professionals also use tests to measure employee performance and determine employee performance ratings. A more detailed discussion of how tests are used in organizational settings is in Section IV of this text.

IN THE NEWS BOX 2.1
THE NFL AND THE WONDERLIC

American football is a physically demanding game requiring players to coordinate closely to carry out strategies they have learned and practiced on the field. According to TV analyst Mike Fisher (2014) of Fox Sports, NFL executives who select players for professional football teams hold in high regard one psychological test, the Wonderlic Personnel Test. For three decades, executives have found the Wonderlic to be an important selection tool for the NFL—as important as an NFL player's bench press and hand width. Using the Wonderlic, whose 50 questions take just over 10 minutes to answer, football executives can measure potential NFL players' cognitive ability. Fisher shared a previous conversation with a former NFL executive who revealed that "serious red flags" go up if a potential NFL player scores "below 10 or 12" on the Wonderlic.

How do players typically score? Although the average score is about 20, scores vary significantly, with some NFL players scoring in the teens and others earning almost perfect scores. For example, Terry Bradshaw and Dan Marino, popular NFL quarterbacks, scored 15 on the Wonderlic. However, Ryan Fitzpatrick, who signed with the Buffalo Bills in 2009, scored 48 on the Wonderlic, which is equal to an intelligence quotient of about 150. And Pat McInally, a Harvard graduate and former Cincinnati Bengals wide receiver and punter, scored the NFL's only perfect score of 50.

Use of the test is controversial. Gil Brandt, former vice president of player personnel for the Dallas Cowboys, had a bias against players who scored exceptionally well on the Wonderlic. "When you have a player who is really extraordinarily smart, he's probably not as aggressive as a player with a lesser intelligence quotient," Brandt said. "I'm not sure that's correct—but I think it is" (as cited in Shipley, 2011, p. D03).

Lyons, Hoffman, and Michel (2009) investigated this question and published their study of 762 players from three NFL draft classes. They found no correlation between intelligence, as measured by the Wonderlic, and performance on the field. There was, however, a negative correlation between football performance and Wonderlic score for tight ends and defensive players. Yes, you understood correctly—the lower their scores on the Wonderlic, the better performance they achieved on the field! Even at the quarterback position, many think cognitive abilities are needed, there was no significant relationship between high scores and high performance.

Source: Shipley, A. (2011, October 26). Smart guy. *The Washington Post*. Met 2 Edition, D03.

PSYCHOLOGICAL TESTING CONTROVERSIES

As we discussed in Chapter 1, psychological testing today is a big business and a part of the American culture. Thousands of psychological tests are available. Many individuals take tests and many professionals use others' test scores to make important and informed decisions. These decisions, of course, are meant to benefit people. The widespread use of tests suggests that, in general, psychological tests do serve their purpose. Nonetheless, psychological testing has always been, and probably always will be, controversial. Although some of this controversy stems from the general public's misunderstandings about the nature and use of psychological tests and can be easily eliminated through education, some of the controversy is deeply rooted in ongoing debates and occurs among professionals themselves.

One of the largest and most deeply rooted controversies pertains to discrimination. For years, some test professionals, educational organizations, and civil rights groups have expressed repeated concern that psychological tests unfairly discriminate against certain racial and economic groups, resulting in qualified members of these groups being passed over for admission to educational programs or not being hired at the same rate as members of other groups. The American public really began to express its concern that psychological tests were discriminatory when psychological testing became widespread during the 20th century. Much of this concern was, and continues to be, targeted at standardized tests of intelligence, aptitude, and achievement. As shared by Lemann (1999) in his book *The Big Test*,

> In the 1940s standardized educational tests created a ranking of Americans, one by one from top to bottom on a single measure. If one analyzed the ranking by social or ethnic group, then at the bottom, always, were Negroes. Living mostly in the benighted, educationally inferior South, consigned to separate schools that operated only sporadically with ill-trained teachers, historically denied by law even the chance to learn to read and write and figure, disproportionately poor, ill-nourished, and broken-familied, Negroes as a group were in a uniquely bad position to perform well on tests designed to measure such school-bred skills as reading and vocabulary and mathematics fluency. So whenever goods were distributed on the basis of test scores, Negroes got a disproportionately low share of them. (pp. 155–156)

Today, the discrimination controversy continues. One very visible case started in 2003, when the city of New Haven, Connecticut, administered a promotional examination for firefighters aspiring to achieve the ranks of lieutenant and captain. When the tests were scored, the city made the decision to scrap the results for fear that the city would be sued for discrimination if they used the results because no African Americans and only 2 Hispanics had scores high enough to be eligible for promotion. Subsequently, 1 Hispanic and 19 White firefighters sued the city, claiming they were discriminated against when they were denied promotions as a result of the city's refusal to use the test results. The firefighters claimed city officials denied them promotions because of the fear of potential Civil Rights Act violations rather than how they performed on the promotional exams (Associated Press, 2009). The case was elevated to the Supreme Court in June 2009. We talk in detail about this case and the Supreme Court ruling in the "How Are Tests Used in Organizational Settings?" chapter.

The Controversy Over Intelligence Tests

Intelligence Testing in Education

Researchers have documented that middle- and upper-class White people, on average, score higher on intelligence tests than do members of other economic and racial groups (Lemann, 1999). Early in the 20th century, believing that this difference in intelligence was due to heredity, elementary schools began administering intelligence tests to students and using the results to place those with higher intelligence quotient (IQ) scores in special academic programs and those with lower scores in more vocationally related programs (Hunt, 1993). Individuals who believed that intelligence was inherited had no problem with using psychological tests in this manner. They believed that people who do better on such tests naturally have superior intellects. In their view, if intelligence is indeed inherited, using psychological tests in this manner is fair and in the best interest of individuals and society.

However, what if intelligence is not inherited but rather is the result of the environment in which one is raised? If this were the case, all people would be born with the same potential, but only those who grew up in favorable backgrounds would, in general, score higher on intelligence and academic ability tests. Those who had disadvantaged backgrounds would score lower. In this case, using intelligence test scores, which are thought to reflect innate abilities, to determine an individual's educational opportunities would be unfair. Hence, we are sure you can understand the debate and the public's concern over the use of intelligence tests.

Over the years, activists who believe that intelligence is determined primarily by environment have worked to eliminate what they consider to be the unfair use of such tests. During the 1960s, in the heat of the civil rights movement, activist groups demanded that schools abandon the use of intelligence tests. New York, Los Angeles, and Washington, D.C., did just that (Hunt, 1993). For Your Information Box 2.1 includes discussion of a court case in which, for exactly this reason, schools in California were ordered not to use intelligence tests for student placement. However, continued efforts to eliminate intelligence testing failed when it became apparent that the placement of children with learning or physical disabilities in the same classrooms as average and gifted children slowed learning (Hunt, 1993).

Intelligence Testing in the Army

In an effort to improve the credibility of psychological testing and establish psychology as a true scientific movement, during World War I, Robert Yerkes came across an opportunity to promote the use of mental testing. The American military gave Yerkes permission to administer mental tests to more than 1.75 million U.S. Army recruits. As a result, believing that individuals might be intelligent but not literate or proficient in English, Yerkes (1921) designed the Army Alpha and Beta tests, the first mental tests designed for group testing. The Army Alpha test was developed for use with literate groups, and the Army Beta test for use with those who were unable to read, write, or speak English. Yerkes argued that both tests measured native intellectual abilities—abilities unaffected by culture or educational opportunities. By the end of the war, the Army Alpha and Beta tests were being used to screen Army recruits for officer training.

During the 1920s, Walter Lippmann, a popular newspaper columnist, criticized the Army Alpha and Beta tests as having a great potential for abusing the psychological testing process—a process that could be of great benefit to the Army (Lippmann, 1922a, 1922b, 1922c, 1922d, 1922e). Like others, Lippmann questioned whether intelligence tests such as the Army Alpha and Beta tests actually measured intelligence and whether intelligence was determined by heredity (or innate) or through life experiences (or learned). The heredity or experience question is what we refer to as the **nature-versus-nurture controversy**. Seventeenth-century philosophers such as René Descartes may have supported that intelligence occurs naturally and is influenced little by the environment. On the other hand, philosophers such as John Locke likely would have supported that we are born with a "blank slate," or tabula rasa, and our environment shapes our intelligence.

Data collected using Army recruits suggested that average intelligence scores of African American men were much lower than average scores of White men. In addition, when scores of foreign-born recruits were sorted by their countries of origin, those from Turkey, Greece, Russia, Italy, and Poland produced large numbers of scores that indicated a mental age of younger than 11 years, which for an adult was an indication of low intelligence (Yerkes, 1921). Political groups that opposed the immigration of large numbers of families from Europe following World War I used these data to support their arguments that immigration was harmful to the United States.

Later in the 20th century, Gould (1982) also criticized such mass intelligence testing, claiming that the intelligence tests were culturally biased. For immigrants, the language and customs of the United States were unfamiliar, and what appeared to be stupidity was just lack

FOR YOUR INFORMATION BOX 2.1
CAN IQ TESTS BE ILLEGAL?

Unless you live in California, you are probably not aware of the controversy surrounding the use of IQ scores as a method for placing children in educable mentally retarded (EMR) classes. In 1979, in the case of *Larry P. v. Riles*, testimony suggested that IQ tests are biased against African American children. The plaintiff, the party bringing the suit, showed that six African American children who scored low on one intelligence test scored much higher on the same test when it was revised to reflect the African American children's cultural background. The African American children's first scores placed them in the range labeled "retarded"; however, the scores from the revised test labeled them as "normal." In addition, evidence was given that a higher proportion of African American children, compared with the rest of the student body, were in EMR classes. This information caused the judge to rule that schools in California may not use IQ test scores to place African American children in EMR classes or their "substantial equivalent."

California abolished EMR classes, and in 1986, the same judge modified his ruling, this time banning the use of IQ tests to evaluate African American children referred for any special assessment. This ruling did not please all parents. For instance, Wendy Strong, the mother of a 7-year-old, tried to get help for her daughter, Brianna, who had problems learning. Because her race was shown as African American on school records, school psychologists were not able to administer an IQ test to Brianna. Brianna's mother threatened to have her daughter's racial category changed so that she could be tested. Such a change was possible because Brianna had one African American parent and one White parent.

Eventually, another suit was brought by African American parents who wished to have their children tested. In 1994, the appeals court ruled that parents such as the Strongs were not adequately represented in the 1986 proceedings. Therefore, the court canceled the 1986 ruling but upheld the original 1979 ruling.

of cultural knowledge and experience. Consider the following three examples from the Army Alpha test (Gould, 1982, para. 21):

1. Crisco is a
   a. patent medicine.
   b. disinfectant.
   c. toothpaste.
   d. food product.

2. *Washington* is to *Adams* as *first* is to _____.

3. Christy Mathewson is famous as a
   a. writer.
   b. artist.
   c. baseball player.
   d. comedian.

How did you do on those questions? Did you know that Crisco is a popular vegetable shortening and butter substitute? Washington was the first president of the United States, and Adams was the second. At the time these questions were used, Christy Mathewson was a well-known baseball player; however, his name is no longer general knowledge.

Critics' concern was that immigrants would not have the cultural knowledge and experience to answer such questions correctly. In addition, the tests themselves and the instructions given when administering them were usually incomprehensible to uninformed test takers. The Army Alpha and Beta tests, for example, required test takers to follow directions and perform a series of ballet movements that were confusing and distracting.

The Army Alpha and Beta tests were discontinued following World War I, but the nature-versus-nurture debate continued. Its connection to psychological tests and intelligence raised public controversy again nearly 50 years later, at a time when the civil rights movement was changing the American experience.

In 1969, Arthur Jensen published an article in the *Harvard Educational Review* that again pointed out a difference in average intelligence scores between Blacks and Whites. Although there have been numerous explanations for these findings, Jensen caused an uproar by implying that this difference in intelligence was due almost exclusively (80%) to genetic factors. This time, Jensen used later and more sophisticated tests than those the Army had used during World War I, but the basic pro-heredity argument was still the same.

The debate that followed Jensen's (1969) article led professionals and the public to question how psychologists and test developers define and measure intelligence. A number of psychologists (e.g., Eells, Davis, Havighurst, Herrick, & Tyler, 1951; Harrington, 1975, 1976) also have pointed out that the intelligence tests administered to Blacks were invalid for measuring their intelligence because the tests had been developed for middle-class White children, whose experiences are different from those of children from other ethnic groups and socioeconomic classes. Furthermore, Hilliard (1984) questioned Jensen's underlying assumptions regarding an operational definition of race.

The same debate arose again in 1994, when Richard Herrnstein and Charles Murray published their book *The Bell Curve: Intelligence and Class Structure in American Life*, which reiterated many of the conclusions that Jensen drew in 1969. Herrnstein and Murray argued that IQ is extremely important, that it is somewhere between 40% and 80% heritable, and that it is related not only to school performance but also to jobs, income, crime, and illegitimacy. Herrnstein and Murray used intelligence research to substantiate their claim that some of the difference in average IQ scores between Whites and Blacks is likely attributable to genetic factors, suggesting that Blacks are genetically inferior in intellectual abilities and capabilities.

In response to the publication of *The Bell Curve*, the American Psychological Association (APA) convened a task force of psychologists representing the prevalent attitudes, values, and practices of the psychology profession. Based on the work of this task force, the APA published the report "Intelligence: Knowns and Unknowns" (Neisser et al., 1996). The report did not disagree with the data presented in *The Bell Curve*; however, it interpreted the data differently and concluded that although no one knows why the difference exists, there is no support for the notion that the 15-point IQ difference between Black and White Americans is due to genetics (Neisser et al., 1996; Yam, 1998). Furthermore, in a review of *The Bell Curve* in *Scientific American*, Leon Kamin (1995) stated "The caliber of the data in *The Bell Curve* is, at many critical points, pathetic. Further, the authors repeatedly fail to distinguish between correlation and causation and thus draw many inappropriate conclusions" (p. 99).

Nisbett et al. (2012) published a review that discussed the most current research findings on intelligence. Although the review observed that Neisser et al.'s (1996) article remains a good summary of the state of our knowledge in intelligence, there have been some important new findings since then. Improvements in brain imaging techniques have enabled us to learn much more about the relationship between brain physiology and intelligence. We also now know much more about the roles of both heredity and environment in intelligence. In spite of these advances, there is still much we do not know about the nature of intelligence and its correlates.

For an interesting news story about IQ scores and the Flynn effect, see In the News Box 2.2.

The Controversy Over Aptitude and Integrity Tests

As with intelligence tests, the American public has expressed concern over the use of aptitude and integrity tests.

Aptitude Tests and the U.S. Employment Service

During the 1940s, before the Equal Employment Opportunity Act became law, the U.S. Employment Service (USES) developed the General Aptitude Test Battery (GATB) to assist with career counseling and job referral. An occupationally oriented, multiaptitude test, the GATB consists of 12 tests measuring nine cognitive and manual aptitudes: general learning ability, verbal aptitude, numerical aptitude, spatial aptitude, form perception, clerical perception, motor coordination, finger dexterity, and manual dexterity.

As with intelligence tests, research showed that average GATB scores of minority groups were well below those of the other groups. Because the USES and many of its state and local offices used GATB scores to make referrals to employers, more Whites were being referred for particular jobs than were African Americans or Hispanics (Hunt, 1993). The amended Civil Rights Act of 1991 made it illegal to use GATB scores in this way because national policy required giving the disadvantaged compensatory advantages (Wigdor, 1990). Rulings by the Equal Employment Opportunity Commission and several court decisions resulted in a solution called **within-group norming** or "race norming"—the practice of administering the same test to every test taker but scoring the test differently according to the race of the test taker. Using within-group norming, test users would not be able to refer test takers for jobs using their raw test scores—the scores calculated according to the test instructions—or based on how their scores compared with those of others in the overall norm group. Instead, the test users were required to compare each test taker's score with the scores of other test takers only within the same racial or ethnic group. (We talk more about norms in the chapter "How Do Test Users Interpret Test Scores?") Using race norming, a minority test taker who scored the same as a White test taker would in fact rank higher than the White test taker. Employment services in 38 states used this race norming.

Many psychologists were outraged about the use of race norming. They claimed that it was a disgrace to the psychological testing industry, a distortion of a test's measure of job fitness (L. S. Gottfredson, 1991), and an illegal quota system that unfairly discriminated against Whites. Nonetheless, in 1989 the National Research Council conducted a study that supported the use of race norming. However, the council recommended that referrals by employment services be based not only on an applicant's GATB score but also on the applicant's experience, skills, and education. Several years later, race norming was outlawed, but not because it was unfair. In a struggle to pass the Civil Rights Act of 1991, members of Congress who favored race norming needed to yield to those who did not. As passed, Section 106 of the Civil Rights Act of 1991 prohibited discriminatory use of test scores, keeping employers from adjusting scores on the basis of race, color, religion, sex, or national origin when the sole purpose was to refer or select people for jobs. Use of the GATB in the United States declined considerably not only because it became evident that parts of the GATB discriminated against minorities but also because the test has not been updated since the 1980s, and there are other more suitable tests (National Center for O*NET Development, 2014). However, Canadians continue to use the GATB as a pre-employment test and for vocational counseling and rehabilitation.

The U.S. Armed Forces now uses a similar instrument, the Armed Services Vocational Aptitude Battery (ASVAB), a series of tests used primarily by the military to help determine

IN THE NEWS BOX 2.2
THE FLYNN EFFECT

You may have read or heard of the book, *The Better Angels of Our Nature: Why Violence Has Declined*, written by a well-known psychologist, Steven Pinker (2011). In 800 pages, Pinker presents evidence that the inhabitants of our world are not as violent as they once were. He discusses many types of sociological data (e.g., calculations of soldiers killed in wars 2,000 years ago compared with today) to make his case. We do not have space to discuss all his arguments here; however, we would like to discuss a little-known testing phenomenon called the *Flynn effect* that Pinker uses to make his point.

The Flynn effect refers to James Flynn's 1984 published discovery that over time, IQ scores become greater. Flynn's original study compared the same group of participants who had taken either the Wechsler or Stanford–Binet IQ test two or more times over the course of many years. He examined the data from 73 studies containing 7,500 participants, ages 2 to 48 years, and concluded that between 1932 and 1978, White Americans had gained 14 IQ points.

Flynn's research indicates that each new generation scores significantly higher on IQ tests, and the effect is observed all over the world. According to Flynn (2013), if we scored individual's IQ tests from 10 years ago using IQ testing norms of today, our ancestors would have scored an average IQ of about 70—a score nearing mental retardation. If we scored individuals' IQ tests today using IQ testing norms a decade ago, we would have an average IQ of about 130—a score indicating giftedness. The Flynn effect holds true for people of various cultural and racial backgrounds and for IQ tests written in various languages. Various explanations exist for why intelligence scores all over the world continue to increase. Rather than believing that our ancestors were on the verge of mental retardation, or that we are on the verge of becoming gifted, Flynn hypothesizes that the difference in scores is a result of changes in the way members of each new generation think, or our mental artillery. According to Flynn (2013),

> We've gone from people who confronted a concrete world and analyzed that world primarily in terms of how much it would benefit them to people who confront a very complex world, and it's a world where we've had to develop new mental habits—new habits of mind—and these include things like clothing that concrete world with classification, introducing abstractions that we try to make logically consistent, and also taking the hypothetical seriously—that is wondering about what might have been rather than what is.

Now we can return to Pinker and his optimistic forecasts for our world. Pinker (2011) argues that enhanced powers of reasoning—suggested by research on the Flynn effect—enable us to detach ourselves from our immediate experience or perspective and frame our ideas in more abstract, universal terms. This detachment leads to a more overall view of others' interests as well as our own. Finally, this universal view leads to better moral commitments, including nonviolence. Pinker suggests that the 20th century has seen, and the 21st century will see, a "moral Flynn effect" in which an acceleration of reasoning ability moves the world away from violence, persecution, and exploitation.

Source: Singer, P. (2011, October 9). Kinder and gentler. *New York Times Book Review.* BR 1–3.

whether individuals qualify for service in certain military branches and, if so, what jobs they qualify for (Military Advantage, 2014). For more information on the ASVAB, read On the Web Box 2.2.

In 1964, the U.S. Congress passed the Civil Rights Act. Intended to bring about equality in hiring, transfers, promotions, compensation, access to training, and employment-related decisions, Title VII of the act made it unlawful to discriminate or segregate based on race,

ON THE WEB BOX 2.2
THE ARMED SERVICES VOCATIONAL APTITUDE BATTERY (ASVAB)
www.military.com/join-armed-forces/asvab

The U.S. Department of Defense developed and maintains the ASVAB, which is an aptitude test administered at over 14,000 schools and military processing stations across the United States. A person's ASVAB scores are used to determine qualification for certain military occupations and are also used to determine enlistment bonuses. Individuals seriously interested in joining the military often take the ASVAB practice tests to determine strengths and areas of improvement to better prepare for the ASVAB test.

To learn more about the ASVAB, take available practice tests, and receive some tips and strategies, go to www.military.com/join-armed-forces/asvab. To find out more about minimum scores for specific military jobs in the Air Force, Army, Marine Corps, and Navy, go to https://www.military.com/join-armed-forces/asvab/asvab-scores-and-military-jobs.html

color, national origin, or gender in all terms and conditions of employment. Issued as an interpretation of Title VII in 1978, the *Uniform Guidelines on Employee Selection Procedures* (1978) recommended that employers analyze their hiring and promotion processes to determine whether their selection procedures (including the use of tests) were discriminatory. If the selection rate for any race, sex, or ethnic group was less than four fifths (or 80%) of the selection rate for the group with the highest selection ratio (i.e., the proportion of the job qualified job applicants that are selected for employment), the selection process could be considered potentially discriminatory even if there were no discriminatory intent on the part of the employer because it results in adverse impact for the underselected groups. (A more detailed discussion of using psychological tests in compliance with the Civil Rights Act of 1964 is in the "How Are Tests Used in Organizational Settings?" chapter of this text.)

Aptitude Testing in Education

During the 1960s and 1970s, Americans noticed a decline in SAT scores (Turnball, 1985). National averages for the SAT between 1952 and 1963 stayed approximately the same despite the fact that 7% more students took the SAT during those years. However, between 1964 and 1970, national average scores began to decline significantly. Between 1963 and 1975, the College Board reported that college-bound high school students answered approximately 5% fewer SAT questions correctly—a 60- to 90-scale-point decline in aggregate SAT scores. By 1977, both the SAT math and verbal scores had declined (College Entrance Examination Board, 2018).

Many people believed the decline was a result of poor schooling and therefore expressed concern about how much American students were learning in public schools. As a result, the College Board and Educational Testing Service convened a special panel that concluded that a 14-year decline in average scores was due to two factors (Turnball, 1985). First, more students were taking the SAT, and these students not only had weaker academic records but also were coming from more diverse backgrounds. Again, the implication was that the traditional test takers, middle- and upper-class White students, were more likely to make high grades. Second, the type of educational experience students had during the late 1960s and early 1970s had caused a decrease in performance on standardized tests. Among the reasons given for a decline in educational experience were a "diminished seriousness of purpose and attention" and a "marked diminution in young people's learning motivation" (Haney, 1981, p. 1026).

However, Berliner and Biddle (1995) stated,

> So although critics have trumpeted the "alarming" news that aggregate national SAT scores fell during the late 1960's and the early 1970's, this decline indicates nothing about the performance of American schools. Rather, it signals that students from a broader range of backgrounds were then getting interested in college, which should have been cause for celebration, not alarm. (p. 21)

Integrity Testing in Organizations

Yet another concern has been integrity testing. **Integrity tests** measure individual attitudes and experiences toward honesty, dependability, trustworthiness, reliability, and prosocial behavior (Society for Industrial and Organizational Psychology, 2014). Typically, integrity tests require test takers to answer questions about the following:

- Illegal use of drugs or engagement in unacceptable theft or criminal activities

- Opinions about illegal or inappropriate activities

- Personality or beliefs

- Reactions to theoretical and/or hypothetical situations

There are two basic types of integrity tests. One type requires individuals to respond to questions about previous experiences related to ethics and integrity. These tests are overt and include very straightforward questions. The other type requires individuals to respond to questions about their preferences and interests. These tests are more personality based and measure propensity to engage in unacceptable work behaviors. From the preferences and interests, inferences are drawn about how the individual may behave in the future. Both types are used by organizations to identify individuals who are likely to engage in inappropriate, dishonest, and antisocial behavior at work.

Employers have used integrity tests for many years both to screen job applicants and to keep existing employees honest. According to research, their use is justified. For example, in 2009, according to the National White Collar Crime Center, organizations were losing anywhere from $20 billion to $240 billion annually to workplace theft, including intellectual theft (with 30% to 50% of business failures being due to such theft). And the problem doesn't seem to be getting any better. In 2013, survey results indicated that in the retail industry alone, 78,085 employees were caught stealing, which was a 6.5% increase from 2012 (Jack L. Hayes International, Inc., 2014). According to a study the National Retail Federation (NRF) and the University of Florida conducted, the U.S. retail industry lost $44 billion in 2014, with over 70% of the loss due to shoplifting or employee/internal theft (NRF, 2018). Results of a 2017 Hiscox study revealed that U.S. businesses lost an average of $1.13 million, with 68% of losses occurring in smaller organizations with fewer than 500 employees. The must significant loses occurred due to funds theft and check fraud.

Although the use of integrity tests might be justified by alarming figures associated with employee theft, many individuals and labor groups oppose their use because they believe that integrity tests (a) lack evidence of reliability and validity for intended use and therefore falsely classify some honest people as dishonest, (b) are an invasion of privacy, and (c) have a different and more inhibiting effect on minorities, eliminating higher percentages of minorities than Whites from job opportunities (U.S. Congress, Office of Technology Assessment, 1990). In the early 1990s, the APA expressed concern about the reliability and validity of such tests. After 2 years of research, an APA task force concluded that for most integrity tests, publishers have little information regarding whether the tests actually predict honesty (American Psychological Association Task Force on the Prediction of Dishonesty and Theft in Employment Settings, 1991). However, the task force also determined that some integrity tests have useful levels of validity. As a result, the APA urged employers to stop using those integrity tests for which little validity information was available (American Psychological Association Science Directorate, 1991). Instead, the APA suggested that employers rely on only those tests that have substantial evidence of their predictive validity. (A detailed discussion of integrity tests is found in the chapter, "How Are Tests Used in Occupational Settings?" In the chapter "How Do We Gather Evidence of Validity Based on Test–Criterion Relationships?," we discuss predictive validity in more detail).

The Controversy Over High-Stakes Testing in Education

In the 21st century, one of the most significant controversies has been the use of high-stakes testing in education. As shared in the previous chapter, in 2009 the Common Core State Standards were introduced into the U.S. educational system. To address students' lack of academic progress (primarily in math) and the differing academic standards of states, the Common Core made math and English and language arts learning goals consistent across states by introducing a standard set of knowledge and skills students should be able to demonstrate at the end of each grade throughout their K–12 education to ensure they have the knowledge and skills they need to succeed in beginning college courses, in entry-level jobs, and in life after graduating from high school (Common Core State Standards Initiative, 2014; Silva, 2013). Providing consistent learning goals for educators, and created through collaboration by school administrators, teachers, and other experts, the Common Core standards had, by 2010, been voluntarily adopted by educational systems in most states (42 states, including the District of Columbia, 4 territories, and the Department of Defense school system).

Standardized testing has played a critical role in the Common Core standards, as states that have adopted the Common Core standards have used a common and comprehensive set of standardized tests to measure student performance and teacher progress (Common Core State Standards Initiative, 2014). As schools have made changes to meet Common Core standards and the outcomes of standardized tests have been evaluated, controversy has existed and continues over whether the Common Core standards initiative has achieved its promise of alleviating low student achievement.

As with integrity tests, the APA also has advocated its position on the use of high-stakes testing given mandates by many school districts to use standardized tests to assess student performance and provide teachers with feedback. Although not specific to standardized testing associated with the Common Core standards, the APA's position is clear: Tests are an objective means for measuring performance when used properly because test results can help teachers understand how well students are learning critical knowledge, skills, and abilities. Tests can also help teachers themselves understand the effectiveness of their teaching methods and materials (APA, 2017). Both are critical to strengthening schools. According to the APA,

> Measuring what and how well students learn is an important building block in the process of strengthening and improving our nation's schools. Tests, along with student grades and teacher evaluations, can provide critical measures of students' skills, knowledge, and abilities. Therefore, tests should be part of a system in which broad and equitable access to educational opportunity and advancement is provided to all students. Tests, when used properly, are among the most sound and objective ways to measure student performance. But, when test results are used inappropriately or as a single measure of performance, they can have unintended adverse consequences. (para. 1)

So how do school districts know when they are using tests properly? To avoid unintended consequences and to help improve student and school system performance, it is important that tests provide meaningful assessments of student learning—they must be developed and used properly. Meaningful assessment can come from tests that "are sound, are scored properly, and are used appropriately" (APA, 2017, para. 3). According to the APA (2017), officials must ensure three things. First, students must have a fair opportunity to learn the curriculum that they will be tested on. Second, no subgroup of students (e.g., students with disabilities, English language learners, minority students) should be disadvantaged by the test or test-taking conditions. Third, no important decisions should be made based on one test score. Further, school officials must ensure that the tests used have evidence of validity—or provide useful information—for the intended purpose. For example, if a test is designed and has been validated to help measure what a student does and does not know, school districts should not use the test to evaluate a school's educational quality. School districts must understand the specific purpose of the tests they are using and review test publishers' information on the tests' limitations, including how to properly use the test scores.

Overall, the APA supports the use of high-stakes testing in our nation's schools. However, the APA is clear that school districts must take the steps necessary to ensure that test scores are properly used. They must ensure that tests are not the only method for ensuring quality learning. They must ensure that they use tests that do not disadvantage any specific student groups. They must ensure that a focus on passing tests does not inhibit students from mastering knowledge, skills, and abilities taught in an entire curriculum. They must implement remedial programs to help students who do not perform well on the tests. In addition, policy makers should support further research to learn more about the long-term consequences of testing in our nation's schools (e.g., student achievement and learning, graduation rates, student drop-out rates, anxiety).

To promote fairness in testing and to avoid unintended consequences, school districts using tests to make important decisions should be familiar with the newly released Standards for Educational and Psychological Testing (American Educational Research Association, APA, & National Council on Measurement in Education, 2014). The *Standards* include very clear guidelines that individuals involved in test development or use should follow. As they are involved in the use of test scores, according to the *Standards*, school district professionals who select and interpret tests must possess the testing knowledge, skills, and abilities necessary to fulfill their roles. Because school district professionals are increasingly using tests to make important decisions, the *Standards* include additional guidelines for using tests for accountability purposes. In the "What Are the Ethical Responsibilities of Test Publishers, Test Users, and Test Takers?" chapter, we discuss the *Standards* in much more detail.

Chapter Summary

By now, you should understand that psychological testing is important because psychological tests are used to make important decisions. Both individuals and institutions use the results of psychological tests to make decisions. Individual decisions are those made by the person who takes a test, and institutional decisions are made by others who use an individual's performance on a test to make a decision about that individual. Furthermore, institutions make decisions using either a comparative method or an absolute method. Comparative decisions involve comparing an individual's score with other people's scores to see who has the best score. Absolute decisions involve setting a minimum score that test takers must achieve to qualify.

Testing is also important because different professionals, in a variety of clinical, educational, and

(Continued)

(Continued)

organizational settings, use psychological tests for many purposes. In educational settings, administrators, teachers, school psychologists, and career counselors use psychological tests to make a variety of educational decisions, including admissions, grading, and career decisions. In clinical settings, clinical psychologists, psychiatrists, social workers, and other health care professionals use psychological tests to make diagnostic decisions, determine interventions, and assess the outcomes of treatment programs. In organizational settings, human resources professionals and industrial and organizational psychologists use psychological tests to make decisions such as whom to hire for a particular position, what training an individual needs, and what performance rating an individual will receive.

Even given their widespread use, psychological tests are not without their critics. Controversy will likely always exist about the use of psychological tests to make important decisions. Much of the past controversy has focused on intelligence, aptitude, and integrity tests, with one of the most current controversies being the use of high-stakes testing in education. These controversies have influenced social movements, laws, and guidelines on how test users should and should not use psychological tests.

Engaging in the Learning Process

Learning is the process of gaining knowledge and skills through schooling or studying. Although you can learn by reading the chapter material, attending class, and engaging in discussion with your instructor, more actively engaging in the learning process may help you better learn and retain chapter information. To help you actively engage in the learning process, we encourage you to access our new supplementary student workbook. The workbook contains critical thinking activities to help you understand and apply information and help you make progress toward learning and retaining material. If you do not have a copy of the workbook, you can purchase a copy through sagepub.com.

Key Concepts

After completing your study of this chapter, you should be able to define each of the following terms. These terms are bolded in the text of this chapter and defined in the Glossary.

absolute decisions	institutional decisions	nature-versus-nurture
comparative decisions	integrity tests	controversy
individual decisions		within-group norming

Critical Thinking Questions

The following are some critical thinking questions to support the learning objectives for this chapter.

Learning Objectives	Critical Thinking Questions
Describe different types of decisions that are made using the results of psychological tests.	• After reflecting on what constitutes a psychological test, make a list of tests you have taken up until this point in your life. How would you classify the types of decisions made using the results of each psychological test? • What would happen if psychological tests were outlawed? How would common decisions get made? Would the decisions made without the use of psychological tests be better decisions?
Explain which professionals use psychological tests, in what settings, and for what reasons.	• What do you think are the most important decisions made in educational, clinical and counseling, and organizational settings? • What might be the consequences of abolishing standardized testing in educational settings?
Describe common controversies of psychological testing.	• Identify and document the main points of a current controversy associated with psychological testing. What is your opinion of the controversy and why do you have that opinion? What facts exist that do and do not support your opinion?

3

WHAT ARE THE ETHICAL RESPONSIBILITIES OF TEST PUBLISHERS, TEST USERS, AND TEST TAKERS?

LEARNING OBJECTIVES

After completing your study of this chapter, you should be able to do the following:

- Define ethics and the importance of acting ethically by following professional practice standards.
- Identify the professional practice standards of associations and societies most relevant to psychological testing.
- Distinguish professional practice standards from certification and licensure.
- Explain the general responsibilities of test publishers, test users, and test takers.
- Explain the issues associated with testing special populations.

"My roommate is taking a personality class. Last week, after a long night of studying, she decided to give me a personality test. I came out neurotic. Since then, I've been too upset to go to class."

"My company hired an industrial-organizational psychologist to assess all employees to determine their personality types. Instead of using information about personality type to train employees how to work together, which is how we thought the company would use the test results, my boss went around asking people to transfer to other departments, telling them that he did not want employees with certain personality types working for him."

"Can I please get a copy of the Wechsler Intelligence Scale for Children? My son is going to be taking the test next week to determine if he should be put in a gifted program. I'd like to show him the test and give him a little experience."

"For an assignment in my Tests and Measurements class, I need to learn as much as I can about a psychological test and write a test critique. I'd like to critique the Minnesota Multiphasic Personality Inventory (MMPI). I called the test publisher to purchase the test and they told me I couldn't because I didn't have a "C" level qualification. What's a "C" level qualification and why can't I purchase the test for my assignment?"

You might have personally experienced situations or heard of situations similar to those described in these anecdotes. At first, you might not see anything wrong; however, knowledgeable test users and consumers know that each one of these remarks illustrates a potential misuse of a psychological test.

Psychological tests are used by many professionals in a variety of settings, including educational, clinical, and organizational settings. Unfortunately, misuse by those administering and taking tests, as well as those scoring and interpreting test results, is a chronic and disturbing problem that can harm individuals and society. For individuals, test misuse may result in inappropriate decisions and improper diagnoses. Test misuse reflects poorly on professional organizations and properly trained test users, and it results in poor decisions that harm the public economically and mentally.

Often people who administer tests and people who take tests do not misuse tests intentionally; rather, they do so because of inadequate technical knowledge and misinformation about proper testing procedures. To prevent test misuse, psychologists have developed technical and professional guidelines, principles, and standards for constructing, evaluating, administrating, scoring, and interpreting psychological tests. Test misuse can be overcome by understanding guidelines, principles, and standards that exist for psychological testing. This chapter introduces you to those guidelines, principles, and standards. The information in this chapter will enable you, at a very general level, to evaluate your own experience taking tests such as the SAT and the ACT to gain entrance into college, or intelligence tests to determine your eligibility for gifted or honors programs, or perhaps classroom tests to determine your mastery of course material.

To enhance your understanding of proper test use, we begin by introducing you to the concept of ethics. After sharing the story of Michael Elmore, we discuss what we mean by ethics and professional standards, summarizing some of the most commonly referenced and discussed professional practice standards relevant to the field of psychological testing. Following a discussion of the responsibilities of test publishers, test users, and test takers, we discuss issues related to testing special populations.

WHAT ARE ETHICS?

One day in 1954, Charlotte Elmore became concerned because her 6-year-old son, Michael, was not receiving the same instruction in reading as was her neighbor's daughter. Both attended first grade at the same school, but Michael's class was just starting reading lessons, and the girl next door was already reading to her parents. Mrs. Elmore contacted the school principal, who made a shocking revelation. The school had administered an intelligence test to all students, and Michael's score, the principal said, indicated that he was borderline "retarded." Furthermore, the principal informed her that Michael would need to repeat first grade. When Mrs. Elmore asked why she and her husband had not been told of Michael's score, the principal explained that most parents have difficulty in really understanding intelligence tests and that it was best for their children if parents left such matters to school authorities. When Mrs. Elmore asked to have Michael retested, the principal refused, explaining that scores rarely change by more than a few points.

Fortunately, Mrs. Elmore put more faith in her observations of Michael and his accomplishments than she did in the school's interpretation of one test score. She asked an outside psychologist to retest Michael, and the boy's intelligence quotient score on the retest was 90. Although 100 is the mean of most intelligence tests, 90 is not considered low; on many tests, scoring 10 to 15 points below or above the mean is typical. The outside psychologist did not agree that Michael needed to repeat first grade, and he contacted the principal on Mrs. Elmore's behalf. Eventually, with the help of remedial reading classes and a change of schools, Michael caught up with his classmates.

In high school, Michael was recommended for college preparatory classes, where he earned As and Bs and became a member of the honor society. In 1965, he was accepted as a premed student at Indiana University. While he was in medical school, he took another intelligence test and earned a score of 126—an above-average score. He completed medical school and began practicing medicine as a gastroenterologist, a doctor who treats diseases of the digestive tract (Elmore, 1988).

Although Michael Elmore's story had a happy ending, there were ethical issues associated with the intelligence test administered to Michael. A number of questionable ethical practices on the part of his elementary school could have prevented him from reaching his full potential and becoming a successful contributor to society.

According to the American Psychological Association (APA), "**ethics** [emphasis added] express the professional values foundational to a profession" (APA, 2018a, para. 1). These values influence members' decision-making processes in terms of "doing the right thing." In other words, ethics reflect the morals—what is considered "right" or "wrong." To ensure they are doing what is commonly agreed to as right, members of a profession are expected follow their profession's standards to demonstrate commonly agreed upon ethical behaviors to ensure they do no harm to the individuals with whom they work.

Most professional associations and societies have sets of published professional practice standards that guide the work of these organizations' members. Some associations and societies also have professional practice standards intended for anyone who practices in a specific field. Some of these associations and societies refer to their standards as ethical principles and codes of conduct. Others refer to the standards as codes of ethics or just standards themselves. For example, while the APA has *Ethical Principles of Psychologists and Code of Conduct*, the Society for Human Resource Management (SHRM) has a *Code of Ethical and Professional Standards in Human Resource Management*.

What is important to know is that associations and societies have published guidelines to guide the work of members and/or nonmembers who practice in the field. **Ethical standards** are not laws established by governmental bodies. Violation of ethical standards, however, has various penalties—including possible expulsion of a member from the organization or negative consequences to individuals or organizations. No one can be tried or sued in a court of law for violating ethical standards; rather, these standards are statements by professionals regarding what they believe are appropriate and inappropriate behaviors when practicing their profession. Members of professional societies and associations vote on and adopt these standards after a good deal of discussion and debate. In many cases, the professional practice standards are developed to ensure individuals behave in a way that does not break laws and minimize the likelihood of lawsuits.

Psychological testing plays an important role in individuals' opportunities for education, employment, and mental health treatment. When people use tests improperly, there is great potential for harm to individuals—often without the victims' awareness. Therefore, ethical use of psychological tests—and following professional practice guidelines—is of paramount importance to psychologists and other professionals who use or rely on psychological tests.

PROFESSIONAL PRACTICE STANDARDS

As previously shared, most professional associations and societies publish professional practice standards to guide the work of members and nonmembers who practice in the field. Some of the most commonly referenced and discussed professional practice standards in the field of psychological testing, and where you can find additional information about these standards, are included in On the Web Box 3.1. These standards are also summarized below.

The APA's Ethical Principles of Psychologists and Code of Conduct

In 1953, the APA published the first ethical standards for psychologists. This document, *Ethical Standards of Psychologists* (APA, 1953), was the result of much discussion and study by the APA committee that developed it as well as many persons in the general membership. Since then, the ethical principles of the APA have been revised and updated several times. In December 2002, the APA membership approved and adopted the most current version—the *Ethical Principles of Psychologists and Code of Conduct*. The APA amended the 2002 version in 2010.

The *Ethical Principles of Psychologists and Code of Conduct* is an 18-page document. After an introduction and preamble, the document is organized into three parts: general principles, ethical standards, and the 2010 amendments. The general principles are goals, intended to help psychologists act ethically, while the standards are enforceable rules for psychologists (APA, 2010).

The 10 ethical standards are as follows:

1. Resolving ethical issues

2. Competence

3. Human relations

4. Privacy and confidentiality

5. Advertising and other public statements

6. Record keeping and fees

7. Education and training

8. Research and publication

9. Assessment

10. Therapy

ON THE WEB BOX 3.1
WHERE TO ACCESS PROFESSIONAL PRACTICE STANDARDS

Most professional associations and societies publish professional practice standards to ensure that members and others who select, develop, or use standardized psychological tests do so ethically. Open your web browser and copy and paste the website URLs below to find out more about the professional practice standards most relevant to psychological testing.

Standards	Publisher	Website
APA's *Ethical Principles of Psychologists and Code of Conduct*	American Psychological Association	http://www.apa.org/ethics/code/principles.pdf
Code of Fair Testing Practices in Education	American Psychological Association	http://www.apa.org/science/programs/testing/fair-testing.pdf
Standards for Educational and Psychological Testing	American Educational Research Association	http://www.aera.net/Publications/OnlineStore
SHRM Code of Ethical and Professional Standards in Human Resource Management	Society for Human Resource Management	http://www.shrm.org/about/pages/code-of-ethics.aspx#sthash.gcyad0s5.dpu
Principles for the Validation and Use of Personnel Selection Procedures	Society for Industrial and Organizational Psychology	http://www.siop.org/_Principles/principles.pdf
Uniform Guidelines on Employee Selection Procedures	Equal Opportunity Employment Commission	http://www.gpo.gov/fdsys/pkg/CFR-2013-title29-vol4/xml/CFR-2013-title29-vol4-part1607.xml

Although the ninth set of standards, assessment, is most directly related to the use of psychological tests, the goals set forth in the five general principles also are relevant for test users. Compliance with the standards for privacy and confidentiality is critical to ethical testing.

The *Ethical Principles* are reproduced in Appendix D, and are also available for download on the APA's website at the URL included in On the Web Box 3.1.

The Code of Fair Testing Practices in Education

The APA also publishes another important document, called the *Code of Fair Testing Practices in Education*. The Joint Committee on Testing Practices, a consortium of professional organizations and test publishers, developed the *Code* in 1988 and later published a revised version in 2005. Designed to be consistent with the 1999 Standards (not the 2014 Standards), the *Code* includes standards for professionals who develop and use tests in educational settings to make admission, educational assessment, educational diagnosis, and student placement decisions. The standards make clear the obligations of educational test developers and users for ensuring that tests used in educational settings are "fair to all test takers regardless of age, gender, disability, race, ethnicity, national origin, religion, sexual orientation, linguistic background, or other personal characteristics" (Joint Committee on Testing Practices, 2004, p. 2). The *Code* does not directly apply to teacher-made tests, though teachers who develop their own tests are encouraged to follow the relevant standards.

The *Code* is an 11-page document, organized into three parts. Each part has categories of standards, and each category consists of multiple standards. The *Code* is reproduced in Appendix C, and is also available for download for download on the APA's website at the URL included in On the Web Box 3.1.

The Standards for Educational and Psychological Testing

The APA also collaborates with other organizations to provide detailed guidance on ethical issues associated with psychological tests. Perhaps the most important document is the *Standards for Educational and Psychological Testing*, originally published in 1966. The American Educational Research Association (AERA), APA, and National Council on Measurement in Education (NCME) collaborated for the fifth time to publish the most recent version of the *Standards* during the summer of 2014. The *Standards* provide psychologists and others who develop and use standardized psychological tests and assessments with criteria for evaluating tests and testing practices (AERA, APA, & NCME, 2014). According to the AERA et al. (2014), unless those who develop and use standardized psychological tests and assessments have a very sound professional reason for not following the standards, they should not only make a reasonable effort to abide by the *Standards*, but they should encourage others to follow the *Standards* as well.

The *Standards* are a complete 230-page book, organized into three parts. Each part has categories of standards, and each category consists of multiple standards. The parts and categories are shown below. The *Standards* are available for purchase through the AERA online store at the URL included in On the Web Box 3.1.

Part I: Foundations
Category
1. Validity
2. Reliability/Precision and Errors in Measurement
3. Fairness in Testing

Part II: Operations
Category
1. Test Design and Development
2. Scores, Scales, Norms, Score Linking, and Cut Scores
3. Testing Administration, Scoring, Reporting, and Interpretation
4. Supporting Documentation for Tests
5. The Rights and Responsibilities of Test Takers
6. The Rights and Responsibilities of Test Users

Part III: Testing Applications
Category
1. Psychological Testing and Assessment
2. Workplace Testing and Credentialing
3. Educational Testing and Assessment
4. Uses of Tests for Program Evaluation, Policy Studies, and Accountability

SHRM's Code of Ethical and Professional Standards in Human Resource Management

SHRM published its *Code of Ethical and Professional Standards in Human Resource Management* in 2007. The *Code of Ethical and Professional Standards* includes standards for human resources professionals to follow when working in the human resources profession. The *Code* is approximately four web pages long, organized into six sections, each with a core principle, the intent of the principle, and guidelines for demonstrating the principle:

1. Professional Responsibility

2. Professional Development

3. Ethical Leadership

4. Fairness and Justice

5. Conflicts of Interest

6. Use of Information

The *Code of Ethical and Professional Standards* is available on SHRM's website at the URL included in On the Web Box 3.1.

The Society for Industrial and Organizational Psychology's Principles for the Validation and Use of Personnel Selection Procedures

In 2003, the Society for Industrial and Organizational Psychology (SIOP) published the fourth edition of the *Principles for the Validation and Use of Personnel Selection Procedures* to reflect current research and to be consistent with the *Standards for Educational and Psychological Testing*. The *Principles* reflect the official statement from SIOP regarding professionally accepted practices for selecting, developing, and using testing instruments to make employment-related decisions to "hire, train, certify, compensate, promote, terminate, transfer, and/or take other actions that affect employment" (SIOP, 2003, p. 3).

The *Principles* include four main sections:

- Overview of the Validation Process

- Sources of Validity Evidence

- Generalizing Validity Evidence

- Operational Considerations in Personnel Selection

Because the *Principles* are designed to be consistent with the *Standards for Educational and Psychological Testing*, which were revised in 2014, in 2018 SIOP is expected to publish a fifth edition to ensure consistency. The *Principles for the Validation and Use of Personnel Selection Procedures* is a 76-page document available on SHRM's website at the URL included in On the Web Box 3.1.

The Uniform Guidelines on Employee Selection Procedures

The U.S. Equal Employment Opportunity Commission (EEOC) published the *Uniform Guidelines on Employee Selection Procedures* in 1978. The *Uniform Guidelines* are regulations published as Part 1607 of Title 29 of the Code of Federal Regulations (EEOC, 2014). The *Uniform Guidelines* were created to help those who may use tests and/or use other hiring procedures to make employment decisions (i.e., employers, labor organizations, employment agencies, and licensing and certification boards) comply with federal law prohibiting discriminatory employment practices based on race, color, religion, sex, and national origin.

The *Uniform Guidelines* are over 50 pages long, organized into 18 sections, each with subsections containing specific guidelines.

Section 1: Statement of Purpose

Section 2: Scope

Section 3: Discrimination Defined: Relationship Between Use of Selection Procedures and Discrimination

Section 4: Information on Impact

Section 5: General Standards for Validity Studies

Section 6: Use of Selection Procedures Which Have Not Been Validated

Section 7: Use of Other Validity Studies

Section 8: Cooperative Studies.

Section 9: No Assumption of Validity

Section 10: Employment Agencies and Employment Services

Section 11: Disparate Treatment

Section 12: Retesting of Applicants

Section 13: Affirmative Action

Section 14: Technical Standards for Validity Studies

Section 15: Documentation of Impact and Validity Evidence

Section 16: Definitions

Section 17: Policy Statement on Affirmative Action

Section 18: Citations

The *Uniform Guidelines* are available on the EEOC's website at the URL included in On the Web Box 3.1.

Other Testing Guidelines

Some of the professional practice standards discussed above apply to the members of the organizations that published the codes of ethics. For example, the APA's (2010) *Ethical Principles of Psychologists and Code of Conduct* apply only to members of the APA. Many individuals who use psychological tests do not belong to any professional organization, and membership in such an organization is not a requirement. These people include test publishers, test administrators, managers, and teachers, among others. To provide those outside the membership of professional organizations with a set of standards, several organizations have developed guidelines that apply to everyone in the field of testing—licensed and unlicensed, professional as well as other test users.

The International Test Commission (ITC), which is made up of national psychological associations, test commissions, and test publishers, was established in 1978 to facilitate the exchange of information on problems related to the construction, development, and use of tests and other diagnostic tools. The ITC published the original *International Guidelines for Test Use* in 2000 (updated in 2013) and the *International Guidelines on Computer-Based and Internet Delivered Testing* in 2005.

Both sets of guidelines were developed for the following individuals (ITC, 2013):

- The purchasers and holders of test materials

- Those responsible for selecting tests and determining the use to which tests will be put

- Those who administer, score, or interpret tests

- Those who provide advice to others on the basis of test results (e.g., recruitment consultants, educational and career counselors, trainers, succession planners)

- Those concerned with the process of reporting test results and providing feedback to people who have been tested

The *International Guidelines for Test Use* include the knowledge, understanding, and skills test users need to use tests appropriately, professionally, and ethically, as well as guidelines for ethical test use.

The six main areas of knowledge, understanding, and skills are listed below. Each area is further defined by more specific knowledge, understanding, and skills. Complete definitions can be found at https://www.intestcom.org/files/guideline_test_use.pdf

1. Relevant declarative knowledge

2. Instrumental knowledge and skills

3. General personal task-related skills

4. Contextual knowledge and skills

5. Task management skills

6. Contingency management skills

The guidelines are presented in two parts, each with subsections that include more specific guiding behaviors of test users.

Part 1: Take responsibility for ethical test use
    1.1 Act in a professional and ethical manner
    1.2 Ensure they have the competence to use tests
    1.3 Take responsibility for their use of tests
    1.4 Ensure that test materials are kept securely
    1.5 Ensure that test results are treated confidentially

Part 2: Follow good practice in the use of tests
    2.1 Evaluate the potential utility of testing in an assessment situation
    2.2 Choose technically sound tests appropriate for the situation

2.3 Give due consideration to issues of fairness in testing

2.4 Make necessary preparations for the testing session

2.5 Administer the tests properly

2.6 Score and analyze test results accurately

2.7 Interpret results appropriately

2.8 Communicate the results clearly and accurately to relevant others

2.9 Review the appropriateness of the test and its use

The *International Guidelines on Computer-Based and Internet Delivered Testing* include international guidelines for best practices in computer-based and Internet-delivered testing. In addition to applying to the test users discussed above, the current *Guidelines* apply to developers, publishers of computer-based and Internet tests, as well as consultants to developers and publishers (ITC, 2005, p. 7).

The *Guidelines* are organized into four sections, each with subsections that include specific guidelines for test developers, test publishers, and test users (ITC, 2005):

1. Give due regard to technological issues in Computer-based (CBT) and Internet Testing

2. Attend to quality issues in CBT and Internet testing

3. Provide appropriate levels of control over CBT and Internet testing

4. Make appropriate provision for security and safeguarding privacy in CBT and Internet testing

The entire *Guidelines* can be found at https://www.intestcom.org/files/guideline_computer_based_testing.pdf.

Although both sets of ITC guidelines are not as extensive as the APA's *Standards for Educational and Psychological Testing* (AERA et al., 2014) or *Code of Fair Testing Practices in Education* (Joint Committee on Testing Practices, 2004), they do call attention to the need for everyone involved in the testing process to take responsibility for ethical test use and fair testing practices.

In the 1980s, the APA Science Directorate published *Test User Qualifications: A Data-Based Approach to Promoting Good Test Use* (Eyde, Moreland, Robertson, Primoff, & Most, 1988), a 143-page technical report that includes various models for screening qualifications of test users. Later, the directorate published the *Report of the Task Force on Test User Qualifications* (APA, 2000). The latter report contains guidelines that inform test users about the qualifications that the APA deems essential for the optimal use of psychological tests. The guidelines are relevant today and identify two kinds of qualifications: generic, which apply to most testing situations, and specific, which apply to specific situations such as testing people with disabilities. Unlike the APA's publications of ethical standards that it intends for compliance of its members, the *Report of the Task Force on Test User Qualifications* describes its guidelines as "aspirational"; that is, the purpose is to inspire achievement in best testing practices.

For Your Information Box 3.1 contains the core knowledge and skills for test users taken from these guidelines. On the Web Box 3.2 provides an overview of the APA Science Directorate's Testing and Assessment website.

FOR YOUR INFORMATION BOX 3.1
REPORT OF THE TASK FORCE ON TEST USER QUALIFICATIONS

If you have looked ahead on your class syllabus or in this textbook, you may be wondering why there are chapters devoted to topics such as reliability and validity. In fact, the material covered in this book was chosen to provide you with the information you will need in order to use and understand psychological tests. As you recall from Chapter 1, we all are, at one time or another, users and consumers of the results of psychological testing.

As you review the following list of the knowledge and skills a test user should have, you might find it helpful to locate the chapter or passage in this book that addresses each requirement.

1. Psychometric and Measurement Knowledge

It is important for test users to understand classical test theory and, when appropriate or necessary, item response theory (IRT). The essential elements of classical test theory are outlined below. When test users are making assessments on the basis of IRT, such as adaptive testing, they should be familiar with the concepts of item parameters (e.g., item difficulty, item discrimination, and guessing), item and test information functions, and ability parameters (e.g., theta).

1.1   *Descriptive statistics.* Test users should be able to define, apply, and interpret concepts of descriptive statistics. For example, means and standard deviations are often used in comparing different groups on test scales, whereas correlations are frequently used for examining the degree of convergence and divergence between two or more scales. Similarly, test users should understand how frequency distributions describe the varying levels of a behavior across a group of persons.

Test users should have sufficient knowledge and understanding of descriptive statistics to select and use appropriate test instruments, as well as score and interpret results. The most common descriptive statistics relevant to test use include the following:

    1.1.1   Frequency distributions (e.g., cumulative frequency distributions)

    1.1.2   Descriptive statistics characterizing the normal curve (e.g., kurtosis, skewness)

    1.1.3   Measures of central tendency (e.g., mean, median, and mode)

    1.1.4   Measures of variation (e.g., variance and standard deviation)

    1.1.5   Indices of relationship (e.g., correlation coefficient)

1.2   *Scales, scores, and transformations.* Test results frequently represent information about individuals' characteristics, skills, abilities, and attitudes in numeric form. Test users should understand issues related to scaling, types of scores, and methods of score transformation. For example, test users should understand and know when to apply the various methods for representing test information (e.g., raw scores, standard scores, and percentiles). Relevant concepts include the following:

    1.2.1   Types of scales

        a. Nominal scales

        b. Ordinal scales

        c. Interval scales

        d. Ratio scales

    1.2.2   Types of scores

        a. Raw scores

        b. Transformed scores

            i.   Percentile scores

            ii.   Standard scores

            iii. Normalized scores

    1.2.3   Scale score equating

    1.2.4   Cut scores

1.3   *Reliability and measurement error.* Test users should understand issues of test score reliability and measurement error as they apply to the specific test being used, as well as other factors that may be influencing test results. Test users should also understand the appropriate interpretation and application of different measures of reliability (e.g., internal consistency, test–retest reliability, interrater reliability, and parallel forms reliability). Similarly, test users should understand the standard error of measurement, which presents a numerical estimate of the range of scores consistent with the individual's level of performance. It is important that test users have knowledge of the following:

1.3.1 Sources of variability or measurement error

    a. Characteristics of test taker (e.g., motivation)

    b. Characteristics of test (e.g., domain sampling, test length, and test heterogeneity)

    c. Characteristics of construct and intended use of test scores (e.g., stability of characteristic)

    d. Characteristics and behavior of test administrator (e.g., importance of standardized verbal instructions)

    e. Characteristics of the testing environment

    f. Test administration procedures

    g. Scoring accuracy

1.3.2 Types of reliability and their appropriateness for different types of tests and test use

    a. Test–retest reliability

    b. Parallel or alternative forms reliability

    c. Internal consistency

    d. Scorer and interrater reliability

1.3.3 Change scores (or difference scores)

1.3.4 Standard error of measurement (i.e., standard error of a score)

1.4 *Validity and meaning of test scores.* The interpretations and uses of test scores, and not the test itself, are evaluated for validity. Responsibility for validation belongs both to the test developer, who provides evidence in support of test use for a particular purpose, and to the test user, who ultimately evaluates that evidence, other available data, and information gathered during the testing process to support interpretations of test scores.

Test users have a larger role in evaluating validity evidence when the test is used for purposes different from those investigated by the test developer.

Contemporary discussions of validity have focused on evidence that supports the test as a measure of a construct (sometimes called construct validity). For example, evidence for the uses and interpretations of test scores may come through evaluation of the test content (content representativeness), through evidence of predictions of relevant outcomes (criterion-related validity), or from a number of other sources of evidence. Test users should understand the implications associated with the different sources of evidence that contribute to construct validity, as well as the limits of any one source of validity evidence.

1.4.1 Types of evidence contributing to construct validity

    a. Content

    b. Criterion related

    c. Convergent

    d. Discriminant

1.4.2 *Normative interpretation of test scores.* Norms describe the distribution of test scores in a sample from a particular population. Test users should understand how differences between the test taker and the particular normative group affect the interpretation of test scores.

    a. Types of norms and relevance for interpreting test taker score (e.g., standard scores and percentile norms)

    b. Characteristics of the normative group and the generalizability limitations of the normative group

    c. Type of score referent

      i. Norm referenced

      ii. Domain referenced (criterion referenced)

      iii. Self-referenced (ipsative scales)

    d. Expectancy tables

ON THE WEB BOX 3.2

APA SCIENCE DIRECTORATE: TESTING AND ASSESSMENT

www.apa.org/science/programs/testing/index.aspx

The APA has a long and continuing interest in the ethical and effective use of psychological tests. This web page provides access to the APA's latest publications on how to find and ethically use psychological tests.

One of the most helpful and interesting links on this page is "FAQ/Finding Information About Psychological Tests." This link provides "how-to" information on locating and purchasing published tests as well as information on directories of unpublished tests.

Other links of interest on the Testing and Assessment page include the following:

- The Standards for Educational and Psychological Testing

- Appropriate Use of High-Stakes Testing in Our Nation's Schools

- Rights and Responsibilities of Test Takers: Guidelines and Expectations

You are likely to find the "Rights and Responsibilities of Test Takers" to be particularly interesting because these apply to you. According to the preamble of this document, "The intent . . . is to enumerate and clarify the expectations that test takers may reasonably have about the testing process, and the expectations that those who develop, administer, and use tests may have of test takers" (para. 1). In other words, in this document the APA has set out to educate the test taker, the test user, and the test publisher about the responsibilities of each in ensuring that the assessment is developed, administered, scored, and interpreted with the highest ethical and professional standards in mind.

Source: APA (2018e).

CERTIFICATION AND LICENSURE

Although professional practice standards guide the behavior of individuals within a field, certification and licensure are credentials demonstrating individuals are qualified to practice in their fields. Many fields offer **certification**—a professional credential individuals earn by demonstrating that they have met predetermined qualifications (e.g., that they have specific knowledge, skills, and/or experience). Certification is a voluntary process and is generally offered by private, nongovernmental state or national organizations. Typically, certification requires passing an exam.

One organization that oversees certification for counselors is the National Board for Certified Counselors (NBCC), an independent nonprofit credentialing body. The NBCC was created by the American Counseling Association to establish and monitor a national certification system that would identify and maintain a register of counselors who have voluntarily sought and obtained certification. Because certified counselors may have training in various fields, such as psychology, education, and counseling, the NBCC (2012) has its own *Code of Ethics*, which is a minimum ethical standard for all national certified counselors. Of 95 directives in the *Code of Ethics*, 14 are most directly related to ethical use of psychological tests (25, 31, 34–37, 48–50, 62, 65, 79, 80, and 91).

Another organization that oversees certification for human resources professionals is the HR Certification Institute (HRCI). In partnership with the Professional Examination Service and Prometric, HRCI (2018) screens for, administers, scores, and provides certificates to individuals wishing to obtain one or more professional in human resources credentials (e.g., Associate Professional in Human Resources, Associate Professional in Human Resources - International, Professional in Human Resources, Senior Professional in Human Resources, or Global Professional in Human Resources credential). The HRCI (n.d.) has its own *Code of Ethical and Professional Responsibility*, which is a set of standards for all who hold an HRCI credential.

Although certification is a voluntary process, **licensure** is a mandatory credential individuals must obtain to practice within their professions. The purpose of licensure is generally (but not always) to protect the health and safety of the public. The licensure process is typically established by a state-level government entity, and it is illegal for individuals in specific professions to practice without licenses. A specific state's requirements for obtaining a license might differ from those of other states, so individuals who desire to practice their professions in different states often must seek licensure in more than one state, except when there is a state reciprocity agreement.

In the News Box 3.1 includes a discussion of jobs you may not know need licenses.

GENERAL RESPONSIBILITIES OF TEST PUBLISHERS, TEST USERS, AND TEST TAKERS

Because individuals and institutions use test scores to make important decisions about people, test publishers, test users, and test takers must work together to ensure that test scores are accurate and that good decisions are made using the test scores. Bad practices, on the part of test publishers, test users, or test takers, can compromise the quality of decisions—as in the case of Michael Elmore—and can have undesirable and harmful consequences for individuals, organizations, and society as a whole. Bad practices can affect the reliability/precision of measurement (which we discuss in detail in the "What Is Test Reliability/Precision?" chapter) and the validity of test score interpretation (which we discuss in detail in the validity chapters).

Although we have already discussed published professional practice standards that guide the work of those involved in testing, below we discuss the specific responsibilities of test publishers, test users, and test takers. Test developer responsibility is discussed in more detail in the "How Do We Develop a Test?" and "How Do We Assess the Psychometric Quality of a Test?" chapters, where we discuss test development and piloting in detail, and in the reliability and validity chapters where we discuss procedures for gathering evidence of reliability/precision and validity.

Test Publisher Responsibilities

In the first chapter of the text, we discussed how psychological testing is a multibillion dollar business, with thousands of published, commercially available tests. In On the Web Box 1.1, we included some of the names and web addresses of some of the most well-known test publishers, including some of the tests they publish. Whether well known or not, all test publishes have a responsibility to demonstrate the highest level of professionalism and ethics when selling and marketing psychological tests.

The Sale of Psychological Tests

Sometimes professionals need to purchase psychological tests for their businesses or for research projects. For example, a clinical psychologist may need to purchase a test to help diagnose disorders. An industrial and organizational psychology practitioner may need to

IN THE NEWS BOX 3.1
JOBS YOU DIDN'T KNOW NEED LICENSES

Many jobs in the United States require employees to have undergraduate college degrees. Some jobs also require employees to have graduate degrees. However, there are some jobs where having an undergraduate or even an advanced degree is not enough. To work in some professions, employees must be licensed to demonstrate that they are competent to practice their professions. For example, most people know that physicians with MDs, to demonstrate their competence to practice medicine in the United States, must pass the United States Medical Licensing Examination administered by the Federation of State Medical Boards and the National Board of Medical Examiners. Likewise, most people know that attorneys, to demonstrate their competence to practice law, must pass state-administered bar exams administered by their states' bar licensing agencies. And depending on the field of psychology pursued, and in which state an individual will practice, an individual may or may not need to become licensed to practice.

According to an Institute for Justice's national study (Carpenter, Knepper, Erickson, & Ross, 2012), one in three jobs in the United States now requires licensure, and some of these jobs may surprise you! The institute's Angela C. Erickson shared 10 occupations for which some states require individuals to be licensed before practicing:

Occupation	Requirement
Makeup artist	"Makeup artists are licensed in 36 states which consistently require three to nine months of education and experience, two exams and an average of $116 in fees to get a license," Erickson said. "In several states, an exception is made for make up artists working in theaters, while those in salons, spas or making house calls are required to be licensed."
Security guard	"Security guards are currently licensed in 37 states. Michigan's barriers are the most onerous, requiring an applicant to be at least 25 years old, have three years of training and pay $200 in fees, but those requirements may soon be removed in regulatory reforms sweeping through the state."
Auctioneers	"Auctioneers are licensed in 33 states, with requirements varying from just a $15 fee in Hawaii to $650 in fees, two exams and over two years lost to education and an apprenticeship in Tennessee. Auctioneers are another occupation Michigan is considering deregulating."
Residential painting contractor	"In 10 states, an individual who paints home or apartment walls must have a government-issued license. In three of those states, painters are expected to have a year or more of experience while the other states require zero to 12 days."
Funeral attendant	"Funeral attendants place caskets in the parlor, arrange the flowers around it and direct mourners, among other simple duties. They are only licensed in nine states, which on average require two days of training and $167 in fees."
Interior designer	"The four states that license interior designers require six years of education and apprenticeship."
Travel agent	"Despite the ease of booking travel over the Internet, eight states license travel agents who are charged fees ranging from $15 to $375 in order to obtain a license."
Shampooer	"Five states license shampooers who only shampoo and rinse customers' hair in salons. Tennessee has the most onerous requirements at 70 days of training, two exams and $140 in fees."
Home entertainment installer	"Someone who goes into homes to set up stereo systems and audio or television receivers is required to have a government-issued license in three states. Louisiana has the most onerous requirements, where applicants must have two years of training and pass two exams."
Florist	"Florists are only licensed in Louisiana, which requires them to pay $225 and pass an exam."

purchase a test to use as part of an organization's selection process. Likewise, sometimes students (both undergraduate and graduate) may need to purchase psychological tests for class assignments. In a tests and measurements class, for example, an instructor may require that students evaluate a psychological test. A thorough evaluation requires not only library research but also sometimes access to the test and the test manual. Students also may be interested in conducting independent research studies. They may wish to explore the relationship between some psychological attribute and an outcome, for example, self-esteem and grade point average. To conduct the research, students might want to purchase a psychological test to measure self-esteem.

Publishers market their tests in test catalogues and on their websites. According to the *Standards for Educational and Psychological Testing* (AERA et al., 2014), publishers should sell psychological tests they market only to individuals who are appropriately trained to administer, score, and interpret the tests. Publishers should also market psychological tests truthfully, provide all test information (including evidence of validity) to test users before purchase, and provide comprehensive test manuals for each psychological test after purchase.

For each test they are marketing or selling, test publishers have a responsibility to include statements of **user qualifications**—the background, training, and/or certifications the test purchaser must meet. Not all publishing firms place the same restrictions on the sale of psychological tests, but in general, reputable publishers require purchasers to have appropriate credentials for test use.

To purchase most psychological tests, test users must meet minimum training, education, and experience qualifications. For example, Pearson, one test publishing company, has test user qualification levels for each of the tests it sells (Pearson Education, 2018b). If you go to Pearson's website, you will find that Pearson classifies its tests into one of three levels: A, B, and C.

- Level A: To purchase Level A products, no special qualifications are required.

- Level B: To purchase Level B products, an individual must meet one of four criteria:
  - Have a master's degree in psychology, education, occupational therapy, social work, or a field closely related to the intended use of the assessment and formal training in the ethical administration, scoring, and interpretation of clinical assessments
  - Be certified by or have full active membership in a professional organization (such as ASHA, AOTA, AERA, ACA, AMA, CEC, AEA, AAA, EAA, NAEYC, or NBCC) that requires training and experience in the relevant area of assessment
  - Have a degree or license to practice in the health care or allied health care field
  - Have formal, supervised mental health, speech/language, and/or educational training specific to assessing children, or in infant and child development, and formal training in the ethical administration, scoring, and interpretation of clinical assessments

- Level C: To purchase Level C products, an individual must have a high level of expertise in test interpretation, and meet one of three criteria:
  - Have a doctorate degree in psychology, education, or a closely related field, with formal training in the ethical administration, scoring, and interpretation of clinical assessments related to the intended use of the assessment
  - Be licensed or certified to practice in the individual's state in a field related to the purchase
  - Be certified by or full active membership in a professional organization (such as APA, NASP, NAN, or INS) that requires training and experience in the relevant area of assessment

The qualification level required to purchase each test can be found in the test catalogue or on the web. Although there are some exceptions, test purchasers must complete a qualification form (such as the one below) in order to purchase a test. Once the form has been accepted, test users are allowed to purchase the test.

Because publishers recognize how valuable reviewing and using psychological tests can be to the learning experience, they often allow a student to purchase a test if the student provides a letter from a qualified instructor or completes a qualification form signed by the instructor. By signing the letter or the qualification form, the instructor assumes responsibility for the proper use of the test purchased by the student. You can find qualification forms for various test publishers on their websites.

The Marketing of Psychological Tests

Test publishers should properly and truthfully market the psychological tests that they publish. They should ensure **test security** so that the content of psychological tests does not become public. Test security includes not publishing psychological tests in newspapers, magazines, and popular books. Not only does a lack of test security invalidate future use of a test, but it also may result in psychological injury to individuals who take and attempt to interpret the test. Such test misuse creates further resistance on the part of the public toward psychological testing.

An exception to this rule occurs when test developers wish to share their tests with the research community. In such cases, peer-reviewed journals will often publish test questions along with validation studies and scoring instructions. Tests published in scholarly journals are considered to be in the public domain.

It is common, however, for test publishers to print examples of outdated test items. For example, the Educational Testing Service releases previously administered tests in the form of practice tests. All portions of tests shown in this textbook have been published with the permission of the respective test publishers.

Availability of Comprehensive Test Manuals

Publishers should ensure that every psychological test has an accompanying test manual, which should contain psychometric information based on research. The manual should include the following:

1. Information that a test purchaser can use to evaluate the psychometric characteristics of the test (e.g., how the test was constructed, evidence of reliability/precision and validity, composition of norm groups)

2. Detailed information about proper administration and scoring procedures

3. Information about how to compare test scores with those of norm groups

If they are aware of ways a test is being misused, test publishers have the responsibility to caution test users and researchers about such misuse. For example, if a publisher knows that using a specific test in a specific context cannot be justified (e.g., using a particular personality test for selection), the publisher should clearly communicate this information to avoid test misuse.

Although test publishers try to comply with these objectives, sometimes the system fails. Sometimes unqualified people may purchase and use psychological tests, or a test may be released before it is complete or may be released with misleading or incomplete information

QUALIFICATION POLICIES & USER ACCEPTANCE FORM

PEARSON

Questions?
Call 800.627.7271

Qualifications Policy

Please establish your qualification level for this and future purchases by completing the User Acceptance Form. For faster service, fax form to 800.232.1223, or send this form along with your order. You may also complete the form online at PearsonClinical.com.

Pearson is committed to maintaining professional standards in testing as presented in the *Standards for Educational and Psychological Testing* published by the American Educational Research Association (AERA), American Psychological Association (APA), and the National Council on Measurement in Education (NCME). A central principle of professional test use is that individuals should use only those tests for which they have the appropriate training and expertise. Pearson supports this principle by stating qualifications for the use of particular tests, and selling tests to individuals who provide credentials that meet those qualifications. The policies that Pearson uses to comply with professional testing practices are described below.

The "User" is the individual who assumes responsibility for all aspects of appropriate test use, including administration, scoring, interpretation, and application of results. Some tests may be administered or scored by individuals with less training, as long as they are under the supervision of a qualified User.

Each test manual will provide additional detail on administration, scoring and/or interpretation requirements and options for the particular test.

We accept orders from individuals when a User Acceptance Form has been submitted and accepted. All tests are classified by a User qualification code. See the specific test descriptions in the catalog or on the Web for these qualification levels.

QUALIFICATION LEVEL A:

There are no special qualifications to purchase these products.

QUALIFICATION LEVEL B:

Tests may be purchased by individuals with:

• A master's degree in psychology, education, occupational therapy, social work, or in a field closely related to the intended use of the assessment, and formal training in the ethical administration, scoring, and interpretation of clinical assessments.
OR
• Certification by or full active membership in a professional organization (such as ASHA, AOTA, AERA, ACA, AMA, CEC, AEA, AAA, EAA, NAEYC, NBCC) that requires training and experience in the relevant area of assessment.
OR
• A degree or license to practice in the healthcare or allied healthcare field.
OR
• Formal, supervised mental health, speech/language, and/or educational training specific to assessing children, or in infant and child development, and formal training in the ethical administration, scoring, and interpretation of clinical assessments.

QUALIFICATION LEVEL C:

Tests with a C qualification require a high level of expertise in test interpretation, and can be purchased by individuals with:

• A doctorate degree in psychology, education, or closely related field with formal training in the ethical administration, scoring, and interpretation of clinical assessments related to the intended use of the assessment.
OR
• Licensure or certification to practice in your state in a field related to the purchase.
OR
• Certification by or full active membership in a professional organization (such as APA, NASP, NAN, INS) that requires training and experience in the relevant area of assessment.

We are committed to supporting the professional standards of our clients, the integrity of our respected assessments, and the ethical obligations outlined by the American Psychological Association.

User Acceptance Form

*Name_____

*Organization Name _____

*Telephone _____ *Fax _____ *E-mail _____

*Address _____

*City _____ *State ___ *Zip_____ *Country_____

1. Professional *Title

☐ Audiologist
☐ Consultant/Specialist–Education
☐ Counselor–Family/Mental Health/Substance Abuse
☐ Counselor–Vocational/Academic
☐ Director–Clinical Training
☐ Early Childhood Professional
☐ Education Professional
☐ Educational Diagnostician
☐ Human Resources Professional
☐ Nurse
☐ Occupational Therapist
☐ Physical Therapist
☐ Physician
☐ Principal
☐ Professor
☐ Psychiatrist

☐ Psychologist–Clinical
☐ Psychologist–Forensic
☐ Psychologist–Industrial/Occupational
☐ Psychologist–Neuro
☐ Psychologist–School
☐ Psychometrist
☐ Public Safety Official
☐ School Social Worker
☐ Social Worker
☐ Special Education Professional
☐ Speech Language Pathologist
☐ Student/Intern
☐ Teacher
☐ Testing Coordinator
☐ Training Development Professional
☐ Other: _____

2. Primary Work Setting:

Education
☐ Public School
☐ Private School
☐ Post-Secondary 4-year
☐ Post-Secondary 2-year
☐ Technical/Vocational College
☐ Headstart
☐ Daycare/Preschool
☐ Other: _____

Government
☐ Corrections
☐ Public Safety/High-Risk
☐ Military/VA
☐ CMHC
☐ Federal/State/Local Org
☐ Other (please specify) _____

Mental Health & Counseling
☐ Psychology & Counseling
☐ Hospital/University Hospital
☐ Neuropsychology
☐ Forensic Practice
☐ Psychiatric Practice
☐ Speech and Language
☐ Audiology
☐ Substance Abuse
☐ Career Counseling
☐ Occupational Therapy
☐ Physical Therapy
☐ Nursing Home/Assisted Living

Medical Specialty
(e.g., Pain, Bariatrics, Rehab)
☐ _____

3. Highest professional degree attained:

*Degree_____ *Major Field _____ *Year _____

*Institution _____

4. Course work completed in Tests and Measurement: yes or no

If yes *Date_____ *Course _____

*Institution _____

☐ graduate level   ☐ undergraduate level

5. Valid license or certificate issued by a state regulatory board:

*Certificate/License Type _____ *Number _____

*Certifying or Licensing Agency_____

*State_____ *Expiration Date _____

6. Full and Active Membership in Professional Organization(s) Status:

☐ASHA ☐AOTA ☐APA ☐AERA ☐ACA ☐AMA ☐NASP ☐NAN ☐INS ☐CEC ☐AEA ☐AAA ☐EAA ☐NAEYC ☐NBCC ☐OTHER _____

Member No. _____ Member Type _____

I agree that:
• I agree to update the information upon request.
• I am qualified to properly use any Pearson Products I order, and I have provided Pearson with only accurate and true qualification information.
• Any Pearson Products purchased under my account will be used by me and/or under my supervision.
• Any Pearson Products purchased under my account will be used in accordance with all applicable legal and ethical guidelines.
• I have read and hereby agree to Pearson's Terms and Conditions of Sale and Use of Pearson Products to all orders for my account and will abide by the Pearson Terms and Conditions and Qualification Policies (as may be modified or amended at PearsonClinical. com). I agree I will not resell any Pearson Products.
• I understand that violation of any Pearson's Terms and Conditions of Sale and Use may result in the revocation of my right to purchase as a qualified customer. If there are any changes that may affect my qualification to purchase, I will immediately notify Pearson of such changes.

*Signature _____ *Date _____
* Required fields

Phone **800.627.7271** | Fax **800.232.1223** | **PearsonClinical.com** in the manual. For this reason, responsibility for proper test use ultimately resides with the individual using the psychological test.

Test User Responsibilities

A **test user** is a person who participates in purchasing, administering, interpreting, or using the results of a psychological test. It is easy to understand what we mean by test user if you think of the various stages that are involved in the psychological testing process:

1. An individual or group determines a need for psychological testing.

2. An individual or group selects the psychological test(s) to use.

3. An individual administers a test to the test taker.

4. An individual scores the test.

5. An individual interprets the test for the test taker.

Sometimes the same person carries out each step of this process. For example, in the case of Michael Elmore, the outside psychologist may have (a) determined that Michael's intelligence needed to be retested, (b) selected which intelligence test to administer, (c) administered the intelligence test, (d) scored the test, (e) interpreted the results, and (f) communicated the results to Michael's family and the school principal. Sometimes there are various people involved. For example, the outside psychologist probably determined that Michael should be retested and selected the appropriate intelligence test, and one of the psychologist's assistants may have administered the intelligence test. The test may have been mailed to a test publishing company for scoring. The psychologist may have taken Michael's raw score, along with other information, to interpret the test results. Michael's psychologist most likely communicated these results to Michael's parents and perhaps to the school principal. Thus, there may be various professionals involved in the testing process. Each involved party is a test user and must act responsibly to contribute to the effective delivery of testing services. Acting responsibly means ensuring that each person in one or more of the roles just described is qualified to perform that role.

Acting responsibly also means that test users use tests according to the professional practice standards previously discussed. Given that so many different professionals in organizational, educational, as well as clinical and counseling settings are involved in the testing process, it would be difficult to discuss all of the responsibilities of test users. Regardless of where they work, what tests they use, or how they use test results, test users should understand and abide by the professional practice standards within their professions, as well as the testing guidelines that apply to all professions. For example, an industrial-organizational psychologist who is a member of SIOP and the APA, who works with organizations to identify and/or develop tests to be used for selecting individuals for jobs, should abide by the APA's (2010) *Ethical Principles of Psychologists and Code of Conduct*, SIOP's (2003) *Principles for the Validation and Use of Personnel Selection Procedures*, and the EEOC's *Uniform Guidelines on Employee Selection Procedures* (1978).

Test Taker Responsibilities

A **test taker** is person who responds to test questions or whose behavior is measured. As a test taker yourself—someone who has taken tests—chances are you think your role in the testing process is to merely take a test. Although the test taker's primary responsibility is to take a test, test takers have many other responsibilities. Test takers themselves play a significant role in ensuring that test scores are accurate and used to make good decisions.

Although other resources exist, APA's (2018d) *Rights and Responsibilities of Test Takers* and the *Standards for Educational and Psychological Testing* (AERA et al., 2014) include perhaps the most comprehensive discussion of the personal and legal responsibilities of test takers. These responsibilities are summarized below.

Test takers have the responsibility to:

- Be prepared to take a test, including knowing where and when the test will be given, paying for a test if required, and showing up on time with required materials.

- Understand and accept the consequences of not taking a test.

- Carefully read or listen to, as well as follow, test administrator instructions.

- Respectfully inform the appropriate individuals, in a timely manner, if they believe the testing conditions may have affected their results or they have other concerns about the testing process or results.

- Protect test security and copyrights by not sharing test content with others and not reproducing materials without authorization.

- Represent themselves honestly, avoiding cheating, using unapproved aids, or arranging for another person to take the test.

- Request testing accommodations if they have a physical condition, illness, or language issue that may interfere with their performance.

- Ask questions if they are uncertain about why they are taking a test, how the test will be administered, what they will be asked to do, how others will use the results, or the confidentiality of test results.

- Treat others with courtesy and respect by not interfering with the performance of other test takers in group settings.

Test Taker Rights

The common purpose of the professional practice guidelines related to testing is to protect the rights of individuals who take tests. Although test taker rights are described in detail in professional practice guidelines such as the *Standards* (AERA et al., 2014) and the *Ethical Principles of Psychologists and Code of Conduct* (APA, 2010), the APA (2018d) nicely summarizes test taker rights on its website in the *Rights and Responsibilities of Test Takers: Guidelines and Expectations*. These rights are listed below, followed by a discussion of some of the issues of most concern.

According to the APA (2018d), a test taker has the right to the following:

1. Be informed of your rights and responsibilities as a test taker.

2. Be treated with courtesy, respect, and impartiality, regardless of your age, disability, ethnicity, gender, national origin, religion, sexual orientation, or other personal characteristics.

3. Be tested with measures that meet professional standards and that are appropriate, given the manner in which the test results will be used.

4. Receive a brief oral or written explanation prior to testing about the purpose(s) for testing, the kind(s) of tests to be used, if the results will be reported to you or to others, and the planned use(s) of the results. If you have a disability, you have the right to inquire and receive information about testing accommodations. If you have difficulty in comprehending the language of the test, you have a right to know in advance of testing whether any accommodations may be available to you.

5. Know in advance of testing when the test will be administered, if and when test results will be available to you, and if there is a fee for testing services that you are expected to pay.

6. Have your test administered and your test results interpreted by appropriately trained individuals who follow professional codes of ethics.

7. Know if a test is optional and learn of the consequences of taking or not taking the test, fully completing the test, or canceling the scores. You may need to ask questions to learn these consequences.

8. Receive a written or oral explanation of your test results within a reasonable amount of time after testing and in commonly understood terms.

9. Have your test results kept confidential to the extent allowed by law.

10. Present concerns about the testing process or your results and receive information about procedures that will be used to address such concerns.

Issue 1: Right to Privacy

The concepts of individual freedom and privacy are integral to the cultural heritage of Americans. The *Ethical Principles* (APA, 2010) and *Standards* (AERA et al., 2014) affirm the rights of individuals to privacy, confidentiality, and self-determination. The *Ethical Principles* indicate an obligation to maintain and discuss the limits of confidentiality (Ethical Standards 4.01 and 4.02), minimize intrusions on privacy (Ethical Standard 3.04), and not release test data to others unless required by law or ordered by the court (Ethical Standard 9.04). **Confidentiality** means that individuals are assured that all personal information they disclose will be kept private and will not be disclosed to others without their explicit permission.

Sometimes test users are tempted to violate ethical standards regarding confidentiality. Managers, for instance, may believe it is in the best interest of their companies to have psychological information about employees. Teachers may also seek test scores of students with the good intention of understanding students' performance problems. Sometimes researchers may simply be careless about safeguarding files that contain test scores and personal information about research participants. However, APA ethical standards emphasize that regardless of good intentions or the apparently trivial nature of data collected, assessment information should not be disclosed without obtaining consent (Ethical Standard 3.10).

A related concept is **anonymity**—the practice of administering tests or obtaining information without obtaining the identity of the participant. Anonymous testing is often found in double-blind studies—those in which the researchers do not know the names of the participants or the experimental conditions to which they are assigned. Some research suggests that persons who complete surveys or tests anonymously might be more honest about themselves. On the other hand, it is often important for researchers to identify individuals so as to correlate test scores with other variables. Hence, there is a strong temptation for investigators to code test materials or surveys in such a way that participants can be identified without the participants' knowledge. Such practices violate ethical standards that ensure individual privacy. The *Ethical Principles* (APA, 2010) acknowledge that other obligations (e.g., knowledge that failure to disclose information would result in danger to others) may lead to conflict of ethical standards. For most psychologists and test administrators, however, there are no ethical reasons for violating rights of confidentiality or anonymity.

Issue 2: Right to Informed Consent

Individuals have the right of self-determination. According to the *Ethical Principles* (APA, 2010) and the *Standards* (AERA et al., 2014) those who use tests and assessments have an obligation to provide test takers with information prior to testing so the test takers can make an informed choice about whether to continue with testing. This information is typically delivered during the informed consent process. **Informed consent** refers to the process of explaining to individuals such things as why they are being tested, the purpose of a test, if and how third parties might be involved, if and what fees might be involved, and limits to confidentiality. When the validity of interpretations of the results will not be compromised, in some cases, the informed consent process might also include sharing with test takers helpful materials such as study guides or sample questions and tests (AERA et al., 2014). Furthermore, depending on the purpose of the test, individuals might be provided with test taking strategies (such as time management strategies).

However, informed consent is not always required. Informed consent is not required if the testing purpose is to evaluate a person's capacity to make decisions, if state law or governmental regulations require the testing, or if consent is implied. Consent is implied when a person voluntarily participates in an assessment or test as part of an organizational, educational, or institutional activity. An example of implied consent is when a person takes a test when applying for a job.

Professional standards make it clear that obtaining informed consent becomes increasingly important when the consequences of testing to the test taker increase. In the case of minors or persons of limited cognitive ability, both the test takers and their parents or guardians must give informed consent. In the case of Michael Elmore, school administrators did not inform his parents about administering the intelligence test, and they assumed that the Elmores were not capable of understanding the test and its implications. It is important to note that parental permission is not the same as informed consent. It is the test user's responsibility to confirm that both the child and the parent understand, to the best of their ability, the requirements and implications of the psychological test before the test is administered.

Issue 3: Right to Know and Understand Results

In addition, according to Ethical Standard 9.10 of the *Ethical Principles* (APA, 2010), the test taker—or a designated representative such as a parent if the test taker is a minor—is entitled to an explanation of test results. And, as reinforced by Ethical Standard 9.07, only a qualified professional should explain test results.

Issue 4: Right to Protection From Stigma

Likewise, in communicating test results to the test taker, guardian, or others, the test user should refrain from using stigmatizing labels such as *feebleminded* and *addictive personality*. In other words, the test results provided to anyone should facilitate positive growth and development.

TESTING SPECIAL POPULATIONS

Individuals who have minority status in terms of disabilities or ethnicity might need special accommodations when testing so that they can perform to the best of their abilities. Three of those special populations are people with physical or mental challenges, people with learning disabilities, and people from cultural backgrounds different from those for whom the test was designed.

Test Takers With Physical or Mental Challenges

Some people who have physical or mental challenges might need special accommodations during testing to ensure that their test scores are accurate. By physical and mental challenges, we mean sensory, motor, or cognitive impairments. **Sensory impairments** include deafness and blindness. **Motor impairments** include disabilities such as paralysis and missing limbs. **Cognitive impairments** are mental challenges that include intellectual disabilities, learning disabilities, and traumatic brain injuries.

The *Standards for Educational and Psychological Testing* (AERA et al., 2014) address testing individuals with disabilities. According to the *Standards*, test users should ensure that the test outcomes indicate the intended skills or attributes accurately and that the test scores have not been altered because of disabilities. When testing individuals with disabilities for diagnostic and intervention purposes, test users should not rely solely on test scores. Test users must consider other sources of information, such as interviews and behavioral measures, in addition to test scores. Various laws also protect persons who are physically or mentally challenged, for example, the Rehabilitation Act of 1973 (which was amended in 1978, 1986, and 1987), the Americans With Disabilities Act of 1990, and the Education for All Handicapped Children Act of 1990.

These ethical standards and laws guide our understanding of what a test user must consider when testing someone who has physical or mental challenges. Often such test takers have special needs that require modifications to the testing process. Test users must modify the testing format and the test interpretation process to accurately reflect the skill or attribute that the psychological test measures. In other words, an individual's impairment must not influence the test outcome when the test is measuring a concept unrelated to the disability.

On the Web Box 3.3 provides some history and directions for online access to *Test Access: Guidelines for Computer-Administered Testing* (Allan, Bulla, & Goodman, 2003), which provides information on modifying and adapting tests for individuals who are blind.

The modifications that a test developer or user makes depend on the specific disability. For Your Information Box 3.2 highlights some of the major administration and interpretation modifications for four categories of disabilities: visual impairment, hearing impairment, motor impairment, and cognitive impairment. Of course, not all psychological tests can be appropriately modified using these methods. Therefore, psychologists have designed some alternative tests for individuals with disabilities. Table 3.1 shows appropriate alternative tests for measuring various attributes in individuals with disabilities in one of the four categories.

Test Takers With Learning Disabilities

Some people have learning disabilities. Unlike the physical and mental disabilities already discussed, such as paralysis and visual impairment, a **learning disability** does not have visible

ON THE WEB BOX 3.3
GUIDELINES FOR TESTING THE BLIND
www.aph.org/tests/access/index.html

In the 1970s, Larry Skutchan, a young college student who had lost his sight, quickly gained familiarity with the problems of assessing the blind. Traditional assessment methods in the 1970s relied on printed tests and handwritten answers. "I was very lucky that many of the professors at the University of Arkansas at Little Rock were patient and caring enough to provide alternate means of assessment, usually with the professor himself reading the questions and accepting my responses orally," Skutchan recalled (as cited in Allan et al., 2003, "Foreword," para. 1). Skutchan, however, also experienced alternative techniques that were not nearly so comfortable or fair:

> I particularly recall an assessment where a freshman work study student read me the questions and wrote my responses, and it was clear that the material was far above the knowledge level of that student. This situation

is particularly troublesome in advanced course studies where the pool of candidates qualified to render such an examination shrinks in direct proportion to the complexity of the material on which the student is assessed. On the other hand, one has to wonder, especially with oral assessments, if the student or professor sometimes inadvertently conveys information about the material. None of these situations makes for an accurate assessment of the student's knowledge and ability. (para. 2)

Skutchan was technology project leader for the American Printing House for the Blind when it published the *Test Access: Guidelines for Computer-Administered Testing* (Allan et al., 2003). You can access the guidelines online by going to www.aph.org/tests/access/index .html.

FOR YOUR INFORMATION BOX 3.2
GUIDELINES FOR ACCOMMODATING TEST TAKERS WITH DISABILITIES

Visual Impairment (Totally or Partially Blind)

- The room should be free of distractions because the visually impaired are easily distracted by extraneous events.

- The test taker should be given ample time for testing to allow for dictation of instructions, slower reading of instructions, or time for the test taker to touch the testing materials.

- All materials should be put within reach of the test taker.

- The room lighting should be modified for optimal vision for the partially blind.

- The size of the test print should be increased for the partially blind.

- The appropriate writing instruments and materials (e.g., thicker writing pens) should be available for the partially blind.

- The test should be administered in Braille if the test taker uses Braille to read.

- Test scores of modified standardized tests should be interpreted cautiously unless there are norms for visually impaired test takers.

Hearing Impairment (Totally or Partially Deaf)

- A test taker who has a mild hearing impairment should be given the option of amplifying the test administrator's voice using an electronic amplification apparatus.

(Continued)

(Continued)

- A test taker who has a severe hearing impairment should be provided with the option of having written instructions and questions pantomimed or having an interpreter sign instructions, questions, and the test taker's responses. The test administrator, however, should be aware that substituting written instructions for verbal instructions introduces another variable (reading proficiency) into the testing situation and that pantomiming can compromise the standardization of instructions.

- When interpreting scores, test users should understand that the communication of the deaf is often fragmented, similar to that of individuals who are not very intelligent or who have mental disabilities, but in this case the fragmentation does not indicate low intelligence or a mental disability.

Motor Impairment

- Test administrators should select tests that do not need to be modified because of the test taker's motor impairment or that require very little modification. (Often intelligence tests include verbal and motor performance measures. Not using the motor performance measures could put too much emphasis on verbal intelligence.)

- The test administrator should have a writer available to enter responses on paper-and-pencil tasks that require fine motor coordination.

Cognitive Impairment

- Test takers with cognitive impairments should, in many cases, be tested using a structured interview, usually with family members or friends of the test takers present.

Source: Adapted from Cohen, Swerdlik, and Phillips (1996).

TABLE 3.1 ■ Tests Developed Specifically for Persons With Physical or Mental Challenges		
Disability	**Attribute Measured**	**Name of Test**
Visual impairment	Intelligence	Haptic Intelligence Scale
	Intelligence	Intelligence Test for Visually Impaired Children
	Intelligence	Perkins–Binet Tests of Intelligence for the Blind
	Cognitive ability	Cognitive Test for the Blind and Visually Impaired
	Development	Skills Inventory
	Learning/job success	Non-Language Learning Test
	Learning potential	The Blind Learning Aptitude Test
	Personality	Adolescent Emotional Factors Inventory
	Personality	Sound Test
	Vocational functioning	Comprehensive Vocational Evaluation System
	Vocational functioning and interest	PRG Interest Inventory
Hearing impairment	Cognitive ability	Test of Nonverbal Intelligence
	Intelligence	Child Behavior Checklist
	Behavior	Devereaux Adolescent Behavior Rating Scale
	Behavior disorders	Walker Problem Behavior Identification Checklist

Disability	Attribute Measured	Name of Test
Motor disabilities	Perceptual–motor skills	Purdue Perceptual–Motor Survey
	Sensory–motor skills	Frostig Movement Skills Test Battery
Cognitive disabilities	Adaptive behavior	Vineland Adaptive Behavior Scales
	Career assessment	Career Assessment Inventories for the Learning Disabled
	Sexual knowledge and attitudes	Socio-Sexual Knowledge and Attitudes Test
	Vocational preference	Reading Free Vocational Inventory

signs. A learning disability is a difficulty in any aspect of learning. According to the National Institute of Neurological Disorders and Stroke (2011), "learning disabilities are disorders that affect the ability to understand or use spoken or written language, do mathematical calculations, coordinate movements, or direct attention" (para. 1). There are a variety of learning disabilities, and Table 3.2 includes some examples of the most common ones.

To compensate for physical and mental impairments and learning disabilities, students can develop learning and test-taking strategies. The specific strategies required depend on the type and severity of the impairment or disability and vary from one person to the next, with some people requiring more help than others. Given the appropriate resources and support, most people with learning disabilities are very capable of performing well in school.

Students with learning disabilities have an important resource in their instructors, who can make adjustments that allow these students to learn and test more effectively. However,

TABLE 3.2 ■ Three Broad Categories of Learning Disabilities

The term *learning disabilities* includes a variety of disorders that affect the ability to learn. Some examples are below.

- Reading disability is a reading and language-based learning disability, also commonly called dyslexia. For most children with learning disabilities receiving special education services, the primary area of difficulty is reading. People with reading disabilities often have problems recognizing words that they already know. They may also be poor spellers and may have problems with decoding skills. Other symptoms may include trouble with handwriting and problems understanding what they read. About 15 percent to 20 percent of people in the United States have a language-based disability, and of those, most have dyslexia.

- Dyscalculia is a learning disability related to math. Those with dyscalculia may have difficulty understanding math concepts and solving even simple math problems.

- Dysgraphia is a learning disability related to handwriting. People with this condition may have problems forming letters as they write or may have trouble writing within a defined space.

- Information-processing disorders are learning disorders related to a person's ability to use the information that they take in through their senses—seeing, hearing, tasting, smelling, and touching. These problems are not related to an inability to see or hear. Instead, the conditions affect the way the brain recognizes, responds to, retrieves, and stores sensory information.

- Language-related learning disabilities are problems that interfere with age-appropriate communication, including speaking, listening, reading, spelling, and writing.

Source: National Institute of Child Health and Human Development. (2018). Learning disabilities. Retrieved from https://www.nichd.nih.gov/health/topics/learningdisabilities

instructors cannot help students who have not self-declared their disabilities—informed the school administration or their instructors—and presented their diagnoses by professionals in education, psychology, or medicine. Even physical impairments are not always apparent to teachers and testing administrators.

Persons applying for jobs might not be as likely as students to have trained professional advocates to assist them with test modifications. Therefore, applicants who have any types of disabilities, including learning disabilities, need to self-declare their disabilities and, when appropriate, present their diagnoses by professionals in education, psychology, or medicine to their prospective employers.

Test Takers From Multicultural Backgrounds

Test takers vary considerably in terms of their experiences and backgrounds. For example, the U.S. Census Bureau reported that almost 18% of the U.S. population was Hispanic in 2016 (U.S. Census Bureau, 2018). Other minority groups, especially those from Asia, are also growing. In this textbook, we refer to test takers from **multicultural backgrounds** as those who belong to various minority groups based on race, cultural or ethnic origin, sexual orientation, family unit, primary language, and so on. As we move further into the 21st century, identifying racial differences will become more difficult as the number of families with two or more racial backgrounds increases.

This advance in diversity requires test users and test developers to attend to the demographic characteristics of the people for whom a test was developed. When test takers differ from the original test takers that the developer used to develop the test, minority scores can differ significantly from those of the majority of test takers. For instance, a vocabulary test in English is likely to be more difficult for test takers whose primary language is not English but rather is Spanish, Arabic, or Japanese. In this case, the test user should not compare English speakers with those who speak other languages. Decisions based on "high" or "low" scores or on "passing" or "failing" scores will depend on the purpose of the test.

Although attention to multicultural clinical assessment and its accompanying ethical or measurement problems has grown, the quality and quantity of research studies do not match the current need for information. Studies of American minorities and non-Americans are scarce for many popular assessment techniques, ranging from well-researched objective tests, such as the Personality Assessment Inventory, to projective techniques, such as the Thematic Apperception Test.

Studies conducted on the Rorschach inkblot test provide a good example. The Rorschach, which was developed in the early 20th century by Swiss psychologist Hermann Rorschach, is a projective personality test that is often used to identify personality disorders and assess emotional functioning. Although various methods for scoring the Rorschach are used, the Exner scoring system appears to be the most popular method in the United States, as it addresses many criticisms of skeptics. Several studies indicate that scores for relatively normal community samples of Mexicans, Central Americans, and South Americans on the Rorschach test often differ strikingly from the norms of Exner's system for scoring this test. These findings raise the issue of whether the test can be used ethically with Hispanic adults and children in the United States (Wood, Nezworski, Lilienfeld, & Garb, 2003). More detail about the Rorschach inkblot test can be found in the "How Are Tests Used in Clinical and Counseling Settings?" chapter.

A positive example of multicultural relevance is demonstrated by the Minnesota Multiphasic Personality Inventory–2 (MMPI-2). The MMPI

More detail about the Personality Assessment Inventory can be found in **Test Spotlight 6.1** in Appendix A.

was originally developed in the 1930s at the University of Minnesota to help identify personal, social, and behavioral problems in psychiatric patients. The test takers who participated in the development of the original MMPI were White residents of Minnesota, a largely rural state. As the MMPI became widely used for people of all races from diverse backgrounds, psychologists questioned whether the test provided accurate information for persons of color and urban populations. A major impetus for revising the MMPI came from these questions. Recent research suggests that the revised test, the MMPI-2, is a suitable measure for Blacks and Hispanics in the United States because the distribution of scores for these minorities is similar to the distribution of scores for Whites. The revision of the original MMPI provides a model for improving older tests that are not suitable for use with minorities (Wood et al., 2003).

> More detail about the MMPI can be found in **Test Spotlight 12.1** in Appendix A.

Although the tests discussed in this section are appropriate primarily for clinical diagnosis, these and other tests have also been administered in the workplace. Using tests that are inappropriate for test takers in the workplace can cause people to be refused jobs, passed over for promotions, or perceived as ineligible for merit increases. In educational settings, inappropriate testing of minorities can cause students to be denied access to college or assigned to remedial classes.

Chapter Summary

Psychological testing plays an important role in individuals' opportunities for education, employment, and mental health treatment. Improper test use can cause harm to individuals. Therefore, it is critical that those who use tests use them ethically by following professional practice standards. Some of the most relevant professional practice standards are the *Standards for Educational and Psychological Testing*, the *Code of Fair Testing Practices in Education*, the *Code of Ethical and Professional Standards in Human Resource Management*, the *Principles for the Validation and Use of Personnel Selection Procedures*, the *Uniform Guidelines on Employee Selection Procedures*, the *International Guidelines for Test Use*, and the *International Guidelines on Computer-Based and Internet Delivered Testing*.

Individuals and institutions use test scores to make important decisions. Test publishers, test users, and test takers all have a responsibility for ensuring that test scores are accurate and that good decisions are made. Test publishers should follow professional practice standards by selling tests only to qualified users, marketing tests truthfully, and providing a comprehensive test manual for each test. Test users should understand and abide by the professional practice standards within their professions, as well as the testing guidelines that apply to all professions. Test takers also have responsibilities, ranging from being prepared to take a test to treating others with courtesy and respect. In addition to having responsibilities, test takers have rights, such as the right to privacy, to informed consent, to know and understand results, and to be protected from stigma.

Persons who have physical or mental challenges might have special needs when taking tests that require modifying the testing process. The modifications that a test user makes depend on the specific disability of a test taker. When testing someone who has physical or mental challenges, ethical standards and certain laws require that the test user modify the test or the interpretation to ensure that the individual's impairment does not influence the test outcome. Another group whose members might need test modifications are those with learning disabilities. Students and their instructors can work together to develop learning and test-taking strategies.

Engaging in the Learning Process

Learning is the process of gaining knowledge and skills through schooling or studying. Although you can learn by reading the chapter material, attending class, and engaging in discussion with your instructor, more actively engaging in the learning process may help you better learn and retain chapter information. To help you actively engage in the learning process, we encourage you to access our new supplementary student workbook. The workbook contains critical thinking activities to help you understand and apply information and help you make progress toward learning and retaining material. If you do not have a copy of the workbook, you can purchase a copy through sagepub.com.

Key Concepts

After completing your study of this chapter, you should be able to define each of the following terms. These terms are bolded in the text of this chapter and defined in the Glossary.

anonymity	informed consent	test security
certification	learning disability	test taker
cognitive impairments	licensure	test user
confidentiality	motor impairments	user qualifications
ethical standards	multicultural backgrounds	
ethics	sensory impairments	

Critical Thinking Questions

The following are some critical thinking questions to support the learning objectives for this chapter.

Learning Objectives	Critical Thinking Questions
Define ethics and the importance of acting ethically by following professional practice standards.	• Identify two professional associations or societies that have published guidelines that guide the work of members who use psychological tests to make important decisions. What evidence can you find of the consequences for violating the published guidelines? • How might the unethical practices of someone administering a test affect test takers?
Identify the professional practice standards of associations and societies most relevant to psychological testing.	• What might happen if professional practice standards did not exist to guide those who use psychological tests? • What are the similarities and differences of the professional practice standards discussed in Chapter 3? • What practices do you believe are most critical to acting ethically when using psychological tests?

Learning Objectives	Critical Thinking Questions
Distinguish professional practice standards from certification and licensure.	• How would you distinguish between professional practice standards, certification, and licensure? • Identify two tests that are used for certification and two that are used for licensure and discuss why each is properly classified (certification vs. licensure).
Explain the general responsibilities of test publishers, test users, and test takers.	• Who has more responsibility for using tests properly—test publishers, test users, or test takers? • What are the similarities and differences in three test publisher's processes for selling tests to test users?
Explain the issues associated with testing special populations.	• What kinds of testing accommodations do you think individuals with visual, hearing, motor, and cognitive impairment might need? • What might be the consequences of not providing accommodations to those with learning disabilities? • Why is it important to understand the multicultural background of test takers?

PSYCHOMETRIC PRINCIPLES

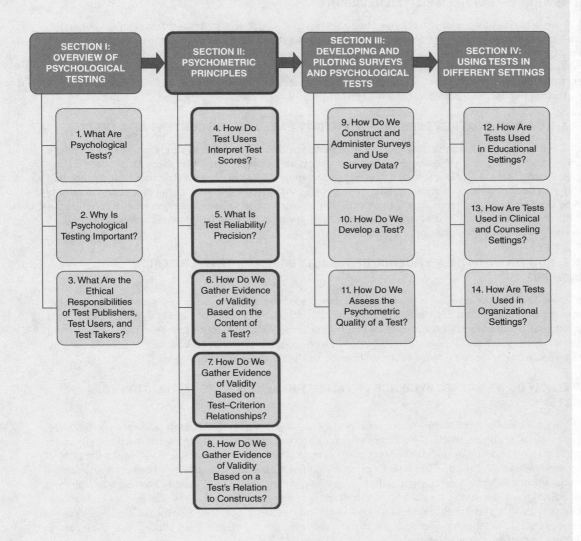

SECTION I: OVERVIEW OF PSYCHOLOGICAL TESTING

1. What Are Psychological Tests?

2. Why Is Psychological Testing Important?

3. What Are the Ethical Responsibilities of Test Publishers, Test Users, and Test Takers?

SECTION II: PSYCHOMETRIC PRINCIPLES

4. How Do Test Users Interpret Test Scores?

5. What Is Test Reliability/Precision?

6. How Do We Gather Evidence of Validity Based on the Content of a Test?

7. How Do We Gather Evidence of Validity Based on Test–Criterion Relationships?

8. How Do We Gather Evidence of Validity Based on a Test's Relation to Constructs?

SECTION III: DEVELOPING AND PILOTING SURVEYS AND PSYCHOLOGICAL TESTS

9. How Do We Construct and Administer Surveys and Use Survey Data?

10. How Do We Develop a Test?

11. How Do We Assess the Psychometric Quality of a Test?

SECTION IV: USING TESTS IN DIFFERENT SETTINGS

12. How Are Tests Used in Educational Settings?

13. How Are Tests Used in Clinical and Counseling Settings?

14. How Are Tests Used in Organizational Settings?

SECTION II

CHAPTER 4: HOW DO TEST USERS INTERPRET TEST SCORES?

In Chapter 4, we focus on increasing your understanding of the procedures used to interpret test scores. Because these procedures depend on the type of data that a test produces, we begin with a discussion of the four levels of measurement of psychological test data. We then discuss frequency distributions, measures of central tendency, measures of variability, and measures of relationship. After discussing how to convert raw scores into more meaningful units (e.g., z scores, T scores), we discuss the role of norms in interpreting test scores.

CHAPTER 5: WHAT IS TEST RELIABILITY/PRECISION?

In Chapter 5, we describe three methods of estimating a test's reliability/precision: test–retest reliability or stability over time, internal consistency or homogeneity of the test questions, and scorer reliability or agreement. We provide an introduction to classical test theory and describe the relationship between reliability/precision and random measurement error. We discuss how to calculate an index of reliability called the *reliability coefficient*, an index of error called the *standard error of measurement*, and an index of agreement called *Cohen's kappa*. Finally, we discuss factors that increase and decrease the reliability of test scores.

CHAPTER 6: HOW DO WE GATHER EVIDENCE OF VALIDITY BASED ON THE CONTENT OF A TEST?

In Chapter 6, we introduce you to the different types of evidence that are used to evaluate whether a proposed interpretation of a test score is valid. We discuss how validity is discussed in the *Standards for Educational and Psychological Testing* (American Educational Research Association [AERA], American Psychological Association [APA], & National Council on Measurement in Education [NCME], 2014). We begin with a brief discussion of validity as defined by the *Standards*. We focus most of our attention on evidence of validity based on an evaluation of the content of the test. We show how test developers collect evidence of validity while the test is being developed, as well as how they collect evidence after having developed the test.

CHAPTER 7: HOW DO WE GATHER EVIDENCE OF VALIDITY BASED ON TEST–CRITERION RELATIONSHIPS?

In Chapter 7, we describe the processes psychologists use to ensure that tests perform properly when they are used for making predictions and decisions. We begin by discussing the concept of validity evidence based on a test's relationships to other variables, specifically external criteria. We also discuss the importance of selecting a valid criterion measure, how to evaluate validity coefficients, and the statistical processes such as linear and multiple regression that provide evidence that a test can be useful for making predictions.

CHAPTER 8: HOW DO WE GATHER EVIDENCE OF VALIDITY BASED ON A TEST'S RELATION TO CONSTRUCTS?

In Chapter 8, we define and illustrate the terms *psychological construct*, *theory*, and *nomological network*. Because establishing evidence of construct validity involves accumulating and relating all of the psychometric information known about a test, we show how familiar concepts, such as reliability/precision, evidence of validity based on test content, and evidence of validity based on a test's relationships with other variables, are linked together. In addition, we discuss how convergent evidence of validity and discriminant evidence of validity are two other factors used for establishing validity based on a test's relationships with other variables and how this evidence of validity can be evaluated using a statistical tool called a multi-method, multi-trait matrix. Finally, we describe experimental methods used to establish evidence of construct validity for a test, including two procedures: exploratory factor analysis and confirmatory factor analysis.

HOW DO TEST USERS
INTERPRET TEST SCORES?

"My professor wrote all our midterm exam scores on the whiteboard. She asked us to review the scores and then describe to her how the class performed as a whole and how each of us performed in comparison to the rest of the class. Besides saying that everyone did 'okay,' and calculating the average exam score, none of us had much to say. Our professor then spent the entire class period helping us understand the different ways to describe a group of scores and compare one score to a group of scores. I didn't know there were so many ways to describe the results of a test."

"For a class assignment, I had to select a psychological test and critique it. As I was searching through the test manual for my chosen test, I noticed that in addition to what they call raw scores, some tests report their scores in T-scores and z-scores. What are these?"

"I recently received my SAT results. According to the results, nationally I scored in the 70th percentile, but in my state I scored in the 78th percentile. What do those numbers mean?"

If your friend told you she correctly answered 20 problems on her math midterm, correctly identified 18 of the organisms on her biology exam, or correctly answered 67 questions on her psychology exam, what would you think about her performance? Although your friend's attitude would probably give you a clue about how well (or poorly) she did, her raw scores (20 problems, 18 organisms, 67 questions) would actually tell you little about her performance. You would not know if the 20 correct problems on her math midterm or the 67 correct answers on the psychology exam were a good or bad thing. To properly understand and interpret raw scores, you need additional information.

In this chapter, our goal is to increase your understanding of the procedures used to interpret test scores. Because these procedures depend on the type of data that a test produces, and not all data are created or treated equally, we begin with a discussion of the four levels of measurement of psychological test data. We then discuss the most common procedures for interpreting test scores (frequency distributions, measures of central tendency, measures of variability, and measures of relationship). After discussing how we convert raw test scores into more meaningful standard scores, we discuss the role of norms in interpreting test scores.

LEVELS OF MEASUREMENT

Recall from Chapter 1 that measurement involves following rules for assigning numbers to attributes. We assign numbers so that we can analyze and make better sense of information. We assign numbers to information, sometimes arbitrarily, and the numbers often serve as placeholders and do not represent amounts or magnitudes of anything. When we speak about **level of measurement**, we are referring to the relationship among the numbers we have assigned to the information.

Understanding levels of measurement is critical to describing and interpreting psychological test and measurement results because we use numbers, at the item level, the scale level, and the test result level. Tests and surveys are made up of items. For example, it's likely that for a test you've taken in the past you had to answer multiple-choice questions. Each question is an item. After a person takes a test, we score the individual items. For psychological tests, the individual items are typically combined to produce a score on a scale and/or combined to produce a test result, which may be a test score or a description. For example, a knowledge test may include multiple-choice test items that are individually scored as correct or incorrect, and then the number of correct items is summed to create an overall raw test score. A personality test may include test items where an individual must choose from one of two possible answers, and then the answers are scored to reveal a description of a person's personality.

How we describe or report item-level results and the claims we can make about psychological test results depends on the properties (the level of measurement) of these numbers. For example, with the appropriate level of measurement, we may be able to say that Johnny is twice as intelligent as Susan. However, if the level of measurement does not allow this type of explanation, we may only be able to say that Johnny's intelligence is simply different from Susan's intelligence, or that Johnny is more intelligent than Susan.

Let's take a look at how we might assign numbers to specific test items. Recall from Chapter 1 that the behaviors test takers perform vary by test. For example, a test may require an individual to answer a multiple-choice question, rate his or her agreement with statements, or complete a puzzle. Each of these test items has a level of measurement. Imagine we designed a 10-item multiple-choice test to measure knowledge of the material in Chapter 2 of the current textbook. Here is one possible multiple-choice item:

When Lauren received her SAT results, she decided to apply for admission to two very selective colleges because she scored in the 90th percentile. What type of decision did Lauren make based on her SAT results?

A) An individual decision

B) An institutional decision

C) An absolute decision

D) A comparative decision

For the question above, we might assign numbers to each of the four potential response options as follows:

A = 1

B = 2

C = 3

D = 4

Now, imagine we designed a test to measure marital satisfaction, and as a part of the test, individuals had to respond to the test items below:

Please indicate how frequently you and your spouse agree on how to make the following important decisions:

	Always agree	Almost always agree	Sometimes agree	Frequently disagree	Almost always disagree	Always disagree
How to spend and save money						
How many children you will have						
How much free time to spend together						

For the items above, we might assign numbers to each of the six potential response options as follows:

1 = Always agree

2 = Almost always agree

3 = Sometimes agree

4 = Frequently disagree

5 = Almost always disagree

6 = Always disagree

We would assign the numbers so we could quantify each important decision.

For each of the two tests above, in addition to using numbers at the item level, we might also use numbers to represent the final test outcome. For example, with the knowledge test, we might report a final test score as the number of items answered correctly (e.g., 7 of 10) or a percentage (e.g., 70%). For the marital satisfaction test, we might use numbers to represent a group of items (e.g., we might calculate the average number for each important decision and then add the averages together to create a scale score), and/or we might calculate a final marital satisfaction score for a person who takes the test by summing their responses to all items. As you can see, numbers play an important role in testing. Understanding levels of measurement plays a critical role in determining what types of mathematical calculations (e.g., totals, percentages, ratios) we may perform on those numbers to describe the test results.

So what are the levels of measurement we use when describing and interpreting the results of psychological tests? Most measurement experts continue to think in terms of four levels of measurement based on the mathematical operations that can be performed with the data at each level (S. Stevens, 1946, 1951, 1961). The four levels are nominal, ordinal, equal interval, and ratio. As we move from one level of measurement to the next, we are able to perform more statistical calculations that allow us to interpret and make more and different claims regarding test results. Table 4.1 provides definitions and some examples of the four levels of measurement, including the statistical calculations we might use when analyzing test or survey data.

TABLE 4.1 ■ Levels of Measurement			
Level of Measurement	Definition	Examples	Some Appropriate Statistics
Nominal	At the nominal level, numbers are assigned to represent labels or categories of data only.	Are you currently happy? 1 = Yes 2 = No What do all psychological tests require that you do? A = Answer questions B = Fill out a form C = Perform a behavior D = Sign a consent form	Frequency, mode, chi-square
Ordinal	At the ordinal level, numbers are assigned to rank-order data. However, the distances or values between numbers are not equal; they can vary.	Please rank the following colors in terms of the color you like most (1) to the color you like least (6). Please use each number (1–6) once. ____blue ____green ____yellow ____orange ____black ____white	Frequency, mode, median, percentile, rank-order correlation

Level of Measurement	Definition	Examples	Some Appropriate Statistics
Interval	At the interval level, numbers are also assigned to rank-order data, *and* the distance between numbers is judged to be equal. However, there is no absolute zero point (a number that indicates the complete absence of what is measured).	To what extent do you and your spouse agree on how to spend and save money? A = Always agree B = Almost always agree C = Sometimes agree D = Frequently disagree E = Almost always disagree F = Always disagree How would you rate your current health? 1 = Poor 2 = Fair 3 = Good 4 = Very good 5 = Excellent	Frequency, mean, mode, median, standard deviation, Pearson product–moment correlation, *t* test, *F* test
Ratio	At the ratio level, numbers are also assigned to rank-order data, *and* the distance between numbers is also equal, *and* there is an absolute zero point.	How many children do you have? ____ How many years of experience do you have in the hospitality industry? ____	Frequency, mean, mode, median, standard deviation, Pearson product–moment correlation, proportion, *t* test, *F* test

Nominal Scales

The most basic level of measurement is the **nominal scale**. With nominal scales, we assign numbers to represent groups or categories of information. Numbers in the nominal scale serve as labels only—they are not intended for use in calculations. You can easily remember this level of measurement, as *nominal* comes from the French word for "name"—you are just naming data. Nominal scales are frequently used for demographic data such as grouping people based on their gender, race, or place of residence. For example, we can assign a 0 to women and a 1 to men, or we can assign a 0 to Whites, a 1 to Hispanics, a 2 to Blacks, and so on. Although a researcher may assign a 0 to women and a 1 to men, these numbers do not represent quantitative values; in other words, men are not worth more than women because the number assigned to them is higher or vice versa. Instead, the numbers simply give the categories numerical labels. Another example is the number marked on a football, basketball, or baseball player's uniform. Again, such numbers are labels used for identification. For example, during the 2018 Super Bowl, Patriots' quarterback Tom Brady had the number 12 on his jersey, and Eagles' player Nick Foles had the number 9. Tom Brady's number on his jersey does not indicate he is superior to Nick Foles—the number merely helps us identify each quarterback.

Now, let's look at some examples within the field of psychological testing. Let's say a clinical psychologist administers an intelligence test and a personality test to a group of individuals. The psychologist may use the intelligence test results to classify each individual as "average" or "gifted." Average individuals could be assigned a label of 1 and gifted individuals a label of 2. The psychologist may use the personality test results to determine whether each individual has a psychological disorder. We may assign each psychological disorder a number, for example, 1 for manic depressive, 2 for bipolar disorder, and so on.

Because nominal scales yield only **categorical data**—data grouped according to a common property—there are few ways to describe or manipulate the data they yield. Usually, researchers report nominal data in terms of the number of occurrences in each category—or frequencies. For example, a clinical psychologist might report how many individuals he assigned a 1 (average) and a 2 (gifted) or how many individuals he diagnosed as manic depressive (1) or bipolar (2). The psychologist might also report the most frequent diagnosis (what we refer to as the *mode*).

Ordinal Scales

Ordinal scales are the second level of measurement. In addition to having all of the qualities of nominal scales, with ordinal scales the numbers are assigned to order or rank objects on the attribute being measured. You can easily remember this level of measurement because the first three letters are *ord*, which are also the first three letters of *order*.

If a teacher asks children to line up in order of their height, placing the shortest child first and the tallest child last, the teacher can then assign numbers based on each child's height. The shortest child may be assigned a 1, the next shortest child a 2, and so on. If there are 20 children, the tallest child would be assigned a 20. In this case, the teacher has created an ordinal scale based on the children's height. An ordinal scale indicates an individual's or object's value based on its relationship to others in the group. If another child—smaller than the others—joins the group, that child will be labeled 1, and the number assigned to each of the other children would change in relationship to the new child.

There are a number of practical uses for ordinal scales. Car dealerships often rank their salespeople based on the number of cars they sell each month. High schools and colleges rank students by grade point average (GPA), yielding a measure of class standing. Publications such as *U.S. News & World Report* and the *Financial Times* rank colleges and universities. For example, when *U.S. News & World Report* released its 2017 list of best colleges and universities, it ranked Rollins College number 2 out of 113 southern regional universities (*U.S. News & World Report*, 2018).

Applied to psychological testing, a clinical psychologist may create ordinal-level data by ordering each of 10 individuals who take an intelligence test from highest score to lowest score. The person who scores the highest may be assigned a label of 1, and the person who scores the lowest may be assigned a label of 10. Other individuals would be assigned labels of 2 through 9, depending on their test scores.

On the Web Box 4.1 provides an example of another practical use of ordinal scales, ranking states in terms of health and well-being.

You should remember two important points about ordinal scales. First, the number or rank has meaning only within the group being compared and provides no information about the group as a whole. For instance, the top student in your class may have a GPA of 3.98, but next year another student may receive the top ranking with a GPA of only 3.75. Similarly, the individual who was labeled number one in the group who took the intelligence test may have had an intelligence score of 110, but at any given time, the highest scoring individual (and

ON THE WEB BOX 4.1
THE GALLUP-HEALTHWAYS WELL-BEING INDEX
http://info.healthways.com/wellbeingindex

Beginning in 2008, Gallup began surveying thousands of adults, as part of their Well-Being Index, to gather data on the health and well-being of U.S. residents. Business leaders at the national, state, city, and organizational levels use these findings to understand the well-being of citizens and employees. They use the data to inform decisions and develop strategies related to such things as health benefits, work environments, corporate culture, and community investment—with the overall objective of enhancing health, happiness, and productivity.

The survey results are widely used. For example, U.S. leaders can use the data collected from this survey to develop strategies for improving health, increasing productivity, and lowering health care costs. Academics and medical experts might use the data to inform their own research. Journalists might use the results to inform their reporting of the health and well-being of U.S. residents.

Based on data collected in 2017, all 50 U.S. states were ranked according to their citizens' well-being (Sharecare, Inc., 2018):

(1) South Dakota, (2) Vermont, (3) Hawaii,
(4) Minnesota, (5) North Dakota, (6) Colorado,

(7) New Hampshire, (8) Idaho, (9) Utah,
(10) Montana, (11) Massachusetts, (12) Florida,
(13) Texas, (14) California, (15) Arizona,
(16) Wyoming, (17) Nebraska, (18) Virginia,
(19) North Carolina, (20) Connecticut, (21) Iowa,
(22) Washington, (23) New York, (24) Maine,
(25) Alaska, (26) New Mexico, (27) Wisconsin,
(28) New Jersey, (29) Tennessee, (30) Maryland,
(31) Georgia, (32) Michigan, (33) Kansas,
(34) Pennsylvania, (35) Oregon, (36) Illinois,
(37) South Carolina, (38) Alabama, (39) Missouri,
(40) Delaware, (41) Rhode Island, (42) Indiana,
(43) Nevada, (44) Ohio, (45) Kentucky,
(46) Oklahoma, (47) Mississippi, (48) Arkansas,
(49) Louisiana, (50) West Virginia.

Detailed results and a downloadable report are available at http://www.well-beingindex.com. The results are reported for overall well-being, life evaluation, emotional health, physical health, healthy behavior, work environment, and basic access.

Source: Sharecare, Inc. (2018).

---

therefore the highest ranking individual) may have a higher or lower intelligence score. The ranks are assigned based on the comparison group and have little meaning outside the group.

Second, an ordinal scale gives no information about how closely two individuals or objects are related. The student with the highest GPA (ranked first) may be only a little better or a lot better than the student with the next highest GPA (ranked second). If the top student has a GPA of 3.98, the student ranked next will be second whether his or her GPA is 3.97 or 3.50, as long as the student's GPA is higher than the GPAs of the rest of the students. Similarly, the individual with the highest intelligence test score may have just a slightly higher intelligence score than the next-ranked individual; however, the gap between the second-ranked person and third-ranked person may be much larger.

Age equivalents, grade equivalents, and percentile scores (which we discuss later in this chapter) all represent ordinal-level data. In fact, most psychological scales produce ordinal data. However, because we cannot add, subtract, multiply, or divide ordinal scores (nor can we compute means or standard deviations, which we talk about later in this chapter), ordinal scales are limited in their usefulness to psychologists. Therefore, some test developers make the assumption that these instruments produce equal interval data.

Interval Scales

Interval scales are the next level of measurement. These scales have all the qualities of the previous scales, but each number represents a point that is an equal distance from the points adjacent to it. You can easily remember this level of measurement because *interval* means gap or distance, and with this level of measurement we can determine the gap or distance between numbers.

For instance, an increase of 1 degree on a temperature scale represents the same amount of increase in heat at any point on the scale. A good example of what some assume to be an interval scale is a Likert-type scale. For example, assume that a test required you to indicate the extent to which you agreed with a number of statements, where 1 = *strongly disagree*, 2 = *disagree*, 3 = *somewhat agree*, 4 = *agree*, and 5 = *strongly agree*. Although professionals and researchers debate whether Likert-type scales are ordinal or interval, many treat the scales as interval scales, assuming that each point on the Likert-type rating scale represents an equal distance or amount of the construct being measured (Trochim, 2006). We assume that everyone responding has the same understanding of what *somewhat agree* and *agree* represent as well as the distance between the two.

The advantage of an interval scale is that we can perform more statistical calculations, including means and standard deviations, for these scores. These statistics allow comparison of the performance of one group with the performance of another group, or the score of one individual with the score of another individual, on the same test. We also use these statistics to calculate test norms and standard scores.

A drawback of the interval scale (and of the previous two scales) is that it does not have a point that indicates an absolute absence of the attribute being measured. For example, temperature scales (both Fahrenheit and Celsius) have a point that is labeled 0 (zero), but that point does not represent a total absence of heat. In other words, the zero point on an equal interval scale is arbitrary and does not represent the point at which the attribute being measured does not exist.

When we think about psychological constructs, this property makes sense. Although we can measure an individual's level of anxiety, intelligence, or mechanical aptitude, it is difficult to establish the point at which an individual totally lacks anxiety, intelligence, or mechanical aptitude. The interval scale allows comparisons of groups and individuals, even though the point at which the attribute is totally absent cannot be specified. In a joking manner, we sometimes tell our students that a 0% score on an exam does not really mean that they have no knowledge of the subject matter; rather, the exam simply did not sample the knowledge they do have. This makes our students feel better for perhaps a minute!

Ratio Scales

Ratio scales are the fourth level of measurement. Ratio scales have all of the qualities of the previous scales, and they also have a point that represents an absolute absence of the property being measured—that point is called *zero*. You can easily remember this level of measurement because the last letter is *o*, which is similar to zero.

Most measurement scales used in everyday life for physical measurements are ratio scales. For instance, stepping on your bathroom scale gives a measure of your weight in pounds. You might weigh 150 pounds, and your roommate might weigh 165 pounds. If each of you gains 1 pound, you have gained the same amount. When nothing is on the scale, it registers 0 (zero)—an absence of any weight. Because there is a true zero point, ratio scales also allow ratio comparisons. For example, we can say that a person who weighs 160 pounds is twice as heavy as a person who weighs 80 pounds.

Although most measures of psychological constructs do not meet the requirements of a ratio scale, those that use common measures of time or distance do qualify as ratio measures.

For instance, the time required to complete a task or the distance between two individuals might be used to infer attributes such as performance or preference, respectively.

Why is it important for you to understand the differences in the levels of measurement? The answer is simple: The level of measurement tells you about the statistical operations you can perform and what you can and cannot say about test scores. For example, let us say that three of your best friends score 75, 50, and 25 on a test that measures introversion. If the test scores were on an ordinal scale, all we can determine from the scores is who is more or less introverted. (In fact, we cannot even say that unless we know whether a high or low score indicates the presence of introversion.) We can say that Corrine (who scored 75) is more introverted than Jean (who scored 50) when a high score indicates a high level of introversion. We cannot say that Jean (who scored 50) is twice as introverted as John (who scored 25). We cannot compare ordinal scores using multiples, because ordinal scales do not have a true zero point that indicates an absence of introversion. We can compare using multiples only with a ratio level of measurement.

PROCEDURES FOR INTERPRETING TEST SCORES

Now that you have a better understanding of how the type of data a test produces can vary (that is, the data's level of measurement), we'll turn our attention to the most common procedures we use for making sense of test scores. These procedures all depend on raw test scores. **Raw scores** are the most basic scores calculated from a psychological test. They tell us very little about how an individual has performed on a test, how an individual has performed in comparison with others who took the test, or how an individual performed on one test compared with another test. Raw scores are not very useful at all without additional interpretive information. For example, we might score a 7 on a test. Used alone, the 7 has little meaning.

To make sense of raw test scores, we rely on a number of techniques. For example, we often arrange groups of raw scores from the same test into frequency distributions, or calculate descriptive statistics from raw scores, such as measures of central tendency, variability, or relationship. We also convert raw scores into more informative standard scores so that we can make comparisons between test scores and compare converted scores with those from what we call a **norm group**—a previously tested group of individuals. (We talk more about norm groups later in this chapter.)

Unfortunately, many test users do not understand how to properly make sense of raw test scores or interpret test scores. When tests are interpreted improperly, people are likely to make the wrong decisions about themselves and others. Some historical examples, from Lyman (1998), can help you understand what can happen when test scores are not properly interpreted:

> A college freshman, told that she had "average ability," withdrew from college. Her counselor had not added "when compared with other students at her college where standards are exceptionally high." The freshman reasoned that if she had only average ability compared with people in general, she must be very unintelligent when compared with college students. Rather than face the situation, she dropped out of college. (p. 2)

> "When am I going to start failing?" a student once asked me. On being questioned, he told me this story: "My high school teacher told me that I had an IQ [intelligence quotient] of only 88. She said that I might be able to get into college because I was an All-State football player but that I'd be certain to flunk out—with an IQ like that!" I pointed out to Don that he had been doing well in my course. I discovered that he had earned a B+ average during his first 2 years at our university. I reminded Don that the proof of a pudding lies in its eating—and that the proof of scholastic achievement

lies in earned grades, not in a single test designed to predict grades. Two years later, Don graduated with honors. (p. 2)

Although there are a variety of questions we want to ask about the use of these tests (Is there evidence of validity for the intended purpose? Is there evidence of reliability/precision? Were the tests administered properly? Were the tests scored properly?), one question is most important to the current chapter: Were the test scores properly interpreted? In the situations Lyman (1998) described, it seems likely that the test users may have made unacceptable errors in interpreting the students' test scores. Is it possible that if the college counselor had compared the college freshman's ability with that of college students, she may have scored "above aver-age"? Given that he was doing so well in school, is it possible that Don's IQ might have been a percentile rank instead of a raw score (discussed later in this chapter)?

Frequency Distributions

When a group of people take a test, we can summarize their scores using a **frequency distribution**—an orderly arrangement of a group of numbers (or test scores). Frequency distributions show the actual number (or percentage) of observations that fall into a range or category; they provide a summary and picture of group data. Although there are numerous ways to portray frequency distributions, two of the most frequently used methods are tables and histograms.

To create frequency tables and histograms, we begin with raw scores. For example, let us imagine that we have raw test scores for the 27 children in Table 4.2. To construct a frequency table, the first step is to identify the minimum and maximum test scores and arrange the test scores from highest to lowest or vice versa. The second step is to count and document the number of individuals who earned each particular score. The third step is to document this information in the form of a frequency table, as shown in Table 4.3.

TABLE 4.2 ■ Raw Test Scores for 27 Children			
Child	Test Score	Child	Test Score
1	21	15	29
2	22	16	16
3	25	17	23
4	14	18	27
5	25	19	27
6	26	20	28
7	28	21	30
8	17	22	24
9	22	23	19
10	10	24	31
11	34	25	31
12	36	26	32
13	37	27	40
14	20		

TABLE 4.3 ■ Frequency Table of 27 Test Scores Presented in Table 4.2		
Score	Frequency	Percentage
40	1	3.7%
39	0	0%
38	0	0%
37	1	3.7%
36	1	3.7%
35	0	0%
34	1	3.7%
33	0	0%
32	1	3.7%
31	2	7.4%
30	1	3.7%
29	1	3.7%
28	2	7.4%
27	2	7.4%
26	1	3.7%
25	2	7.4%
24	1	3.7%
23	1	3.7%
22	2	7.4%
21	1	3.7%
20	1	3.7%
19	1	3.7%
18	0	0%
17	1	3.7%
16	1	3.7%
15	0	0%
14	1	3.7%
13	0	0%
12	0	0%
11	0	0%
10	1	3.7%

Sometimes we create frequency tables using grouped test scores instead of individual raw scores. To do this, the first step is to create **class intervals**, which are a way to group raw scores so as to display them. Lyman (1998) suggested that when creating class intervals in frequency tables, we should aim for approximately 15 groups of scores. To determine the width of each group, and hence the number of groups, take the highest score and subtract the lowest score. Then divide this number by 15. If the calculated width is an even number, add 1 so that each interval will have a midpoint. Table 4.4 shows how to calculate the class intervals and construct the grouped frequency distribution for the raw test scores presented in Table 4.2.

In psychological testing, it is common to display these distributions graphically as a **histogram**—a bar graph used to represent frequency data in statistics. The horizontal axis represents all of the possible values of some variable (class intervals), and the vertical axis represents the number of people (frequency) who scored each value on the horizontal axis. It is also common to display distributions graphically as stem-and-leaf plots, which are similar to histograms. Although they look like histograms on their sides, stem-and-leaf plots are constructed in a somewhat different manner. The first digit of each raw score is placed in the left "stem" column. The second digit of each number is then placed in the second "leaf" column. Figure 4.1 shows a histogram created from the data in Table 4.4 and a stem-and-leaf plot from the data in Table 4.3.

If the distribution of scores in a histogram is symmetrical (balanced on both sides), the frequency distribution might form a bell-shaped curve or what we call a normal curve. Distributions often become more symmetrical when the sample of test scores is large because they more closely represent the entire population of scores.

TABLE 4.4 ■ Grouped Frequency Distribution of Test Scores Presented in Table 4.2	
High score = 40	1. Class interval width = 40 (high score) − 10 (low score) = 30
Low score = 10	2. 30 (difference)/15 (ideal number of intervals) = 2
	3. Because 2 is an even number, we add 1 to create an interval width of 3
Class Interval	**Frequency**
10–12	1
13–15	1
16–18	2
19–21	3
22–24	4
25–27	5
28–30	4
31–33	3
34–36	2
37–39	1
40–42	1

FIGURE 4.1 ■ Histogram and Stem-and-Leaf Plot of Data Presented in Tables 4.3 and 4.4

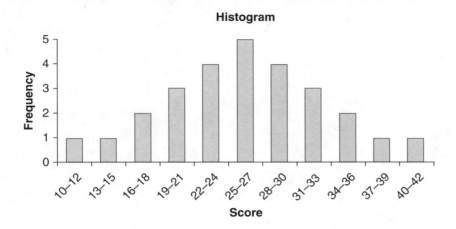

Histogram

Stem	Leaf
1	0 4 6 9 7
2	0 1 2 3 4 5 5 6 7 7 8 8 9
3	0 1 1 2 4 6 7
4	0

Stem-and-leaf plot

The Normal Curve

When we administer a psychological test to a group of individuals, we obtain a distribution of real scores from real people. Unlike this real distribution of scores (or what we call the obtained distribution of scores), **normal probability distributions** (also referred to as **normal curves**) are theoretical distributions that exist in our imagination as perfect and symmetrical, and actually consist of a family of distributions that have the same general bell shape—high in the middle and tapering to the ends. Figure 4.2 shows some examples of normal distributions.

Notice how each distribution in Figure 4.2 forms a bell-shaped curve. Each distribution is symmetrical, with scores more concentrated in the middle than at the tails. Although the area under each distribution is the same, the distributions differ in terms of how spread out they are or how tall or short the shape is. What a graph of a normal distribution of test scores looks like depends on two descriptive statistics—the mean from a distribution of test scores and the standard deviation. The mean of the distribution determines the location of the center of the graph. The standard deviation determines the width and the height of the graph. With smaller standard deviations, the curve is narrow and tall. With larger standard deviations, the curve is wider and shorter.

FIGURE 4.2   ■   Examples of Normal Distributions

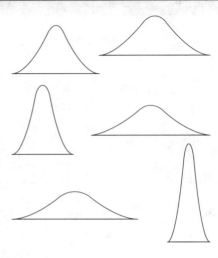

The normal probability distribution has a number of characteristics that are important for interpreting test scores. These characteristics are explained below and graphically shown in the distribution pictured in Figure 4.3.

- Most test scores cluster or fall near the middle of the distribution, forming what we refer to as the average or the central tendency. The farther to the right or left you move from the average, the fewer scores there are.

- Most people will score near the middle of the distribution, making the center of the distribution the highest point.

- The curve can continue to infinity, and therefore the right and left tails of the curve will never touch the baseline.

- Approximately 34.1% of the population will score between the mean and 1 standard deviation (we explain this term later in this chapter) above the mean, and approximately 34.1% will score between the mean and 1 standard deviation below the mean. Approximately 13.6% of the population will score between 1 and 2 standard deviations above the mean, and approximately 13.6% will score between 1 and 2 standard deviations below the mean. Approximately 2.1% of the population will score between 2 and 3 standard deviations above the mean, and approximately 2.1% will score between 2 and 3 standard deviations below the mean. This curve will capture most of the scores in a population.

- The curve is convex at its highest point and changes to concave at 1 standard deviation above the mean and 1 standard deviation below the mean.

Most distributions of human traits, from height and weight to aptitudes and personality characteristics, would form a normal curve if we gathered data from the entire population. For example, although some people are as short as 4 feet and some are as tall as 7 feet, most men and women are between 5 feet 2 inches and 5 feet 9 inches. The scores on most psychological tests, when administered to large groups of individuals, approximate the normal curve.

FIGURE 4.3 ■ Normal Probability Distribution

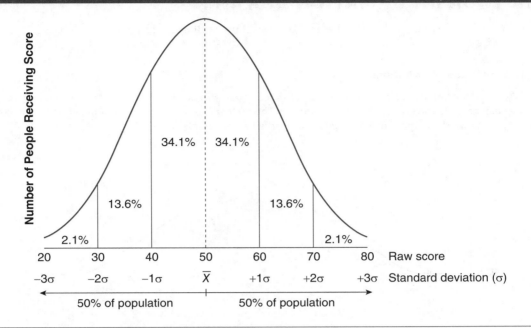

Not all psychological measurements, however, yield normal or bell-shaped curves. Some are negatively skewed (there is one peak, with many high scores). Some are positively skewed (there is one peak, with many low scores). Some are sharply peaked (there is one peak, and most individuals have the same score). Finally, some are bimodal (there are two distinct peaks, typically with many low scores and many high scores). For Your Information Box 4.1 provides an example of evenly distributed, skewed, peaked, and bimodal distributions using test scores from groups of children.

Descriptive Statistics

Another way we make sense of raw test scores is by calculating descriptive statistics. Have you ever told a friend about a movie you saw? Instead of telling your friend every little detail, you probably summarized the movie by sharing just the main points. That is what **descriptive statistics** are all about. Although frequency distributions provide a visual image of a distribution of scores, descriptive statistics help us describe or summarize a distribution of test scores using numbers. Descriptive statistics allow us to determine the main points of a group of scores. The descriptive statistics we typically rely on in psychological testing are measures of central tendency, measures of variability, and measures of relationship.

Measures of Central Tendency

A **measure of central tendency** is a value that helps us understand the middle of a distribution or set of scores. Three common measures of central tendency are the mean (the arithmetic average), the median, and the mode. The **mean** is the average score in a distribution or sample. There are two symbols

FOR YOUR INFORMATION BOX 4.1
EVENLY DISTRIBUTED, SKEWED, PEAKED, AND BIMODAL DISTRIBUTIONS

Evenly Distributed Distributions

In evenly distributed distributions, most test scores cluster or fall near the middle of the distribution, forming what we refer to as the average or central tendency. The farther a point is to the right or left from the central tendency, the fewer the number of individuals represented at that point.

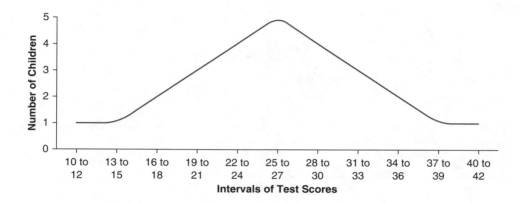

Positively Skewed Distributions

Positively skewed distributions have one high point and are skewed to the right. In positively skewed distributions, there are more low scores than high scores.

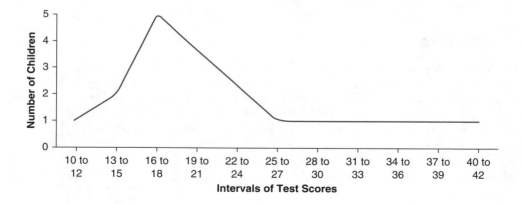

Negatively Skewed Distributions

Negatively skewed distributions have one high point and are skewed to the left. In negatively skewed distributions, there are more high scores than low scores.

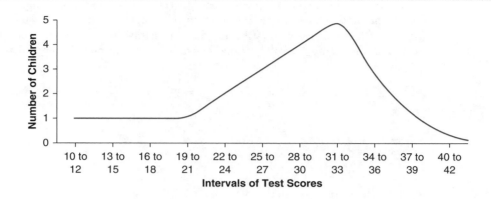

Peaked Distributions

Peaked distributions have one high point and result when many individuals score near the center of the distribution.

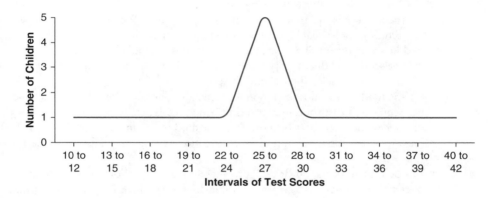

Bimodal Distributions

Bimodal distributions have two high points and result when many people score low, many people score high, and few people score in the middle.

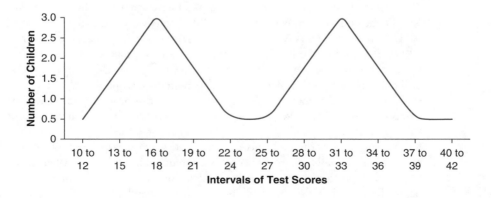

we use to indicate the mean. One symbol (μ) represents the mean of a population, and the other symbol ($\bar{x}$ or x-bar) represents the mean of a sample. When describing test scores, many times we are concerned with an entire group or distribution of test scores (a population of scores). In those cases, we will be using the symbol μ. The formula for a population mean is

$$\mu = \frac{\sum x}{N}$$

where

Σ = "sum of"

x = each raw test score in the distribution

N = the total number of test scores in the distribution

We calculate the mean by adding all of the raw scores in a group or distribution (x) and dividing by the total number of scores (N). You probably learned to calculate averages in elementary school; this is the same thing.

The **median** is the middle score in a group of scores. We find the median by putting all the raw scores in order (e.g., from lowest to highest or from highest to lowest) and selecting the middle score. If there is an even number of scores, we find the middle score by adding the two middle scores and dividing by 2. Be careful with this one; students sometimes forget to order the scores before selecting the middle score.

The **mode** is the most common score in a distribution. We calculate the mode by ordering the scores in a distribution and seeing which score occurs most often. While there is often just one mode, there may be more than one mode or no mode at all. When there is more than one mode, the distribution is often referred to as being bimodal (two modes) or multimodal (more than two modes).

For Your Information Box 4.2 provides an example of how to calculate the three measures of central tendency. As a reminder, Table 4.1 shows which measures of central tendency can be calculated at each level of measurement.

What is the best measure of central tendency? It depends. Let us answer this question by looking at some examples. When Kia, the daughter of one of this textbook's authors, lost her first tooth, there was a question about how much money the tooth fairy should leave under her pillow. We could have collected data to help us make this decision. We could have asked a sample of parents how much money they left under their children's pillows when their children lost teeth. Using these amounts, we could have calculated the average amount and paid Kia the mean. However, what if 2 of the 20 parents we asked had wealthy tooth fairies who paid $20 per tooth, and everyone else's tooth fairy paid between $2 and $4 per tooth? The two $20 tooth fairies would have raised the mean to a level that would have made it appear that most people paid more for a lost tooth than they really did. The point is this: The mean is the best measure of central tendency when distributions of scores are relatively symmetric. However, for skewed distributions, the central tendency can be greatly influenced by the extreme scores (in this case, the two parents who paid $20 per tooth) or what we call **outliers**—a few values that are significantly higher or lower than most of the values. There is another story that nicely demonstrates the problems that can arise when making decisions using the mean. A researcher in a small town of 20 people was interested in finding out whether it was necessary to provide food to some of the poorer residents of the town. So he asked all 10 of the richest people how much bread they had and found that they had 1 loaf each. He them asked the

FOR YOUR INFORMATION BOX 4.2
CALCULATING MEASURES OF CENTRAL TENDENCY

The following scores represent the going rate for a lost tooth according to 10 "tooth fairies."

Tooth Fairy	Going Rate	Measures of Central Tendency
1	$1.00	**Mean = $1.65**
2	$1.25	• Add the raw scores together ($1.00 + $1.25+ $1.00 + $1.25 + $1.00 + $1.50 + $5.00 + $2.00 + $1.25 + $1.25 = $16.50)
3	$1.00	• Divide the sum by the total number of scores ($16.50/10 = $1.65)
4	$1.25	**Mode = $1.25**
5	$1.00	• Order the raw scores from highest to lowest ($1.00 $1.00 $1.00 $1.25 $1.25 $1.25 $1.25 $1.50 $2.00 $5.00)
6	$1.50	• Identify the most frequent score ($1.25)
7	$5.00	**Median = $1.25**
8	$2.00	• Order the raw scores from highest to lowest ($1.00 $1.00 $1.00 $1.25 $1.25 $1.25 $1.25 $1.50 $2.00 $5.00)
9	$1.25	• Identify the middle score
10	$1.25	• If an even number of scores, average the middle two scores and divide by 2 ($1.25 + $1.25/2 = $1.25)

poorest residents how much bread they had and found than none of them had any bread at all. Based on this research, he concluded that no food assistance was necessary for the town because *on average,* the town's residents had one-half load of bread each! So you can see, when dealing with skewed distributions, the median and/or the mode often would be a more informative statistic than the mean.

If a distribution of scores is symmetric and approaches the normal curve, the mean, mode, and median will be the same. As you can see by looking at the first example in Figure 4.4, if a distribution of scores is positively skewed (there are many low scores), the mean will be higher than the median. As you can see by looking at the second example, if a distribution is negatively skewed (there are many high scores), the mean will be lower than the median.

Measures of Variability

Like measures of central tendency, **measures of variability** describe a set of scores in numerical form. However, measures of central tendency tell about the center of a distribution of scores, and measures of variability represent how spread out a group of scores is and provide more information about individual differences. For example, the two frequency distributions in Figure 4.5 represent the scores of 18 students on two quizzes. Although the mean of both sets of scores is 5.6, notice that the distributions look very different; the scores in the first

FIGURE 4.4 ■ Measures of Central Tendency and Skewed Distributions

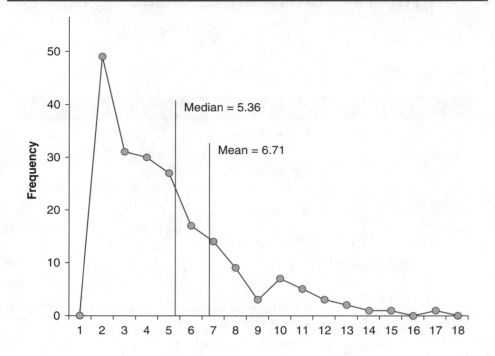

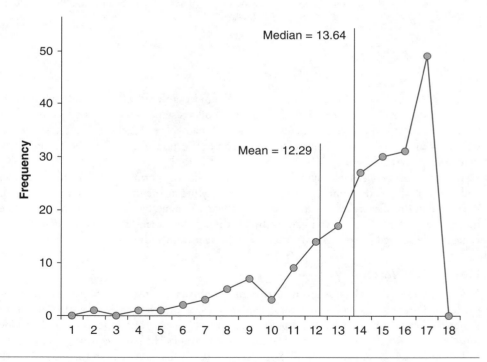

Source: HyperStat Online. (n.d.). *The effect of skew on the mean and median*. Retrieved from http://davidmlane.com/hyperstat/A92403.html. Reprinted by permission of David Lane, Rice University, Houston, Texas.

FIGURE 4.5 ■ **Variability in Distributions of Test Scores**

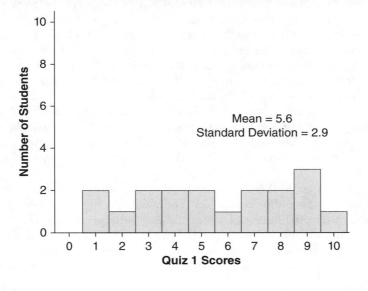

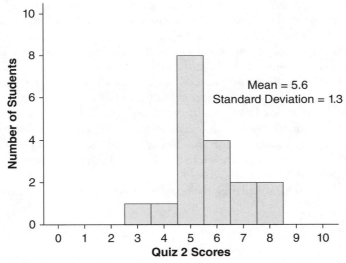

graph are more spread out, and the curve is flatter, compared with the scores in the second graph. Although students scored very similar on Quiz 2, the differences between students' scores are much greater on Quiz 1.

Three commonly used measures of variability are the range, variance, and standard deviation. We already introduced you to the range. Remember when we determined the class intervals for our histogram? The first thing we did was calculate the **range**—the highest score in a distribution minus the lowest score in a distribution. The range of the distribution of scores presented in For Your Information Box 4.2 would be $5.00 (highest score) − $1.00 (lowest score) = $4.00.

How does calculating the range of a distribution of scores help us? Let us say that an elementary school decides to administer a 150-question math test to all incoming second grade students to measure their math skills. When we calculate the average math test score of the students in each of the two 2nd grade classes, we find that each class has a mean of 100 correct answers. Does this mean that students in both 2nd grade classes have about the same math skills? Yes and no. Yes, both of the classes have the same mean math knowledge. But no, the individuals in each class do not necessarily all have similar math skills. Although the mean informs us about the average math knowledge of each class, it tells us nothing about how varied the math knowledge is within each of the classes. It is very possible that students in one of the end grade classes scored as low as 50 and as high as 150 (a range of 100) and the other 2nd grade class had scores as low as 90 and as high as 110 (a range of 20). Although the mean of these two classes may have been the same, one class has a larger variance and will require more diverse math instruction than the other class.

Although the range is easy to calculate, be careful using it when a distribution of scores has outlying low and/or high scores. The low and/or high scores do not accurately represent the entire distribution of scores and may misrepresent the true range of the distribution. For example, although most of the tooth fairies in For Your Information Box 4.2 reported that the going rate for a lost tooth was between $1.00 and $1.25, one tooth fairy reported that the going rate was $5.00. A range of $4.00 may be misleading in this case.

Like the range, the variance and standard deviation tell us about the spread in a distribution of scores. However, the variance and standard deviation are more satisfactory indexes of variability than is the range. The **variance** (σ^2) tells us whether individual scores tend to be similar to or substantially different from the mean. In most cases, a large variance tells us that individual scores differ substantially from the mean, and a small variance tells us that individual scores are very similar to the mean. What is a "large" variance, and what is a "small" variance? Large and small depend on the range of the test scores. If the range of test scores is 10, then 7 would be considered a large variance and 1 would be considered a small variance. In most cases, a large variance tells us that individual scores differ substantially from the mean. In some cases, however, a large variance may be due to outliers. For example, if there are 100 scores and 99 of them are close to the mean and 1 is very far from the mean, there may be a large variance due to this one outlier score.

A common formula for calculating the population variance of a distribution or group of test scores is

$$\sigma^2 = \frac{\sum(x - \mu)^2}{N},$$

where

σ^2 = the variance

Σ = sum of the values

x = a raw score

μ = mean of a distribution of test scores

^{2} = squared or multiplied by itself

N = the total number of test scores in the distribution of test scores

The formula for the variance requires squaring the sum of the deviations (differences) of each score from the mean. This calculation changes the unit of measurement, making it difficult to interpret the variance. Therefore, we often take the square root of the variance, which gives us what we call the **standard deviation** (s or σ)—the most commonly used measure of variability in a distribution of test scores.

A common formula for calculating the standard deviation for a distribution of test scores is

$$\sigma = \sqrt{\frac{\sum (x - \mu)^2}{N}}$$

You may recall from a statistics course that the denominator of the standard deviation (and variance) formula is sometimes given as $n - 1$. This value is used when you want to estimate the standard deviation of a population based on a sample drawn from it. When you are calculating the standard deviation of a known population, like a single group of test scores and these scores are the only scores of interest, you use N instead of $n - 1$. In general, you would use the population formula when you only wish to describe the variability of a single set of data. On the other hand, if you wish to make an inference about the variability of the larger population from which your data was drawn, you would use the formula for the sample standard deviation (using $n - 1$ in the denominator). This principle also applies to more complex statistical formulas that use the standard deviation, such the correlation coefficient. You would use the population standard deviations when calculating the correlation coefficient if you were only describing the correlation between two groups of scores. You would use the sample standard deviations when calculating the correlation coefficient if you wanted to have an estimate of what the correlation was in the population from which those scores were drawn. The symbol s is used instead of σ when referring to a sample standard deviation. (We discuss the correlation coefficient a little later in this chapter.) Most of the numerical examples in this textbook use the population standard deviation in calculations because we are only describing the characteristics of the data used in the examples and not making inferences about the nature of the populations from which the data were drawn.

If a distribution of test scores approximates a normal distribution, knowing the standard deviation will provide you a lot of information about how the scores are distributed. This is because in a normal distribution, 1 standard deviation *above and below* the mean will always contain approximately 68% (34.1% + 34.1%) of the test scores. Two standard deviations *above and below* the mean will always contain approximately 95% (13.6% + 34.1% + 34.1% + 13.6%) of the test scores. Approximately 99% of the test scores will be included at 3 standard deviations *above and below* the mean (2.1% + 13.6% + 34.1% + 34.1% + 13.6% + 2.1%). So if you knew that the mean of a group of normally distributed test scores was 100 and the standard deviation was 15, you would be able to estimate that about 68% of the test scores would fall between 85 and 115 (±1 standard deviation from the mean). Although theoretically they can go on forever, standard deviations often stop at 3 because very few scores typically fall outside 3 standard deviations from the mean.

For Your Information Box 4.3 explains, step by step, how to calculate the standard deviation of a distribution of test scores from 11 children.

The standard deviation is an extremely useful descriptive statistic because it allows us to understand how similar or dissimilar scores are. For example, imagine that your professor administered a 100-item multiple-choice exam to two different classes and the highest possible score on the exam was 100. Now imagine that your professor wanted to compare how well the students in both classes performed. First, your professor could calculate the mean of both distributions of scores. Let us say that the mean was calculated to be 75% for both

FOR YOUR INFORMATION BOX 4.3

CALCULATING THE POPULATION STANDARD DEVIATION OF A DISTRIBUTION OF SCORES

Child	Raw Score (x)	Deviation From Mean $(x - \mu)$	Squared Deviation $(x - \mu)^2$
1	20	$20 - 14 = 6$	$6 \times 6 = 36$
2	18	$18 - 14 = 4$	$4 \times 4 = 16$
3	15	$15 - 14 = 1$	$1 \times 1 = 1$
4	15	$15 - 14 = 1$	$1 \times 1 = 1$
5	14	$14 - 14 = 0$	$0 \times 0 = 0$
6	14	$14 - 14 = 0$	$0 \times 0 = 0$
7	14	$14 - 14 = 0$	$0 \times 0 = 0$
8	13	$13 - 14 = -1$	$-1 \times -1 = 1$
9	13	$13 - 14 = -1$	$-1 \times -1 = 1$
10	10	$10 - 14 = -4$	$-4 \times -4 = 16$
11	8	$8 - 14 = -6$	$-6 \times -6 = 36$
Sum	154		108

Formula for Standard Deviation of a Distribution

$$\sigma = \sqrt{\frac{\Sigma(x - \mu)^2}{N}}$$

1. List each child's raw score (x).

2. Calculate the mean (μ) test score of the distribution by adding all of the raw scores and dividing by the total number of test scores $(\mu = 154/11 = 14)$.

3. Subtract the mean from each child's raw score $(x - \mu)$ to determine the deviation from the mean.

4. Square $(^2)$ (multiply number by itself) each deviation.

5. Sum (Σ) the squared deviations (108).

6. Divide the sum of the squared deviations by the number of test scores $(108/11 = 9.82)$. This equals the variance.

7. Take the square root of the variance to determine the standard deviation $(\sqrt{9.82} = 3.1)$.

classes; that is, the average score for both classes was a solid C grade. Second, your professor could calculate the standard deviation for each class. Let us say that the standard deviation of one class was 17 and the standard deviation of the second class was 8. The standard deviation would allow your professor to understand that although the average score was the same for both classes, the scores in the first class were more varied than the scores in the second class.

FOR YOUR INFORMATION BOX 4.4
USING THE MEAN AND STANDARD DEVIATION TO PLOT A DISTRIBUTION

Using the mean and standard deviation of a distribution, we can draw what the distribution most likely looks like, assuming that these statistics are calculated from a large sample and the distribution is nearly bell shaped, or normal.

For example, if the mean is 14 and the standard deviation is 3.1, we can plot the distribution by doing the following:

1. Draw an *x* axis (horizontal axis) and place the mean (14) at the center.

2. Add the standard deviation (3.1) to the mean, and place this number 1 standard deviation above the mean (14 + 3.1 = 17.1). Add the standard deviation (3.1) to this number (17.1), and place the sum 2 standard deviations above the mean (17.1 + 3.1 = 20.2). Add the standard deviation (3.1) to this number (20.2) and place the sum 3 standard deviations above the mean (20.2 + 3.1 = 23.3). Do the same to label the opposite side of the distribution, but subtract the standard deviation from the mean (14 − 3.1 = 10.9, 10.9 − 3.1 = 7.8, 7.8 − 3.1 = 4.7).

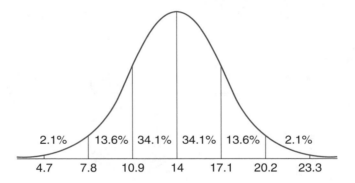

| 2.1% | 13.6% | 34.1% | 34.1% | 13.6% | 2.1% |
| 4.7 | 7.8 | 10.9 | 14 | 17.1 | 20.2 | 23.3 |

According to the characteristics of the normal distribution, approximately 34.1% of the population will score between 14 and 17.1, 34.1% will score between 14 and 10.9, and so on.

Furthermore, when we know the mean and standard deviation of a distribution of scores, we can draw a picture of what the distribution of scores probably looks like. For Your Information Box 4.4 shows how to draw a distribution of scores.

Measures of Relationship

Measures of relationship also help us describe distributions of test scores. However, unlike measures of central tendency and measures of variability, we must have at least two sets or distributions of scores, from the same individuals, to calculate measures of relationship. The **correlation coefficient** is a statistic that we typically use to describe the relationship between two or more distributions of scores. Using a correlation coefficient, we can relate one set of scores to another set to see whether the same individuals scored similarly on two different tests. (For example, if individuals scored low on one test, did they also score low on another test?) Such a relationship is described as a positive correlation. On the other hand, if people who score high on one test scored low on the other test and vice versa, the relationship is described as a negative correlation. Figure 4.6 shows two scatterplots: one of a positive correlation and one of a negative correlation.

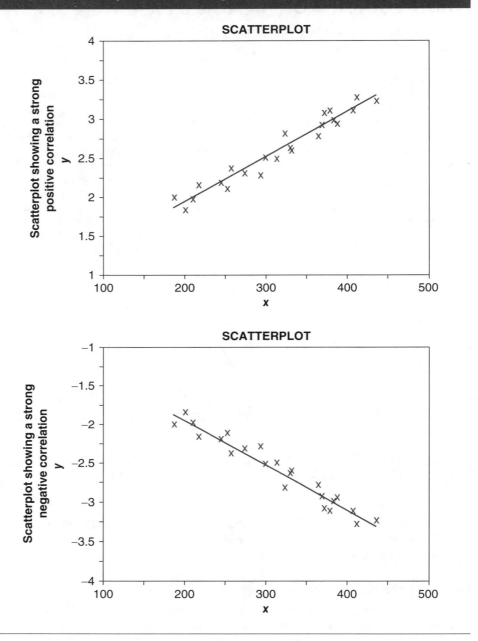

FIGURE 4.6 ■ Sample Positive and Negative Correlations

There are several ways to determine the association between two distributions of test scores. The most common technique yields an index called the **Pearson product–moment correlation coefficient**. Signified by either r (representing the correlation coefficient of a sample) or ρ (referred to as rho, which is the correlation coefficient in a population), the coefficient measures the linear association between two variables, or sets of test scores, that have been measured on interval or ratio scales. In almost all actual cases, the symbol r is used to indicate a correlation coefficient. This is because we usually calculate the correlation coefficient on a sample to estimate what the correlation coefficient would most likely be in a full population (if we could measure it). One useful formula for hand calculating the Pearson product–moment correlation coefficient between two sets of scores is:

$$r = \frac{(\sum xy)}{\sqrt{\left(\sum x^2 \sum y^2\right)}}$$

where

r = correlation coefficient

Σ = sum of the values

x = deviation of each score from the mean for the first set of scores

y = deviation of each score from the mean for the second set of scores

x^2 = deviation of each score from the mean squared for the first set of scores

y^2 = deviation of each score from the mean squared for the second set of scores

However, in practice, most people usually will use Excel or one of the many commercially available statistical packages such as SPSS or SAS, to do the computations. There are also many online calculations that will do the job as well. A simple to use calculator can be found at http://www.socscistatistics.com/tests/pearson/default2.aspx.

The correlation (r) between two distributions of scores is expressed in terms of a coefficient that can range from −1.00 to +1.00, with −1.00 indicating a perfect negative (or inverse) correlation, 0.00 indicating a complete lack of a relationship, and +1.00 indicating a perfect positive correlation. When correlating two sets of test scores, you will observe one of three types of relationships. First, there might be a positive correlation. With positive correlations, as the value of one variable (e.g., the weight of a diamond in carats) increases, the value of the other variable (e.g., the cost of the diamond) also increases. Second, there might be a negative correlation. With negative correlations, as the value of one variable (e.g., your age) increases, the value of the other variable (e.g., your visual acuity) decreases. Third, there might be no correlation, where there is no relationship at all between the variables (e.g., there is no relationship between height and academic ability).

For Your Information Box 4.5 shows, step by step, how to calculate the correlation between two sets of test scores (student test scores from a midterm exam and a final exam) using the Pearson product–moment correlation coefficient formula above.

STANDARD SCORES

We calculate measures of central tendency, measures of variability, and measures of relationship using raw test scores. These measures help us understand distributions of test scores. However, another way we can make sense of raw test scores is by using standard scores, which involves converting (or transforming) raw test scores into more meaningful units. Why? First, raw test scores are sometimes difficult to interpret in and of themselves. For example, if a friend told you that he earned a raw score of 19 on his midterm exam, would you say, "Great job" or "Better luck next time"? If you are like most people, you would ask your friend, "How

FOR YOUR INFORMATION BOX 4.5

CALCULATING THE CORRELATION BETWEEN TWO SETS OF TEST SCORES

Student	Midterm Exam Score X	Final Exam Score Y	Deviation From the Mean on the Midterm x	Deviation From the Mean on the Midterm Squared x^2	Deviation From the Mean on the Final y	Deviation From the Mean on the Final Squared y^2	Product of Midterm and Final Deviations From the Mean (x)(y)
1	95	90	15.3	234.1	11.4	130.0	174.4
2	86	80	6.3	39.7	1.4	2.9	8.8
3	76	66	−3.7	13.7	−12.6	158.8	46.6
4	55	70	−24.7	610.1	−8.6	74.0	212.4
5	67	67	−12.7	161.3	−11.6	134.6	147.3
6	90	89	10.3	106.1	10.4	108.2	107.1
7	100	92	20.3	412.1	13.4	179.6	272.0
8	56	67	−23.7	561.7	−11.6	134.6	274.9
9	78	80	−1.7	2.9	1.4	2.0	−2.4
10	94	85	14.3	204.5	6.4	41.0	91.5
Sum				**2,346.1**		**964.4**	**1,332.8**

This is the formula that we will use to calculate the correlation coefficient from these data:

$$r = \frac{(\sum xy)}{\sqrt{\left(\sum x^2 \sum y^2\right)}}$$

1. List each student's score on the midterm exam and final exam (X and Y).

2. Calculate the deviations from the mean (x and y) for all scores and the squared deviations (x^2 and y^2) for all scores on the midterm and the final.

3. Multiply the deviation from the mean of each score on the midterm by the deviation of each score from the mean on the final to arrive at the product of the deviation scores.

4. Add the products of all the deviation scores to get the sum of those products (= 1,332.8).

5. Multiply the sum of the squared deviation scores from the mean on the midterm (= 2346.1) by the sum of the squared deviation scores on the final (= 964.4) and take the square root of the result (= 1504.19).

6. Divide the result from step 4 by the results of step 5 (1332.8 / 1504.19) to get the correlation coefficient r (= .886).

$$r = \frac{(\sum xy)}{\sqrt{\left(\sum x^2 \sum y^2\right)}} = \frac{1332.8}{\sqrt{(2346.1)(964.4)}} = .886$$

many points were possible on the midterm exam?" This information allows you to give more meaning to your friend's score. If there were 20 points possible on the exam, you could quickly calculate that your friend earned a 95% (19/20 = 95). Now you could say, "Great job." Second, we often convert raw test scores into more meaningful units because we often have a need to compare scores so we can draw helpful inferences about how an individual performed on multiple tests. When raw test scores are expressed in different units (e.g., one test score is the number correct out of 50 and the other test score is the number correct out of 75), it is difficult to make comparisons between the two tests and make inferences.

The more meaningful units we transform test scores into are called **standard scores**—universally understood units in testing that allow test users to evaluate, or make inferences about, a person's performance.

For example, if a student brought home a report that showed she had scored a 47 on her arithmetic test and a 63 on her English test, the first question we would ask her is "What kind of scores did the other students earn?" Does a 47 on her arithmetic test mean she did well? Although this raw score is concrete, it is not necessarily informative. If we knew that the mean on the arithmetic test was 40 and the mean on the English test was 60, all we would know is that the student did better than average on both tests. We would not know whether her raw score entitled her to a C+ or an A.

When we transform raw test scores, we create a more informative scale to help us interpret a particular score in terms of where the score fits in an overall distribution of test scores. There are two types of transformations: linear and area. **Linear transformations** change the unit of measurement, but do not change the characteristics of the raw data in any way. **Area transformations**, on the other hand, change not only the unit of measurement, but also the unit of reference. Area transformations rely on the normal curve. They magnify the differences between individuals at the middle of the distribution and compress the differences between individuals at the extremes of the distribution. The most popular linear transformations include percentages, standard deviation units, z scores, and T scores, the latter two of which are based on the standard deviation. The most common area transformations are the percentile rank and the stanine.

Linear Transformations

Percentages

You are likely very familiar with percentages. Most of the time, your professors probably transform the raw test scores from classroom exams into percentages. For example, if you answered 90 items correctly (your raw test score) on a 100-item test, your professor might have shared that you earned a 90% on the test. To calculate a **percentage** you first divide a raw score by the total possible score and then multiply the answer by 100. So if you correctly answered 90 of 100 questions, your transformed percentage score would be 90% ([90/100 = .90] × 100 = 90%).

Standard Deviation Units

Recall our discussion of the normal distribution. In a normal distribution, the mean is the same as the median, and therefore 50% of the scores will fall below or at the mean and 50% will fall above or at the mean. We said that if we take the mean of a distribution and add 1 standard deviation, 34% of the population will score in this range. If we add 2 standard deviations to the mean, 47% of the population will score in this range. If we add 3 standard deviations to the mean, 49% of the population will score in this range. The same is true when we subtract the standard deviation from the mean. **Standard deviation units** refer to how many standard deviations an individual score falls away from the mean. The mean always has a standard deviation unit of 0, 1 standard deviation above the mean has a standard deviation unit of 1, 2 standard deviations above the mean has a standard deviation unit of 2, and 3 standard deviations above the mean has a standard deviation unit of 3. Standard deviation units below the mean are represented with a negative (−) sign.

For example, if the mean of a distribution is 6 and the standard deviation is 2, then 1 standard deviation unit would represent a raw score of 8. Therefore, approximately 34% of the population will score between 6 and 8. If an individual scores 7, her score falls within 1 standard deviation of the mean. If another individual scores 9, his score falls between 1 and 2 standard deviations above the mean. If another individual scores 5, her score falls within 1 standard deviation below the mean.

z Scores

A **z score** is similar to a standard deviation unit except that it is represented as a whole number with a decimal point. A z score helps us understand how many standard deviations an individual test score is above or below the distribution mean. As with standard deviation units, the mean of a distribution of test scores will always have a z score of 0. A z score of 1 is always 1 standard deviation above the mean. A z score of −1 is always 1 standard deviation below the mean. The formula for the z score of a distribution of scores is

$$z \text{ score} = \frac{x - \mu}{\sigma},$$

where

x = a raw score

μ = mean of a distribution of test scores

σ = standard deviation

T Scores

T scores are similar to z scores in that they help us understand how many standard deviations an individual test score is above or below the distribution mean. However, T scores are different than z scores in that they always have a mean of 50 and a standard deviation of 10. They are also always positive, unlike z scores. So if an individual's raw test score was converted to a T score of 60, we would know that the individual scored 1 standard deviation above the mean. If an individual's raw test score was converted to a T score of 30, we would know that the individual scored 2 standard deviations below the mean. Once you know a person's z score, you can easily calculate the T score using the following formula:

$$T \text{ score} = (z \times 10) + 50.$$

Area Transformations

Percentile

Percentiles, like the linear transformations discussed above, allow us to determine a person's relative standing compared with others in a distribution of scores. There are two different definitions of percentiles. (This term is sometimes also referred to as percentile rank when referring to the numerical result of the calculation of a percentile. In practice, however, the terms are often use interchangeably.) The first definition is the percentage of scores in a distribution that fall *at* or *below* a given raw score. The second definition is the percentage of scores in a distribution falls *below* a given raw score. We will be using the first definition in this book—the number of scores in a distribution that fall *at* or *below* a given raw score.

For example, you may have taken the SAT prior to applying to colleges. Your SAT report likely included two types of percentile scores—one based on a comparison of your score to individuals who took the SAT during the same year as you, and another based on a comparison of your score to all Grade 11 and 12 students in the United States who have taken the SAT. If your report indicated for one of these that you scored in the 60th percentile, this would mean that 60% of the individuals in the comparison group scored at or below your score. Another way of saying the same thing is that you scored equal to or better than 60% of the individuals in the comparison group.

To calculate an individual's percentile rank (based on the first definition), you would use the following formula:

$$\frac{(B+.5E)}{N} \times 100$$

where

B = number of scores below the individual's score

E = number of scores equal to the individual's score

N = the number of people who took the test

Here are the steps you would use to calculate a percentile rank for a set of test scores:

1. Sort the distribution of scores from lowest to highest.

2. Count the number of scores that fall below the raw score of interest (B).

3. Count the number of scores equal to the raw score of interest (E).

4. Count the total number of scores (N).

5. Substitute the values obtained in Steps 2, 3, and 4 into the formula for percentile rank.

Here is an example. Suppose you had the following distribution of test scores:

47 62 68 74 76 76 81 82 83 83 84 86 90 90 92 93 94 97 99 99

Calculate the percentile rank for a raw score of 90.

1. Sort the distribution (already done for you).

2. Count the number of scores below 90: $B = 12$.

3. Count the number of scores equal to 90: $E = 2$.

4. Count the total number of scores: $N = 20$.

5. Percentile rank = 65

A score of 90 is at the 65th percentile. This percentile (or percentile rank) indicates that 65% of the scores in the distribution were at or below a score of 90 or, alternatively, that a score of 90 was equal to or better than 65% of the scores. Alternatively, you could say that 35% of the scores were higher than 90.

The median of a normal distribution always has a percentile rank of 50. If a person scored in the 50th percentile, this percentile would mean that he or she scored equal to or better than 50% of the population.

Stanines

Although stanines are not as common as percentiles, sometimes you will encounter the standard score of a stanine. **Stanines** are a standard score scale with nine points that allows us to describe a distribution in words instead of numbers (from 1 = *very poor* to 9 = *very superior*). They are expressed in whole numbers from 1 to 9. Stanine scores of 1, 2, and 3 typically represent performance below the mean. Stanine scores of 4, 5, and 6 usually are considered to be average or close to the mean. Stanine scores of 7 and 8 are considered to be above average, and a stanine score of 9 is typically thought of as exceptional. As shown in Figure 4.7, in a normal distribution, 4% of the population will score a stanine of 1, 7% a stanine of 2, 12% a stanine of 3, 17% a stanine of 4, 20% a stanine of 5, 17% a stanine of 6, 12% a stanine of 7, 7% a stanine of 8, and 4% a stanine of 9. For Your Information Box 4.6 provides an example of linear and area transformations.

THE ROLE OF NORMS

Yet another way we sometimes interpret test sores is by using norms. Because few psychological tests produce ratio scale measures, we cannot say how much of an attribute, trait, or characteristic a person has. For example, we cannot say how much intelligence Robert has. Most test scores provide us with relative measures that allow us to conclude only that Robert

FIGURE 4.7   ■   Stanines and the Normal Distribution

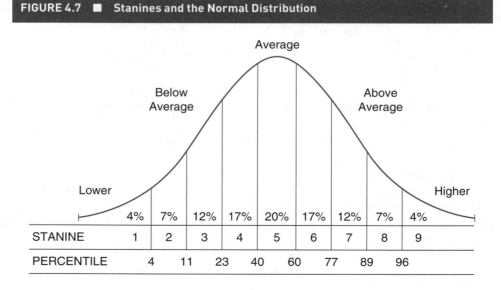

	4%	7%	12%	17%	20%	17%	12%	7%	4%
STANINE	1	2	3	4	5	6	7	8	9
PERCENTILE	4	11	23	40	60	77	89	96	

FOR YOUR INFORMATION BOX 4.6

LINEAR AND AREA TRANSFORMATIONS

Imagine that your class took a test of 50 questions, each worth 1 point. Given the following information, we can draw a picture of what the distribution of the test scores would look like, using standard scores, assuming that the results are normally distributed:

Number of questions = 50

Mean = 31

Range = 36

Variance = 36

Standard deviation = 6

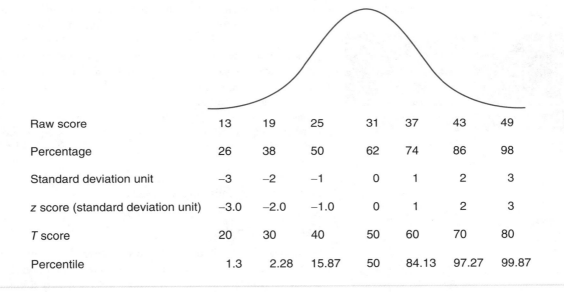

Raw score	13	19	25	31	37	43	49
Percentage	26	38	50	62	74	86	98
Standard deviation unit	−3	−2	−1	0	1	2	3
z score (standard deviation unit)	−3.0	−2.0	−1.0	0	1	2	3
T score	20	30	40	50	60	70	80
Percentile	1.3	2.28	15.87	50	84.13	97.27	99.87

is more intelligent than John, Robert scored 3 standard deviations above the mean, or Robert scored equal to or better than 75% of the people who took the test.

To help interpret test scores, we will sometimes compare an individual's test score to **norms**, which are test scores achieved by some identified group of individuals. These norms provide us with a standard against which we can compare individual test scores. The process of comparing an individual's test score to a norm group is referred to as **norm-based interpretation**, which helps us answer the question "Where does a test taker stand in comparison with a group that defines the standards?" Such norm-based interpretation is appropriate only for standardized tests, which we discussed in an earlier chapter.

Norms are often reported in charts or tables that describe the performance of a large group of individuals who were administered the test in the past (referred to as the norm group). When a person takes a test, his or her score is then compared to this norm group as a means of interpreting the test score—to determine the relative standing of the individual compared to those who have taken the test in the past. Norms are created, typically, during test construction by administering a test to a large number of individuals who are carefully selected to be representative of the population that the test is intended to serve. Professional test publishers update their tables of norms as they collect data on additional individuals who have taken the test. For some tests, norms can consist of data on many thousands of individuals. As we discuss below, when there is enough data for meaningful interpretation, norms can also be broken down by specific demographics. For example, test publishers might provide separate norms for men and women or different age groups.

There are a number of different types of norms. In what follows, we consider and provide examples of three popular norms: age norms, grade norms, and percentile ranks.

Types of Norms

Age Norms and Grade Norms

Age norms and **grade norms** are common types of norms because they allow us to determine at what age level or grade level an individual is performing. That is, they allow us to determine whether an individual's test score is similar to, below, or above the scores of others at the same age or grade level. Frequently used in educational settings, these types of norms are typically developed by administering a test to the targeted age or grade (e.g., 10-year-olds or fourth graders) as well as to test takers with ages and grades immediately below and immediately above the targeted age or grade (e.g., 9-year-olds or third graders and 11-year-olds or fifth graders). Although age and grade norms typically present scores for a broader age and grade than that mentioned previously, sometimes the scores that are presented in the norms are only estimates of what a younger student (e.g., an 8-year-old or a second grader) or older student (e.g., a 12-year-old or a sixth grader) would be likely to obtain.

For Your Information Box 4.7 provides an example of grade norms from the California Achievement Tests.

Percentile Ranks

As we have already discussed, the **percentile rank** is a very common type of norm because it provides us with a way to rank individuals on a scale from 1% to 100%, making it relatively easy to interpret. With percentile rank norms, scores can range from the 1st percentile to the 99th percentile, with the average individual's score set at the 50th percentile. If an individual's raw score of 11 corresponds to a percentile rank of 98, we can say that the individual scored equal to or higher than 98% of the test takers in the norm group. Because percentile ranks make it easy for individuals to interpret test scores, many developers of standardized tests, particularly tests of academic achievement, provide conversion tables showing the percentile ranks in the norm group of all possible raw scores. Table 4.5 provides an example of a simple norms table for a hypothetical 11-item Technician's Aptitude and Proficiency Test. As you can see, the raw scores convert to percentile ranks, making it much easier to interpret a test taker's score meaningfully.

Originally developed in 1975, the Mini-Mental State Examination (MMSE) is a fairly short cognitive ability test often used to screen individuals for and estimate the severity of cognitive impairment. It is also used to measure cognitive changes over time—for example, how an individual is responding to treatment. On the Web Box 4.2 provides actual normative data for the MMSE.

TABLE 4.5 ■ Sample Norms Table for a Hypothetical Technician's Aptitude and Proficiency Test	
Raw Score	Percentile Rank
11	98
10	96
9	85
8	75
7	62
6	48
5	34
4	23
3	18
2	10
1	4
0	1

Source: From Lyman, Howard B. *Test Scores and What They Mean*, 6th ed. Published by Allyn & Bacon, Boston, MA. Copyright © 1998 by Pearson Education.

More detail about the MMSE can be found in **Test Spotlight 4.1** in Appendix A.

FOR YOUR INFORMATION BOX 4.7
CALIFORNIA ACHIEVEMENT TESTS GRADE NORMS

The California Achievement Tests measure student achievement in various subject areas, including vocabulary. Below are grade norms for the Vocabulary subtest (which consists of two parts) from the 1970 edition of the tests. The overall score is determined by summing the subtest scores. The total score can range from 0 to 40.

Vocabulary Score	Grade Equivalent	Vocabulary Score	Grade Equivalent	Vocabulary Score	Grade Equivalent
0–12	0.6	29	2.6		5.1
	0.7	30–31	2.7		5.2
	0.8		2.8	39	5.3
14	0.9	32	2.9		5.4
	1.0	33	3.0		5.5
15	1.1	34	3.1		5.6
	1.2		3.2		5.7
16	1.3	35	3.3		5.8
17	1.4		3.4		5.9
	1.5		3.5		6.0
18	1.6	36	3.6		6.1
19	1.7		3.7		6.2
20	1.8		3.8		6.3
21	1.9		3.9	40	6.4
22	2.0	37	4.0		6.5
23–24	2.1		4.1		6.6
25	2.2		4.2		6.7
26	2.3		4.3		6.8
27	2.4		4.4		6.9
28	2.5		4.5		7.0
		38	4.6		7.1
			4.7		
			4.8		
			4.9		
			5.0		

Source: Adapted from McGraw-Hill (1970).

(Continued)

(Continued)

Based on these norms, the median score for children just beginning Grade 3 is approximately 33 (see the shaded boxes). What would you think if a Grade 3 student obtained a score of 40? Would you automatically think that this child belongs in Grade 6? What these results mean is that this Grade 3 student has achieved a score that we would expect a typical Grade 6 student to obtain. It does not mean that the Grade 3 student has the same overall achievement level as a student who is in Grade 6. Just because the Grade 3 student obtained a score that we would expect a Grade 6 student to obtain does not mean that the Grade 3 student is achieving at the level of a Grade 6 student or that the Grade 3 student should be advanced to Grade 6. To determine if this Grade 3 student were achieving at the level of Grade 6 student, a broader assessment would be necessary. Such an assessment would need to include a number of skills tests to determine whether the student would be able to achieve at the sixth grade level in other achievement areas (e.g., math) and to determine whether the student would be able to cope with the social and emotional issues faced by students in higher grades.

The Careful Use of Norms

Norms can be very valuable for helping us interpret individual test scores. However, as reinforced in the *Standards for Educational and Psychological Testing* (AERA et al., 2014), to properly interpret test scores, we must use an appropriate reference group. Using an inappropriate norm group can result in very important decisions being made based on poor interpretation of test data. Consider the following example.

Alan Alexakis, a graduate assistant in philosophy at Athol University, answered 210 items correctly on the hypothetical Orange Omnibus Test (OOT) of 300 items. His raw score of 210 on the OOT means that he did as well as or better than

- 99% of the seventh-grade pupils in the Malone Public Schools

- 92% of the Athol High School seniors

- 91% of the high school graduates in Worcester Academy

- 85% of the entering freshmen at Patricia Junior College

- 70% of the philosophy majors at Lamia College

- 55% of the graduating seniors at the University of Thessaloniki

- 40% of the graduate assistants at [the] American College of Athens

- 15% of the English professors at the University College London (Lyman, 1998, p. 82)

Although Alan's raw score on this test (210 of 300) remains the same, our interpretation of his performance will differ depending on the norm group with which we compare his test score. This is an extreme example, but it makes a point. If we compare Alan's score with the scores of seventh graders, it would appear that he did very well. If we compare his score with the scores of English professors, it would appear that he did poorly. The person who interprets test scores must choose the norm group that most closely resembles the test

ON THE WEB BOX 4.2
NORMATIVE DATA ON THE MINI-MENTAL STATE EXAMINATION
http://tinyurl.com/lrhm2ef

The MMSE is a 10-minute standardized test widely used in clinical settings to detect cognitive impairment in adults. The MMSE is also useful for monitoring cognitive changes over time. It was originally published in 1975 and is currently published by PAR. The MMSE assesses orientation, immediate and short-term recall, language, and the ability to follow simple verbal and written commands. It also provides a total score that places an individual on a scale of cognitive function. For more information on the MMSE, go to the website above. As you will learn at www.minimental.com, an individual's cognitive status is determined by comparing his or her MMSE raw score with the descriptive statistics of a norm group of test takers of similar ages and educational levels. Notice that there is a positive relationship between MMSE scores and grade, and there is an inverse relationship between MMSE scores and age. As individuals progress in their education, their scores increase. However, as individuals age, their scores decline, as shown in the following table.

Education	Age (years)													
	18–24	25–29	30–34	35–39	40–44	45–49	50–54	55–59	60–64	65–69	70–74	75–79	80–84	>84
Fourth grade	22	25	25	23	23	23	23	22	23	22	22	21	20	19
Eighth grade	27	27	26	26	27	26	27	26	26	26	25	25	25	23
High school	29	29	29	28	28	28	28	28	28	28	27	27	25	26
College	29	29	29	29	29	29	29	29	29	29	28	28	27	27

Source: From Crum, R. M., Anthony, J. J., Bassett, S. S., & Folstein, M. F. (1993). Population-based norms for the mini-mental state examination by age and educational level. *JAMA, 18,* 2386–2391. Published by the American Medical Association.

takers. The norm group chosen can have a significant impact on the interpretation of an individual's score.

Test users should also be careful to look at the size of the norm group. The accuracy of interpretation depends on whether the norms chosen accurately summarize the performance of the norm group population. When the population is large and the norm group small, there is greater chance that the norm group is not representative of the entire target population. It is critical that we create and use norms that include a sufficient number of test takers and that the test takers are a representative sample of the population (AERA et al., 2014). What is an adequate size for a norm group? This is a difficult question to answer. Many norm groups for educational tests contain thousands of individuals. Norm groups for research instruments are often smaller—in the hundreds.

Test users should also be careful to use up-to-date norms. Over time, the characteristics and sizes of populations change, and therefore their test scores change. When populations change, tests must be renormed to ensure continued value of the norms and to facilitate proper interpretation (AERA et al., 2014). What was average in the past might no longer be average today. Likewise, over time, tests are modified and updated. It is not appropriate, or fair to test takers, to compare and interpret their test scores on revised tests using norms from previous versions of tests. When tests are modified or updated, new norms must be developed, and these new norms should serve as the standard for comparison.

Test users should also be careful when using age and grade norms. If an individual child scores at a higher age or grade level, we should not automatically assume that the child is ready to be placed with older students or in a higher grade. A broader assessment and more than one test score are necessary to determine whether a child would be able to cope with the social and emotional issues the child would face in the company of older students or students in higher grades.

There is not always just one right norm group for interpreting test scores (AERA et al., 2014). For example, a human resources professional at a specific organization might interpret cognitive ability test scores using local norms based on sampling from their local offices to make local selection decisions. Or the professional might use regional norms to make regional selection decisions. What is important is that those who interpret test scores using norm-based interpretation have a good rationale for using a specific norm group (AERA et al., 2014).

Chapter Summary

Most psychological tests produce raw scores. The claims we can make using these scores depend on the scores' level of measurement. Four common levels of measurement are nominal, ordinal, interval, and ratio. As we move from one level of measurement to the next, we are able to perform more mathematical operations (addition, subtraction, multiplication, and division) that allow us to make more and different claims regarding test results.

To make sense of raw scores, we rely on a number of techniques. For example, we plot frequency distributions and calculate measures of central tendency, variability, and relationship. Each technique we use has a different purpose. Frequency distributions provide us with a picture of a distribution of scores. Measures of central tendency (mean, mode, and median) help us identify the center of a distribution of scores. Measures of variability (range, variance, and standard deviation) help us understand the spread

of scores in a distribution. Measures of relationship (correlation coefficients) help us determine the relationship between distributions of test scores.

We also convert raw scores into standard units of measurement (e.g., percentage, standard deviation unit, z score, T score, percentile) to provide more meaning to individual scores and so that we can compare individual scores with those of a previously tested group or norm group. Norms provide us with a standard against which we can compare individual test scores and make accurate inferences. There are a number of different types of norms, and test users must select and use the norm group that is most similar to the test takers. Test users should also be careful to use up-to-date norms and be sure that the norm group is representative of the target population. Those who interpret test scores using norm-based interpretation should have a good rationale for using a specific norm group.

Engaging in the Learning Process

Learning is the process of gaining knowledge and skills through schooling or studying. Although you can learn by reading the chapter material, attending class, and engaging in discussion with your instructor, more actively engaging in the learning process may help you better learn and retain chapter information. To help you actively engage in the learning process, we encourage you to access our new supplementary student workbook. The workbook contains critical thinking activities to help you understand and apply information and help you make progress toward learning and retaining material. If you do not have a copy of the workbook, you can purchase a copy through sagepub.com.

Key Concepts

After completing your study of this chapter, you should be able to define each of the following terms. These terms are bolded in the text of this chapter and defined in the Glossary.

age norms	measures of relationship	percentage
area transformations	measures of variability	percentile rank
categorical data	median	range
class intervals	mode	ratio scales
correlation coefficient	nominal scale	raw score
descriptive statistics	normal curve	standard deviation
frequency distribution	normal probability	standard deviation unit
grade norms	distribution	standard scores
histogram	norm-based interpretation	stanines
interval scales	norm group	T scores
level of measurement	norms	variance
linear transformations	ordinal scales	z score
mean	outliers	
measure of central	Pearson product–moment	
tendency	correlation coefficient	

Critical Thinking Questions

The following are some critical thinking questions to support the learning objectives for this chapter.

Learning Objectives	Critical Thinking Questions
Discriminate between different levels of measurement.	• How would you classify the level of measurement of the test questions on some of your most recent classroom exams? • What might be the implications of a test user not understanding levels of measurement when interpreting test results for individuals or groups?

(Continued)

(Continued)

Learning Objectives	Critical Thinking Questions
Differentiate the procedures for interpreting test scores.	• What test score interpretation procedure(s) would you recommend to a faculty member who wanted to help a student thoroughly understand how he performed on his midterm exam? • What similar and different test interpretation procedure(s) would you use to interpret how one individual performed on a test compared to how a group of students performed on one or more tests?
Explain the purpose of and calculate standard scores.	• Which standard score(s) would be most meaningful to you as a parent of a child who took a standardized test? Explain your answer. • How might you use standard scores to compare a person's performance on a 10-item multiple-choice test with a 100-item multiple-choice test?
Explain the role and proper use of norms when interpreting test scores.	• What are some instances where it would be inappropriate to use norms? • What advice would you provide a test user who was going to use norm-based interpretation to make important decisions?

5

WHAT IS TEST RELIABILITY/PRECISION?

LEARNING OBJECTIVES

After completing your study of this chapter, you should be able to do the following:

- Define reliability/precision, and describe three methods for estimating the reliability/precision of a psychological test and its scores.

- Describe how an observed test score is made up of the true score and random error, and describe the difference between random error and systematic error.

- Calculate and interpret a reliability coefficient, including adjusting a reliability coefficient obtained using the split-half method.

- Differentiate between the KR-20 and coefficient alpha formulas, and understand how they are used to estimate internal consistency.

- Calculate the standard error of measurement, and use it to construct a confidence interval around an observed score.

- Identify four sources of test error and six factors related to these sources of error that are particularly important to consider.

- Explain the premises of generalizability theory, and describe its contribution to estimating reliability.

"My statistics instructor let me take the midterm exam a second time because I was distracted by noise in the hallway. I scored 2 points higher the second time, but she says my true score probably didn't change. What does that mean?"

"I don't understand that test. It included the same questions—only in different words—over and over."

"The county hired a woman firefighter even though she scored lower than someone else on the qualifying test. A man scored highest with a 78, and this woman only scored 77! Doesn't that mean they hired a less qualified candidate?"

"The psychology department surveyed my class on our career plans. When they reported the results of the survey, they also said our answers were unreliable. What does that mean?"

Have you ever wondered just how consistent or precise psychological test scores are? If a student retakes a test, such as the SAT, can the student expect to do better the second time without extra preparation? Are the scores of some tests more consistent than others? How do we know which tests are likely to produce more consistent scores?

If you have found yourself making statements or asking questions like these, or if you have ever wondered about the consistency of a psychological test or survey, the questions you raised concern the reliability of responses. As you will learn in this chapter, we use the term **reliability/precision** to describe the consistency of test scores. All test scores—just like any other measurement—contain some error. It is this error that affects the reliability, or consistency, of test scores.

In the past, we referred to the consistency of test scores simply as reliability. Because the term *reliability* is used in two different ways in the testing literature, the authors of the *Standards for Educational and Psychological Testing* (American Educational Research Association [AERA], American Psychological Association [APA], & National Council on Measurement in Education [NCME], 2014) have revised the terminology, and we follow the revised terminology in this book. When we are referring to the consistency of test scores in general, the term *reliability/precision* is preferred. When we are referring to the results of the statistical evaluation of reliability, the term *reliability coefficient* is preferred. In the past, we used the single term *reliability* to indicate both concepts.

We begin the chapter with a discussion of what we mean by reliability/precision and classical test theory. Classical test theory provides the conceptual underpinnings necessary to fully understand the nature of measurement error and the effect it has on test reliability/precision. Then we describe the three categories of reliability coefficients and the methods we use to estimate them. We first consider *test–retest* coefficients, which estimate the reliability/precision of test scores when the same people take the same test form on two separate occasions. Next, we cover *alternate-form* coefficients, which estimate the reliability/precision of test scores when the same people take a different but equivalent form of a test on two independent testing sessions. Finally, we discuss *internal consistency* coefficients, which estimate the reliability/precision of test scores by looking at the relationships between different parts of the same test given on a single occasion. This category of coefficients also enables us to evaluate *scorer reliability* or agreement when raters use their subjective judgment to assign scores to test taker responses.

In the second part of this chapter, we define what each of these categories and methods is in more detail. We show you how each of the three categories of reliability coefficients is calculated. We also discuss how to calculate an index of error called the standard error of measurement (SEM), and a measure of rater agreement called *Cohen's kappa*. Finally, we discuss factors that increase and decrease a test's reliability/precision.

WHAT IS RELIABILITY/ PRECISION?

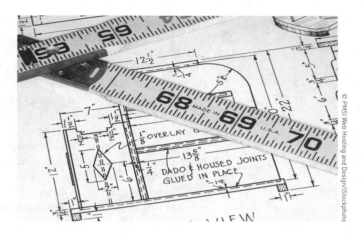

As you are aware, psychological tests are measurement instruments. In this sense, they are no different from yardsticks, speedometers, or thermometers. A psychological test measures how much the test taker has of whatever skill or quality the test measures. For instance, a driving test measures how well the test taker drives a car, and a self-esteem test measures whether the test taker's self-esteem is high, low, or average when compared with the self-esteem of similar others.

The most important attribute of a measurement instrument is its reliability/precision. A yardstick, for example, is a reliable measuring instrument over time because each time it measures an object (e.g., a room), it gives approximately the same answer. Variations in the measurements of the room—perhaps a fraction of an inch from time to time—can be referred to as **measurement error**. Such errors are probably due to random mistakes or inconsistencies of the person using the yardstick or because the smallest increment on a yardstick is often a quarter of an inch, making finer distinctions difficult. A yardstick also has internal consistency. The first foot on the yardstick is the same length as the second foot and third foot, and the length of every inch is uniform. It wouldn't matter which section of the yardstick you used to make the measurement, as the results should always be the same.

Reliability/precision is one of the most important standards for determining how trustworthy data derived from a psychological test are. A **reliable test** is one we can trust to measure each person in approximately the same way every time it is used. A test also must be reliable if it is used to measure attributes and compare people, much as a yardstick is used to measure and compare rooms. Although a yardstick can help you understand the concept of reliability, you should keep in mind that a psychological test does not measure physical objects as a yardstick does, and therefore a psychological test cannot be expected to be as reliable as a yardstick in making a measurement.

Keep in mind that just because a test has been shown to produce reliable scores, that does not mean the test is also *valid*. In other words, evidence of reliability/precision does not mean that the inferences that a test user makes from the scores on the test are correct or that the test is being used properly. (We explain the concept of validity in the next three chapters of the text.)

CLASSICAL TEST THEORY

Although we can measure some things with great precision, no measurement instrument is perfectly reliable or consistent. For example, clocks can run slow or fast—even if we measure their errors in microseconds. Unfortunately, psychologists are not able to measure psychological qualities with the same precision that engineers have for measuring speed or physicists have for measuring distance.

For instance, did you ever stop to think about the obvious fact that when you give a test to a group of people, their scores will vary; that is, they will not all obtain the same score? One reason for this is that the people to whom you give the test differ in the amount of the attribute the test measures, and the variation in test scores simply reflects this fact. Now think about the situation in which you retest the same people the next day using the same test. Do you think that each individual will score exactly the same on the second testing as on the first? The answer is that they most likely wouldn't. The scores would probably be close to the scores they obtained on the first testing, but they would not be exactly the same. Some people would score higher on the second testing, while some people would score lower. But assuming that the amount of the attribute the test measures has stayed the same in each person (after all, it's only 1 day later), why should the observed test scores have changed? Classical test theory provides an explanation for this. According to classical test theory, a person's test score (called the observed score) is made up of two independent parts. The first part is a measure of the amount of the attribute that the test is designed to measure. This is known as the person's **true score** (T). The second part of an observed test score consists of random errors that occur anytime a person takes a test (E). It is this **random error** that causes a person's test score to change from one administration of a test to the next (assuming that his or her true score hasn't changed). Because this type of error is a random event, sometimes it causes an individual's test score to go up on the second administration, and sometimes it causes it to go down. So if you could know what a person's true score was on a test, and also know the amount of random error, you could easily determine what the person's actual observed score on the test would be. Likewise, error in measurement can be defined as the difference between a person's observed score and his or her true score. Formally, classical test theory expresses these ideas by saying that any observed test score (X) is made up of the sum of two elements: a true score (T) and random error (E). Therefore,

$$X = T + E.$$

True Score

An individual's true score (T) on a test is a value that can never really be known or determined. It represents the score that would be obtained if that individual took a test an infinite number of times and then the average score across all the testings was computed. As we discuss in a moment, random errors that may occur in any one testing occasion will actually cancel themselves out over an infinite number of testing occasions. Therefore, if we could average all the scores together, the result would represent a score that no longer contained any random error. This average is the true score on the test and represents the amount of the attribute the person who took the test actually possesses without any random measurement error.

One way to think about a true score is to think about choosing a member of your competitive video gaming team. You could choose a person based on watching him or her play a single game. But you would probably recognize that that single score could have been influenced by a lot of factors (random error) other than the person's actual skill playing video games (the true score). Perhaps the person was just plain lucky in that game, and the observed score was really higher than his or her actual skill level would suggest. So perhaps you might prefer that the person play three games so that you could take the average score to estimate his or her true level of video gaming ability. Intuitively, you may understand by asking the person to play multiple games that some random influences on performance would even out because sometimes these random effects will cause his or her observed score to be higher than the true score, and sometimes it will cause the observed score to be lower. This is the nature of random error. So you can probably see that if somehow you could get the person to play an infinite number of games and average all the scores, the random error would cancel itself out entirely and you would be left with a score that represents the person's true score in video gaming.

Random Error

Random error is defined as the difference between a person's actual score on a test (the observed score) and that person's true score (T). As we described above, because this source of error is random in nature, sometimes a person's observed score will be higher than his or her true score and sometimes the observed score will be lower than his or her true score. Unfortunately, in any single test administration, we can never know whether random error has led to an observed score that is higher or lower than the true score. An important characteristic of this type of measurement error is that, because it is random, over an infinite number of testings the error will increase and decrease a person's score by exactly the same amount. Another way of saying this is that the mean or average of all the error scores over an infinite number of testings will be zero. That is why random error actually cancels itself out over repeated testings. Two other important characteristics of measurement error is that it is normally distributed, and it is uncorrelated with (or independent of) true scores. (See the previous chapter for a discussion of normal distributions and correlations.) Clearly, we can never administer a test an infinite number of times in an attempt to fully cancel out the random error component. The good news is that we don't have to. It turns out that making a test longer also reduces the influence of random error on the test score for the same reason—the random error component will be more likely to cancel itself out (although never completely in practice). We will have more to say about this when we discuss how reliability coefficients are actually computed.

Systematic Error

Systematic error is another type of error that obscures a person's true score on a test. When a single source of error always increases or decreases the true score by the same amount, we call it **systematic error**. For instance, if you know that the scale in your bathroom regularly adds 3 pounds to anyone's weight, you can simply subtract 3 pounds from whatever the scale says to get your true weight. In this case, the error your scale makes is predictable and systematic. The last section of this chapter discusses how test developers and researchers can identify and reduce systematic error in test scores.

Let us look at an example of the difference between random error and systematic error proposed by Nunnally (1978). If a chemist uses a thermometer that always reads 2 degrees warmer than the actual temperature, the error that results is *systematic*, and the chemist can predict the error and take it into account. If, however, the chemist is nearsighted and reads the thermometer with a different amount and direction of inaccuracy each time, the readings will be wrong and the inconsistencies will be unpredictable, or *random*.

Systematic error is often difficult to identify. However, two problems we discuss later in this chapter—practice effects and order effects—can add systematic error as well as random error to test scores. For instance, if test takers learn the answer to a question in the first test administration (practice effect) or can derive the answer from a previous question (order effect), more people will get the question right. Such occurrences raise test scores systematically. In such cases, the test developer can eliminate the systematic error by removing the question or replacing it with another question that will be unaffected by practice or order.

Another important distinction between random error and systematic error is that random error lowers the reliability of a test. Systematic error does not; the test is reliably inaccurate by the same amount each time. This concept will become apparent when we begin calculating reliability/precision using correlation.

The Formal Relationship Between Reliability/Precision and Random Measurement Error

Building on the previous discussion of true score and error, we can provide a more formal definition of reliability/precision. Recall that according to classical test theory, any score that a person makes on a test (his or her observed score, X) is composed of two components, his or her true score, T, and random measurement error, E. This is expressed by the formula $X = T + E$. Now for the purposes of this discussion, let's assume that we could build two different forms of a test that measured the exactly the same construct in exactly the same way. Technically, we would say that these alternate forms of the test were parallel. As we discussed earlier, if we gave these two forms of the test to the same group of people, we would still not expect that everyone would score exactly the same on the second administration of the test as they did on the first. This is because there will always be some measurement error that influences everyone's scores in a random, nonpredictable fashion. Of course, if the tests were really measuring the same concepts in the same way, we would expect people's scores to be very similar across the two testing sessions. And the more similar the scores are, the better the reliability/precision of the test would be.

Now for a moment, let's imagine a world where there was no measurement error (either random or systematic). With no measurement error, we would expect that everyone's observed scores on the two parallel tests would be exactly the same. In effect, both sets of test scores would simply be a measure of each individual's true score on the construct the test was measuring. If this were the case, the correlation between the two sets of test scores, which we call the **reliability coefficient**, would be a perfect 1.0, and we would say that the test is perfectly reliable. It would also be the case that if the two groups of test scores were exactly the same for all individuals, the variance of the scores of each test would be exactly the same as well. This also makes intuitive sense. If two tests really were measuring the same concept in the same way and there were no measurement error, then nobody's score would vary or change from the first test to the second. So the total variance of the scores calculated on the first test would be identical to the total variance of the scores calculated for the second test. In other words, we would be measuring only the true scores, which would not change across administrations of two parallel tests.

Now let's move back to the real world, where there is measurement error. Random measurement error affects each individual's score in an unpredictable and different fashion every time he or she answers a question on a test. Sometimes the overall measurement error will cause an individual's observed test score to go up, sometimes it will go down, and sometimes it may remain unchanged. But you can never predict the impact that the error will have on an individual's observed test score, and it will be different for each person as well. That is the nature of random error. However, there is one thing that you can predict. The presence of random error will always cause the variance of a set of scores to increase over what it was *if there were no measurement error*. A simple example will help make this point clear.

Suppose your professor administered a test and everyone in the class scored exactly an 80 on the test. The variance of this group of scores would be zero because there was no variation at all in the test scores. Now let's presume that your professor was unhappy about that outcome and wanted to change it so that the range of scores (the variance) was a little larger. So he decided to add or subtract some points to everyone's score. In order that he not be accused of any favoritism in doing this, he generates a list of random numbers that range between −5 and +5. Starting at the top of his class roster and at the top of a list of random numbers, he adjusts each student's test score by the number that is in the same position on random number list as the student in on the class roster. Each student would now have had a random number of points added or subtracted from his or her score, and the test scores would now vary between 75 and 85 instead of being exactly 80. You can immediately see that if you calculated the variance on this adjusted group of test scores, it would be higher than the original group of scores. But now, your professor has obscured the students' actual scores on the test by adding additional random error into all the test scores. As a result, the reliability/precision of the test scores would be reduced because the scores on the test now would contain that random error. This makes the observed scores different from the students' true scores by an amount equal to random error added to the score. Now let's suppose that the students were given the option to take the test a second time and no random error was added to the results on the second testing. The scores on the two testing occasions might be similar, but they certainly would not be the same. The presence of the random error, which the professor added to the first test, will have distorted the comparison. In fact, the more random error that is contained in a set of test scores, the less similar the test results will be if the same test is given to the same test takers a second time. This would indicate that the test is not a consistent, precise measure of whatever the test was designed to measure. Therefore the presence of random error reduces the estimate of reliability/precision of the test.

Formally, the reason why the addition of random error reduces the reliability of a test is because reliability is about estimating the proportion of variability in a set of observed test scores that is attributable only to true scores.

In classical test theory, reliability is defined as true-score variance divided by total observed-score variance:

$$r_{xx} = \sigma_t^2 / \sigma_x^2,$$

where

r_{xx} = reliability

σ_t^2 = true-score variance

σ_x^2 = observed-score variance

Recall that according to classical test theory, observed-score (X) variance is composed of two parts. Part of the variance in the observed scores will be attributable to the variance in the true scores (T), and part will be attributable to the variance added by measurement error (E). Therefore, if observed-score variance σ_x^2 were equal to true-score variance σ_t^2, this would mean that there is no measurement error, and so, using the above formula, the reliability coefficient in this case would be 1.00. But any time observed-score variance is greater than true-score variance (which is always the case because of the presence of measurement error), the reliability coefficient will become less than 1. Unfortunately, we can never really know what the true scores on a test actually are. We can only estimate them using observed scores and that is why we always refer to calculated reliability coefficients as *estimates* of a test's reliability.

To make these important ideas more concrete for you, we have simulated 10 people's scores on two parallel tests to directly demonstrate, using a numerical example, the relationship between true scores, error scores, and reliability. See the In Greater Depth box 5.1 for this simulation and discussion.

THREE CATEGORIES OF RELIABILITY COEFFICIENTS

Earlier we told you that we can never really determine a person's true score on any measure. Remember, a true score is the score that a person would get if he or she took a test an infinite number of times and we averaged the all the results, which is something we can never

IN GREATER DEPTH BOX 5.1

NUMERICAL EXAMPLE OF THE RELATIONSHIP BETWEEN MEASUREMENT ERROR AND RELIABILITY

Below you will find an example that will help make the relationship between measurement error and reliability more concrete for you. The example includes simulated results for 10 test takers who have taken two tests, which for the purpose of this example, we will assume are parallel. That means both tests measure the same construct in exactly the same way for all test takers. It also means that the participant's true scores are exactly the same for both tests and

that the amount of error variance is also the same for both tests. As you have learned, we can never really know an individual's true score on a test, but for the purposes of this example, we will assume we do. So for each individual in the simulation, we show you three pieces of data for each test: the true score, the error score, and the observed score. We can then easily demonstrate for you how these data influence the calculated reliability of a test.

	Simulated Scores on Two Tests for 10 People					
	Test 1			Test 2		
Person	True Score	Error	Observed Score	True Score	Error	Observed Score
1	75	−1	74	75	2	77
2	82	−2	79	82	2	84
3	83	0	82	83	−2	80
4	79	1	80	79	−2	76
5	83	3	86	83	1	85
6	76	2	78	76	1	77
7	82	2	84	82	3	85
8	83	−1	83	83	−3	81
9	77	1	78	77	−3	74
10	80	−4	76	80	1	80

Important Individual Statistics for Test 1 and Test 2	Test 1	Test 2
True Score Variance:	8.10	8.10
Error Variance	4.50	4.50
Observed Score Variance	12.60	12.60
Average Error	0.00	0.00
Correlation of True Score and Error	.00	.00
True Score Variance/ Observed Score Variance	.64	.64

Important Combined Statistics for Test 1 and Test 2	
Correlation of Errors (Test 1 and Test 2)	.00
Correlation of True Scores (Test 1 and Test 2)	1.00
Correlation of Observed Scores (Test 1 and Test 2) (This is also the test reliability coefficient)	.64

Observations From the Data

There are quite a few observations that one can make from the data presented above. The first thing to note about the data is that each individual's true score is the same on Test 1 and Test 2. This follows from the fact that the data represent scores on parallel tests. One of the assumptions of parallel tests is that the true scores will be the same within test takers on both tests. (Remember, we can never really know the true scores of people who have taken a test.)

The next thing to look at in these simulated data is the observed score made by each person on the tests. You can easily see that the observed scores are different from the true scores. As you have learned, the reason why the observed scores are not the same as the true scores is because of random measurement error that occurs each time a person answers a question (or any other measurement is made) on a test. You can also see that the amount of error for a person on each test is simply the observed score minus the true score. This is just a restatement of the basic equation from classical test theory that states the observed score (X) is equal to the true score (T) plus error (E).

The most important thing to note about the observed scores is that they are not the same on each test even though the true scores were the same. The reason why this is the case is because measurement error is a random phenomenon and will vary each time a person takes a test. As an example, look at the first person's observed score on Test 1. That person's observed score was 74. This was because her true score was 75, but the error score was -1, making her observed score 74. Now look at the same person's score on Test 2. It is 77—three points higher than her score on Test 1 even though her true score was exactly the same on Test 2 as it was on Test 1. The reason why her observed score was higher on Test 2 than it was on Test 1, was that on Test 2, random measurement error resulted in a three point increase in her observed score rather than a one point decrease.

Now let's look at the error scores in more detail as they demonstrate some important characteristics of measurement error. First, notice how the average measurement error for each test is zero. This is the nature of measurement error. It will cancel itself out in the long run. That is why a longer test will, on average, contain less measurement error than a shorter test and therefore be a more precise estimate of the true score than a shorter test.

Second, remember that sometimes measurement error will increase the observed score on a test, and sometimes it will decrease it. In the long run, measurement error will be normally distributed and more frequently result in a small change in observed scores and less frequently result in a large change.

Third, look at the relationship between the true scores and the error. We can do that by correlating the two quantities across all the test takers. For each test, the correlation between true scores and error is zero. This is always the case because measurement error is random and any random phenomena will always have a zero correlation with any other phenomena. If we correlate the error for Test 1 with the error for Test 2 will also see that the correlation is zero. This demonstrates that each time a test is given the amount of error will vary in an unpredictable manner that is not related to the error that occurs on any other administration of the test. One way we describe this is to say that the errors are independent of each other. This is one reason why individual test scores will vary from one administration of the same test to another when they are given to the same group of people. As we are about to demonstrate, this fact is what test reliability is all about. The less the scores vary from one testing occasion to another for each individual, the less measurement error exists, and the higher the reliability/precision of a test will be.

Putting It All Together

You will recall that earlier in this chapter we said that in classical test theory, one way reliability can be defined is true-score variance divided by total observed-score variance. From our simulated data above, we have all the information we need to calculate the reliability of the tests using this method. For either test, the true score variance is 8.10, and the observed score variance is 12.60. Therefore, the reliability coefficient of both tests would be 8.10/12.60 = .64. In words, this reliability coefficient would mean that 64% of the variance in the observed scores on the tests can be accounted for by the true scores. The remaining 36% of the variance in the observed scores is accounted for by measurement error.

It may have occurred to you that our calculations of the reliability coefficient that we have just demonstrated are based on knowing the true scores of all the people who have taken the test. But we have also said that in reality, one can never know what the true scores actually are. So you may be wondering how we can compute a reliability coefficient if we don't know the true scores of all the test takers. Fortunately, the answer is simple. There is another definition of reliability/precision that is mathematically equivalent to the formula that uses true score variance and observed score variance to calculate reliability. That

(Continued)

(Continued)

definition is as follows: Reliability/precision is equal to the correlation between the observed scores on two parallel tests (Crocker & Algina, 1986).

As you will see in the next section on the different methods we use to calculate reliability/precision, this is the definition we will often rely on to make those calculations. Let's now apply that definition to our simulated data and compare the results that we obtain to the results we obtained using true score and observed score variances. In our simulation, Test 1 and Test 2 were designed to be parallel. As a reminder, you can

confirm this from the fact that the true scores on Test 1 and Test 2 are the same for all test takers, and the error variances on both tests are equal. If we correlate the observed scores on Test 1 with the observed scores on Test 2, we find that the correlation (reliability/precision) is .64. This is exactly the same result that we found when we used the formula that divided the true score variance by the observed score variance from either of the two tests to compute the reliability coefficient. We will have much more to say about calculating reliability coefficients later in this chapter.

actually do. And because we cannot ever know what a person's true score actually is, we can never exactly calculate a reliability coefficient. The best that we can do is to estimate it using the methods we have described in this chapter. That is why throughout this chapter, we have always spoken about reliability coefficients as being estimates of reliability/precision. In this section, we will explain the methods that are used to estimate the reliability/precision of a test and then we will show you how estimates of reliability/precision and related statistics are actually computed using these methods.

If you measured a room but you were unsure whether your measurement was correct, what would you do? Most people would measure the room a second time using either the same or a different tape measure.

Psychologists use the same strategies of remeasurement to check psychological measurements. These strategies establish evidence of the reliability/precision of test scores. Some of the methods that we will discuss require two administrations of the same (or very similar) test forms, while other methods can be accomplished in a single administration of the test. The *Standards for Educational and Psychological Testing* (AERA et al., 2014) recognize three categories of reliability coefficients used to evaluate the reliability/precision of test scores. Each category uses a different procedure for estimating the reliability/precision of a test. The methods are (a) the test–retest method, (b) the alternate-forms method, and (c) the internal consistency method (split-half, coefficient alpha methods, and methods that evaluate scorer reliability or agreement). Each of these methods takes into account various conditions that can produce inconsistencies in test scores. Not all methods are used for all tests. The method chosen to estimate reliability/precision depends on the test itself and the conditions under which the test user plans to administer the test. Each method produces a numerical reliability coefficient, which enables us to estimate and evaluate the reliability/precision of the test.

Test–Retest Method

To estimate how reliable a test is using the **test–retest method**, a test developer gives the same test to the same group of test takers on two different occasions. The scores from the first and second administrations are then compared using **correlation**. This method of estimating reliability allows us to examine the stability of test scores over time and provides an estimate of the test's reliability/precision.

The interval between the two administrations of the test may vary from a few hours up to several years. As the interval lengthens, test–retest reliability will decline because the number of opportunities for the test takers or the testing situation to change increases over time. For example, if we give a math achievement test to a student today and then again tomorrow, there probably is little chance that the student's knowledge of math will change overnight. However, if we give a student a math achievement test today and then again in 2 months, it is very likely that something will happen during the 2 months that will increase (or decrease) the student's knowledge of math. When test developers or researchers report test–retest reliability, they must also state the length of time that elapsed between the two test administrations.

Using test–retest reliability, the assumption is that the test takers have not changed between the first administration and the second administration in terms of the skill or quality measured by the test. On the other hand, changes in test takers' moods, levels of fatigue, or personal problems from one administration to another can affect their test scores. The circumstances under which the test is administered, such as the test instructions, lighting, or distractions, must be alike. Any differences in administration or in the individuals themselves will introduce error and reduce reliability/precision.

It is the test developer who makes the first estimates of the reliability/precision of a test's scores. A good example of estimating reliability/precision using the test–retest method can be seen in the initial reliability testing of the Personality Assessment Inventory (PAI). The PAI, developed by Leslie Morey, is used for clinical diagnoses, treatment planning, and screening for clinical psychopathology in adults. To initially determine the PAI's test–retest reliability coefficient, researchers administered it to two samples of individuals not in clinical treatment. (Although the test was designed for use in a clinical setting, using a clinical sample for estimating reliability would have been difficult because changes due to a disorder or to treatment would have confused interpretation of the results of the reliability studies.) The researchers administered the PAI twice to 75 normal adults. The second administration followed the first by an average of 24 days. The researchers also administered the PAI to 80 normal college students, who took the test twice with an interval of 28 days. In each case, the researchers correlated the set of scores from the first administration with the set of scores from the second administration. The two studies yielded similar results, showing acceptable estimates of test–retest reliability for the PAI.

> More detail about the PAI can be found in **Test Spotlight 5.1** in Appendix A.

An important limitation in using the test–retest method of estimating reliability is that the test takers may score differently (usually higher) on the test because of practice effects. **Practice effects** occur when test takers benefit from taking the test the first time (practice), which enables them to solve problems more quickly and correctly the second time. (If all test takers benefited the same amount from practice, it would not affect reliability; however, it is likely that some will benefit from practice more than others will.) Therefore, the test–retest method is appropriate only when test takers are not likely to learn something the first time they take the test that can affect their scores on the second administration or when the interval between the two administrations is long enough to prevent practice effects. In other words, a long time between administrations can cause test takers to forget what they learned during the first administration. However, short intervals between testing implementations may be preferable when the test measures an attribute that may change in an individual over time due to learning or maturation, or when the possibility that changes in the testing environment that occur over time may affect the scores.

Alternate-Forms Method

To overcome problems such as practice effects, psychologists often give two forms of the same test—designed to be as much alike as possible—to the same people. This strategy requires the test developer to create two different forms of the test that are referred to as **alternate forms**. Again, the sets of scores from the two tests are compared using correlation. This method of estimating reliability/precision provides a test of equivalence. The two forms (Form A and Form B) are administered as close in time as possible—usually on the same day. To guard against any **order effects**—changes in test scores resulting from the order in which the tests were taken—half of the test takers may receive Form A first and the other half may receive Form B first.

An example of the use of alternate forms in testing can be seen in the development of the Test of Nonverbal Intelligence, Fourth Edition (TONI-4; PRO-ED, n.d.). The TONI-4 is the fourth version of an intelligence test that was designed to assess cognitive ability in populations that have language difficulties due to learning disabilities, speech problems, or other verbal problems that might result from a neurological deficit or developmental disability. The test does not require any language to be used in the administration of the test or in the responses of the test takers. The items are carefully drawn graphics that represent problems with four to six possible solutions. The test takers can use any mode of responding that the test administrator can understand to indicate their answers, such as nodding, blinking, or pointing. Because this test is often used in situations in which there is a need to assess whether improvement in functioning has occurred, two forms of the test needed to be developed—one to use as a pretest and another to use as a posttest. After the forms were developed, the test developers assessed the alternate-forms reliability by giving the two forms to the same group of subjects in the same testing session. The results demonstrated that the correlation between the test forms (which is the reliability coefficient) across all ages was .81, and the mean score difference between the two forms was one half of a score point. This is good evidence for alternate-forms reliability of the TONI-4.

More detail about the TONI-4 can be found in **Test Spotlight 5.2** in Appendix A.

The greatest danger when using alternate forms is that the two forms will not be truly equivalent. Alternate forms are much easier to develop for well-defined characteristics, such as mathematical ability, than for personality traits, such as extroversion. For example, achievement tests given to students at the beginning and end of the school year are alternate forms. Although we check the reliability of alternate forms by administering them at the same time, their practical advantage is that they can also be used as pre- and posttests if desired. There is also another term, which we discussed earlier in this chapter, that we sometimes use to describe different forms of the same test. This term is **parallel forms**. Although the terms *alternate forms* and *parallel forms* are often used interchangeably, they do not have exactly the same technical meaning. The term parallel forms refers to two tests that have certain identical (and hard to achieve) statistical properties. So it will usually be more correct to refer to two tests that are designed to measure exactly the same thing as alternate forms rather than parallel forms.

Internal Consistency Method

What if you can give the test only once? How can you estimate the reliability/precision? As you recall, test–retest reliability provides a measure of the test's reliability/precision over time, and that measure can be taken only with two administrations. However, we can measure another type of reliability/precision, called internal consistency, by giving the test once to one group of people. **Internal consistency** is a measure of how related the items (or groups of items) on the test are to one another. Another way to think about this is whether knowledge of how a person answered one item on the test would give you information that would help you correctly predict how he or she answered another item on the test. If you can (statistically) do that across the entire test, then the items must have something in common with each other. That commonality is usually related to the fact that they are measuring a similar attribute, and therefore we say that the test is internally consistent. Table 5.1 shows two pairs of math questions. The first pair has more commonality for assessing ability to do math calculations than the second pair does.

TABLE 5.1 ■ Internally Consistent Versus Inconsistent Test Questions			
A. Questions with higher internal consistency for measuring math calculation skill:			
Question 1:	7 + 8 = ?	Question 2:	8 + 3 = ?
B. Questions with lower internal consistency for measuring math calculation skill:			
Question 1:	4 + 5 = ?	Question 2:	150 × 300 = ?

Can you see why this is so? The problems in Pair A are very similar; both involve adding single-digit numbers. The problems in Pair B, however, test different arithmetic operations (addition and multiplication), and Pair A uses simpler numbers than Pair B does. In Pair A, test takers who can add single digits are likely to get both problems correct. However, test takers who can add single digits might not be able to multiply three-digit numbers. The problems in Pair B measure different kinds of math calculation skills, and therefore they are less internally consistent than the problems in Pair A, which both measure the addition of single-digit numbers. Another way to look at the issue is that if you knew that a person correctly answered Question 1 in Pair A, you would have a good chance of being correct if you predicted that the person also would answer Question 2 correctly. However, you probably would be less confident about your prediction about a person answering Question 1 in Pair B correctly also answering Question 2 correctly.

Statisticians have developed several methods for measuring the internal consistency of a test. One traditional method, the **split-half method,** is to divide the test into halves and then compare the set of individual test scores on the first half with the set of individual test scores on the second half. The two halves must be equivalent in length and content for this method to yield an accurate estimate of reliability.

The best way to divide the test is to use random assignment to place each question in one half or the other. Random assignment is likely to balance errors in the score that can result from order effects (the order in which the questions are answered), difficulty, and content.

When we use the split-half method to calculate a reliability coefficient, we are in effect correlating the scores on two shorter versions of the test. However, as mentioned earlier, shortening a test decreases its reliability because there will be less opportunity for random measurement error to cancel itself out. Therefore, when using the split-half method, we must mathematically adjust the reliability coefficient to compensate for the impact of splitting the test into halves. We will discuss this adjustment—using an equation called the **Spearman–Brown formula**—later in the chapter.

An even better way to measure internal consistency is to compare individuals' scores on all possible ways of splitting the test into halves. This method compensates for any error introduced by any unintentional lack of equivalence that splitting a test in the two halves might create. Kuder and Richardson (1937, 1939) first proposed a formula, KR-20, for calculating internal consistency of tests whose questions can be scored as either right or wrong (such as multiple-choice test items). Cronbach (1951) proposed a formula called coefficient alpha that calculates internal consistency for questions that have more than two possible responses such as rating scales. We also discuss these formulas later in this chapter.

Estimating reliability using methods of internal consistency is appropriate only for a **homogeneous test**—measuring only one trait or characteristic. With a **heterogeneous test**—measuring more than one trait or characteristic—estimates of internal consistency are likely to be lower. For example, a test for people who are applying for the job of accountant may measure knowledge of accounting principles, calculation skills, and ability to use a computer spreadsheet. Such a test is heterogeneous because it measures three distinct factors of performance for an accountant.

It is not appropriate to calculate an overall estimate of internal consistency (e.g., coefficient alpha, split-half) when a test is heterogeneous. Instead, the test developer should calculate and report an estimate of internal consistency for each homogeneous subtest or factor. The test for accountants should have three estimates of internal consistency: one for the subtest that measures knowledge of accounting principles, one for the subtest that measures calculation skills, and one for the subtest that measures ability to use a computer spreadsheet. In addition, Schmitt (1996) stated that the test developer should report the relationships or correlations between the subtests or factors of a test.

Furthermore, Schmitt (1996) emphasized that the concepts of internal consistency and homogeneity are not the same. Coefficient alpha describes the extent to which questions on a test or subscale are interrelated. Homogeneity refers to whether the questions measure the same trait or dimension. It is possible for a test to contain questions that are highly inter-related, even though the questions measure two different dimensions. This difference can happen when there is some third common factor that may be related to all the other attributes that the test measures. For instance, we described a hypothetical test for accountants that contained subtests for accounting skills, calculation skills, and use of a spreadsheet. Even though these three subtests may be considered heterogeneous dimensions, all of them may be influenced by a common dimension that might be named general mathematical ability. Therefore, people who are high in this ability might do better across all three subtests than people lower in this ability. As a result, coefficient alpha might still be high even though the test measures more than one dimension. Therefore, a high coefficient alpha is not proof that a test measures only one skill, trait, or dimension.

Earlier, we discussed the PAI when we talked about the test–retest method of estimating test reliability/precision. The developers of the PAI also conducted studies to determine its internal consistency. Because the PAI requires test takers to provide ratings on a response scale that has five options (*false*, *not at all true*, *slightly true*, *mainly true*, and *very true*), they used the coefficient alpha formula. The developers administered the PAI to three samples: a sample of 1,000 persons drawn to match the U.S. census, another sample of 1,051 college students, and a clinical sample of 1,246 persons.

Table 5.2 shows the estimates of internal consistency for the scales and subscales of the PAI. Again, the studies yielded levels of reliability/precision considered to be acceptable by the test developer for most of the scales and subscales of the PAI. Two scales on the test—Inconsistency and Infrequency—yielded low estimates of internal consistency. However, the test developer anticipated lower alpha values because these scales measure the care used by the test taker in completing the test, and careless responding could vary during the testing period. For instance, a test taker might complete the first half of the test accurately but then become tired and complete the second half haphazardly.

Scorer Reliability

What about errors made by the person who scores the test? An individual can make mistakes in scoring, which add error to test scores, particularly when the scorer must make judgments about whether an answer is right or wrong. When scoring requires making judgments, two or more persons should score the test. We then compare the judgments that the scorers make about each answer to see how much they agree. The methods we have already discussed pertain to whether the test itself yields consistent scores, but scorer reliability and agreement pertain to how consistent the judgments of the scorers are.

Some tests, such as those that require the scorer to make judgments, have complicated scoring schemes for which test manuals provide the explicit instructions necessary for making

TABLE 5.2 ■ **Estimates of Internal Consistency for the Personality Assessment Inventory**

Scale	Alpha		
	Census	College	Clinic
Inconsistency	.45	.26	.23
Infrequency	.52	.22	.40
Negative Impression	.72	.63	.74
Positive Impression	.71	.73	.77
Somatic Complaints	.89	.83	.92
Anxiety	.90	.89	.94
Anxiety-Related Disorders	.76	.80	.86
Depression	.87	.87	.93
Mania	.82	.82	.82
Paranoia	.85	.88	.89
Schizophrenia	.81	.82	.89
Borderline Features	.87	.86	.91
Antisocial Features	.84	.85	.86
Alcohol Problems	.84	.83	.93
Drug Problems	.74	.66	.89
Aggression	.85	.89	.90
Suicidal Ideation	.85	.87	.93
Stress	.76	.69	.79
Nonsupport	.72	.75	.80
Treatment Rejection	.76	.72	.80
Dominance	.78	.81	.82
Warmth	.79	.80	.83
Median across 22 scales	.81	.82	.86

Source: From *Personality Assessment Inventory* by L. C. Morey. Copyright © 1991. Published by Psychological Assessment Resources (PAR).

these scoring judgments. Deviation from the scoring instructions or a variation in the interpretation of the instructions introduces error into the final score. Therefore, **scorer reliability** or **interscorer agreement**—the amount of consistency among scorers' judgments—becomes an important consideration for tests that require decisions by the administrator or scorer.

More detail about the WCST can be found in **Test Spotlight 5.3** in Appendix A.

A good example of estimating reliability/precision using scorer reliability can be seen in the Wisconsin Card Sorting Test (WCST). This test was originally designed to assess perseveration and abstract thinking, but it is currently one of the most widely used tests by clinicians and neurologists to assess executive function (cognitive abilities that control and regulate abilities and behaviors) of children and adults. Axelrod, Goldman, and Woodard (1992) conducted two studies on the reliability/precision of scoring the WCST using adult psychiatric inpatients. In these studies, one person administered the test and others scored the test. In the first study, three clinicians experienced in neuropsychological assessment scored the WCST data independently according to instructions given in an early edition of the test manual (Heaton, 1981). Their agreement was measured using a statistical procedure called intraclass correlation, a special type of correlation appropriate for comparing responses of more than two raters or of more than two sets of scores. The scores that each clinician gave each individual on three subscales correlated at .93, .92, and .88—correlations that indicated very high agreement. The studies also looked at **intrascorer reliability**—whether each clinician was consistent in the way he or she assigned scores from test to test. Again, all correlations were greater than .90.

In the second study, six novice scorers, who did not have previous experience scoring the WCST, scored 30 tests. The researchers divided the scorers into two groups. One group received only the scoring procedures in the test manual (Heaton, 1981), and the other group received supplemental scoring instructions as well as those in the manual. All scorers scored the WCST independently. The consistency level of these novices was high and was similar to the results of the first study. Although there were no significant differences between groups, those receiving the supplemental scoring material were able to score the WCST in a shorter time period. Conducting studies of scorer reliability for a test, such as those of Axelrod and colleagues (1992), ensures that the instructions for scoring are clear and unambiguous so that multiple scorers arrive at the same results.

We have discussed three methods for estimating the reliability/precision of a test: test–retest, alternate forms, and internal consistency, which included scorer reliability. Some methods require only a single administration of the test, while others require two. Again, each of these methods takes into account various conditions that could produce differences in test scores, and not all strategies are appropriate for all tests. The strategy chosen to determine an estimate of reliability/precision depends on the test itself and the conditions under which the test user plans to administer the test.

More detail about the Bayley Scales of Infant and Toddler Development can be found in **Test Spotlight 5.4** in Appendix A.

Some tests have undergone extensive reliability/precision testing. An example of such a test is the Bayley Scales of Infant and Toddler Development, a popular and interesting test for children that has extensive evidence of reliability. According to Dunst (1998), the standardization and the evidence of reliability/precision and validity of this test far exceed generally accepted guidelines.

The test developer should report the reliability method as well as the number and characteristics of the test takers in the reliability study along with the associated reliability coefficients. For some tests, such as the PAI, the WCST, and the Bayley Scales, more than one method may be appropriate. Each method provides evidence that the test is consistent under certain circumstances. Using more than one method provides strong corroborative evidence that the test is reliable.

The next section describes statistical methods for calculating reliability coefficients, which estimate the reliability/precision of a test. As you will see, the answer to how reliable a test's scores are may depend on how you decide to measure it. Test–retest, alternate forms, and internal consistency are concerned with the test itself. Scorer reliability involves an examination of how consistently the person or persons scored the test. That is why test publishers may need to report multiple reliability coefficients for a test to give the test user a complete picture of the instrument.

THE RELIABILITY COEFFICIENT

As we mentioned earlier in this chapter, we can use the correlation coefficient to provide an index of the strength of the relationship between two sets of test scores. To calculate the reliability coefficient using the test–retest method, we correlate the scores from the first and second test administrations; in the case of the alternate-forms and split-half methods, we correlate the scores of the first test and the second test.

The symbol that stands for a correlation coefficient is r. To show that the correlation coefficient represents a reliability coefficient, we add two subscripts of the same letter, such as r_{xx} or r_{aa}. Often authors omit the subscripts in the narrative texts of journal articles and textbooks when the text is clear that the discussion involves reliability, and we follow that convention in this chapter. Remember that a reliability coefficient is simply a Pearson product–moment correlation coefficient applied to test scores.

Adjusting Split-Half Reliability Estimates

As we mentioned earlier, the number of questions on a test is directly related to reliability; the more questions on the test, the higher the reliability, provided that the test questions are equivalent in content and difficulty. This is because the influence of random measurement error due to the particular choice of questions used to represent the concept is reduced when a test is made longer. Other sources of measurement error can still exist, such as inconsistency in test administration procedures or poorly worded test instructions. When a test is divided into halves and then the two halves of the test are correlated to estimate its internal consistency, the test length is reduced by half. Therefore, researchers adjust the reliability coefficient (obtained when scores on each half are correlated) using the formula developed by Spearman and Brown. This formula is sometimes referred to as the prophecy formula because it designed to estimate what the reliability coefficient would be if the tests had not been cut in half, but instead were the original length. We typically use this formula when adjusting reliability coefficients derived by correlating two halves of one test. Other reliability coefficients, such as test–retest and coefficient alpha, should not be adjusted in this fashion. For Your Information Box 5.1 provides the formula Spearman and Brown developed and shows how to calculate an adjusted reliability coefficient.

The Spearman–Brown formula is also helpful to test developers who wish to estimate how the reliability/precision of a test would change if the test were made either longer or shorter. As we have said, the length of the test influences the reliability of the test; the more homogeneous questions (questions about the same issue or trait) the respondent answers, the more information the test yields about the concept the test is designed to measure. This increase yields more distinctive information about each respondent than fewer items would yield. It produces more variation in test scores and reduces the impact of random error that is a result of the particular questions that happened to be chosen for inclusion on the test.

Other Methods of Calculating Internal Consistency

As you recall, a more precise way to measure internal consistency is to compare individuals' scores on all possible ways of splitting the test in halves (instead of just one random split of test items into two halves). This method compensates for error introduced by any lack of

FOR YOUR INFORMATION BOX 5.1

USING THE SPEARMAN–BROWN FORMULA

The Spearman–Brown formula below represents the relationship between reliability and test length. It is used to estimate the change in reliability/precision that could be expected when the length of a test is changed. It is often used to adjust the correlation coefficient obtained when using the split-half method for estimating the reliability coefficient, but it is also used by test developers to estimate how the reliability/precision of a test would change if a test were made longer or shorter for any reason.

$$r_{xx} = \frac{nr}{1+(n-1)(r)},$$

where

r_{xx} = estimated reliability coefficient of the longer or shorter version of the test

n = number of questions in the revised (often longer) version divided by the number of questions in the original (shorter) version of the test

r = calculated correlation coefficient between the two short forms of the test

Suppose that you calculated a split-half correlation coefficient of .80 for a 50 question test split randomly in half. You are interested in knowing what the estimated reliability coefficient of the full-length version of the test would be. Because the whole test contains 50 questions, each half of the test would contain 25 questions. So the value of n would be:

50 (the number of questions in the longer, or full, version of the test) divided by 25 (the number of questions in the split, or shorter, version of the test).

Thus n in this example would equal 2.

You can then follow these steps to adjust the coefficient obtained and estimate the reliability of the test.

Step 1: Substitute values of r and n into the equation:

$$r_{xx} = \frac{2(.80)}{1+(2-1)(.80)},$$

Step 2: Complete the algebraic calculations:

$$r_{xx} = .89.$$

Our best estimate of the reliability coefficient of the full-length test is .89.

---

equivalence in the two halves. The two formulas researchers use for estimating internal consistency are KR-20 and coefficient alpha.

Researchers use the KR-20 formula (Kuder & Richardson, 1937, 1939) for tests whose questions, such as true/false and multiple choice, can be scored as either right or wrong. (Note that although multiple-choice questions have a number of possible answers, only one answer is correct.) Researchers use the coefficient alpha formula (Cronbach, 1951) for test questions, such as ratings scales, that have more than one correct answer. Coefficient alpha may also be used for scales made up of questions with only one right answer because the formula will yield the same result as does the KR-20.

How do most researchers and test developers estimate internal consistency? Charter (2003) examined the descriptive statistics for 937 reliability coefficients for various types of tests. He found an increase over time in the use of coefficient alpha and an associated decrease in the use of the split-half method for estimating internal consistency. This change is probably due to the availability of computer software that can calculate coefficient alpha. Charter also reported that the median reliability coefficient in his study was .85. Half of the coefficients examined were above what experts recommend, and half were below what experts recommend. For Your Information Box 5.2 provides the formulas for calculating KR-20 and coefficient alpha.

FOR YOUR INFORMATION BOX 5.2
FORMULAS FOR KR-20 AND COEFFICIENT ALPHA

Two formulas for estimating internal reliability are KR-20 and coefficient alpha. KR-20 is used for scales that have questions that are scored either right or wrong, such as true/false and multiple-choice questions. The formula for coefficient alpha is an expansion of the KR-20 formula and is used when test questions have a range of possible answers, such as a rating scale. Coefficient alpha may also be used for scales made up of questions with only one right answer:

$$r_{KR20} = \left(\frac{k}{k-1}\right)\left(1 - \frac{\sum pq}{\sigma^2}\right)$$

where

r_{KR20} = KR-20 reliability coefficient

k = number of questions on the test

p = proportion of test takers who gave the correct answer to the question

q = proportion of test takers who gave an incorrect answer to the question

σ^2 = variance of all the test scores

The formula for coefficient alpha (α is the Greek symbol for alpha) is similar to the KR-20 formula and is used when test takers have a number of answers from which to choose their response:

$$r_{\alpha} = \left(\frac{k}{k-1}\right)\left(1 - \frac{\sum \sigma_i^2}{\sigma^2}\right)$$

where

r_a = coefficient alpha estimate of reliability

k = number of questions on the test

σ_i^2 = variance of the scores on one question

σ^2 = variance of all the test scores

Calculating Scorer Reliability/Precision and Agreement

We can calculate scorer reliability/precision by correlating the judgments of one scorer with the judgments of another scorer. When there is a strong positive relationship between scorers, scorer reliability will be high.

When scorers make judgments that result in nominal or ordinal data, such as ratings and yes/no decisions, we calculate **interrater agreement**—an index of how consistently the scorers rate or make decisions. One popular index of agreement is **Cohen's kappa** (Cohen, 1960). In For Your Information Box 5.3 we describe kappa and demonstrate how to calculate it.

When one scorer makes judgments, the researcher also wants assurance that the scorer makes consistent judgments across all tests. For example, when a teacher scores essay exams, we would like the teacher to judge the final essays graded in the same way that he or she judged the first essays. We refer to this concept as **intrarater agreement**. (Note that *inter* refers to "between," and *intra* refers to "within.") Calculating intrarater agreement requires that the same rater rate the same thing on two or more occasions. In the example mentioned above, a measure of intrarater agreement could be computed if a teacher graded the same set of essays on two different occasions. This would provide information on how consistent (i.e., reliable) the teacher was in his or her grading. One statistical technique that is used to evaluate intrarater reliability is called the intraclass correlation coefficient, the discussion of which goes beyond the scope of this text. Shrout and Fleiss (1979) provided an in-depth discussion of this topic. Table 5.3 provides an overview of the types of reliability we have discussed and the appropriate formula to use for each type.

TABLE 5.3 ■ Methods of Estimating Reliability		
Method	**Test Administration**	**Formula**
Test–retest reliability	Administer the same test to the same people at two points in time.	Pearson product–moment correlation
Alternate forms or parallel forms	Administer two forms of the test to the same people.	Pearson product–moment correlation
Internal consistency	Give the test in one administration, and then split the test into two halves for scoring.	Pearson product–moment correlation corrected for length by the Spearman–Brown formula
Internal consistency	Give the test in one administration, and then compare all possible split halves.	Coefficient alpha or KR-20
Interrater reliability	Give the test once, and have it scored (interval- or ratio-level data) by two scorers or two methods.	Pearson product–moment correlation
Interrater agreement	Create a rating instrument, and have it completed by two judges (nominal- or ordinal-level data).	Cohen's kappa
Intrarater agreement	Calculate the consistency of scores for a single scorer. A single scorer rates or scores the same thing on more than one occasion.	Intraclass correlation coefficient

When you begin developing or using tests, you will not want to calculate reliability by hand. All statistical software programs and many spreadsheet programs will calculate the Pearson product–moment correlation coefficient. You simply enter the test scores for the first and second administrations (or halves) and choose the correlation menu command. If you calculate the correlation coefficient to estimate split-half reliability, you will probably need to adjust the correlation coefficient by hand using the Spearman–Brown formula because most software programs do not make this correction.

Computing coefficient alpha and KR-20 are more complicated. Spreadsheet software programs usually do not calculate coefficient alpha and KR-20, but the formulas are available in the larger, better known statistical packages such as SAS and SPSS. Consult your software manual for instructions on how to enter your data and calculate internal consistency. Likewise, some statistical software programs calculate Cohen's kappa; however, you may prefer to use the matrix method demonstrated in For Your Information Box 5.3.

INTERPRETING RELIABILITY COEFFICIENTS

We look at a correlation coefficient in two ways to interpret its meaning. First, we are interested in its sign—whether it is positive or negative. The sign tells us whether the two variables increase or decrease together (positive sign) or whether one variable increases as the other decreases (negative sign).

FOR YOUR INFORMATION BOX 5.3

COHEN'S KAPPA

Cohen's kappa provides a nonparametric index for scorer agreement when the scores are nominal or ordinal data (Cohen, 1960). For example, pass/fail essay questions and rating scales on personality inventories provide categorical data that cannot be correlated. Kappa compensates and corrects interobserver agreement for the proportion of agreement that might occur by chance. Cohen developed the following formula for kappa (κ):

$$\kappa = \frac{p_o - p_c}{1 - p_c}$$

where

p_o = observed proportion

p_c = expected proportion

An easier way to understand the formula is to state it using frequencies (f):

$$\kappa = \frac{f_o - f_c}{N - f_c},$$

where

f_o = observed frequency

f_c = expected frequency

N = overall total of data points in the frequency matrix

Many researchers calculate Cohen's kappa by arranging the data in a matrix in which the first rater's judgments are arranged vertically and the second rater's judgments are arranged horizontally. For example, assume that two scorers rate nine writing samples on a scale of 1 to 3, where 1 indicates very poor writing skills, 2 indicates average writing skills, and 3 indicates excellent writing skills. The scores that each rater provided are shown below:

Scorer 1: 3, 3, 2, 2, 3, 1, 2, 3, 1

Scorer 2: 3, 2, 3, 2, 3, 2, 2, 3, 1

As you can see, Scorers 1 and 2 agreed on the first writing sample, did not agree on the second sample, did not agree on the third sample, and so on. We arrange the scores in a matrix by placing a check mark in the cell that agrees with the match for each writing sample. For example, the check for the first writing sample goes in the bottom right cell, where excellent for Scorer 1 intersects with excellent for Scorer 2, the check for the second writing sample goes in the middle right cell where excellent for Scorer 1 intersects with average for Scorer 2, and so on:

		Scorer 1		
		Poor (1)	**Average (2)**	**Excellent (3)**
Scorer 2	Poor (1)	✓		
	Average (2)	✓	✓✓	✓✓
	Excellent (3)			✓✓✓

To calculate kappa, each cell in the matrix must contain at least one agreement. Unfortunately, our N of 9 is too small. As you can see, our nine writing samples do not fill all of the cells in the matrix. The following is another matrix containing data for 36 writing samples:

(Continued)

(Continued)

		Scorer 1			
		Poor (1)	Average (2)	Excellent (3)	Row Totals
Scorer 2	Poor (1)	9	3	1	13
	Average (2)	4	8	2	14
	Excellent (3)	2	1	6	9
	Column totals	15	12	9	36

In this matrix for 36 writing samples, Scorers 1 and 2 agreed a total of 23 times (the sum of the diagonal cells). The sum of the row totals (S rows) is 36, and the sum of the column totals (S columns) is 36, in agreement with the overall total of 36.

To calculate the expected frequency (f_c) for each diagonal, we use the following formula:

$$f_c = \frac{\text{Row Total} \times \text{Column Total}}{\text{Overall Total}},$$

where

f_c for the first cell in the diagonal = $(13 \times 15)/36 = 5.42$

f_c for the second cell in the diagonal = 4.67

f_c for the third cell in the diagonal = 2.25

Now we can calculate the sum of the expected frequencies of the diagonals (Σf_c):

$\Sigma f_c = 5.42 + 4.67 + 2.25 = 12.34.$

When we plug the sum of the expected frequencies of the diagonals into the frequencies formula for kappa, we can calculate the value of kappa:

$$\kappa = \frac{\Sigma f_o \Sigma f_c}{N - \Sigma f_c} = \frac{23 - 12.34}{36 - 12.34} = .45$$

In this example, kappa (κ) equals .45.

Kappa ranges from −1.00 to +1.00. The higher the value of kappa, the stronger the agreement among the judges or raters. The scorers of the 36 writing samples are in moderate agreement. They should discuss how they are making their judgments so that they can increase their level of agreement.

Second, we look at the number itself. As you also recall, correlation coefficients range from −1.00 (a perfect negative correlation) to +1.00 (a perfect positive correlation). Most often, the coefficient's number will fall in between. Therefore, if a test's reliability coefficient is +.91, we know that its sign is positive; people who made high scores on the first administration made similarly high scores on the second, and people who made low scores on the first administration made similarly low scores on the second. Furthermore, the coefficient .91 is very close to +1.00 or perfect agreement, so the test appears to be very reliable. Likewise, a correlation can be negative. A correlation coefficient of −.91 would also be very reliable, but the interpretation would be different. In a negative correlation, those who scored high on one test would score low on the second test, and those who scored low on the first test would consistently score high on the second test. While correlations can range from −1.00 to +1.00, reliability coefficients are considered to range from 0.00 to 1.00. Tests can range from not at all reliable ($r_{xx} = 0.00$) to perfectly reliable ($r_{xx} = 1.00$). To better understand the amount of error in a test score, we use the reliability coefficient to calculate another statistic called the standard error of measurement.

FOR YOUR INFORMATION BOX 5.4
CALCULATING THE STANDARD ERROR OF MEASUREMENT

The formula for calculating the standard error of measurement is

$$SEM = \sigma\sqrt{1 - r_{xx}},$$

where

SEM = standard error of measurement

σ = standard deviation of one administration of the test scores

r_{xx} = reliability coefficient of the test

For this example, we will use the data in Table 5.4, which provides data on two administrations of the same test for 10 test takers. The calculated reliability coefficient (r_{xx}) for this test is .91. The standard deviation (σ) for the first administration of the test is 14.327.

With $s = 14.327$ and $r_{xx} = .91$, you can calculate the SEM by substituting these values into the equation and completing the algebraic calculations as follows:

$$SEM = 14.327\sqrt{1 - .91};$$

$$SEM = 4.2981 \text{ or } 4.3.$$

The SEM can be used to construct a confidence interval around a test score to provide a better estimate of the range in which the test taker's true score is likely to fall. This process is demonstrated in For Your Information Box 5.5.

Calculating the Standard Error of Measurement

Psychologists use the **standard error of measurement (SEM)** as an index of the amount of inconsistency or error expected in an individual's observed test score. In other words, the SEM is an estimate of how much the individual's observed test score (X) might differ from the individual's true test score (T). As you recall, the true test score is the theoretical score that a person would obtain if there were no measurement errors. For Your Information Box 5.4 shows how to calculate the SEM.

Interpreting the Standard Error of Measurement

To understand what the SEM means, we must apply it to an individual's test score. As you now know, if an individual took a particular test two times, the scores on the first and second administrations of the test would likely be different because of random errors in measurement. If the person took the test 10 times, we would probably observe 10 similar but not identical scores. Remember, we are assuming the person's true score has not changed across the administrations, but rather the observed differences in scores are due to random measurement error. The important point to understand is that a person's observed score on a test is really only an estimate of his or her true score on the construct that the test was designed to measure.

Also recall that random error is assumed to be normally distributed. What this means is that each time a person takes a test, the amount of influence that measurement error will have on that person's observed score can vary. Sometimes measurement error can create a large difference between a person's observed and true scores; sometimes the difference will be small. It depends on the magnitude of the measurement error present in the test. And because random error is normally distributed (if graphed, it would look like a normal curve), its influence on the observed score will vary from one test administration to another. The SEM enables us to quantify the amount of variation in a person's observed score that measurement error would most likely cause.

Because of the characteristics of the normal distribution, we can assume that if the individual took the test an infinite number of times, the following would result:

- Approximately 68% of the observed test scores (X) would be within ±1 SEM of the true score (T).

- Approximately 95% of the observed test scores (X) would be within ±2 SEM of the true score (T).

- Approximately 99.7% of the observed test scores (X) would be within ±3 SEM of the true score (T).

(To understand this assumption, refer to our discussion of the properties of the normal curve earlier in the "How Do Test Users Interpret Test Scores?" chapter of the textbook.)

Confidence Intervals

We can then use the preceding information to construct a **confidence interval**—a range of scores that we feel confident will include the test taker's true score. For Your Information Box 5.5 shows how to calculate a confidence interval for an observed score.

Confidence intervals are important because they give us a realistic estimate of how much error is likely to exist in an individual's observed score, that is, how big the difference between the individual's observed score and his or her (unobservable) true score is likely to be. The wider the confidence interval, the more measurement error is present in the test score.

Understanding confidence intervals is important any time we make decisions based on people's test scores, such as whether to hire them or admit them to a special educational program or whether they may be at risk for a particular medical disorder. The presence of error in the test scores could cause the decision to be incorrect. The more confident we are that the observed score on a test is really close to the person's true score, the more comfortable we can be that we are making a correct decision about the meaning of the score.

For Your Information Box 5.5 shows you how to calculate a confidence interval that is likely to contain an individual's true score using the data presented in Table 5.4. That table presents

TABLE 5.4 ■ Test Scores for 10 Candidates on Two Administrations		
Test Taker	**First Administration**	**Second Administration**
Adams	90	95
Butler	70	75
Chavez	50	65
Davis	100	95
Ellis	90	80
Franks	70	75
Garrison	60	65
Hart	75	80
Isaacs	75	80
Jones	85	80

FOR YOUR INFORMATION BOX 5.5
CALCULATING A 95% CONFIDENCE INTERVAL
AROUND AN ESTIMATED TRUE TEST SCORE

The formula for calculating a 95% confidence interval around a score is

$$95\% \text{ CI} = X \pm 1.96(\text{SEM}),$$

where

95% CI = the 95% confidence interval

X = an individual's observed test score (this is the estimate of the person's true score.)

±1.96 = the 2 points on the normal curve that include 95% of the scores

SEM = the standard error of measurement for the test

For this example, we will use the data in Table 5.4 for the first administration of a test. The calculated SEM is 4.3 (see For Your Information Box 5.4). If we wanted to calculate the 95% confidence interval for an observed score of 90 on that first administration, the calculation is performed as follows:

$$95\% \text{ CI} = X \pm 1.96(\text{SEM})$$

$$95\% \text{ CI} = 90 - (1.96 \times 4.3) \text{ and } 90 + (1.96 \times 4.3)$$

$$= (90 - 8.428) \text{ and } (90 + 8.428)$$

$$= 81.572 \text{ and } 98.428$$

$$95\% \text{ CI} = 81.572 \text{ to } 98.428.$$

Therefore, we would say that there is a 95% chance that this confidence interval will contain the true test score (T), which falls between 81.572 and 98.428.

the observed test scores for 10 people who took the same test on two occasions. The reliability coefficient of the test is .91, the standard deviation (σ) for the first administration of the test is 14.327, and the SEM is 4.3 points. When we calculate the 95% confidence interval for the true scores on the first administration of the test, it is ±8.4 points of the observed score. This means that 95% of the time, this confidence interval will include the person's true score. So a person who has an observed score of 75 on the test will most likely have a true score between 66.6 and 83.4—a relatively wide interval of about 17 points. Let's see what the implications of this are in practice. If we calculated the 95% confidence interval for a person who had an observed score of 70 on the test, we see that we can be 95% confident that the person's true score is between 61.6 and 78.4. Can you see the potential problem this creates? Assume that we had set the passing score on the test at 73. Without knowledge of the SEM and confidence interval, we would conclude that the person who scored 75 passed, and the person who scored 70 did not. But based on the 95% confidence interval, the true score of the person with the score of 75 could be as low as 66.6, and the true score of the person who scored 70 could be as high as 78.4. So it is possible that the person with the observed score of 70 might have really passed (based on his or her true score), while the person with the observed score of 75 might have actually failed. Unfortunately, as we have stated before, there is no way to know the precise true score. So when making a judgment about the meaning of two different observed scores, it is important to evaluate the confidence intervals to see whether they overlap like they do in this case. When the true-score confidence intervals for two different observed scores overlap, it means that you cannot be sure that the observed scores' differences reflect equivalent differences in true scores. In that case, the two observed scores should be treated as if they are the same score. While our example used a 95% confidence interval, it is not uncommon to use the 90% confidence interval when dealing with test scores. Using the 90% confidence interval will produce a narrower band of test scores than the 95% confidence interval does, but statistically we will be less certain that the person's true score falls within the interval.

An applied example of how the estimation of measurement error is used occurs when a political poll suggests that one candidate will win an election by 2%, but the stated margin of error in the poll is 3%. In this case, the race would be considered to be a statistical tie despite the fact that the poll showed that one candidate was ahead by 2% because the estimated 2% difference is smaller than the margin of error.

One of the issues that is usually not mentioned in textbooks on psychological testing when confidence intervals around true scores are discussed is that the calculated confidence interval is almost always centered on an observed score—not a true score. We also follow that practice in this book. As you now know, any observed score is only an estimate of a true score that will be more or less precise depending on the amount of measurement error present in the test. Some authors, such as Nunnally and Bernstein (1994), have suggested that the observed score around which the confidence interval is to be constructed should be statistically adjusted to account for measurement error before the confidence interval is calculated. By doing so, the confidence interval for the true scores will be a more precise estimate because it will be centered on an estimated true score, not the original observed score. However, other authors, such as Harvill (1991), have indicated that centering the confidence interval on an unadjusted observed score will provide a satisfactory estimate so long as the reliability/precision of the test is reasonably high and the observed score is not an extreme score relative to the mean score on the test.

Finally, it is important to mention that the standard error of measurement as we have presented it here is an average across all the observed scores on a test. But it can be shown that the SEM may not be exactly the same at all score levels on a test. Raw (untransformed) scores near the mean of the score distribution tend to have a larger SEM than very high or very low scores, but scaled scores that have been transformed from the raw scores for easier interpretation can sometimes show the opposite pattern (Brennan & Lee, 1999). This becomes a very important consideration when test scores are used to make any kind of selection or placement decision. As you have learned, when confidence intervals around the true scores overlap, you may not be sure that differences in observed test scores actually correspond to differences in true scores. In those cases, you might have to consider the two different observed scores equivalent for decision-making purposes. You also have learned that the width of the confidence interval is dependent upon the SEM. So if the SEM differs at different observed scores, the confidence interval around the true scores will also differ. If you are using a predetermined passing or cut score for selection or classification of individuals, it is important to calculate the SEM at the passing score when possible, as it might be different than the SEM averaged across all the scores. An SEM calculated at a specific score is known as a conditional standard error of measurement, because its value is conditioned upon, or calculated at, a particular observed score. The *Standards for Educational and Psychological Testing* (AERA et al., 2014) suggest that where possible, conditional standard errors of measurement should be reported at several score levels unless there is evidence that the standard error of measurement is constant across a wide range of scores. The calculation of a conditional standard error of measurement requires some advanced statistical techniques that we will not be able consider here.

As a general statement, remember that when the reliability/precision of the test scores is high, the SEM is low. This is because high reliability/precision implies low random measurement error. As that reliability/precision decreases, random measurement error increases and the SEM increases. Although high reliability/precision is always important, it is especially so when test users use test scores to distinguish among individuals. For instance, when hiring, the answer to whether one candidate really had a lower test score than another can be found by using the SEM to calculate a 95% confidence interval around each candidate's score. Often there will be a substantial overlap of confidence intervals for observed scores that are close to each other, suggesting that although there is a difference in observed scores, there might not be a difference in true scores of candidates.

Next we discuss how the reliability estimate—and thus the reliability of the test scores—may be increased or decreased.

FACTORS THAT INFLUENCE RELIABILITY

Because reliability is so important to accurate measurement, we need to consider several factors that may increase or decrease the reliability of the test scores. Error that can increase or decrease individual scores, and thereby decrease reliability, comes from four sources:

- The *test itself* can generate error by being poorly designed; by containing trick questions, ambiguous questions, or poorly written questions; or by requiring a reading level higher than the reading level of the test takers.

- The *test administration* can generate error when administrators do not follow instructions for administration in the test manual or allow disturbances to occur during the test period. For example, the test administrator might misread the instructions for the length of the test period; answer test takers' questions inappropriately; allow the room to be too hot, cold, or noisy; or display attitudes that suggest the test is too difficult or unimportant.

- The *test scoring* can generate error if it is not conducted accurately and according to the directions in the test manual. For example, scorers might make errors in judgment or in calculating test scores. Although computer scoring is likely to decrease scoring errors, it is important to enter the correct scoring scheme into the computer software.

- *Test takers* themselves also can contribute to test error. Fatigue, illness, or exposure to test questions before taking the test can change test scores. In addition, test takers who do not provide truthful and honest answers introduce error into their test scores.

Six factors related to these sources of error—test length, homogeneity of questions, test–retest interval, test administration, scoring, and cooperation of test takers—stand out as particularly important and worthy of consideration in detail. Test developers and administrators focus on these factors to increase the reliability and accuracy of the test scores.

Test Length

As a rule, adding more questions that measure the same trait or attribute can increase a test's reliability. Each question on a test serves as an observation that indicates the test taker's knowledge, skill, ability, or trait being measured. The more observations there are on the construct that the test is designed to measure, the less random error will contribute to the observed scores and the more accurate the measure is likely to be.

Adding more questions to a test is similar to adding finer distinctions to a measuring tape, for example, adding indications for each 16th of an inch to a tape that previously had indications only for each 8th of an inch. Likewise, shortening a test by skipping or dropping questions causes the test to lose reliability. An extreme example is the test that has only one question—a most unreliable way to measure any trait or attitude.

As you recall, the Spearman–Brown formula adjusts the reliability estimate for test length. Test developers can also use the Spearman–Brown formula to estimate the number of questions to add to a test so as to increase its reliability to the desired level.

Embretson (1996) pointed out an important exception to this rule when using adaptive tests (e.g., the computer-based version of the GRE). A short adaptive test can be more reliable than a longer version. In an adaptive test, the test taker responds to questions selected based on his or her skill or aptitude level, and therefore the SEM decreases. As a result, the test taker answers fewer questions without sacrificing reliability. This circumstance, however, does not suggest that a test made up of one question or only a few questions would be reliable.

Homogeneity

Another important exception to the rule that adding questions increases reliability is that an increase in test questions will increase reliability only when the questions added are homogeneous (very much alike) with other questions on the test. That is, to increase reliability, the test developer must add questions that measure the same attribute as the other questions on the test. Heterogeneous (very different or diverse) tests can be expected to have lower reliability coefficients. As you recall, estimating reliability by calculating internal consistency is not appropriate for heterogeneous tests. If you have ever taken a test in which it seemed you were asked the same questions a number of times in slightly different ways, you have experienced a test that is homogeneous and probably very reliable.

Test–Retest Interval

The longer the interval between administrations of a test, the lower the reliability coefficient is likely to be. A long interval between test administrations provides more opportunity for test takers to change in terms of the factor being measured. Such changes cause a change in individuals' true scores. In addition, the longer time increases the possibility of error through changes in test administration, environment, or personal circumstances. A long interval may lessen practice effects; however, a better way to decrease practice effects would be to use alternate forms.

Test Administration

Proper test administration affects the reliability estimate in three ways. First, carefully following all of the instructions for administering a test ensures that all test takers experience the same testing situation each time the test is given. In other words, test takers hear the same instructions and take the test under the same physical conditions each time. Treating all test takers in the same way decreases error that arises from creating differences in the way individuals respond. Second, constancy between two administrations decreases error that arises when testing conditions differ. Third, effective testing practices decrease the chance that test takers' scores will be contaminated with error due to poor testing conditions or poor test instructions.

Scoring

Even tests scored by computer are subject to incorrect scoring. Test users must be careful to use the correct scoring key, to check questions that have unusually large numbers of correct or incorrect answers for mistakes in scoring, and to exercise considerable care when scoring tests that require judgments about whether an answer is right or wrong. Frequent checks of computations—including those made by computers—also decrease the chance of scoring errors. Scorers who will make qualitative judgments when scoring tests, such as using a rating scale, must receive training together to calibrate their judgments and responses.

Cooperation of Test Takers

Some tests, such as the PAI, have a built-in method for determining whether test takers guessed, faked, cheated, or in some other way neglected to answer questions truthfully or to the best of their ability. Many times, however, it is up to the test administrator to observe and motivate respondents to cooperate with the testing process. For instance, test administrators need to be aware of individuals who complete the test in an unusually short amount of time. These individuals might have checked answers without reading the questions or skipped whole pages either deliberately or by mistake. Although respondents cannot be forced to participate honestly, their tests can be dropped from the group of tests used to calculate reliability when there are doubts about the truthfulness of their answers.

GENERALIZABILITY THEORY

Up to now in this chapter, we have used classical test theory to describe the processes for measuring a test's consistency or reliability. Another approach to estimating reliability/precision is **generalizability theory**, proposed by Cronbach, Gleser, Nanda, and Rajaratnam (1972). This theory concerns how well and under what conditions we can generalize an estimation of reliability/precision of test scores from one test administration to another. In other words, the test user can predict the reliability/precision of test scores obtained under different circumstances, such as administering a test in various plant locations or school systems. Generalizability theory proposes separating sources of systematic error from random error to eliminate systematic error.

Why is the separation of systematic error and random error important? As you recall, we can assume that if we were able to record the amount of random error in each measurement, the average error would be zero, and over time random error would not interfere with obtaining an accurate measurement. However, systematic error does affect the accuracy of a measurement; therefore, using generalizability theory, our goal is to eliminate systematic error.

For example, if you weigh yourself once a week in the gym, your weight will consist of your true weight and measurement error. One possible source of measurement error would be random error in the scale or in your precision in reading the scale. But another source of the measurement error could be the weight of your clothes and shoes. Another source might be the time of day when you weigh yourself; generally speaking, you will weigh less in the morning than you will later in the day. These sources of error would not be random, but would be more systematic because each time they occurred, they would have the same influence on the measurement.

Using generalizability theory, you could look for systematic or ongoing predictable error that occurs when you weigh yourself. For instance, the weight of your clothes and shoes will vary systematically depending on the weather and the time of the year. Likewise, your weight will be greater later in the day. On the other hand, variations in the measurement mechanism and your ability to read the scale accurately vary randomly. We would predict, therefore, that if you weighed yourself at the same time of day wearing the same clothes (or, better yet, none at all), you would have a more accurate measurement of your weight. When you have the most accurate measurement of your weight, you can confidently assume that changes in your weight from measurement to measurement are due to real weight gain or loss and not to measurement error.

IN GREATER DEPTH BOX 5.2
GENERALIZABILITY THEORY

Consider the situation where 20 employees participate in three business simulations all designed to measure the same set of leadership skills. The employees are all observed and scored by the same two raters. So, we have the scores of each of two raters scoring 20 employees on three simulations, or 120 scores. As you would expect, these scores will not all be the same, but rather they will vary. The question becomes, "Why do the scores vary?" Intuitively you probably realize that employees' scores might vary because of the differing levels of leadership skills present in the employee group. This is what is termed *the object of our measurement*. But is the level of leadership skills each employee possesses the only reason why the scores on the simulations might vary? Probably not in this example.

Another reason that could cause the scores to vary is that although the simulations were all designed to measure the same leadership skills, perhaps the simulations are not equally difficult. Or perhaps one of the simulations is easier for employees who happen to have a background in finance, while another of the simulations is easier for employees with a background in sales. Yet another possibility is that one of the raters might be systematically more lenient or stringent than the other raters across all the simulations when rating the performance of the employees. Finally, a combination of conditions could contribute to the variance in the scores, as would happen if a particular rater tended to give employees evaluated earlier in the day higher ratings than those evaluated later in the day.

The beauty of generalizability theory is that it allows you to actually quantify each of these (and other) possible sources of variation so that you can determine whether the results you obtain are likely to generalize (thus the name) to a different set of employees evaluated by different raters on different occasions. Using this approach, you would be able to tell the degree to which each of the facets (simulations, raters, and their interaction) contributed to the variations in the leadership skill scores of the employees. In this case, we would hope that the main contributor to the variation in scores was the skill level of the employees because that is the focus or object of our measurement. In other cases, we might be more interested in the variation in scores attributable to the simulations themselves or the consistency of the raters.

As you have learned, at the heart of the concept of reliability/precision is the idea of consistency of measurement. If the same employees went through the same set of simulations a second time, we would like to expect that their scores would be similar to what they were in the first administration. If the scores were not, we might conclude that the simulations were not reliable measures of the leadership skills they were designed to measure. However, if the reason why the scores were different on the second administration was that we used a different set of raters who differed in the way they scored the simulations from the original set of raters, it would be incorrect to conclude that the simulations were unreliable. The actual source of the unreliability in this case would be error caused by scoring differences between the first and second sets of raters. Using generalizability would enable us to separate the variance in the employee's scores that was attributable to the raters from the variance in the scores that was due to the simulations themselves.

This approach is conceptually different from the classical measurement of the reliability of a test, because classical reliability measurement focuses on the amount of random measurement error and cannot separately evaluate error that may be systematic. The actual calculations are somewhat complicated and beyond the scope of this book, but we wanted to give you an idea of another approach that can be used to evaluate the reliability of a measure.

Researchers and test developers identify systematic error in test scores by using the statistical procedure called analysis of variance. As you recall, we discussed four sources of error: the test itself, test administration, test scoring, and the test taker. Researchers and test developers can set up a generalizability study in which two or more sources of error (the independent variables) can be varied for the purpose of analyzing the variance of the test scores (the dependent variable) to find systematic error. In Greater Depth Box 5.2 presents an example of how generalizability theory looks for and quantifies sources of systematic error.

Chapter Summary

Psychological tests are measurement instruments. An important attribute of a measurement instrument is its reliability/precision or consistency. We need evidence that the test yields the same score each time a person takes the test unless the test taker has actually changed. When we know a test is reliable, we can conclude that changes in a person's score really are due to changes in that person. Also, we can compare the scores of two or more people on a reliable test.

No measurement instrument is perfectly reliable or consistent. We express this idea by saying that each observed test score (X) contains two parts: a true score (T) and error (E). Two types of error appear in test scores: random error and systematic error. The more random error present in a set of test scores, the lower the reliability coefficient will be. Another way of saying the same thing is that the higher the proportion of true score variance is of the observed scores, the higher the reliability coefficient will be. Test developers use three methods for checking reliability. Each takes into account various conditions that could produce differences in test scores. Using the test–retest method, a test developer gives the same test to the same group of test takers on two different occasions. The scores from the first and second administrations are then correlated to obtain the reliability coefficient. The greatest danger in using the test–retest method of estimating reliability/precision is that the test takers will score differently (usually higher) on the test because of practice effects. To overcome practice effects and differences in individuals and the test administration from one time to the next, psychologists often give two forms of the same test—alike in every way—to the same people at the same time. This method is called alternate or if certain statistical assumptions are met, parallel forms.

If a test taker can take the test only once, researchers divide the test into halves and correlate the scores on the first half with the scores on the second half. This method, called split-half reliability, includes using the Spearman–Brown formula to adjust the correlation coefficient for test length. A more precise way to measure internal consistency is to compare individuals' scores on all possible ways of splitting the test into halves. The KR-20 and coefficient alpha formulas allow researchers to estimate the reliability of the test scores by correlating the answer to each test question with the answers to all of the other test questions.

The reliability of scoring is also important. Tests that require the scorer to make judgments about the test takers' answers and tests that require the scorer to observe the test takers' behavior may have error contributed by the scorer. We estimate scorer reliability by having two or more persons score the same test and then correlating their scores to see whether their judgments are consistent or have a single person score two occasions of the same test.

To quantify a test's reliability/precision estimate, we use a reliability coefficient, which is another name for the correlation coefficient when it estimates reliability/precision. This statistic quantifies the estimated relationship between two forms of the test. The statistical procedure we use most often to calculate the reliability coefficient is the Pearson product–moment correlation. All statistical software programs and many spreadsheet programs will calculate the Pearson product–moment correlation. Coefficient alpha and KR-20, both of which also use correlation, are available in statistical packages only.

To interpret the meaning of the reliability coefficient, we look at its sign and the number itself. Reliability coefficients range from –0.00 (a completely unreliable test) to +1.00 (a perfectly reliable test). Psychologists have not set a fixed value at which reliability can be interpreted as satisfactory or unsatisfactory.

Psychologists use the standard error of measurement (SEM) as an index of the amount of inconsistency or error expected in an individual's test score. We can then use the SEM to construct a confidence interval—a range of scores that most likely includes the true score. Confidence intervals provide information about whether individuals' observed test scores are statistically different from each other. Six factors—test

(Continued)

(Continued)

length, homogeneity of questions, the test–retest interval, test administration, scoring, and cooperation of test takers—are important factors that influence the reliability of the test scores.

Another approach to estimating reliability is generalizability theory, which concerns how well and under what conditions we can generalize an estimation of reliability from one test to another or on the same test given under different circumstances. Generalizability theory seeks to identify sources of systematic error that classical test theory would simply label as random error. Using analysis of variance, researchers and test developers can identify systematic error and then take measures to eliminate it, thereby increasing the overall reliability of the test.

Engaging in the Learning Process

Learning is the process of gaining knowledge and skills through schooling or studying. Although you can learn by reading the chapter material, attending class, and engaging in discussion with your instructor, more actively engaging in the learning process may help you better learn and retain chapter information. To help you actively engage in the learning process, we encourage you to access our new supplementary student workbook. The workbook contains critical thinking activities to help you understand and apply information and help you make progress toward learning and retaining material. If you do not have a copy of the workbook, you can purchase a copy through sagepub.com.

Key Concepts

After completing your study of this chapter, you should be able to define each of the following terms. These terms are bolded in the text of this chapter and defined in the Glossary.

alternate forms	intrarater agreement	scorer reliability
Cohen's kappa	intrascorer reliability	Spearman–Brown formula
confidence interval	measurement error	split-half method
correlation	order effects	standard error of
generalizability theory	parallel forms	measurement (SEM)
heterogeneous test	practice effects	systematic error
homogeneous test	random error	test–retest method
internal consistency	reliability coefficient	true score
interrater agreement	reliability/precision	
interscorer agreement	reliable test	

Critical Thinking Questions

The following are some critical thinking questions to support the learning objectives for this chapter.

Learning Objectives	Critical Thinking Questions
Define reliability/precision, and describe three methods for estimating the reliability/precision of a psychological test and its scores.	• What are some practical issues that require us to have more than one way to estimate the reliability/precision of a test? • Can you think of some common examples where scorer reliability is an important issue that is not related to formally taking a written test, such as scoring in certain Olympic events? • If you were told only that the reliability of a test was evaluated by the test–retest method, what questions would you want to ask before concluding that the test was sufficiently reliable/precise?
Describe how an observed test score is made up of the true score and random error, and describe the difference between random error and systematic error.	• Why is it important to understand the concept of "true scores" even though we can never really know what any person's true score on a test is? • How is the concept of error in a test score different from the everyday concept of error, which is about making a mistake? In what way might the two concepts actually be similar?
Calculate and interpret a reliability coefficient, including adjusting a reliability coefficient obtained using the split-half method.	• Why is the reliability/precision of a test sometimes referred to as the correlation of a test with itself? • If your professor gave a midterm test consisting of only one item, what would you tell him or her about how that might pose a problem for acceptable test reliability? • What are some of the questions you would ask if someone told you that the reliability coefficient of a test was negative?
Differentiate between the KR-20 and coefficient alpha formulas, and understand how they are used to estimate internal consistency.	• Why might calculating coefficient alpha for a test give you a similar result to dividing a test into two parts to estimate reliability? • What might it mean if you computed both KR20 and test-retest reliability and found that KR-20 was quite low, but test-retest reliability was much higher?
Calculate the standard error of measurement, and use it to construct a confidence interval around an observed score.	• Imagine your score on the honors program admissions test was 89 and Jane's score on the same test was 90. Assume the passing score for admission was set at 90, so Jane was admitted to the honors program while you weren't. What information would you want to know about the test to understand whether the decision was justified? • Why could it be a problem if two people had different scores on a test but the confidence intervals around both scores overlapped? • What difficulties might a professor face when calculating a reliability coefficient on a classroom test? Should the test be still be given if the reliability coefficient is not known?

(Continued)

(Continued)

Learning Objectives	Critical Thinking Questions
Identify the four sources of test error and six factors related to these sources of error that are particularly important to consider.	• What do you think would happen to the reliability/precision of at test if the test takers were not given sufficient time to answer all the questions on it and all the questions that they did not get a chance to answer were scored as incorrect? • Why might the question, "Does England have a 4th of July" have a negative effect on the reliability/precision of a test? • Why might it not be a good idea to use a lot of humor when writing test questions? • What steps could you take to ensure the reliability/precision of a test is not adversely affected by the person who is administering it?
Explain the premises of generalizability theory, and describe its contribution to estimating reliability.	• How does using generalizability theory potentially give a researcher more information about reliability than classical test theory does?

6

HOW DO WE GATHER EVIDENCE OF VALIDITY BASED ON THE CONTENT OF A TEST?

"I purchased an intelligence test at the bookstore. I showed it to my psychology professor, and he told me to be careful. He said that just because the test is called an intelligence test doesn't necessarily mean that it does a good job of measuring intelligence. How do you know whether a test measures what it says it measures?"

"I took the driving portion of my driver's license test yesterday. It took about an hour. I had to show the evaluator how to use the blinkers, flashers, and lights. I also had to make a right turn,

left turn, parallel park, merge into traffic, and drive in the city and on the highway. Why did they make me do so many things?"

"We have a psychology midterm exam next week. The psychology professor showed us what he called a test plan. He said that the test would cover five chapters. He said we would need to know the terms and be able to apply the principles. He also said that there would be 50 questions on the test. Why would he give us this information?"

"I applied for an administrative job last week. As part of the selection process, they gave me a written test. The test didn't seem very professional, and it didn't appear to measure anything related to an administrative job. The test form was dirty and crumpled, the questions were confusing, and I had to answer questions that were totally unrelated to administrative work. What is the deal?"

If you are like many individuals, when you take a test you don't think twice about whether the test you are taking is accurate or predictive. You likely assume that the test measures what it says it measures or predicts what it says it predicts. We encourage you to not automatically make such assumptions and to remember that the title of a test actually tells us very little. A test may measure some broader, narrower, or even different attribute, trait, or characteristic than the test developer claims or than is implied by the title. A test titled the Math Achievement Test may measure academic achievement (which is broader), achievement in geometry (which is narrower), or general intelligence (which is a different attribute altogether). Although measures of reliability/precision tell us whether a test measures whatever it measures consistently, only measures of validity can provide us with confidence that the interpretations or inferences we make about test takers from their test scores are likely to be correct. And it is the correctness of these inferences that is central to the evaluation of test validity.

It is a commonly held but incorrect belief that the issue of test validity is *only* concerned with determining whether a test measures what it was designed to measure. In the next three chapters, you will learn that while that question is always important to answer, the issue of test validity is more involved than that. In discussing this broader conception of test validity, we will be focusing on answering the question, "What *evidence* is available that might cause you to conclude that a test is valid?" As you will learn, there are many different types of evidence that you might be able to point to. Whether the test measures what it is designed to measure is only one of them. But all the types of evidence will have one thing in common. They all will speak to whether the inferences we are going to make about test takers from their test scores are appropriate.

In this chapter, we begin our discussion of the different types of evidence that we can use to evaluate whether a proposed interpretation of the meaning of a test score is correct and appropriate. We also describe how the concept of **validity** is discussed in the *Standards for Educational and Psychological Testing* (American Educational Research Association [AERA], American Psychological Association [APA], and National Council on Measurement in Education [NCME], 2014). Although the title of this chapter is "How Do We Gather Evidence of Validity Based on the Content of a Test?," it is important that we begin this chapter with a brief, somewhat broader discussion of how validity is defined in general by the *Standards*

(AERA et al., 2014). Therefore, other types of evidence of test validity, such as evidence based on the relationship of the test scores to other variables (what traditionally is referred to as criterion-related validity) and the overarching concept of construct validity, are briefly mentioned in this chapter but are more thoroughly discussed in the next two chapters.

SOURCES OF EVIDENCE OF VALIDITY

As we suggested above, when we speak of the validity of a test, we are asking, "Are the inferences I am going to draw from a person's score on a test appropriate?" Test validity is a function of how the scores are used—the inferences that will be made about the meaning of a person's test scores (or the conclusions that will be drawn from the test scores). According to the 2014 *Standards* (AERA et al., 2014), "It is incorrect to use the unqualified phrase 'the validity of the test'" (p. 11). According to the *Standards* (AERA et al., 2014), *validity* refers to whether there is evidence supporting the interpretation of the resulting test scores for their proposed use. Furthermore, validity is not to be thought of as a characteristic of the test. In other words, we should not refer to a test as valid; rather we should discuss whether there is evidence that supports the proposed use of the resulting test scores.

Here is a simple example of why defining validity based on whether or not there is evidence to support the interpretation and use of the scores on a test is important. In the past, validity was often defined as an evaluation of whether the test measures what it was designed to measure. Under this definition, a new test could be designed to measure a group of personality traits based on some well-researched theory of personality. After the test was constructed, the test developer evaluates how well the test was measuring what it had been designed to measure by comparing test takers' results on the new test with their results on a different test known to measure the same personality characteristics. If the results on the two tests were similar, the test developer would report that the test was valid because there was evidence to support the fact that the test was measuring what it was designed to measure.

When test developers declare a test as being valid, test users could assume that the test is good for measuring almost anything. Here is an example of why this assumption can cause a very practical problem. Imagine that a personnel manager finds a personality test online, sees the claim that it is valid, and decides to use it to help select salespeople for his or her organization. The manager reasons that personality characteristics are important for success in selling, so it makes logical sense to use a test to measure these characteristics. Do you see the issue here? The personnel manager wants to use the test scores to make an inference or prediction about likely future sales performance of job applicants who take the test. However, such an inference or prediction would be inappropriate unless the test developer or publisher has provided evidence that the test would be valid for predicting which test takers would be good salespeople and which wouldn't. Although the test publisher has declared that the test is a valid measure of personality traits identified and defined by a personality theorist, his or her research results may not indicate that the test scores are useful for identifying successful salespeople. Unfortunately, it is still a common misconception that when we speak about validity, we are speaking about evaluating a characteristic of the test, implying that a particular test can be judged as being valid or invalid. An important source of information in addition to the *Standards* (AERA et al., 2014) for anyone interested in understanding more about test validity as it is related primarily to employee selection is *Principles for the Validation and Use of Personnel Selection Procedures* (Society for Industrial and Organizational Psychology, 2003).

Having said that the current view of validity centers on the correct interpretations that will be made from a test's scores, we do not mean to imply that investigating whether a test measures what it is supposed to measure is not important. In fact, a critical part of the development of any test revolves around investigating whether the concepts or characteristics that the test developer is interested in measuring are actually being measured. Without that evidence, test users who have a need to measure particular attributes would have no way of determining which tests to choose for their specific purposes. The important point is that a test can measure exactly what it is intended to measure and yet not be valid to use for a particular purpose.

The AERA et al. 2014 *Standards*, as well as the 1999 *Standards*, view validity as a unitary or single concept. The *Standards* focus on the importance of evaluating the interpretation of test scores and "the degree to which the accumulated evidence supports the intended interpretation of test scores for the proposed use" (AERA et al., 2014, p. 14). The 2014 *Standards* describe the following five sources of evidence of validity:

1. *Evidence based on test content:* Previously referred to as **content validity**, this source of validity evidence involves logically examining and evaluating the content of a test (including the test questions, format, wording, and tasks required of test takers) to determine the extent to which the content is representative of the concepts that the test is designed to measure without either underrepresenting those concepts or including elements that are irrelevant to their measurement. This is the type of evidence for validity we will focus on in this chapter.

2. *Evidence based on response processes:* This source of validity evidence involves observing test takers as they respond to the test and/or interviewing them when they complete the test. We use these observations and interviews to understand the mental processes that test takers use to respond. For instance, if the test was designed to measure logical reasoning, test takers should report mentally processing the test information while they solve the test problems as opposed to relying on memorized answers. If the test is scored by using trained observers or judges, this source of validity evidence also involves exploring whether those observers or judges used the criteria that were defined to document and evaluate test taker behaviors or performances.

3. *Evidence based on internal structure:* This type of evidence was previously considered part of what was termed **construct validity** (which we discuss in detail in a later chapter). It focuses on whether the conceptual framework used in test development could be demonstrated using appropriate analytical techniques. For instance, if a test was designed to measure a single concept (such as anxiety), we would analyze the test results to find out how many underlying concepts account for the variations in test taker scores. (One such analysis that we discuss later is factor analysis.) If the test was designed to measure one concept only, the analysis should show that only one concept (presumably anxiety in our example) accounts for a majority of the information the test takers provided. If the analysis suggests that the scores were affected by more than one underlying concept or factor, then we would question whether we had evidence of validity of the test based on its underlying single concept structure.

Studies of the internal structure of the test are also used to determine whether certain items on the test are more difficult for some groups of people than for others, such as would be the case if minority test takers responded to certain items differently than nonminority test takers. This type of analysis may show whether test takers with the same ability, but belonging to different groups, have different probabilities of correctly answering a test question. For example, men and women would probably score quite differently on a test that measures knowledge of childbirth.

4. *Evidence based on relations with other variables:* Traditionally referred to as **criterion-related validity** (which we will discuss in the next chapter) and also another

part of construct validity, this source of validity evidence typically involves correlating test scores with other measures to determine whether those scores are related to other measures to which we would expect them to relate. Likewise, we would want to know that the test scores are not related to other measures to which we would not expect them to relate. For instance, a test designed to be used in employee selection should correlate with measures of job performance (criterion-related validity). A test of mechanical aptitude should correlate with another test of mechanical aptitude, while not correlating with a vocabulary test (construct validity).

5. *Evidence based on the consequences of testing:* Any time we make a psychological measurement, both intended and unintended consequences may occur. For example, an intended consequence of a test for personnel selection would be obtaining accurate information for hiring. However, if the test is biased, an unintended consequence might be that test scores appear to favor one group over another. However, it is also important to understand that just because different groups score differently on a test does not automatically mean that the test is biased. If, for instance, the higher scoring group actually possessed more of the skills that the test was designed to measure than the lower scoring group, then the test scores would simply be properly reflecting the differing skill levels between the two groups. (We discuss the issue of test bias in a later chapter, "How Do We Assess the Psychometric Quality of a Test?" which covers the psychometric properties of tests.) Therefore, test users need to be aware that it is important to distinguish between consequences of testing associated with the validity of the test itself (i.e., whether correct inferences are being made from the interpretation of the test scores) versus other outcomes not related to the purpose for which the scores will be used.

Although the latest version of the *Standards* (AERA et al., 2014) no longer directly uses the terms *content*, *construct*, and *criterion-related validity*, these terms are still widely used in professional practice. Therefore, we may from time to time use these more traditional terms in this chapter and following chapters. In our opinion, a student would not be able to interpret decades of testing literature without a strong understanding of these terms. However, it is important to understand that although multiple terms may still be used to describe approaches to gathering evidence of test validity, validity is a unitary or single concept with multiple sources of evidence available to demonstrate it. It would be incorrect to assume that one type of validity is better or more scientific than another type of validity. Ultimately, it is the combined evidence from multiple sources and research approaches that will determine whether any particular inference made about the meaning of a test score is appropriate and defensible.

USE OF VARIOUS SOURCES OF EVIDENCE OF VALIDITY

As you just learned, in order for the inferences made from a test score to be appropriate, it is important that the test measure the attribute, trait, or characteristic it was designed to measure or predict the outcome it claims to predict. Developing different types of evidence of validity helps determine whether a test measures what it says it measures or predicts what it says it predicts.

If you are like most students, you might be wondering whether it is necessary to gather all the different sources of evidence of validity for all tests. It is sometimes possible, but not always necessary, to do so for a single test. The appropriate strategy for gathering validity evidence often depends on the purpose of the test.

Some tests measure concrete constructs such as knowledge of psychological testing and the ability to play the piano. **Concrete attributes** are attributes that can be clearly described in terms of observable and measurable behaviors. Most people would agree that there are specific observable and measurable behaviors associated with being able to play the piano. Other tests measure abstract attributes such as personality, intelligence, creativity, and aggressiveness. **Abstract attributes** are those that are more difficult to describe in terms of behaviors because people may disagree on what these behaviors represent. For example, what does it mean to be intelligent? If your friend is a high academic achiever, does that mean she is highly intelligent? If your friend has common sense, does that mean he is intelligent? Is creativity part of intelligence?

Evidence of validity using test content is easiest to develop for tests such as achievement tests that measure concrete attributes. Such tests are easier because the job of an achievement test is to measure how well someone has mastered the content of a course or training program. To feel confident that the test measures what it is designed to measure, we can compare the content of the test with the content of the course. We do so by making sure that the questions on the test are representative of all the relevant information covered and match the instructional objectives of the course. Gathering evidence of validity based on test content is more difficult (but not necessarily less appropriate) when the attribute being measured, such as personality or intelligence, is abstract because such attributes need to be carefully defined and linked to observable behaviors. (We will have much more to say about how we gather evidence of validity when we are dealing with abstract attributes in the "How Do We Gather Evidence of Validity Based on a Test's Relation to Constructs?" chapter.)

Evidence of validity based on relationships with other variables, criterion-related validity, is most appropriate for tests that claim to predict outcomes such as success on the job. If an employment test needs to forecast who is likely to be successful on the job, its purpose is to predict future job performance rather than to determine how well certain concepts have been mastered. Gathering this type of validity evidence is therefore appropriate for employment tests, college admissions tests, and diagnostic clinical tests.

Evidence of validity based on relationships with other variables, or construct validity, is appropriate when a test measures an abstract construct such as marital satisfaction.

Although it is not always necessary to gather all evidences of validity for a single test, researchers try to gather more than one type of evidence. While it's acceptable to rely on one strategy at first, the more evidence you can gather to support the validity of a test, the better.

Now that we have presented the important background information necessary to understand the basic nature of test validity, for the remainder of this chapter, we are going to focus on one type of evidence for validity: evidence based on test content. We will consider the other types of evidence for validity in the next two chapters.

EVIDENCE OF VALIDITY BASED ON TEST CONTENT

With our brief introduction to test validity completed, we are now ready to jump into the principle focus of this chapter—how we develop evidence of validity based on test content. All tests are designed to measure something, and the test must contain test items (such as multiple-choice questions) that relate to the "something" that you want to measure. The *Standards for Educational and Psychological Testing* (AERA et al., 2014) uses the term **construct** to indicate any concept or characteristic that a test is designed to measure. However, many testing professionals, as well as psychological researchers, use the term in a slightly different manner. A construct, in the more traditional usage, is an attribute, trait, or characteristic that is not directly observable, but can be inferred only by looking at observable behaviors believed to indicate the presence of that construct. For instance, if a test was designed to measure a construct called "sales ability," you would not be able to directly observe sales ability. Rather, you would want to observe whether a test taker demonstrates specific behaviors that indicate the amount of sales ability he or she has. These behaviors might be things like refocusing potential customers on the value of a product or service instead of the price or effectively addressing customer objections. Remember in the first chapter of the book we said that in a broad sense, a psychological test is a procedure, an instrument, or a device that measures samples of behaviors in order to make inferences. We can't directly measure constructs, but we can directly measure behaviors.

Whether you are using the newer or more traditional definition of a construct, any test must contain test items from a broad domain of content believed to relate to the construct being measured. This is the essence of evidence of validity based on test content. If a midterm exam that is intended to assess your understanding of the material covered during the first half of a course does indeed contain a representative sample of the material covered during the first half of the course, the exam demonstrates evidence of validity based on test content. As another example, consider a test called the Fundamental Interpersonal Relations Orientation–Behavior (FIRO-B), sometimes used by organizations to help people improve their interactions with others. The test is designed to measure needs in three areas—inclusion, control, and affection—believed to relate to three fundamental dimensions of interpersonal relationships. Test takers are asked to respond to behavioral statements that are expected to be related to each of these needs.

See **Test Spotlight 6.1** in Appendix A for more detail about the Fundamental Interpersonal Relations Orientation–Behavior.

As you just learned, evidence of validity based on test content is one type of evidence that can be used to demonstrate the validity of a test. This evidence of validity reflects the extent to which the questions on the test are representative of the attribute being measured. Theoretically, if a test is designed to measure a specific attribute, it demonstrates evidence of validity based on its content when the items in the test are a representative sample of the universe of items that represent the attribute's entire domain. For example, if we designed a test to measure your knowledge of the material presented in this textbook, the test would demonstrate more evidence of validity based on content if we included test items that measured your knowledge of material presented in all the chapters versus material presented in just one or two chapters. The entire textbook is the universe, and therefore evidence of validity of the test would be demonstrated by including test items that measure your knowledge across the entire textbook.

Although all types of evidence of validity share the common purpose of helping us make appropriate inferences from the scores on a test, the ways the different types of evidence are gathered differ from one another (as you will see in "How Do We Gather Evidence of Validity Based on Test–Criterion Relationships?" and the "How Do We Gather Evidence of Validity Based on a Test's Relation to Constructs?" chapters). Evidence of validity based on test content involves examining the questions or behaviors required on the test and making a judgment regarding the degree to which the test provides an adequate sample of the construct being measured. Evidence of validity based on relationships with other variables (criterion or construct validity) involves correlating the test scores to a measure of performance or another test.

Evidence of validity based on test content is important to many types of psychological tests. Here are some examples:

- A paper-and-pencil test of "attitude toward life" includes questions that adequately represent the wide-ranging situations in which people can demonstrate their attitudes toward life—in the home, on the job, and in social situations.

- An employment test intended to measure mechanics' aptitude contains test questions that represent not just one or two tasks but rather the many tasks a mechanic must perform.

- A classroom math achievement test shows evidence of validity based on test content when the proportion and type of math questions on the exam represent the proportion and type of material read and/or covered in the class.

- An employment interview shows evidence of validity based on content when it contains questions directly associated with the knowledge, skills, or abilities needed to successfully perform a job.

How do you obtain this kind of evidence of validity? Evidence of validity based on test content is demonstrated in two ways. The first way involves performing a series of systematic steps as a test is being developed—steps to ensure that the construct being measured is clearly defined and that the items used to measure the construct are representative of the construct's domain. This method does not result in any final number (quantitative value) that represents the evidence of validity of the test; rather, it provides the test developer and user with confidence that the questions on the test are representative of a clearly defined domain.

The second way for obtaining evidence of validity based on content involves evaluating the content of a test after the test has been developed. This method may be done by the test developer as part of the validation process or by others using the test. This method may result in a number that can be used to quantify the content validity of the test.

Demonstrating Evidence of Validity Based on Test Content During Test Development

Again, the first method for obtaining evidence of validity based on the content of a test involves performing a series of systematic steps as a test is being developed. Although we discuss the process of test development in more detail in a later chapter, here we provide a brief summary of these steps.

Defining the Testing Universe

The first step in ensuring a content-valid test is to carefully define the **testing universe**—the body of knowledge or behaviors that a test represents. This step usually involves reviewing other instruments that measure the same construct, interviewing experts who are familiar with the construct, and researching the construct by locating theoretical or empirical research on the construct. The purpose is to ensure that you clearly understand and can clearly define the construct you will be measuring. Evidence of validity based on test content requires that the test cover all major aspects of the testing universe (of the construct) in the correct proportion (Groth-Marnat, 1997).

For example, let's say you are interested in designing a test to measure the abstract attribute of self-esteem. Before writing test items, you would need to clearly understand what self-esteem is and the behaviors people demonstrate when they have high or low self-esteem. To increase your understanding, one of the first things you might do is review various theories and studies of self-esteem. You might also review other tests of self-esteem, and you might choose to interview experts in self-esteem.

On the other hand, if you were interested in developing a test to measure a more concrete attribute such as an employee's job knowledge, you should review other tests that measure the same job knowledge, training manuals, and job descriptions, and you could interview job incumbents and managers for a job analysis. (The chapter "How Are Tests Used in

Organizational Settings?" explains the concept of job analysis and how it serves as content-based evidence of validity.)

Developing the Test Specifications

After the testing universe has been defined, the second step in developing a content-valid test is to develop the **test specifications**—a documented plan containing details about a test's content. Test specifications are very similar to the blueprints that are prepared prior to building a home. Although the contents of test plans vary depending on the type of test being developed, many test specifications, especially those for knowledge tests, include not only a clearly defined testing universe but also the **content areas**—the subject matter that the test will measure—and the number of questions that will be included to assess each content area. The *Standards for Educational and Psychological Testing* (AERA et al., 2014) more broadly define the definition of test specifications to also include the documentation of the purpose and intended use of the test; the format; the length of the test; psychometric characteristics of the items; how the test is delivered, administered, and scored; as well as details of the content.

Establishing a Test Format

Once the testing universe has been defined and the test specifications have been documented, the third step in designing a test is to decide on its format. For example, will it be a **written test**, a paper-and-pencil test in which a test taker must answer a series of questions; a computerized test; or a **practical test**, which requires a test taker to actively demonstrate skills in specific situations? If it is a written test, the test developer must also decide what types of questions (multiple choice, true/false, matching, and so on) to use.

For Your Information Boxes 6.1 and 6.2 provide examples of test specifications for different tests—one measuring job knowledge and the other measuring academic achievement. For Your Information Box 6.3 discusses the importance of content-based evidence of validity to competency exams.

Constructing Test Questions

After the testing universe has been defined, the test specifications have been developed, and the test format has been established, the fourth step in test development is to write the test questions or items, being careful that each question represents the content area and objective it is intended to measure.

A frequently encountered need to demonstrate evidence of validity based on content occurs during the development of tools used for making employment decisions. In 1978, the federal government published the *Uniform Guidelines on Employee Selection Procedures* (1978), which courts still rely on today when deciding cases regarding discrimination in the workplace. These guidelines provide a uniform set of principles that employers are expected to follow when using any instrument (not just written tests) to make employment decisions. This would include interviews, performance appraisals, application forms, physical requirements, or anything else that an employer uses as part of the decision process. If job applicants (or employees) demonstrate to the court that they have good reason to believe that the employer discriminated against them, even unintentionally, because of race, color, sex, religion, or national origin, the employer would be required to produce evidence that the tools that were used as part of the selection system were valid. This type of evidence for validity is frequently gathered during the time that the selection tools are being developed.

Content-based evidence of validity is a common type of evidence used by employers to defend against legal challenges. You may be wondering if one can demonstrate evidence of validity based on content of a selection tool such as employment interview. The answer is that

FOR YOUR INFORMATION BOX 6.1

TEST SPECIFICATION TABLE OF A 43-ITEM JOB KNOWLEDGE TEST

When one of this textbook's authors was asked to develop a series of job knowledge tests for a local organization, she knew that one of the first things she needed to do for each test was to define the testing universe and create test specifications. Below are the test specifications for one job. As you can see, these specifications are very much like a blueprint; among other things, they contain detailed information about the testing universe, the content areas, and the number of questions. Creating these test specifications helped the author clearly understand and document the body of knowledge that the test needed to measure. It provided the foundation for the writing of test questions that sampled the testing universe representatively.

Type of Test: Job Knowledge	Job: Universal Processer		Item Format: Multiple Choice	Test Length: 43 items

Testing Universe: This test is intended to measure the technical and professional expertise and knowledge required to successfully perform the role of the Universal Processer—expertise and knowledge required to accurately process cash, invoices, and policies according to company standards.

			Knowledge of Terms and Concepts	Application (Process/Procedures)
Mail Distribution and Handling	Mail delivery and distribution methods	9% (4 Qs)	1	1
	Mail prioritization and distribution			1
	Ordering of documentation			1
Cash and Invoice Processing	Log In and Envelope creation	40% (17 Qs)	1	1
	Cash handling ✓ Entering checks		2	2
	✓ Entering Invoice /statement documentation		2	1
	✓ Applying payments		1	6
	Completing envelopes			1
Policy Processing	Associating policies to checks	35% (15 Qs)		2
	Entering policy information		3	10
End of Day Processing	Individual Deposit List	16% (7Qs)	1	3
	Tape			3
Total		**100%**	**11**	**32**

FOR YOUR INFORMATION BOX 6.2
TEST SPECIFICATION TABLE OF A 70-ITEM ACADEMIC ACHIEVEMENT TEST

When test developers design academic achievement tests, they write instructional objectives and include them in the test specification tables. (The learning objectives in this textbook are the instructional objectives that appear in the test specification table for the test bank.) Below is a test specification table similar to those that this textbook's authors use to write questions for an exam intended to measure students' knowledge of reliability and validity. As you can see, the content areas are test–retest reliability, alternate-forms reliability, split-half reliability, interrater reliability, and evidence of validity based on content. The **instructional objectives** guide students' learning of the terms and concepts of *reliability/precision* and *validity*. (The activities associated with each learning or instructional objective in this book help students apply the concept in the learning objective.) As you can see, the specification table indicates that a different number of questions will be asked to measure students' knowledge of each of the content areas and each of the instructional objectives.

Instructional Objectives

Content Area	Knowledge of Terms and Concepts	Application of Concepts	Number of Questions
Test–retest reliability	5	2	7
Alternate-forms reliability	5	2	7
Split-half reliability	5	2	7
Interrater reliability	2	1	3
Evidence of validity based on content	5	5	10
Total questions	22	12	34

you can if you develop the right types of interview questions. Perhaps you have had a job interview where you were asked questions such as "What is your favorite hobby?" or "Do you have any brothers or sisters?" A favorite of one of this book's authors is, "If you could be any animal that you wanted to be, which one you would choose?" Remember that validity is all about the correctness of the inferences that you are going to make from a test score or, in this example, the answers to the interview questions. In other words, we are asking whether there is evidence to suggest that job applicants or employees who answer these questions in one manner are more likely to perform better on the job than applicants or employees who answer in a different manner. The questions listed above are very unlikely to be valid for that purpose.

On the other hand, consider questions such as "Tell me about a time when you had to deal with an unhappy customer" or "Tell me about a time when you went out of your way to help a colleague complete a task at work." Presuming the job for which these questions were being asked requires dealing with customers or colleagues, then on the surface, at least, it is easy to see that these questions look to be more job related than the previous ones. But providing solid evidence of validity based on content requires more evidence than just a surface analysis. Sometimes it requires a technique called **job analysis**—a process that identifies the

FOR YOUR INFORMATION BOX 6.3

EVIDENCE OF VALIDITY BASED ON TEST CONTENT AND COMPETENCY EXAMS

Because training plays a critical role in developing employees, many organizations invest significant funds, time, and energy to develop and administer training programs. To help training directors make informed decisions about which training programs to offer or modify, organizations also invest funds, time, and energy in evaluating the effectiveness of training programs.

Although there are a variety of methods to evaluate the effectiveness of training, some organizations do so by administering competency exams at the end of training programs (J. Smith & Merchant, 1990). Competency exams attempt to measure how well a person learned the knowledge and skills taught during training. These can be paper-and-pencil or web-based exams, or they can be practical hands-on or web-based assessments. (Paper-and-pencil exams require test takers to answer questions on paper, and practical exams require individuals to demonstrate their knowledge or display their new skills in real-life situations.)

When competency exams are developed and administered properly, they help organizations in a variety of ways. For example, they can determine the following:

- Whether employees can use the new computer software they have been trained to use

- Whether customer service representatives can provide the correct information to customers

If competency exam scores indicate that students do not have the necessary knowledge or cannot demonstrate the necessary skills, organizations will often reevaluate the content and delivery of their training programs.

Like other types of tests, competency-based tests are useful only if they contain content that is appropriate for their intended purpose. Therefore, the developers of competency-based training programs must ensure that their exams can show evidence of their validity—that they measure trainees' knowledge, skills, and behaviors adequately (J. Smith & Merchant, 1990). To develop and administer a competency exam that will be able to demonstrate this evidence, test developers perform the following steps:

1. *Determine the learning objectives of the training program:* These objectives come from an in-depth analysis of the knowledge, skills, and abilities required for a particular job. The requirements of a job can be determined by conducting a job analysis, reviewing job descriptions, or interviewing job incumbents.

2. *Outline the content areas of the exam:* An outline ensures that relevant subject matter is neither omitted nor emphasized inappropriately on an exam.

3. *Establish the format for the exam:* Test developers must decide whether the exam will be a written exam or a practical exam and what types of items will be included on the exam (e.g., multiple choice, true/false).

4. *Write the exam items:* Using the learning objectives and content areas as a guide, test developers must develop questions or problems that measure the content areas and meet the learning objectives.

The following table provides a sample outline of the content for a manufacturing orders training module competency exam.

Content General Categories	Areas Subcategories	Weight (percentage of total score)	Question Number Written Questions (paper and pencil)	Question Number Practical Questions (work samples and simulations)
Manufacturing repair process–II		25	1, 2, 3, 4, 5	

Content General Categories	Areas Subcategories	Weight (percentage of total score)	Question Number Written Questions (paper and pencil)	Question Number Practical Questions (work samples and simulations)
Manufacturing repair process–II	A. Concepts B. Netting logic and application C. Bill Of Materials	50	9, 10, 11, 13, 18, 19, 25, 26, 27, 6, 7, 17, 28	1, 2, 4, 3, 5, 6, 7, 11, 13, 8, 9, 10, 12, 14, 15, 16
Maintenance transactions	A. Creating an order B. Allocating material C. Releasing order	25	20, 21, 22, 23, 24, 29, 30, 31	17, 18, 21, 19, 20, 22, 23, 24, 25, 26

Source: Adapted from J. Smith & Merchant (1990).

When the developers finish writing the exam, they reevaluate the content of the exam by asking the following questions (J. Smith & Merchant, 1990):

1. Are all exam items job related? Knowledge or skills that are not needed on the job should not be included on the competency exam.

2. Are the knowledge and skills being tested adequately covered in the training program?

3. Is the exam comprehensive, and does it weight areas appropriately?

Competency exams can provide organizations with valuable information about whether their training programs are teaching the knowledge, skills, and abilities necessary to be successful on a job. However, the usefulness of competency exams, like all psychological tests, depends on showing evidence that the tests are valid for their intended purpose.

knowledge, skills, abilities, and other characteristics required to perform a job. Some types of job analysis also provide details of the actual tasks and activities that are performed on the job. Often these data are gathered through interviews and direct observations by trained observers of the job being analyzed. (See the chapter "How Are Tests Used in Organizational Settings?" for more details on job analysis.) However, in recent years an increasingly common approach for gathering content-based evidence of validity for employee selection tools has been a less intensive process called **competency modeling** (Shippmann et al., 2000). Competency modeling is a procedure that identifies the knowledge, skills, abilities, and other characteristics most critical for success on some or all of the jobs in an organization (Lievens & Sanchez, 2007). It also defines the behaviors that, when performed well, indicate that a person possesses each of those competencies. While this may sound similar to job analysis, in practice it is usually an easier process for an organization to undertake, and the results are often more generalizable to multiple jobs within the organization. For instance, a typical competency model for leadership positions in organizations might contain competencies such as decision making, problem solving, planning, organizing, and communication skills. These competencies could be applicable to a wide range of leadership roles. Also, once the critical competencies have been identified, you can construct interview questions to measure them.

However, because competency models are frequently designed to apply to multiple functions or a family of jobs within an organization (such as leadership or sales; Campion et al., 2011), they usually do not contain descriptions of the specific tasks that must be performed on a particular job. Also, competency models may not focus on the specific technical knowledge or skills necessary to perform a job. Instead, many competency models concentrate on what are often termed "soft skills," such as communication, decision making, planning and organizing, time management, and the like. Because the process used in the development of competency models is usually less scientifically rigorous than that used for a formal job analysis (Shippmann et al., 2000), competency modeling may not always be the appropriate method to use to develop content-based evidence of validity for tests used in personnel selection. For instance, when we develop selection or promotional exams for police or firefighters, a complete job analysis is usually conducted because of the complex nature of these jobs. This job analysis will determine the tasks performed on the job, the technical knowledge needed to perform those tasks as well as the skills, abilities, and other personal characteristics that are important contributors to success in the roles. This kind of detailed information would be required to develop legally defensible selection tools for public safety related positions.

So how would you gather the evidence necessary to demonstrate exactly which competencies are most important for any particular role if you wished to use a competency modeling approach instead of a full job analysis? Here is an example how one of the authors of this textbook accomplished this for a client interested in developing a validated interview for the role of department manager in their organization.

The process began with a large general leadership competency model that had already been shown to have applicability to a wide range of leadership positions in other similar organizations. Then, leadership experts from the client's organization reviewed the model and selected those competencies that they felt were most important to their role of department manager. As an example, some of the competencies that they chose were decisiveness, delegating decisions, strategic planning, motivating employees, and building teams. Each of these competences also had about six observable behaviors associated with them.

The next step in the validation process was to identify a larger group (about 30) of people in leadership positions who were familiar with the job requirements for a department manager. These individuals were asked to participate in a survey to determine how critical each behavior in the proposed competency model was to successful performance of the department manager job. Behaviors that were rated as not being critical were dropped from the model. After the survey was completed and the data analyzed, the results were used to determine the behaviors that were most important to be evaluated via interview questions. Then interview questions were written specifically to evaluate these behaviors. The entire validation process was carefully documented to provide the content-based evidence of validity that would be necessary in the event of a legal challenge.

For Your Information Box 6.4 contains a portion of the behavior survey that was used to collect content-based evidence of validity for the development of interview questions for the department managers.

Demonstrating Evidence of Validity Based on Test Content After Test Development

Although ensuring that a test will be able to provide evidence of validity based on its content is aided by performing a series of systematic steps during test development, often test developers and others assess content validity after a test has been developed. One technique involves examining the extent to which experts agree on the relevance of the content of the test items (Lawshe, 1975). With this technique, experts review and rate how essential test items are to the attribute the test measures. Then a **content validity ratio** is calculated, providing a measure of agreement among the judges. Based on minimum values, questions that experts agree

FOR YOUR INFORMATION BOX 6.4
BEHAVIOR VALIDATION SURVEY

The purpose of this survey is to confirm the job relevance and criticality for job performance of the behaviors for department manager positions in your company.

Below you will find a list of behaviors that may or may not be performed by most department managers. The behaviors are the observable indicators of a number of different competencies. Please carefully read and rate each behavior in terms of how critical it is to the successful performance of a department manager's job.

When you think about how critical each behavior is, please think about

- how important each behavior is to successful job performance for a department manager,
- the frequency with which the behavior is likely to be performed, and
- the consequence to the company if the behavior is performed poorly. For instance, there may be some behaviors that are performed very infrequently, but when they are performed, the consequence of performing them poorly would have significant impact to the organization. This behavior might still be considered a critical behavior even though a department manager might not be frequently called upon to demonstrate it.

You will be using the following nine-point scale to rate the behaviors. The more critical you believe the behavior to be, the higher number you should use. Anchors are provided for rating scale points at 1, 3, 5,

7, and 9, but you may also use 2, 4, 6, or 8 for criticality ratings that you feel are in between the anchored points on the scale. Here are the rating scale anchors:

1. This behavior is not at all critical to the job performance of a department manager. Failure to perform this behavior adequately would have little or no impact on a department manager's ability to adequately perform the job.

3. This behavior is somewhat critical to the job performance of a department manager. Failure to perform this behavior adequately would have a minor impact on a department manager's ability to adequately perform the job.

5. This behavior is moderately critical to the job performance of a department manager. Failure to perform this behavior adequately would have a significant impact on a department manager's ability to adequately perform the job.

7. This behavior is very critical to the job performance of a department manager. Failure to perform this behavior adequately would have a major impact on a department manager's ability to adequately perform the job.

9. This behavior is extremely critical to the job performance of a department manager. Failure to perform this behavior adequately would make it nearly impossible for a department manager to adequately perform the job.

1 = Not at all critical 3 = Somewhat critical 5 = Moderately critical 7 = Very critical 9 = Extremely critical	1	2	3	4	5	6	7	8	9
Perceives relationships between and among information, data, and events that reveal both actual and potential problems	O	O	O	O	O	O	O	O	O
Seeks out additional information when necessary to define or clarify issues	O	O	O	O	O	O	O	O	O
Differentiates critical from noncritical issues	O	O	O	O	O	O	O	O	O
Gathers data from a variety of sources	O	O	O	O	O	O	O	O	O

(Continued)

(Continued)

1 = Not at all critical 3 = Somewhat critical 5 = Moderately critical 7 = Very critical 9 = Extremely critical	1	2	3	4	5	6	7	8	9
Ensures that data are up to date before using them	O	O	O	O	O	O	O	O	O
Identifies the data that are most salient to the issues at hand	O	O	O	O	O	O	O	O	O
Makes effective and timely decisions, even when data are limited or ambiguous	O	O	O	O	O	O	O	O	O
Does not delay in making decisions that may produce unpleasant consequences	O	O	O	O	O	O	O	O	O
Makes decisions as quickly as necessary even when others disagree with them	O	O	O	O	O	O	O	O	O
Communicates the connection of the tasks with the strategy of the work unit	O	O	O	O	O	O	O	O	O
Ensures that subordinates clearly understand the tasks that need to be performed	O	O	O	O	O	O	O	O	O
Assigns tasks to subordinates based on multiple criteria (e.g., skill level, developmental needs, schedules)	O	O	O	O	O	O	O	O	O
Provides sufficient resources for the task to be completed	O	O	O	O	O	O	O	O	O
Ensures that good performance will lead to outcomes that are valued by the individual	O	O	O	O	O	O	O	O	O
Designs reward systems that reinforce desired behaviors	O	O	O	O	O	O	O	O	O
Advocates for continuous improvement of practices with management and colleagues	O	O	O	O	O	O	O	O	O

Source: Wilson Learning Corporation.

are essential are considered as evidence of validity, and items that experts do not agree are essential are not considered evidence of validity.

For example, to develop evidence of validity based on the content of the job knowledge test in For Your Information Box 6.1, one of this textbook's authors created and administered the content validation survey. Five managers who were very familiar with the job were provided with a copy of the test and asked to rate whether the knowledge measured by each test item was *essential, useful but not essential,* or *not necessary* for successful performance of the job. As shown in Figure 6.1, ratings of each panelist were documented in a spreadsheet.

FIGURE 6.1 ■ Content Validation Ratings From Validation Survey

Q#	Panelist 1 Essential	Panelist 1 Useful	Panelist 1 Not Necessary	Panelist 2 Essential	Panelist 2 Useful	Panelist 2 Not Necessary	Panelist 3 Essential	Panelist 3 Useful	Panelist 3 Not Necessary	Panelist 4 Essential	Panelist 4 Useful	Panelist 4 Not Necessary	Panelist 5 Essential	Panelist 5 Useful	Panelist 5 Not Necessary	Content Validity Ratio Numerator	Content Validity Ratio Denominator	CVR
1	1			1			1			1			1			2.5	2.5	1
2	1			1			1			1			1			2.5	2.5	1
3	1					1	1				1		1			0.5	2.5	0.2
4	1			1			1			1			1			2.5	2.5	1
5	1			1			1			1			1			2.5	2.5	1
6	1				1		1			1			1			1.5	2.5	0.6
7	1			1			1			1			1			2.5	2.5	1
8	1			1			1			1			1			2.5	2.5	1
9	1			1			1			1			1			2.5	2.5	1
10	1			1			1			1			1			2.5	2.5	1
11	1			1			1			1			1			2.5	2.5	1
12	1			1			1			1			1			2.5	2.5	1
13	1				1		1			1			1			1.5	2.5	0.6
14	1			1			1			1			1			2.5	2.5	1
15		1		1			1			1			1			1.5	2.5	0.6
16	1			1			1			1			1			2.5	2.5	1
17	1			1			1			1			1			2.5	2.5	1
18	1				1		1			1			1			1.5	2.5	0.6
19	1				1		1			1			1			1.5	2.5	0.6
20	1				1		1			1			1			1.5	2.5	0.6
21	1			1			1			1			1			2.5	2.5	1
22	1			1			1			1			1			2.5	2.5	1
23	1			1			1			1			1			2.5	2.5	1
24	1			1			1			1			1			2.5	2.5	1
25	1			1			1			1			1			2.5	2.5	1
26	1			1			1			1			1			2.5	2.5	1
27	1			1			1			1			1			2.5	2.5	1
28	1			1			1			1			1			2.5	2.5	1
29	1			1			1			1			1			2.5	2.5	1
30	1			1			1			1			1			2.5	2.5	1
31	1			1			1				1		1			1.5	2.5	0.6
32	1			1			1			1			1			2.5	2.5	1

The content validity ratio for each question was then calculated using the following formula (Lawshe, 1975):

where

CVR_i = value for an item on the test

n_e = number of experts indicating that an item is essential

N = total number of experts in the panel

Notice how the content validity ratios can range between –1.00 and 1.00, where 0.00 means that 50% of the experts believe that an item is essential. To determine whether an item is essential, its minimum value is compared with minimum values, shown in Table 6.1, that depend on the number of experts who contributed ratings. Highlighted items did not meet the minimum value required (.99) for five raters, and therefore they were not rated as essential by enough experts to be considered evidence of validity. These items were eliminated from the test.

Content validity ratios have been used to provide the evidence of validity based on a test's content of employment tests (Ford & Wroten, 1984), measures of the work behavior of psychiatric aides (Distefano, Pryer, & Erffmeyer, 1983), mathematics achievement tests (Crocker, Llabre, & Miller, 1988), and assessment centers.

Evidence of Validity Based on Test Content Summary

Although not all tests (e.g., the Minnesota Multiphasic Personality Inventory, MMPI-2, discussed in the next chapter, "How Do We Gather Evidence of Validity Based on Test–Criterion Relationships?") have evidence of validity based on their content, most psychological tests, particularly in educational settings, should show that evidence. When purchasing a test, users should not make any assumptions about whether the test can show evidence of validity based on its content. The purchaser has the responsibility of comparing the specifications of the purchased test with the content domain of the test. Furthermore, the test user must consider whether different aspects of the content domain are underrepresented or overrepresented in the test based on its intended use and must make adjustments accordingly.

TABLE 6.1 ■ Minimum Values for Lawshe's (1975) Content Validation Ratings	
Number of Experts	**Minimum Value**
≤5	0.99
6	0.99
7	0.99
8	0.75
9	0.78
10	0.62
20	0.42
40	0.29

The usefulness of evidence of validity based on the content of a test is clear in educational and organizational settings. In educational settings, this evidence plays an important role in validating educational achievement tests that assess how well a student has learned the content of a course. In organizational settings, this evidence is essential for tests used in personnel selection to establish that a test is job related. Although less clear, evidence of validity based on content has come to play more of a role in clinical and personality assessment because test developers are constantly working to define their constructs (Butcher, Graham, Williams, & Ben-Porath, 1990; Haynes, Richard, & Kubany, 1995; Millon, 1994).

FACE VALIDITY

At the beginning of this chapter, we introduced you to five types of evidence that can be used to demonstrate test validity. *Face validity* is another term that is often used when discussing tests that has nothing to do with evaluating the constructs that are being measured by a test. **Face validity** answers the question, "Does it appear to the test taker that the questions on the test are related to the purpose for which the test is being given?" As such, face validity is concerned only with how test takers perceive the attractiveness and appropriateness of a test.

Despite the fact that the concept of face validity does not have anything to do with the evaluation of test validity, it sometimes can be an important consideration in choosing a test that might be used in an applied setting. Consider the case of using a personality test as part of an employee selection system. The test might ask job applicants to indicate how well statements such as "I sympathize with others' feelings" or "I have a soft heart" describe them. Questions like these may be reflective of certain personality characteristics that have been demonstrated to be predictive of job performance on the job for which applicants are applying. But if the test takers cannot perceive the connection between the test questions and the requirements for the job, the test is said to lack face validity. This can result in the applicants' not taking the test seriously or, in the worst case, viewing the hiring process as being unfair. As a result, making a decision on what kind of test to use may involve consideration of the face validity of the instrument.

Although it is helpful for a test to have face validity in circumstances like those we described, face validity is never an acceptable means of demonstrating evidence of the validity of a test. To learn more about what supporters and challengers say about face validity, see On the Web Box 6.1.

ON THE WEB BOX 6.1
SUPPORTING AND CHALLENGING THE IMPORTANCE OF FACE VALIDITY
www.jalt.org/test/rob_1.htm
www.jalt.org/test/new_2.htm

Face validity has nothing to do with whether a test measures what it says it measures; rather, it is concerned with how test takers perceive the attractiveness and appropriateness of a test. In the past, and even more so today, testing experts have debated the importance and usefulness of face validity. To learn more about face validity and why some experts support the notion while others challenge it, visit the websites listed above.

Chapter Summary

Because decisions are made using psychological tests, it is important that the inferences made from the scores on psychological tests be justified and that test users administer tests only for their intended purposes. The validity of a test helps us understand whether the conclusions we are going to draw from test scores are appropriate and defensible. Traditionally, testing experts have evaluated three primary measures of validity: content, criterion related, and construct. The latest revision of the *Standards for Educational and Psychological Testing* (AERA et al., 2014) no longer refers to these traditional types of validity; instead, it cites five sources of evidence that a test is valid. It is usually not appropriate, or even possible, to estimate the validity of a test using all of these validation procedures. The strategy chosen to provide evidence of validity depends on the nature and purpose of the psychological test.

There are two methods for determining content-based evidence of validity of a test. The first involves performing a series of systematic steps during test development to ensure that the test samples the construct being measured representatively. The second method involves reviewing test items after the test development and determining the extent to which experts agree that test items are essential.

Although different from other evidence of validity, face validity—the perception of the test taker that the test questions are appropriate—is sometimes important to consider, especially in applied settings.

Engaging in the Learning Process

Learning is the process of gaining knowledge and skills through schooling or studying. Although you can learn by reading the chapter material, attending class, and engaging in discussion with your instructor, more actively engaging in the learning process may help you better learn and retain chapter information. To help you actively engage in the learning process, we encourage you to access our new supplementary student workbook. The workbook contains critical thinking activities to help you understand and apply information and help you make progress toward learning and retaining material. If you do not have a copy of the workbook, you can purchase a copy through sagepub.com.

Key Concepts

After completing your study of this chapter, you should be able to define each of the following terms. These terms are bolded in the text of this chapter and defined in the Glossary.

abstract attributes	content validity	practical test
competency modeling	content validity ratio	test specifications
concrete attributes	criterion-related validity	testing universe
construct	face validity	validity
construct validity	instructional objectives	written test
content areas	job analysis	

Critical Thinking Questions

The following are some critical thinking questions to support the learning objectives for this chapter.

Learning Objectives	Critical Thinking Questions
Explain what test validity is.	• How would you explain to someone that while reliability is largely a function of the test itself, validity is not? • What would be some of the nonstatistical things you would consider to determine if your final exam in this course could be considered to be valid? • What do you think the drawback would be to no longer defining validity as whether a test actually measures what it was designed to measure?
Understand the five sources of evidence of validity described in the *Standards* (AERA et al., 2014).	• What is the value of conceptualizing validity in terms of the various types of evidence that can be established for it as opposed to using the traditional terms content, criterion-related, and construct validity? • Why is it important to consider the types of attribute a test is attempting to measure when deciding on what the best evidence of validity for the test might be? • What misconceptions might a person draw regarding test validity if they did not understand the idea that validity is considered to be a unitary or single concept?
Explain, at a general level, the appropriate use of various validation strategies.	• Why is it probably a problem from an evidence of validity based on content perspective, if you were asked in a job interview, "If you needed to move Mount Fuji, how would you do it?" • Take a look at a recent classroom test you took and evaluate how you think it demonstrated evidence of validity based on test content. • Can you describe a type of test where it would be very difficult to establish evidence of validity based on test content and provide the reasons why it would be so difficult?
Describe methods for generating validity evidence based on the content of a test.	• What steps would you want your professor to take while developing his or her final examination to ensure that there was evidence for the test's validity based on content? • If the test were already developed, how might your professor confirm that the test demonstrates some evidence of validity based on its content?
Understand the steps involved in ensuring that a test demonstrates evidence of validity based on its content.	• Think about a hobby, special interest or talent that you wanted to promote to others. Suppose you wanted to assemble a group of friends to help you in this endeavor, but you needed to be certain that they were all experts in the area. So you decide to create a test that will help you determine their level of expertise. What steps would you take while you are designing the test to ensure that the test would demonstrate evidence of validity based on its content?
Explain the nature and importance of face validity and why it does not provide evidence for interpreting test scores.	• Suppose you were applying for a customer service job after graduation. One of the requirements of the job was attaining an acceptable score on a handwriting analysis test. Why might the requirement raise an issue to you regarding the face validity of the test?

7

HOW DO WE GATHER EVIDENCE OF VALIDITY BASED ON TEST–CRITERION RELATIONSHIPS?

LEARNING OBJECTIVES

After completing your study of this chapter, you should be able to do the following:

- Identify evidence of validity of a test based on its relationships to external criteria, and describe two methods for obtaining this evidence.

- Read and interpret validity studies.

- Discuss how restriction of range occurs and its consequences.

- Describe the differences between evidence of validity based on test content and evidence based on relationships with external criteria.

- Describe the difference between reliability/precision and validity.

- Define and give examples of objective and subjective criteria, and explain why criteria must be reliable and valid.

- Interpret a validity coefficient, calculate the coefficient of determination, and conduct a test of significance for a validity coefficient.

- Understand why measured validity will be reduced by unreliability in the predictor or criterion measure and what statistical correction can be applied to adjust for this reduction.

- Explain the concept of operational or "true" validity and how it is calculated.

- Explain the concept of regression, calculate and interpret a linear regression formula, and interpret a multiple regression formula.

"The graduate school I'm applying to says they won't accept anyone who scores less than 1,000 on the GRE. How did they decide that 1,000 is the magic number?"

"Before we married, my fiancée and I went to a premarital counselor. She gave us a test that predicted how happy our marriage would be."

"My company uses a test for hiring salespeople to work as telemarketers. The test is designed for people selling life insurance and automobiles. Is this a good test for hiring telemarketers?"

Have you ever wondered how psychological tests really work? Can we be comfortable using an individual's answers to test questions to make decisions about hiring him for a job or admitting her to college? Can mental disorders really be diagnosed using scores on standard questionnaires?

Psychologists who use tests for decision making are constantly asking these questions and others like them. When psychologists use test scores for making decisions that affect individual lives, they, as well as the public, want substantial evidence that the correct decisions are being made.

This chapter describes the processes that psychologists use to ensure that tests perform properly when they are used for making predictions and decisions. We begin by discussing the concept of validity evidence based on a test's relationships to other variables, specifically external criteria. As we discussed in the previous chapter, "How Do We Gather Evidence of Validity Based on the Content of a Test?" this evidence has traditionally been called *criterion-related evidence of validity*. We also discuss the importance of selecting a valid criterion measure, how to evaluate validity coefficients, and the statistical processes that provide evidence that a test can be used for making predictions.

WHAT IS EVIDENCE OF VALIDITY BASED ON TEST–CRITERION RELATIONSHIPS?

In the last chapter, we introduced you to the concept of evidence of validity based on a test's relationship with other variables. We said that one method for obtaining evidence is to investigate how well the test scores correlate with observed behaviors or events. When test scores correlate with specific behaviors, attitudes, or events, we can confirm that there is evidence of validity. In other words, the test scores may be used to predict those *specific* behaviors, attitudes, or events. But as you recall, we cannot use such evidence to make an overall statement that the test is valid. We also said that this evidence has traditionally been referred to as *criterion-related validity* (a term that we use occasionally in this chapter, as it is still widely used by testing practitioners).

For example, when you apply for a job, you might be asked to take a test designed to predict how well you will perform the job. If the job is clerical and the test really predicts how well you will perform, your test score will be related to your skill in performing clerical duties such as word processing and filing. To provide evidence that the test predicts clerical performance, psychologists correlate test score with a measure of each individual's performance on clerical tasks such as supervisor's ratings. The measure of performance that we correlate with test scores is called the **criterion**. If higher test scores relate to higher performance ratings, the test shows evidence of validity based on the relationship between these two variables, traditionally referred to as **criterion-related validity**. Educators use admissions tests to forecast how successful an applicant will be in college or graduate school. The SAT and the Graduate Record Examination (GRE) are admissions tests used by colleges. The criterion of success in college is often the student's first-year grade point average (GPA). In a clinical setting, psychologists often use tests to diagnose mental disorders. In this case, the criterion is the diagnoses made by several psychologists or psychiatrists independent of the test. Researchers then correlate the diagnoses with the test scores to establish evidence of validity.

METHODS FOR PROVIDING EVIDENCE OF VALIDITY BASED ON TEST–CRITERION RELATIONSHIPS

There are two methods for demonstrating evidence of validity based on test–criterion relationships: the predictive method and the concurrent method. This section defines and gives examples of each method.

The Predictive Method

When it is important to show a relationship between test scores and a future behavior, researchers use the predictive method to establish evidence of validity. In this case, a large group of people take the test (the predictor), and their scores are held for a predetermined time interval, such as 6 months. After the time interval passes, researchers collect a measure of some behavior, for example, a rating or other measure of performance, on the same people (the criterion). Then researchers correlate the test scores with the criterion scores. If the test scores and the criterion scores have a strong relationship, the test has demonstrated **predictive evidence of validity**.

Researchers at Brigham Young University used the predictive method to demonstrate evidence of validity of the PREParation for Marriage Questionnaire (PREP-M). For Your Information Box 7.1 describes the study they conducted.

Psychologists might use the predictive method in an organizational setting to establish evidence of validity for an employment test. To do so, they administer an employment test (predictor) to candidates for a job. Researchers file test scores in a secure place, and the company *does not* use the scores for making hiring decisions. The company makes hiring decisions based on other criteria, such as interviews or different tests. After a predetermined time interval, usually 3 to 6 months, supervisors evaluate the new hires on how well they perform the job (the criterion). To determine whether the test scores predict the candidates who were successful and unsuccessful, researchers correlate the test scores with the ratings of job performance. The resulting correlation coefficient is called the **validity coefficient**, a statistic used to infer the strength of the evidence of validity that the test scores might demonstrate in predicting job performance.

To get the best measure of validity, everyone who took the test would need to be hired so that all test scores could be correlated with a measure of job performance (something that it is not usually practical to do). This is because it is desirable to get the widest range of test scores possible (including the very low ones) to understand fully how all the test scores relate to job performance. Therefore, gathering predictive evidence of validity can present problems for some organizations because it is important that everyone who took the test is also measured

FOR YOUR INFORMATION BOX 7.1

EVIDENCE OF VALIDITY BASED ON TEST–CRITERION RELATIONSHIPS OF A PREMARITAL ASSESSMENT INSTRUMENT

In 1991, researchers at Brigham Young University (Holman, Larson, & Harmer, 1994) conducted a study to determine the evidence of validity based on test–criterion relationships of the PREParation for Marriage Questionnaire (PREP-M; Holman, Busby, & Larson, 1989). Counselors use the PREP-M with engaged couples who are participating in premarital courses or counseling. The PREP-M has 206 questions that provide information on couples' shared values, readiness for marriage, background, and home environment. The researchers contacted 103 married couples who had taken the PREP-M a year earlier as engaged couples and asked them about their marital satisfaction and stability.

© Kati Neudert/iStockphoto

The researchers predicted that those couples who had high scores on the PREP-M would express high satisfaction with their marriages. The researchers used two criteria to test their hypothesis. First, they drew questions from the Marital Comparison Level Index (Sabatelli, 1984) and the Marital Instability Scale (Booth, Johnson, & Edwards, 1983) to construct a criterion that measured each couple's level of marital satisfaction and marital stability. The questionnaire showed internal consistency of .83. The researchers also classified each couple as "married satisfied," "married dissatisfied," or "canceled/delayed" and as "married stable," "married unstable," or "canceled/delayed." These classifications provided a second criterion.

The researchers correlated the couples' scores on the PREP-M with their scores on the criterion questionnaire. The husbands' scores on the PREP-M correlated at .44 ($p < .01$) with questions on marital satisfaction and at .34 ($p < .01$) with questions on

marital stability. The wives' scores on the PREP-M were correlated with the same questions at .25 ($p < .01$) and .20 ($p < .05$), respectively. These correlations show that the PREP-M is a moderate to strong predictor of marital satisfaction and stability—good evidence of the validity of the PREP-M. (Later in this chapter, we discuss the size of correlation coefficients needed to establish evidence of validity.)

In addition, the researchers compared the mean scores of those husbands and wives classified as married satisfied, married dissatisfied, or canceled/delayed and those classified as married stable, married unstable, or canceled/delayed. As predicted, those who were married satisfied or married stable scored higher on the PREP-M than did those in the other two respective categories. In practical terms, these analyses show that counselors can use scores on the PREP-M to make predictions about how satisfying and stable a marriage will be.

on the criterion. Some organizations might not be able to hire everyone who applies regardless of qualifications, and there are usually more applicants than available positions, so not all applicants can be hired. Also, organizations frequently will be using some other selection tool such as an interview to make hiring decisions, and typically, only people who do well on the interview will be hired. Therefore, even predictive studies in organizations may only have access to the scores of a portion of the candidates who applied for the job. Because those actually hired are likely to be the higher performers, a **restriction of range** in the distribution of test scores is created. In other words, if the test is a valid predictor of job performance and the other selection tools that are used to make a hiring decision are also valid predictors, then people with lower scores on the test will be less likely to be hired. This causes the range of test scores to be reduced or restricted to those who scored relatively higher. Because a validity study conducted on these data will not have access to the full range of test scores, the validity coefficient calculated only from this restricted group is likely to be lower than if all candidates had been hired and included in the study.

Why would the resulting validity coefficient from a range-restricted group be lower than it would be if the entire group was available to measure? Think of it like this: The worst case of restricted range would be if everyone obtained exactly the same score on the test (similar to what would happen if you hired only those people who made a perfect score on the test). If this situation occurred, the correlation between the test scores and any other criteria would be zero. This is because if the test scores do not vary from person to person, high performers and lower performers would all have exactly the same test score. We cannot distinguish high performers from low performers when everybody gets the same score, and therefore these test scores cannot be predictive of job performance. Using the full range of test scores enables you to obtain a more accurate validity coefficient, which usually will be higher than the coefficient you obtained using the restricted range of scores. However, a correlation coefficient can be statistically adjusted for restriction of range, which, when used properly, can provide a corrected estimate of the validity coefficient of the employment test in the unrestricted population. We have much more to say about corrections to measured validity coefficients later in the chapter when we cover the relationship between reliability and validity. These problems exist in educational and clinical settings as well because individuals might not be admitted to an institution or might leave during the predictive study. For Your Information Box 7.2 describes a validation study that might have failed to find evidence of validity because of restriction of range.

The Concurrent Method

The method of demonstrating **concurrent evidence of validity** based on test–criteria relationships is an alternative to the predictive method. In the concurrent method, test administration and criterion measurement happen at approximately the same time. This method does not involve prediction. Instead, it provides information about the present and the status quo (Cascio, 1991). A study by Maisto and colleagues (2011), described in For Your Information Box 7.3, is a good example of a study designed to assess concurrent (as well as predictive) evidence of validity for an instrument used in a clinical setting.

The concurrent method involves administering two measures, the test and a second measure of the attribute, to the same group of individuals at as close to the same point in time as possible. For example, the test might be a paper-and-pencil measure of American literature, and the second measure might be a grade in an American literature course. Usually, the first measure is the test being validated, and the criterion is another type of measure of performance such as a rating, grade, or diagnosis. It is very important that the criterion test itself be reliable and valid (we discuss this further later in this chapter). The researchers then correlate the scores on the two measures. If the scores correlate, the test scores demonstrate evidence of validity.

In organizational settings, researchers often use concurrent studies as alternatives to predictive studies because of the difficulties of using a predictive design that we discussed earlier. In this setting, the process is to administer the test to employees currently in the position for which the test is being considered as a selection tool and then to collect criterion data on the same people (such as performance appraisal data). In some cases, the criterion data are specifically designed to be used in the concurrent study, while in other cases recent, existing data are used. Then the test scores are correlated with the criterion data and the validity coefficient is calculated.

Barrett, Phillips, and Alexander (1981) compared the two methods for determining evidence of validity based on predictor–criteria relationships in an organizational setting using

FOR YOUR INFORMATION BOX 7.2
DID RESTRICTION OF RANGE DECREASE THE VALIDITY COEFFICIENT?

Does a student's academic self-concept—how the student views himself or herself in the role of a student—affect the student's academic performance? Michael and Smith (1976) developed the Dimensions of Self-Concept (DOSC), a self-concept measure that emphasizes school-related activities and that has five subscales that measure level of aspiration, anxiety, academic interest and satisfaction, leadership and initiative, and identification versus alienation.

Researchers at the University of Southern California (Gribbons, Tobey, & Michael, 1995) examined the evidence of validity based on test–criterion relationships of the DOSC by correlating DOSC test scores with GPA. They selected 176 new undergraduates from two programs for students considered at risk for academic difficulties. The students came from a variety of ethnic backgrounds, and 57% were men.

At the beginning of the semester, the researchers administered the DOSC to the students following the guidelines described in the DOSC manual (Michael, Smith, & Michael, 1989). At the end of the semester, they obtained each student's first-semester GPA from university records. When they analyzed the data for evidence of reliability/precision and validity, the DOSC showed high internal consistency, but scores on the DOSC did not predict GPA.

Did something go wrong? One conclusion is that self-concept as measured by the DOSC is unrelated to GPA. However, if the study or the measures were somehow flawed, the predictive evidence of validity of the DOSC might have gone undetected. The researchers suggested that perhaps academic self-concept lacks stability during students' first semester. Although the internal consistency of the DOSC was established, the researchers did not measure the test–retest reliability/precision of the test. Therefore, this possibility cannot be ruled out. The researchers also suggested that GPA might be an unreliable criterion.

Could restriction of range have caused the validity of the DOSC to go undetected? This is a distinct possibility for two reasons. First, for this study the researchers chose only those students who were at risk for experiencing academic difficulties. Because the unrestricted population of students also contains those who are expected to succeed, the researchers might have restricted the range of both the test and the criterion. Second, the students in the study enrolled in programs to help them become successful academically. Therefore, participating in the programs might have enhanced the students' academic self-concept.

This study demonstrates two pitfalls that researchers designing predictive studies must avoid. Researchers must be careful to include in their studies participants who represent the entire possible range of performance on both the test and the criterion. In addition, they must design predictive studies so that participants are unlikely to change over the course of the study in ways that affect the abilities or traits that are being measured.

cognitive ability tests. They found that the two methods provide similar results. However, this may not always be the case. For Your Information Box 7.3 describes a recent example of the two approaches producing different results.

SELECTING A CRITERION

A criterion is an evaluative standard that researchers use to measure outcomes such as performance, attitude, or motivation. Evidence of validity derived from test–criteria relationships provides evidence that the test relates to some behavior or event that is independent of the psychological test. As you recall from For Your Information Box 7.1, the researchers at Brigham Young University constructed two criteria—a questionnaire and classifications on marital satisfaction and marital stability—to demonstrate evidence of validity of the PREP-M.

FOR YOUR INFORMATION BOX 7.3

DEVELOPING CONCURRENT AND PREDICTIVE EVIDENCE OF VALIDITY FOR THREE MEASURES OF READINESS TO CHANGE ALCOHOL USE IN ADOLESCENTS

Maisto and his colleagues (2011) were interested in motivation or readiness to change and how it relates to alcohol use in adolescents. They felt that if a good measure of this construct could be identified, it would help in the design of clinical interventions for the treatment of alcohol abuse. They noted that there was little empirical evidence to support the validity of any of the existing measures of motivation or readiness to change, especially in an adolescent population.

The researchers identified three existing measures of "readiness to change" frequently used in substance abuse contexts. The first was the Stages of Change and Treatment Eagerness Scale (SOCRATES). This tool was designed to measure two dimensions of readiness to change called Problem Recognition and Taking Steps concerning alcohol use (Maisto, Chung, Cornelius, & Martin, 2003). The second measure they evaluated was the Readiness Ruler (Center on Alcoholism, Substance Abuse and Addictions, 1995). This measure is a simple questionnaire that asks respondents to rate on a scale of 1 to 10 how ready they are to change their alcohol use behavior using anchors such as *not ready to change*, *unsure*, and *trying to change*. The third measure they investigated is called the Staging Algorithm (Prochaska, DiClemente, & Norcross, 1992), which places people into five stages based on their readiness to change: pre-contemplation, contemplation, preparation, action, and maintenance.

The research question was whether these instruments would show concurrent and/or predictive evidence of validity. That is, would high scores on the readiness-to-change instruments be associated with lower alcohol consumption reported when both measures were taken at the same point in time (concurrent evidence), and would high scores on the instruments taken at one point in time predict lower alcohol consumption measured at a later point in time (predictive evidence)?

The participants were adolescents aged 14 to 18 years who were recruited at their first treatment session from seven different treatment programs for adolescent substance users. Two criteria were used for the study. The first was the average percentage of days that the participants reported being abstinent from alcohol (PDA). The second was the average number of drinks they consumed per drinking day (DDD). These criteria were measured three times during the study—on the first day of treatment (concerning the previous 30 days) and at 6-month and 12-month follow-up sessions. The three "readiness-to-change" measures were filled out by the participants each time.

Concurrent evidence of validity was gathered by correlating the scores on each readiness-to-change instrument with the average alcohol consumption criteria reported by the participants at the same time. The correlation between baseline alcohol consumption and the initial readiness change measure taken at the same time for PDA was positive and statistically significant for the Readiness Ruler (.35), the Staging Algorithm (.39), and the SOCRATES Taking Steps dimension (.22). Higher scores on each of the readiness measures were associated with a larger percentage of days that the participants reported being abstinent from alcohol. Likewise, higher scores on the readiness instruments were significantly associated with lower numbers on the DDD measure. The correlations were −.34 for the Readiness Ruler, −.40 for the Staging Algorithm, and −.22 for the SOCRATES Taking Steps dimension. The scores from the SOCRATES Problem Recognition measure were not correlated with either PDA or DDD. Therefore, all the instruments with the exception of SOCRATES Problem Recognition demonstrated evidence of concurrent validity. A similar pattern of results was observed when data collected at the 6-month follow-up were analyzed.

Predictive evidence of validity was gathered using a statistical technique, discussed in this chapter, called multiple regression. This technique can be applied to evaluate the relationship between a criterion variable and more than one predictor variable. While the researchers in this study were interested only in evaluating how well the readiness-to-change scores predicted later alcohol consumption (the criterion variable), they recognized that there were other variables present in the study that might also be related to alcohol consumption. Some of these other variables were age, gender, race, and how much alcohol each participant reported consuming at the beginning of the study. By using multiple regression, the researchers were able to statistically "control for" the effects of these other variables. Then they could estimate how well the readiness-to-change measures by themselves predicted future alcohol consumption. This is called incremental validity because it shows how much additional variance is accounted for by the readiness-to-change measures alone, over and above the variance accounted for by the other variables used in the regression.

The researchers performed two regressions. First, the initial readiness-to-change scores on each instrument were used to predict alcohol consumption after 6 months of treatment. Then the readiness-to-change scores taken at 6 months of treatment were used to predict alcohol consumption after 12 months of treatment. The results showed that only the Readiness Ruler had significant predictive evidence of validity for both measures of alcohol consumption (PDA and DDD) at 6 months and 12 months of treatment.

The interesting finding in this study is that while all the measures showed concurrent evidence of validity, only the Readiness Ruler showed both concurrent and predictive evidence. There may be a number of plausible explanations for these seemingly contradictory results. Can you think of some of those reasons?

In a business setting, employers use pre-employment tests to predict how well an applicant is likely to perform a job. In this case, supervisors' ratings of job performance can serve as a criterion that represents performance on the job. Other criteria that represent job performance include accidents on the job, attendance or absenteeism, disciplinary problems, training performance, and ratings by **peers**—other employees at the work site. None of these measures can represent job performance perfectly, but each provides information on important characteristics of job performance.

Objective and Subjective Criteria

Criteria for job performance fall into two categories: objective and subjective. An **objective criterion** is one that is observable and measurable, such as the number of accidents on the job, the number of days absent, or the number of disciplinary problems in a month. A **subjective criterion** is based on a person's judgment. Supervisor and peer ratings are examples of subjective criteria.

Each has advantages and disadvantages. Well-defined objective criteria contain less error because they are usually tallies of observable events or outcomes. Their scope, however, is often quite narrow. For instance, dollar volume of sales is an objective criterion that might be used to measure a person's sales ability. This number is easily calculated, and there is little chance of disagreement on its numerical value. It does not, however, take into account a person's motivation or the availability of customers. On the other hand, a supervisor's ratings of a person's sales ability may provide more information on motivation, but in turn ratings are based on judgment and might be biased or based on information not related to sales ability, such as expectations about race or gender. Table 7.1 lists a number of criteria used in educational, clinical, and organizational settings.

DOES THE CRITERION MEASURE WHAT IT IS SUPPOSED TO MEASURE?

The concept of validity evidence based on content (addressed in the prior chapter) also applies to criteria. Criteria must be representative of the events they are supposed to measure. Criterion scores have evidence of validity to the extent that they match or represent the events in

TABLE 7.1 ■ Common Criteria	Objective	Subjective
Educational settings		
Grade point average (GPA)	X	
Withdrawal or dismissal	X	
Teacher's recommendations		X
Clinical settings		
Diagnosis		X
Behavioral observation	X	
Self-report		X
Organizational settings		
Units produced	X	
Number of errors	X	
Ratings of performance		X

question. Therefore, a criterion of sales ability must be representative of the entire testing universe of sales ability. Because there is more to selling than just having the highest dollar volume of sales, several objective criteria might be used to represent the entire testing universe of sales ability. For instance, we might add the number of sales calls made each month to measure motivation and add the size of the target population to measure customer availability.

Subjective measures such as ratings can often demonstrate better evidence of their validity based on content because the rater can provide judgments for a number of dimensions specifically associated with job performance. Rating forms are psychological measures, and we expect them to be reliable and valid, as we do for any measure. We estimate their reliability/precision using the test–retest or internal consistency method, and we generate evidence of their validity by matching their content to the knowledge, skills, abilities, or other characteristics (such as behaviors, attitudes, personality characteristics, or other mental states) that are presumed to be present in the test takers. (A later chapter contains more information on various types of rating scales and their uses in organizations: "How Are Tests Used in Organizational Settings?") By reporting the reliability of their criteria, researchers provide us with information on how consistent their outcome measures are. As you may have noticed, the researchers at Brigham Young University (Holman, Busby, & Larson, 1989) who conducted the study on the predictive validity of the PREP-M reported high reliability/precision for their questionnaire, which was their subjective criterion.

Sometimes criteria do not represent all of the dimensions in the behavior, attitude, or event being measured. When this happens, the criterion has decreased evidence of validity based on its content because it has underrepresented some important characteristics. If the criterion measures *more* dimensions than those measured by the test, we say that **criterion contamination** is present. For instance, if one were looking at the test–criterion relationship of a test

IN THE NEWS BOX 7.1
WHAT ARE THE CRITERIA FOR SUCCESS?

Choosing criteria for performance can be difficult. Consider the criteria for teacher performance in Tennessee. In 2010, Tennessee won a federal Race to the Top Grant worth about $501 million for the state's public school system. As part of the program outlined in the grant application, the criteria for evaluating teachers would be students' test scores on state subject matter tests (e.g., writing, math, and reading) and observations by school principals.

Think a minute about these criteria. Are these criteria objective or subjective? Are they well defined? Can these criteria be reliably measured? Is there likely to be error in the measures of these criteria? Are they valid measures of teacher performance?

Let's look closely at these criteria. One criterion is objective and one is subjective. Can you tell which is which? If you answered that the test scores are objective and the observations are subjective, you are correct. The test scores have good attributes. They provide data that can be analyzed using statistical procedures. They can be collected, scored, and secured efficiently. If the tests are constructed correctly the scores will be reliable and valid. On the other hand, if the tests are not developed correctly, their scores can contain error and bias.

What about the principals' observations? What are their attributes likely to be? We say that the observations are subjective, because they are based on personal opinion. They will probably be affected by each principal's preconceived notions and opinions. One way those errors can be avoided is by training the principals to use a valid observation form that relies only on behaviors. Such forms would identify behaviors and form the basis for ratings. Under the grant guidelines, teachers would receive at least four 10-minute evaluations each year.

The federal grant requirements outline a plan that, if carried out correctly, can yield useful results for improving the education of Tennessee's students. These evaluations, however, are most important to the individual teachers in Tennessee because they will be used to decide which teachers will be retained, given pay raises, promoted, and granted tenure. As you might expect, some principals and teachers have serious complaints. Those who teach subjects for which there are no state tests, such as art, music, physical education, and home economics, are allowed to choose the subjects under which they wish to be evaluated. A physical education teacher could choose to be evaluated using the school's scores on the state writing test. Some principals who once did classroom visits regularly now feel compelled to observe teachers only when they are formally evaluating them.

Has something gone wrong here? Should the state provide more regulations and rules to govern the evaluation procedures? The state board is looking into the evaluation process. "Evaluations shouldn't be terribly onerous, so complex you get lost among the trees," board chairman Fielding Rolston has said. "We don't want there to be so many checkmarks you can't tell what's being evaluated" (Crisp, 2011).

Sources: Crisp (2011), Winerip (2011), and Zehr (2011).

of sales aptitude, a convenient criterion might be the dollar volume of sales made over some period of time. However, if the dollar volume of sales of a new salesperson reflected both his or her own sales as well as sales that resulted from the filling of back orders sold by the former salesperson, the criterion would be considered contaminated.

As you can see, when evaluating a validation study, it is important to think about the criterion in the study as well as the predictor. When unreliable or inappropriate criteria are used for validation, the true validity coefficient might be under- or overestimated. In the News Box 7.1 describes some issues associated with identifying appropriate criteria to evaluate the performance of school teachers needed to meet the requirements for a large federal grant.

To close this section, we thought it would be useful for you to see some information about the predictive validity of a test than many of you may have taken as a requirement for college admission—the SAT. To learn more about the evidence that has been gathered to support the validity of the SAT, see On the Web Box 7.1.

CALCULATING AND EVALUATING VALIDITY COEFFICIENTS

You may recall that the correlation coefficient is a quantitative estimate of the linear relationship between two variables. In validity studies, we refer to the correlation coefficient between the test and the criterion as the validity coefficient and represent it in formulas and equations as r_{xy}. The x in the subscript refers to the test, and the y refers to the criterion. The validity coefficient represents the amount or strength of the evidence of validity based on the relationship of the test and the criterion.

Validity coefficients must be evaluated to determine whether they represent a level of validity that makes the test useful and meaningful. This section describes two methods for evaluating validity coefficients and how researchers use test–criterion relationship information to make predictions about future behavior or performance.

Tests of Significance

A validity coefficient is interpreted in much the same way as a reliability coefficient, except that our expectations for a very strong relationship are not as great. We cannot expect a test to have as strong a relationship with another variable (test–criterion evidence of validity) as it does with itself (reliability). Therefore, we must evaluate the validity coefficient by using a test of significance and by examining the coefficient of determination.

The first question to ask about a validity coefficient is, "How likely is it that the correlation between the test and the criterion resulted from chance or sampling error?" In other words, if the test scores (e.g., SAT scores) and the criterion (e.g., college GPA) are completely unrelated, then their true correlation is zero. If we conducted a study to determine the relationship between these two variables and found that the correlation was .4, one question we would need to ask is, "What is the probability that our study would have yielded the observed correlation by chance alone, even if the variables were truly unrelated?" If the probability that the correlation occurred by chance is low—less than 5 chances out of 100 ($p < .05$)—we can be reasonably sure that the test and its criterion (in this example, SAT scores and college GPA) are truly related. This process is called a **test of significance**. In statistical terms, for this example we would say that the validity coefficient is significant at the .05 level. In organizational settings, it can be challenging for validity studies to have statistically significant results at $p < .05$ because of small sample sizes and criterion contamination.

Because larger sample sizes reduce sampling error, this test of significance requires that we take into account the size of the group (N) from which we obtained our data. Appendix E can be used to determine whether a correlation is significant at varying levels of significance. To use the table in Appendix E, calculate the degrees of freedom (df) for your correlation using the formula $df = N - 2$, and then determine the probability that the correlation occurred by chance by looking across the row associated with those degrees of freedom. The correlation coefficient you are evaluating should be larger than the critical value shown in the table. You can determine the level of significance by looking at the column headings. At the level

ON THE WEB BOX 7.1
VALIDITY AND THE SAT

To help make admissions decisions, many colleges and universities rely on applicants' SAT scores. Because academic rigor can vary from one high school to the next, the SAT—a standardized test—provides schools with a fair and accurate way to put students on a level playing field to compare one student with another. However, whether the SAT truly predicts success in college— namely, 1st-year college grades—is controversial.

To learn more about the validity of the SAT, visit the following websites:

Website	Description
General Information	
www.fairtest.org/facts/satvalidity.html	General discussion of the following: <ul><li>What the SAT is supposed to measure</li><li>What SAT I validity studies from major colleges and universities show</li><li>How well the SAT I predicts success beyond the freshman year</li><li>How well the SAT I predicts college achievement for women, students of color, and older students</li><li>How colleges and universities should go about conducting their own validity studies</li><li>Alternatives to the SAT</li></ul>
Research Studies	
https://research.collegeboard.org/sites/default/files/publications/2012/7/researchreport-2008-5-validity-sat-predicting-first-year-college-grade-point-average.pdf	Research study exploring the predictive validity of the SAT in predicting 1st-year college grade point average (GPA)
www.ucop.edu/news/sat/research.html	Research study presenting findings on the relative contributions of high school GPA, SAT I scores, and SAT II scores in predicting college success for 81,722 freshmen who entered the University of California from fall 1996 through fall 1999
www.collegeboard.com/prod_downloads/sat/newsat_pred_val.pdf	Summary of research exploring the predictive value of the SAT Writing section
www.psychologicalscience.org/pdf/ps/frey.pdf	A paper that looks at the relationship between SAT scores and general cognitive ability

at which your correlation coefficient is smaller than the value shown, the correlation can no longer be considered significantly different from zero. For Your Information Box 7.4 provides an example of this process.

When researchers or test developers report a validity coefficient, they should also report its level of significance. You might have noted that the validity coefficients of the PREP-M (reported

FOR YOUR INFORMATION BOX 7.4

TEST OF SIGNIFICANCE FOR A CORRELATION COEFFICIENT

Here we illustrate how to determine whether a correlation coefficient is significant (evidence of a true relationship) or not significant (no relationship). Let's say that we have collected data from 20 students. We have given the students a test of verbal achievement, and we have correlated students' scores with their grades from a course on creative writing. The resulting correlation coefficient is .45.

We now go to the table of critical values for Pearson product–moment correlation coefficients in Appendix E. The table shows the degrees of freedom (df) and alpha (α) levels for two-tailed and one-tailed tests. Psychologists usually set their alpha level at 5 chances out of 100 (p < .05) using a two-tailed test, so we use that standard for our example.

Because we used the data from 20 students in our sample, we substitute 20 for N in the formula for degrees of freedom (df = N − 2). Therefore, df = 20 − 2 or 18. We then go to the table and find 18 in the df column. Finally, we locate the critical value in that row under the .05 column.

A portion of the table from Appendix E is reproduced in the table below, showing the alpha level for a two-tailed test. The critical value of .4438 (bolded in the table) is the one we use to test our correlation. Because our correlation (.45) is greater than the critical value (.4438), we can infer that the probability of finding our correlation by chance is less than 5 chances out of 100. Therefore, we assume that there is a true relationship and refer to the correlation coefficient as significant. Note that if we had set our alpha level at a more stringent standard of .01 (1 chance out of 100), our correlation coefficient would have been interpreted as not significant.

If the correlation between the test and the predictor is not as high as the critical value shown in the table, we can say that the chance of error associated with the test is above generally accepted levels. In such a case, we would conclude that the validity coefficient does not provide sufficient evidence of validity.

CRITICAL VALUES FOR PEARSON PRODUCT–MOMENT CORRELATION COEFFICIENTS

df	.10	.05	.02	.01	.001
16	.4000	.4683	.5425	.5897	.7084
17	.3887	.4555	.5285	.5751	.6932
18	.3783	.4438	.5155	.5614	.6787
19	.3687	.4329	.5034	.5487	.6652
20	.3598	.4227	.4921	.5368	.6524

Source: From *Statistical Tables for Biological, Agricultural and Medical Research* by R. A. Fisher and F. Yates. Copyright © 1963. Published by Pearson Education Limited.

earlier in this chapter) are followed by the statements $p < .01$ and $p < .05$. This information tells the test user that the likelihood a relationship was found by chance or as a result of sampling error was less than 5 chances out of 100 ($p < .05$) or less than 1 chance out of 100 ($p < .01$).

The Coefficient of Determination

Another way to evaluate the validity coefficient is to determine the amount of variance that the test and the criterion share. We can determine the amount of shared variance by squaring the validity coefficient to obtain r^2—called the **coefficient of determination**. For example, if the correlation (r) between a test and a criterion is .30, the coefficient of determination (r^2) is .09. This means that the test and the criterion have 9% of their variance in common. Larger validity coefficients represent stronger relationships with greater overlap between the test and the criterion. Therefore, if $r = .50$, then $r^2 = .25$—or 25% shared variance.

We can calculate the coefficient of determination for the correlation of husbands' scores on the PREP-M and the questionnaire on marital satisfaction and stability. By squaring the original coefficient, .44, we obtain the coefficient of determination, $r^2 = .1936$. This outcome means that the predictor, the PREP-M, and the criterion, the questionnaire, shared (or had in common) approximately 19% of their variance.

Unadjusted validity coefficients rarely exceed .50. Therefore, you can see that even when a validity coefficient is statistically significant, the test can account for only a small portion of the variability in the criterion. The coefficient of determination is important to calculate and remember when using the correlation between the test and the criterion to make predictions about future behavior or performance.

How Confident Can We Be About Estimates of Validity?

Conducting one validity study that demonstrates a strong relationship between the test and the criterion is the first step in a process of validation, but it is not the final step. Studies that provide evidence of a test's validity should continue for as long as the test is being used. No matter how well designed the validation study is, elements of chance, error, and situation-specific factors that can over- or underinflate the estimate of validity are always present. Ongoing investigations of validity include cross-validation (where the results that are obtained using one sample are used to predict the results on a second, similar sample) and meta-analyses (where the results from many studies are statistically combined to provide a more error-free estimate of validity). Psychologists also inquire about whether validity estimates are stable from one situation or population to another—a question of validity generalization. We have more to say about these topics in later chapters.

THE RELATIONSHIP BETWEEN RELIABILITY AND VALIDITY

You have already learned in your study of reliability that according to classical test theory, observed scores on a test can be thought of as the sum of two components—the individual's true score on the construct that the test was designed to measure and a random component, which we call measurement error. You have also learned that the reliability coefficient can be conceived of as a test's correlation with itself or another parallel test. That is why we often indicate the reliability coefficient as R_{xx}, where the two subscripts are the same. The reason why random error will always reduce the reliability coefficient is that any event that is random will have a zero correlation with any other event. That is simply another way of saying that knowledge of one random event will give you no information that would enable you to predict any other event. So the more that random events affect a test score, the less that score can correlate with any other measurement—even itself.

You have now learned that one way we provide evidence of validity is to correlate the scores on a test with the scores on a criterion measure. This is called a validity coefficient. You also know that test scores always contain random error so they are never perfectly reliable. And now you have also learned that reliability is also a concern when we develop criteria measures. So if the correlation of a test with itself is reduced from the maximum theoretical value 1.0 due to measurement error, what happens to the correlation coefficient when we correlate test scores that contain random error with a criterion measure which also contains random error? The answer is that just as in the case of reliability, the random error in both measures will reduce the degree to which the two sets of scores can correlate with each other no matter how well the construct that is measured by the test actually predicts the construct measured by the criterion. This reduction in the validity coefficient is referred to as **attenuation due to unreliability**.

It is a simple matter to quantify the degree to which unreliability can affect (attenuate or reduce) the validity coefficient. Mathematically, the square root of the reliability coefficient of test will set the upper limit of the validity coefficient. So if a test has a reliability of .64, the maximum correlation that the test could have with a perfectly reliable criterion is the square root of the reliability coefficient. In this example that would be $\sqrt{.64} = .8$, so the maximum validity coefficient would be .8.

If the criterion is less than perfectly reliable (which will always be the case), the maximum possible correlation between the test and criteria will be even lower. The maximum validity coefficient between a test and criteria can also be easily calculated if you know the reliability of both. It is simply the product of the square roots of both reliability coefficients. So if the reliability of the criterion measure was .7, the *maximum* observed correlation the criterion could have with a test that had a reliability coefficient of .64 would be $\sqrt{.64} \times \sqrt{.7} = .67$ if the constructs being measured were perfectly related, which also will never be the case. If the "true" correlation between the constructs were actually .5 (which, like true scores in reliability calculations, you can never really know), the observed correlation (the validity coefficient) between the test and criterion for this example would be further reduced and is equal to $.5 \times \sqrt{.64} \times \sqrt{.7} = .34$. The general formula that demonstrates that the correlation between a test and a criterion is dependent upon the "true" correlation between the predictor and criterion constructs and the reliability of the observed scores is:

$$r_{x_o y_o} = r_{x_t y_t} \sqrt{R_{xx} R_{yy}}$$

where

$r_{x_o y_o}$ = the observed correlation between the predictor measure (test) and criterion measure

$r_{x_t y_t}$ = the "true" correlation between the predictor construct and criterion construct

R_{xx} = the reliability coefficient of the predictor measure (test)

R_{yy} = the reliability of the criterion measure

This attenuation of the "true" validity coefficient due to the unreliability of the test and the criterion is the reason why observed validity coefficients often range between .2 and .4 while reliability coefficients for well-designed tests are often greater than .8. Even though both coefficients are correlations, the reliability coefficient is the correlation between the test and itself that will always be higher than the correlation of the test with a less than perfectly reliable criterion measure. The measurement error that is present in both will attenuate the observed correlation.

Psychometricians have developed a method for "correcting" validity coefficients for attenuation due to unreliability. These methods can be controversial because if they are used inappropriately, they will misrepresent the relationship between a test and criterion (i.e., validity) and could lead to incorrect inferences being made from the test scores. In Greater Depth Box 7.1 discusses the correction of validity coefficients for attenuation due to unreliability in more detail, some of the interpretive challenges such corrections present, and an important concept called operational validity.

IN GREATER DEPTH BOX 7.1
OPERATIONAL VALIDITY AND THE CORRECTION FOR ATTENUATION IN VALIDITY DUE TO UNRELIABILITY

Consider the following (not so) hypothetical example. A large company wishes to use a personality test to predict job performance to help select their employees. In particular, they are interested in the personality trait of conscientiousness that they believe will be related to overall job performance. So they decide to conduct a predictive validity study in which everybody hired takes the personality test to measure their level of conscientiousness, but these results are not used as part of the selection process. One year later, they collect performance evaluation data on everyone who took the test. To compute a validity coefficient, they correlate the scores on the conscientiousness scale of the personality test with the scores on the performance evaluations and find that it is .29. This would be called the observed validity of conscientiousness to predict job performance

But what if the performance evaluation they used as a criterion measure was unreliable? As we discussed earlier, the observed validity coefficient will be attenuated or reduced due to this unreliability. Before discussing how the validity coefficient can be statistically adjusted to account for the unreliability in the criterion, we need to discuss the difference between the observed validity and something called the true score validity.

You learned in our discussion of reliability that all observed scores consist of two components—true scores and random error. The true scores represent the degree to which a person possess a particular knowledge or trait if we could measure it without error. We refer to this knowledge or trait as the construct that the test was designed to measure. In our example, there are two constructs that the company needed to measure as part of their validity study. The first was the personality trait of conscientiousness. This construct was measured via a personality test and can be called the predictor construct. The second construct was overall job performance, which was measured via job performance evaluation data. This can be called the criterion construct. If we could, we would really like to know everyone's true scores at the construct level. Then we could correlate the true scores on the predictor with the true scores on the criterion and obtain the true score validity coefficient. But unfortunately, we can't do that. All we can

do is correlate the scores on the imperfect observed measures that are designed to assess each construct to obtain an observed validity coefficient. Because these observed scores contain random error (they are not perfectly reliable), the observed validity coefficient will always be lower than what the true score validity coefficient would have been. The relationships between the constructs and the observed measures of those constructs are depicted graphically in Figure 7.1.

The fact that the observed validity coefficient will always be less that the hypothetical true score validity raises some important questions: Since the observed validity coefficient will be reduced because of the presence of measurement error, how are we to properly interpret it? Does the attenuated validity coefficient really accurately describe the predictive relationship between the predictor and the criterion?

To answer these questions, let's go back to our example. The predictive validity study that we described above used performance evaluation data as its measure of overall job performance. The observed validity coefficient between conscientiousness scores on the personality test and the job performance scores was measured to be .29. However, research has demonstrated that the reliability/precision of performance evaluations as a measure of overall job performance is relatively poor, with a mean meta-analytic reliability coefficient across many studies of only .52 (Viswesvaran, Ones, & Schmidt, 1996). This means that while 52% of the variance in job performance ratings is due to the true scores on the construct, 48% of the variance is attributable to measurement error. Therefore, the observed correlation of .29 between conscientiousness overall job performance measured by performance evaluation data level will be lower than it would be if we could measure both without error at the construct level. The true correlation has been attenuated due to measurement error (unreliability) in the observed criterion measure. The implications of this is that the personality trait of conscientiousness may actually be a better predictor of overall job performance than the validity coefficient suggests!

There is a correction that can be applied to estimate what the validity coefficient would be if we were able to measure the criterion construct without error.

(Continued)

(Continued)

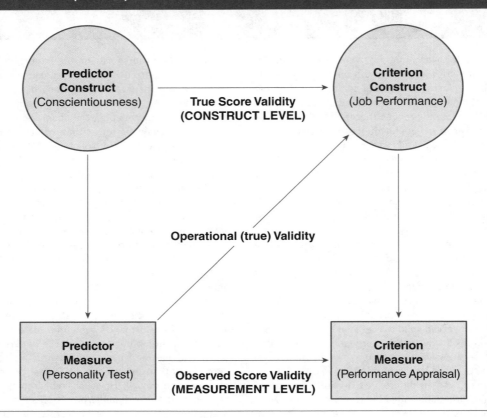

FIGURE 7.1 ■ **Graphical Representation of True Score, Observed Score, and Operational Validity**

Source: Copyright © 2014 by Society for Industrial and Organizational Psychology.

It is called the **correction for attenuation**. The formula is quite simple:

$$r_{xy(corrected)} = \frac{r_{xy(as\ measured)}}{\sqrt{R_{yy}}}$$

where:

$r_{xy(corrected)}$ = the validity coefficient corrected for attenuation

$r_{xy(as\ measured)}$ = the original measured validity coefficient

$\sqrt{R_{yy}}$ = the estimated reliability of the observed criterion

In our example, the measured validity coefficient was determined to be .29. The estimated reliability of the criterion (the job performance evaluation data) was estimated via previous research to be .52 (Viswesvaran et al., 1996). Therefore, the validity coefficient corrected for attenuation due to the unreliability in the criterion would be $\frac{.29}{\sqrt{.52}} = .40$. The corrected validity coefficient can be interpreted to be the correlation between the predictor (conscientiousness in our example) and the criterion *construct* (job performance), not the criterion *measure* (performance evaluation data). We call this correlation the **operational validity** or the true validity of the predictor for predicting the criterion *construct* (Viswesvaran et al., 2014). It is an attempt to reflect the true relationship between the predictor and the criterion once the error in measurement is removed from the criterion variable. In our example, it suggests that in actual operation, the construct of conscientiousness is better predictor of the *construct* of job performance than is apparent when you simply look at the correlation between conscientiousness and performance evaluation data based on the observed data.

It may have occurred to you that while the validity coefficient is the correlation between a predictor variable and a criterion variable, we have only applied the correction to the criterion variable. While we could have also applied the correction to the predictor variable as well, it would not have been appropriate to do so in this case (Society for Industrial and Organizational Psychology, 2003). This is because once we choose a test, we are interested in how well that test (with all its error) predicts the criterion. If a test has a lot of error, (i.e., is not very reliable) it will do a poor job of prediction because of that error. There is no reason to correct for that as the correlation between the unreliable test and the criterion accurately represents the degree to which the test can or cannot predict the criterion. However, if the criterion measure is unreliable, then the conclusions or inferences we will draw from the validity coefficient could be very flawed. While the test might be a poor predictor of the criterion at the measurement level because of criterion unreliability, as you have seen, it might actually be a much better predictor at the construct level. That is, the operational validity of the test-criterion relationship might be very good while the observed validity is poorer. The benefit or utility of a test actually comes from its operational validity. This is a measure of how well the criterion will be predicated by the test in actual practice. That's why operational validity is sometimes also referred to as true validity (Viswesvaran et al., 2014). Measurement error in the criterion serves to mask the true relationship between the two.

In closing this section, it is important for us to state that the practice of correcting validity coefficients is something of a controversial area and there are differing opinions about the appropriateness of the corrections. For a dissenting view, the interested student should see LeBreton, Scherer, and James, (2014). Also, we have only discussed correcting validity coefficients for unreliability in the criterion measure. Validity coefficients can also be corrected for range restriction. As we mentioned earlier in this chapter, restriction in range can also reduce a validity coefficient when tests are used for selection purposes because we only have access to the test and criterion scores for those people who are actually selected, not the full range of people who might have taken the test. Also, because test scores will often be correlated with other criteria used to select employees (such as the scores on interviews), those with the lowest test scores will often not be selected even if the test scores themselves are not used as a selection criterion as would be the case in a predictive validity study. This will result in an indirect restriction of range on the test scores that will then artificially reduce the observed validity coefficient. A comprehensive review of the statistical issues that are present when conducting criterion-related validity studies to gather evidence for validity based on a test's relationship with other variables can be found in Van Iddekinge and Ployhart (2008). Finally, the corrections we have described in this section are most often used when large scale psychometric meta-analyses are conducted that combine the results of many smaller individual studies to arrive at a more accurate estimates of validity for a particular predictor variable. They are less often used to correct the results obtained in individual studies like our example because the small sample sizes usually present in these studies would likely result in unstable corrected estimates that would vary significantly if the study were repeated on a different sample.

USING VALIDITY INFORMATION TO MAKE PREDICTIONS

When a relationship can be established between a test and a criterion, we can use test scores from other individuals to predict how well new individuals will perform on the criterion measure. For example, some universities use students' scores on the SAT to predict the students' success in college. Organizations use job candidates' scores on pre-employment tests that have demonstrated evidence of validity to predict those candidates' scores on the criteria of job performance.

Linear Regression

We use the statistical process called **linear regression** when we use one set of test scores (X) to predict one set of criterion scores (Y'). While a full description of linear regression is beyond the scope of this book, we can show you the basic process.

We start by constructing the following linear regression equation:

$$Y' = a + bX,$$

where

Y' = the predicted score on the criterion

a = the intercept

b = the slope (also called a b weight, regression weight, or regression coefficient)

X = the score the individual made on the predictor test

You may recognize this formula from previous math courses you have taken as the equation for a straight line. In linear regression, we refer to this line as the regression line. We calculate the **slope** or b **weight** (b) of the regression line—the expected change in Y for every one-unit change in X—using the following formula:

$$b = r \frac{s_y}{s_x}$$

where

r = the correlation coefficient

s_x = the standard deviation of the distribution of X

s_y = the standard deviation of the distribution of Y

The **intercept** is the place where the regression line crosses the y-axis. The intercept (a) is calculated using the following formula:

$$a = \bar{Y} - b\bar{X},$$

where

$\bar{Y}$ = the mean of the distribution of Y

b = the slope

$\bar{X}$ = the mean of the distribution of X

You may have noticed that we are using the symbols for the sample standard deviation (s_x and s_y) and the sample mean ($\overline{X}$ and $\overline{Y}$) here and in For Your Information Box 7.5 instead of the symbols for the population values. This is because a regression equation is usually used to make predictions about a population based on sample data.

A test for statistical significance can be performed on b, the regression weight. This is a test that evaluates whether the slope of the regression line is statistically significantly different from zero. If b is significantly different from zero, it means that X can be considered to be a valid predictor of the criterion, Y. Mathematically, a test of b in a simple linear regression will give you exactly the same results as a test of the correlation between X and Y. If this correlation is statistically significant, then it also means that the slope of the regression line that predicts Y from X is statistically significantly different from zero as well. If the correlation between X and Y is not statistically significant, there would be no reason to perform a regression, as that would mean that the predictor (X) does not provide any predictive information about criterion (Y).

For Your Information Box 7.5 shows the calculation of a linear regression equation and how it is used to predict scores on a criterion.

The process of using correlated data to make predictions is also important in clinical settings. For Your Information Box 7.6 describes how clinicians use psychological test scores to identify adolescents at risk for committing suicide.

Multiple Regression

Complex criteria, such as job performance and success in graduate school, are often difficult to predict with a single test. In these situations, researchers frequently use more than one test to make a more accurate prediction. A technique called multiple regression is often used in this situation.

We use the statistical process of **multiple regression** when we have more than one set of test scores ($X_1, X_2, \ldots X_n$) used for predicting a criterion (Y). A multiple regression equation expands the familiar linear regression equation to include more than one predictor or test as follows:

$$Y' = a + b_1 X_1 + b_2 X_2 + b_3 X_3 \ldots b_n X_n,$$

where

Y' = the predicted score on the criterion

a = the intercept (where the regression line crosses the y-axis)

X_i = the predictor

b_i = the expected change in Y for every one-unit change in X_i, when all the other predictors in the equation do not vary or remain constant. As in simple linear regression, these are also called b weights or regression weights. The b weight is also related to slope, but when there are more than two predictors, this cannot be graphically represented because you would actually need to graph in more than three dimensions to see it.

FOR YOUR INFORMATION BOX 7.5

MAKING PREDICTIONS WITH A LINEAR REGRESSION EQUATION

Research suggests that academic self-efficacy (ASE) and class grades are related. We have made up the following data to show how we could use the scores on an ASE test to predict a student's grade. We have also done the various calculations for you. (Note: Our fake data set is small, to facilitate this illustration.)

For instance, we can ask, "If a student scores 65 on the ASE test, what course grade would we expect the student to receive?" We have assigned numbers to each grade to facilitate this analysis, therefore, 1 = D, 2 = C, 3 = B, and 4 = A.

Step 1: Calculate the means and standard deviations of X and Y.

$$\bar{X} = 63.2$$

$$\bar{Y} = 2.6$$

$$s_x = 20.82$$

$$s_y = .97$$

Step 2: Calculate the correlation coefficient (r_{xy}) for X and Y.

$$r_{xy} = .67$$

Step 3: Calculate the slope (b) and intercept (a).

$$b = r\frac{s_y}{s_x},$$

$$b = .67 \times \frac{.97}{20.82}$$

$$b = .031$$

$$a = \bar{Y} - b\bar{X}$$

$$a = 2.6 - (.031)(63.2)$$

$$a = .64$$

Step 4: Calculate Y' (the predicated grade) when $X = 65$.

$$Y' = a + bX$$

$$Y' = .64 + (.031)(65)$$

$$Y' = .64 + 2.02 = 2.66$$

Step 5: Translate the number calculated for Y' back into a letter grade.

Student	ASE (X)	Grade (Y)
1	80	3
2	62	2
3	90	4
4	40	2
5	55	2
6	85	2
7	70	4
8	75	3
9	25	1
10	50	3

Therefore, a predicted numerical grade of 2.66 convert to a letter grade of between C and B, perhaps a C+.

The best prediction we can make is that a person who scored 65 on an ASE test would be expected to earn a course grade of C+. Note that by substituting any test score for X, we will receive a corresponding prediction for a score on Y.

This equation actually provides a predicted score on the criterion (Y') for each test score (X). When the Y' values are plotted, they form the linear regression line associated with the correlation between the test and the criterion.

FOR YOUR INFORMATION BOX 7.6
EVIDENCE OF VALIDITY OF THE SUICIDE PROBABILITY SCALE USING THE PREDICTIVE METHOD

Although the general incidence of suicide has decreased during the past two decades, the rate for people between 15 and 24 years old has tripled. Suicide is generally considered to be the second or third most common cause of death among adolescents, even though it is underreported (O'Connor, 1997–2014).

If young people who are at risk for committing suicide or making suicide attempts can be identified, greater vigilance is likely to prevent such actions. Researchers at Father Flanagan's Boys' Home, in Boys Town, Nebraska, conducted a validity study using the predictive method for the Suicide Probability Scale (SPS) that provided encouraging results for predicting suicidal behaviors in adolescents (Larzelere, Smith, Batenhorst, & Kelly, 1996).

The SPS contains 36 questions that assess suicide risk, including thoughts about suicide, depression, and isolation. The researchers administered the SPS to 840 boys and girls when they were admitted to the Boys Town residential treatment program from 1988 through 1993. The criteria for this study were the numbers of suicide attempts, suicide verbalizations, and self-destructive behaviors recorded in the program's daily incident reports completed by supervisors of the group homes. (The interrater reliabilities for reports of verbalizations and reports of self-destructive behaviors were very high at .97 and .89, respectively. The researchers were unable to calculate a reliability estimate for suicide attempts because only one attempt was recorded in the reports they selected for the reliability analysis.)

After controlling for a number of confounding variables, such as gender, age, and prior attempts at suicide, the researchers determined that the total SPS score and each of its subscales differentiated ($p = .05$) between those who attempted suicide and those who did not. In other words, the mean SPS scores of those who attempted suicide were significantly higher than the mean SPS scores of those who did not attempt suicide. The mean SPS scores of those who displayed self-destructive behaviors were also significantly higher ($p = .01$) than the mean SPS scores of those who did not attempt self-destructive behaviors. Finally, the total SPS score correlated at .25 ($p = .001$) with the suicide verbalization rate. Predictions made by the SPS for those at risk for attempting suicide showed that each 1-point increase in the total SPS score predicted a 2.4% greater likelihood of a subsequent suicide attempt.

The researchers suggested a cutoff score of 74 for those without prior suicide attempts and a cutoff score of 53 for those with prior suicide attempts. In other words, if an adolescent who has no history of suicide attempts scores above 74 on the SPS, the youth would be classified as at risk for suicide and treated accordingly. If an adolescent who has a history of a suicide attempt scores below 53, the youth would be classified as not at risk for suicide.

The researchers emphasized, however, that although the SPS demonstrated statistically significant validity in predicting suicide attempts, it is not a perfect predictor. A number of suicide attempts were also recorded for those with low scores, and therefore a low SPS score does not ensure that an adolescent will not attempt suicide. The SPS does, however, provide an instrument for accurately identifying adolescents at risk for committing suicide.

The subscripts following each b and X are used to identify each predictor in the regression equation.

In multiple regression, there is still one criterion (Y), as in simple linear regression, but there are now multiple predictors. There are a number of different statistics we can use when interpreting the results of a multiple regression. One of the statistics is analogous to the correlation coefficient (r) used in simple regression. It is called the multiple correlation coefficient and is indicated by a capital letter R. R describes the overall relationship between more than one predictor and a criterion. R is interpreted in a similar fashion to the usual correlation coefficient. Like any correlation coefficient, R can be subjected to a test of significance. If R is significant, it indicates that all the predictors in the equation taken together explain a statistically significant amount of variance in the criterion. However, an even more useful statistic for interpreting the results of a multiple regression is called the **coefficient of multiple determination** (R^2). Earlier in this chapter we discussed the coefficient of determination. You will recall that the coefficient of determination (r^2) is simply the square of a correlation coefficient between a single predictor and a criterion. It is interpreted as the proportion of variance that is shared by the two variables. Likewise, the coefficient of multiple determination (R^2) is the square of the multiple correlation coefficient. R^2 is a statistic that is obtained through multiple regression analysis, which is interpreted as the total proportion of variance in the criterion variable that is accounted for by *all* the predictors in the multiple regression equation.

In multiple regression, we usually expect that all of the included predictors will be correlated with the criterion—that's why we chose them as predictors in the first place. However, in most cases, the predictors will also be correlated with each other as well as with the criterion. This correlation among the predictor variables in a multiple regression is called multicollinearity and can create difficulty in interpreting the results. As you know, when variables are correlated, it indicates that they share something in common. When we have two or more predictors that are both correlated among themselves *and* are also correlated with the criterion, we may not know whether each predictor is accounting for a separate, unique portion of the variance in the criterion. Sometimes, both predictors may be accounting for the same variance in the criterion. If this is the case, using two predictors would not provide any more predictive power than simply using either one by itself. This can complicate the interpretation of the results of a multiple regression equation. The issue often arises when you need to answer the question of whether adding an additional test to a test battery is worth the effort and expense. Here is an example.

Suppose a college admissions officer wanted to investigate the degree to which he could predict students' 1st-year college GPA (the criterion) using measures of the student's success in high school as predictors. One of the predictors that he decides to use is the students' self-reported high school GPAs stated on their applications for admission. The other predictor he decides to use is the students' GPAs that are reported on their official high school transcripts. You probably can immediately see that the two predictors would be extremely highly correlated, because they are both measuring exactly the same thing. As a result, using both predictors in a multiple regression would not provide any independent predictive information regarding 1st-year college GPA. Therefore, there would be no reason to include them both as predictors. Anytime we use multiple predictors to predict a criterion, it is important to evaluate the extent to which they are predicting unique, nonoverlapping parts of the variance in the criteria. Multiple regression can help us to make that determination.

In Greater Depth Box 7.2 explores in more detail the interpretation of multiple regression results.

IN GREATER DEPTH BOX 7.2
INTERPRETING MULTIPLE REGRESSION RESULTS

When we interpret the results of a multiple regression analysis, the first thing that we typically look for is whether the value of R^2 is statistically significant. If it is significant, it indicates that all the predictors taken together are able to predict a significant amount of variance in the criterion. Next we look at the size of R^2 because the size tells us how much variance in the criterion is accounted for simultaneously by all the predictors that were included in the regression. Finally, we look at which of the b weights (if any) are significant. When a b weight is statistically significant, this means that the predictor associated with that b weight is explaining a unique, nonredundant amount of variance in the criterion that isn't already accounted for by any of the other predictors in the regression.

This ability of multiple regression to provide information on the amount of unique variance a predictor accounts for in a criterion after the variance accounted for by the other predictors is taken into account is one of its most important features. We use this information to establish evidence of validity when more than one predictor is used to predict a criterion. We do this by entering the predictors one at a time in a predetermined order into the regression. After each predictor is entered into the regression, the total variance accounted for in the criterion (R^2) is recomputed. If R^2 significantly increases when a new predictor is entered, there is evidence that the new predictor is accounting for additional variance in the criterion. If R^2 does not significantly increase when the new predictor is entered, it means that the predictor does not explain any variance in the criterion that has not already been explained by the predictors that have already been entered into the regression. This increment in R^2 is called R^2 change or, more simply, $R^2\Delta$ and is also referred to as **incremental validity.**

It is important to understand that the change in R^2 observed each time a new variable is entered into the regression will depend on the order we enter the predictors. When the predictors are correlated (which they almost always are), it will mean that they are both partially explaining the same variance in the criterion. As a result, the predictor entered first into the regression will be able to account for the largest amount of criterion variance. The next predictor entered into the regression will be able to account only for that variance in the criterion that wasn't already accounted for by the first predictor. If the two predictors are highly correlated, then most of the variance in the criterion that the second predictor could account for in the criterion would already have been accounted for by the first predictor. Therefore, the $R^2\Delta$ for the second predictor would be very low. However, if the order of entry of the predictors were reversed and the second predictor were entered first into the regression, it would now account for the larger portion of the variance in the criterion, and the original first predictor would now account for only a little additional variance. Therefore, the decision on the order that the predictors will be entered into the regression when investigating incremental validity is critical and must be carefully considered and explained by the researcher. The conclusions that are reached about the relative importance of the predictors might be very different just because of the order in which they were entered into the regression.

A small example will help clarify what we have explained above. Presume that a human resources (HR) manager wants to use two well-designed personality tests (call them Test H and Test N) to predict performance in a particular job. From prior research, she knows that both tests have independently been shown to be valid predictors of job performance in similar jobs, with validity coefficients of .30. So her thinking is that using both of the tests would be more predictive than using only one of them. To make sure of this, she gives all employees currently in the job both personality tests, and also collects the employees' performance ratings. She analyzes her data using multiple regression, using the test scores as the predictor and the performance ratings as the criterion. First she enters Test H into the regression and is pleased to see that R^2 is statistically significant for predicting the performance ratings. Next, she enters Test N into the regression and is surprised to see that the change in R^2 that occurs ($R^2\Delta$) is not significant. Test N doesn't seem to be adding any predictive ability at all. Just to check her results, she repeats the regression. But this time she enters Test N into the regression first. Now, R^2 for Test N

(Continued)

(Continued)

is significant, so she proceeds to add Test H into the equation, and again, R^2 does not increase significantly. What the HR manager has discovered is that both Test H and Test N are explaining the same variance in the criterion. Whichever test is entered into the regression first is explaining all the variance that can be explained in the criterion by these personality tests, leaving nothing for the second test to explain. Therefore, there is no incremental validity that will be gained by using the second test. Therefore, there is no reason to include the second test to select employees. The HR manager will need to decide which of the two tests she wants to include based on some other factor, such as cost.

We have a final observation about the example above. We discussed only the R^2 value that resulted from the regression, not the b weights associated with each predictor. This is because our interest was in determining the incremental validity of the predictors (the tests). Earlier in this section, we said that when a b weight is statistically significant, it means that the predictor associated with that b weight is explaining a unique, nonredundant amount of variance in the criterion after all of the variance accounted for in the criterion by every other predictor is taken into account. In the example above, although R^2 was significant, neither b weight would have been significant. This is because

b weights reflect only the amount of variance in the criterion that is not already explained by any other predictor in the regression. In our example, Test H and Test N accounted for the same variance in the criterion. That is, neither test was accounting for any unique variance over and above what the other test wasn't already accounting for. Therefore, although the overall regression was able to account for a significant amount of variance in the criterion, the variance that each test was individually accounting for was redundant. As a result, neither b weight would have been statistically significant.

The study described next is a good example of how researchers use multiple regression to gather evidence of incremental validity when using more than one predictor.

Chibnall and Detrick (2003) published a study that examined the usefulness of three personality inventories—the Minnesota Multiphasic Personality Inventory–2 (MMPI-2), the Inwald Personality Inventory (IPI; an established police officer screening test), and the Revised NEO Personality Inventory (NEO PI-R)—for predicting the performance of police officers. They administered the inventories to 79 police recruits and compared the test scores with two criteria: academic performance and physical performance. Tables 7.2 shows the outcome of the study for the academic performance criterion.

TABLE 7.2 ■ Multiple Regression Model for Predicting Academic Performance of Police Recruits (R^2 = .55)			
Step 1 **Demographic Variables**	**Step 2** **IPI Scales**	**Step 3** **MMPI-2 Scales**	**Step 4** **NEO PI-R Scales**
Recruit class	Trouble law	Depression	Assertiveness
Marital status	Antisocial	Hypomania	Ideas
Race	Obsessiveness		Depression
$R^2\Delta$ = .20	$R^2\Delta$ = .16	$R^2\Delta$ = .08	$R^2\Delta$ = .11

Source: Reprinted with permission from J. T. Chibnall and P. Detrick. (2003). "The NEO PI-R, Inwald Personality Inventory, and MMPI-2 in the prediction of police academy performance: A case for incremental validity." *American Journal of Criminal Justice*, 27(2), 33–248.

Note: Step refers to the order that a predictor is entered into the regression equation for predicting academic performance. Step 1 is the first predictor entered, Step 2 is the second, and so on. The predictors are the individual demographic characteristics or the subscales that reached significance. IPI = Inwald Personality Inventory, MMPI-2 = Minnesota Multiphasic Personality Inventory–2, NEO PI-R = Revised NEO Personality Inventory. $R^2\Delta$ is the percentage of incremental variance in academic performance contributed by each predictor when entered into the equation in the order shown.

When the researchers entered the demographic variables of recruit class, marital status, and race into the regression first, they jointly accounted for 20% of

the prediction of academic performance. In the second step, the researchers entered the test scores from three IPI scales. Table 7.2 shows the contribution of the IPI scales that contributed significantly to the prediction. Together, the three scales of the IPI contributed an additional 16% of the variance in the criterion ($R^2\Delta$). In the third step, the researchers entered two scales of the MMPI-2, and together they accounted for an additional 8% of the variance in the criterion. Finally, the researchers entered three scales of the NEO PI-R, and together they accounted for another

11% of the variance. Altogether, the demographic characteristics and the three inventories accounted for 55% of the variance in academic performance (R^2).

Physical performance was not predicted by demographic characteristics or most of the other tests included in the study. Only three dimensions of the NEO PI-R accounted for a significant amount of variance in physical performance (20%).

Chapter Summary

Evidence of validity based on test–criteria relations—the extent to which a test is related to independent behavior or events—is one of the major methods for obtaining evidence of test validity. The usual method for demonstrating this evidence is to correlate scores on the test with a measure of the behavior we wish to predict. This measure of independent behavior or performance is called the criterion.

Evidence of validity based on test–criteria relations depends on evidence that the scores on the test correlate significantly with an independent criterion—a standard used to measure some characteristic of an individual, such as a person's performance, attitude, or motivation. Criteria may be objective or subjective, but they must be reliable and valid. There are two methods for demonstrating evidence of validity based on test–criteria relations: predictive and concurrent.

There is a strong relationship between reliability and validity. If a test is not reliable, it will not correlate well with any criterion due to random measurement error. The resulting reduction of the validity coefficient over

what it would have been if there were less measurement error in the predictor is called attenuation. There are statistical procedures that can be used to correct for attenuation but their use can be controversial.

We use correlation to describe the relationship between a psychological test and a criterion. In this case, the correlation coefficient is referred to as the validity coefficient. Psychologists interpret validity coefficients using tests of significance and the coefficient of determination. Statistical artifacts such as unreliability and restriction can result in a reduction of the observed validity coefficient.

Either a linear regression equation or a multiple regression equation can be used to predict criterion scores from test scores. Predictions of success or failure on the criterion enable test users to use test scores for making decisions about hiring. When we use multiple regression we have to be aware that the predictors are likely to be correlated with one another and that can complicate the interpretation of the results.

Engaging in the Learning Process

Learning is the process of gaining knowledge and skills through schooling or studying. Although you can learn by reading the chapter material, attending class, and engaging in discussion with your instructor, more actively engaging in the learning process may help you better learn and retain chapter information. To help you actively engage in

the learning process, we encourage you to access our new supplementary student workbook. The workbook contains critical thinking activities to help you understand and apply information and help you make progress toward learning and retaining material. If you do not have a copy of the workbook, you can purchase a copy through sagepub.com.

Key Concepts

After completing your study of this chapter, you should be able to define each of the following terms. These terms are bolded in the text of this chapter and defined in the Glossary.

attenuation due to
    unreliability
b weight
coefficient of determination
coefficient of multiple
    determination
concurrent evidence
    of validity
correction for attenuation

criterion
criterion contamination
criterion-related validity
incremental validity
intercept
linear regression
multiple regression
objective criterion
operational validity

peers
predictive evidence
    of validity
restriction of range
slope
subjective criterion
test of significance
validity coefficient

Critical Thinking Questions

The following are some critical thinking questions to support the learning objectives for this chapter.

Learning Objectives	Critical Thinking Questions
Identify evidence of validity of a test based on its relationships to external criteria and describe two methods for obtaining this evidence.	• What is the benefit of making a distinction between the predictive and concurrent methods of establishing evidence of validity based on test content? • What do you think the impact would be on the results of a predictive validity study conducted in an organization if an unexpected layoff of personnel occurred before the study was completed?
Read and interpret validity studies.	• If you were a test publisher and a client who bought your test reported that a concurrent validity study they conducted didn't show evidence of validity, what are some of the question you would want to ask them to help understand their results? • If you were asked to do an in-class presentation on the topic of test validity based on a test's relationship with other variables, what are some of the criteria you would want to be included in your professor's evaluation of your presentation? Why?
Discuss how restriction of range occurs and its consequences.	• Under what circumstances would restriction of range not be of concern when conducting a validity study based on test-criterion relationships? • Do you think that restriction of range could also be a problem when estimating the reliability of a test? Explain.
Describe the differences between evidence of validity based on test content and evidence based on relationships with other variables.	• Do you think it would be possible for a test that had evidence for validity based on content to not show evidence of validity based on test-criterion relationships? Why or why not?

Learning Objectives	Critical Thinking Questions
Describe the difference between reliability/precision and validity.	• How would you explain, in your own words, how reliability affects validity? • Why is the following statement true: "A test can be reliable but not valid, but it can't be valid if it is not reliable."
Define and give examples of objective and subjective criteria, and explain why criteria must be reliable and valid.	• If you had to develop an objective criterion to use in a test validity study, what steps would you take to demonstrate that the criteria itself was valid?
Interpret a validity coefficient, calculate the coefficient of determination, and conduct a test of significance for a validity coefficient.	• If test X was shown to have a validity coefficient of .4, and test B had one of .3, how could you use the concept of the coefficient of determination to quantify the differences between the validities of the two tests? • If you were tutoring a classmate on the topic of validity, how would you explain the meaning of a statistically non-significant validity coefficient?
Understand why measured validity will be reduced by unreliability in the predictor or criterion measure and what statistical correction can be applied to adjust for this reduction.	• Job performance reviews are a usually a subjective criterion which have been shown to have a fairly low reliability coefficient of about .52. Nonetheless, they are a frequently used criteria to validate tests used for employee selection. Why might this fact be of concern in these types of validity studies? • How might the conclusions drawn form a validity study be affected if the correction for attenuation is applied to *both* the predictor measure and the criterion measure instead of only to the criterion measure as is usually recommended?
Explain the concept of operational or "true" validity and how it is calculated.	• Why is the concept of operational validity sometimes called "true validity"? In what sense is the validity "true"?
Explain the concept of regression, calculate and interpret a linear regression formula, and interpret a multiple regression formula.	• What are some of the characteristics that are shared between linear regression and multiple regression? What are some of the differences? • Why do you think that it is important for a researcher who is trying to develop a battery of tests to predict a psychological disorder to understand the concept of incremental validity? • A linear regression equation includes a number of important elements that help us understand the relationship between a predictor variable and a criterion variable. What are they and how does each one help us understand the relationship? • Some people may think that if we want to predict an outcome using tests, the more tests we use, the better the prediction will be. Why is this statement often false? When might it be true?

8

HOW DO WE GATHER EVIDENCE OF VALIDITY BASED ON A TEST'S RELATION TO CONSTRUCTS?

LEARNING OBJECTIVES

After completing your study of this chapter, you should be able to do the following:

- Discuss the concept of a construct, and give examples of theoretical constructs.

- Explain how the 2014 *Standards for Educational and Psychological Testing* treatment of constructs in testing differs from the more traditional usage of the term *construct validity*.

- Explain and give examples of the three steps of construct explication.

- Explain the process of establishing evidence of validity based on a test's relationship with other constructs.

- Explain how Campbell and Fiske's (1959) multitrait–multimethod matrix provides evidence of validity based on a test's relationship with other constructs.

- Discuss the roles of exploratory and confirmatory factor analysis in establishing validity.

"What does it mean when individuals have a dependency on alcohol? Does it mean they drink every day? Or when they drink they get very drunk? Do you have to lose your job, your house, and your family to be classified as an alcoholic?"

"My professor says that spanking can be classified as child abuse. I disagree! Child abusers are people who torture children and use them for their sexual pleasure. Discipline is something else."

"My 8-year-old has an IQ of 130. She makes good grades, but sometimes she says and does really silly things. I thought she was supposed to be smart."

Another chapter on validity? How many kinds of validity can there be? As you remember from our earlier chapters on validity, psychologists now think of validity as a single concept that can be demonstrated using various kinds of evidence. Evidence of validity may be drawn from a relationship of test scores with test content or from the relationship of test scores with other variables. So it is really not correct to speak of multiple types of validity, only different sources of *evidence* of validity.

So why do we need a chapter on validity based on the relationship of test scores with constructs when we already devoted a chapter to evidence of validity based on a test's relationship to other variables, specifically external criteria? To understand that, we first need to review what a construct is.

We previously told you that a **construct** is an attribute, trait, or characteristic that in itself is not directly observable but can only be inferred by looking at observable behaviors, which are hypothesized to indicate the presence of that construct. For example, we never really observe the construct of aggression, but we do observe behaviors that would lead us to conclude that a person might be demonstrating the construct of aggression. Likewise, if a test were designed to measure the construct of aggression, it might have questions relating to the frequency and intensity of these aggressive behaviors. Then a score on this test would be interpreted as indicating the test takers' standing on this hypothetical construct called aggression. The question of validity of this test then becomes a question of whether there is evidence that this inference is valid. Traditionally, this type of evidence was referred to as an indication that the test possessed **construct validity**.

The most current *Standards for Educational and Psychological Testing* (American Educational Research Association [AERA], American Psychological Association [APA], and National Council on Measurement in Education [NCME], 2014) no longer mentions the traditional term *construct validity* in the chapter on validity. Instead, most of what previously was referred to as evidence for construct validity is included under the topics of evidence of validity based on internal structure and evidence of validity based on relations with other variables. So why would we still have this chapter in our textbook? Because the ideas underlying the concept of constructs are crucially important to psychologists, even if our formal definitions have changed. Various tests designed to measure the same construct all ought to be measuring similar things, and we need to understand how we gather evidence for validity regardless of our terminology. Therefore, we take a more traditional approach to describing the role that psychological constructs play in testing, with the understanding that when we use the term *construct validity*, we are only using it for convenience and do not mean to imply that it is a separate type of validity.

This chapter defines and illustrates the terms *psychological construct*, *theory*, and *nomological network*. Because establishing evidence of validity involves accumulating and relating all of the psychometric information known about a test, we show how familiar concepts, such as reliability, evidence of validity based on test content, and evidence of validity based on a test's relationships with other variables, are linked together. In addition, we discuss how convergent evidence of validity and discriminant evidence of validity are two other strategies used for establishing validity based on a test's relationships with other variables. This evidence focuses on the constructs that a test is designed to measure as opposed to the test's relationship to an external criterion. Finally, we discuss experimental methods used to establish evidence of validity for a test based on its internal structure, including two procedures: exploratory factor analysis and confirmatory factor analysis.

THE NOTION OF CONSTRUCT VALIDITY

What Is a Construct?

Before discussing how to establish evidence of construct validity, we need to define what we mean by a theoretical or hypothetical construct. Psychologists gain their understanding of people and other organisms by focusing their attention on concrete and abstract constructs. **Behavior**—actions that are observable and measurable—are concrete constructs. Underlying attitudes or attributes that exist in our imaginations are abstract constructs. Intelligence, beauty, love, and self-esteem all are psychological constructs, but your instructor cannot "see" constructs like intelligence or self-esteem or bring a bucket of intelligence or a big box of self-esteem to class. These constructs exist in theory. We cannot observe or measure them directly. They are hypothetical.

We can, however, observe and measure the behaviors that show evidence of these constructs. Psychological theories propose the presence of constructs, such as intelligence, beauty, love, and self-esteem, and make predictions about behaviors that are related to them. By observing and measuring those behaviors, we assume that we have measured the abstract construct. As an example of this process, Kevin Murphy and Charles Davidshofer (1994) used the theoretical construct of gravity. Before Isaac Newton, the notion of gravity did not exist. Newton theorized that apples fall to the earth because of a concept he called *gravity*. We cannot see gravity, but we see what we assume to be its result—falling apples!

As you can see from the statements at the beginning of this chapter, definitions of constructs can vary from person to person. Many times the definitions that professionals use for constructs such as alcoholism, child abuse, and intelligence differ from those used by the general population. Psychologists even disagree among themselves, so they must clearly define constructs before they can measure them. To illustrate this process in terms of testing, let's consider a classic and still important abstract construct proposed by Albert Bandura, a well-known cognitive psychologist. Bandura (1977) suggested the existence of a construct he called *self-efficacy*—a person's expectations and beliefs about his or her own competence and ability to accomplish an activity or a task. He proposed that "expectations of personal efficacy determine whether coping behavior will be initiated, how much effort will be expended, and how long it will be sustained in the face of obstacles and aversive experiences" (p. 191).

Figure 8.1 illustrates Bandura's theory of self-efficacy. People form their opinions about their own self-efficacy from their own performance accomplishments, their experiences watching others perform (vicarious experience), the messages they receive from others about their performance (verbal persuasion), and their emotional arousal. "Mode of Induction" in the model shows the various ways a person receives information. The test developer can use this model as a test plan for constructing an instrument that measures self-efficacy. For instance, the instrument may ask test takers questions about their experiences with each source of information.

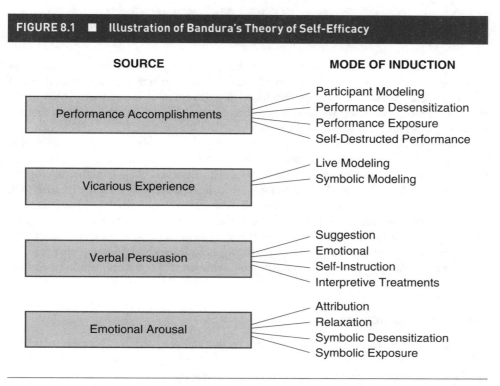

FIGURE 8.1 ■ Illustration of Bandura's Theory of Self-Efficacy

Source: Bandura, A. (1977). Self-efficacy: Toward a unifying theory of behavioral change. *Psychological Review, 84,* 191–215. Copyright © 1977 by the American Psychological Association.

Since Bandura published his self-efficacy theory, researchers have developed numerous tests that measure general self-efficacy—individuals' expectations of competency and resulting coping behaviors and extended effort in general (Lee & Bobko, 1994; Sherer et al., 1982; Tipton & Worthington, 1984). In addition to general measures, researchers have developed tests that measure self-efficacy for specific tasks such as mathematics (Pajares & Miller, 1995), computer skills (Murphy, Coover, & Owen, 1989), social interactions (Wheeler & Ladd, 1982), and career choice (Betz & Hackett, 1986), to name only a few.

Most research using tests of self-efficacy has borne out Bandura's predictions about coping behavior (Bandura, Barbaranelli, Caprara, & Pastorelli, 1996). In addition, researchers have found self-efficacy to be a good predictor of performance (Sharpley & Ridgway, 1993; Tam, 1996; Weinberg, Gould, & Jackson, 1979). Test Spotlight 8.1 in Appendix A describes a test that measures the self-efficacy concept specifically in the area of mathematics.

In the past, psychologists had gathered evidence of the validity of tests by pursuing two of the methods we discussed in earlier chapters—validity based on test content and validity based on a test's relationship to external criteria. A number of theorists, however, challenged these strategies because this evidence of validity did not link the testing instrument to an accepted theory of psychological behavior (T. B. Rogers, 1995). In 1954, the APA published recommendations that established a new method for establishing validity in which the researcher provides evidence that the testing instrument measures behavior predicted by a psychological theory. The APA (1954) called this evidence *construct validity* and defined it as the extent to which the test measures a theoretical

See **Test Spotlight 8.1** in Appendix A for details about the Mathematics Self-Efficacy Scale.

construct. The process of establishing construct validity for a test is a gradual accumulation of evidence that the scores on the test relate to observable behaviors in the ways predicted by the underlying theory.

The process of establishing evidence of construct validity implies one important consideration pointed out by Cronbach and Meehl (1955): When test users accept evidence of construct validity, they must accept the underlying definition of the construct used in the validation process. In other words, test users accept the definition of the construct used by those who developed and validated the test.

At first glance, this consideration does not seem to be a problem. Recall, however, that definitions of a construct may vary from theorist to theorist. An example of this variation is the numerous definitions given to the construct of intelligence. Who is highly intelligent? Is it someone who always receives perfect grades? Is it someone who is highly creative? Is it someone who is perfectly rational and logical? Is it someone who displays knowledge and skills greater than those displayed by others of the same chronological age? Is intelligence inherited? Is it a series of learned behaviors? Is it a combination of some or all of these traits? As you can see, choosing a test to measure intelligence means choosing a test that matches your definition of intelligence. Without this consideration, the test scores would be confusing or meaningless.

Construct Explication

Measurement of an abstract construct depends on our ability to observe and measure related behavior. Murphy and Davidshofer (1994) described three steps for defining or explaining a psychological construct, referred to as **construct explication**:

1. Identify the behaviors that relate to the construct.

2. Identify other constructs that may be related to the construct being explained.

3. Identify behaviors related to similar constructs, and determine whether these behaviors are related to the original construct.

A construct validation study of the Self-Efficacy Scale conducted by Mark Sherer and colleagues (1982) illustrates these principles of construct explication. These researchers were interested in validating a scale that measures self-efficacy. They reviewed the research of Bandura and others and determined that positive correlations exist between therapeutic changes in behaviors and changes in self-efficacy. In other words, as an individual's self-efficacy increases, the individual's behavior in treatment is likely to improve as well (Step 1). Sherer and colleagues also noted that past performance or expectations are related to self-efficacy (Step 2). In addition, individuals who have experienced numerous successes in the past are likely to have developed high self-efficacy, as demonstrated by their persistence in pursuing goals with which they have limited experience (Step 3). Figure 8.2 provides a model of this explication process.

The process of construct explication is a critical part of test development. After all, if we can't clearly define what we mean when we speak of abstract constructs, how can we build a test that reliably measures them? Sometimes this process of construct explication results in new ways to view and define existing constructs. For instance, the abstract concepts of anxiety and anger are familiar to us all. If you were asked to engage in a construct explication exercise, you probably could easily identify what observable behaviors you believe are associated with these constructs and name some related (and unrelated) constructs.

FIGURE 8.2 ■ The Process of Construct Explication

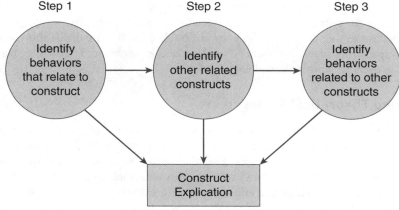

When Charles Spielberger (1966) and his associates were doing their long-term research on anxiety, anger, and curiosity, they realized that there might be another dimension that helped define these constructs beyond what they had considered in the past. The new dimension was the concept of trait duration. Working from a conceptualization of anxiety initially proposed by Cattel and Scheier (1961), they asked, "Is the attribute a temporary state or an ongoing part of a person's personality and therefore a trait?" Two well-known tests that came out of this research are the State–Trait Anger Expression Inventory-2 (STAXI-2) and the State–Trait Anxiety Inventory (STAI). The STAI attempts to distinguish between a temporary condition of anxiety—perhaps brought on by situational circumstances—and a long-standing quality of anxiety that has become a part of the person's personality. Likewise, the STAXI-2 assesses temporary anger (state anger) and angry temperament and angry reaction (trait anger). The way Spielberger explicated the constructs of anxiety and anger now allows us to differentiate between two different conceptualizations of them: **state** and **trait**.

Test Spotlight 8.2 in Appendix A describes the STAXI-2 in more detail.

As theorists identify more constructs and behaviors that are interrelated, they construct what Cronbach and Meehl (1955) referred to as a **nomological network**—a method for defining a construct by illustrating its relation to as many other constructs and behaviors as possible. (Cronbach [1988] later amended his earlier vision of a nomological network, noting that actually identifying a complex model of associations for a construct had proved to be difficult in practice.) However, a listing of a particular construct's relations and non-relations with other constructs and tests can provide a number of **hypotheses**—educated guesses or predictions—about the behaviors that people who have small or large quantities of the construct should display. For instance, based on the research on self-efficacy, we expect people with high self-efficacy to express positive attitudes regarding their own competence and to display persistence in accomplishing new and difficult tasks. Establishing evidence of construct validity, then, is the process of testing the predictions made by that model.

GATHERING EVIDENCE OF CONSTRUCT VALIDITY

To understand the process of establishing evidence of construct validity, we apply the scientific method for testing the hypotheses proposed by theories. We can divide this process into two parts: gathering theoretical evidence and gathering psychometric evidence. Figure 8.3 provides an overview of this methodology.

Gathering Theoretical Evidence

The first step in the validation process is establishing a listing of associations the construct has with other constructs. As we illustrated with the example of self-efficacy, researchers seek to find relationships with other constructs. They then review as many studies of the construct as possible to establish the construct's relation with observable and measurable behaviors. Establishing evidence of construct validity requires a thorough understanding of the construct in question, and there is no substitute for careful reading of all available literature—both theoretical observations and empirical studies. Researchers then develop a model of the construct that links it to other constructs and observable behaviors.

Second, researchers propose one or more experimental hypotheses using the test as an instrument for measuring the construct. If the test is a true or valid measure of the construct, scores on the test should perform in accordance with the predictions made for the construct.

Let's return to the validation of the Self-Efficacy Scale (Sherer et al., 1982) to examine how this process works. A review of theoretical and empirical studies of self-efficacy revealed that self-efficacy is linked to a number of personality characteristics: locus of control, social

FIGURE 8.3 ■ Methodology for Establishing Construct Validity

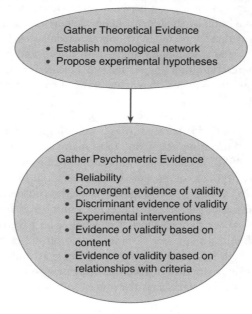

desirability, ego strength, interpersonal competency, and self-esteem. Sherer and colleagues hypothesized that scores on the Self-Efficacy Scale would be significantly correlated with personality tests measuring each of these constructs but that the correlation would not be strong enough to suggest that the scales were measuring exactly the same construct. Consequently, the researchers designed a study to test this hypothesis.

Note that Sherer and colleagues (1982) proposed a specific hypothesis based on the accepted definition of self-efficacy and the nomological network they constructed. According to Cronbach (1988, 1989), the preferred method for establishing evidence of construct validity is to propose a hypothesis based on the nomological network and to test it. He referred to the alternative as *dragnet empiricism*, which involves collecting evidence based on convenience rather than a specific hypothesis. Dragnet empiricism, as you probably realize, is not an acceptable way to establish evidence of construct validity.

Gathering Psychometric Evidence

As you recall, establishing evidence of construct validity for a test involves an ongoing process of gathering evidence that the scores on the test relate to observable behaviors in the ways predicted by the underlying theory and the nomological network. There are a number of ways to establish quantitative evidence to suggest that the test has construct validity.

Reliability/Precision

As you recall, reliability/precision is an essential characteristic for a psychological test. Evidence of reliability/precision is important; otherwise, the test scores may correspond to theoretical predictions one time but might not do so again. In addition, the theory underlying psychological testing suggests that a test cannot have a stronger correlation with any other variable than it does with itself, and therefore we can use estimates of reliability/precision to evaluate the strength of correlations with other variables that are related to the theoretical construct.

Convergent Evidence of Validity

If the test is measuring a particular construct, we expect the scores on the test to correlate strongly with scores on other tests that measure the same or similar constructs. This correlation provides us with **convergent evidence of validity**. For example, researchers have developed a number of tests to measure general self-efficacy as well as self-efficacy related to a specific task. We would expect two measures of general self-efficacy to yield strong, positive, and statistically significant correlations. They may also correlate with scores from task-specific tests, but not to as great an extent.

This concept always raises a very good question: If there is already a test that measures the construct, why develop another one? A test author might develop another test to create parallel forms, create a test for specific populations (e.g., children, people who speak another language), revise the test to increase reliability and validity, reproduce the test in another format (e.g., for administration by computer or in a shortened version), or develop a test that represents an altered definition of the underlying construct. In each of these cases, the original test and the new test would yield different scores, but we would expect the two sets of scores to correlate strongly.

If the test scores correlate with measures of constructs that the underlying theory says are related, we would also describe those correlations as convergent evidence of validity. For example, Bandura's (1977) theory of self-efficacy suggests that self-efficacy is related to measures of competency. Sherer and colleagues (1982) administered their measure of self-efficacy and a measure of interpersonal competency to 376 students and found a moderate correlation

(r = .45) between the two tests. This correlation coefficient, or validity coefficient, describes the extent of convergent evidence of validity for their measure of general self-efficacy.

Sometimes students confuse *convergent evidence of validity* with the *concurrent method of gathering evidence of validity*. Convergent evidence of validity is gathered when a researcher reviews the literature for other tests that claim to measure constructs that are the same as, or similar to, the construct in which the researcher is interested. If the tests are given to the same group of people and there is a significant correlation between the scores, then convergent evidence of validity has been demonstrated. On the other hand, the concurrent method is a strategy for establishing validity evidence based on the correlation that the test scores have with a specific external criterion measure gathered around the same time that the test is administered. Criteria, as you recall, are objective or subjective measures of behavior, such as job performance ratings, course grades, and results of interviews.

Discriminant Evidence of Validity

Just as we would expect some tests to correlate with our new tests, there are other tests we would *not* expect to correlate with our test. When the test scores do not correlate with unrelated constructs, we can say that the test is demonstrating **discriminant evidence of validity**. For example, a test that measures skill at performing numerical calculations would not be expected to correlate with a test that measures reading comprehension. If the correlation between the numerical calculations test and a test of reading comprehension is zero (or not statistically significant), there is discriminant evidence of validity for the numerical calculations test.

Coombs and Holladay (2004) are test authors who researched a new test, the Workplace Aggression Tolerance Questionnaire, which assesses workplace aggression behaviors such as physical and verbal, active and passive, and direct and indirect forms of aggression. The authors correlated the test scores with the scores from the Marlowe–Crowne Social Desirability Scale, which measures a person's need for being perceived favorably. They found a weak relationship (r = −.18, p < .01) between aggressive behaviors and wishing to be perceived favorably. The researchers presented this weak relationship as discriminant evidence of validity because it is not likely that aggressive persons are worried about being perceived favorably by others.

Multitrait–Multimethod Design

Donald Campbell and Donald Fiske (1959) cleverly combined the need to collect evidence of reliability/precision, convergent evidence of validity, and discriminant evidence of validity into one study. They called it the **multitrait–multimethod (MTMM) design** for investigating construct validity. Using this approach, investigators test for "*convergence* across *different* measures . . . of the same 'thing' . . . and for *divergence* between measures . . . of related but conceptually distinct 'things'" (Cook & Campbell, 1979, p. 61). In other words, the researcher chooses two or more constructs that are unrelated in theory and two or more types of tests—such as objective, projective, and a peer rating—to measure each of the constructs. Data are collected on each participant in the study on each construct using each method. Figure 8.4 shows an MTMM correlation matrix adapted from Campbell and Fiske's article.

The figure shows all the correlations between three different traits when each are measured by three different methods. Extraversion is labeled as Trait A, impulse control is labeled as Trait B, and creativity is labeled as Trait C. A self-report is Measurement Method 1, a peer evaluation is Measurement Method 2, and an objective test is Measurement Method 3. So, for instance, if you wanted to know the correlation between extraversion and creativity when both are measured by a self-report, you would look at the top of the table to locate the trait of extraversion under the method heading of self-report, A_1 (which is the first column of the

FIGURE 8.4 ■ A Multitrait–Multimethod Correlation Matrix

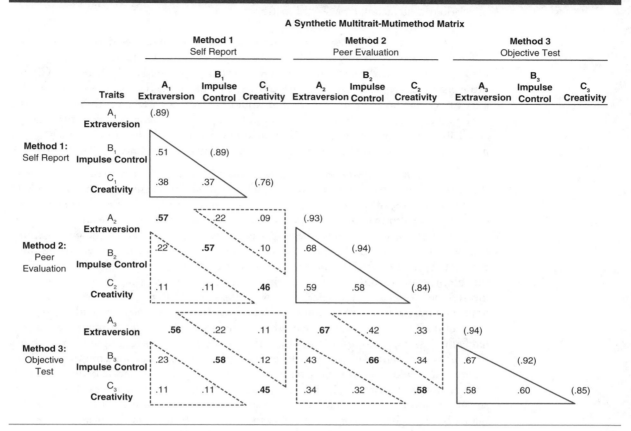

Source: Adapted from Campbell and Fiske (1959).

Note: The validity diagonals are the three sets of bolded values. The reliability diagonals are the three sets of values in parentheses. Each heterotrait–monomethod triangle is enclosed by a solid line. Each heterotrait–heteromethod triangle is enclosed by a broken line.

table). Then you would move down the rows until you located the trait of creativity as also measured by a self-report. This is found in row 3 of the table (C_1). The correlation listed the intersection of column 1 and row 3 is the correlation of extraversion and creativity when both are measured by a self-report. The correlation is .38. For another example, if you wanted to know the correlation between impulse control when measured by a peer evaluation (B_2) and impulse control when it is measured by an objective test (B_3), you would find that correlation at the intersection of column 5 and row 8 of the table. That correlation is .66 in our example. You probably also have noticed that some of the correlations are enclosed by broken or solid triangles, others are in parentheses, and some others are bolded. This is to make it easy to identify correlations that have similar meanings when the matrix is used to provide evidence for construct validity. We will explain each of these groupings in the next section.

As we have discussed, a **multitrait–multimethod correlation matrix** presents all the correlations between a group of different traits, attributes, or constructs, each measured by two or more different measurement methods or tests. While at first glance, an MTMM correlation matrix may seem complicated to interpret, there are really only four different pieces of information contained in the matrix. Each one of those pieces of information is a simple correlation coefficient. We will explain each of those correlations and how taken together, they provide a wealth of information pertaining to evidence of construct validity. Here are the four types of correlations contained in an MTMM matrix:

1. *Heterotrait–heteromethod correlations:* These are the correlations between two different (hetero) traits measured by two different (hetero) methods. An example from Figure 8.4 would be the correlation between creativity measured by a self-report (C_1) and extraversion measured by an objective test (A_3). In this case, the measures share neither a trait nor a method in common, so you would expect this correlation to be low relative to the other correlations in the table. In our example MTMM matrix, the correlation is .11. This correlation is considered discriminant evidence for validity. In Figure 8.4, all the heterotrait–heteromethod correlations are enclosed by a broken line.

2. *Heterotrait–monomethod correlations:* These are correlations between two different (hetero) traits measured by the same (mono) method. An example from our MTMM would be the correlation between impulse control measured by a peer evaluation (B_2) and creativity (C_2) also measured by a peer evaluation. In this case, the correlations are measuring the relationship between *different* traits that were measured using the *same* method. Can you guess whether the correlations should be large or small relative to the other correlations in the table? If you guessed moderately large, you would be correct. Even though the traits are different, the fact that both were evaluated using the same method of measurement can create a correlation between the scores. This correlation is often referred to as method variance, or sometimes method bias. In this example, it would occur if the peer's rating on the first trait influenced his or her rating on the second trait. So if a peer tended to give high ratings on impulse control, then the same peer might be more likely to also give high ratings of creativity (even if the person being rated were not that creative). The reverse would occur when the rating was low, causing the correlation between impulse control and creativity to be higher than it should have been if it were based only on the actual relationship between the traits. In our example, the correlation in our MTMM matrix is .58, higher than one might expect two traits to be that, on the surface, don't seem to be related. In Figure 8.4, all the heterotrait–monomethod correlations are enclosed by a solid line. You can see that in general, they are larger than the heterotrait–heteromethod correlations. This is due to the variance the scores share because of the common method of measurement.

3. *Monotrait–heteromethod correlations:* These are the correlations between the same (mono) traits measured by two different (hetero) methods. An example of this would be the correlation of extraversion as measured by peer evaluation (A_2) with extraversion measured by an objective test (A_3). In this case, we are correlating two traits, which are both supposed to measure the same construct using two different methods. We would expect this correlation to be larger than most in the MTMM matrix. This is our convergent evidence for validity. In an MTMM matrix, these correlations appear on what is referred to as the validity diagonal, and are printed in boldface type in Figure 8.4.

4. *Monotrait–monomethod correlations:* These are the correlations between the same (mono) traits using the same (method). This is equivalent to correlating a test with itself, so it is really a reliability coefficient. Because a test should not be able to correlate more highly with any other variable than it does with itself, these correlations will be the highest in an MTMM matrix. In Figure 8.4, monotrait–monomethod correlations appear in parenthesis along what is called the reliability diagonal. An example of this would be the correlation between creativity as measured by a self-report (C_1) with itself, which in our MTMM is .76.

Later in this chapter we will describe how researchers actually used an MTMM approach to provide both convergent and discriminant evidence for validity in a new test they developed.

Experimental Interventions

Experimental interventions in which the test is used as a dependent variable (the variable that is being measured by the research) make a substantial contribution to the argument for evidence of construct validity. If the underlying theory predicts that a course of treatment or training will increase or decrease the psychological construct, a significant difference between pretest scores and posttest scores would be evidence of construct validity for the test used to measure the construct. For example, if a clinician conducted a 12-week course of treatment intended to raise participants' self-efficacy, she might administer Sherer and colleagues' (1982) Self-Efficacy Scale, along with other reliable and valid measures of self-efficacy, to participants at the beginning of treatment and at the end of treatment. If the other measures indicated that the treatment successfully raised individual participants' perceptions of self-efficacy and the Self-Efficacy Scale showed comparable results, we could say that the study provided evidence of construct validity for the Self-Efficacy Scale.

Another study that provides evidence of construct validity for a test would be one that verifies a prediction that group membership affects the construct. For instance, if the underlying theory predicts that one group will have higher or lower mean test scores than another group and the data yield such a result, the study provides evidence of construct validity.

For example, researchers administered the Counselor Self-Efficacy Scale (CSES) to 138 participants who were either students enrolled in graduate counseling courses or licensed professional psychologists (Melchert, Hays, Wiljanen, & Kolocek, 1996). Because Bandura's (1977) theory states that experience with a particular activity is likely to raise self-efficacy for that activity, the researchers hypothesized that those who had higher levels of training and experience would score higher on the CSES. Their data yielded four groups—1st-year master's students, 2nd-year master's students, post-master's doctoral students, and professional psychologists—who were differentiated by scores on the CSES that increased as levels of training and experience increased. These data provide evidence of construct validity for the CSES.

Evidence of Validity Based on Content

A test demonstrates evidence of validity based on its content when its questions are a representative sample of a well-defined test domain. This type of evidence is usually the appropriate approach for math, reading, or other test domains with known boundaries. Because psychological constructs exist primarily in our imaginations and are not observable, it is more difficult to define a test domain well enough to construct a test that contains a representative sample from the construct. In some cases, however, psychological constructs do lend themselves to content validation, and when evidence of validity based on content can be provided, it greatly strengthens the case for construct validity.

Cronbach (1989) distinguished between content-based evidence and construct-based evidence of validity in this way:

> Content validation stops with a demonstration that the test conforms to a specification; however, the claim that the specification is well chosen embodies a CV [construct validity] claim. . . . Any interpretation invokes constructs if it reaches beyond the specific, local, concrete situation that was observed. (p. 151)

Bandura's (1977) construct of self-efficacy is one that lends itself to content-based evidence of validity because it specifies four sources of self-efficacy: performance accomplishments, vicarious experience, verbal persuasion, and emotional arousal. To develop a test plan for an instrument that measures self-efficacy, the test developer would stipulate that an equal number of questions would represent a connection to each source of self-efficacy (Fritzsche & McIntire, 1997). Showing that the test questions do indeed reflect the four sources of self-efficacy, however, is a matter of construct validity. Such information, in addition to evidence of reliability, convergent evidence of validity, and discriminant evidence of validity, substantially strengthens the argument that the test measures the theoretical construct it was designed to measure.

Evidence of Validity Based on Relationships With External Criteria

Likewise, although evidence of validity based on a test's relationship with external criteria relies solely on the statistical relationship between the test and that criterion, it too can provide evidence of construct validity. If the underlying theory predicts that a psychological construct is related to observable behaviors, such as job performance or a cluster of behaviors that denote a mental disorder, evidence of that relationship adds to the evidence of construct validity as well. In other words, when an underlying theory *explains* the relation between a predictor and a criterion, there is evidence of construct validity.

There are numerous examples of this validation strategy for tests of self-efficacy. Bandura's (1977) theory predicts that persons who have high self-efficacy will perform better than persons with low self-efficacy, and many validation studies of measures of self-efficacy include evidence of validity based on this relationship as well as convergent evidence of validity and reliability. For instance, Sherer and colleagues (1982), in addition to demonstrating convergent evidence of validity for their measure of general self-efficacy, demonstrated criterion-based evidence of validity by finding significant correlations between self-efficacy scores (predictor) and current employment, number of jobs quit, and number of times fired (criteria). Because Bandura's theory predicts these relationships, evidence of criterion-related validity strengthens the argument that the instrument is construct valid.

Multiple Studies

Because gathering evidence of construct validity is an ongoing process, the argument that there is evidence for the construct validity is strengthened when the test demonstrates one or all of these characteristics in a number of studies conducted on different samples of participants by different researchers. Cross-referencing of such studies suggests that individual studies were not unduly affected by biases related to the experimenter or to special characteristics of the sample, and therefore test users can conclude that the test faithfully represents and measures the underlying construct.

FACTOR ANALYSIS

Over the past three decades, the introduction and availability of computer software to psychological researchers and test developers has allowed them to broaden studies of the constructs that tests are measuring by identifying the **factors**—the underlying concepts or constructs that the tests or groups of test questions are measuring. To investigate underlying aspects of constructs, researchers use a statistical technique called **factor analysis**—an advanced procedure based on the concept of correlation that helps investigators explain why items within a test are correlated or why two different tests are correlated (Murphy & Davidshofer, 1994).

Factor analysis is a statistical procedure that can be used to identify whether the pattern of correlations among all the questions on a test can be more simply explained by a smaller number of underlying constructs, or factors. For instance, if we review the correlations among all the items on a test that contains 200 arithmetic questions, we would probably see that certain items are more correlated with a group of other items while also being less correlated with a different group of items. The pattern of these correlations might be explainable if certain items were more related to one underlying construct, while other items were more related to a different construct. For instance, you might observe that a division item was more correlated with other division items, but not as correlated with addition items. This pattern of results could be explainable based on a person's standing on the four underlying constructs that the test was designed to measure—addition, subtraction, multiplication, and division. Not all tests or measures have multiple underlying factors. Some tests or measures are referred to as unidimensional because there is only a single underlying factor that can explain most of the variance in the scores. In our arithmetic test example, it is also possible that there might be only a single factor that can explain the full pattern of correlations between the individual questions—general mathematical ability. These tests are sometimes called homogenous. On the other hand, other tests may be multidimensional in nature because there is more than one underlying factor that explains the variance in test scores. These measures are sometimes referred to as heterogeneous.

Although early researchers calculated factor analyses by hand laboriously or later, with the help of calculators, we can now conduct factor analyses using statistical software such as SPSS, SAS, and LISREL. The researcher enters the raw data (usually individual answers to test questions), and the software program calculates a correlation matrix of all variables or test questions. The software program then uses the correlation matrix to calculate a factor solution based on each test question's relationship to the other test questions. As we explained above, factors are formed by finding groups of questions that are more correlated with each other than they are with other questions on the test.

Here is another example. If we had a test that contained both reading and arithmetic questions, we might expect it to produce two factors—one for the verbal factor (as represented by the reading questions) and one for the mathematical factor (as represented by the arithmetic questions). This is because we would expect that each person's answers to the arithmetic questions would be more correlated with their answers to other arithmetic questions than with their answers to the reading questions. As the test questions group together, they form factors—underlying dimensions that measure the same trait or attribute.

There is also a subjective element to factor analysis. Once the program produces the statistical results which show which items group together to form a factor, the researcher must review the groupings to see if they make sense based on the constructs the test items were designed to measure. For instance, if a test developer is creating items for a personality test that were designed to measure the constructs of conscientiousness and extraversion, she would first create items that she believes are related to these constructs based on prior research or some underlying theory. The expectation would be that a factor analysis conducted after many people took the test would show that the items designed to measure conscientiousness will form one factor, and the extraversion items will form a separate and distinct factor. The test developer would evaluate this by actually looking at the content of all the items that grouped together. If the developer finds that that some of the conscientious items seemed to be more related to the extraversion factor or vice versa, the developer would need to carefully review those items to try to determine why this happened. Perhaps the items are worded poorly, or perhaps they were incorrectly classified when the test was designed. Sometimes, the factor analysis shows that certain items don't seem to share anything in common with any of the other items. In these cases, the items need to be rewritten or deleted from the test altogether as they may be measuring something unique that is not related to the any of the constructs that the test is designed to measure. If these items are left in the test, they would adversely affect the test's construct validity.

Exploratory Factor Analysis

Besides using factor analysis as an aid to test development, researchers can also use factor analysis as a means of exploring underlying factors of psychological tests. In an **exploratory factor analysis**, researchers do not propose a formal hypothesis about the factors that underlie a set of test scores, but instead use the procedure broadly to help identify underlying components.

Although it is well beyond the scope of this book to provide a comprehensive explanation of exploratory factor analysis, we want to give you an idea of how some of the information that exploratory factor analysis provides can be used to help understand the constructs that underlie a test or measurement instrument. The notion that tests items are designed to reflect the presence of specific underlying constructs lies at the heart of construct validity and is why factor analysis is a frequently used statistical technique to help establish evidence for its presence. What is generally referred to as factor analysis actually is a group of related statistical techniques, which also includes a technique called principal-components analysis. Although there some technical differences between the approaches, we will not cover them in this section. A classic text on factor analysis, which covers the subject in detail, is Gorsuch's (1983) *Factor Analysis*.

When we analyze the responses to a set of properly performing test questions, we see that people's responses to the questions are not the same; rather, they vary. We would expect this because people differ on the amount of the underlying construct(s) that the test is designed to measure. Also, as we discussed in our chapter on reliability, there is always additional variance in the scores due to measurement error. The basic question that exploratory factor analysis seeks to answer is the degree to which this variance in the responses on all the test questions can be accounted for by a smaller number of underlying constructs. In the language of factor analysis, these underlying constructs are referred to as either factors or components. Because of this, factor analysis is frequently viewed as a data reduction technique. The reason why it is "exploratory" is that the researcher is not hypothesizing that a specific factor structure is present in the data. Rather, the analysis is literally designed to help him explore and understand the factor structure(s) that may be present in the existing data.

In order to perform a factor analysis, you first need to compute the correlations between all the items on the test, survey, or other measurement instrument that you are analyzing. Fortunately, all factor analysis programs will compute this correlation matrix for you as the first part of the process. If you were to look at such a correlation matrix, you would be able to see that some of the items on the test are more highly correlated with some items or groups of items than with others. When an item is correlated with another item, it means that they share something in common (i.e., they are measuring similar things). For instance, on a personality test, you would expect that items that were designed to measure the same trait would be more correlated with one another than they would with items designed to measure a different trait. Another way of saying the same thing is that items designed to indicate the presence of a particular construct will correlate better with other items deigned to indicate the presence of the same construct than they will with items designed to indicate the presence of a different construct. If the test were designed to measure a single construct but the exploratory factor analysis suggested that there were three factors that could account for the correlations among the test items, the test developer would have to look at the test items to understand why this occurred. This result would call into question the construct validity of the test. Therefore, by reviewing the output of an exploratory factor analysis, we can gain valuable insight to the construct structure present in the test, and thereby draw conclusions about its construct validity.

In Greater Depth Box 8.1 provides a more detailed discussion of exploratory factor analysis along with an actual example of its use in an applied setting to provide evidence of construct validity.

IN GREATER DEPTH BOX 8.1
USING EXPLORATORY FACTOR ANALYSIS TO PROVIDE EVIDENCE OF CONSTRUCT VALIDITY

To give you a better sense of exploratory factor analysis and how it is used to establish evidence of construct validity, we are going to present an actual example of how one of your textbook authors used it to investigate evidence of construct validity of a structured interview used for employee selection. This interview was designed to measure four different constructs that a job analysis had determined were important for success in a customer service job. The constructs were communication (four questions), decision making (three questions), problem solving (three questions), and customer focus (six questions). Each question was designed to evaluate a different behavior related to each competency. For instance, the communication competency evaluated the behaviors of clarity of communication, listening skills, and effectively responding to questions asked. Each behavior was rated on a five-point scale of effectiveness. So for each interview, there were 16 different ratings made across the four competencies the interview was designed to measure.

Table 8.1 presents the correlation matrix for all the interview ratings that was the input into the factor analysis program. Looking at the table, we can see that communications questions Q1, Q2, and Q3 seem to be much more highly correlated with one another than they are with the other questions on the interview, but the pattern of correlations among these other questions is much harder to identify. This is because there are so many numbers in the table, and the magnitudes of the differences in the correlation coefficients are smaller than in the communication questions. Finding meaning in the pattern of correlations is exactly the type of problem factor analysis can help us solve.

The first step in an exploratory factor analysis is to decide how many factors to attempt to extract from the data (the correlation matrix in this example). Generally, two approaches are used for the factor extraction. The first is to let the factor analysis program make the decision using a purely statistical criterion. The program continues to attempt to extract factors until the factors no longer account for some minimum amount of variance in the variables, at which point the extraction stops.

The second approach to factor extraction is to tell the factor analysis program to extract a specific

number of factors. The number of factors requested would be based on the researcher's knowledge of the data. In the present example, the interview we were analyzing was designed to measure four specific constructs, so we used that knowledge as a starting point and instructed the program to attempt to extract four factors from the data. What we are hoping is most of the variance in the scores on the 16 questions will be explainable by just these four factors. If this turns out not to be the case, we would continue our exploration (hence the name exploratory factor analysis) by looking at solutions that contain a different number of factors—both more and less. Ultimately, the researcher has to make the somewhat subjective decision of how many factors should be retained as a solution, using some criteria that we discuss next.

When we instructed the program to attempt to extract four factors, we found that we could explain 67%, or two thirds, of the variance of the scores on the 16 interview questions with the four factors the computer extracted. Given the design of the interview, this is exactly what we would like to see. However, even though this looks promising, these results by themselves don't provide sufficient evidence for construct validity. We first have to look at some of the other output from the factor analysis before we reach a conclusion.

We next need to examine which interview questions were most strongly associated with each of the four factors. What we hope for is that all the questions that were designed to measure each construct in the interview are strongly associated with a single factor. Ideally, all the communication questions should be associated with their own factor, all the decision-making questions should be associated with their own factor, and so on. On the other hand, if questions that were designed to measure different constructs were associated with the same factor, it would cast doubt on the construct validity of the interview. After all, what could we call a construct that was strongly associated with questions both from customer focus and decision making?

Let's look at Table 8.2 to see how output from the factor analysis program helps us see which questions were associated most strongly with each of the four factors. The questions in the interview (the variables)

(Continued)

(Continued)

are in the rows of the table, and the four factors that the program extracted from the analysis of the correlation matrix are represented in the columns. (These are referred to as components in the table.) The numbers in the body of the table are called factor loadings. Factor loadings are simply the correlation coefficients between each variable (the interview questions) and each of the factors the program identified. Like all correlation coefficients, the larger the absolute size, the stronger the relationship between the variable and the factor and the more variance they share in common.

The data presented in Table 8.2 show the correlations between the interview questions and each factor after the program has performed a statistical transformation on the data (called a rotation) to help make the results more interpretable. A rotation is a purely statistical transformation and does nothing to change the relationships that are present in original correlation matrix. During rotation, the factor analysis program searches for a solution whereby each variable has a high correlation with only one of the factors, and lower correlations on all the others. The computer tries many different possible solutions and stops when it finds what it considers to be the best one based on statistical criteria.

In our case, the rotation resulted in data that are easily interpretable. As you can see in Table 8.2, almost all of the questions have relatively high correlations with only one of the components and lower correlations with the others. We have shaded the correlations in the table that are most associated with each of the components to make them easier to identify. Let's look at Component 1. The highest correlations are with the focusing on customer questions Q5, Q3, Q1, Q6 and Q2. To understand what the factor or component represents, the researcher looks at these data and asks him- or herself, "What do all these questions have in common?" In this case it is quite clear. The questions with the highest correlations with Component 1 are about customer-focused behaviors. Therefore, Component 1 seems to be some type of customer service factor. For Component 2, we can see that the questions with the highest correlations are with the communicating effectively questions Q3, Q4, Q1, and Q2, all of which are about communication. So Component 2 would be a communication factor. What might you name Component 3 and Component 4? From the table, you can see that the questions with the highest correlations with Component 3 are about problem solving. For Component 4, the highest correlations are with questions that are about decision making.

Although it would be nice if each question in the interview was correlated with only one factor and completely uncorrelated with the others, in practice this is never the case. You can think of it like this. If we had a test that was designed to measure both mathematical and verbal abilities, we would like all the variance of the scores on the all math items to be related only to the underlying construct of mathematical ability. But because the test questions have to be read to be answered, the variability of the scores on the math questions will also be related to some degree to the person's reading ability—a verbal-type skill. So each question on even a well-designed test may share something in common with more than one the test's underlying factors. In factor analysis, this is called cross-loading. Our hope is that any cross-loadings will be much lower in size than the main loadings. Looking again at Table 8.2, you can see examples of cross-loading in our interview example. The question Making Decisions Q1 correlates almost as highly on Component 3, which we named problem solving (.525) as it does with the Component 4, which we named decision making (.563). When this occurs, the researcher needs to go back and examine the test question to assess how well it truly is a measure of the construct it was designed to measure. When the developers of the interview examined Q1 in the decision-making section of the interview, they discovered that the question actually was more targeted to solving a problem than it was to making a decision. The question needed to be revised to make it a better indicator for the construct of decision making. By doing so, the evidence of construct validity of the interview would be improved. The same analysis was conducted for Focusing on Customers Q4, which cross-loaded on the customer service component and the decision-making component. In fact, the correlation with the customer service component was actually somewhat lower that the correlation with the decision-making component, an outcome we would not expect or desire. This source of this cross-loading was traced to the fact that question actually asked about making a decision that resulted in high-quality customer service, so it was actually tapping both constructs. This question also needed to be revised as well to improve the evidence of construct validity of the interview.

Admittedly, factor analysis is a complicated topic. But you should now have a basic understanding of how exploratory factor analysis helps test developers design tests that can demonstrate good evidence of construct validity or gather that evidence after the test is developed.

FIGURE 8.5 ■ **Confirmatory Factor Analysis Model to Provide Evidence of Construct Validity of an Employment Interview**

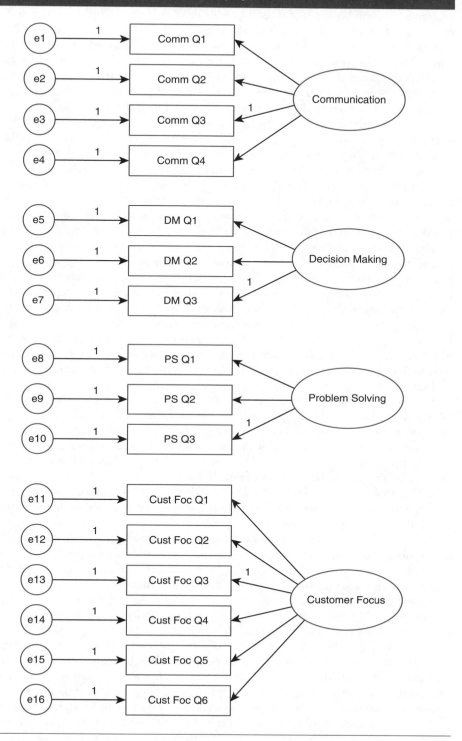

Confirmatory Factor Analysis

Another type of factor analysis is called **confirmatory factor analysis**. In confirmatory factor analysis, the researcher specifies *in advance* what he or she believes the factor structure of the data should look like and then statistically tests how well that model actually fits the data. The researcher relies on either existing theoretical or empirical knowledge to design the model that will be tested. As with exploratory factor analysis, the researcher can specify the number of factors that he or she expects to be able to extract from the data. But unlike exploratory factor analysis, he or she can also specify in advance a large number of other characteristics he believes will be present in the data, such as which variables are most strongly associated with each factor and even whether the factors themselves are correlated (J. Stevens, 2002). He or she can also specify the amount and nature of any measurement error present in the data. After the model is tested, the researcher can review the results and then modify the model if necessary to find a new one that may be a better fit for the data. One of the special aspects of confirmatory factor analysis is that if a new model is specified and tested, the new results can be statistically compared with the initial results to determine which model fits the data best.

Figure 8.5 shows how a confirmatory factor analysis model is depicted graphically. It is based on the same data as presented in the In Greater Depth Box 8.1 used to provide evidence of construct validity of an employment interview. In confirmatory factor analysis, we first specify in advance the factors we believe should underlie the data. You recall that the interview questions were designed to measure four factors: communication skills, decision making, problem solving, and focusing on customers. These factors are represented by the ovals on the right-hand side of the diagram. Each oval has arrows pointing to rectangles to the left. The rectangles represent the questions that were written to tap each one of the factors. For example, you can see that there are four rectangles associated with the communication factor. The rectangles represent the score on each of the four questions that were written to measure communication skills. The arrows from the communication competency to each question indicate that the researcher expects those questions to be most associated with the communication factor and not associated with any of the other three factors. Finally, at the left side of the figure, you can see some circles labeled e1 to e16, with arrows pointing to each of the questions. These labels represent the error in measurement that is associated with the scores on each of the questions. The numbers shown on many the connecting arrows in Figure 8.5 are used by the factor analysis program for proper computation and can be ignored for the purposes of this discussion.

Evidence of construct validity would be provided if the results of the confirmatory factor analysis showed that the interview data collected were a good statistical fit for the model proposed. If not, the model can be revised and retested.

Because you can specify the model to be tested in a confirmatory factor analysis in much greater detail than you can in an exploratory factor analysis, you may get different results if you do both analyses on the same data set. In this case, it would be up to the researcher to investigate further to understand why the difference occurred.

A good example of the process of confirmatory factor analysis is provided by Longshore, Turner, and Stein (1996), who tested the construct validity of a scale developed to measure self-control in a population of offenders in the criminal justice system (Grasmick, Tittle, Bursik, & Arneklev, 1993). A general theory of crime (M. Gottfredson & Hirschi, 1990) suggests that self-control—the degree to which a person is vulnerable to momentary temptation—is important in predicting whether a person will commit a crime. Other researchers have challenged this theory, citing a lack of empirical evidence of self-control as a stable trait. To answer these charges, Grasmick and colleagues (1993) developed a scale measuring self-control as defined by M. Gottfredson and Hirschi (1990). The scale contains 23 statements about noncriminal predispositions, such as impulsiveness and risk seeking, with which test

TABLE 8.1 ■ Correlation Matrix for Interview Question

	Communication				Customer Focus						Decision Making			Problem Solving		
	Q1	Q2	Q3	Q4	Q1	Q2	Q3	Q4	Q5	Q6	Q1	Q2	Q3	Q1	Q2	Q3
Communication Q1	1.000															
Communication Q2	.761	1.000														
Communication Q3	.780	.761	1.000													
Communication Q4	.479	.453	.487	1.000												
Customer Focus Q1	.492	.478	.519	.224	1.000											
Customer Focus Q2	.497	.485	.452	.298	.585	1.000										
Customer Focus Q3	.424	.399	.375	.196	.472	.535	1.000									
Customer Focus Q4	.487	.445	.448	.256	.490	.568	.451	1.000								
Customer Focus Q5	.463	.432	.439	.174	.458	.395	.466	.409	1.000							
Customer Focus Q6	.534	.450	.482	.257	.453	.465	.441	.456	.462	1.000						
Decision Making Q1	.477	.445	.425	.252	.441	.560	.436	.430	.352	.407	1.000					
Decision Making Q2	.551	.489	.512	.344	.431	.515	.399	.482	.374	.426	.672	1.000				
Decision Making Q3	.418	.372	.402	.332	.438	.413	.356	.471	.328	.405	.477	.531	1.000			
Problem Solving Q1	.446	.430	.442	.339	.362	.461	.335	.370	.335	.388	.490	.472	.369	1.000		
Problem Solving Q2	.480	.520	.472	.328	.391	.503	.387	.389	.435	.403	.535	.486	.399	.599	1.000	
Problem Solving Q3	.501	.525	.542	.320	.373	.424	.319	.424	.333	.390	.454	.526	.471	.474	.570	1.000

TABLE 8.2   ■   Rotated Component Matrix for Interview

	Component			
	1	2	3	4
Focusing on Customers Q5	.736	.171	.282	−.032
Focusing on Customers Q3	.700	.053	.179	.271
Focusing on Customers Q1	.645	.233	.093	.368
Focusing on Customers Q6	.594	.286	.195	.222
Focusing on Customers Q2	.540	.153	.304	.471
Communicating Effectively Q3	.380	.768	.246	.146
Communicating Effectively Q4	−.091	.739	.126	.275
Communicating Effectively Q1	.428	.725	.241	.190
Communicating Effectively Q2	.393	.722	.301	.105
Solving Problems Q2	.284	.226	.785	.148
Solving Problems Q1	.188	.209	.757	.189
Solving Problems Q3	.154	.378	.566	.322
Making Decisions Q3	.182	.233	.171	.746
Making Decisions Q2	.219	.280	.420	.615
Making Decisions Q1	.276	.097	.525	.563
Focusing on Customers Q4	.510	.215	.091	.542

Note: Extraction method: principal-components analysis. Rotation method: varimax with Kaiser normalization. Rotation converged in seven iterations.

takers agree or disagree. Studies of the scale by the test developers suggest that it is reliable and valid (Grasmick et al., 1993).

To conduct their confirmatory factor analysis, Longshore and colleagues (1996) used data collected during an evaluation of a program to treat offenders. The researchers hypothesized, based on M. Gottfredson and Hirschi's (1990) theory and previous research conducted by the test developers (Grasmick et al., 1993), that the measure of self-control would have six underlying factors:

1. *Impulsiveness:* People with low self-control seek immediate gratification.

2. *Simple tasks:* People with low self-control prefer simple tasks and lack the diligence and tenacity needed for benefiting from more complex tasks.

3. *Risk seeking:* People with low self-control are drawn to excitement and adventure.

4. *Physical activity:* People with low self-control prefer physical activity to contemplation and conversation.

5. *Self-centeredness:* People with low self-control tend to be indifferent to the needs of others.

6. *Temper:* People with low self-control have low tolerance for frustration and are likely to handle conflict with confrontation.

Longshore and colleagues' (1996) factor analysis provided support for the hypothesis. The data yielded the predicted factors; however, the factors of impulsiveness and self-centeredness combined, resulting in five factors instead of six. Based on these data, the researchers concluded that there was good evidence of construct validity for the measure of self-control.

Putting It All Together

The validation study of the Brief Multidimensional Students' Life Satisfaction Scale (BMSLSS; Seligson, Huebner, & Valois, 2003) provides a real-life example of the validation concepts we have discussed in Section II. According to Seligson and colleagues (2003), as of 2003, there was a shortage of validated instruments that assessed children's and adolescents' perceptions of the quality of their lives. Also, most of the validated measures that did exist were not suitable for use in large-scale studies, in part because they were too long. Therefore, the investigators decided to develop the BMSLSS for adolescents. The BMSLSS contains only five self-report questions. Each of the questions was designed to measure one of the domains included in a previously validated test of life satisfaction called the Multidimensional Students' Life Satisfaction Scale (MSLSS; Huebner, 1991). The MSLSS is a 40-item self-report scale designed to measure students' life satisfaction in each of five dimensions: family, school, friends, self, and living environment.

The researchers carried out their first validation study with 221 middle school students. As part of the overall validation strategy, the students completed a group of different measures, all relating to perceived quality of life, along with the newly developed BMSLSS, the Positive and Negative Affect Schedule–Children (Laurent et al., 1999), the Students' Life Satisfaction Scale (Huebner, 1991), the MSLSS (Zulig, Huebner, Gilman, Patton, & Murray, 1994), and the Children's Social Desirability Questionnaire (Crandall, Crandall, & Katkovsky, 1965). They also provided one rating of global life satisfaction on a seven-point scale.

Evidence for convergent and discriminant validity was provided using an MTMM analysis. The "traits" that were included were the five dimensions that the BMSLSS was designed to measure (perceived satisfaction with family, school, friends, self, and living environment). The methods that were included were the BMSLSS and, for comparison, the MSLSS. These are two different tests or "methods" designed to measure the same five dimensions.

Table 8.3 shows a multitrait–multimethod matrix contrasting the MSLSS with the BMSLSS. As you can see, this matrix contrasts two methods, each measuring the same five traits.

The note at the bottom of Table 8.3 will help you identify the tests (methods) and dimensions (traits). The bold numbers in the table are the correlations that provide the convergent evidence of validity. They are the correlations between the same dimensions on the two tests. All of these correlations are positive and have moderate strength. Convergent evidence of validity is demonstrated when these correlations are significant and are also larger than the other correlations in the table. This makes sense because these are the correlations between the measures of the traits on the new, shorter test (the BMSLSS) with the equivalent traits on the test with which it is being compared (the MSLSS). These should be correlated if they are measuring the same constructs. As we mentioned earlier in the chapter, the location of these correlations in the matrix is called the validity diagonal.

The underlined numbers show the correlations between the dimensions or traits *within* each test (top left quadrant for the MSLSS and bottom right quadrant for the BMSLSS).

| TABLE 8.3 ■ Multitrait–Multimethod Matrix for the Brief Multidimensional Students' Life Satisfaction Scale (BMSLSS) and the Multidimensional Students' Life Satisfaction Scale (MSLSS) |

MTMM Matrix for Middle School Students

	Method 1: MSLSS					Method 2: BMSLSS				
	A1	B1	C1	D1	E1	A2	B2	C2	D2	E2
A1										
B1	0.43									
C1	0.26	0.27								
D1	0.39	0.38	0.36							
E1	0.55	0.51	0.34	0.25						
A2	**0.55**	0.26	0.08	0.31	0.24					
B2	0.24	**0.52**	0.23	0.32	0.23	0.41				
C2	0.25	0.26	**0.53**	0.35	0.21	0.31	0.40			
D2	0.26	0.27	0.17	**0.60**	0.17	0.39	0.41	0.40		
E2	0.35	0.33	0.13	0.14	**0.47**	0.42	0.34	0.30	0.24	

Source: From Seligson, J. L., Huebner, S., & Valois, R. F. (2003). Preliminary validation of the Brief Multidimensional Students' Life Satisfaction Scale (BMSLSS). *Social Indicators Research*, *61*(2), 121–145. Published by Springer Science and Business Media.

Note: Traits = Perceived Satisfaction with: A = family, B = friends, C = school, D = living environment, E = self. The numbers in bold are the validity coefficients. The heterotrait–monomethod correlations are underlined. The heterotrait–heteromethod correlations are in italics.

These are the heterotrait–monomethod correlations because they are measuring the relationship between the different (i.e., hetero) traits using the same (i.e., mono) method or test. If the test is truly multidimensional, these correlations should be small. These correlations should only be attributable to the fact that the dimensions were all measured on the same test, so they share a method in common. These correlations should also be small relative to the size of the correlations on the validity diagonal.

The numbers in italics are the heterotrait–heteromethod correlations because they show the correlations between different (i.e., hetero) dimensions in different (i.e., hetero) tests. These are the correlations that provide discriminant evidence of validity. They should also be low relative to the other correlations in the table because they share neither a trait nor a method in common. As you can see, the discriminant coefficients are lower than the convergent coefficients. Overall therefore, the matrix provides strong evidence of construct validity for the BMSLSS.

For Your Information Box 8.1 contains another good example of how researchers use multiple approaches when gathering evidence of construct validity for a new test. This study is particularly interesting because the initial data used to pilot the test and revise the items were collected on the Internet via a website that was publically accessible. Anybody who wanted to could participate in the data collection.

In conclusion, it is important to remember Cronbach's (1989) advice about construct validation: "To call Test A valid or Test B invalid is illogical. Particular interpretations are what we validate. . . . Validation is a lengthy, even endless process" (p. 151).

FOR YOUR INFORMATION BOX 8.1
DEMONSTRATING CONSTRUCT VALIDITY OF A DELAY-OF-GRATIFICATION SCALE

Michael Hoerger and his colleagues were interested in developing an instrument that would measure gratification delay, which they defined as a person's ability to put off immediate satisfaction for the sake of long-term rewards (Hoerger, Quirk, & Weed, 2011). Although there had been a significant amount of prior research on the construct of gratification delay, the researchers believed that none of the prior instruments had measured the full construct of gratification delay, which they believed consisted of five domains: food, physical pleasures, social interactions, money, and achievement.

The researchers began by developing and pilot testing a large pool of possible items that they thought represented all five of the hypothesized domains. They then had a large number of participants respond to all the items using the Internet. The researchers created a website that was linked to other research websites, search engines, Wikipedia pages, Facebook, discussion forums, and blogs. Anyone who was interested could access the study website and participate. As a result, the researchers were able to pilot test the items with more than 10,000 participants! They used these data to revise items and create the two final delay-of-gratification scales. One scale contained 35 items, and the other contained 10 items. Both scales were designed to measure all five delay-of-gratification domains. The researchers also requested additional information from the participants that would be useful for collecting discriminant and convergent evidence of validity. They asked participants to rate themselves on a group of 30 personality trait descriptors, such as conscientiousness, patience, and altruism. They also asked the participants to rate themselves on a number of behavioral tendencies, such as "I pay bills on time" and "I party excessively." In two additional studies, they asked participants who completed their Delay of Gratification Inventory (DGI) to complete a number of other existing tests that were also designed to measure delay-of-gratification–type constructs. In addition, participants completed measures of psychopathology such as the Minnesota Multiphasic Personality Inventory (MMPI; see Test Spotlight 11.1 in Appendix A for a description of the MMPI-2).

The researchers conducted a confirmatory factor analysis (CFA) of the DGI to see if they could confirm the five-factor structure they had hypothesized. The results of the CFA supported the hypothesized five-factor model. In addition, the pattern of correlations between responses on the DGI and the responses on the trait descriptions and behavioral tendencies varied in an interpretable fashion. For instance, the food domain scores on the DGI correlated most highly with measures of fast food consumption—thinking about food, health, exercise, and soda drinking—but did not correlate with excitement seeking, risk taking, or excessive partying. The other domain scores in the DGI also showed a pattern of correlations with the behavioral tendencies and traits that one would expect. The correlations between the DGI and other tests of delay of gratification were also strong, demonstrating evidence of convergent validity. Finally, those individuals whose scores on the DGI suggested that they could delay gratification well also scored highly on measures of achievement striving, self-control, and conscientiousness. High DGI scorers also showed reduced levels of depression, binge eating, anxiety, and interpersonal problems.

This study is a good example of how researchers use multiple approaches to demonstrate evidence of construct validity. It is also an important study because of the way that Hoerger and his colleagues (2011) used the Internet to recruit a very large number of people to participate in their test development efforts and validation research. But there might be methodological issues associated with collecting data in this manner. For example, data accuracy does not increase as the sample size grows larger. Can you identify other issues? Do you think that using Facebook or other public websites to recruit participants for research purposes is a good idea? Why or why not?

In Section II we have discussed the basic psychometric principles associated with establishing test reliability and validity. As you can see, these research-based activities provide cumulative evidence regarding a test's usefulness and interpretation. In Section III we discuss the process of developing psychological tests and surveys and describes in more detail how researchers conduct validation studies.

Chapter Summary

Psychologists measure behaviors (activities that are observable and measurable) and constructs (underlying attitudes or attributes that exist only in our imaginations). Although we cannot observe or measure constructs directly, we can predict behaviors that influence and measure those behaviors.

Because definitions of constructs vary from person to person, psychologists define and explain constructs carefully. Construct explication is the process of relating a construct to a psychological theory and proposing a nomological network of the constructs and behaviors to which the construct is related.

We gather theoretical evidence of construct validity by proposing the nomological network and experimental hypotheses. We then gather psychometric evidence by establishing evidence that the test is reliable and correlates with other tests measuring constructs in the nomological network (convergent evidence of validity) and by confirming that it is not correlated with constructs to which it is theoretically unrelated (discriminant evidence of validity). In addition, evidence of validity based on test content or a test's relationship with other criterion measures also bolsters the argument that we have strong evidence of validity. Finally, researchers can propose and conduct experiments using the test to measure the construct.

Exploratory factor analysis takes a broad look at test data to determine how many underlying components are likely. Confirmatory factor analysis is a method that tests theoretical predictions about underlying variables or factors that make up a construct. Although some constructs are unidimensional or homogeneous, many constructs are multidimensional. The process of confirmatory factor analysis involves proposing underlying factors and then verifying their existence using the statistical procedure of factor analysis.

Engaging in the Learning Process

Learning is the process of gaining knowledge and skills through schooling or studying. Although you can learn by reading the chapter material, attending class, and engaging in discussion with your instructor, more actively engaging in the learning process may help you better learn and retain chapter information. To help you actively engage in the learning process, we encourage you to access our new supplementary student workbook. The workbook contains critical thinking activities to help you understand and apply information and help you make progress toward learning and retaining material. If you do not have a copy of the workbook, you can purchase a copy through sagepub.com.

Key Concepts

After completing your study of this chapter, you should be able to define each of the following terms. These terms are bolded in the text of this chapter and defined in the Glossary.

behavior
confirmatory factor analysis
construct
construct explication
construct validity
convergent evidence
    of validity

discriminant evidence
    of validity
exploratory factor analysis
factor analysis
factors
hypotheses

multitrait–multimethod
    correlation matrix
multitrait–multimethod
    (MTMM) design
nomological network
state
trait

Critical Thinking Questions

The following are some critical thinking questions to support the learning objectives for this chapter.

Learning Objectives	Critical Thinking Questions
Discuss the concept of a construct and give examples of theoretical constructs.	• Recall a time when you described someone you know in terms of a hypothetical construct. What was that construct and what made you think the description applied to that person? • Why do you think it is important to make a distinction between hypothetical constructs and observable behaviors? • What is a real life example where two people have defined or explicated a hypothetical construct in different fashions? What might be the consequences of this?
Explain how the current *Standards for Educational and Psychological Testing* treatment of constructs in testing differs from the more traditional usage of the term *construct validity*.	• Explain in your own words how the *Standards* now connects the concept of construct validity with the other types of evidence of validity you have learned about.
Explain and give examples of the steps involved in construct explication.	• What are some hypothesis that you might draw about a person described as being talented in some area? What are some of the constructs that you think might be related to being talented, and what are some that might be unrelated?
Explain the process of establishing evidence of validity based on a test's relationship with other constructs.	• Why is it important to establish a nomological network when developing theoretical evidence for construct validity? • How does gathering evidence of reliability help in establishing psychometric evidence for construct validity? • How does gathering evidence of validity based on test content and evidence based on relationships with other variables strengthen the argument that a test shows evidence of construct validity as well?
Explain how Campbell and Fiske's (1959) multitrait-multimethod provides evidence of validity based on a test's relationship with other constructs.	• What value does the multitrait–mutlimethod matrix have in demonstrating construct validity? • What are two different everyday constructs that should be related to each other (convergent validity) and two that should be unrelated (discriminant validity)?
Discuss the role of exploratory and confirmatory factor analysis in establishing construct validity.	• Describe in your own words how the process of factor analysis can help establish evidence of construct validity of a test. What would be the difference between using an exploratory versus confirmatory factor analysis approach to establish this evidence? • What do you think a test developer should do if a factor analysis of her test, which was designed to measure the construct of emotional stability, suggested there were three identifiable factors contained in the test?

DEVELOPING AND PILOTING SURVEYS AND PSYCHOLOGICAL TESTS

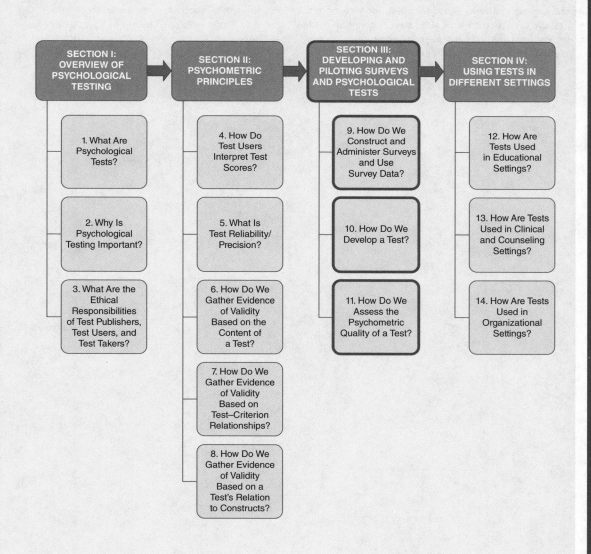

SECTION I: OVERVIEW OF PSYCHOLOGICAL TESTING	SECTION II: PSYCHOMETRIC PRINCIPLES	SECTION III: DEVELOPING AND PILOTING SURVEYS AND PSYCHOLOGICAL TESTS	SECTION IV: USING TESTS IN DIFFERENT SETTINGS
1. What Are Psychological Tests?	4. How Do Test Users Interpret Test Scores?	9. How Do We Construct and Administer Surveys and Use Survey Data?	12. How Are Tests Used in Educational Settings?
2. Why Is Psychological Testing Important?	5. What Is Test Reliability/ Precision?	10. How Do We Develop a Test?	13. How Are Tests Used in Clinical and Counseling Settings?
3. What Are the Ethical Responsibilities of Test Publishers, Test Users, and Test Takers?	6. How Do We Gather Evidence of Validity Based on the Content of a Test?	11. How Do We Assess the Psychometric Quality of a Test?	14. How Are Tests Used in Organizational Settings?
	7. How Do We Gather Evidence of Validity Based on Test–Criterion Relationships?		
	8. How Do We Gather Evidence of Validity Based on a Test's Relation to Constructs?		

CHAPTER 9: HOW DO WE CONSTRUCT AND ADMINISTER SURVEYS AND USE SURVEY DATA?

In Chapter 9, we have included a dedicated discussion of surveys. We begin by defining what a survey is. We then discuss the popularity of surveys, including some of the most popular survey software. After reviewing a five-phase scientific approach to constructing and administering surveys and analyzing the resulting data, we discuss survey reliability and validity.

CHAPTER 10: HOW DO WE DEVELOP A TEST?

In Chapter 10, we discuss the steps for developing psychological tests. We look at the process of constructing a test plan, various formats for writing questions (e.g., multiple choice, true/false), the strengths and weaknesses of different formats, and how test takers' perceptions and preconceived notions can influence test scores. We present guidelines on how to write test questions and discuss the importance of the instructions that accompany a test. Finally, we discuss the importance of "testing the test" by conducting a pilot test before the test is released for use.

CHAPTER 11: HOW DO WE ASSESS THE PSYCHOMETRIC QUALITY OF A TEST?

In Chapter 11, we continue to describe the test development process by discussing analyzing the items in terms of their difficulty, their ability to discriminate among respondents, and their likelihood of introducing error into the test results. We take a close look at how we determine if a test is equally predictive for different subgroups in the population. We also describe the process of revising the test and gathering evidence of reliability and validity. Finally, we briefly discuss the contents of the test manual.

9

HOW DO WE CONSTRUCT AND ADMINISTER SURVEYS AND USE SURVEY DATA?

LEARNING OBJECTIVES

After completing your study of this chapter, you should be able to do the following:

- Describe the similarities and differences between a survey and a psychological test.
- Recognize some of the most popular survey software providers.
- Apply the five-phase scientific approach to constructing administering and using survey data.
- Describe survey reliability/precision and validity.

"I'm confused. My professor told me that a survey is different than a psychological test. Why then do the names of some tests have the word survey in them?"

"I am taking a Survey Research Methods class. The instructor told us we needed a foundation in the scientific method before we studied surveys. She said that survey construction is both a science and an art. I wanted to learn how to construct a survey—not what science is all about. What is the deal?"

"Our human resources department was interested in finding out how employees feel about our company benefits program. They wanted to know whether employees were aware of the medical, retirement, and flexible spending plans that were available to them—and if so, whether the plans are valuable to them. They wanted this information to find out whether the existing

benefits program needed to be modified to fit employees' needs. It took the human resources staff about 2 months to design this survey. Why did it take so long?"

"I had to complete a course evaluation survey for my Research Methods class. One of the questions on the survey was 'Was the teacher available and responsive to your needs?' Another question was 'How much time did you spend studying for this class?' My teacher said that these were not very good survey questions. Why not?"

You may be wondering why we've included a chapter on surveys in a psychological testing textbook. We've done so for two primary reasons. First, like psychological tests, surveys are very popular measurement instruments and important decisions are often made based on survey results. While some similarities exist between the methods we use to construct, administer, and use psychological test and survey data, there are also differences. We want to increase your awareness of these differences. Second, many of our adopters use this textbook as a part of a research or measurement course. These adopters have shared how valuable they find this chapter. Many of the techniques that are necessary to learn to write high quality survey questions are also applicable to writing high quality test questions. The material we present in this chapter will also add to your knowledge of how to develop high quality test questions should you ever have to do so. Finally, and perhaps most importantly, even if you never have to design a survey yourself, by understanding how surveys are designed and results are interpreted, you will become a more informed consumer of the many different types of surveys that all of us frequently encounter in the media, especially in election years!

We begin by defining what a survey is and discussing how surveys are popular research tools. Knowing that how we collect information affects data quality, we present an overview of the different ways to collect and acquire data. We focus on one approach, the scientific method, which is the very essence of collecting accurate survey data. After briefly reviewing the scientific method, we focus on a five-phase scientific approach to constructing and administering surveys and analyzing their results. Finally, we discuss survey reliability/precision and validity.

Although this chapter contains an excellent overview of surveys, we encourage those interested in constructing and administering surveys and analyzing their data to consult the additional sources mentioned throughout the chapter.

SIMILARITIES AND DIFFERENCES BETWEEN SURVEYS AND PSYCHOLOGICAL TESTS

If you search the Internet or review survey research methods textbooks, you will find various definitions of what a survey is. At the broadest level, **surveys** are instruments used to collect important information from individuals. As we shared in the "What Are Psychological Tests?" chapter, surveys differ from psychological tests in two important ways. First, psychological tests focus on individual outcomes, whereas surveys focus on group outcomes. When we administer a test, the results are reported at the individual level (i.e., each person receives a test score) and sometimes at the aggregate level (e.g., the scores of many individuals may be summarized to report the results at the group level). When we administer a survey, the results are more typically presented at the group level only. For example, we might ask students to rate their satisfaction with a new college program and then report the overall results. Second, the results of a psychological test are often reported in terms of an overall derived score or scaled scores. Results of surveys, on the other hand, are often reported at the question level by providing the percentage of respondents who selected each answer alternative. The distinction between surveys and tests is not always clear. For example, Hogan Assessment Systems (2018) developed and sells the Hogan Development Survey, an 11-scale instrument that measures personality characteristics that may interfere with a person's interpersonal success and productivity when in conditions of increased tension. While the instrument is used to measure the construct of personality, includes scales, and is reported at the individual level using an overall score and scale scores, the instrument has the word *survey* in the title. What is important is not whether the instrument has the word survey in the title or not but rather that the instrument is well designed and has evidence of reliability/precision and validity for the intended use.

Overall, surveys allow us to collect information so that we can describe and compare how people feel about things (attitudes), what they know (knowledge), and what they do (behaviors). We use surveys, like psychological tests, for various reasons. For example, it is not uncommon for elementary schools to administer surveys to better understand how parents feel about the implementation of a new policy (how they feel), how much parents know about the school's curriculum (what they know), or what parents do with their children to facilitate the learning process (what they do). Every 4 years, television news stations administer surveys (or what they call political polls) to learn how people plan to vote so that they can make predictions about whom the next president of the United States will be. Organizations use surveys to measure employee satisfaction and organizational effectiveness. Mayors, governors, city managers, and other administrators even use surveys to determine whether the people living in their towns, cities, or districts are happy. See In the News Box 9.1 for a few examples.

The U.S. government conducts the Current Population Survey monthly with households across the nation to determine the unemployment rate (U.S. Bureau of Labor Statistics [BLS], 2018b), the Consumer Expenditure Survey to determine how people spend their money (BLS, 2018a), and the National Health Interview Survey to collect information about people's health conditions, their use of health services, and the behaviors that affect their risk for illness (Centers for Disease Control and Prevention, 2012). To learn more about one of the nation's most important surveys, the Current Population Survey, read On the Web Box 9.1.

One of the earliest known surveys was the first census of the population of the United States conducted in 1790 by the federal government. Since that time, surveys have become very popular research tools, and millions of them are conducted each year in the United States. As a result of their popularity, there are thousands of **survey research firms**—companies that specialize in the construction and administration of surveys and analysis of survey data. Some of the larger, well-known survey research firms are highlighted in On the Web Box 9.2.

As with psychological tests, we use the data collected from surveys to make important decisions. For example, an elementary school may require children to wear uniforms to school if the results of a survey indicate that parents believe this would be a positive move. An organization may decide to invest significant training dollars in a management development program when survey results suggest that lack of management skill plays a significant role in organizational turnover. A network news organization may decide to broadcast who will be elected president, prior to the closing of the polls, based on the results of exit polls.

IN THE NEWS BOX 9.1
ARE YOU HAPPY?

In recent years, mayors, governors, city managers, and other administrators have become interested in whether the people living in their towns, cities, or districts are happy. This new area of research is taking place globally in countries such as China, Bhutan, Australia, the United Kingdom, and the United States. Why are governments researching happiness? What do they expect to do with that knowledge?

In China, Lingnan University's dedication to assessing Chinese people's happiness and mental health conditions led to a collaboration with ING LIFE, a life and health insurance subsidiary in Bangkok, Thailand. Lennard Yong of ING LIFE said,

> Happiness is the best insurance in life. ING believes that promoting happiness is one of the key objectives of insurance. Thus, the goal of our sponsorship of the survey is to raise public awareness about happy living. This is also the mission and rationale behind our insurance services and product design—to work for the best interests of our clients, and thus help them lead worry-free and happier lives. We are delighted to collaborate with Lingnan University to design the survey and analyse the results, so as to attain more insightful findings for this meaningful initiative. ("Wan Chai the 'Happiest' District," 2011, para. 4)

The government of Bhutan believes that happiness should take priority over economic growth, and it has acted on this belief. When Bhutan's government was deciding whether to join the World Trade Organization, it considered whether trade within the organization would affect the happiness of the Bhutanese. The government officials determined that membership (which is coveted by many countries) would result in a net loss of well-being, and it decided against joining (de Graaf & Musikanski, 2009).

Seonaid Anderson distributed a happiness survey in Australia in 2009 and concluded that a more relaxed lifestyle and a higher level of happiness overall were spin-offs of the global financial crisis ("Fed: Many Australians," 2009). In Great Britain, another happiness survey, according to Forsyth (2010), made members of the Conservative party unhappy. They worried that in a time of economic hardship, the results of a happiness survey would show that the voters were not happy under the Conservatives.

In Somerville, Massachusetts, officials hoped to use the results of their happiness survey to see how parks and bike paths affected the happiness of people living nearby and how people's feelings changed when mass transit services were improved. Daniel T. Gilbert, a Harvard professor, developed Somerville's happiness survey, which the city distributed with its census questionnaire in 2011. Over 7,500 people returned the survey. Responding to the question "How satisfied are you with your life in general?" one respondent gave himself a 6, explaining, "I would like to be three inches taller and speak Quechua fluently" (Tierney, 2011, p. A1).

Did the respondents take this survey seriously? It is hard to tell. However, the officials are taking the respondents' answers seriously, and policies may change as a result.

SURVEY SOFTWARE

Prior to advances in technology, those who needed to design and implement surveys typically created paper-based surveys and then administered the surveys by either handing out the surveys to respondents or distributing the surveys via email as attachments. Individuals then typically manually entered results into some type of data analysis software (such as Microsoft Excel or SPSS) to analyze the results. They typically then transferred the results into reports using either word processing software or Microsoft PowerPoint. However, with advancing technology, we now have survey software available, automating much of the survey process.

ON THE WEB BOX 9.1

THE CURRENT POPULATION SURVEY

www.bls.gov/cps/home.htm

On a monthly basis, the BLS measures the unemployment rate of the U.S. civilian noninstitutionalized population (BLS, n.d.-b). The noninstitutionalized population includes those individuals who are over the age of 16 and who live in the United States, but who are not housed in institutions (e.g., psychiatric facilities, prisons, nursing homes) or who are not on active duty.

In April 2018, the average unemployment rate of the civilian noninstitutionalized population was 3.9%, down from the 2013 average unemployment of 7.4% (BLS, 2018b). Annual average unemployment rates of noninstitutionalized persons 16 years of age and older from 2000 to 2017 are shown below.

2000	2001	2002	2003	2004	2005	2006	2007	2008	2009	2010	2011	2012	2013	2014	2015	2016	2017
4.0%	4.7%	5.8%	6.0%	5.5%	5.1%	4.6%	4.6%	5.8%	9.3%	9.6%	8.9%	8.1%	7.4%	6.2%	5.3%	4.9%	4.4%

Have you ever wondered where statistics on the unemployment rate come from? The Current Population Survey (CPS) is a monthly household survey conducted by the U.S. Census Bureau for the BLS. The CPS data are gathered through personal and telephone interviews from a sample of approximately 60,000 households. The primary purpose of the survey is to provide comprehensive data on the employment and unemployment experiences of the nation's population classified by age, sex, race, and other characteristics.

The CPS provides data that are used by lawmakers, researchers, and the general public. These data include the following:

- Employment status of the civilian noninstitutionalized population age 16 years or older by age, sex, race, Hispanic origin, marital status, family relationship, and Vietnam-era veteran status

- Employed persons by occupation, industry, class of worker, hours of work, full- or part-time status, and reasons for working part-time

- Employed multiple jobholders by occupation, industry, number of jobs held, and full- or part-time status of multiple jobs

- Unemployed persons by occupation, industry, class of worker of last job, duration of unemployment, reason for unemployment, and methods used to find employment

- Discouraged workers and other persons not in the labor force

- Information on weekly and hourly earnings by detailed demographic group, occupation, education, union affiliation, and full- or part-time employment status

- Special topics such as the labor force status of particular subgroups of the population, such as women maintaining families, working women with children, displaced workers, and disabled veterans

Data are also available on work experience, occupational mobility, job tenure, educational attainment, and school enrollment of workers.

Source: BLS (n.d.-a).

Just as there are companies dedicated to constructing and administering surveys and analyzing survey data, there are firms dedicated to providing survey software so that individuals and companies can design, collect, analyze, and report their own data. And just as you have many choices for where to shop for such things as food and clothing, those interested in finding and perhaps purchasing survey software have many choices as well. Where you shop for food and clothing likely depends on your personal needs and desires,

ON THE WEB BOX 9.2
POPULAR SURVEY RESEARCH FIRMS

Thousands of survey research firms are dedicated to constructing and administering surveys and/or analyzing survey data. Although most of these firms are small companies that specialize in interviewing people, there are a number of full-service companies that design surveys, collect survey data, tabulate survey answers, interpret survey data, and report survey results to organizational sponsors. Some of the larger, well-known survey research firms are highlighted below.

Gallup (www.gallup.com): Established more than 70 years ago and employing many of the world's leading scientists in management, economics, psychology, and sociology, Gallup helps organizations increase customer engagement and maximize employee growth. Gallup provides measurement tools (surveys), coursework, and strategic advisory services to client organizations via the web, at Gallup University campuses, and in 40 offices around the world.

J. D. Power & Associates (www.jdpower.com): Established in 1968, J. D. Power & Associates, a business unit of the McGraw-Hill Companies, is a global marketing information firm that conducts independent surveys of customer satisfaction, product quality, and buyer behavior.

Westat (www.westat.com): Established in 1961 and employee owned, Westat is a contract research organization that provides custom research and program evaluation studies to organizations. Its surveys cover a broad range of topics, including health conditions and expenditures, academic achievement and literacy, medical treatments and outcomes, exposure assessments, program participation, employment and earnings, and respondents' knowledge, attitudes, and behaviors.

University of Michigan Institute for Social Research (www.isr.umich.edu): The Institute for Social Research (ISR) is one of the largest and oldest (more than 50 years old) academic survey and social research organizations in the world. ISR is dedicated to advancing public understanding of human behavior by directing and conducting some of the longest running and most widely cited and used empirical research studies in the United States.

As with psychological tests, the data collected from surveys are used to make important decisions. Therefore, survey developers must pay careful attention to the design and administration of surveys and the analysis of data gathered. Unfortunately, although surveys are popular and valuable research tools, like psychological tests they are also often misunderstood or misinterpreted. Surveys, like psychological tests, are not error free, and how one approaches their design, administration, and analysis can affect how well the survey data describe what they are intended to describe.

Pew Research Center (www.pewresearch.org): Established in 2004 by the Pew Charitable Trusts, the Pew Research Center describes themselves as a "fact tank" that is nonpartisan, and nonadvocacy. They conduct public opinion polling around a wide range of topics including U.S. politics and policy as well as global demographic trends. You will frequently hear them cited in the media as a source of public opinion polling data during election seasons in the United States.

as well as constraints, such as how much money you have to spend. The same is true when making survey software choices. There are many different survey software providers available, and while there are some similarities across the software packages, there are also differences. For the names and web addresses of some of survey software providers see On the Web Box 9.3.

There really is no one best survey software. While some survey software providers may be more well known than others (such as SurveyMonkey and Qualtrics), the choice of software depends on a person or company's specific needs, desires, and constraints. For example, while one individual may have an immediate need to design and implement only one, relatively

ON THE WEB BOX 9.3
NAMES AND WEB ADDRESSES OF ONLINE SURVEY SOFTWARE PROVIDERS

Open your web browser, go to your favorite search engine, and conduct a search for "survey software." You will find pages and pages of companies providing online survey software services. Some of these publishers, the software they offer, and their website addresses are listed here:

Publisher	Software	Website
SurveyMonkey	SurveyMonkey	https://www.surveymonkey.com
Qualtrics	Qualtrics	http://www.qualtrics.com
Widgix	SurveyGizmo	http://www.surveygizmo.com
Inquisite	Inquisite	https://inquisite.chevron.com
KwikSurveys	KwikSurveys	https://kwiksurveys.com
Creative Research Systems	The Survey System	http://www.surveysystem.com/index.htm
Speedwell	KeyPoint	http://www.speedwellsoftware.com/surveys
Snap Surveys	Snap Surveys	http://www.snapsurveys.com/survey-software/
StatPac	StatPac Web Survey Software	https://www.statpac.com/online-surveys/Web-survey-software.htm
Golden Hills Software	SurveyGold	http://www.surveygoldsolutions.com
William Steinberg Consultants	Survey Tools for Windows	http://surveytools4windows.com/product/survey-tools-for-windows/

simple survey, another may need to design and implement more complex surveys on an ongoing basis. Some individuals may have limited to no funds available, while others may have funding to help support their survey needs. Understanding how survey software differs can be helpful for choosing the right survey software.

While we can purchase some survey software in stores selling electronics and download other software onto a computer, perhaps the more popular software is that which is available on a company's server and accessed by users over the Internet (such as SurveyMonkey and Qualtrics). Some of the providers who offer access to users over the Internet allow users to create, deploy, analyze, and report survey findings free of charge, though the capabilities are often limited. For example, anyone can sign up for a free account on SurveyMonkey. With a free account, users can create short surveys (up to 10 survey items) and collect data from a limited number of respondents (up to 100 people). With the free service, users can analyze and report survey results, though the options are limited (SurveyMonkey, 2018a). Those who need to design longer surveys, gather data from more respondents, and/or use more advanced survey formatting, data collection, and data analysis features can sign up for one of four pay plans (Basic, Standard, Advantage, and Premier), each with increasing features (SurveyMonkey, 2018b). Some advanced design features often include the option of selecting from an extensive library of survey templates, choosing from a variety of survey question types (e.g., multiple choice, ranking, matrix/rating scales), choosing already written questions from a question bank, and setting question skip logic. Users can often also customize survey colors and logos, and design surveys in multiple languages. Some software allows users to collect data using multiple data collection methods (creating web links to insert in social media sites, sending the survey directly through email by adding email addresses, posting surveys directly on Facebook, or embedding surveys directly on websites).

For an additional fee, some providers even provide users with access to millions of potential survey respondents who meet the criteria for the survey. For example, to study novice nurses' preparedness to effectively use electronic health records, Miller et al. (2014) needed to find a significant number of survey respondents who were new registered nurses and nurse managers. To do so, they sought the help of MarketTools ZoomPanel, which was at the time a division of Zoomerang, which was acquired by SurveyMonkey. With the assistance of Zoom-Panel, Miller et al. were able to send surveys to more than 70,000 new registered nurses and 1,900 nurse managers.

Some survey software offers advanced data analysis and reporting options. For example, question-level data can be summarized using descriptive statistics and reported in different types of charts and tables. The colors and labels of the charts and tables can sometimes be customized. Data within and between questions can also often be compared. The charts and tables created can then be exported in a variety of formats, such as Excel, PDF, and PowerPoint.

Some providers offer survey software designed to help individuals and organizations implement custom 360° (multirater) surveys. Organizations often deploy 360° surveys so that employees can receive developmental feedback. The surveys are typically sent to those individuals an employee works with on a day-to-day basis (e.g., his or her manager, peers, direct reports, and customers), requiring those individuals to rate the employee's demonstration of competencies or behaviors identified as critical to successful performance of the job. While the rating scales used may differ, often 360° surveys require individuals to rate the extent to which a person demonstrates the competencies or behaviors (e.g., from *limited extent* to *great extent*). Typically, the employee rates himself or herself as well (see Figure 9.1).

All except the employee's own ratings and the manager rating is aggregated to provide the employee with information on behavioral strengths and development areas. For more information on several such 360° software providers (e.g., 36 Dollar 360), see On the Web Box 9.4.

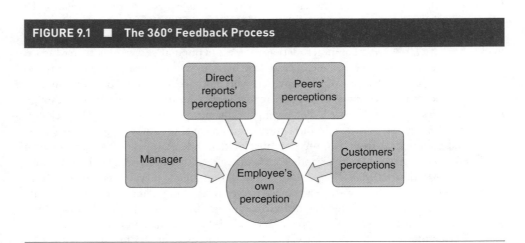

FIGURE 9.1   ■   The 360° Feedback Process

ON THE WEB BOX 9.4
NAMES AND ADDRESSES OF 360° FEEDBACK SOFTWARE PROVIDERS

Open your web browser, go to your favorite search engine, and conduct a search for "360-degree survey software." You will find the names of many companies providing online 360° survey software services. Some of these publishers, the software they offer, and their website addresses are listed here:

Publisher	Software	Website
Qualtrics	Qualtrics	http://www.qualtrics.com
SVI	36 Dollar 360	http://www.36dollar360.com
Halogen Software	Halogen 360 Multirater	http://www.halogensoftware.com/products/360-feedback
CustomInsight	Focal 360	http://www.custominsight.com/360-degree-feedback/
HR-Survey	360 Degree Feedback	http://www.hr-survey.com/360Feedback.htm

THE SCIENTIFIC APPROACH TO CONSTRUCTING, ADMINISTERING, AND USING SURVEY DATA

Many people believe that constructing a survey is a simple and quick process. To demonstrate how quickly a survey can be designed, we constructed the course evaluation survey in For Your Information Box 9.1 in only 5 minutes. The survey looks okay, doesn't it? In fact, the survey is not very good at all. It has several weaknesses, which are almost guaranteed to result in inaccurate measurement, meaningless results, and poor decisions. First, we did not take the time to think through the objectives or purpose of the survey. Second, we did not take the time to carefully construct the survey questions to ensure we met the objectives. Third, we did not pretest the survey to determine whether students would understand the questions as we intended. Fourth, we did not take the time to carefully format the survey—including instructions and professional formatting—to make the survey easy to complete and score. This is not a complete list of the weaknesses of this very quickly constructed survey, but we hope we have made our point. Although the survey in For Your Information Box 9.1 may, at first glance, appear to be a good one, it probably does not measure what we need it to measure, or measure whatever it measures consistently. We hope that no one would want to make any decisions (e.g., promotion of a faculty member, elimination of a course) based on the results of this survey.

Constructing a good survey, and demonstrating evidence of reliability and validity, takes time. It is as much a science as it is an art. Surveys are a science because science is a process—and good surveys follow a scientific process (method). Survey research is an art because knowing how much rigor to put into the design and writing good questions takes years of practice.

For Your Information Box 9.2 includes a much better course evaluation survey. By the end of this chapter, you should be able to determine what makes this one better than the survey in For Your Information Box 9.1.

FOR YOUR INFORMATION BOX 9.1
QUICKLY DEVELOPED COURSE EVALUATION SURVEY

1. How did you hear about this course?

   _____ Another student

   _____ College catalog

   _____ Faculty member

2. Did the professor show preferential treatment to certain students?

   _____ Yes

   _____ No

3. What treatment did you observe?

   _____

   _____

4. Please give your overall opinion of the course.

	Excellent	Okay	Mediocre	Poor
Course organization	_____	_____	_____	_____
Course content	_____	_____	_____	_____
Clarity of presentation	_____	_____	_____	_____
Audiovisual aids	_____	_____	_____	_____
Syllabus materials	_____	_____	_____	_____

5. Overall, did you enjoy and would you recommend this course to other students?

   _____ Yes

   _____ No

Experienced **survey researchers**—people who design and conduct surveys and analyze their results—generally would tell you the same things about what makes a good survey. First, they would probably tell you that good surveys share the following characteristics:

- They have specific and measurable objectives

- They contain straightforward questions that can be understood similarly by most people

- They have been pretested to ensure that there are no unclear questions or incorrect skip patterns

- They have been administered to an adequate sample of respondents so that the results are reflective of the population of interest

- They include the appropriate analysis to obtain the objectives

- They include an accurate reporting of results (both verbal and written)

- They have evidence of reliability and validity

Second, experienced survey researchers would probably tell you that using a scientific approach to survey research increases the chances that a survey will have these features. A scientific approach to surveys involves five general phases that correspond to the five steps of the scientific method. For more information on the scientific method, see For Your Information Box 9.3.

FOR YOUR INFORMATION BOX 9.2
BETTER COURSE EVALUATION SURVEY

The purpose of this survey is to gather your feedback on the success of the course. Please take a few moments to answer the following questions to the best of your ability. Your comments are essential for the planning of future courses.

1. How did you hear about this course? (*Please select one of the following.*)

    _____ Another student

    _____ College catalog

    _____ Faculty member

    _____ Other (please specify) _____

    _____

2. Did the professor show preferential treatment to certain students?

    _____ Yes

    _____ No (skip to Question 4)

3. What preferential treatment did you observe?

    _____

    _____

4. Please rate each of the following as being excellent, good, fair, or poor. (Please make a check mark on the appropriate line.)

	Excellent	Good	Fair	Poor
Course organization	_____	_____	_____	_____
Course content	_____	_____	_____	_____
Clarity of presentation	_____	_____	_____	_____
Audiovisual aids	_____	_____	_____	_____
Syllabus materials	_____	_____	_____	_____

5. Overall, did you enjoy this course?

    _____ Yes

    _____ No

6. Would you recommend this course to other students?

    _____ Yes

    _____ No

The scientific method involves several ways of collecting information, which can be categorized as experimental research techniques and descriptive or correlation-based research techniques. In general, **experimental research techniques** help us determine cause and effect, and **descriptive research techniques** help us describe a situation or a phenomenon. Most surveys are descriptive—used to describe, or even compare, a situation or phenomenon; for example, a class evaluation survey might indicate that your tests and measurements professor was an effective professor or even that this professor appeared to be more effective than your cognitive psychology professor. Surveys are not commonly used for determining cause and effect; for example, survey data cannot establish that having Professor Miller teach your tests and measurements class will cause you to learn more than having Professor Lovler teach the same class! A true experiment (in which there is a control group and an experimental group and participants are randomly assigned to these groups) must be set up to establish cause and effect. In some cases, however, surveys can be used as data collection instruments within an experimental technique.

FOR YOUR INFORMATION BOX 9.3

KNOWLEDGE ACQUISITION AND THE SCIENTIFIC METHOD

Every day we are bombarded with information—including information generated from the results of surveys. As we scan the web for news, we might read an article describing a miracle cure for a common disease or an article claiming that the unemployment rate has increased. Later in the day, we might watch a television commentary suggesting that television viewing increases teenage violence and that attending preschool improves children's intelligence. On our way home from work or school, we might drop by the drugstore, where a pharmacist might tell us that a certain brand of aspirin is more effective than another brand for alleviating headaches.

Usually we take this information for granted and use it to make decisions about ourselves and others. For example, we might decide that our children will watch very little television or that we will change the brand of aspirin we use. Unfortunately, some of the information we hear and learn about is misleading and, if taken as fact, could result in poorly informed decisions.

Before making decisions that are based on what we hear or see, we must verify that the information is accurate. To do this, we must look at how the information was obtained. How did the pharmacist come to the conclusion that one brand of aspirin is more effective than another brand? How did the radio talk show host come to the conclusion that watching television increases teenage violence?

In 1970, Helmstadter identified different methods we use to obtain knowledge: through tenacity, intuition, authority, rationalism, empiricism, and the scientific method. These methods continue to be referred to today and are summarized in Table 9.1.

TABLE 9.1 ■ Helmstadter's Six Methods for Acquiring Knowledge	
Method	**Definition**
Tenacity	We acquire information based on superstition or habit, leading us to continue believing something we have always believed. For example, we come to believe that one brand of aspirin is better than another because we have always used that brand and it has always worked for us.
Intuition	We acquire information without any reasoning or inferring. For example, we come to believe that one brand of aspirin is more effective than another brand just because we believe it is so.
Authority	We acquire information from a highly respected source. For example, we come to believe that one brand of aspirin is better than another brand because a pharmacist tells us so.
Rationalism	We acquire information through reasoning. For example, we come to believe that one brand of aspirin reduces headaches more effectively than another brand because the first brand includes ingredients that are similar to another medicine we use that really works for us.
Empiricism	We acquire information through personal experience. For example, we come to believe that one brand of aspirin reduces headaches more effectively because we have used it and it works for us.
Scientific method	We acquire information by testing ideas and beliefs according to a specific testing procedure that can be observed objectively. This method is without personal beliefs, perceptions, biases, values, attitudes, and emotions. For example, we come to believe that one brand of aspirin is more effective at reducing headaches than another brand because systematic research has accumulated evidence of its effectiveness.

Source: Helmstadter (1970).

Although the first five methods help us gain knowledge, they are not necessarily the best means for gaining *accurate* knowledge. The sixth, the **scientific method**—a process that scientists use to generate knowledge—often allows us to obtain more accurate information through systematic and objective observations. Although there is some disagreement among researchers regarding the exact elements of the scientific method, many researchers speak of five steps associated with it:

1. Identifying a problem or an issue and forming a hypothesis

2. Designing a study to explore the problem or issue and test the hypothesis

3. Conducting the study

4. Analyzing and interpreting the data

5. Communicating the research results

Table 9.2 shows the five steps in the scientific method, the corresponding steps of survey design, and the competencies a survey researcher needs to be able to perform each step.

Third, experienced survey researchers would probably tell you to choose a level of detail appropriate for the purpose of the survey project. Regardless of the purpose of a survey, it is important to identify the objectives of the survey carefully, construct the survey carefully,

TABLE 9.2 ■ A Scientific Approach to Survey Design		
Step in the Scientific Method	**Corresponding Step for Designing Surveys**	**Competencies of the Survey Researcher**
1. Identify a problem and form a hypothesis	Presurvey issues	• Know how to conduct a literature review • Know how to gather people who are knowledgeable about the survey topic • Know how to conduct focus groups
2. Design a study to explore the problem and test the hypothesis	Construct the survey	• Know the different types of surveys • Know the different types of survey questions • Know how to write effective survey questions • Know how to assemble questions into a survey instrument • Know the various methods for pretesting surveys • Know how to interpret data to revise and finalize the survey
3. Conduct the study	Administer the survey	• Know the methods for sampling respondents • Understand the logistics of administering various surveys
4. Analyze the research data	Analyze the survey data	• Know how to code survey data • Know how to enter survey data into a database • Know the methods for analyzing survey data
5. Communicate the research findings	Communicate the findings of the survey	• Know how to write a report • Know how to prepare presentation materials • Know how to present information to a group

Source: Adapted from *The Survey Handbook* by Arlene Fink. Copyright © 1995 by SAGE Publications, Inc.

enter and analyze survey data carefully, and present the findings clearly. However, because the scientific approach to survey research requires detailed planning, is complex and time-consuming, and can be expensive, the amount of energy and time you spend on each of these phases may vary depending on the objectives of the survey. For example, designing and administering a class evaluation survey is less complex and therefore requires less planning, time, and money than designing and administering the **decennial census survey**—a survey that is administered by the U.S. Census Bureau every 10 years, primarily to determine the population of the United States.

Preparing for the Survey

The first phase in developing a survey involves identifying the objectives of the survey, defining the objectives operationally, and constructing a plan for completing the survey.

Identifying the Objectives

The first step in preparing the survey is to define the **survey objectives**—the purpose of the survey and what the survey will measure. For example, one survey's objective may be to determine why there is a high degree of turnover in an organization. Another survey's objective may be to assess public opinion regarding a new product or service. The objective of a third survey may be to determine whether students thought a college course was beneficial.

Where do the objectives come from? They come from a particular need, from literature reviews, and from experts. For example, suppose that your college's administrators decide that they need to know whether their courses are fulfilling students' needs. They may ask the college's institutional research office to design a course evaluation survey to be administered in each class at the end of the semester. There is an obvious need here, and the exact objectives of the survey would come from discussions with college administrators, faculty, and students.

Survey objectives can also come from **literature reviews**—systematic examinations of published and unpublished reports on a topic. By reviewing the literature on a specific topic, survey researchers find out what is known about the topic. They then use this information to identify important aspects of a topic or gaps in knowledge about the topic. The survey objectives can also come from **experts**—individuals who are knowledgeable about the survey topic or who will be affected by the survey's outcomes. By talking to experts, you can take an idea about a survey (e.g., I just want to design a class evaluation survey) and define exactly what information the survey should collect—its specific objectives (e.g., determine whether faculty are treating some students preferentially, determine whether faculty are meeting students' needs, determine whether faculty are presenting information in an organized manner). For a class evaluation survey, your experts might be faculty, college administrators, or students.

Defining the Objectives Operationally

After identifying the objective(s) of the survey, the next step is to define the objective(s) operationally and determine how many questions are needed to gather the information to meet the objective(s). For Your Information Box 9.4 lists the objectives, the operational definitions for each objective, and the number of questions used to measure each objective of a class evaluation survey designed by students in a survey research methods course taught by one of this textbook's authors. The objectives are listed separately in the first column. The **operational definitions**—specific behaviors that represent the purpose—are listed in the second column for each objective. The number of questions used to measure the objectives is in the third column. Note how similar this table is to the test specification table for ensuring that a psychological test can demonstrate evidence for validity based on its content.

FOR YOUR INFORMATION BOX 9.4
OPERATIONAL DEFINITIONS FOR A CLASS EVALUATION SURVEY

As part of a survey research methods course, one of this textbook's authors required students to develop a college-level course evaluation survey. Discussions with subject matter experts (faculty, administrators, and students), reviews of course evaluations used by other colleges, and a literature review helped students clearly define the survey objectives. After defining the objectives, students operationally defined each one and determined how many questions would be developed to measure each objective. The objectives, operational definitions, and number of questions are shown below:

Objective	Operational Definition	Number of Questions
To measure student opinions of course learning materials	• Did the course include relevant reading material to contribute to students' intellectual growth? • Did exams assess the information included in reading material and presented by the instructor in class?	2
To measure the instructor's preparedness for class	• Did the instructor come to class on time? • Did the instructor have a clear agenda for each class meeting? • Did the instructor make learning objectives clear?	3
To measure the instructor's knowledge of subject matter and ability to convey knowledge	• Was the instructor able to answer questions about the material? • Did the instructor present information in a clear and logical sequence? • Did the instructor provide clear examples?	3
To determine the overall effectiveness of the course	• Was the instructor effective overall? • Was the course a good course?	2

Constructing a Plan

The next step is to construct a plan for completing the survey. Such a plan includes a list of all the phases and steps necessary to complete the survey, an estimate of the costs associated with the survey's development and administration and analysis of the survey data, and a timeline for completing each phase of the survey.

Constructing the Survey

The second phase in developing a survey involves selecting the type of survey to be constructed, writing survey questions, preparing the survey instrument, and pretesting the survey.

Selecting the Type of Survey

Before starting from scratch, developers find that it is always a good idea to search for an existing survey that meets the survey's objectives. They find existing surveys by conducting literature reviews and speaking with subject matter experts.

If an appropriate survey does not exist, developers must design their own survey, first deciding what type to develop. Surveys take many forms. **Self-administered surveys** are those that individuals complete themselves. These include **mail surveys** (mailed to respondents with instructions for completing and returning them) and **individually administered surveys** (administered by a facilitator in person for respondents to complete in the presence of the facilitator). At one time or another, you have probably received a survey in the mail. Likewise, you have probably been stopped in a shopping mall and asked to complete a survey. These are examples of mail and individually administered surveys, respectively.

Personal interviews are surveys that involve direct contact between the survey researcher and the respondents in person or by phone. Personal interviews include **face-to-face surveys**, in which an interviewer asks a series of questions in respondents' homes, a public place, or the researcher's office. These also include **telephone surveys**, in which an interviewer calls respondents and asks them questions over the phone. You have probably been stopped at one time or another and asked a few questions about a product. Likewise, you may have been contacted on the phone and asked to indicate whether you like, have heard enough of, or dislike various music segments. These are examples of face-to-face and telephone surveys, respectively. For both, interviewers can read survey questions from a paper-and-pencil form or a laptop. We are even beginning to see instances in which computers dial and ask survey questions over the telephone by themselves!

Writing Survey Questions

After selecting the type of survey, researchers write survey questions that match the survey's objectives. Just as there are different types of surveys, there are also various types of survey questions. These are some of the most popular:

- Open ended
- Closed ended
- Yes/no questions
- Fill in the blank
- Implied no choice
- Single-item choice
- Enfolded
- Free choice
- Multiple choice
- Ranking
- Rating
- Guttman format
- Likert and other intensity scale formats
- Semantic differential
- Paired comparisons and constant-referent comparisons

The type of questions chosen depends on the kind of information needed. For Your Information Box 9.5 provides examples of various types of survey questions.

FOR YOUR INFORMATION BOX 9.5

EXAMPLES OF SURVEY QUESTIONS

Different types of survey questions serve different purposes, and each has strengths and weaknesses. Below are some examples of the types of survey questions. Although it is an older reference, the U.S. General Accounting Office's (1993) *Developing and Using Questionnaires* is a very valuable resource for not only planning and using surveys but also understanding the strengths and weaknesses of different survey question types.

Open-Ended

Last year you were a member of student government. Please comment on your experience.

_____

Closed-Ended

Did you attend last week's biology study group?

_____ Yes _____ No

Row Format

Please indicate how many hours per week you study for each of the following courses.

Course	Hours	Course	Hours
Psychology	_____	Calculus	_____
Biology	_____	Art history	_____

Column Format

For each of the courses listed below, identify how many hours you study per week and how many pages you read for the course per week.

Course	Hours per week you study	Pages per week you read
Psychology	_____	_____
Biology	_____	_____
Calculus	_____	_____
Art history	_____	_____

Implied No Choice

Why didn't you pass your psychology exam?

_____ I did not study.

_____ I did not feel well.

_____ I don't know.

Did your professor review the following materials before your exam?

	Yes	No
Test–retest reliability	_____	_____
Alternate forms reliability	_____	_____
Split-half reliability	_____	_____
Content validity	_____	_____
Criterion-related validity	_____	_____
Construct validity	_____	_____

Single-Item Choice

There are two methods that can be used to evaluate your understanding of course material. One method is to give you an in-class exam, and the other method is to have you write a term paper. The question is, which method do you prefer?

_____ In-class exam

_____ Term paper

Fill in the Blank

How many brothers and sisters do you have? _____

(Continued)

(Continued)

Free Choice

If the psychology department started a psychology club, would you attend the meetings?

_____ Yes   _____ Probably not

_____ Probably   _____ No

_____ Uncertain

Multiple Choice

Which of the following statements best explains why you decided to transfer to another college/university? (Select one only.)

_____ I could not afford the tuition.

_____ I did not like the other students.

_____ I did not like the faculty.

_____ Other (describe) _____

_____

Ranking

Students select colleges for various reasons. Consider each of the following items that may influence a student's decision to apply to a specific college. Rank-order each of the items from *most important* (1) to *least important* (5).

Cost _____   Faculty _____

Location _____   Clubs/organizations _____

Majors _____

Rating

How organized was your professor?

_____ Very organized

_____ Somewhat organized

_____ Marginally organized

_____ Not organized at all

Likert-Type Format

Being able to approach your professors is a major advantage of attending a small college. Please indicate the extent to which you agree or disagree with the following statements about your professors.

	Strongly agree	Agree	Neither agree nor disagree	Disagree	Strongly disagree
Has set office hours					
Is approachable					

Semantic Differential

Please circle the number representing the demeanor of your professor.

Happy   1   2   3   4   5   6   7   **Grumpy**

No matter the type of questions, writing survey questions is not an easy task because of the complex cognitive processes a respondent goes through to answer a survey question. For Your Information Box 9.6 offers an explanation of the cognitive aspects of answering questions.

Although less common, **structured record reviews**, which are forms that guide data collection from existing records (e.g., using a form to collect information from personnel files), and **structured observations**, which are forms that guide an observer in collecting behavioral information (e.g., using a form to document the play behaviors of children on the playground), are also considered to be surveys.

Each type of survey has advantages and disadvantages. The type that is appropriate depends on the objectives of the research and the target audience. For further information about the

FOR YOUR INFORMATION BOX 9.6
COGNITIVE ASPECT OF ANSWERING QUESTIONS

For years, cognitive psychologists and survey researchers have acknowledged that answering survey questions can be a complex cognitive task (e.g., see Cannell, Miller, & Oksenberg, 1981; Groves, 1989; Kahn & Cannell, 1957; Miller, Mullin, & Herrmann, 1990; Tourangeau, 1984). Research suggests that when people answer survey questions, they go through at least four stages:

> Comprehension → Retrieval → Judgment → Response communication

First, they must comprehend the question. Second, they must retrieve the answer to the question. Third, they must judge the appropriate answer to the question. Fourth, they must communicate the answer.

Comprehension

When respondents are asked a question, they must first understand each word in the question and what the entire question is asking. To comprehend or understand a survey question, respondents must have long enough attention spans to pay attention to the question, a certain level of language ability so that they can understand the vocabulary and the entire question, and the appropriate general knowledge so that they can understand certain concepts contained in the question.

Retrieval

Once the respondents understand the meaning of the question, they must search their memories for the appropriate answer. When answer choices are presented to respondents, they must recognize the most appropriate answer. When answer choices are not presented to respondents, they must search their memories in a more thorough fashion for the correct answer. When the appropriate cues or hints are available, respondents will probably find the answer. When inappropriate cues are available, respondents will take bits and pieces of the information and reconstruct an answer to fit what is most likely to be the answer.

Judgment

After the respondents have retrieved answers from memory, they must judge or decide whether the information meets the objectives of the question. For example, if the question asks respondents to recall events from a specific time period, they will judge whether the events occurred during the appropriate time frame (i.e., if the question asks for their expenditures over the past 3 months, they will judge whether their answers include all of their expenditures over the past 3 months).

Response Communication

Once the respondents have comprehended the question, searched for and found answers, and judged their answers for appropriateness, they must communicate the answers to the question. If a question involves response choices, respondents must match their answers to the available choices. If the question requires that respondents articulate responses, they must construct understandable responses. However, before they communicate their response, respondents will evaluate whether the answers to the question meet their own personal motives and objectives. If respondents believe that their answers are threatening or not socially desirable, they may choose not to provide the correct answers. In other words, they may refuse to answer or may provide fake answers.

---

advantages and disadvantages of different types of surveys, read the U.S. General Accounting Office's (1993) *Developing and Using Questionnaires.*

Survey developers must pay careful attention to writing understandable, readable, and appealing survey questions because there are many chances for error in understanding a question, formulating an answer, and providing a response. To facilitate the question-answering process and increase the likelihood of obtaining accurate information, survey developers make sure their survey questions have the characteristics described in the following subsections.

Survey questions should be purposeful and straightforward. The relationship between what the question is asking and the objectives of the survey should be clear.

In fact, the survey researcher should begin with an explanation of the purpose of a group of questions. This helps the survey respondent focus on the appropriate issue(s). An example is provided below.

> Now we would like to ask you about the instructor. Please indicate whether you strongly agree (SA), agree (A), neither agree nor disagree (N), disagree (D), or strongly disagree (SD) with each of the following statements by placing a circle around the number that best represents your response.

The instructor . . .	SA	A	N	D	SD
• **presented material in an organized fashion**	5	4	3	2	1
• seemed well prepared for class	5	4	3	2	1
• explained assignments clearly	5	4	3	2	1
• allowed ample time for completion of assignments	5	4	3	2	1
• kept students informed about their progress/grades in the course	5	4	3	2	1
• was available outside of class time	5	4	3	2	1
• had a thorough knowledge of course content	5	4	3	2	1
• showed enthusiasm for the subject	5	4	3	2	1
• used teaching methods that were well suited for the course	5	4	3	2	1

Survey questions should be unambiguous. All survey questions should be concrete and should clearly define the context of the question. Questions should not contain jargon or acronyms unless all respondents to a particular survey are familiar with the jargon and acronyms.

Unacceptable	**Better Alternative**
Do you go out often?	Which of the following best describes how often you have gone out to dinner during the past three months? (Please select one.)

_____ Yes	_____ Not at all	_____ 3 or 4 times
_____ No	_____ 1 or 2 times	_____ 5 or more times

The question above and to the left is unacceptable because it does not clearly define what information the survey developer is seeking. Is the survey developer asking whether you go outside often, to the movies often, or what? The question to the right makes the exact meaning clearer.

Survey questions should be written in correct syntax. That is, all survey questions should be complete sentences with an orderly arrangement of words.

Unacceptable	**Better Alternative**
School attended? _____	What graduate school did you attend? _____

Survey questions should use appropriate rating scales and response options. Many questions ask respondents to rate their attitudes about something on a rating scale. The rating scale should always match the type of information being requested. Look at the following question from a local hotel satisfaction survey. Do you see a problem?

How satisfied were you with the overall quality of the services you received?

_____ Excellent _____ Very good _____ Average _____ Below average _____ Poor

The rating scale does not match the type of information the question is seeking. In other words, the rating scale describes "quality of services," although the question asks about the customer's level of satisfaction. A better alternative would be the following:

How satisfied were you with the overall quality of the services you received?

_____ Extremely satisfied

_____ Very satisfied

_____ Somewhat satisfied

_____ Not very satisfied

_____ Not satisfied at all

For Your Information Box 9.7 displays the types of rating scales identified by Mercer, a leading human resources consulting firm specializing in the design and delivery of assessments using state-of-the-art technology.

An important decision we must make when determining anchor points in a survey question is whether to include a midpoint category. A midpoint category offers respondents an opportunity to select a neutral response or be indifferent. Below is an example of a response scale without and with a mid point category.

Without midpoint category	With midpoint category
1—Strongly agree	1—Strongly agree
2—Agree	2—Agree
3—Somewhat agree	3—Somewhat agree
4—Somewhat disagree	**4—Neither agree or disagree**
5—Disagree	5—Somewhat disagree
6—Strongly disagree	6—Disagree
	7—Strongly disagree

Experts have in the past, and continue to, debate about whether to include a mid-point category. Some experts believe that including a midpoint category is important as it increases scale reliability, while others believe that including a mid point category can result in individuals satisficing; that is, taking the easy way out by not investing the time needed to really think about and provide a high quality answer. Whether to include a midpoint category is not an easy decision. Some people may genuinely have a neutral attitude, and not having a midpoint category may force these individuals to select a response that does not truly reflect how they feel, reducing the precision of measurement. If an individual selects a response

FOR YOUR INFORMATION BOX 9.7
DIFFERENT TYPES OF RATING SCALES

Industrial-organizational psychologists have researched the pros and cons of alternative response scales for many years, but there is no consensus on the "one best scale." What works best depends on the purpose of the survey and on the types of items included. However, there is consensus on the basic criteria for what constitutes a good response scale:

- The scale is simple and easy to understand.
- To the extent possible, raters have a common understanding about what the scale means—they interpret the scale in a similar fashion.
- The words used to define the levels are clearly ordered (e.g., it may not be clear which is higher, *excellent* or *outstanding*).
- The scale is suitable for the types of items in the survey (e.g., a scale in which one of the levels is *always* may or may not be appropriate, depending on the types of items).
- The scale leads to variance in ratings (competencies and participants are not all rated the same; there is a good spread in ratings).
- The scale is aligned with the main purpose of feedback (e.g., different scales would be appropriate when the purpose is developmental versus evaluating performance against expectations/ requirements).

Three other general conclusions can be drawn from the research:

1. Increasing the number of rating levels will, up to a point, lead to a greater spread in ratings (which is desirable). In most situations, having at least five levels is preferable. However, scales with more than seven levels can lead to more error being introduced.
2. The labels or anchor terms tend to confuse raters when there are more than six levels and each level is labeled.
3. In many cases, regardless of the themes or number of levels used, raters tend to inflate ratings, and there is less variance in scores than one would desire.

Listed below are the general types of response scales, based on the main theme or aspect on which the ratings are made:

- *Simple qualitative:* How would you rate the person in this area? (e.g., from *poor* to *excellent*)
- *Extent:* To what extent does the statement describe the person? (e.g., from *very little extent* to *very great extent*)
- *Frequency:* How often does the person demonstrate effective use of the behavior or skill? (e.g., from *almost never* to *almost always*)
- *Developmental (strength/development need):* How would you rate the person's capabilities in this area? (e.g., from *significant development need* to *exemplary—a role model*)

- *Comparison with others:* Compared with others with whom I have worked, this person is _____ in this area (e.g., from *significantly below average* to *the best I've ever worked with*)
- *Performance:* How would you rate his or her performance in this area? (e.g., from *does not meet expectations to far exceeds expectations*; note that this theme would make sense for performance appraisal purposes, but probably not for development purposes where peers and subordinates also provide ratings)

It is possible to construct a response scale that has more than one theme. For example, an anchor point of *the best I've ever worked with* combines the qualitative and comparison themes. However, unless this is carefully done, there is a danger of the response scale becoming too complex and thereby confusing.

As a final comment on general types of response scales, it is important that each level in a scale relate to the same theme(s). It is not appropriate, for example, that some levels of a scale relate to frequency and other levels relate to capability (developmental). This is a common failing of many "home-grown" response scales.

Anchor Points

Response scales vary in terms of two main factors—the number of levels (5 point, 6 point, etc.) and the theme or themes captured by the anchor terms and scale definitions. There is obviously a very large number of possible scales. Normally, each level in the scale has a descriptive anchor when there are four or fewer levels, but all the levels do not necessarily have to be anchored when there are five or more levels. Here is an example:

5—Exceptional strength
4
3—Competent
2
1—Weak

The theme for the 5-point scale above is developmental, and only three of the levels are anchored. It is highly questionable whether adding anchors for the second and fourth levels, using intermediate terms, would lead to more accurate and valid ratings. Raters implicitly form a mental image of the scale and its meaning and are able to easily understand that a rating of 4 is halfway between *competent* and *exceptional strength*.

The response scale below is an example of a 5-point frequency scale in which only three points are anchored:

Never		**Sometimes**		**Always**
1	2	3	4	5

There are many different types of response scales, including the following:

Qualitative Scales

4—Excellent	5—Outstanding	6—Extraordinary
3—Good	4—Very good	5—Superior
2—Fair	3—Good	4—Very good
1—Poor	2—Fair	3—Good
	1—Poor	2—Fair
		1—Poor

Extent Scales

4—Exactly descriptive	5—Very great extent	6—Completely true description
3—Very descriptive	4—Great extent	5—Largely true
2—Somewhat descriptive	3—Some extent	4—Somewhat true
1—Not descriptive	2—Little extent	3—Somewhat false
	1—Very little extent	2—Largely false
		1—Completely false description

Frequency Scales

4—Almost always	5—Almost always	6—100% of the time
3—Usually	4—Most of the time	5—90+% of the time
2—Sometimes	3—Often	4—80+% of the time
1—Seldom	2—Sometimes	3—70+% of the time
	1—Seldom	2—60+% of the time
		1—Less than 60% of the time

Developmental Scales

4—Towering strength	5—Exemplary, best possible	6—No room for improvement
3—Strength	4—Real strength	5—Significant strength
2—Competent	3—Fully competent	4—Strength
1—Development need	2—Development need	3—Competent
	1—Weakness	2—Development need
		1—Significant development need

Comparison Scales

4—One of the very best	5—Far above average	6—Top 5%
3—Better than most	4—Above average	5—80–95th percentile
2—Better than some	3—Average	4—50–80th percentile
1—Not as good as most	2—Below average	3—20–50th percentile
	1—Far below average	2—5–20th percentile
		1—Bottom 5%

Performance Scales

4—Commendable	5—Far above requirements	6—Exceeds all standards
3—Exceeds	4—Above requirements	5—Exceeds most, meets others
2—Meets	3—Meets requirements	4—Meets most, exceeds others
1—Does not meet	2—Below requirements	3—Meets all
	1—Far below requirements	2—Meets most, below on some
		1—Below on many standards

Source: From *INSIGHT: 360 Survey Response Scales Corporation*, by Censeo Corporation. Copyright © 2005 by Censeo Corporation. Reprinted by permission of Censeo Corporation.

that does not truly reflect how he or she feels, the validity of the survey results will also be affected because the inferences a researcher draws from the results (e.g., the proportion of respondents who truly agree or disagree with a question) will likely not be correct. However, if we include a midpoint category, individuals who are not motivated to accurately answer the question may be encouraged to satisfice. Another issue that has to be considered when deciding whether a midpoint category should be included is whether the midpoint might be treated as a "don't know" response. If the option of "don't know" is not explicitly included as one of the response options, the midpoint could be appropriately used to express that opinion. Sometimes that may be appropriate, sometimes not, depending on the context.

The best advice we can offer you is to review each question on the survey and ask yourself whether a midpoint response such as "neither agree nor disagree" could reflect a meaningful opinion that a survey respondent might hold. If so, then a middle option should be included in the scale. The consequences of not doing so is to force survey respondents to endorse an option on either side of the scale—an option they don't really agree with. This is especially true if the survey is administered online and the participants are not allowed to skip any questions. In that case, they would have to either endorse one of the options presented or decide not to complete the survey at all. A good resource for additional information on many of the topics we cover in this chapter is Marsden and Wright's (2010), *Handbook of Survey Research*, second edition.

Survey questions should include the appropriate categorical alternatives. When you are asking a question for which you have no idea of the possible responses, you should leave the question open ended. If you do provide alternatives, the question should include an inclusive list of response alternatives or an "other" category. For example, if you are interested in finding out whether students enjoyed their psychology class, it would not be appropriate to allow them to respond only *Yes, extremely* or *No, not at all*.

Unacceptable	**Better Alternative**
Did you enjoy your introductory psychology course?	Did you enjoy your introductory psychology course?
_____ Yes, extremely	_____ Yes, extremely
_____ No, not at all	_____ Yes, for the most part
	_____ No, for the most part
	_____ No, not at all

Survey questions should ask one and only one question. Be careful not to ask a **double-barreled question**—a question that is actually asking two or more questions in one. Here are two examples of double-barreled questions (really a triple-barreled question in one case) that we found in a hotel satisfaction survey:

1. Was our staff well informed, knowledgeable, and professional?

2. Were we responsive to your needs, solving any problems you may have had efficiently and to your satisfaction?

If a survey respondent says "yes" to either of these questions, it is impossible to tell whether the respondent is saying "yes" to the entire question or to only part of it. The same is true when a survey respondent says "no" to either of these questions. It would have been more appropriate to ask one or more of the following questions:

Was our staff well informed?	_____ Yes _____ No
Was our staff knowledgeable?	_____ Yes _____ No
Was our staff professional?	_____ Yes _____ No
Was our staff responsive to your needs?	_____ Yes _____ No
Did our staff efficiently solve any problems you may have had?	_____ Yes _____ No
Did our staff solve any problems you may have had to your satisfaction?	_____ Yes _____ No

Survey questions should be written at a comfortable reading level. Survey developers try to write questions that are easy to read (low readability level) so that respondents will be more likely to understand and interpret questions appropriately. Microsoft Word and similar software will calculate the reading level of any passage you write.

Preparing the Survey Instrument

Once the survey developer has written the questions, he or she must put them together into a package. The goal is to catch survey respondents' attention and motivate respondents to complete the survey so as to reduce the errors associated with incomplete surveys. Figure 9.2 displays the course evaluation survey developed by a research methods class taught by one of this textbook's authors. This survey highlights each of the items discussed subsequently.

FIGURE 9.2 ■ A Course Evaluation Survey Developed by Students

COURSE EVALUATION SURVEY

At the conclusion of each course, Rollins College administers a course evaluation survey to all students. Responses to this survey are used by the instructor to refine and improve the course, and by Rollins administration to evaluate instructor performance as well as make decisions about tenure, promotions, and other personnel issues.

Rollins College would like your feedback on the course and the effectiveness of the instructor. It is very important that you complete the entire survey. Your name will not be associated with your response.

PART I—COURSE

First, we would like to ask you about the course. Please indicate whether you strongly agree (SA), agree (A), neither agree nor disagree (N), disagree (D), or strongly disagree (SD) with each of the following statements by placing a circle around the number that best represents your response.

The course . . .	SA	A	N	D	SD
• contributed to my intellectual growth	5	4	3	2	1
• was useful to my work/career	5	4	3	2	1
• used a current text	5	4	3	2	1
• included helpful text readings	5	4	3	2	1
• exams tested my understanding of the material	5	4	3	2	1

(Continued)

FIGURE 9.2   ■   (Continued)

PART II—INSTRUCTOR

Now we would like to ask you about the instructor. Please indicate whether you strongly agree (SA), agree (A), neither agree nor disagree (N), disagree (D), or strongly disagree (SD) with each of the following statements by placing a circle around the number that best represents your response.

The instructor . . .	SA	A	N	D	SD
• presented material in an organized fashion	5	4	3	2	1
• seemed well prepared for class	5	4	3	2	1
• explained assignments clearly	5	4	3	2	1
• allowed ample time for completion of assignments	5	4	3	2	1
• kept students informed about their progress/grades in the course	5	4	3	2	1
• was available outside of class time	5	4	3	2	1
• had a thorough knowledge of course content	5	4	3	2	1
• showed enthusiasm for the subject	5	4	3	2	1
• utilized teaching methods that were well suited for the course	5	4	3	2	1

Since the instructors are very interested in identifying ways to improve the content of each course and their effectiveness as instructors, please comment below for those statements listed above that you have circled a 2 or below.

_____

_____

Next, please comment on each of the following questions. Your opinion counts, so please be candid with your response!

1. Overall, why was the instructor effective or ineffective?

_____

2. Overall, why would you classify this as a good course or a poor course?

_____

3. Overall, on a scale of 1 to 10 (with 10 being the highest), how would you rate this course?

_____

4. Add any other comments.

_____

THANK YOU FOR YOUR FEEDBACK

Title and seal. The front page of the survey should always have a title, in a large font, centered at the top of the page so that it stands out from the survey questions. The title should indicate what the questionnaire is about (e.g., "Course Evaluation Survey"). Many times, survey researchers also identify the target audience (e.g., "Survey of Employees Regarding Child Care Arrangements"). When possible, the first page should also include a seal or a company logo to lend more credibility.

Appeal and instructions. The front page should include an appeal to the respondent and instructions on how to complete the survey. The instructions should do the following both concisely and courteously:

1. State the purpose of the survey.

2. Explain who is sponsoring or conducting the survey.

3. Explain why it is important for respondents to complete the survey to the best of their ability.

4. Explain how to complete the form.

5. Assure respondents that their answers are confidential and will be reported in group format only.

6. Thank respondents for their cooperation. (U.S. General Accounting Office, 1993)

When the survey is a mail survey, the instructions should also include information about how to return it. If a professional administers the survey, he or she should read these instructions to respondents.

Headings and subheadings. The survey should include headings and subheadings to help guide respondents through the survey. These should be short phrases that tell respondents what each part of the survey is about and should stand out from the survey questions.

Transitions. Survey respondents should be introduced to each new section with a topic heading that informs them about the next section of the survey. The transition should also include any specific instructions about how to answer the questions when the type of question changes.

Response instructions. Survey developers should provide response instructions that tell respondents how to answer appropriately or that lead them to another part of the questionnaire. Response instructions should be short directions, often in parentheses and italics. For example, some response forms that will be scanned electronically require that respondents complete the forms with a pencil.

Bold typeface. Survey researchers often use bold typeface to emphasize key points in directions or questions.

Justification of response spaces. A common practice is to justify the response spaces (e.g., a line, a checkbox) to the left of response choices and columns to the right.

Shading. When there are spaces on the survey that you want respondents to leave blank, it is a good idea to use shading in these spaces to discourage respondents from writing in them. You might also separate rows of text on a horizontal layout to guide respondents across a page of text.

White space. Survey designers should also make sure that there is adequate white (blank) space on the survey. A crowded survey does not look inviting and is often difficult to complete. For instance, designers leave margins of at least 1 inch and ample space between questions and sections of the survey. Some designers are tempted to try to fit the entire survey on one sheet of paper. Although surveys should be printed on as few pages as possible, the designer must balance the need for white space with the need to conserve paper and printing costs.

Printing. Surveys fewer than three pages in length are usually printed on two sides of a sheet of paper. When it is necessary for the survey to be longer, pages should be stapled in the upper left corner. Extremely long surveys may be spiral bound or printed in a booklet format.

Font. Survey designers should use an attractive, businesslike, and readable font and should make sure the overall format is organized and inviting. This makes the survey look professional and easier to complete—and, in turn, makes respondents pay more attention to the survey, decreasing survey completion time and respondents' effort.

Pretesting the Survey

The third task in the survey construction phase is to pretest the survey. **Pretesting** allows you to do the following:

1. Identify sources of **nonsampling measurement errors**—errors associated with the design and administration of the survey.

2. Examine the effectiveness of revisions to a question or an entire survey.

3. Examine the effect of alternative versions of a question or survey.

4. Assess the final version of a survey for respondent understanding, time to complete, and ease of completion.

5. Obtain data from the survey and make changes to the format that might make data entry or analysis more efficient.

The methods may differ for pretesting surveys. The method the survey developer chooses depends on the objectives of the pretest and the available resources, such as time, funds, and staff. Some pretesting methods are more appropriate for the preliminary stages of survey development. For example, the following methods are useful for providing survey designers with knowledge of respondent understanding of survey concepts and wording (qualitative analysis).

One-on-One Interviews

- *Concurrent "think-aloud" interviews:* Respondents describe their thoughts as they think about and answer the survey questions.

- *Retrospective "think-aloud" interviews:* Typically, these are one-on-one interviews during which the interviewer asks respondents how they went about generating their answers after they complete the survey.

- *Paraphrasing:* The interviewer asks respondents to repeat questions in their own words.

- *Confidence ratings:* After answering survey questions, respondents rate how confident they are that their responses are correct.

Respondent focus groups. A **focus group** brings together people who are similar to the target respondents in order to discuss issues related to the survey. Usually, each person in the group completes the survey, and then the respondents discuss the survey experience with the test developer or a trained facilitator. Some pretesting methodologies evaluate the drafted survey under conditions that mimic the actual survey process. These methodologies help researchers identify problems, such as respondent fatigue, distraction, hostility, and lack of motivation, that are difficult to identify using other pretesting methods.

Behavior coding of respondent–interviewer interactions. Behavior coding involves assigning numbers or letters to the interchange between an interviewer and a survey respondent. Coding provides a systematic technique for identifying problems with questions. Behavior coding helps identify the types and frequencies of interviewer behaviors (e.g., the interviewer reads the question exactly as written, the interviewer reads the question with a major change in meaning) and respondent behaviors (e.g., the respondent provides an adequate response, the respondent asks for clarification) that can compromise the reliability and validity of a survey. Behavior coding is most useful for personal interviews; however, it can be modified for other types of surveys. Behavior coding is a popular pretesting technique for government surveys.

Interviewer and respondent debriefings. This method involves asking interviewers or respondents questions following a **field test**—an administration of the survey or test to a large representative group of individuals to identify problems with administration, item interpretation, and so on. (We discuss the field or pilot test in more detail in the "How Do We Develop a Test?" chapter.)

Split-sample tests. This method involves field-testing two or more versions of a question, sets of questions, or surveys. The objective is to determine which version of the question, set of questions, or survey provides the most accurate results.

Item nonresponse. This method involves distributing the survey and then calculating the **item nonresponse rate**—how often an item or question was not answered.

It is very important that a survey be pretested to ensure that the questions are appropriate for the target population. Most survey questions need to be revised multiple times before they are finalized. Before moving on to the survey administration phase, the survey should meet the following criteria:

- The questions reflect the purpose of the survey.

- There is no technical language or jargon (unless you are sure that it will be understood universally).

- There are no long and complex questions that may be difficult to understand.

- The meanings of all key terms are explained.

- There are no double-barreled questions.

- Adequate, explicit, and inclusive alternatives are presented for multiple-choice questions.

- The survey vocabulary is appropriate for all respondents.

- There are no misspelled words or grammatical errors.

- The survey has a title and headings.

- The survey includes instructions.

- The survey layout includes adequate white space.

- The type on the survey is large enough to be read comfortably.

- There are introductory and transition statements between questions.

- The directions for answering are clear.

- The style of the items is not too monotonous.

- The survey format flows well.

- The survey items are numbered correctly.

- The skip patterns are easy to follow.

- The survey is not too long.

- The survey is easy to read and is attractive.

When pretesting surveys, asking oneself the questions in For Your Information Box 9.8 might be valuable. The questions are categorized by the type of survey being used.

Administering the Survey

The third phase in developing a survey requires administering the survey to the target population. This phase involves three steps: selecting the appropriate respondents, determining the sample size, and distributing the survey.

Selecting the Appropriate Respondents

Although the survey might be administered to the entire **population**—all members of the target audience—it is more typical to administer the survey to a representative subset of the population, known as a **sample**. The decision often depends on the survey's purpose, the cost of administering the survey, and the availability of respondents.

If you were interested in designing a class evaluation survey to measure the success of a particular class, your population would be all of the members of the class. Because it would be easy to do, you would probably choose to administer the survey to the entire population (all class members). However, if you were interested in designing a survey to determine how high school seniors feel about the usefulness of the SAT as a college admissions test, your population would be all high school seniors who have completed the SAT and plan to attend college. Because it would be very expensive and infeasible to distribute your survey to all high school seniors who have completed the SAT, you would probably sample all high school seniors who have completed the SAT and who plan to attend college.

A good sample would be a representative group of the population of high school seniors. If the sample is not representative, it is difficult to generalize the survey results to the entire population—that is, to say that the results would be the same if we had given the survey to the entire population. The goal is to use a sampling technique that allows you to give everyone— or nearly everyone—in your population an equal chance of being selected and to end up with a sample that is truly representative of the population. There are various methods for selecting a sample. Most can be classified into two categories: probability sampling and nonprobability sampling. Trochim's Research Methods Knowledge Base, available online, includes a complete description of different sampling techniques (Trochim, 2006).

FOR YOUR INFORMATION BOX 9.8
QUESTIONS TO ASK WHEN PRETESTING SURVEYS

Mail and Other Self-Administered Surveys

- Are instructions for completing the survey clearly written?

- Are the questions easy to understand?

- Do respondents know how to indicate their answers (e.g., circle or mark the response, use a special pencil, use the space bar)?

- Are the response choices mutually exclusive (not double-barreled)?

- Are the response choices exhaustive?

- Do respondents understand what to do with completed questionnaires (e.g., return them by mail in a self-addressed envelope, fax them)?

- Do respondents understand when to return the completed survey?

- If it is a computer-assisted survey, can respondents use the software commands correctly?

- If it is a computer-assisted survey, do respondents know how to change (or "correct") their answers?

- If an incentive is given for completing the survey, do respondents understand how to obtain it (e.g., it will automatically be sent on receipt of the completed survey, it is included with the questionnaire)?

- Is privacy respected and protected?

- Do respondents have any suggestions regarding the addition or deletion of questions, the clarification of instructions, or improvements in format?

Telephone Interviews

- Do interviewers understand how to ask questions and present options for responses?

- Do interviewers know how to get in-depth information, when appropriate, by probing respondents' brief answers?

- Do interviewers know how to record information?

- Do interviewers know how to keep the interview to the time limit?

- Do interviewers know how to return completed interviews?

- Are interviewers able to select the sample using the instructions?

- Can interviewers use the phone logs readily to record the number of times and when potential respondents were contacted?

- Do interviewers understand the questions?

- Do interviewees understand how to answer the questions (e.g., pick the top two, rate items according to whether they agree or disagree)?

- Do interviewees agree that privacy has been protected and respected?

In-Person Interviews

- Do interviewers understand how to ask questions and present options for responses?

- Do interviewers know how to get in-depth information, when appropriate, by probing respondents' brief answers?

- Do interviewers know how to record information?

- Do interviewers know how to keep the interview to the time limit?

- Do interviewers know how to return completed interviews?

- Do interviewees understand the questions?

- Do interviewees understand how to answer the questions (e.g., pick the top two, rate items according to whether they agree or disagree)?

- Do interviewees agree that privacy has been protected and respected?

Probability sampling is a type of sampling that uses statistics to ensure that a sample is representative of a population. Simple random sampling, stratified random sampling, and cluster sampling are examples of probability sampling methods.

With **simple random sampling**, every member of a population has an equal chance of being chosen as a member of the sample. To select a random sample, many people use a table of random numbers. Using this technique, a researcher assigns consecutive numbers to each individual in the population. Then, using a table of random numbers (found in the appendices of many statistics books), the researcher reads the numbers in any direction. When he or she reaches a number that matches one of the assigned numbers, the individual corresponding to that number becomes a member of the sample. Of course, researchers could also write the names of individuals on pieces of paper, throw them into a hat, and select individuals to be included in their sample by randomly pulling pieces of paper out of the hat!

Because each member of a population has an equal chance of being selected, we often presume that a simple random sample will be representative of the characteristics of a population. Unfortunately, simple random sampling does not ensure that the sample will include adequate proportions of individuals with certain characteristics. For example, if a particular population is 75% female and 25% male, simple random sampling will not guarantee the same proportion of female to male respondents in the sample.

A variation of simple random sampling is **systematic sampling**, in which every *n*th (e.g., every fifth) person in a population is chosen as a member of the sample. To sample systematically, the researcher assigns consecutive numbers to each individual in the population and then selects every *n*th person to become a member of the sample. This technique has the same weakness as random sampling; it might not have the same proportion of individuals as the population, and if the list is arranged alphabetically, not everyone will have an equal chance of being chosen.

Unlike simple random sampling, with **stratified random sampling**, a population is divided into subgroups or *strata* (e.g., gender, age, socioeconomic status). A random sample is selected from each stratum. The strata should be based on some evidence that they are related to the issue or problem the survey addresses. For example, if you are interested in exploring how high school seniors feel about the value of the SAT for predicting college success, your population would include all high school seniors. You may wish to stratify your sample by gender because SAT score seems to be a better predictor for female students. This becomes especially important when one of the survey objectives is to make inferences about subgroups (e.g., male vs. female students) in the population. If there is not a sufficient number of respondents in some of the subgroups in which you are interested, any conclusions you reach may not accurately generalize to the full population.

Cluster sampling is used when it is not feasible to list all of the individuals who belong to a particular population and is a method often used with surveys that have large target populations. With cluster sampling, clusters (e.g., regions of the country, states, high schools) are selected and participants are selected from each cluster. For Your Information Box 9.9 includes an example of cluster sampling.

Nonprobability sampling is a type of sampling in which not everyone has an equal chance of being selected from the population. Nonprobability sampling methods are often used because they are convenient and less expensive than probability sampling. One method of nonprobability sampling is **convenience sampling**. With convenience sampling, the survey researcher uses any available group of participants to represent the population. For example, if your population of interest is high school seniors, you might choose to use

FOR YOUR INFORMATION BOX 9.9

AN EXAMPLE OF CLUSTER SAMPLING

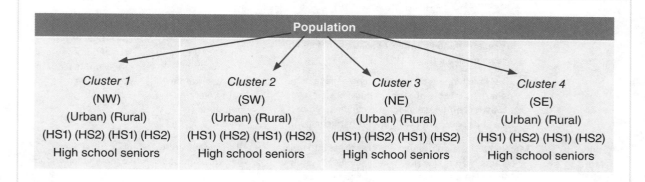

the high school seniors at a local high school as your participants. Table 9.3 includes a summary of different types of samples, how they are drawn, and some strengths and weaknesses of each.

Let us say you were interested in surveying high school seniors. You could divide the population of high school seniors into four initial clusters, namely, the regions of the country where they attend high school: the Northwest, Southwest, Northeast, and Southeast. Then you would divide the high schools in each of these regions into those that are in urban settings and those that are in rural settings. You could then randomly select two high schools from each rural setting and two high schools from each urban setting and administer your survey to each student in the randomly selected high schools or randomly select students in each of these high schools.

Determining the Sample Size

The **sample size** refers to the number of people needed to represent the target population accurately. How many people constitute a good sample size? This is not an easy question, because there are various factors that must be considered when deciding how many people to include in a sample. One thing to consider is the **homogeneity of the population**—how similar the people in your population are to one another. The more similar the members of the population, the smaller the sample that is necessary. The more dissimilar the members of the population, the larger the sample that is necessary to have this variation represented in the sample. Remember that the fewer the people chosen to participate in a survey (the smaller the sample), the more error the survey results are likely to include. This error is referred to as **sampling error**—a statistic that reflects how much error can be attributed to the lack of representation of the target population by the sample of respondents chosen.

TABLE 9.3 ■ Types of Samples

Type of Sample	How to Draw	Strengths	Weaknesses
Simple random	There are different ways to draw a random sample. For example: • Every participant can be assigned a number and a predetermined number of participants can be drawn from a hat. • Every participant can be listed on a piece of paper and a table of random numbers, or a statistical software program, can be used to select a predetermined number of participants.	• Every case in the population has an equal chance of being selected. • The result is in an unbiased, representative sample of the population studied.	• It can be time-consuming. • It is not always practical or feasible to randomly select individuals from the population.
Stratified random	Members of the population are classified into strata or categories (e.g., gender, age, region of country), and then a random sampling technique is used to select participants from within the strata in the same proportion as they exist in the population being studied.	• Participants will be representative of the population.	• It is not always practical to randomly select individuals from the population.
Cluster	Instead of randomly sampling participants, the researcher uses naturally occurring groupings of participants (e.g., participants in Classroom 1 and participants in Classroom 2).	• The method can be used when it is not practical to randomly select individual participants. • It is easy to obtain participants.	• Subjects in the naturally occurring groupings may not be equivalent, making it hard to interpret study results.
Convenience	The researcher uses whatever participants are available, for example, volunteers.	• It is easy to obtain participants.	• Participants are likely not representative of the entire population. • The results likely cannot be generalized to the population.

There are various references that include statistical calculations that researchers use to estimate a sample size. For an online resource for calculating survey sample sizes, see On the Web Box 9.5.

Distributing the Survey

The last step is to distribute the survey. How we distribute the survey depends on the type of survey (e.g., mail survey, face-to-face interview, telephone survey). The survey user who is conducting an individually administered or face-to-face survey must decide when, where,

ON THE WEB BOX 9.5

CALCULATING SAMPLE SIZE

www.surveysystem.com/sscalc.htm

How many people must you sample to represent the entire population accurately? There are various print materials available to help researchers estimate a sample size, and there are also online resources. For example, Creative Research Systems (2012) offers, as a public service, an online sample size calculator. This easy-to-use calculator can help you determine how many people you need to survey to get results that reflect the attitude or knowledge of your target population. This calculator also allows you to find out how precise your results are when you have already sampled a population.

Some surveys are administered to an entire population, and others are administered to a representative sample or a random sample of the population. As you probably have noted, representative samples and random samples are different. A representative sample is chosen so that the demographics of the sample match the demographic characteristics of the population. On the other hand, a random sample contains simply those individuals who were chosen using a random numbers table or by drawing names out of a hat. One of the assumptions we must make when using the Creative Research Systems online sample size calculator is that the sample we choose will be a random sample. Representative samples and convenience samples require far more responses than a simple random sample.

Another thing to remember when estimating sample size is that not everyone who receives a survey will complete and return it. Therefore, when deciding how many surveys to send, the researcher must first estimate the expected response. The expected response rate will be the number the calculator gives you, not the number of surveys to distribute. If you have already administered a survey and wish to know if the number that responded is sufficient, you can put in the number of received responses and calculate how confident you can be that the responses represent the responses you would have received if you had surveyed the entire population.

To use this calculator to determine a sample size, you will need to know the confidence interval and confidence level you are willing to accept. As you learned in the "What Is Test Reliability/Precision?" chapter, the confidence interval is the range of scores that we feel confident includes the true score. For example, if we have a confidence interval of ±5% and 50% of our sample picks a particular answer, we can be certain that if we

Determine Sample Size

Confidence Level: ☐ 95% ◉ 99%

Confidence Interval: 5

Population: 1000

[Calculate]   [Clear]

Sample size needed: 400

Determine Sample Size

Confidence Level: ◉ 95% ☐ 99%

Confidence Interval: 5

Population: 1000

[Calculate]   [Clear]

Sample size needed: 278

had asked the question of the entire population, somewhere between 45% (50 − 5) and 55% (50 + 5) would have selected that answer.

On the other hand, the confidence level is how certain we can be that the true percentage of the population who would pick an answer lies within the confidence level. For example, if our confidence level is 95%, this means that we can be 95% sure. By combining the confidence interval and the confidence level, we can say, for example, that we are 95% certain that the true percentage of the population who answered positively is between 45% and 55%.

(Continued)

(Continued)

When we are willing to accept wider confidence intervals, we can be more certain that the entire population would be within our range. For example, if we asked 500 Florida teenagers to name their favorite fast-food restaurant and 60% named the same one, we could be very certain that between 40% and 80% of all Florida teenagers actually do prefer this fast-food restaurant, but we cannot be so sure that between 59% and 61% of the teenagers prefer this one.

If you know the size of the population, you will want to enter it as well. On the other hand, if the population is unknown or is very large, you can leave it blank. Remember, random samples can be taken only from finite populations, that is, samples for which every individual can be identified and therefore have an equal chance of being chosen.

Here is an example of how the sample size calculator works. If we indicate that we are willing to accept a 99% confidence level, with a confidence interval of 5%, and we know we have a population size of 1,000, the calculator estimates that we would need a random sample of 400. Note that if we leave the population blank, the required sample size increases to 666.

If we estimate that only half of those who receive the survey will complete and return it—a response rate of 50%—then we will need to administer or mail twice as many as we need, or 800.

Many people would say, "If I must administer 800 surveys for a population of 1,000, why not administer them to all 1,000?" However, as the size of the population grows, the proportion of the sample in relation to the population decreases. You can test this assertion by calculating the random sample size needed for a population of 10,000.

One way to decrease the size of the sample needed is to settle for a lower confidence level (e.g., a 95% confidence level instead of a 99% confidence level). For example, if we are willing to accept a confidence level of 95%, we would need a random sample of only 278 respondents. With an expected response rate of 50%, we would need to administer only 556 surveys, and that number would provide considerable savings of administration and analysis costs when compared with surveying the entire population.

For more information on calculating sample sizes, or to use the online sample size calculator, go to www.surveysystem.com/sscalc.htm.

Source: Reprinted by permission of Creative Research Systems.

and how people will meet with the survey researcher. The survey user who is conducting a telephone survey must decide who will make the phone calls, how the participants will be selected, and when the participants will be called. For mail surveys, the survey user must decide when, how, and to whom he or she will mail the surveys. Dillman's (1978) *Mail and Telephone Surveys: The Total Design Method* is an older, yet excellent reference for conducting mail and telephone surveys. Fink's (2002) *The Survey Kit* is another excellent reference for conducting all types of surveys.

Special materials (e.g., special paper on which to print the survey, envelopes for mail surveys, pencils for self-administered surveys, telephones for telephone surveys) might be required. Finally, self-administered surveys must be assembled (stapling papers together and stuffing and addressing envelopes) so that they are ready for respondents to complete.

Coding, Entering, and Analyzing Survey Data

The fourth phase of survey development involves coding and entering the survey data into the computer software for analysis. This process includes coding the survey questions, entering the data into a spreadsheet program, verifying that the data are entered correctly, and conducting the statistical analysis.

Coding the Survey Questions

The answers to all survey questions must be coded before they can be entered into a computer program. Although coding answers to closed-ended survey questions is relatively simple, coding answers to open-ended questions can be difficult. With closed-ended questions, survey researchers typically assign a code or numerical value to each of the response choices. For example, let us say the question was "Why didn't you pass your psychology exam?" (Select one of the following.)

_____ I did not study   _____ I don't know

_____ I did not feel well   _____ Other

The first response option may be coded as a 1, the second as a 2, the third as a 3, and the fourth as a 4. Thus, each person's response would get a 1, 2, 3, or 4. Sometimes researchers use A, B, C, D, and so on, instead of numbers, depending on the level of measurement of the question. Note that these are categorical data; therefore, statistical analyses are limited to calculating frequency of responses and percentage of responses.

If the respondent were allowed to choose more than one answer to a question (e.g., "Please select all that apply"), the data analyst would code the corresponding number to the response options chosen by the respondent. When respondents choose more than one answer to a question, it is often necessary to record the answers to the question as if it were two questions. For more information on coding survey items, see Fink (2003).

Coding becomes more difficult for open-ended questions. Usually the first step is to take all of the answers to a particular open-ended question and sort them based on a criterion. For example, imagine the following survey item: "Last year you were a member of student government. Please comment on your experience." You might sort by positive and negative experiences (the criterion), or you might sort by the contents of the answers (another criterion; Edwards & Thomas, 1993). All open-ended questions need to be coded before they can be entered into the computer program.

Entering and Verifying the Data

Survey researchers usually use statistical software packages, such as SPSS, SAS, and Excel, to record and analyze responses. As the responses are entered into the computer program, the researcher constructs a **database**—a matrix in the form of a spreadsheet that shows the responses given by each participant (row) and for each question (column) in the survey. After entering the data and before starting the data analysis, the researcher verifies that the data have been entered correctly. For instance, if your survey questions have four possible responses numbered 1 to 4, you or the software can check to be sure that there is no datum less than 1 or greater than 4. If such a number is found, it is an entry error and can be corrected.

Conducting the Statistical Analysis

Usually survey developers plan the data analysis at the time of the survey's construction. Having a data analysis plan ensures that the data gathered will be appropriate for meeting the survey's objectives. (Recall our discussion of nominal, ordinal, interval, and ratio data in the "How Do Test Users Interpret Test Scores?" chapter.) The actual analysis is usually a matter of pointing the mouse and clicking a button.

One statistic important for all surveys is the **response rate**—the number of individuals who responded to the survey divided by the total number of individuals to whom the survey was sent. Response rates tend to vary depending on the type of survey. For instance, one-on-one interviews can be expected to have higher response rates than mail surveys.

Survey researchers also calculate and report the reliability (internal consistency) of each of the dimensions on the survey. For example, earlier in this chapter we said that one objective of the course evaluation survey was to measure student opinions of course format. The reliability coefficient (KR-20 or coefficient alpha) shows how strongly the items in the survey that were intended to measure one objective are related (Edwards & Thomas, 1993).

The data analysis also includes calculating the sampling error. Used with means and standard deviations, sampling error tells us how accurately the data reflect what the results would have been if the researchers had surveyed the entire population. Many survey researchers believe that if the results of a survey come within 5 percentage points of what the results would have been if the entire population had been surveyed, the survey has done a good job. For more information on computing sampling errors for surveys, read Fowler (1988).

Next the researcher conducts **univariate analyses**—computation of statistics that summarize individual question responses. Univariate analyses include frequency counts, percentages, means, modes, and medians. Frequency counts are tallies of how many participants chose each of the response options for a question. Percentages are calculated by taking the number of individuals who chose a particular response and dividing that number by the total number of people who responded to the question. For questions that yield interval-level data, such as ratings from 1 to 10, the researcher may wish to calculate the mean, median, or mode. (We discussed these concepts in detail in "How Do Test Users Interpret Test Scores?" chapter.)

The survey objectives may require the researcher to compare the responses given by two or more subgroups of respondents or the responses to two or more questions by all respondents. Such an analysis requires bivariate or multivariate analysis. **Bivariate analyses** provide information on two variables or groups, and **multivariate analyses** provide information on three or more variables or groups. These analyses may include calculating correlation coefficients, cross-tabulations, chi-square comparisons, *t* tests, or analyses of variance. (Some of these statistical tests are beyond the scope of this textbook; however, you will find them explained in most introductory statistics textbooks.) The technique the researcher chooses depends on the objectives of the survey and the level of measurement provided by the survey.

Presenting the Findings

The fifth and final phase involves reporting the survey results to those who commissioned the survey's development and sometimes to the public at large. Whether the report is written or oral, its effectiveness and usefulness depend on how well it is prepared and how well it addresses the questions and general knowledge of its audience (Fink, 2003). For instance, reports that contain numerous tables and statistical jargon will be useful for statisticians, but the general public needs a simpler version in everyday words.

Outlining a Report

In general, a survey report includes a description of the survey's objectives, details about survey construction and administration, and the survey findings. To ensure that each of these areas is covered in the report, the researcher prepares an outline of the information similar to the one shown in Figure 9.3.

FIGURE 9.3 ■ Survey Report Outline

---

1. Survey Objectives—Class Evaluation Survey

   - To measure student opinions of course format and learning materials
   - To measure the instructor's organization and knowledge of the subject matter
   - To determine the overall effectiveness of the course

2. Survey Methods

   - Performed literature review
   - Communicated with subject matter experts
     - Dean of the faculty
     - Faculty
   - Identified survey objectives
   - Operationally defined survey objectives
   - Wrote survey questions
   - Prepared survey instrument
   - Pilot-tested survey
   - Revised and finalized survey
   - Administered survey

3. Survey Findings

   - 80% reported that the reading material was relevant.
   - 90% reported that exams assessed information presented in class.
   - 90% reported that the instructor was prepared for class.
   - 85% reported that the instructor was organized.
   - 90% reported that the instructor made course objectives clear.
   - 100% reported that the instructor was knowledgeable of the material.
   - 80% reported that the course was effective.
   - 90% reported that this was a good course.

4. Implications

   - Students liked the course.
   - Students thought the instructor was organized and knowledgeable.
   - Students thought the course was effective.

Source: Adapted from Fink, A. (2003). *The survey handbook* (2nd ed.). Thousand Oaks, CA: Sage. Copyright © 2003 by SAGE Publications. Reprinted by permission of SAGE Publications, Inc.

Ordering and Determining the Contents of a Presentation

The general headings of the presentation outline provide a summary of the report and can serve as a structure for presenting the survey results. The focus of the presentation and the amount of detail provided should be adjusted to reflect the needs of the audience. For example, if you are presenting to researchers, they might be interested in knowing more about the size of the sample, the response rate, and the methods of analysis than would a general audience that might be more interested in the results and implications of the survey.

Using Slides and Handouts

Professionals use learning aids, such as slides and handouts, to keep the attention of the audience and to increase the audience's understanding of the results. You can use these learning aids to display your presentation outline, major points related to each section of the outline, and charts, tables, and graphs. Typically this information is prepared on a transparency, on a slide, or in a PowerPoint (or some other software) presentation. You can also make copies of the information to provide to the audience as handouts, which help the audience follow the presentation and make notes only as needed.

SURVEY RELIABILITY/ PRECISION AND VALIDITY

Only well-developed and well-administered surveys provide information about attitudes, behaviors, and knowledge that we can feel confident about using. Psychometrics (which we discussed previously in Section II) allows us to determine when a survey is good. What is a good survey? Like a good psychological test, a good survey measures what it says it is measuring consistently and accurately. If a survey does not measure what it is intended to measure consistently and accurately, then it will not collect accurate information. Without accurate information, we tend to make poor decisions.

An unreliable survey cannot be valid because with inconsistent data you cannot have accurate findings. However, a reliable survey can be invalid; it can give you similar information each time you use it, but not information that is related to the purpose of the survey.

Survey Reliability/Precision

In survey research, we often speak of two types of errors: random errors and measurement errors. Random errors are those that are unpredictable, and measurement errors are those that are associated with how a survey performs in a particular population. As you recall from the "What Is Test Reliability/Precision?" chapter, reliability/precision is a statistical measure that tells you how good an instrument is at obtaining similar results each time it is used. A reliable survey is one that gives you similar information each time you use it. A reliable survey is as free as possible from measurement error caused by poorly worded questions, ambiguous terms, inappropriate reading level, unclear directions, and incorrect skip patterns—to name a few potential problems.

As with psychological tests, there are various ways to gather evidence of the reliability/precision of a survey: test–retest, alternate forms, and split-half reliability. Test–retest and split-half reliability are the most common (discussed in detail in "What Is Test Reliability/Precision?" chapter). You can increase a survey's reliability by writing multiple items for each dimension, determining whether other organizational members would assign an item to the same dimension for which it was written, and grouping all items from a single dimension together.

Survey Validity

As you should recall from the earlier chapters on validity, when we speak of test validity, we are asking, "Are the inferences I am going to draw from a person's score on a test appropriate?" *Validity* refers to whether there is evidence to support the interpretation of the test scores. In survey research, when speaking of validity, we often refer to the degree to which the survey reflects or assesses the concept that a researcher is attempting to measure. If a survey is designed to measure students' satisfaction with course content, it should measure only students' satisfaction with course content—not students' satisfaction with their grades!

In survey research, we speak of both internal and external validity. Various methods exist for demonstrating evidence of internal validity. In survey research, we typically assess evidence of validity using four methods discussed in previous chapters: content, criterion-related, construct, and face validity. We are also concerned with external validity, or the extent to which the survey results obtained from a sample are generalizable to other populations, other places and /or other times.

Chapter Summary

Individuals and organizations use surveys to collect important information from individuals. Surveys allow us to collect information so that we can describe and compare how people feel about things (attitudes), what they know (knowledge), and what they do (behaviors). Full-service survey research companies design surveys, collect survey data, tabulate survey answers, interpret survey data, and report survey results for organizational sponsors. Companies also offer free and fee-based survey software so that individuals and companies can design, collect, analyze, and report their own survey data.

The scientific approach to survey development involves five phases: identifying the survey objectives, constructing the survey, administering the survey, entering and analyzing the data, and presenting the findings. During the first phase, the researcher identifies the objectives of the survey, defines the objectives operationally, and constructs a plan for completing the survey. During the second phase, the researcher selects the type of survey to conduct, writes survey questions, prepares the survey, and pretests the survey. During the third phase, the researcher administers the survey. During the fourth phase, the researcher develops coding schemes for entering the data into a computer program, verifies the data, and analyzes the data. During the fifth phase, the researcher presents the results orally or in written format to the survey user. As with psychological tests, it is very important that surveys be reliable and valid.

Engaging in the Learning Process

Learning is the process of gaining knowledge and skills through schooling or studying. Although you can learn by reading the chapter material, attending class, and engaging in discussion with your instructor, more actively engaging in the learning process may help you better learn and retain chapter information. To help you actively engage in the learning process, we encourage you to access our new supplementary student workbook. The workbook contains critical thinking activities to help you understand and apply information, and help you make progress toward learning and retaining material. If you do not have a copy of the workbook, you can purchase a copy through sagepub.com.

Key Concepts

After completing your study of this chapter, you should be able to define each of the following terms. These terms are bolded in the text of this chapter and defined in the Glossary.

bivariate analyses
cluster sampling
convenience sampling
database
decennial census survey
descriptive research
    techniques
double-barreled question
experimental research
    techniques
experts
face-to-face surveys
field test
focus group
homogeneity
    of the population

individually administered
    surveys
item nonresponse rate
literature reviews
mail surveys
multivariate analyses
nonprobability sampling
nonsampling measurement
    errors
operational definitions
personal interviews
population
pretesting
probability sampling
response rate
sample

sample size
sampling error
scientific method
self-administered surveys
simple random sampling
stratified random sampling
structured observations
structured record reviews
survey objectives
survey research firms
survey researchers
surveys
systematic sampling
telephone surveys
univariate analyses

Critical Thinking Questions

The following are some critical thinking questions to support the learning objectives for this chapter.

Learning Objectives	Critical Thinking Questions
Describe the similarities and differences between a survey and a psychological test.	• Imagine you were talking with a faculty member who had just developed an instrument. What questions would you ask the faculty member to determine if the instrument he or she developed was a survey or a psychological test?
	• How would you compare the similarities and differences between a survey and a psychological test?
	• What examples can you find of three surveys and three psychological tests?
Recognize some of the most popular survey software providers.	• What are the similarities and differences between the capabilities/functions of software available from three commercially-available survey software providers?
	• If you were going to design and administer a survey, which survey software would you use and why?

Learning Objectives	Critical Thinking Questions
Apply the five-phase scientific approach to constructing and administering and using survey data.	• What might be the implications of not following the five-step scientific method to survey design? • Imagine you were developing a survey to measure college student attitudes toward recycling. What would be your objectives and how would you operationalize each objective? • Find an existing survey (e.g., your college's course evaluation survey, a hotel customer satisfaction survey, a survey used by a faculty member as part of his or her research). What types of questions are included in the survey? What best practices in question design do you see, and what improvements could be made?
Describe survey reliability/ precision and validity.	• What steps would you follow to gather evidence of reliability/precision for a survey designed to measure high school students' nutritional habits? • What steps would you follow to gather evidence of validity for a survey designed to measure high school students' nutritional habits?

10

HOW DO WE DEVELOP A TEST?

LEARNING OBJECTIVES

After completing your study of this chapter, you should be able to do the following:

- Describe how to define the test domain, the target audience, and the purpose of the test.
- Develop a test plan, including defining the construct or constructs the test measures, choosing the test format, and specifying how to score the test.
- Differentiate between objective and subjective test questions, and describe the strengths and weaknesses of each.
- Describe the important issues in writing instructions for the test administrator and the test taker.
- Understand why it is important to conduct a "test of the test" (called a pilot test) before a test is ready for administration.

"Some of my professors use test questions supplied by the publisher of our text to make up their tests. I don't think that's right, since those questions are much harder than the questions that professors make up themselves."

"I made up a self-esteem test and gave it to my friends. All my friends had high scores, so I know they all have high self-esteem."

"My supervisor at work has a test she put together herself that she gives to everyone who applies for a job. She won't hire anyone who doesn't pass the test. When I looked at the test, I could tell right away what the right answers were even though I don't know anything about the job!"

WHY DEVELOP A NEW TEST?

As you learned in the "What Are Psychological Tests?" chapter, thousands of psychological tests are available from commercial marketers, test publishers, and research journals. The test publishers and research journals discussed in that chapter were limited, however, to U.S. publishers and journals. On the Web Box 10.1 provides information and web addresses for test developers in South Africa, India, South Korea, Malaysia, and Great Britain. Whether published in the United States or overseas, there are plenty of psychological tests from which the user can choose.

As we discussed in Section II, test validity depends on the suitability of a test for a particular audience of test takers, adequate sampling of behaviors from a specific test domain, and the purpose for which test scores are used. Therefore, researchers develop new tests to meet the needs of a special group of test takers, to sample behaviors from a newly defined test domain, or to improve the accuracy of test scores for their intended purpose. For instance, an achievement test may be needed for a special population of individuals with a disability that affects how they perceive or answer the test questions. A new theory may suggest fresh definitions of constructs and require a new test to assess them. Finally, a better defined test domain may generate test scores that predict a critical criterion more accurately.

Sometimes an unusual external event may motivate a test developer to create a new test. In January 2018, U.S. president Donald Trump took the Montreal Cognitive Assessment (MoCA) as part of his annual physical examination. The MoCA is a 30-item test that is designed to detect mild cognitive impairment such as would occur in the early stages of Alzheimer's disease. Because of the media coverage that was generated as a result of the president taking the test, there was a heightened interest in it from the general public in assessing their own cognitive status. However, the MoCA must be administered by a trained professional to obtain valid results. On February 26, 2018, JoNel Aleccia wrote in Kaiser Health News (a nonprofit news service of the Kaiser Family Foundation that covers health issues), that the copyright holder of the MoCA, Dr. Zaid Nasreddine, saw an opportunity to redevelop the test for anyone who wanted to test themselves. As a result of an external event, Dr. Nasreddine committed to developing a shortened, online, self-administered version of the test for individuals who may be worried about their own or a family member's cognitive decline.

In the previous chapter, we discussed the scientific method of survey design. In this chapter and the next, we discuss the steps for developing psychological tests. The scientific method applies to developing and validating psychological tests. This chapter looks at the process of constructing a test plan, various formats for writing questions (e.g., multiple choice, true/false) along with their strengths and weaknesses, and how test takers' perceptions and preconceived notions can influence test scores. Then, we present guidelines on how to write test questions and discuss the importance of the instructions that accompany a test. Finally we discuss the important to "test the test" by conducting a pilot test and analyzing the results before the test is administered to the intended population.

You will find many similarities between developing a scientific survey and developing a psychological test. Both rely on the scientific method, behavior observation, data collection, and analysis. Both require conducting a study to determine the validity of the results.

We have divided the test development process into 10 steps. Figure 10.1 provides a flowchart depicting this process. This chapter discusses the first five steps:

ON THE WEB BOX 10.1

TEST DEVELOPMENT AROUND THE WORLD

Because we wrote this textbook in the United States, most of our examples of psychological testing come from American journals and newspapers. However, psychologists, educators, and organizations develop and use psychological tests around the world. This box introduces you to websites on test development in South Africa, India, South Korea, Malaysia, and Great Britain. These are only a few examples of the many test developers and consultants around the world.

 In South Africa, the Human Sciences Research Council (HSRC; www.hsrc.ac.za) supports applied social scientific research projects and coordinates research that is large scale, collaborative, policy relevant, user driven, and public sector oriented. Research projects of the HSRC include the study of social movements and the dynamics of change and conducting continuing surveys about HIV.

 In India, the social sciences division of the Indian Statistical Institute (www.isical.ac.in/~psy) funds research and training on test development. For example, in March 2010, the Psychology Research Institute of the Indian Statistical Institute held a workshop on reliability in psychological research. Visit this site to find a list of tests that the division has funded and information on ongoing projects.

 In South Korea, the Korea Institute for Curriculum and Evaluation (KICE; http://www.kice.re.kr/main.do?s=english) conducts research on educational curriculum and evaluation. It also promotes and strengthens educational tests using scientific development and implementation. KICE oversees research, development, and implementation of the College Scholastic Ability Test, including scoring and results analysis of the test.

 In Malaysia, McPhee Andrewartha (www.mcpheeandrewartha.com.au) is a consulting firm and counseling and consulting management and psychology group that provides products and services in vocational assessment, human resources evaluation, early assessment of schoolchildren, and employee attitude surveys.

 In Great Britain, the Psychometrics Centre at the University of Cambridge (www.psychometrics.cam.ac.uk) strives to promote excellence in psychological, occupational, clinical, and educational assessment. The focus is on four core areas: research, training, services to industry, and developing new tests.

1. Defining the testing universe, audience, and purpose
2. Developing a test plan
3. Composing the test items
4. Writing the administration instructions
5. Conducting the pilot test

The next chapter covers the last five steps:

6. Conducting the item analysis
7. Revising the test
8. Validating the test
9. Developing norms and identifying cut scores
10. Compiling the test manual

FIGURE 10.1 ■ Flowchart of the Test Development Process

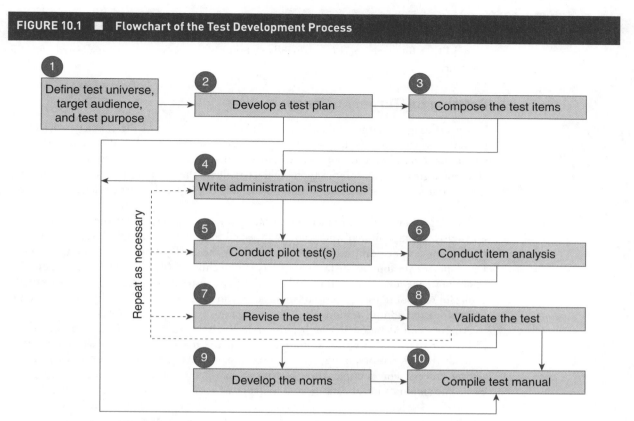

DEFINING THE TESTING UNIVERSE, AUDIENCE, AND PURPOSE

The first step in test development is to define the testing universe, the target audience, and the purpose of the test. As you recall from the chapter of developing evidence for validity based on the content of a test, the testing universe is the body of knowledge or behaviors that the test represents, the target audience is the group of individuals who will take the test, and the purpose of the test is the information that the test will provide to the test user. The 2014 *Standards for Educational and Psychological Testing* (American Educational Research Association [AERA], American Psychological Association [APA], & National Council on Measurement in Education [NCME], 2014) also make it clear that an important part of the initial design of test is a consideration of the expected uses and interpretation of the test scores. After development, it will then be up to the developer to ensure that all the design decisions made support these intended uses. This stage provides the foundation for all other development activities, so it is important to put ample time and thought into these important issues.

Defining the Testing Universe

To define the testing universe, the developer prepares a working definition of the construct that the test will measure. If the test will measure an abstract construct, the developer conducts a thorough review of the psychological literature to locate studies that explain the construct and any current tests that measure the construct. As discussed in the chapters on test validity, we need to define constructs operationally in terms of behaviors that are associated with the construct.

Defining the Target Audience

When defining the target audience, the developer makes a list of the characteristics of the persons who will take the test—particularly those characteristics that affect how test takers will respond to the test questions. For instance, in many cases we cannot just develop a test for children; instead, we must indicate the characteristics of the children, such as age and reading level. A test for sixth graders will differ considerably from a test for first graders, preschoolers, or infants.

Developers must also consider what reading level is appropriate for the target audience. Obviously, young children would not be expected to read a psychological test. They usually require one-on-one administration. As you recall, the Bayley Scales of Infant and Toddler Development are appropriate for testing very young children (Bayley, 1993). Some adults also might not have sufficient reading skills to read test questions and instructions. For example, adults for whom English is a second language or who have a reading disability will also require one-on-one test administration.

Another consideration is whether the individuals in the target audience have any disabilities or characteristics that would require a special test administration or interpretation. Individuals with sensory, motor, or cognitive impairments may require modifications to the testing process. For example, these test takers may require special equipment, such as an electronic amplification apparatus, or a reader or writer to assist them in completing the test.

Finally, developers must consider whether test takers will be motivated to answer the test questions honestly. Sometimes test takers may want to provide false answers to achieve high or low scores on a test. For instance, a dishonest person may wish to "pass" an honesty test, or a mentally ill person may wish to achieve a healthy diagnosis. Researchers have designed special test formats, which we discuss later in this chapter, for such persons who desire to "fake" a test.

Defining the Test Purpose

The purpose includes not only what the test will measure—for instance, self-esteem—but also how the test users will use the test scores. Will the scores be used to compare test takers with other test takers (normative approach), will they be used to compare a test taker standing on one trait with their own standing on other traits (ipsative approach) or will they be used to indicate achievement (criterion approach)?

An example of the normative approach to test interpretation is an employment test in which the applicant who achieves the highest score will receive the job offer (you may recall that this can be a comparative decision). In this case, the individual's actual score is not as important as the individual's score in relation to the scores of others who also took the test. You might be interested to know that the normative approach is used to determine who wins the gold medal in each Olympic event. The athlete does not need to perform better than athletes did during past years to win the gold medal. The athlete simply needs to perform better than the athletes who competed that year.

An example of the criterion approach is the way we interpret achievement test results. In this approach, the individual must achieve a certain score to qualify as passing or excellent (recall that this is an absolute decision). A good example of this is how we often classify student performance using the letter grades A to F. Students who achieve a test score that

qualifies as an A will receive that letter grade. Many or all students may achieve As, or many or all students may achieve Fs. The interpretation of the test score does not depend on the performance of others. (We will discuss the ipsative approach later in this chapter.)

Another question when determining the test purpose is whether the scores will be used cumulatively to test a theory (e.g., to identify a correlation between intelligence and another variable) or individually to provide information about the individual (e.g., his or her intelligence quotient). In the former case, the purpose of the test is to deliver a distribution of scores. In the latter case, the accuracy of the individual scores is most important. In other words, when test users use a large number of test scores to establish a statistical relationship, the accuracy of each score is not as important as when test users' interest is in the score of each individual. Therefore, a shorter test, perhaps with lower reliability/precision, may be sufficient when using many test scores, and a longer, highly reliable test will be necessary when the focus of interest is on individual scores.

Information about the testing universe, target audience, and test purpose provides the basis for making other decisions about the test. For instance, information about the intended test takers and how test scores will be used determines whether the test can be administered to groups, individuals, or both. Special populations may require special types of administration, and characteristics of the test takers, such as reading level, determine whether the construct can be measured in a group setting using a paper-and-pencil format or whether the test should be administered orally in a one-on-one setting.

DEVELOPING A TEST PLAN

Just as survey development requires writing a plan that operationalizes the survey objectives, test development requires writing a test plan. As you recall from the "How Do We Gather Evidence of Validity Based on the Content of a Test?" the **test plan** specifies the characteristics of the test, including an operational definition of the construct and the content to be measured (the testing universe), the format for the questions, and the administration and scoring of the test. Let us consider each part of the test plan in more detail.

Defining the Construct and the Content to Be Measured

After reviewing the literature about the construct and any available tests, the test developer is ready to write a concise definition of the construct. Such a definition includes operationalizing the construct in terms of observable and measurable behaviors. The definition also provides boundaries for the test domain by specifying what content should be tested and excluding content that is not appropriate for testing.

The test plans for clinical tests are based on carefully researched constructs. For example, For Your Information Box 10.1 contains operational definitions of the constructs measured by the College Adjustment Scales (Anton & Reed, 1991), a test designed to measure common developmental and psychological problems experienced by college students.

In organizations, test developers base their test plan on a job analysis that defines the knowledge, skills, abilities, and other characteristics (KSAOs) required to perform a job successfully. These KSAOs are the constructs that the test measures. The job analysis also describes the tasks performed on the job. These tasks are the observable and measurable behaviors associated with each KSAO. (Our chapter on "How Are Tests Used in Organizational Settings?" includes a discussion of job analysis in more detail.) As you may have already learned, the technique of competency modeling can also be used for this purpose.

In educational settings, the curricula (e.g., assigned readings, handouts, lectures) provide the basis for developing a test plan. Test plans are used to provide one source of evidence of validity based on the content of the test.

In addition to defining and operationalizing the construct, the test plan specifies the approximate number of questions needed to sample the test domain. Should the test developer write 5 questions or 50 questions to measure each construct? This decision affects the reliability/precision of the test and depends in part on the test format that the test developer chooses.

Choosing the Test Format

The **test format** refers to the type of questions that the test will contain. Most test developers prefer to use one type of format throughout the test to facilitate the administration and scoring. Sometimes test inventories or batteries that measure several different constructs use different formats in each section. In such cases, it is important to provide administration instructions for each section and to administer each section separately.

Test formats provide two elements: a stimulus to which the test taker responds and a mechanism for response. For instance, a multiple-choice question may provide a question (stimulus) followed by four or five possible answers (mechanisms for response). A multiple-choice format is also an **objective test format** because it has one response that is designated as "correct" or that provides evidence of a specific construct. In other words, the test taker receives credit for choosing only one correct response. Other types of objective test formats include true/false questions and fill-in-the-blank questions. Most test developers prefer objective test formats because the scorer does not need to make any judgment to determine the correct response. Objective test formats also are easily related to the test plan and the construct designated for measurement. These attributes facilitate documentation of the test's reliability and validity.

Subjective test formats, on the other hand, do not have a single response that is designated as "correct." Interpretation of the response as correct or providing evidence of a specific construct is left to the judgment of the person who scores or interprets the test taker's response. **Projective tests**, such as the Thematic Apperception Test (described in detail in

FOR YOUR INFORMATION BOX 10.1

CONSTRUCTS MEASURED BY THE COLLEGE ADJUSTMENT SCALES

Anxiety	*Definition:* A measure of clinical anxiety focusing on common affective, cognitive, and physiological symptoms. *Behaviors:* High anxiety is indicated by muscle tension, increased vigilance and scanning of the environment, rapid and shallow respiration, and excessive concerns and worries about real or expected life events that may be experienced as intrusive and unwanted thoughts.
Depression	*Definition:* A measure of clinical depression focusing on common affective, cognitive, and physiological symptoms. *Behaviors:* Depression is indicated by easy or chronic fatigue, lost interest or pleasure in normally enjoyable activities, feelings of sadness and hopelessness, and social withdrawal or isolation from friends and peers.
Suicidal Ideation	*Definition:* A measure of the extent of recent ideation (ideas) reflecting suicide, including hopelessness and resignation. *Behaviors:* Suicidal ideation is indicated by reports of thinking about suicide or behaviors associated with suicide attempts, including formulating a suicide plan.
Substance Abuse	*Definition:* A measure of disruption in interpersonal, social, academic, and vocational function as a result of substance use and abuse. *Behaviors:* Substance abuse is indicated by difficulty in interpersonal, social, academic, and vocational functioning as a result of substance abuse or by reporting guilt or shame about substance use, including embarrassment about behaviors displayed while abusing drugs or alcohol.
Self-Esteem Problems	*Definition:* A measure of global self-esteem that taps negative self-evaluations and dissatisfaction with personal achievement. *Behaviors:* Self-esteem problems are indicated by self-criticism and dissatisfaction with perceived skills, abilities, or achievement in comparison with peers, including seeing oneself as unassertive, excessively sensitive to criticism from others, and/or physically or sexually unattractive.
Interpersonal Problems	*Definition:* A measure of the extent of problems in relating to others in the campus environment. *Behaviors:* Interpersonal problems are indicated by difficulty in relating to others, including excessive dependence or increased vulnerability and/or a distrustful, argumentative style of relating to others.
Family Problems	*Definition:* A measure of difficulties experienced in relationships with family members. *Behaviors:* Family problems are indicated by difficulty in achieving emotional separation from family and learning to live independently, including worry or concern over problems occurring in a conflicted or tumultuous family.
Academic Problems	*Definition:* A measure of the extent of problems related to academic performance. *Behaviors:* Academic problems are indicated by poor study skills, inefficient use of time, poor concentration ability, and/or test anxiety.
Career Problems	*Definition:* A measure of the extent of problems related to career choice. *Behaviors:* Career problems are indicated by difficulty in setting career goals and making decisions that are important for career goal attainment, including anxiety or worry about selecting an academic major or future career.

the "How Are Tests Used in Clinical and Counseling Settings?" chapter), are subjective test formats because the stimuli for these tests are ambiguous pictures. As we discussed in previous chapters, the test taker provides a story or an explanation (mechanism for response), which the scorer judges to be appropriate or inappropriate. Other examples of subjective test formats are open-ended or essay questions and the traditional employment interview. In each of these, the test taker or interviewee responds with any answer he or she considers appropriate. Documenting the reliability/precision and validity of tests based on a subjective test format is more difficult than doing so based on an objective test format. For this reason, many test developers prefer objective test formats. We discuss these formats in more detail later in this chapter.

Administering and Scoring the Test

After choosing a test format (objective or subjective) and the appropriate type of question (e.g., true/false, multiple choice, open ended), the test developer needs to specify how to administer and score the test. This information is an important part of the test plan that will influence the format and content of the test items. For example, will the test be administered in writing, orally, or by computer? How much time will test takers have to complete the test? Will the test be administered to groups or individuals? Will the test be scored by the test publisher, the test administrator, or the test takers? Finally, what type of data is the test expected to yield? In other words, will the test scores provide the information required by the purpose of the test?

The **cumulative model of scoring** is probably the most common method for determining an individual's final test score. The cumulative model assumes that the more the test taker responds in a particular fashion (with either "correct" answers or ones that are consistent with a particular attribute), the more the test taker exhibits the attribute being measured. To score a test using the cumulative model, the test taker receives 1 point for each correct answer, and the total number of correct answers becomes the raw score on the test. Assuming that the test questions are comparable, the cumulative model of scoring can yield interval-level data. In any case, psychologists traditionally assume that such tests produce interval-level data that can then be interpreted using the norming procedures described in the "How Do Test Users Interpret Test Scores?" chapter.

The **categorical model of scoring** is used to place test takers in a particular group or class. For instance, the test taker must display a pattern of responses that indicates a clinical diagnosis of a certain psychological disorder or the attributes that make up a behavioral trait. The categorical model typically yields nominal data because it places test takers in categories.

The **ipsative model of scoring** differs from the cumulative and categorical models. In an ipsatively scored test, the test taker is usually presented with two to four statements in a forced choice format. (We discuss the forced choice item format in more detail later in this chapter in the section on composing test items.) In personality testing, in which this format is most likely to be used, the test taker is required to indicate which of the items is "most like me" and which of the items is "least like me." The choices in each group are carefully chosen to be equal in desirability. Each test item will contain statements associated with more than one trait or construct. For example, a personality test item might contain the following choices:

a. I try to lead others.

b. I like a leisurely lifestyle.

c. I hold back my opinions.

d. I do a lot in my spare time.

Choices a and c are associated with the trait of assertiveness. Choices b and d are associated with the trait of activity level. (These choices were taken from the International Personality Item Pool [International Personality Item Pool, 2015]). The item is scored by assigning 1 point to the choice that is rated "most like me" and –1 point to the choice rated "least like me." The individual trait or scale scores are then computed based on the total number of points each scale in the test received.

Because of the way in which scores on ipsative items are computed, one cannot simply add up all the points each test taker received, as in the cumulative scoring method. This is because the total score on an ipsative test will be exactly the same for everyone. In fact, this property is one of the defining characteristics of an ipsatively scored test. But this also means that standard statistical tests cannot be performed on the test scores, as there is no variance in scores to analyze. As a result, comparisons among different people who take the test cannot be made. An ipsative test will only provide information regarding where test takers stand relative to themselves on the constructs that the test is designed to measure. That is, for a single individual, an ordered ranking of the scales on which the test taker scored highest to lowest can be made and interpreted. But the interpretation must be limited in scope to the individual test taker. It would not be appropriate to compare the score of one person with the score of another on an ipsative test. But there is an additional benefit that ipsative tests do possess. The forced choice format has been shown to reduce the influence of social desirability and other response sets in the results (Christiansen, Burns, & Montgomery, 2005).

If ipsative tests are used to compare individuals, the results can be problematic. Meade (2004) provided psychometric and statistical evidence that the ipsative method can yield quite different results from those of the cumulative method. He compared forced choice ipsative data with normative data collected from job applicants in an organizational setting. Meade found that the job applicants shown as suitable for hiring by the ipsative method were different from those identified as suitable for hiring by the normative method. He suggested that the decision process that respondents must use to select an item as "most like me" or "least like me" is unknown and inherently alters the psychometric properties of forced choice items. Meade asserted that using the forced choice format in employment testing is inappropriate. However, there have been some recent advances in item-response theory (IRT) models that make may it possible in certain circumstances to compare individuals who have taken ipsatively designed tests. For more information on how IRT models can help us solve problems of ipsative data, read Brown and Maydeu-Olivares (2013).

Developing the Test Itself

After completing the test plan, the test developer is ready to begin writing the test questions and instructions. Because composing the actual testing stimuli is an important and time-consuming activity, we devote the remainder of this chapter to the art of writing the test itself. Again, you will find many similarities between writing survey questions and writing test questions.

Before we discuss writing test questions, you should know that after writing the initial test questions, the test developer conducts a **pilot test**—a scientific evaluation of the test's performance—followed by revisions to determine the final form that the test will take. The test developer then follows up the pilot test with other studies that provide the necessary data for validation and norming. Conducting the pilot test and analyzing its data are integral parts of the test development process.

COMPOSING THE TEST ITEMS

As you can see, test developers have much to do before they begin to write the test itself. Careful definition and review of the constructs, however, makes development much easier and yields more questions that are successful. Many decisions, such as method of administration, are considered and resolved while developing the test plan. Therefore, the test plan becomes the blueprint for proceeding with development. Imagine what it would be like to build a home without a blueprint. Without a detailed blueprint, the home builders would have no clear understanding of what they were building. The same is true for test development.

Throughout this textbook, we have referred to the *stimulus* to which the test taker responds as a *test question*. In reality, test questions are not always questions. Stimuli are frequently presented on tests in the form of statements, pictures, or incomplete sentences, as well as other less common forms. Therefore, psychologists and test developers refer to these stimuli or test questions as **test items**, and we refer to them as such for the remainder of this chapter and in the next chapter.

Test developers choose the item format based on information in the test plan, such as the target audience, method of administration, and requirements for scoring. Following is a discussion of some standard item formats, including strengths or weaknesses that may cause test developers to choose or reject them as appropriate formats in various situations. Recall that the "How Do We Construct and Administer Surveys and Use Survey Data?" chapter provided a list of various types of survey questions. Types of test items include those in that chapter as well as a few more types, such as projective item formats. We consider item formats in terms of whether they are objective or subjective.

Objective Items

Multiple Choice

The item format used most often is **multiple choice**. Because this format is familiar, many people use it for pre-employment tests, standardized achievement tests, and classroom tests. The multiple-choice format consists of a question or partial sentence, called a **stem**, followed by a number of responses (usually four or five), of which only one is correct. The incorrect responses are called **distractors** and are designed to appear correct to someone who does not know the correct answer.

When writing a multiple-choice item, it is important that the developer clearly differentiate the correct response from the distractors. Distractors that are "almost right" can be tricky and confusing to the respondent. Such items rarely yield accurate assessment information. On the other hand, the distractors must be realistic enough to appeal to the uninformed test taker. In no case should funny or unrealistic distractors be included; they decrease the accuracy of the assessment.

Multiple-choice items are popular because having one right answer eliminates confusion or controversy in scoring a correct response. Scoring is also easily accomplished either by a nonprofessional or electronically (e.g., by a computer). One problem, however, is that test takers who do not know the correct answer may obtain credit by guessing. A test taker who does not know the correct answer for a multiple-choice item with four responses has a 1 in 4 (25%) chance of guessing the correct answer. These odds can be decreased if the test taker can eliminate one or two of the distractors, yielding a 1 in 3 (33%) or 1 in 2 (50%) chance of guessing the correct answer. This disadvantage is offset by presenting a large number of items. For instance, although an uninformed test taker may have a 1 in 4 chance of guessing the correct answer on 1 item, those odds are significantly increased by increasing the number of items. The odds of an uninformed test taker's correctly guessing the correct response (when there are four responses) to each of 10 multiple-choice questions are 1 in 1,048,576! See For Your Information Box 10.2 for an example of a multiple-choice question.

True/False

The stem of a **true/false** item asks, "Is this statement true or false?" If a test contains only true/false items, the instructions contain the stem and direct the test takers to mark each statement as true or false. Again, test takers can gain some advantage by guessing, and the odds of guessing correctly on one item are 50% (1 in 2). On a short test containing only true/false items, guessing can have a large impact on the scores. For example, on a 10-item true/false test with a passing score of 70%, of those people who knew the answer to only 5 of the items and guessed on the other five, 81% would pass. In a four-choice multiple-choice format, only 37% would pass.

The Hogan Personality Inventory uses the true/false format. This format converts to a multiple-choice format by presenting four or five statements, from which the test taker chooses the one statement that is true or false. For Your Information Box 10.2 shows two examples of true/false items.

Forced Choice

The **forced choice** format is similar to the multiple-choice format; however, test developers typically use forced choice items for personality and attitude tests rather than for knowledge tests. This format requires the test taker to choose one of two or more words or phrases that appear unrelated but are equally acceptable. The stem of the forced choice question (often included in the test instructions) may ask the respondent, "Which of each pair is most descriptive of you?" Although the words or phrases appear to be unrelated, the test developer must have empirical evidence that the responses yield significantly different responses from different types of people. In other words, people with similar personality traits usually prefer one response to the other.

Researchers during World War II designed forced choice items to yield ratings with less bias (Berkshire & Highland, 1953). This format subsequently became popular, making it more difficult to "fake" a test. This format would be appropriate to use when the potential test takers are likely to answer dishonestly. For Your Information Box 10.2 shows two examples of forced choice items. One version of the Myers–Briggs Personality Inventory has a section of forced choice questions.

The strength of the forced choice format is that the items are more difficult for respondents to guess or fake. Because the paired words or phrases appear to have little in common, the test taker cannot guess what the best response should be. On the other hand, the forced choice format has little face validity, that is, no apparent connection with the stated purpose of the test. As you may recall, lack of face validity may produce poor responses from test takers. Making a number of decisions between or among apparently unrelated words or phrases can become distressing, and test takers who want to answer honestly and accurately often become frustrated with forced choice questions.

Subjective Items

Some test users prefer subjective items to objective items. Although objective items are easy to score and interpret, they also rely on cues provided by the test. Subjective items, on the other hand, give the test taker fewer cues and open wider areas for response.

FOR YOUR INFORMATION BOX 10.2
EXAMPLES OF OBJECTIVE ITEM FORMATS

Multiple Choice

Which one of the following levels of measurement involves ranking from lowest to highest?

  a. Nominal

  b. Ordinal

  c. Interval

  d. Ratio

Forced Choice

Place an X in the space to the left of the word in each pair that best describes your personality:

  1. _____ Sunny

  2. _____ Outgoing

  3. _____ Friendly

  4. _____ Loyal

True/False

Indicate whether the following statements are true or false by placing a T for true or an F for false in the space to the left of the statement:

  1. _____ Proportions can be calculated only from data obtained using a ratio scale.

  2. _____ Equal-interval scales do not have a true zero point.

Essay questions, similar to open-ended survey questions, are popular subjective items in educational settings. Such questions are usually general in scope and require lengthy written responses by test takers. Essays provide a freedom of response that facilitates assessing higher cognitive behaviors such as analysis, synthesis, and evaluation (Hopkins & Antes, 1979). Because the responses that essays generate may vary in terms of breadth and depth of topic, the scorer must make a judgment regarding whether the response is correct. Often the scorer awards points based on how closely the test taker's response matches a predetermined correct response.

Many students prefer essay questions because this format allows them to focus on demonstrating what they have learned rather than limiting them to answering specific questions. Others point out, however, that writing skills, ranging from readability of handwriting to graceful phrasing, may influence scorer judgments. Unless writing skills are part of the testing universe, such considerations may lead to inaccurate judgments and so to inaccurate test scores.

In organizational settings, the traditional subjective test is the employment interview. **Interview questions**, like essay questions, are general in scope. In this case, the interviewer decides what is a "good" or "poor" answer. Again, the interviewee has a wide range of responses; however, as with the essay, the interview format introduces many opportunities for causing inaccurate judgments.

Test developers in the early 20th century developed a number of **projective techniques** for diagnosing mental disorders. This subjective format uses a highly ambiguous stimulus to elicit an unstructured response from the test taker. In other words, the test taker "projects" his or her perspective and perceptions onto a neutral stimulus. Such tests contain a variety of projective stimuli, including pictures and both written and spoken words. Test takers may respond verbally or by drawing pictures. Interpretation of children's play also can be categorized as a projective technique (Krall, 1986).

Another subjective format often used in attitude and personality scales is the **sentence completion** format, which presents an incomplete sentence such as "I feel happiest when

I am _____." The respondents then complete the sentence in any way that makes sense to them. One person might say, "I feel happiest when I am *playing the piano*." Another might respond, "I feel happiest when I am *studying for an important exam*." The person scoring the test will then compare the test taker's responses with responses supplied by the test developer to award points or identify a trait or type.

For Your Information Box 10.3 shows an example of each of these subjective item formats.

By their nature, subjective tests are at risk for introducing judgment error into test scores. Therefore, evidence of interrater reliability is of particular importance for subjective tests. Test developers can reduce scoring errors by providing clear and specific scoring keys that illustrate how various types of responses should be scored. Test users can increase the reliability of scoring essays, interviews, and projective tests by providing training for scorers and using two scorers who make independent evaluations. If not carefully constructed, both objective and subjective test item formats are likely to introduce error into test scores.

Complex Item Formats

The *Standards for Educational and Psychological Testing* (AERA et al., 2014) includes discussion of three other types of item formats used in specialized testing situations.

Performance Assessments

Performance assessments require test takers to directly demonstrate their skills and abilities to perform a group of complex behaviors and tasks. The setting in which these tasks are demonstrated is made as similar as possible to the conditions that will be found when the tasks are actually performed. One example of a performance assessment is an audition of a musician who trying out for a band. The musician who is auditioning usually plays along with all the other band members so that his or her skills can be properly evaluated. Sometimes, the audition will take place in front of an audience to maximize the realism of the setting. To ensure that the inferences that will be made from the performance assessment are appropriate, care must be taken regarding its content. For instance, the level of difficulty of the music played in the audition should be similar to the level of difficulty at which the musician will be expected to perform, and the style of music should be similar to the style of music the band typically plays. It would not make much sense to ask a musician who is auditioning for a band that specializes in country music to demonstrate her expertise playing death metal.

In an employment setting, performance assessments are often called work samples, as they require the person to demonstrate his or her ability to perform a group of tasks that have been identified as critical for successful job performance. For instance, an applicant for the position of auto mechanic might be asked to diagnose and fix an actual problem with a car.

Simulations

A **simulation** is similar to a performance assessment in that it requires test takers to demonstrate their skills and abilities to perform a complex task. However, the tasks are not performed in the actual environment in which the real tasks will be performed, often because of safety or cost-related concerns. Consider the job of a bomb disposal technician. It would be important to evaluate whether an applicant for that position has the skills and abilities to perform the job. However, because of the dangerous nature of the tasks involved, it would be more appropriate to simulate a bomb disposal situation in a safe environment than to conduct a true performance assessment.

FOR YOUR INFORMATION BOX 10.3
EXAMPLES OF SUBJECTIVE ITEM FORMATS

Essay

Compare and contrast the four levels of measurement, and give an example of each.

Interview

Please tell me about a time that you were in disagreement with your colleagues. What was the disagreement about, what did you do, and what was the outcome?

Projective Technique

What do you see when you look at this picture?

Sentence Completion

I am at my best when _____.

Like performance assessments, simulations are often also conducted in organizational settings. In the chapter on how tests are used in organizational settings, you will learn about assessment centers, which are a common type of simulation that businesses use.

Portfolios

A **portfolio** is a collection of work products that a person gathers over time to demonstrate his or her skills and abilities in a particular area. For instance, artists might have portfolios that demonstrate their best paintings, architects might have portfolios that showcase their designs, or singers might have CDs that contain samples of their best performances. When portfolios are required for the purposes of selection, whether it be for admission to an educational program or for a job, the scoring process and criteria should be standardized so that the results are comparable across different applicants.

Finally, there is an important point to keep in mind when using complex item formats such as performance assessments, simulations, and portfolios. They all are subject to and evaluated by the same technical standards as any other test (AERA et al., 2014). All the issues regarding reliability/precision and validity evidence that you have learned about also apply to these types of measures.

Response Bias

A source of error in test scores comes from the test takers themselves. Researchers have found that some people have **response sets** (also known as response styles) for choosing answers to test items. Response sets are patterns of responding that result in false or misleading information. These sources of error limit the accuracy and usefulness of test scores, so test developers need to consider the possible effects of response bias when they develop tests. Social desirability, acquiescence, random responding, and faking are response sets that test developers have researched a great deal. Others, such as poor handwriting, not reading instructions, and inattention to detail, also pose problems for test scorers.

Social Desirability

One problem for test developers is the tendency of some test takers to provide or choose answers that are socially acceptable or that present themselves in a favorable light. This response is called **social desirability**. Research suggests that many people have a desire to make a favorable impression. Crowne and Marlowe (1960, 1964) developed a social desirability scale to assess the extent to which individuals tend to respond in a socially desirable fashion. For Your Information Box 10.4 contains information on identifying test takers who are likely to have the social desirability response set. When writing test items, it is important to consider social desirability. For instance, developers try to balance the social desirability of the correct response and the distractors in multiple-choice questions. When using the forced choice format, developers can pair responses based on their desirability. When social desirability is likely to cause error, test developers may conduct a study to determine how socially desirable each proposed response is to a sample of people who resemble the test's target audience. The developers then discard responses that correlate strongly with a social desirability scale.

Acquiescence

Another response set familiar to test developers is **acquiescence**, the tendency to agree with any ideas or behaviors presented. For instance, someone who labels each statement on a true/false test as true would be demonstrating a response set of acquiescence. Javeline (1999) pointed out how an acquiescence response set may have a cultural basis as well as being an individual inclination. According to Javeline, the inclination to agree is most prevalent in societies that value deference and politeness. If such a bias is not taken into account, conclusions drawn from attitude surveys, such as public opinion polls, may be interpreted incorrectly. For this reason, test and survey developers should balance items for which the correct response would be positive with an equal number of items for which the correct response would be negative. For Your Information Box 10.5 illustrates this strategy and describes how balancing positive and negative items affects cumulative scoring.

Random Responding and Faking

Sometimes test takers are unwilling or unable to respond to test items accurately. In this case, they may engage in **random responding**—responding to items in a random fashion by marking answers without reading or considering them. This response set is likely to occur when test takers lack the necessary skills (such as reading) to take the test, do not wish to be evaluated, or lack the attention span necessary to complete the task.

Earlier in this chapter, we discussed **faking**, which refers to the inclination of some test takers to try to answer items in a way that will cause a desired outcome or diagnosis. For instance, a test taker completing a personality test for a prospective employer may try to answer items in a way that makes him or her appear to be friendly and cooperative (faking good). On the other hand, a test taker who has been charged with a serious crime may wish to appear to be mentally disturbed (faking bad). As you recall, one way to prevent faking is to use a forced choice format for the test items.

Rather than prevention, some test developers include special items in the test to detect which test takers are giving dishonest answers. These items are scored separately from the test, and test developers refer to them as *faking scales* or *validity scales*. A high score on a faking scale identifies test takers who are uncooperative, responding randomly, or faking. The items on a faking scale usually have nothing to do with the test construct and have obvious responses for most of the population. In other words, they will be either true or false for nearly everyone in the target audience. Test takers who respond dishonestly are likely to answer differently from most people on a number of these items, thereby tipping off the scorer that they were not cooperating. The chapter later in the book, "How Are Tests Used in Organizational Settings?" includes a discussion of this issue in more detail as it pertains to socially desirable responding and faking on personality tests.

FOR YOUR INFORMATION BOX 10.4
IDENTIFYING THE SOCIAL DESIRABILITY RESPONSE SET

In 1960, Douglas Crowne, of Ohio State University, and David Marlowe, of the University of Kentucky's College of Medicine, published an article in the *Journal of Consulting Psychology* describing a new scale they had developed to identify persons who have a high need to present themselves in a favorable light. In 1964, they published *The Approval Motive: Studies in Evaluative Dependence*, which details the development of the Marlowe–Crowne Social Desirability Scale. They describe the items in the scale as being "behaviors which are culturally sanctioned and approved but which are improbable of occurrence" (Crowne & Marlowe, 1960, p. 350).

The scale soon became widely used by test developers who wished to identify tests and test items that suggested responses that would appeal to persons who wished to show themselves in a favorable light. The scale, still used in research today, became the accepted operationalization of the social desirability response set.

As you can see from the sample items below, the test provides statements that are very socially acceptable. Those statements, however, are not ones that many people could sincerely attribute as true of themselves. The scale format is true/false, and Crowne and Marlowe provided a key to show which answer (shown in parentheses) a person with a high need for approval is likely to provide. Sample items include the following:

- Before voting, I thoroughly investigate the qualifications of all the candidates. (T)

- I never hesitate to go out of my way to help someone in trouble. (T)

- On occasion, I have had doubts about my ability to succeed in life. (F)

- I sometimes feel resentful when I don't get my way. (F)

Source: From Crowne, D. P., & Marlowe, D. (1960). A new scale of social desirability independent of social psychopathology. *Journal of Consulting Psychology, 24*(4), 349–354. Copyright © 1960 by the American Psychological Association. Reprinted with permission.

Although these scales are useful for detecting uncooperative test takers, many cooperative test takers may resent tests that ask questions about personal feelings and activities that have no relation to the purpose of the test. For instance, job applicants may interpret employment tests that ask personal questions as unfair. As you recall, face validity—what the test appears to measure—is not essential for a test to be valid, but it can enhance the test taker's willingness to cooperate with the testing process.

WRITING EFFECTIVE ITEMS

As you can see, researchers and test developers have thought a lot about how to write test items that will elicit accurate and honest information. Most developers consider item writing to be an art that depends on originality and creativity as well as a science that uses research about how test takers respond to various types of items for constructing reliable items. We discussed how to write effective survey questions in the last chapter, and those guidelines also apply to writing effective test items.

After writing the test items, the developer should administer them as a test, with appropriate instructions for the test administrator and test taker, to a sample of the target audience. This pilot test provides objective data to help determine whether the items yield the desired information.

FOR YOUR INFORMATION BOX 10.5
USING REVERSE SCORING TO BALANCE POSITIVE AND NEGATIVE ITEMS

Some test takers are inclined to give mostly positive responses to questions regardless of the questions' content. The test developer tries to offset the effects of this response set, known as acquiescence, by balancing positive statements with negative statements. Because scoring is usually a cumulative estimate of how much the test taker exhibits or agrees with the test's construct, it then becomes necessary to reverse the responses to negative items.

For example, a test assessing a student's attitude toward studying may ask the test taker to respond using the following five-point scale:

1 = *rarely true*

2 = *sometimes true*

3 = *neither true nor false*

4 = *very often true*

5 = *almost always true*

High responses (4 or 5) to positive statements, such as "I enjoy memorizing vocabulary words," would reflect a positive attitude toward studying. However, high responses to negative items, such as "When I sit down to study, I get depressed," would indicate the opposite—a negative attitude toward studying. Therefore, the test scorer reverses the response numbers of negative items. A response of 5 to a negative item would be changed to 1, and a response of 4 would be changed to 2. A neutral response of 3 would remain the same.

After reversing the responses on the negative items, the test scorer then uses the cumulative model of scoring, in which the numbers indicated for each response are added to arrive at the overall score.

Experienced item writers know that not all of the items they write will end up being good test items—that is, items that measure the construct as expected. Test takers will misinterpret some items. Some items will be too easy or too difficult, and men and women may answer a few items differently. Therefore, developers follow a general rule of thumb: "Write twice as many items as you expect to use in the final test." By writing twice as many items as needed, the developers will be able to discard poor items and use only those items that yield useful information. (In the "How Do We Assess the Psychometric Quality of a Test?" chapter, we also discuss how to choose the best test items using a process called *item analysis*.)

Although there is no set of rules that guarantees that items will perform as expected, we can pass along some suggestions from the test development literature.

- *Identify item topics by consulting the test plan:* In this way, the test developer maximizes the relation between the test plan and the test itself, thereby increasing content validity.

- *Be sure that each item is based on an important learning objective or topic:* Structure the item around one central idea or problem. Do not test for trivial or peripheral information or skills.

- *Write items that assess information or skills drawn only from the testing universe:* This guideline is important for education and training programs. If the test's purpose is to measure how much the test taker learned in a training class, the test developer needs to write items from the course material. Such items should ask questions that respondents are unlikely to be able to answer from general knowledge.

- *Write each item in a clear and direct manner:* Precise words and simple sentence structure, as well as correct grammar and punctuation, enable the item writer to describe the problem or ask the intended question.

- *Use vocabulary and language appropriate for the target audience:* According to Doak, Doak, and Root (1996), the average adult in the United States cannot read above an eighth grade reading level, and 40% of people over 65 years of age read below a fifth grade reading level. Therefore, the developer should research the reading level of the target audience and create appropriate items. Items intended for the general population should be appropriate for an eighth grade reading level or lower. Other test populations may require a lower reading level or a form of administration that does not require the test taker to read either the items or the instructions.

- *Avoid using slang or colloquial language:* In today's multicultural society, test takers will come from diverse backgrounds. The test author should use standard English and avoid figures of speech or frames of reference that may be unfamiliar to segments of the population. A test item that requires knowledge of customs associated with holidays (e.g., foods associated with a traditional Thanksgiving meal) or sports (e.g., tailgating) may be confusing to test takers not familiar with such customs.

- *Make all items independent:* Developers need to check all items to be sure that cues for the correct response to one item are not found elsewhere in the test.

- *Ask someone else—preferably a subject matter expert—to review items in order to reduce unintended ambiguity and inaccuracies:* This step ensures that the test items convey clear information and questions. Questions that have multiple interpretations should be revised or discarded.

Multiple-Choice and True/False Items

The following are some specific guidelines for writing multiple-choice and true/false questions.

- *Avoid using negative stems and responses:* Instead of asking, "Which of the following is NOT true?" it is better to ask, "Which of the following is FALSE?" Likewise, a response that reads "Confidentiality means that individuals are assured that all personal information they disclose will be kept private" is preferable to a negatively worded response such as "Individuals who are NOT assured that all personal information they disclose will be kept private are NOT assured of confidentiality."

- *Make all responses similar in detail and length:* The tendency to make the correct response more detailed can be avoided by making sure that all responses are similar in detail and length.

- *Make sure the item has only one answer that is definitely correct or "best":* To ensure that there is only one correct answer, construct an answer key that contains a brief rationale for the correct answer for each item.

- *Avoid determining words such as always and never:* Instead, use *sometimes* and *often* as qualifiers. You might have noticed that the items on the Marlowe–Crowne Social Desirability Scale in For Your Information Box 10.4 often include *always* or *never*, and therefore the probability that a test taker could truthfully agree is very low.

- *Avoid overlapping responses:* For instance, quantitative responses such as "10 to 20" and "20 to 30" overlap and leave the test taker who wishes to answer "20" confused about how to respond.

- *Avoid using inclusive distractors:* "All of the above," "none of the above," and "both a and c" are called inclusive distractors. This type of response usually makes items very easy or difficult. If you choose to use them, be sure to balance the number of times they appear as the correct or incorrect response.

- *Use random assignment to position the correct response:* Research suggests that test takers often assign the correct response to b or c. Random assignment of the correct response ensures uniformity of response probability and decreases test takers' ability to guess the correct response.

If you would like some additional in-depth information about writing multiple choice items, a good resource is the third edition of Thomas Haladyna's (2015) book titled *Developing and Validating Multiple Choice Test Items.*

Essay and Interview Questions

The following tips provide some guidance in developing and scoring effective essay and interview questions.

- *Use essay items appropriately:* As mentioned earlier in this chapter, essays are most effective for assessing higher order skills such as analysis, synthesis, and evaluation. If the developer wishes to measure simple recall, an objective format may be more efficient.

- *Consider the time necessary for response:* Frame instructions and items in a way that lets the test taker know the expected length of response. In this way, the developer can provide the appropriate number of essay questions for the time allotted for testing. Remember that some individuals will take longer to complete the test than others will because of variations in writing skills. Ample time should be allotted for all test takers to respond to their satisfaction.

- *Prepare an answer key:* The key for open-ended essays and interviews should outline the expected correct response. In addition, it should list other possible responses along with scores based on the appropriateness of the responses. For example, a response that matches the desired response may receive full credit, and other responses that contain unrelated information may receive partial credit. Remember that in subjective testing, it is possible for a test taker to submit an unexpected solution or response that is as correct as, or even better than, the expected response.

- *Score essays anonymously:* Replacing the test taker's name or other identifiers with a number decreases the possibility of bias associated with the scorer's personal knowledge of the respondent or the respondent's characteristics such as sex, race, and age.

- *Use multiple independent scorers:* Using two or more scorers who read essays or conduct interviews provides an opportunity to detect and decrease bias as well as to investigate scorer reliability.

A Comparison of Objective and Subjective Formats

In this section, we draw from the work of Kryspin and Feldhusen (1974) to summarize the strengths and weaknesses associated with objective and subjective item formats. First, we consider how thoroughly the test developer can sample the test domain. Second, we look at ease of construction. Third, we consider the process of scoring. Finally, we look at how the test taker uses response sets.

Sampling

Objective formats with structured responses, such as multiple-choice and true/false items, provide many opportunities to sample the testing universe. Because test takers expend less time and effort to answer these items, the test developer can cover a wider array of topics, thereby increasing the available evidence of validity based on test content. With subjective formats, such as essay and interview questions, the test developer is limited to the number of questions or topics to which the test taker can respond in one session. When the testing universe covers a wide range of topics, evidence of validity based on content usually suffers for the test using subjective formats.

Construction

Objective items, especially multiple-choice items, require extensive thought and development time because the test developer needs to balance responses in terms of content depth, length, and appeal to the test taker. Novice test developers are quick to note that supplying three or four distractors that resemble the correct response is not an easy task. On the other hand, subjective tests require fewer items and those items are easier to construct and revise. Furthermore, some measurement experts suggest that essay and interview questions are better suited for testing higher order skills such as creativity and organization.

Scoring

Scoring of objective items is simple and can be done by an aide or computer with a high degree of reliability and accuracy. Scoring subjective items, however, requires time-consuming judgments by an expert. Essay and interview scoring is most reliable and accurate when there are two independent scorers who have been trained to avoid biased judgments. Scoring keys are important for subjective items. They are, however, more difficult to construct because they need to address as many likely responses as possible.

Response Sets

Test takers have the option of guessing the correct responses on objective tests. They also may choose socially desirable responses or acquiesce to positive statements. For subjective items, such as essays, respondents may bluff or pad answers with superfluous or excessive information. Scorers might be influenced by irrelevant factors such as poor verbal or writing skills.

As you can see, each format has advantages and drawbacks. Objective items require more time and thought during the development phase. When objective questions are developed properly, they have high evidence of validity based on their content and provide reliable and accurate scores. On the other hand, subjective items, such as essays and interviews, may be more appropriate for assessing higher-order skills. In addition, subjective items require less time to develop. This advantage, however, is offset by the time and expertise required to score or interpret subjective responses and their greater susceptibility to scorer bias.

WRITING THE ADMINISTRATION INSTRUCTIONS

Although the test items make up the bulk of the new test, they are meaningless without specific instructions on how to administer and score the test. The test developer needs to write three sets of instructions: one for the person administering the test, another for the person taking the test, and a third for the person scoring the test and interpreting its results.

Administrator Instructions

Administrator instructions should cover the following:

- Whether the test should be administered in a group and/or individually

- Specific requirements for the test administration location, such as privacy; quiet; and comfortable chairs, tables, or desks

- Required equipment such as No. 2 pencils, a computer with a removable storage device such as an SD card or flash drive and/or Internet access

- Time limitations or the approximate time for completing the test when there are no time limits

- A script for the administrator to read to test takers, including answers to questions that test takers are likely to ask

- Credentials or training required for the test administrator

The last point is very important. Not just anyone can administer a test appropriately. Some tests, such as interviews, essays, and projective tests, require that the test administrator satisfactorily complete training on administering the test. In the case of interviews, for instance, the test publisher or the test user should provide training for the administrator on how to ask the interview questions and record the interviewee's replies. Some tests, such as projective tests, may require that the administrator has completed certain graduate courses in psychological testing.

The **testing environment**—the circumstances under which the test is administered—can affect how test takers respond. A standardized testing environment, as you recall, decreases variation or error in the test scores. Specific and concise instructions for administering the test help ensure that it will be administered properly under standardized conditions. For Your Information Box 10.6 provides an example of instructions for a test administrator for a paper and pencil test. A different set of instructions would be used for a test delivered by computer.

Instructions for the Test Taker

The test administrator usually delivers instructions for the test taker orally by reading a prepared script written by the test developer. Instructions also appear in writing at the beginning of the test or test booklet. The test taker needs to know where to respond (on an answer sheet or in the test booklet) and how to respond (blackening the appropriate space on an answer sheet or circling the correct multiple-choice answer). Each type of item (e.g., multiple choice, essay) should be preceded by specific directions for responding.

Instructions for test takers often encourage them to provide accurate and honest answers. The instructions may also provide a context for answering, such as "Think of your current work situation when replying to the following questions." Test instructions need to be simple, concise, and written at a low reading level. Complicated methods for responding are likely to lead to confused test takers and an increased probability of response errors. For Your Information Box 10.7 provides an example of instructions for test takers for a paper and pencil test.

FOR YOUR INFORMATION BOX 10.6
EXAMPLE OF ADMINISTRATOR INSTRUCTIONS FOR A PAPER AND PENCIL TEST

Testing Materials

Assemble a numbered testing booklet, answer sheet, and two No. 2 pencils for each person scheduled to take the test. Test takers cannot use any aids, such as calculators, smartphones, and/or tablets while taking the test.

Testing Location

The testing room must be well lit with temperature control set at approximately 72°F. Each test taker should sit alone at a table approximately 3 feet wide and 2 feet deep. All test takers must face the front of the room, where the administrator's desk is located. The administrator will ask test takers to turn off all cell phones and to place them on their tables.

Testing Time

The test takers will have 60 minutes to read and respond to the test items. Test takers who complete the test in less than 60 minutes should remain in their seats until the 60-minute time period is over and the administrator has collected the testing materials. Test takers who do not complete the test in the 60-minute time period must lay down their pencils and close their test booklets when asked to do so.

Frequently Asked Questions

(Q) When will I find out my test results?

(A) In 3 weeks, the testing company will send your results to you in the mail.

(Q) Can I use my own pen or pencil?

(A) Please use the pencils provided to ensure that your test can be machine scored.

(Q) May I leave the room during the test?

(A) If you leave the room during the testing period, your test will not be scored. Does anyone need to leave the room before we begin?

Scoring Instructions

Finally, the test is not complete without scoring instructions. The scoring instructions and test key ensure that each person who scores the test will follow the same process. The scoring instructions must also explain how the test scores relate to the construct the test measures. For instance, what does a high score mean, and what does a low score mean? Remember that low scores indicate high performance on some tests, so the developer should not assume that the test taker or test user automatically will know what the score indicates.

CONDUCTING THE PILOT TEST

When developers design a new test, they cannot assume that the test will perform as expected. Just as engineers who have designed a new airplane conduct flight tests to find out how well the plane flies, test developers conduct studies to determine how well a new test performs. As we said earlier in this chapter, the pilot test is a scientific investigation of evidence that suggests that the test scores are reliable and valid for their specified purpose. The pilot-testing process involves administering the test to a sample of the test's target audience and analyzing the data obtained from the pilot test. The test developers then revise the test to fix any problems with the test's performance. As you know, it would be unsafe to carry passengers on a new airplane that has not been tested for performance and safety. Likewise, it is improper to rely on the results of a psychological test that has not been studied to ensure

FOR YOUR INFORMATION BOX 10.7

EXAMPLE OF TEST TAKER INSTRUCTIONS FOR A PAPER AND PENCIL TEST

1. This testing booklet contains 100 multiple-choice questions. Please do *not* write your name or make any marks in the test booklet.

2. Write your name on Line 1 of the blue answer sheet. Begin with your last name, followed by your given name.

3. Write the number of your test booklet on Line 2 of your answer sheet. You will find the testing booklet number in the top-right corner of the booklet cover.

4. Read each of the following multiple-choice questions carefully. Decide which response alternative (a, b, c, d, or e) is the *best* answer. Indicate your response by completely blackening the appropriate circle on the answer sheet.

5. You have 60 minutes to complete this test. If you complete the test in less than 60 minutes, please place your answer sheet inside your closed testing booklet. Please remain seated at your table until the testing period expires and the administrator collects your testing booklet. Please sit quietly so that other test takers will not be distracted. If you have not completed the test when the administrator indicates that the testing period has expired, please place your answer sheet inside your closed testing booklet and wait for the administrator to collect your testing booklet and answer sheet.

that its data are valid and reliable—that is, that the results are consistent and that the inferences that will be made from the scores on the test are appropriate. Because a test is actually a linear combination of all the individual items that make it up, reviewing each item for its psychometric properties and correcting or eliminating those items that are poor, is the first necessary (but not sufficient) step to increase the likelihood that the test developers will be able to show that the test is reliable and develop evidence to suggest that the test is valid for its intended purpose.

As we have discussed, new psychological tests are developed from a test plan—similar to an airplane's blueprints. To the extent that the test matches the test plan, we can say that it has demonstrated evidence of validity based on content. However, there are a number of important issues beyond this evidence that the test developer should investigate to ensure that the test scores are accurate and meaningful. For example, are the test items too difficult or too easy? Do the test items differentiate among individuals; in other words, do the test scores vary, or does everyone get approximately the same score? Are the test takers who receive high scores on the test those who possess the greatest amount of the skill or construct being measured? Are any of the items more difficult for a certain group of respondents, such as women or minorities? In addition, developers want to know whether the test instructions for the administrator and respondent are clear and easy to follow. Is the length of time allotted for administering the test adequate? Do respondents react to the test favorably and cooperatively? Finally, can the test user rely on the test scores to provide the information described in the test's purpose? We will discuss these issues in detail in the "How Do We Assess the Psychometric Quality of a Test?" chapter. But before those questions can be answered, test developers must conduct a "test of the test" which is referred to as a pilot test. Just as engineers rely on flight tests to provide evidence of a new plane's safety and performance to specifications, test developers rely on their pilot tests to provide evidence that their new test will produce scores that will be useful for decision making without harming test users or respondents.

© Christoph Ermel/iStockphoto

Setting Up the Pilot Test

Because the purpose of the pilot test is to study how well the test performs, it is important that the test be given in a situation that matches as closely as possible the actual circumstances in which it will be used. Therefore, for the pilot test, developers choose a sample of people who resemble or are a part of the test's target audience.

For example, if the test is designed to diagnose emotional disabilities in adolescents, the participants for the pilot study should be adolescents. Part of the sample should be adolescents who have been determined to have emotional disabilities. The others should be adolescents who have been determined not to have emotional disabilities. In addition, it would be important to ensure that each of those groups contains both male and female participants from various economic and ethnic backgrounds. The sample should be large enough to provide the power to conduct statistical tests to compare the responses of each group. For example, developers need to compare the responses of male adolescents with emotional disabilities with those of female adolescents with emotional disabilities.

Likewise, the test setting of the pilot test should mirror the planned test setting. If school psychologists will use the test, the pilot test should be conducted in a school setting using school psychologists as administrators. Conducting the pilot test in more than one school would be preferable because error introduced by one school's situation can be identified or offset by other schools.

In setting up pilot studies, developers follow the *Standards for Educational and Psychological Testing* (AERA et al., 2014). This means that test takers (and their parents or guardians, where appropriate) understand that they are participating in a research study and that the test scores will be used for research purposes only. Developers observe strict rules of confidentiality and publish only aggregate results of the pilot study.

Conducting the Pilot Study

The depth and breadth of the pilot study usually depend on the size and complexity of the target audience. For instance, tests designed for use in a single company or college program require less extensive studies than do tests designed for large audiences such as students applying for graduate school in the United States and adults seeking jobs as managers. In either case, however, it is important that the test administrators adhere strictly to the test procedures outlined in their test instructions.

In addition, pilot studies often require gathering extra data such as a criterion measure and the length of time needed to complete the test. Developers may use questionnaires or interviews that gather information from respondents about the test. For example, developers may want to know "Did you readily understand the test instructions?" "Were there any questions you did not understand?" "Did you object to the content of any questions?" and "Do you believe the test assessed your skills fairly?" Information on respondents' reactions and thoughts about the test can help developers understand why some questions yielded more useful data than others. This information makes the process of revising the test easier.

Most pilot studies go well and yield useful data that guide developers in making necessary revisions. However, some pilot tests simply might not work. For instance, administrators may ignore test instructions, respondents may complete answer sheets incorrectly, or respondents may exhibit hostility toward the test or the test administrator. In such cases, it is important to recognize the problems with the test administration, make all necessary revisions before continuing, and conduct a new pilot test that yields appropriate results. Also, it may sometimes be necessary to conduct multiple pilot studies to correct deficiencies that are found in the items themselves by removing or revising them before the test is released for publication. In order to make sure that the test content continues to match the test blueprint, the developer will have to add additional items into the test to replace the items that the first pilot study suggests should be eliminated. This is necessary so to maintain the evidence of the test's validity based on content. As a result, it may be necessary to conduct a subsequent pilot test so that the new and revised items can be properly evaluated, and to make sure that these changes and additions don't adversely affect the psychometric properties of the full test.

Analyzing the Results

The pilot test provides an opportunity to gather both quantitative and qualitative data about the test. The developers use statistical procedures to analyze the test responses for information regarding each item's difficulty, ability to discriminate among individuals, and likelihood of introducing bias or error. In addition, developers can estimate internal consistency. When data on an external criterion—such as performance or diagnoses—have been collected, developers may also gather preliminary information about how well the test scores correlate with the external criterion scores. This quantitative information is then reviewed with the qualitative information, such as test takers' reactions, to make revisions that enhance the performance of the test. You will learn how to analyze and evaluate the results of a pilot test in the next chapter.

Chapter Summary

This chapter has discussed the initial steps for developing psychological tests. The first step in test development is defining the testing universe, the target audience, and the purpose of the test. This stage provides the foundation for all other development activities. After a review of the literature, the test developer writes a concise definition of the construct, operationalizing the construct in terms of observable and measurable behaviors. The next step is to write a test plan that specifies the characteristics of the test, including a definition of the construct, the content to be measured (the testing universe), the format for the questions, and instructions for administering and scoring.

The cumulative model of scoring—which assumes that the more the test taker responds in a particular fashion, the more the test taker exhibits the attribute being measured—is probably the most common method for determining an individual's final test score. The categorical model and the ipsative model are other scoring methods.

After completing the test plan, the test developer begins writing the test questions and instructions. The questions, which test developers call *items*, can be in an objective format (multiple choice, true/false, and forced choice) or a subjective format (essays and interviews). Projective tests are another type of subjective format that uses ambiguous stimuli (words or pictures) to elicit responses from the test taker.

Some people have response sets—patterns of responding that result in false or misleading information—such as social desirability, acquiescence, random responding, and faking that cause test scores to contain error. Therefore, test developers need to be aware of these types of responses and guard against them. Although

(Continued)

(Continued)

there is no set of rules that guarantees that items will perform as expected, the test development literature contains a number of suggestions for writing successful items.

Objective items provide ample sampling of the testing universe, but they are more time-consuming to develop. Scoring of objective items is easier and likely to be more accurate and reliable. Subjective items are easier to construct and revise. Some experts suggest that essay and interview questions are better suited for testing higher order skills such as creativity and organization. Scoring of subjective items is more difficult, requiring independent scoring by two experts to increase reliability and accuracy. There also more complex test items such as performance assessments, simulations and portfolios.

These items are subject to the same technical standards as any other test item.

Although the test items make up the bulk of the new test, they are meaningless without specific instructions on how to administer and score the test. The test developer should write three sets of instructions: one for the administrator, another for the test taker, and a third for the person who scores and interprets the test results.

After writing the test items, the test developer conducts a pilot test to determine the final form the test will take. The test developer then follows up the pilot test with other studies that provide the necessary data for validation and norming. Conducting the pilot test and analyzing its data are integral parts of the test development process.

Engaging in the Learning Process

Learning is the process of gaining knowledge and skills through schooling or studying. Although you can learn by reading the chapter material, attending class, and engaging in discussion with your instructor, more actively engaging in the learning process may help you better learn and retain chapter information. To help you actively engage in the learning process, we encourage you to access our new supplementary student workbook. The workbook contains critical thinking activities to help you understand and apply information and help you make progress toward learning and retaining material. If you do not have a copy of the workbook, you can purchase a copy through sagepub.com.

Key Concepts

After completing your study of this chapter, you should be able to define each of the following terms. These terms are bolded in the text of this chapter and defined in the Glossary.

acquiescence	ipsative model of scoring	sentence completion
categorical model of scoring	multiple choice	simulation
	objective test format	social desirability
cumulative model of scoring	performance assessments	stem
	pilot test	subjective test format
distractors	portfolio	test format
essay questions	projective technique	test items
faking	projective tests	test plan
forced choice	random responding	testing environment
interview questions	response sets	true/false

Critical Thinking Questions

The following are some critical thinking questions to support the learning objectives for this chapter.

Learning Objectives	Critical Thinking Questions
Describe how to define the test domain, the target audience, and the purpose of the test.	• What do you think some of the consequences would be if the developers of a test failed to adequately specify the test domain, the target audience, and the purpose of a test before they began their development efforts?
Develop a test plan, including defining the construct or constructs the test measures, choosing the test format, and specifying how to score the test.	• What would you include in a test plan for this chapter in the text? Explain why you made the decisions you did. • What test format would you recommend for assessing student learning of how to develop a test? Explain your answer.
Differentiate between objective and subjective test questions, and describe the strengths and weaknesses of each.	• What would the consequences be if a test developer decided to use objective test questions for a test when it would have been more appropriate to use subjective questions? • Describe a content area for a test that would be best designed using subjective questions, and one where objective questions might be more appropriate. Include your rationale.
Describe the important issues in writing instructions for the test administrator and the test taker.	• What psychometric characteristic of a test would be most affected if the test taker or test administrator instructions were missing or poorly written? Why?
Understand why it is important to conduct a "test of the test" (called a pilot test) before a test is ready for administration.	• Most tests that instructors write for use in a classroom are not pilot tested. Think of a time when you took a test that would have been better if a pilot test had been conducted? What were the issues that might have been found and corrected?

HOW DO WE ASSESS THE PSYCHOMETRIC QUALITY OF A TEST?

LEARNING OBJECTIVES

After completing your study of this chapter, you should be able to do the following:

- Describe the collection, analyses, and interpretation of data for an item analysis, including item difficulty, item discrimination, interitem correlations, item–criterion correlations, item bias, and item characteristic curves.

- Describe how computer adaptive testing works and understand its benefits.

- Describe the collection and interpretation of data for a qualitative item analysis.

- Identify and explain the criteria for retaining and dropping items to revise a test.

- Describe the processes of validation and cross-validation.

- Explain the concepts of differential validity, single-group validity, and unfair test discrimination.

- Describe two different kinds of measurement bias.

- Explain the purpose of a cut score, and describe two methods for identifying a cut score.

"Last week I participated in a study of a new self-esteem test. The test administrator asked us to take the test anonymously. She said she could not be sure the test was a true measure of our self-esteem, so she couldn't tell us our scores. Why can't she tell us our self-esteem scores?"

"I have a copy of a test on organizational values that I took at work. I wanted to give it as a demonstration in class. My instructor objected because he said we could not interpret the *test scores without the test manual. What's so important about having a test manual?"*

"I created a test on math skills to find out which students need tutoring. When I showed it to my supervisor, she asked about the 'cut score.' What's a cut score?"

"My son's class took a standardized math test. There were a number of questions that were answered correctly by more girls than boys. I suggested to the teacher that the test might be biased against boys. She said that comparing the percentage of each group who answered questions correctly is not a good measure of bias. Why not?"

In the previous chapter, we described the process for designing a test, developing the test's items, writing the instructions for the test administrator, test takers, and test scorer, and conducting a pilot test. In this chapter, we continue describing the test development process by discussing how to analyze test items in terms of their difficulty, their ability to discriminate among respondents, and their likelihood of introducing error into the results. We also describe the process of revising the test and gathering evidence of reliability/precision and validity. Finally, we discuss briefly the contents of the test manual.

In the next section, we discuss how developers evaluate the performance of each test item—a process called **item analysis**.

CONDUCTING QUANTITATIVE ITEM ANALYSIS

Each item in a test is a building block that contributes to the test's outcome or final score. Therefore, developers examine the performance of each item to identify those items that perform well, to revise those that could perform better, and to eliminate those items that do not yield the desired information. The major portion of such a study involves **quantitative item analysis**—statistical analyses of the responses test takers gave to individual items. As you recall from the previous chapter, developers usually write twice the number of items they expect to use in the final test. Therefore, they can choose the very best items from the many they have written. The psychometric quality of the items is first evaluated by analyzing the results obtained in the pilot study.

Item Difficulty

The purpose of norm-referenced tests is to compare the test scores of various individuals. Therefore, it is important for there to be variability in individuals' test scores. Items that everyone gets "right" or everyone gets "wrong" provide no basis for comparison and yield similar test scores for all test takers. Therefore, developers analyze each test item for its difficulty. We define **item difficulty** as the percentage of test takers who respond correctly. We calculate each item's difficulty or p value (percentage value) by dividing the number of persons who answered correctly by the total number of persons who responded to the question. (Note that p stands for percentage as well as probability. In previous chapters, we discussed tests of significance, in which p stands for the probability of occurring by chance.) When test developers write items, they can only guess at how difficult each item will be. The pilot test provides the data for judging item difficulty.

Items with difficulty levels or p values of .5 yield distributions of test scores with the most variation. Because difficulty levels can be expected to vary, most developers seek a range of difficulty levels among all items that averages approximately .5. They discard or rewrite items with extreme p values, usually defined as 0 to .2 (too difficult) and .9 to 1 (too easy).

The concept of item difficulty makes intuitive sense for knowledge and skills tests on which there is one right answer. Difficulty levels can also be calculated, however, for tests of personality and attitudes. In these tests, no one answer is "correct." Yet the test developer still needs assurance that items are not likely to be answered in the same direction or with the same answer by everyone. The answer that indicates the presence of a construct or an attitude is labeled as correct for the purpose of the item analysis.

The p value of the item difficulty provides an accurate indication of how difficult the item was for the test takers in the pilot study. However, the p value does not provide information on the usefulness of the item in measuring the test's construct. Those who have more of the attribute being measured are more likely to respond correctly to the item, but this is not always the case. Sometimes an item may be more difficult for those who have a high degree of the test attribute than for those who have little of the test attribute—a situation that would call for revising or discarding the item.

One other thing to keep in mind when interpreting the difficulty of the items on a test is that a high or low p value can result from two different conditions. For instance, if the p value was very high, it could mean that the item was legitimately too easy, or it could mean that the group selected for the pilot test possessed an especially high level of knowledge, skill, or ability in the construct being measured. That is why it is important to carefully review the characteristics of the population participating in the pilot tests and to attempt to select a population that varies as much as possible in ability level. Later in this chapter, we discuss another approach to analyzing test items, called item response theory (IRT). This method uses a complex mathematical process to calculate statistics on test items that are independent of both the skill level of the population being tested and the difficulty of the items.

Discrimination Index

Because inferences regarding the meaning of high test scores versus low test scores will be made by the users of a test, it is important to obtain a measure of how well each item separates those test takers who demonstrate a high degree of skill, knowledge, attitude, or personality characteristic from those who demonstrate little of the same skill, knowledge, attitude, or personality characteristic. If a test is well constructed, each item on it (or on the subtest if the test is designed to measure multiple concepts) should be a measure of the concept of interest. If this is the case, there should be a statistical relationship between how an individual answers a particular item and his or her overall score on the test. For instance, in a test on which each item has one correct answer (such as a test of knowledge), people who answer a question correctly should score statistically higher on the overall test than people who answer the same question incorrectly. One of the ways that test developers evaluate this is by calculating a **discrimination index**, which compares the performance of those who obtained very high test scores (the upper group [U]) with the performance of those who obtained very low test scores (the lower group [L]) on each item. Calculating the percentage of test takers in each group who responded correctly and then obtaining the difference (D) between the two percentages creates the discrimination index. The formulas look like this:

$$U = \frac{\text{Number in upper group who responded correctly}}{\text{Total number in upper group}} \times 100.$$

$$L = \frac{\text{Number in lower group who responded correctly}}{\text{Total number in lower group}} \times 100.$$

$$D = U - L$$

The upper group and lower group are formed by ranking the final test scores from lowest to highest and then taking the upper third and the lower third to use in the analysis. Kevin Murphy and Charles Davidshofer (2005) suggested that any percentage from 25% to 35% may be used to form the extreme groups, with little difference in the resulting discrimination index. A commonly used choice is 27%.

You probably can see that the discrimination index, D, is simply the difference in the percentage of the highest scoring test takers who correctly answered a question and the percentage of the lowest scoring test takers who correctly answered the same question. So if 90% of the highest scoring test takers correctly answered a question, while only 20% of the lowest scoring test takers did, D would be $90 - 20 = 70$. On the other hand, if 50% of the highest scoring test takers answered correctly, while 40% of the lowest scoring test takers did, D would be $50 - 40 = 10$. Finally, if 30% of the highest scorers answered correctly, while 70% of the lowest scorers did, then D would be $30 - 70 = -40$, a very undesirable outcome.

After calculating a D value for each item, test developers look for items that have high positive numbers. It is most desirable for D values to be 30 or higher, but often they will be in the 20–30 range. Negative numbers indicate that those who scored low on the test overall responded to the item correctly and that those who scored high on the test responded incorrectly. Low positive numbers suggest that nearly as many people who had low scores responded correctly, as did those who had high scores. Each of these situations indicates that the item is not discriminating between high scorers and low scorers. Therefore, test developers discard or rewrite items that have low or negative D values. Next, we discuss a second index of an item's ability to discriminate high scorers from low scorers called item-total correlations.

Item-Total Correlations

Another way to assess the ability of individual test items to discriminate high-scoring individuals from lower scoring individuals is to calculate the **item-total correlation**. This is a measure of the strength and direction of the relation between the way test takers responded to one item and the way they responded to all of the items as a whole. We calculate the item-total correlation using the Pearson product-moment correlation formula.

In the case of multiple-choice or other objective formats, the answers for the item are dichotomous. Analysts usually code correct answers as 1 and incorrect answers as 0. Technically, the correlation of a dichotomous item with a continuous total score results in a statistic called the point biserial correlation coefficient; however, the calculation using the Pearson product-moment correlation formula or the correlation procedure on statistical software will provide the same correct answer. Items that have little or no correlation with the total item score may measure a different construct from that being measured by the other items.

Testing practitioners use item-total correlations as an alternative to the discrimination index discussed earlier. When items on a test are all measuring a similar construct, it is reasonable to assume that, on average, individuals who answer a particular question correctly will obtain a higher total score on the test than will individuals who answer the question incorrectly. Because of this, item-total correlations are usually reviewed as part of the process of item analysis. Test developers want to retain those items that strongly differentiate high-scoring individuals from lower scoring individuals. This is indicated by a positive item-total correlation. In the worst case, however, the item-total correlation coefficient can be negative. This would mean that people who answered a question correctly actually did worse on the test than people who got the question wrong. Such an occurrence is often indicative of a question that has been poorly worded and is confusing the more capable test takers. It could also indicate a question where the wrong answer was keyed as being correct. Questions with negative item-total correlations should be either reworked or removed from the test because they will reduce the test's reliability/precision. The item-total correlation coefficient provides one number that is easy to interpret and use to make decisions about retaining or discarding an item based on how well it discriminates high scorers from lower scorers. Item-total correlations for acceptable items usually range in the .2 to .4 range and can be tested for statistical significance if the pilot test has a large enough number of participants.

Interitem Correlations

Another important step in the item analysis is the construction of an **interitem correlation matrix**, which displays the correlation of each item with every other item. Usually each item has been coded as a dichotomous variable—correct (1) or incorrect (0). Therefore, the interitem correlation matrix will be made up of **phi coefficients**, which are the result of correlating two dichotomous (having only two values) variables. These coefficients are interpreted exactly like Pearson product-moment correlation coefficients. Table 11.1 shows an interitem correlation matrix displaying the correlation of six items with each other. As you can see, Item 1 correlates fairly well with the other five items. Item 3 correlates less well with the other items.

The interitem correlation matrix provides important information for increasing the test's internal consistency. Ideally, each item should be correlated with every other item measuring the same construct and should not be correlated with items measuring a different construct. In practice, interitem correlations tend to be relatively small in size, often in the .15 to .20 range, except for those items that are simple restatements of one another. As you recall, one method for increasing a test's reliability/precision is to increase the number of items measuring the same construct. In revising the test, however, the developer faces another problem: Which items can the developer drop without reducing the test's reliability/precision?

The answer is that items that are not correlated with other items measuring the same construct can (and should) be dropped to increase internal consistency. An item that does not correlate with other items (developed to measure the same construct) is probably measuring a different construct from that being measured by the other items. This is not always apparent when writing or reading the items because the item may be interpreted differently by the target audience.

TABLE 11.1 ■ Interitem Correlation Matrix for Pilot Test						
Item	1	2	3	4	5	6
1		.61	.39	.36	.74	.73
2			.11	.55	.14	.08
3				.03	.01	.09
4					.32	.43
5						.72
6						

As we discussed in the chapter on test reliability/precision, a test's overall internal consistency is calculated using the KR-20 formula for dichotomous items (items coded right or wrong) or the coefficient alpha formula for items that have multiple options for answers. The test developer uses the data from the pilot test to calculate an overall estimate of internal consistency, and then the developer consults the interitem correlation matrix to see which items should be dropped or revised to increase the test's overall internal consistency.

Item-Criterion Correlations

Some developers also correlate item responses with a criterion measure such as a measure of job performance for pre-employment tests or a diagnostic measure for clinical tests. Because the responses to the item are usually dichotomous (correct or incorrect), the resulting correlation coefficients are likely to be low and unlikely to reach statistical significance. However, the item-criterion correlation can be used as a guide for determining whether the item contributes to prediction of the criterion. For instance, items that correlate strongly with the criterion would be helpful in predicting the criterion.

Some tests are designed so that test scores can be used to sort individuals into two or more categories based on their scores on the criterion measure. We refer to these tests as **empirically based tests**, because the decision to place an individual in a category is based solely on the quantitative relationship between the predictor (test score) and the criterion (possible categories). One advantage of an empirically based test is that the test questions are not required to reflect the test's purpose, and therefore test takers have difficulty faking responses. Questions that have no apparent relation to the criterion are referred to as **subtle questions**. However, although empirically based tests can lead to optimal correlations with criteria, they are susceptible to bias derived from sample-specific characteristics. That is, the relationship between a question and a criterion might not be the same in a different group of test takers.

The Minnesota Multiphasic Personality Inventory (MMPI), a widely used personality inventory, is an example of an empirically based test. The original developers of the MMPI, Starke Hathaway and John McKinley, wanted to develop a paper-and-pencil test that would distinguish between normal individuals and those with psychological disorders. They developed the MMPI-1 using data from a sample of White adults in Minnesota. The MMPI-2, the revised version, was improved by using data from a more diverse sample representative of the U.S. population.

> **Test Spotlight 11.1** in Appendix A describes the development of the MMPI and some research it has stimulated.

The Item Characteristic Curve

During recent years, test developers have begun to rely on the concepts of **item response theory (IRT)** for item analysis. One of the reasons for this is that IRT can provide estimates of the ability of test takers that is independent of the difficulty of the items presented as well as estimates of item difficulty and discrimination that are independent of the ability of the test takers. This theory relates the performance of each item to a statistical estimate of the test taker's ability on the construct being measured. A fundamental aspect of IRT is the use of **item characteristic curves (ICCs)**. An ICC is the line that results when we graph the probability of answering an item correctly with the level of ability on the construct being measured. The ICC provides a picture of the item's difficulty and how well it discriminates high performers from low performers.

Figures 11.1 and 11.2 show ICCs for hypothetical items that measure verbal ability. In Figure 11.1, test takers with high ability have a higher probability of answering the item correctly than do test takers with low ability. In Figure 11.2, test takers with high ability

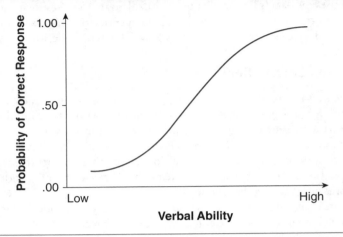

FIGURE 11.2 ■ **Item Characteristic Curve Showing That Test Takers With High Ability Have Only a Slightly Higher Probability of Answering Correctly**

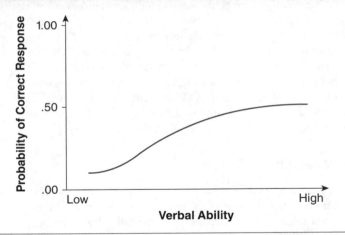

have only a slightly higher probability of answering the question correctly. We can conclude that the item with the greater slope provides better discrimination between high performers (those presumed to have higher ability in reading comprehension) and low performers (those presumed to have lower ability in reading comprehension).

We can determine the difficulty of an item on the ICC by locating the point at which the curve indicates a probability of .5 (a 50/50 chance) of answering correctly. The higher the ability level associated with this point, the more difficult the question. Figure 11.3

FIGURE 11.3 ■ Hypothetical Item Characteristic Curves for Three Items

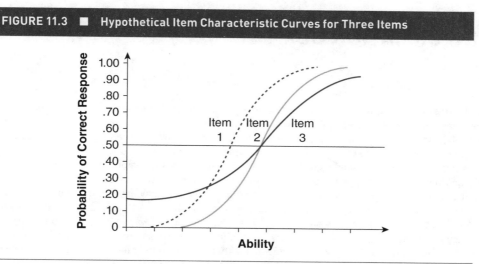

Source: From *Psychological Testing*, 7th ed., by Anne Anastasi and Susana Urbina. Copyright © 1997, pp. 190, 304. Published by Pearson Education Inc., Upper Saddle River, NJ.

shows three ICCs plotted for three different items. Item 1 is easier because less ability is associated with having a 50/50 chance of answering correctly. Items 2 and 3, which have different slopes, both intersect at the same point for having a 50/50 chance of answering correctly. Therefore, these items have the same difficulty level, and both are more difficult than Item 1.

IRT is also important in computerized adaptive testing (CAT). In computerized adaptive tests, all test takers start with the same set of questions. The CAT software then chooses items for individuals based on their level of ability determined from their previous responses. ICCs play a major role in analyzing and scoring test takers' responses. For multiple-choice questions, the CAT software uses a complex statistical technique called maximum likelihood estimation that weights each item by its difficulty, discrimination, and something called the pseudo-guessing parameter. The pseudo-guessing parameter estimates the probability that a test taker with a low ability level will respond correctly simply by guessing. Using IRT and the maximum likelihood parameters, the final test score represents the test taker's entire pattern of responses. According to David Weiss (2004), using this method yields more distinctions among the test takers than does simply adding the number of correct answers. Counting correct answers on a 10-item test provides 11 scores (0-10). Using IRT theory and CAT software on the same 10-item test yields 2^{10} (or 1,024) distinctions.

You may be wondering why IRT is not used for all test item analyses. One reason is that very large sample sizes are required for stable IRT analyses. According to Nunnally and Bernstein (1994), unless the scale you are analyzing is very short, a good IRT analysis requires a minimum sample size of 200 individuals, and could require as many as 500. In many applied settings, not enough test takers are available to perform an item analysis using IRT. The development of ICCs relies on complex methodology and sophisticated computer programming beyond the scope and objectives of this textbook. However, an ability to interpret ICCs can enable test developers and test users to better understand test development data and documentation. See For Your Information Box 11.1 for some more information about how computer adaptive testing works and For Your Information Box 11.2 for some tips on taking computer adaptive tests.

FOR YOUR INFORMATION BOX 11.1
COMPUTER ADAPTIVE TESTING

In **computerized adaptive testing (CAT)**, all test takers start with the same small set of questions—usually those of moderate difficulty. As the test progresses, the computer software chooses and presents each test taker with harder or easier questions depending on how well the test taker answered previous questions. According to test developers, these types of tests provide a fuller profile of a person in a shorter amount of time and the test taker does not need to spend time on questions that are too easy or too difficult. Therefore, a test that once took 4 or 5 hours may take only 2 or 3 hours using the CAT model.

The concept of adaptive testing dates back to the beginning of the 20th century, when Binet developed the Binet intelligence quotient [IQ] test, which was later published as the Stanford–Binet IQ Test (Binet & Simon, 1905). Weiss (2004) related the adaptive testing method to judging an athletic competition, pointing out that it would not be practical to measure athletes' hurdle-jumping ability by having them repeatedly jump over a succession of 2-foot hurdles—similar to answering a succession of multiple-choice questions. Rather, a series of hurdles of increasingly high levels is set up, and the athlete tries to clear each until she or he is no longer able to do so. Then, to determine a more precise indication of the level that the participant can clear, a set of hurdles that vary in a relatively narrow range around the level at which the individual began to miss is constructed. In this way, the task is "adapted" to the individual's performance in order to obtain precise estimates of each athlete's ability. (p. 71)

Adaptive testing for standardized tests remained unfeasible for most of the 20th century, until the advent of computerized testing allowed adaptive testing to be used in nationwide testing situations. CAT allowed psychologists to redesign important tests, Some of the first major implementations of CAT included the national nursing licensure exam administered by the National Council of State Boards of Nursing, the Graduate Record Examination (GRE), the Armed Services Vocational Aptitude Battery, and the achievement testing program used in the Portland, Oregon school system (Weiss, 2004).

CAT software is programmed to begin the test with one to three questions of moderate difficulty. The software is then programmed to select the subsequent test questions based on the test taker's skill level, which is determined by the answers to the previous questions. In a fully adaptive test, the computer scores the response to each item immediately, enabling the software to choose the next question based on whether the test taker correctly answered the prior question. If so, the next question presented will be at a higher level of difficulty. If not, the next question presented will be at a lower level of difficulty (Weiss, 2011). The software is programmed to continuously present questions until it zeros in on the test taker's skill level, at which time the test ends. Because of the way in which the questions are chosen in CAT, there is usually no fixed number of questions that will be presented. The test continues until the software can establish a reliable estimate of the test taker's skill level. Different test takers may receive tests of different lengths. However, sometimes the stopping rule will be based on the number of questions presented (Wainer et al., 2000).

A large number of test items must be available in order to deliver a computerized adaptive test. In addition, those items must be written at a wide range of different levels of difficulty. A computer houses this large bank of questions required by adaptive testing, and the CAT software delivers and scores the exam.

Most paper-and-pencil exams yield scores based on the total number of correct responses. But computerized adaptive tests are scored using the statistical technique IRT, which provides a more precise estimate of a test taker's level of ability than do conventional tests. Unlike traditional scoring, an IRT score represents an estimate of the level of the underlying trait or characteristic that the test is designed to measure rather than a number that represents the percentage of correct responses. This can make the interpretation of the score more difficult for the test taker. For Your Information Box 11.2 presents helpful tips on how to take adaptive tests such as the GRE, the Graduate Management Admission Test, and the Test of English as a Foreign Language.

CAT has many applications. For instance, beginning in the early 21st century, researchers presented convincing evidence that **computerized adaptive rating scales (CARS)** might help managers rate their employees more accurately than do two more popular types of rating scales. In the CARS study (Borman et al., 2001), raters were presented with a pair of behavioral statements (e.g., "This employee arrives on time each day" and "This employee often arrives at work late") and were asked to choose the one that best described the employee they observed in a group of videotaped role-plays. As in CAT, the computer software selected behavioral statements based on the rater's previous responses. The outcomes of the study showed that the CARS format provided more accurate and valid ratings than did graphic rating scales or behaviorally anchored rating scales. (See "How Are Tests Used in Organizational Settings?" for a discussion of these different types of rating scales.)

While CAT provides a great number of psychometric benefits, there may be some unintended consequences that taking a test in a computerized adaptive format creates for a test taker. Ortner, Weisskopf, and Koch (2014) investigated the effect that taking a computerized adaptive test has on a test taker's motivation level while taking the test. Specifically, they looked at test takers' subjective estimations of their probability of success on the test and their fear of failure. In

Germany, 174 secondary students were given either an adaptive or fixed-item (standard format) test of reasoning ability. Test takers were briefly interrupted midway through the testing session so that some motivational variables could be evaluated. Those students who were given the CAT reported a higher level of fear of failure and a lower level of subjective probability of success on the test than those students who were given the fixed-item test. If the level of motivation during the test also influences the performance on the test, then individuals taking the CAT could be disadvantaged by the test format. Additional research is needed to determine how practically significant this issue is. But even the authors of this study still concluded, "CAT is actually the gold standard of achievement testing" (Ortner et al., 2014, p. 55).

Item Bias

Test developers are interested in analyzing responses to individual test items to identify bias that results from various sources so as to correct or delete items that contain systematic error. One important area of analysis is item difficulty. Test items should be of equal difficulty for all groups. Researchers have proposed a number of methods for investigating **item bias**—when an item is easier for one group than for another group. These methods range from comparing scores or passing rates of various groups to comparing group performance in terms of an external criterion (Murphy & Davidshofer, 2005).

The preferred method of researchers, such as Rodney Lim and Fritz Drasgow (1990), involves the computation of item characteristics by group (e.g., men and women) and using the ICCs to make decisions about item bias. By plotting the curves on a graph, differences in difficulty and discrimination can be detected readily. Figure 11.4 shows ICCs for men

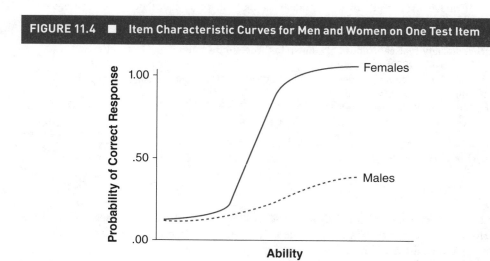

FIGURE 11.4 ■ Item Characteristic Curves for Men and Women on One Test Item

Source: From *Psychological Testing: Principles and Applications*, 6th ed., by Kevin R. Murphy and Charles O. Davidshofer. Copyright © 2005, pp. 214, 215, 223. Published by Pearson Education Inc., Upper Saddle River, NJ.

FOR YOUR INFORMATION BOX 11.2
TIPS FOR TAKING COMPUTERIZED ADAPTIVE TESTS

Are CATs more difficult than traditional standardized tests? What should a student know before taking an adaptive test? How can a student practice for an adaptive test? The Tree Foundation (2012), which offers preparation courses for foreign students who wish to study in the United Kingdom or the United States, has several suggestions that might help students in preparing to take adaptive tests.

First, the Tree Foundation (2012) suggests that students learn how adaptive tests are scored. The foundation emphasizes that an adaptive test does not give the same weight or importance to each question when determining the final score. Questions at the beginning of the test count more than those at the end of the test. Not only are the beginning questions worth more, but they also determine whether the subsequent questions will be more or less difficult. Later questions verify whether the test taker performs at the skill level that the earlier questions identified, and they contribute less to the final score. Therefore, the Tree Foundation suggests that test takers spend more time and effort doing their best on the beginning questions before they begin focusing on the middle questions.

Testing experts at Educational Testing Service (ETS) have a different outlook. They suggest that students who worry too much about the first few questions might hurt their scores. Test takers should pay close attention to the first 10 questions, but they also should pay close attention to the subsequent 10 questions. In truth, they say, test takers should concentrate on each question on the test. Placing too much emphasis on the beginning questions might cause excess anxiety that can reduce test takers' concentration (Guernsey, 2000). According to the Tree Foundation (2012), the ending questions do not count as much, and test takers can use the time left in the testing session to finish the test even if they need to guess. Test takers do need to finish the test, and therefore the Tree Foundation advises them to make intelligent guesses on the last questions. Both the Tree Foundation and ETS agree that the best strategy is "Pace yourself, but don't hurry!"

Second, the Tree Foundation (2012) warns test takers to be cautious. Successful test takers are those who are particularly careful to answer the beginning questions accurately. The test may contain experimental questions—questions that do not count toward the final score. (Tests contain experimental questions because test developers must continue to develop new questions. The best way of finding out whether a question measures accurately is to try it out on current test takers.) Because some questions may be experimental questions, the Tree Foundation advises test takers not to worry about questions that are too difficult or too easy. In other words, "Focus on doing your best!"

Finally, test takers may be glad to know that obtaining an average score is relatively easy. Making a high score, however, can be quite difficult because testing companies continually add scores to their databases as soon as they score each test. Because the majority of test takers will score close to the mean, those who do exceptionally well must score better than 95% of all those who have taken the test. The Tree Foundation (2012) advises test takers against taking a CAT without proper preparation. Guessing on the beginning questions might actually cause the testing software to punish the test takers by awarding easier and easier questions. In other words, "Be prepared!"

The best strategy for doing well on a CAT comes down to three simple rules:

1. Pace yourself and do not hurry.

2. Focus on doing your best.

3. Be prepared.

Source: American Psychological Association (2010).

and women on one test item. As you can see, the item discriminates between high and low performers better for women than for men. The item is also more difficult for men. Such an item should be discarded from a test.

For Your Information Box 11.3 illustrates the advantages of using IRT to detect bias in its discussion of the Golden Rule Insurance Company lawsuit, and For Your Information

FOR YOUR INFORMATION BOX 11.3
THE GOLDEN RULE CASE

During the early 1980s, the Golden Rule Insurance Company sued the Illinois Department of Insurance and ETS, asserting that two insurance licensing exams developed by ETS for the state of Illinois were biased against Black test takers. The basis for their claim was that the percentage of correct responses from Whites was greater than the percentage of correct responses from Blacks on a number of items. The statistic to which the suit referred was the p value, which indicates level of difficulty. This difference in difficulty level for Whites and Blacks resulted in a larger number of Whites' than Blacks' passing the test and obtaining their licenses. The case was settled out of court with the stipulation that ETS would develop subsequent exams using items for which the proportions of correct responses for all test takers were at least .40. Furthermore, the settlement stipulated that items in which the difference between proportions correct for Whites and Blacks exceeded .15 would not be used.

A number of testing experts suggested that there was a problem with the Golden Rule settlement. They noted that comparing item difficulty levels in the form of p values failed to take into consideration the level of ability of test takers. In other words, was the failure to give the correct answer because the item was poorly written or simply because the test taker did not know how to answer the question correctly?

As researchers noted in a symposium at an American Psychological Association (APA) annual meeting (Bond, 1987; Faggen, 1987; Linn & Drasgow, 1987) and in an official statement by the APA, IRT provides a better way to detect items that are more difficult for one group than for another group. As you recall, ICCs associate item difficulty with test takers' ability. Comparing ICCs provides a better way to evaluate item difficulty because it takes test taker ability into account. Furthermore, Rodney Lim, in his master's thesis, demonstrated this principle empirically by using both methods to evaluate item responses from a simulated data set (Lim & Drasgow, 1990). He found that the Golden Rule procedure identified 90% of the items as biased, in contrast to the IRT method, which found that approximately 25% of the items were biased when ability was taken into account.

Source: Adapted from Van de Vijver, F. J. R., & Phalet, K. (2004). Assessment in multicultural groups: The role of acculturation. *Applied Psychology: An International Review, 53,* 215–236.

Box 11.4 discusses bias associated with **acculturation**—the degree to which an immigrant or a minority member has adapted to a country's mainstream culture.

CONDUCTING QUALITATIVE ITEM ANALYSIS

In addition to conducting a quantitative analysis of test takers' responses, test developers often ask test takers to complete a questionnaire about how they viewed the test itself and how they answered the test questions. Such questionnaires enable developers to conduct a **qualitative item analysis**. Test developers might also use individual or group discussions with test takers for understanding how test takers perceived the test and how changes in the test content or administration instructions would improve the accuracy of the test results. Finally, test developers can also ask a panel of experts—people knowledgeable about the test's content or about testing in general—to review the test and provide their opinions on possible sources of error or bias.

FOR YOUR INFORMATION BOX 11.4
THE ROLE OF ACCULTURATION ASSESSMENT

When we conduct a quantitative item analysis, our purpose is to identify sources of error that may be introduced into final test scores by the test itself, its scoring scheme, administration, or interpretation. Therefore, we examine test responses to determine whether an item is easier for one group than for another group, and we examine responses to ensure that an item distinguishes among test takers only on the construct being measured.

Until recently, those test developers who analyzed items for cultural bias did so by including minority members in the norming sample and following up using ICCs or qualitative measures to identify biased items. At that point, the discovery of cultural bias usually led to editing or deleting biased items. Although this methodology is good, it is not sufficient for identifying culture bias in a very diverse population. The populations of the United States and Europe in the 21st century will be truly multicultural, in the sense that many individuals will have behaviors and traditions associated with two or more cultures. Furthermore, one individual might have varying degrees of acculturation in two or more cultures. For example, one young person living in a bicultural family, such as Mexican American or Chinese American, may have embraced one culture more than has another person from a similar bicultural family. Conducting item analyses for every minority group with members acculturated to various degrees in a diverse population is likely to become cumbersome and potentially ineffective.

Two researchers from the Netherlands (Van de Vijver & Phalet, 2004) proposed taking a different approach to dealing with item and test bias associated with the degree to which test takers understand and conform to mainstream culture. They proposed administering a test that measures the degree to

which each test taker belongs to the mainstream culture and then using those test scores to adjust raw scores for error in the test score caused by lack of acculturation. Current measures of acculturation are usually short surveys (about 20 items) that examine test takers' sense of belonging to one or more groups and their attitudes toward those groups.

According to Van de Vijver and Phalet (2004), three types of cultural bias arise in tests:

1. *Construct bias* arises when items do not have the same meaning from culture to culture or subculture. For example, the behaviors associated with being a good daughter or son (filial piety) are different in various cultures.

2. *Method bias* arises when the mechanics of the test work differently for various cultural groups. For example, individuals schooled in North America and Europe may be more familiar with using an electronic scan sheet or a computerized test than others who are used to writing essays or verbally answering questions asked by the test administrator or an examiner.

3. *Differential item functioning* arises when test takers from different cultures have the same ability level on the test construct, but the item or test yields very different scores for the two cultures. For example, a history test that contains a large proportion of questions on the history and geography of the original 13 colonies of the United States might favor test takers from New England over test takers from California and Mexico—even though both groups are equally familiar with American history overall.

Source: Adapted from Van de Vijver and Phalet (2004).

Questionnaires for Test Takers

Ronald Jay Cohen, Mark Swerdlik, and Suzanne Phillips (1996) provided a comprehensive list of questions for test takers, shown in Table 11.2. Some or all of these topics can be addressed in an open-ended survey, or the test developers may wish to construct Likert-type rating scales (discussed in "How Do We Construct and Administer Surveys and Use Survey Data?") to make responding easier for the pilot test participants. The open-ended format yields more information; however, the participants might not have enough time

TABLE 11.2 ■ Potential Areas of Exploration by Means of Qualitative Item Analysis	
Topic	**Sample Question**
Cultural sensitivity	Did you feel that any item or aspect of this test was discriminatory with respect to any group of people? If so, why?
Face validity	Did the test appear to measure what you expected it would measure? If not, what about this test was contrary to your expectations?
Test administrator	Did the presence of the test administrator affect your performance on this test in any way? If so, how?
Test environment	Did any conditions in the room affect your performance on this test in any way? If so, how?
Test fairness	Do you think the test was a fair test of what it sought to measure? Why or why not?
Test language	Were there any instructions or other written aspects of the test that you had difficulty understanding?
Test length	How did you feel about the length of the test with respect to (a) the time it took to complete and (b) the number of items?
Test taker's guessing	Did you guess on any of the test items? About what percentage of the items would you estimate you guessed on? Did you use any particular strategy for guessing, or was it basically random guessing?
Test taker's integrity	Do you think that there was any cheating during this test? If so, please describe the methods you think may have been used.
Test taker's mental/ physical state upon entry	How would you describe your mental state going into this test? Do you think that your mental state in any way affected the test outcome? If so, how? How would you describe your physical state going into this test? Do you think that your physical state in any way affected the test outcome? If so, how?
Test taker's overall impressions	How would you describe your overall impression of this test? What suggestions would you offer the test developer for improvement?
Test taker's preferences	Was there any part of the test that you found entertaining or otherwise rewarding? What specifically did you like or dislike about the test? Was there any part of the test that you found anxiety provoking, condescending, or otherwise upsetting? If so, why?
Test taker's preparation	How did you prepare for this test? If you were going to advise others as to how to prepare for it, what would you tell them?

Source: From R. J. Cohen, M. E. Swerdlik, and S. M. Phillips. (1996). *Psychological testing and assessment: An introduction to tests and measurement*, 3rd ed. Reproduced with the permission of The McGraw-Hill Companies.

to answer a lengthy questionnaire. If Likert-type scales are used, discussion groups with a sample of participants can focus on portions of the test that are targeted for revision. For instance, test takers may find the test length to be appropriate; however, they may express concerns about face validity. Therefore, discussion would focus on face validity, not test length.

Table 11.2 includes sample topics and questions of possible interest to test users. The questions could be raised either orally or in writing shortly after a test's administration. Additionally, depending on the objectives of the test user, the questions could be placed into other formats, such as true/false or multiple choice. Depending on the specific questions to be asked and the number of test takers being sampled, the test user may wish to guarantee the anonymity of the respondents.

Expert Panels

Test developers also find the information provided by experts to be helpful in understanding and improving test results. One group of experts would be people who are knowledgeable about the test's constructs. For example, if the test measures job skills such as financial planning or systems analysis, people who perform these jobs well can be recruited to review the test and provide their opinions on the test's content.

Another area of expertise is psychological measurement. Review by another test developer who has not been involved in the development process can provide a fresh look at issues of test length, administration instructions, and other issues not related to test content.

REVISING THE TEST

Revision of the test is a major part of the test development process. Test developers write more items than are needed. They use the quantitative and qualitative analyses of the test to choose those items that together provide the most information about the construct being measured. Because the instructions for test takers and test administrators are an essential part of the test, the information provided by test takers and experts provides a basis for revising the instructions in a way that facilitates the process of test administration.

Choosing the Final Items

Choosing the items that make up the final test requires the test developer to weigh each item's evidence of validity, item difficulty and discrimination, interitem correlation (a measure of reliability/precision), and bias. Issues such as test length and face validity must also be considered.

Many test developers find that constructing a matrix makes choosing the best items easier. Table 11.3 lists each item, followed by its performance in terms of internal consistency (item-total correlation), validity (item-criterion correlation), difficulty, discrimination, and bias.

TABLE 11.3 ■ Item Statistics Matrix for Items From a Hypothetical Reading Comprehension Test						
Item Number	Content Construct*	Item-Total Correlation	Item-Criterion Correlation	Difficulty (*p*)	Discrimination (*D*)	Bias
1	T	−.20	.00	.50	−10	No
2	T	.35	.00	.20	35	No
3	T	.40	.08	.60	55	No
4	I	.80	.12	.65	40	No
5	I	.25	.01	.50	15	Yes
6	I	−.05	−.02	.50	−35	No
7	E	.56	.25	.49	30	No
8	E	.84	.20	.70	70	No
9	E	.03	−.05	.90	−20	Yes

*The test plan calls for items that measure translation (T), interpretation (I), and extrapolation (E).

The test developer's job is to choose the best-performing items, taking care that each area of content is represented in the proportion required by the test plan. In addition to the matrix, developers can review the ICCs to make visual comparisons of items.

As you recall, positive interitem correlation coefficients and item-total correlations suggest that the item is measuring the same construct as are other items—evidence of internal consistency. The best items will have higher positive correlation coefficients. They will also be close to .5 in difficulty with discrimination indexes that are positive and high. Items that have evidence of bias are not acceptable unless they can be rewritten to relieve that problem. (Such rewrites may require further testing to ensure that bias no longer exists.) It is unusual for all items to meet all of the criteria for a "good" item, and therefore the test developer has the complicated job of weighing the merits of each item and choosing a set of final items that work well together to provide accurate test results for all participants.

As you can see from the data in Table 11.3, the items represented have varying merits. Item 1 has appropriate difficulty and is not biased; however, both its discrimination index and item-total correlation are negative, suggesting that poor performers were more likely to get this item right and good performers were more likely to get it wrong. Also, this item is not correlated with a criterion. Item 2, on the other hand, has a good item-total correlation and shows no bias, but it is very difficult, with only 20% of the test takers correctly answering it. Item 3 has the best data of the items measuring translation. Its item-total correlation is high, its difficulty level is close to .5, its discrimination index is high and positive, and it shows no evidence of bias. Therefore, Item 3 would be a better choice than Items 1 or 2.

Now you can see why the test developer must write many more items for a test than are required. Each item must be judged as acceptable on a number of criteria to be chosen for inclusion in the test. Of the remaining items in Table 11.3, which ones would you choose to include in the final test? If you chose Items 4, 7, and 8, you agree with the authors of this textbook.

When test developers have written an ample number of test items, the task of compiling the final test is simply a matter of choosing the correct number of "good" items that meet the requirements of the test plan. When test items must be rewritten to increase or decrease difficulty or discrimination or to avoid bias, those items should be piloted again to be sure that the changes made produced the desired results. Extensive changes or rewrites signal the need for another pilot test.

Revising the Test Instructions

No matter how well the final items work together, the test cannot produce accurate results unless the instructions for test takers and test administrators are concise and understandable. Clear and comprehensive directions ensure that the test will be administered in the same way for all participants and under circumstances that are advantageous for test taking. Likewise, directions for test takers help prevent test takers from giving useless responses. The qualitative information obtained from test takers and administrators provides a useful guide for revising instructions to promote maximum performance.

Instructions to the test administrator should provide guidance on topics such as choosing the testing room (a quiet place where interruptions are unlikely), answering questions (clarify instructions, but do not elaborate or provide help), equipment or supplies needed (No. 2 pencils), and test length (a specified time period or unlimited time). The instructions may include a section on answering frequently asked questions—information obtained during the pilot test.

Instructions to test takers should include directions for responding (for example, "Darken the box next to the answer you have chosen with a No. 2 pencil"), instructions on guessing (whether or not guessing is penalized), and special instructions (e.g., "Think of how you interact with people at work when answering these questions"). Often tests include sample questions that test takers complete with the test administrator to be sure that directions for responding are clearly understood.

VALIDATING THE TEST

When the final test has been compiled, it is time to move to the next stage of test development—conducting the validation study. In previous chapters, we've described the various types of evidence that demonstrate validity in detail. Therefore, this section simply provides an overview of designing the validation study.

The first part of the validation process—establishing evidence of validity based on test content—is carried out as the test is developed. Evidence that the test measures one or more constructs (construct validity) and has the ability to predict an outside criterion such as performance (evidence of validity based on relationships with an external criterion) must be gathered during another round of data collection.

Standards for setting up the validation study are similar to those suggested for designing the pilot study. The validation study should take place in one or more situations that match the actual circumstances in which the test will be used. Using more than one test site will provide evidence that the results are **generalizable**, meaning the test can be expected to produce similar results even though it has been administered in different locations. Likewise, developers choose as test takers a sample of people who resemble or are part of the test's target audience. The sample should be large enough to provide the power to conduct the desired statistical tests. The test developers continue to follow the *Standards for Educational and Psychological Testing* (American Educational Research Association [AERA], American Psychological Association [APA], & National Council on Measurement in Education [NCME], 2014) by observing strict rules of confidentiality and by affirming their intentions to publish only aggregate results of the validation study. Again, as in the pilot study, the scores resulting from the administration of the test should not be used for decision making or evaluation of individuals. The sole purpose of the validation study is to affirm the test's ability to yield meaningful results.

Test developers collect data on the test's reliability/precision, its correlation with any appropriate outside criteria such as performance evaluations, and its correlation with other measures of the test's construct. In addition, the developers collect data on the demographic characteristics of the test takers (e.g., sex, race, age). Test developers also conduct another item analysis similar to that conducted in the pilot study to affirm that each item is performing as expected. Minor changes in the test, such as dropping items that do not contribute to prediction of an outside criterion and further clarifying test instructions, may be made at this time.

Replication and Cross-Validation

If the final revision yields scores with sufficient evidence of reliability/precision and validity, the test developers conduct a final analysis called **replication** for tests that rely on criterion-related evidence of validity to make predictions. The process of replication involves a final round of test administration to another sample of test takers representative of the target audience. Because of chance factors that contribute to random error, this second administration can be expected to yield lower correlations with criterion measures. In other words, the validity coefficient will be lower than the one found in the original validation study. This decrease in correlation with an outside criterion—referred to as *shrinkage*—is largest when the sample size for the initial validation study is small. However, attention to prediction of the criterion in the pilot study and initial validation study can reduce shrinkage during replication (Cascio, 1991).

A process called **cross-validation** can also be conducted to investigate whether the results of the regression performed to validate the test would be likely to generalize to a new sample of test takers. This can be done without having to administer the test to a second group of test takers (as a replication would require) if the original validation group is large enough. What cross-validation does is to break the original sample used in the original validation study into two parts. One part is called the screening sample and consists of the majority of the test takers, often about 70%. The remaining 30% of the test takers are called the validation sample (J. Stevens, 2002). The way cross-validation works is that a regression is first performed *only* on the people in the screening sample using the test scores from the original validation study as the predictor and the criterion scores from that study as the criterion. This will result in a regression equation that quantifies the relationship between the test scores and the criterion variable for the people within the screening sample. The object of this step is to create a new regression equation that can then be used to predict criterion scores for the people who are in the validation sample.

Recall from the chapter where we discussed regression that a simple regression equation takes the form of

$$Y' = a + bX,$$

where

Y' = the predicted score on the criterion

a = the intercept

b = the slope

X = the score each individual made on the test

The regression computed on the screening sample will produce values for the a (intercept) and b (slope) parameters as well as a value for R^2 (the amount of variance in the criterion measure that is accounted for by the test scores in the screening sample). We can use these values of the intercept (a) and the slope (b) to calculate predicted criterion scores for each individual in the validation sample. These predicted scores are calculated by substituting the a and b values obtained from the regression on the screening sample into the equation $Y' = a + bX$ using each person's actual test score (in the validation sample) as the value for X.

Because we also have the *actual* criterion scores for each person in the validation sample from the original validation study, we can examine how closely they match the scores that were predicted using the regression equation derived *only* from the individuals who were included in the screening sample. We do this by correlating the predicted criterion scores using the values obtained from the regression we ran on the validation sample with the same individual's actual criterion score. This prediction would be considered to be good when the correlation between these two sets of scores is as large as the value of R (or R^2) that was found in the regression conducted on the screening sample. This would mean that the regression equation conducted on the screening sample would accurately predict the criterion on a new group of people. When this is the case, we would have a high level of confidence that the results of our original validity study will generalize to a new group of test takers.

Unfortunately, in most cases, the correlation (or the r^2) between the predicted criterion scores and their actual criterion scores of the people in the validation sample will be lower than the R (or the R^2) that was observed when the regression was conducted only on the people in the screening sample. This is because the prediction equation calculated from the screening sample will not be a perfect predictor of the criterion scores in the validation sample. This is another example of shrinkage in the validity coefficient. It is an indicator of how much smaller the validity coefficient would be when computed for a different sample of people than those in the original validation study. There are no specific amounts of shrinkage universally considered to be acceptable. But the general rule is that less is better.

Shrinkage in the validity coefficient is so predictable that researchers have developed formulas to predict the amount of shrinkage that can be expected (Cattin, 1980; Wherry, 1931). When resources are not available to carry out a cross-validation study, estimation of shrinkage statistically is acceptable or even preferred (Cascio, 1991).

While conducting a cross validation by splitting a single sample of test takers into two parts is a useful technique, it may not be identical to what one might find if a replication were done on an entirely new sample instead. This is because any systematic variance that may exist in the full sample used for the cross validation will still exist both in the screening sample and the validation sample even if the two samples are chosen randomly. The shared systematic variance will tend to inflate the correlation between the screening sample and the validation sample. Therefore, the results of the cross validation may look better than it actually would look if the outcome hadn't been influenced by the presence of this systematic variance.

In Greater Depth Box 11.1 provides a numerical example that demonstrates how a cross-validation of a regression described in this section is performed.

Measurement Bias

When the scores on a test taken by different subgroups in the population (e.g., men, women) need to be interpreted differently because of some characteristic of the test not related to the construct being measured, we say that **measurement bias** is present in the test (AERA et al., 2014). Measurement bias can take a number of different forms. We have already spoken about differential item functioning. When different groups of people have different scores on a group of items or an entire test even though they possess the identical quantities of the construct being measured by the test, we call that differential test functioning (AERA et al., 2014). But probably the most commonly observed (and studied) type of measurement bias is called predictive bias (AERA et al., 2014). Predictive bias occurs when the predictions made about a criterion score based on a test score are different for subsets of test takers (e.g., minority vs. majority, men vs. women). Predictive bias is indicated when a test has different validity coefficients for different groups. For example, a test may be a better predictor for women than for men or for Blacks than for Whites. When a test yields significantly different validity coefficients for subgroups, we say it has **differential validity**. When a test is valid for one group but not for another group (e.g., valid for Whites but not for Blacks), it has **single-group validity**.

Predictive bias is studied by using regression analysis. This type of analysis of test bias was first discussed in a seminal paper published by T. Anne Cleary in 1968, and it is still sometimes referred to as the Cleary approach. The premise that underlies this view of bias is that identical scores on a test should result in identical predicted scores on the criterion regardless of the subgroup to which the test taker belongs. So for instance, if a regression analysis done on the men's test scores shows that men who score a 50 on a test of numerical reasoning are predicted to receive a B in a statistics course, the same prediction should be made if the regression is done on the women's test scores. If instead, women who scored 50 on the test are predicted to receive an A in the course, predictive bias would be present because the meaning or inferences that can be drawn from identical test scores are not the same for both men and women. However, it is important to recognize that the source of the bias may not always be with the test. The source could be the criterion. As we discussed in a prior chapter, it is always important to evaluate the psychometric quality of a criterion measure to insure that it is adequately measuring the intended construct and is not influenced by construct

IN GREATER DEPTH BOX 11.1
CROSS-VALIDATION EXAMPLE

The example reported here demonstrates how we would cross validate a regression used to provide predictive evidence of validity for an employee selection test. For this example, keep the following in mind:

- Performance evaluation scores were used as the criterion.

- Test scores could range from 0 to 100, while performance evaluation scores could range from 1 to 10.

- One hundred individuals were included in the original validation study.

As the first step in the process, we randomly selected 70% of the test takers to serve as the screening sample. The remaining 30% of test takers formed the validation sample. We then performed a regression to predict using the test scores as the predictor and the performance evaluations scores as the criterion in the screening sample. This resulted in the following regression results:

$$\text{Predicted Evaluation Score} = 3.387 + (.033 \times \text{Test Score})$$
$$R = .327$$
$$R^2 = .107$$

These results show that the correlation between the test scores and the performance evaluation scores in the screening sample was .327, and that the test scores accounted for 10.7% of the variance in the performance evaluation scores. This is a typical result that one might see in a successful validation study as described above.

We then used that regression equation to calculate a predicted evaluation score for the 30% of the test takers who weren't used in the regression. Below is an example of how we used the regression equation to calculate a predicted score for the first three test takers in the validation sample.

Test Taker ID	Test Score	Calculation	Predicted Evaluation Score
1	73	Predicted = 3.387 + (.033 × 73)	5.8
2	81	Predicted = 3.387 + (.033 × 81)	6.0
3	93	Predicted = 3.387 + (.033 × 93)	6.4

As the final step we can now correlate the predicted performance evaluation scores that we calculated using the regression equation on the screening sample with the actual performance evaluation scores that we have on the three test takers. Below is a table that shows the actual evaluation scores for the same test takers long with their predicted scores we calculated above.

Test Taker ID	Predicted Evaluation Score	Actual Evaluation Score
1	5.8	6.1
2	6.0	5.7
3	6.4	6.0

When we correlated the actual and predicted evaluation scores for all 30 test takers in the validation sample, we found that it was .225. This makes the coefficient of determination (r^2) equal to .05. This indicates that the test scores now only accounted for 5% of the variance in predicted evaluation scores in the validation sample. When we compare this value to the value that we obtained in the screening sample, we see that the validity coefficient has shrunk from .327 to .225. The amount of variance that the test accounts for in the evaluation score has shrunk from 10.7% to only 5%. The conclusion is that the test might not be as good a predictor in a new sample of test takers as it was in the sample used in the original validation study.

This shrinkage in the validity coefficient is a very common occurrence when the results of a regression analysis are applied on a new sample. In this example, the amount of shrinkage was a little large because our sample size in the validation sample was small (only 30 test takers). Therefore, our results will be unstable. If we repeated the regression drawing a different random sample to create the screening and validation groups, our results might be very different. That is one of the reasons why it is important to have the largest possible sample sizes when we conduct a validation study. Otherwise, we might not be able to develop sufficient confidence that our validation results will actually generalize to a new group of test takers.

irrelevant variance. In our example above, if for some reason the person assigning the grades in the course tended to systematically give higher grades to the women (independent of their numerical reasoning scores), then the source of the predictive bias could be the criterion, not the test. (See Meade and Fetzer, 2008, for a discussion of a statistical approach that can be used to help identify the source of this type of predictive bias.)

The presence of predictive bias is analyzed using regression analysis. The object of the analysis is to answer the question of whether it is appropriate to use the same regression line (and therefore regression equation) to model the relationship between a predictor and criterion across different groups of people. When the same regression line is used to predict a criterion for two different groups, it is referred to as a common regression line. The usual presumption is that if test is unbiased, a common regression line should be equally applicable to different groups of people. The appropriateness of a common regression line is a critical question to answer when a regression equation is used to make decisions about people based on their test scores. The basic question is whether one regression equation predicts outcomes equally well for all populations on which it is intended to be used.

To demonstrate how this question is answered, consider this hypothetical example. Suppose a university has a highly competitive program for which there are now more applicants than available openings. When the program was first developed, everyone who applied was admitted. As part of the admission procedure, everyone was also given a particular aptitude test, even though it was not formally used in the admission process. Now that the program can no longer admit everyone who applies, the director asks the university's institutional research department to investigate whether they could start using the aptitude test as a valid predictor of who is most likely to succeed in the program. If so, the test would then be used as part of the selection process. The program director's idea is that they would develop a regression equation to predict the performance of new students based a regression equation developed by using the 200 existing students' aptitude test scores as the predictor and their program performance results as the criteria. This equation would then be applied to the new students' aptitude test scores to predict who would be most likely to succeed in the program. The program's director knows from prior research that the correlation between the aptitude test and ratings of 1st-year performance in the program was .32, so there is evidence of validity established for the test. (You may recognize this type of research as it is the procedure used to gather predictive evidence of validity.) Although there is evidence of validity for the test, the question whether there is any predictive bias present in the regression results requires additional investigation.

Figure 11.5 presents a scatterplot of the hypothetical data that the institutional research department is given to do the analysis. It presents the aptitude test scores of 200 students currently in the program on the *x*-axis and standardized performance scores that students received when they completed their 1st year of the program on the *y*-axis. The aptitude test scores range from about 50 to 150. The performance scores range from 1 to 10. There are three regression lines shown in this figure. The broken line in the center is the combined regression line for all 200 of the students. This is referred to a common regression line. The upper line is the regression line calculated on only the male students. The lower regression line is calculated on only the female students. There are exactly 100 students in each group. As you can see, the common regression line (the one in the middle) is different from the upper (male students) or lower (female students) line. Let's explore the implications of the differences between the lines in terms of the predictions that would be made for each group regarding their performance.

Looking at the regression lines, we can see that the line for the male students differs from the line for the female students in two important respects. The first is that the lines do not have the same slope as the common regression line. Also, the slope of the regression line for male students is different from the slope of the regression line for female students. We can tell

FIGURE 11.5 ■ Predicted Program Performance From Aptitude Test Scores

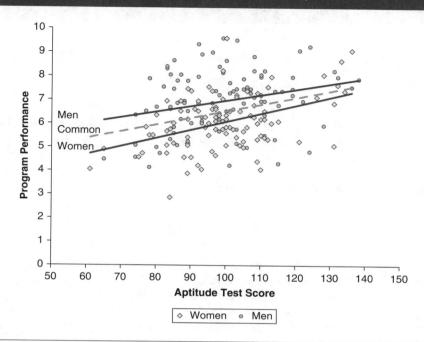

this without any calculations by the fact that the lines are not parallel to each other. They are closer together on the right-hand side of the scatterplot then they are on the left-hand side.

The second way in which the regression lines are different can be seen if you extend the lines on the left-hand side of the scatterplot to the *y*-axis. You can see that they will not cross it in the same location. This means that the intercepts are also different. Taken together, this indicates that the regression equations for male and female students must be different from each other, and they are. Table 11.4 presents the regression equations for the male, female, and combined groups. The fact that the regression lines appear different for male and female students (and both are different from the common regression line) suggests that it may not be appropriate to use the same regression equation to make predictions about the likelihood of success of male and female students in the program based on their test scores.

From the regression equations presented in Table 11.4, we can see that as expected, both the slopes and the intercepts are different for men and women. The intercept of the regression line for men is 4.60, while for women it is 2.62. The slope of the regression line for men is .0237, and for women it is .0346. Thus, there is evidence that two different types of predictive bias may be operating here: slope bias and intercept bias. The effect that these biases have on our ability to predict a criterion are different. We will consider **intercept bias** first.

Looking at Figure 11.5, you can see that the regression line for women is the lower line in the scatterplot. This makes sense, as the intercept shown for women in Table 11.4 is lower for women than it is for men. You can also see that at every level of aptitude test score, the predicted performance of women is lower than it is for men. The difference narrows at the higher ranges of test scores, and is wider at the lower ranges. It is a simple calculation to use the regression equation for women to calculate a predicted performance score for a new woman who enters the program using her aptitude test score as the predictor. Let's assume a

TABLE 11.4 ■ Regression Equations for the Male, Female, and Combined Groups From Figure 11.5	
Male students	$Y' = 4.60 + .0237x$
Female students	$Y' = 2.62 + .0346x$
Combined group	$Y' = 3.67 + .0285x$

female applicant for the program scores a 100 on the aptitude test (remember, the actual scores range from about 50 to 150). Her predicted performance score using the regression equation for women would be

$$\text{Predicted performance score } (Y') = 2.62 + (.0346 \times 100)$$
$$= 2.62 + 3.46$$
$$= 6.08$$

Thus, a woman who scored a 100 on the aptitude test would be expected to have a 1st-year performance score of 6.08. But let's suppose we did not have the separate regression equation for women. Instead, presume that the only regression equation we had was the common regression equation for men and women, and we used that to predict 1st-year performance in the program. In that case, the predicted performance score for a woman who scored 100 on the aptitude test would be

$$\text{Predicted performance score } (Y') = 3.67 + (.0285 \times 100)$$
$$= 3.67 + 2.85$$
$$= 6.52$$

Using the common regression line to calculate the predicted performance score for a woman scoring 100 on the aptitude test gives us an estimated 1st-year performance score of 6.52, about half a point higher than what we found when we used the regression equation based on the women alone. So using a common regression equation *overpredicts* a women's performance score by .5 points. We would find the opposite effect if we used the common regression line to predict a man's score. Using the common regression line to predict a man's performance score based on an aptitude test score of 100 would *underpredict* the score based on the men-only regression equation by about half a point.

This is the nature of intercept bias. It means that using a common regression equation to predict a criterion for two groups will result in a different prediction than if a separate regression equation, calculated within each group, were used. One group may be overpredicted while the other group may be underpredicted. As in this example, it means that the predicted performance for any given level of test score will be different depending on the group to which the person belongs. In other words, equal test scores between two groups do not predict equal levels of performance. If (and this may be a big if) the performance measure is unbiased, then the problem must be the predictive bias of the test.

As we suggested earlier, there is another type of predictive bias. It is called **slope bias**. It occurs when the slopes of the separate regression lines that relate the predictor to the criterion are not the same for one group as another (Society for Industrial and Organizational Psychology, 2003).

The slopes of the regression lines in Figure 11.5 are also different for men and women and are also different from the common regression line. This difference has a couple of important implications. The first is that the differences in the predicted criterion scores using separate regression lines versus using a common regression line will not be constant across all levels of the predictor. As an example, a man with an aptitude test score of 70 would be predicted to have a performance score of 5.7 if the common regression equation were used to calculate the prediction. If the separate regression equation for men were used, his predicted score would be 6.3. This is a .6-point underprediction from the common regression equation. On the other hand, a man with an aptitude test score of 140 would be predicted to have a performance score of 7.7 if the common regression equation were used and a score of 7.9 if the separate equation for men were used. This is only a .2-point underprediction from the common regression equation. The same issue would be present for women: The difference in prediction using the common regression equation versus the separate regression equation for women would be different at different levels of aptitude test scores.

But a more serious issue with slope bias is that it means that the test may be more valid for one group than another. Earlier in this chapter, we told you that when a test yields significantly different validity coefficients for subgroups, we say that it has differential validity. In a linear regression, the slope of the regression line (the *b* weight) is related to the correlation between the predictor and the criterion. Generally, the larger the slope of the line, the larger the correlation between the variables. In the data used in Figure 11.5, the correlation between the aptitude test scores and the performance rating across all the students was .32, which is statistically significant. As you know, this would be considered criterion-related evidence for validity. But what do you think the correlation would be between the aptitude test scores of only the women and their performance ratings or only the men and their performance ratings? Would there be a difference between the groups? Based on the fact that the slope of the regression equation for the women was larger (.0346) than the slope for the men (.0237), you might expect the correlation between the test score and the ratings to be larger for the women than for the men, and you would be correct. The correlation between the test scores and the ratings for the women was .43, while for the men it was .28. This suggests that the test is a more valid predictor for the women than for the men. So the question becomes whether the school should use this test as part of its admission process to select new students or eliminate it because of slope bias (differential validity) and intercept bias.

The question may not be as easy to answer as it appears. The overall regression equation was based on a sample size of 200 students, 100 male and 100 female. The overall validity coefficient of .32 is statistically significant ($p < .05$). But the *difference* between the correlation coefficients for the men (.28) and the women (.43) is not significant ($p > .05$). So statistically, we cannot conclude that slope bias or differential validity is present in the population based on these sample data.

Regarding the presence of intercept bias, a statistical test can be conducted to check for it. Although a discussion of the technique goes beyond our scope, when we conducted the test on this hypothetical data, we found that the intercept bias was not statistically significant either. So the bottom line is that we have no statistical evidence to conclude that there is significant slope or intercept bias in the population from which this sample was drawn. However, it is very important to understand that the statistics were based on a relatively small sample, so we may not have had sufficient statistical power to detect a significant effect, even if one were really present in the data.

In general, a substantial amount of past research has concluded that predictive bias is rare (Kuncel & Sackett, 2007). Based on a large number of empirical investigations, researchers generally have agreed that differential validity is not a widespread phenomenon. The only statistic for which there has been consistent evidence of difference is the intercept of regression lines when they are calculated separately for Whites and minorities (Bartlett, Bobko, Mosier, & Hannan, 1978; Cleary, Humphreys, Kendrick, & Wesman, 1975; Gael, Grant, & Richie, 1975; Hartigan & Wigdor, 1989; Linn, 1982). When differential prediction takes place, the result is usually a slight overprediction of minority group performance. In other words, tests may predict that minorities will do better on the job than they actually do (Cascio, 1991).

However, in 2010, Aguinis, Culpepper, and Pierce strongly challenged this view. They argued that intercept bias is actually present in the population far less frequently than prior research has suggested. They also suggested that slope bias is present far more frequently than previously thought. They presented statistical evidence from large-scale simulation studies that demonstrated that the previous research findings on predictive bias might have been caused by small sample sizes, range restriction, unequal group sizes, low reliability, and other artifacts present in those prior studies. Therefore, they called for a revival of research on predictive bias, since there are so many ethical, legal, and social issues connected to our ability to accurately predict important criteria via testing.

Differential Validity in Tests of Cognitive Ability

The claim that differential validity was a rare occurrence in professionally developed tests has been very frequently applied to tests of cognitive ability in particular. However, in 2011 a large-scale meta-analysis combined the results of 166 previous studies on well over 1 million subjects to evaluate whether there was any evidence for differential validity based on race or ethnicity when cognitive ability tests were used to predict job performance (Berry, Clark, & McClure, 2011). This meta-analysis is the largest one conducted to date designed to look for the presence of racial and ethnic differential validity in cognitive ability tests. The meta-analysis covers three organizational settings where cognitive ability tests are commonly used: civilian employment, the military, and educational admissions. In each setting, the results show that the validity of cognitive ability tests for the prediction of performance was highest for the White subgroup and lowest for the Black subgroup. Validity for the Hispanic subgroup was also lower than for the White subgroup, but the data were available only for educational settings. Validity for the Asian subgroup was approximately the same as for the White subgroup, but as with the Hispanic subgroup, data were available only for educational settings. The average validity of cognitive ability tests for predicting performance of Whites was .33, while the average validity for Blacks was .24. For Hispanics, the average validity was .30. These differences were not the same in all the settings studied. The largest Black–White differences were found in military settings (.17). But the differences were much smaller in employment and educational settings, .03 and .04, respectively.

While the differences in employment and educational settings may seem small, Berry et al. (2011) observed that these small absolute differences in validity equate to much larger relative validity differences among the groups. In percentage terms, the validity of cognitive ability tests for Blacks is 15.8% lower than for Whites in civilian employment settings. In addition, even very small differences in validity can make a large difference in *test utility*—the economic usefulness of the test—to the organization in terms of employee output or the dollar value of performance (Roth, Bobko, & Mabon, 2001). Small differences in validity can also make important differences in the rates of false negatives (rejecting someone who would have been successful) and false positives (accepting someone who will fail) when the tests are used to make selection decisions (Aguinis & Smith, 2007).

The reasons for differential validity are not clear and require additional study. One of the possible explanations suggested by Berry et al. (2011) is bias in the performance ratings used as the criteria for the studies included in the meta-analysis. Racial or ethnic bias of this kind could result in differential validity. One of the ways that this possibility can be tested is by doing a separate differential validity analysis for subjective ratings (e.g., supervisory performance evaluations) versus objective ratings (e.g., production rates, frequency of errors, dollar volume of sales). When Berry and colleagues (2011) performed this analysis on the samples that used subjective ratings, they found that the ability–performance correlation was .05 higher for Whites than for Blacks. But for samples using objective ratings, the ability–performance correlation was .07 higher for Blacks than for Whites. The fact that the relationship between cognitive ability and subjective ratings seems to be more valid for Whites than Blacks suggests that there could be bias in the subjective performance ratings. This possibility needs to be investigated further to determine the degree to which it is a contributing factor to the differential validity findings.

The overall findings of Berry et al.'s (2011) research cast some doubt on the frequently cited view that cognitive ability tests are equally predictive for all ethnic and racial groups (Schmidt, 1988; Schmidt & Hunter, 1981). Since this research was published in 2011, researchers have conducted a number of additional studies to attempt to explain these findings. For example, Roth et al. (2013) conducted a group of simulations to see whether range restriction might explain the difference in validity on the cognitive ability test for Whites and Blacks. This is a particularly important question, as Berry and colleagues' (2011) meta-analysis did not correct for range restriction, because of the lack of the data necessary to perform the correction. The reason that range restriction is a plausible explanation for the results has to do with the frequently reported finding that minority subgroups have lower mean scores on cognitive ability tests than majority subgroups (Roth, Bevier, Bobko, Switzer, & Tyler, 2001). This difference in mean scores between majority and minority subgroups can create a statistical artifact that could make it *look* like differential validity is present in the tests when the observed results are really only due to range restriction. For a more detailed explanation of how this can occur, see the In Greater Depth Box 11.2.

While Roth and colleagues' (2013) study focused on statistical simulations to understand what might be causing the differential validity in observed cognitive ability test scores between Blacks, Hispanics, and Whites, two other studies looked at whether there was actually evidence of this type of range restriction when real data were used for the analysis. The first of these studies was conducted by Berry, Sackett, and Sund (2013). These researchers were able to collect data on the SAT scores and college grades (both overall grade point average [GPA] and grades in individual courses) for 140,000 Asian, Black, Hispanic, and White test takers from 41 different colleges. Because the SAT is taken prior to college entry, this enabled them to evaluate both the unrestricted and restricted ranges of SAT scores. The unrestricted range would be the standard deviation of all the SAT scores, while the restricted range would be the standard deviation of the SAT scores of only those individuals admitted to colleges. Because they had both sets of data, they were able to directly correct for the effect that range restriction has on observed validity coefficients when SAT scores were used to predict freshman-year GPA for Asian, Black, Hispanic, and White students.

The initial data analysis (before correcting for range restriction) showed a slightly lower but similar pattern and direction of differential validity when the SAT scores were used to predict freshman-year GPA as in Berry et al.'s (2011) meta-analysis. The validity was .32 for the Black subgroup and .316 for the Hispanic subgroup. But the validity was higher for both the White and Asian subgroups, at .337 and .316, respectively. However, the more important research question was whether the differences in the observed validities would be reduced or eliminated when they were corrected for the effects of range restriction as suggested by Roth et al.'s (2013) simulations. Surprisingly, the results showed that when the observed validity coefficients were corrected for range restriction, the differential validity did not disappear. Rather, it became more pronounced. When corrected for range restriction, the correlation between SAT scores and freshman-year GPA for the Black subgroup was .432 and for the

IN GREATER DEPTH BOX 11.2

WHY MEAN DIFFERENCES IN TEST SCORES CAN CAUSE THE APPEARANCE OF DIFFERENTIAL VALIDITY

Hunter, Schmidt, and Hunter (1979) demonstrated why the difference in mean scores between majority and minority groups can give the appearance that differential validity is present when it may not truly exist. Let's imagine that an organization sets a cutoff score on a cognitive ability test so that 40% of the majority candidates are selected. Because scores on cognitive ability tests are normally distributed, we can easily determine from statistical tables or online calculators that 40% the scores in a normal distribution will occur at or above .25 standard deviations above the mean of the group. So in order to ensure that the required 40% of the majority test takers will be eligible for hire, we would need to set the cutoff score to be .25 standard deviations above the group's mean score. But as we mentioned, research has shown that minority test takers score on average 1 standard deviation lower than majority test takers on standardized tests of cognitive ability (Hunter et al., 1979). Because the cutoff score was set so that 40% of the majority group would be hired (equivalent to .25 standard deviations above *their* mean), in order to have the same absolute cutoff score for the minority group, the cutoff score for the minority group would have to be set at 1.25 standard deviations above *their* mean score. Thus, the actual cutoff scores would be the same for both groups, but the position of the cutoff score relative to each groups mean score would be different. Referring to an area under the curve table or online calculator, we find that only 11% of the scores in a normal distribution are at or above 1.25 standard deviations above the mean. As a result, only the top 11% of the minority test takers would be eligible for hire whereas the to 40% of the majority group would be eligible even though the same absolute cutoff score was used for both groups. The effect is that compared with the full possible range of scores, the minority group would experience more severe restriction of range because only the top 11% of that group would make the cut. For the majority group on the other hand, the restriction would be much less severe, because the top 40% would make the cut. We know that the correlations between two variables will decrease with increased restriction in range. So the fact that the restriction of range is greater for the minority group would make the observed correlation between their cognitive ability test scores and the criterion lower than the observed correlation for the majority group even when the true correlation between the test score and criterion is actually the same for both groups in the full, unrestricted population.

As an example, lets presume that the validity coefficient were exactly the same in both groups (i.e., no differential validity actually existed). Let's further presume that the full (unrestricted) population correlation between the cognitive ability test and the criterion (i.e., the validity coefficient) for *both groups* were actually .5. This actual observed correlation between test scores and the criterion will be reduced by range restriction we described above in both groups and we can estimate the amount of reduction that would occur in the observed correlation by statistical means. When we do the estimation, we find that the observed correlation between the cognitive ability test scores and the criterion in the *range restricted* majority group would be reduced from .5 to .31 because of the range restriction. But because the range restriction in the minority group is larger than the range restriction in the majority group, the observed correlation between the cognitive ability test and the criterion would be reduced *more* than it was reduced for the majority group. The range restriction would reduce the observed correlation between test score and criterion in the minority group correlation from its true value of .5 to .23. This translates to an 8-point or 26% lower correlation (validity coefficient) for the minority group as compared to the majority group. Thus, it would appear that there was significant differential validity between the two groups when there really was none in the population. Based on this type of analysis, the authors of the study argued that the differential validity of the cognitive ability test between Blacks and Whites that Berry et al. (2011) found could have been accounted for by nothing more than the difference in range restriction between the two groups when combined with the known difference in mean cognitive ability scores between the groups. Research is continuing to determine whether range restriction or other factors was responsible for the differential validity in cognitive ability tests.

Hispanic subgroup was .462. But for the White subgroup, the correlation was .532, and for the Asian subgroup it was .517. This means that in percentage terms, the validity of the SAT in the prediction of freshman-year GPA is 18% lower for Blacks than for Whites. For Hispanics, it is 13% lower than for Whites. The researchers call these differences "quite sizeable" (Berry et al., 2013, p. 352). One of the reasons cited for this unexpected result was that the data showed that the range restriction of the White subgroup was actually greater than that of the Black subgroup. A possible reason given for this was that the variety of affirmative action steps that colleges take to increase the enrollment of minority students might have actually increased the range of the SAT scores of the Black students who were admitted making range restriction a less important issue.

In a 2014 study, Berry, Cullen, and Meyer gathered data from hundreds of validity studies of cognitive ability tests that included more than 1 million persons to extend the research on whether the differential validity of cognitive ability tests previously observed could be explained by range restriction. This research is notable because it also included those data from Berry et al.'s (2011) meta-analysis that could be analyzed for range restriction. Therefore, it also speaks to the question of whether the differential validity found in that study could be explained by range restriction. Like Berry and colleagues' (2013) study described above, this study also found that the differences in the validity of cognitive ability tests to predict criteria across different racial and ethnic groups could not be explained by range restriction. After correcting for range restriction, Berry et al. (2014) found validity differences between Black and Hispanic subgroups still to be 11.3% to 18% lower than the validity for the White subgroup. However, follow-up research conducted in 2017 to their 2013 article, Roth, Le, Oh, Van Iddekinge, and Robins cast doubt on the contention that range restriction cannot account for the differential validity between majority and minority subgroups on cognitive ability tests. The issue that they identified is that in order to correct for range restriction, researchers need to find an estimate of what the unrestricted range would be so they can compare it with the restricted range. It is usually very difficult to find what the unrestricted range actually is. Different procedures used to estimate the unrestricted range can result in corrected validity estimates that are different enough to explain the differential validity findings. Therefore, the question of whether or not there is really differential validity in cognitive ability tests that is explainable by factors over and above that of simple range restriction is still an open question.

It is important to note that although in some studies there was evidence shown that cognitive ability tests are not equally predictive for all groups studied, they are still predictive of many criteria in many different settings (academia, business, and the military). Some corrected validity coefficients reported in these large-scale studies were over .50. Thus, tests of cognitive ability are still among the strongest, if not the strongest, predictors of performance that psychologists have at their disposal.

Test Fairness

When psychological tests are used to compare individuals, their purpose is to identify or illuminate the differences among individuals. That identification, however, should be the result of individual differences on the trait or characteristic being measured. When group membership by itself influences or contaminates test scores, test bias exists, and members of some groups might be treated unfairly as a result.

Guion (1966) stated that employment tests discriminate unfairly "when persons with equal probabilities of success on the job have unequal probabilities of being hired for the job" (p. 26). In other words, performance on both the predictor and the criterion must be taken into consideration. Cascio (1991) stated that a selection measure cannot be said to discriminate unfairly if inferior predictor performance by some group also is associated with inferior job performance by the same group. . . . A selection measure is unfairly discriminatory only when some specified group performs less well than a comparison group on the measure, but performs just as well as the comparison group on the job for which the selection measure is a predictor. (p. 179)

The issue of test fairness often comes up when the issue to test validity is discussed. It is important to understand that although a test can certainly be unfair based on statistical grounds, often the concept of fairness is based on societal values rather than statistics. For instance, statistically a fair test would be unbiased in the sense that it predicts an outcome equally well for the different groups who take it. However, whether a particular individual or group will consider that test fair will also be related to whether the outcome that resulted from the use of test score was favorable or unfavorable to that person or group (Halpern, 2000). On the other hand, the notion of test validity is a statistical and scientific concept, not a social one. But just because a test has been demonstrated to be valid doesn't mean it will be considered to be fair by everyone. (For a discussion of different ethical positions that influence people's perception of fairness and bias, we recommend the article by Hunter and Schmidt, 1976, "A Critical Analysis of the Statistical and Ethical Implications of Various Definitions of Test Bias.")

We have already discussed some of the important general concepts related to test fairness that the *Standards for Educational and Psychological Testing* (AERA et al., 2014) describe when we spoke in "How Do We Gather Evidence of Validity Based on a Test's Relation to Constructs?" about ethical issues in testing, specifically accessibility and universal design. The 2014 *Standards* (AERAet al., 2014) also present four more specific views regarding fairness in testing, all of which are covered in more detail throughout this textbook. The first view is fairness in treatment during the testing process. This view concerns providing all test takers with adequate opportunity to demonstrate the constructs being measured by the test through proper standardization of the testing environment (e.g., time limits, directions), administration (e.g., proctors, security procedures), and scoring procedures. The second view is fairness as a lack of measurement bias. The third view is fairness in access to the construct(s) measured. This view has to do with ensuring that test takers are not disadvantaged in their ability to demonstrate their standing on the constructs being measured by the test by issues such as ethnicity, gender, age, language, or anything else that is irrelevant to the construct that the test is designed to measure. The fourth view is fairness as the validity of individual test score interpretations for the intended uses.

As important as it is to understand what fairness in testing means, it is equally important to understand what it doesn't mean. A commonly held view is that a test is unfair if the results of the test are not the same for all groups of people who are tested. The 2014 *Standards* (AERA et al., 2014) very clearly disagree with this view: "group differences in outcomes do not in themselves indicate that a testing application is unfair or biased" (p. 54). Nonetheless, it is still always important to carefully look for evidence of bias when there are unexplained group differences in test scores. But presuming that there is evidence for validity for the test in question, this is an example of a situation in which test validity and perceptions of test fairness may be at odds.

ETHICAL ISSUES ASSOCIATED WITH TEST VALIDATION

Although we have dedicated an entire chapter in Section I of the text to the ethical responsibilities of test publishers, test users, and test takers, because decisions based on test predictions have far-reaching consequences, we wanted to briefly discuss some of the ethical issues associated with test validation. Each day in the United States and other industrialized nations, individuals are hired or rejected by organizations that base their decisions on employment tests. Therefore, test users must rely on validity studies to ensure that the tests they use make accurate predictions.

In addition, educators use test results to admit or refuse admittance to programs based on predictions made by educational ability tests, and clinicians use tests to screen clients for residential or outpatient treatment and to admit them to specific treatment programs based on diagnoses made by tests. As you may recall from the chapter on the ethical responsibilities of test publishers, test users, and test takers, Michael Elmore's teacher used Michael's score on an intelligence test to decide that Michael was borderline retarded even though he was not.

The increasing diversity of the population in the United States presents questions about the suitability of tests for students, clinical clients, employees, and job seekers from various minority groups. Also, as the use of psychological assessment spreads to countries whose primary languages are not English, questions arise concerning translations and norms associated with translations of standardized tests developed in the United States and Great Britain. When test takers are members of minorities, especially those who do not speak standard English as their primary language, test users must be aware of test bias and how it affects test validity. Cofresi and Gorman (2004) asserted that the test users' responsibilities include testing assessment tools to ensure that they are valid for the minority population who will be the test takers. Appropriate assessments, they emphasize, should be free of questions that require a specific cultural background (e.g., knowledge of sports, holidays, or foods; etiquette related to specific cultures, races, or religions)—unless, of course, that is the knowledge the test is designed to measure. Using test norms that were developed without inclusion of the minority being tested is likely to be inappropriate for interpreting test scores of the minority group.

The 2014 revision of the *Standards for Educational and Psychological Testing* (AERA et al., 2014) has added two additional concepts concerning fairness in testing that test developers and test users must consider before implementing a test. The first is called **accessibility**. As you learned about earlier in the text, all tests are designed to measure one or more constructs. Accessibility pertains to the opportunity tests takers have to demonstrate their standing on the construct(s) the test is designed to measure. This opportunity should not be obstructed by some characteristic of the test that is not related to what the test is measuring. In general, accessibility can be evaluated by comparing the knowledge, skills, and/or abilities that indicate the presence of the construct(s) that the test was designed to measure with the knowledge, skills and/or abilities that are required to respond to the test questions, but are *not* designed to be measured by the test. For instance, if a person is visually impaired, his or her performance on a test of critical thinking might be obstructed because of difficulty in reading the test material, not because of a deficiency in the construct of critical thinking. If this occurs, inferences drawn from the test scores may not be appropriate (i.e., valid). Likewise, if a test is poorly translated into a language different from that in which it was developed, the translation itself can make it difficult for a test taker to demonstrate the construct the test was actually designed to measure. In other words, a poor quality translation restricts accessibility and would interfere with the validity of the measurement.

The second concept that has been added to the 2014 *Standards* is called **universal design**. The idea behind universal design is that tests should be constructed from the outset in such a way that accessibility is maximized for all individuals who may take the test in the future. This means that the constructs a test is designed to measure must be well defined, and the purposes for which the test is to be used should be clearly understood by the developers. Most important, the goal in the design of the test should be that the only thing that will influence a person's score is the degree to which he or she possesses the construct the test is supposed to measure. Any other factors that might influence test performance, such as race, ethnicity, age, gender, cultural background, or socioeconomic status (to name just a few), are referred to as construct-irrelevant sources of variance and must be eliminated. In addition, developers should strive to identify potential sources of construct irrelevant variance in all stages of test development. These would also include administration, scoring, and test interpretation. These considerations are important for both the fairness and validity of the test.

With each decision, the test user is ethically and morally responsible for ascertaining that the test instrument shows acceptable evidence of reliability/precision and validity. The 2014 *Standards* do not suggest a minimum level of reliability/precision or validity, as the necessary levels can vary depending on the use for which the test is intended. In some cases, such as employment decisions where there is discrimination against protected classes, test users might be held legally liable for improper test use. Test users are also responsible for ensuring that proper test administration procedures are followed and for providing appropriate testing conditions. Test users rely on researchers and test publishers to provide full information about tests. Test publishers have a particular responsibility to prevent test misuse by making test manuals and validity information available and accessible *before* test users purchase their tests. Publishers should also refuse to provide test materials to persons who do not have testing credentials or who are likely to misuse the tests. Finally, psychologists in general have a responsibility to increase public awareness about the importance of test reliability and validity so that the public can understand the role that tests play in decisions that affect individuals' lives.

DEVELOPING NORMS AND IDENTIFYING CUT SCORES

Both norms and **cut scores**—decision points for dividing test scores into pass/fail groupings—provide information that assists the test user in interpreting test results. Not all tests have published norms or cut scores. The development of norms and cut scores depends on the purpose of the test and how widely it is used.

Developing Norms

As you recall from "What Is Test Reliability/Precision?" norms—distributions of test scores—are one aid for interpreting an individual's test score. Comparing an individual's score with the test norms, such as the mean and standard deviation, provides information about whether the person's score is high or low. For instance, if Roberto scores 70 on the final exam, we would like to know the mean and standard deviation of that exam. If Roberto scores 70 on an exam that has a mean of 80 and a standard deviation of 10, we can interpret his score as low. If Roberto scores 70 on an exam that has a mean of 60 and a standard deviation of 5, he has done very well.

The purpose of test norms is to provide a reference point or structure for understanding one person's score. Ideally, the test norms would contain a test score for each person in the target audience or the population for which the test has been developed. Such a case, however, is rarely possible. Instead, test developers must rely on constructing norms from a sample of the target audience.

The next best situation would be for test developers to obtain a random sample of the target audience. As you know, the larger and more representative the sample is of the population, the less error is associated with its measurement. Again, this is rarely possible. Random sampling requires that each member of the population have an equal chance of being selected. To obtain a true random sample, researchers must have a list of all members of the population—an unlikely circumstance for tests with large target audiences.

Therefore, test developers rely on administering the test to people in the target audience in various locations, usually constructing a large database from which various statistics can be computed to be used as norms. Test developers may start with data obtained during the validation process and then supplement those scores with new data as the test begins to be used. Although it is not appropriate to use test scores obtained during the validation process for making decisions about individuals, it is appropriate to use these scores as a basis for calculating norms. Likewise, scores from tests administered for use by individuals can be added to the database used for calculating norms. As the size of the database grows, the statistics used for norms will become more stable or unchanging. At this point, test developers can publish the norms with some confidence that the sample in the database is representative of the test's target audience.

Larger databases also allow **subgroup norms**—statistics that describe subgroups of the target audience—to be developed for demographic characteristics, such as race, sex, and age, or for locations, such as regions and states. Again, a large sample is needed for each subgroup so that the statistics it yields will be stable or unchanging as new scores are added.

The test norms—means, standard deviations, percentile rankings, and so on—are published in the test manual. When there are indications that norms are changing because of changes in the target audience or the test environment, publishers should publish new norms. This has been the case with the SAT, published by ETS.

Identifying Cut Scores

When tests are used for making decisions (e.g., whether to hire an individual, whether to recommend a person for clinical treatment), test developers and test users often identify a cut score—the score at which the decision changes. For example, an employer may decide that the minimum score needed for hiring is 60 on a test that yields possible scores of 0 to 100. Those who score at least 60 will be eligible for hire, and those who score less than 60 will be ineligible for hire. Therefore, we would refer to 60 on this particular test as the cut score. Not all tests have cut scores, and sometimes it is appropriate for the test user (e.g., an employer), rather than the test developer, to set the cut score.

Setting cut scores is a difficult process and should be done objectively and very carefully as there are legal, professional, and psychometric implications beyond the scope of this textbook (Cascio, Alexander, & Barrett, 1988). Randomly setting the score one must achieve (such as 70% or 80%), without strong supporting rationale, provides us little confidence that someone who achieves that score has the acceptable level of the construct being measured.

There are generally two approaches to setting cut scores. One approach used for employment tests as well as tests used for professional licensure or certification involves a panel of expert judges who provide an opinion or rating about the number of test items that a *minimally qualified* person is likely to answer correctly The concept of a minimally qualified person may seem strange to you. Why would we want to set a cut score at such a seemingly low level? The answer is that a minimally qualified person is an individual who is able to perform his or her job at a level that is considered to be satisfactory. When test scores are used for decision making, it would not be appropriate to exclude from consideration individuals who can perform the tasks required by their job or profession at a satisfactory level. Therefore, test developers can use this information to arrive at a cut score that represents the lowest score that is still considered to be acceptable.

The other general approach is more empirical and uses the correlation between the test and an outside criterion to predict the test score that a person who performs at a minimum level of acceptability is likely to make. For example, if the validation study correlates test scores with supervisor ratings (5 = *excellent*, 4 = *very good*, 3 = *good*, 2 = *fair*, 1 = *unacceptable*), we can use a regression formula to predict the score that persons rated 2 (*fair*) are likely to make. This score then becomes the cut score.

Often the expert panel approach and the empirical approach are combined. Experts identify a minimum level of test and criterion performance, and then the consequences of using the cut score are tested empirically. Cut scores on employment tests are also affected by external variables such as the labor market. Cut scores are also used with some educational and clinical tests. For example, many graduate programs use a score on the GRE of 1,000 as the minimum score acceptable for admission, and clinical tests suggest diagnoses based on cut scores.

A major problem with setting cut scores is that test scores are not perfectly reliable. Any test score has error inherent in it. As you recall from a previous chapter, the standard error of measurement is an indicator of how much error exists in an individual's test score. It is possible that a person who scores only a few points below the cut score might score above the cut score if that person took the test again. The difference in the two scores would be due to test error, not to the person's performance. For this reason, Anastasi and Urbina (1997) suggested that the cut score should be a band of scores rather than a single score. Using this method, the cut score of 60 proposed in our first example might be expanded to a 5-point band, from 58 to 62. The standard error of measurement provides the information necessary for establishing the width of that band. In the News Box 11.1 contains a recent example of the consequences that can occur if cut scores are not set in a professionally appropriate manner.

A good resource for learning more about some of the different methods that can be used to set cut scores is the pamphlet *Setting Cut Scores for College Placement* (Morgan & Michaelides, 2005). The resource can be retrieved from https://research.collegeboard.org/ sites/default/files/publications/2012/7/researchreport-2005-9-setting-cut-scores-college -placement.pdf.

COMPILING THE TEST MANUAL

As we have pointed out in previous chapters, the test manual is an important part of the test itself. The manual should include the rationale for constructing the test, a history of the development process, and the results of the reliability and validation studies. In addition, it should include the appropriate target audience and instructions for administering and scoring the test. Finally, the manual contains norms and information on interpreting individual scores.

Although we have left the discussion of the test manual to the end of our discussion of test development, we must emphasize that writing the test manual is an ongoing process that begins with the conception of the test. This process continues throughout development as a source of documentation for each phase of test construction. After the processes of piloting, revising, and validating the test are complete, test developers compile the information they have accumulated into a readable format. This compilation of information then is published as the test manual.

IN THE NEWS BOX 11.1
WHAT'S IN A CUT SCORE? THE U.S. SUPREME COURT WANTED TO KNOW

In 1995, the City of Chicago administered an examination to 26,000 applicants for an entry-level firefighter position. In order to advance to the next step in the hiring process, applicants had to pass this exam. The city made the decision to classify applicants into one of three categories based on their test scores. Candidates scoring between 89 and 100 were classified as being "well qualified." Those who scored between 65 and 88 were classified as being "qualified." These applicants were told that their applications would be kept on file but that their chances of hire were small because of the large number of applicants in the well-qualified group. Applicants who scored below 65 were classified as having failed the test and were eliminated from further consideration. Exceptions to these rules were made for military veterans and certain paramedics who scored between 65 and 88.

The city selected the candidates who were to move on to the next step in the hiring process randomly from the "well-qualified" list. This process continued for many years until 2001, when all candidates on that list were exhausted. The city then started using the "qualified" list to select candidates. However, in 1997, six African American candidates who had scores in the "qualified" range but who were not selected alleged that the cut score used by the city violated Title VII of the Civil Rights Act because it produced an adverse impact on African American applicants.

The case first came to court in January 2004. At that time, the plaintiffs (the African American job applicants) produced evidence that demonstrated that the White applicants scored, on average, 1 standard deviation higher on the test than the African American applicants. And while only 2.2% of the African American applicants scored 89 or above on the test, 12.6% of the White applicants did. This meant that White applicants were 5 times more likely to advance to the next stage in the hiring process than African American applicants.

The city argued that the cut score used was consistent with business necessity. They said that a cut score of 89 was chosen to reduce the administrative burden that would have resulted from having a larger number of candidates selected for further processing and not because they thought that that those scoring 89 or higher were necessarily always better qualified than those scoring lower. However, in setting 89 as the cut score, the city ignored the recommendation of its own testing expert. The expert had told the city that candidates scoring within a 13-point band could not be statistically differentiated in terms of their ability to successfully perform the job and that there was no justification for setting a cut score anywhere within any 13-point band. The expert had also told the city that a cut score of 89 would place it within a 13-point band. To make matters worse, evidence was produced at trial that showed that those candidates who had scores between 65 and 88 but who were subsequently hired anyway (those applicants who were selected from the "qualified" list in 2001, plus the military and paramedic candidates for whom exceptions were made) performed equally well on the job as those candidates who had scored 89 and higher. As a result, the court found the city's selection method to be unlawful under Title VII of the Civil Rights Act.

But the case was not over yet. The city appealed the decision to the Seventh Circuit Court, claiming that the plaintiffs' case should have been dismissed because their original filing did not meet the Equal Opportunity Commission's 300-day limitation to file a claim of discrimination. The Seventh Circuit Court agreed and reversed the district's court decision. The plaintiffs then appealed to the Supreme Court, claiming that each time a hiring decision was made based on the cut score, the 300-day time limit to file should start again. In February 2010, the Supreme Court unanimously agreed. The court observed that without this protection, employers who adopt a hiring practice that results in adverse impact could use the practice virtually forever, as long as no one challenged it within the first 300 days of implementation. Ultimately, the decision cost the City of Chicago $78.4 million. The majority of the money ($54.1 million) went to the 5,850 African Americans who were not given the opportunity to be selected because of the city's discriminatory practices regarding the setting of the cut score for the entrance exam.

The lesson of this case is that cut scores that result in an adverse impact against a protected class need to be justified as being job related and consistent with business necessity. This is the same requirement that is placed on any selection procedure. It is unwise, and potentially expensive, to set cut scores simply for administrative convenience without evidence that candidates scoring below the cut score are less likely to be able to successfully perform the job than candidates scoring at or above it.

Sources: Steinmann (2011), *Lewis v. City of Chicago* (2005), and Speilman (2013).

Chapter Summary

Each item in a test is a building block that contributes to the test's outcome or final score. Therefore, developers examine the performance of each item to identify those items that perform well, revise those that could perform better, and eliminate those that do not yield the desired information. Developers analyze each item for its difficulty (the percentage of test takers who respond correctly), discrimination (how well it separates those who show a high degree of the construct from those who show little of the construct), correlation with other items (for reliability/precision) and with an outside criterion (for evidence of validity), and bias (whether it is easier for one group than for another group). ICCs provide pictures of each item's difficulty and discrimination. If the number of test takers involved in the validation study is big enough, the ICC can be used to provide the information necessary to construct a computer adaptive test in which a test takers response to earlier questions dictate which questions they are presented with later in the test. ICCs also can provide information about whether an item is biased against a subgroup of test takers. Test developers might also use individual or group discussions with test takers or experts to gather qualitative information about how to revise the test to improve its accuracy.

After the test has been revised, developers conduct the validation study by administering the test to another sample of people. The validation study provides data on the test's reliability/precision, its correlation with any appropriate outside criteria such as performance evaluations (evidence of validity), and its correlation with other measures of the test's construct (evidence of the construct that the test measures). The study also evaluates whether the test is equally valid for different subgroups of test takers. If the validation study provides sufficient evidence of reliability/precision and validity, the test developers conduct a final analysis called replication and cross-validation—either via regression or via a final round of test administration to yet another sample of test takers. This second administration can be expected to yield lower validity coefficients. When resources are not available to carry out a cross-validation study, statistical estimation of the decrease in the validity coefficients is acceptable.

After validation is complete, test developers can develop norms (distributions of test scores used for interpreting an individual's test score) and cut scores (decision points for dividing test scores into pass/fail groupings). Their development depends on the purpose of the test and how widely it is used.

At the end of the validation process, the test manual is assembled and finalized. Contents of the manual include the rationale for constructing the test, a history of the development process, the results of the validation studies, a description of the appropriate target audience, instructions for administering and scoring the test, and information on interpreting individual scores.

Engaging in the Learning Process

Learning is the process of gaining knowledge and skills through schooling or studying. Although you can learn by reading the chapter material, attending class, and engaging in discussion with your instructor, more actively engaging in the learning process may help you better learn and retain chapter information. To help you actively engage in the learning process, we encourage you to access our new supplementary student workbook. The workbook contains critical thinking activities to help you understand and apply information and help you make progress toward learning and retaining material. If you do not have a copy of the workbook, you can purchase a copy through sagepub.com.

Key Concepts

After completing your study of this chapter, you should be able to define each of the following terms. These terms are bolded in the text of this chapter and defined in the Glossary.

accessibility

acculturation

computerized adaptive rating
    scales (CARS)

computer adaptive
    testing (CAT)

cross-validation

cut scores

differential validity

discrimination index

empirically based tests

generalizable

intercept bias

interitem correlation matrix

item analysis

item bias

item characteristic
    curve (ICC)

item difficulty

item response theory (IRT)

item-total correlation

measurement bias

phi coefficient

qualitative item analysis

quantitative item analysis

replication

single-group validity

slope bias

subgroup norms

subtle questions

universal design

Critical Thinking Question

The following are some critical thinking questions to support the learning objectives for this chapter.

Learning Objectives	Critical Thinking Questions
Describe the collection, analyses, and interpretation of data for an item analysis, including item difficulty, item discrimination, interitem correlations, item–criterion correlations, item bias, and item characteristic curves.	• What would an item with a difficulty value of 1.0 tell you about that item? • What are some of the conclusions you would draw if all of the items on a test had a difficulty value of 0? • Why is it important to know how well an item discriminates between test takers? • How does item discrimination differ from item bias?
Describe how computer adaptive testing works and understand its benefits.	• Would you prefer to take a computer adaptive test or the same test in the traditional format? Why? • Download and read the article "A Framework for the Development of Computerized Adaptive Tests" by Nathan A. Thompson, and David J. Weiss, which can be found at http://pareonline.net/pdf/v16n1.pdf. • Based on that article, in what circumstances would you recommend designing a computer adaptive test? When might it not be appropriate to use a computer adaptive test?
Describe the collection and interpretation of data for a qualitative item analysis.	• How is a qualitative item analysis different from a quantitative item analysis relative to the kind of data that are collected for each? Do you think that you can substitute one for another?

(Continued)

(Continued)

Learning Objectives	Critical Thinking Questions
Identify and explain the criteria for retaining and dropping items to revise a test.	• What are some of the most important indicators that an item should be dropped from a test? • What would be some characteristics of a test item that would indicate that it unquestionably should be dropped from a test? • What would some of the consequences be if a test developer did not bother to identify how well each item in a test was functioning both quantitatively and qualitatively?
Describe the processes of validation and cross-validation.	• What are the similarities and differences between the concept of test validation and the concept of cross validation?
Explain the concepts of differential validity, single-group validity, and unfair test discrimination.	• When test results show that one ethnic group does better on the test than another group, is that always an indicator of bias? Why or why not? • Considering the concept of fairness in testing and the concept of bias in testing, which do you think is more important? • How are the concepts of test bias and accessibility similar and different?
Describe two different kinds of measurement bias.	• How do slope bias and intercept bias differ? • What are the conclusions you would draw about how a test is performing if it showed evidence of slope bias? How about intercept bias?
Explain the purpose of a cut score, and describe two methods for identifying a cut score.	• What would you want to know to justify the decision of setting a classroom test cut score at 60%?

USING TESTS IN DIFFERENT SETTINGS

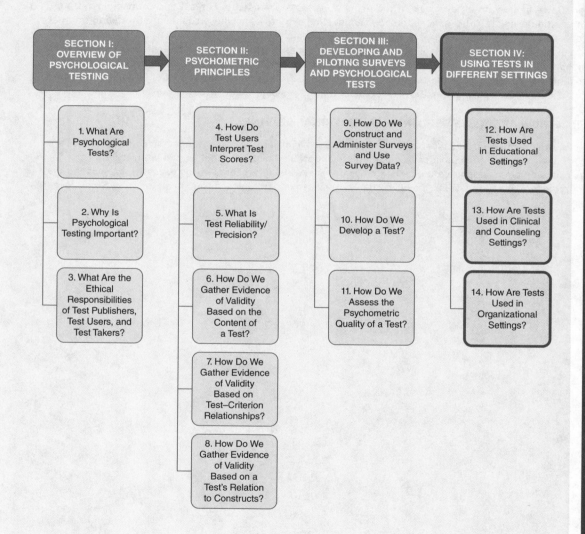

SECTION I: OVERVIEW OF PSYCHOLOGICAL TESTING
- 1. What Are Psychological Tests?
- 2. Why Is Psychological Testing Important?
- 3. What Are the Ethical Responsibilities of Test Publishers, Test Users, and Test Takers?

SECTION II: PSYCHOMETRIC PRINCIPLES
- 4. How Do Test Users Interpret Test Scores?
- 5. What Is Test Reliability/Precision?
- 6. How Do We Gather Evidence of Validity Based on the Content of a Test?
- 7. How Do We Gather Evidence of Validity Based on Test–Criterion Relationships?
- 8. How Do We Gather Evidence of Validity Based on a Test's Relation to Constructs?

SECTION III: DEVELOPING AND PILOTING SURVEYS AND PSYCHOLOGICAL TESTS
- 9. How Do We Construct and Administer Surveys and Use Survey Data?
- 10. How Do We Develop a Test?
- 11. How Do We Assess the Psychometric Quality of a Test?

SECTION IV: USING TESTS IN DIFFERENT SETTINGS
- 12. How Are Tests Used in Educational Settings?
- 13. How Are Tests Used in Clinical and Counseling Settings?
- 14. How Are Tests Used in Organizational Settings?

CHAPTER 12: HOW ARE TESTS USED IN EDUCATIONAL SETTINGS?

In Chapter 12, we begin with an overview of the types of decisions educational professionals make in educational settings based on the results of psychological tests. We discuss educational professionals as test users and specific practice standards educational professionals are expected to follow. Following a discussion of exactly how tests are used in the classroom, we highlight how tests are used in educational settings to make selection and placement decisions, counseling and guidance decisions, and curriculum and administrative policy decisions. We end with a discussion of norm- and criterion-referenced tests and authentic assessment in educational settings.

CHAPTER 13: HOW ARE TESTS USED IN CLINICAL AND COUNSELING SETTINGS?

In Chapter 13, we begin with an overview of the many ways tests are used in clinical and counseling settings, such as in psychotherapists' offices, hospitals, and counseling centers—anywhere clients are treated for mental health problems or problems in daily living. We then review the kinds of tests, and the specific tests, that are used. Following a discussion of how psychological testing is used in the assessment of three common conditions (autism spectrum disorders, depression, and Alzheimer's disease), we review the technical issue of incremental validity and the meaning of evidence-based assessment. We end with a discussion of the product of test use—providing feedback to clients and preparing a written report about the results of psychological testing.

CHAPTER 14: HOW ARE TESTS USED IN ORGANIZATIONAL SETTINGS?

In Chapter 14, we examine various types of tests that are used in organizational settings. We cover tests that are used for hiring employees, such as interviews and tests of performance, personality, and integrity. We consider legal constraints on employment testing legislated by Congress and interpreted by the executive branch and the federal court system. Finally, we describe how organizations use psychological assessment to evaluate employee performance.

HOW ARE TESTS USED IN EDUCATIONAL SETTINGS?

"I asked my teacher why she always identifies and discusses learning objectives before she begins teaching. She said that she needs the objectives to guide her teaching and to determine what material she should include on our exams. I always wondered how teachers choose what to put on the exams."

"This year in school I had to take a number of tests, but only a few of them were used to make grading decisions. Why do teachers make us take all of these tests? Do they use my scores on the tests that don't affect my grade for something else?"

"Last year my little brother was really struggling in elementary school. Based on his teacher's recommendation, my parents took him to see the school psychologist, who conducted an assessment, which included a few psychological tests. Based on the results, the school psychologist worked closely with my parents and his teachers to address the challenges my brother was having—he's now doing much better in school."

"One of my elementary school teachers once told me that she did not believe that tests can by themselves accurately measure a student's understanding of material. What other options do teachers have for measuring student learning and achievement?"

If you are like many students, before reading this textbook, you probably believed that the primary purposes of psychological tests were to determine when someone is psychologically disturbed and to measure someone's intelligence. You probably thought that clinical psychologists administered most psychological tests. By now you should realize that psychological tests are used for more than diagnosing psychological disorders and measuring intelligence. In this final section of the text, we discuss in more detail exactly who uses psychological tests and how. We discuss how tests are used in three settings: educational, clinical and counseling, and organizational.

In this chapter, we focus on how individuals use psychological tests in educational settings. We begin with an overview of the types of decisions made in educational settings based on the results of psychological tests. We then discuss how educational administrators, teachers, and other educational professionals use tests to make a variety of decisions. We discuss why educational administrators, teachers, and school psychologists are all test users, and discuss some professional practice standards specific to those who use tests in educational settings. We end with a discussion of norm- and criterion-referenced tests and authentic assessment in educational settings.

TYPES OF DECISIONS MADE IN THE EDUCATIONAL SETTING

Every day, professionals in educational settings make important decisions using the results of psychological tests. Sometimes the tests are standardized tests available to a broad group, while other times the tests are teacher-made tests. In educational settings, the tests range from traditional multiple-choice tests to performance assessments such as portfolios (which we discuss later in this chapter). The professionals making decisions using test results include educational administrators, teachers, and testing professionals such as school psychologists. These individuals use tests to measure concrete and abstract constructs such as knowledge and skills, learning, cognitive ability, and intelligence. The educational professionals use the test scores to make judgments and decisions about student learning, classroom instruction, eligibility for gifted or special education programs, and educational policy. They use test scores to make inferences about the accomplishments or progress of students, teachers, schools, school districts, states, and nations. The inferences help inform educational professionals about teaching, learning, and outcomes. The consequences resulting from administrators, teachers, and school psychologists using test scores to make judgments and decisions can be significant, influencing such things as the programs students are placed in, student grades, acceptance into college, and school funding.

As you can see, administrators, teachers, and school psychologists make many different types of decisions using psychologist tests. Some of the decisions teachers make quite frequently in class, while other decisions administrators or testing professionals (such as school psychologists) make less frequently. Table 12.1 includes a summary of the most typical decisions.

TABLE 12.1 ■ Types of Decisions Made in Educational Settings Based on Psychological Test Results			
Type of Decision	Individuals Who Typically Make the Decision	Type of Test Typically Used to Make the Decision	Example
Instructional decisions	Classroom teacher	Teacher made	Teachers use the test results to determine the pace of their courses (e.g., should they slow down, speed up, continue their teaching pace, or skip a topic altogether?).
Grading decisions	Classroom teacher	Teacher made	Teachers use the test results to assign grades to students (e.g., teachers administer quizzes, midterm exams, and final exams).
Diagnostic decisions	Classroom teacher	Teacher made	Teachers use the results of tests to understand students' strengths and difficulties (e.g., a test may reveal a student can write a complete sentence but only a simple sentence).
Selection decisions	Specialist or administrator	Standardized	Specialists such as school psychologists or administrators use the results of tests to make group-, program-, or institutional-level admissions decisions (e.g., a test may reveal that a student has a very high intelligence and would benefit from a gifted program).
Placement decisions	Specialist or administrator	Standardized	Specialists or administrators use tests to place individuals into the proper level of a course (e.g., colleges and universities may use test scores to determine the math course in which individuals should be placed).
Counseling and guidance decisions	Specialist or administrator	Standardized	Specialists such as career counselors or administrators use test scores to help students select majors and careers that match the students' strengths and interests.
Program and curriculum decisions	Specialist or administrator at the district level	Standardized	Specialists or administrators use test scores to determine the success of a program or curriculum (e.g., are students who go through the new curriculum learning more than students who go through the old curriculum?) and to determine whether a program or curriculum should be implemented or dropped.
Administrative policy decisions	Specialist or administrator at the district, state, or national level	Standardized	Specialists or administrators use the results of tests to determine where money should be spent and what programs should be implemented to improve the achievement scores of a school, district, state, or nation.

Source: Adapted from Thorndike, Cunningham, Thorndike, and Hagen (1991). *Measurement and evaluation in psychology and education.* New York: Macmillan.

EDUCATIONAL PROFESSIONALS AS TEST USERS

As you can see, a variety of individuals—from classroom teachers to district-level administrators—use psychological tests in educational settings to make a wide range of important decisions. Because educational administrators, teachers, and other educational professionals (such as school psychologists and school counselors) create, administer, score, and use the results of psychological tests, they are considered test users. As test users, all educational professionals who participate in any part of the testing process should be properly trained on the appropriate use of psychological tests. When educational professionals who use psychological tests are not properly informed and trained, the consequences to students, teachers, and schools can be significant.

The following two dialogues demonstrate what can happen when educational professionals are not sufficiently trained on the proper use of psychological tests. The first dialogue occurs between one of the authors of *Educational Testing and Measurement: Classroom Application and Practice* (Kubiszyn & Borich, 2007) and a classroom teacher. The second dialogue, from the same book, occurs between "Ms. Wilson" (a sixth grade teacher) and some of her colleagues at school.

Dialogue 1

Teacher: Hi, I'm Jeff's second-grade teacher. What can I do for you so early in the year?

Author: Jeff says he's in the low reading group, and I am curious about why he is. Could you explain that to me?

Teacher: Oh, don't worry—we don't label kids at this school. I think that would be a terrible injustice.

Author: I see, but could you explain why Jeff is in the "Walkers" instead of the "Runners"?

Teacher: Oh, those are just names, that's all.

Author: Are both groups at the same level in reading?

Teacher: They're both at the first-grade level, yes.

Author: I'm beginning to catch on. Are they reading in the same-level books in the same reading series?

Teacher: Of course not! Some children are further along than others—that's all—but the kids don't know.

Author: Let me guess—the "Runners" are further ahead?

Teacher: Yes, they're in Book 9.

Author: And the "Walkers" are in. . .

Teacher: Book 5. But they are grouped for instructional purposes. I have twenty-five students, you know!

Author: I'm confused. Jeff's reading scores on the California Achievement Test last May were above the ninetieth percentile.

Teacher:	[chuckles to herself] I can understand your confusion. Those test scores are so hard to understand. Why, even we professionals can't understand them.
Author:	A score at the ninetieth percentile means the score was higher than the score of 90 percent of the students who took the test all across the country.
Teacher:	Oh, really? It is very complicated. As I said, even professional educators don't understand testing.
Author:	Some do, Mrs. B.

Dialogue 2

Ms. Wilson:	I know you all feel we've covered a tremendous amount this year. Well, you're right. We have. And now it's time to find out how much you've learned. It's important for you to know how well you're doing in each subject so you can work harder in the areas where you might need improvement. It's also nice to know in what areas you might be smarter than almost everyone else. So, next week, I want you to be ready to take tests over all the material we have covered so far. [A few students groan in unison.] Remember, this will be your chance to show me how smart you are. I want you to get plenty of sleep Sunday night so you'll be fresh and alert Monday. [As the bell rings, Ms. Wilson shouts over the commotion of students leaving the classroom.] Don't forget, I'll be collecting homework on Monday! [As Ms. Wilson collapses into her chair, Ms. Palmer, an experienced teacher, walks in.]
Ms. Palmer:	Glad this grading period is just about over. Next week will be a nice break, don't you think? Just reviewing and giving tests. It'll sure be nice to have this weekend free without any preparations to worry about.
Ms. Wilson:	You mean you won't be making up tests this weekend?
Ms. Palmer:	No. I have tests from the last three years that I've been refining and improving. With only a few modifications, they'll do fine.
Ms. Wilson:	You're awfully lucky. I'm afraid I haven't had a chance to even think about how I'm going to test these kids. All these subjects to make tests for, and then all the scoring and grading to do by next Friday. I think I'm going to have an awful weekend.
Ms. Palmer:	Will you be giving criterion-referenced or norm-referenced tests?
Ms. Wilson:	Umm. . . well. . . I don't know. I remember hearing those terms in a tests and measurements class I once took, but I guess I just haven't had time to worry about those things until now. I suppose I'm going to have to get my old textbook out tonight and do some reviewing. Gosh! I hope I can find it.
Ms. Palmer:	Well, if you use norm-referenced tests, there are some available in Ms. Cartwright's office. You know, she's the counselor who is always so helpful with discipline problems. In fact, she has a whole file full of tests.
Ms. Wilson:	Will you be using norm-referenced tests next week?
Ms. Palmer:	Not really. For these mid-semester grades, I like to make my tests very specific to what I've been teaching. At this point in the year, it seems to provide better

feedback to the kids and parents—especially the parents. Anyway, the parents aren't really interested in where their kid scores in relation to other students until later in the semester, when I've covered more content and the kids have had a chance to get their feet on the ground.

Ms. Wilson:	You mean these norm-referenced tests don't cover specifically what you've taught?
Ms. Palmer:	[trying to be tactful] Well, no. Not exactly. I guess you have forgotten a few things since you took that tests and measurements course.
Ms. Wilson:	I guess so.
Ms. Palmer:	Why don't you make a test blueprint and compare it to some of the items in Ms. Cartwright's test file?
Ms. Wilson:	A test what print?
Ms. Palmer:	A test blueprint. You know, where you take the objectives from your lesson plans and construct a table that shows the content you've been teaching and the level of complexity—knowledge, comprehension, applications—that you're shooting for. Then see how Ms. Cartwright's tests match the test blueprint.
Ms. Wilson:	But what if I didn't write down all my objectives? I had objectives, of course, but I just didn't write them down all the time, or when I did, I usually didn't keep them for long. You know what I mean? [no comment from Ms. Palmer] And I don't think I wrote them so they included levels of complexity according to the taxonomy-of-objectives thing I think you're referring to.
Ms. Palmer:	But I'm afraid that without objectives, you won't know if the items on Ms. Cartwright's tests match what you've taught. Would you believe that last year a teacher in this school flunked half his class using a test that didn't match what he taught? Boy, what a stir that caused.
Ms. Wilson:	[looking worried] I guess I'll have to start from scratch, then. It looks like a very long weekend.
Ms. Palmer:	Of course, you might consider giving some essay items.
Ms. Wilson:	You mean long answer, not multiple choice, questions?
Ms. Palmer:	Yes, but you'll have to consider the time it will take to develop a scoring guide for each question and the time you'll spend grading all those answers. And then, of course, only some of your objectives may be suited to an essay format.
Ms. Wilson:	[trying to sort out all of what Ms. Palmer just said without sounding too stupid] By scoring guide, do you mean the right answer?
Ms. Palmer:	Well, not quite. As you know, essay items can have more than one right answer. So, first you will have to identify all the different elements that make an answer right and then decide how to assign points to each of these elements, depending on what percentage of the right answer they represent.
Ms. Wilson:	How do you decide that?
Ms. Palmer:	[trying to be polite and being evasive for the sake of politeness] Well. . . very carefully.

Ms. Wilson:	I see. [long pause] Well, maybe my old tests and measurements book will have something on that.
Ms. Palmer:	I'm sure it will.
Ms. Wilson:	Sounds as though I have my work cut out for me. I guess I'll just have to organize my time and start to work as soon as I get home.
	[Ms. Palmer and Ms. Wilson leave the classroom and meet Mr. Smith, another teacher.]
Mr. Smith:	You won't believe the meeting I just had with Johnny Haringer's parents!
Ms. Palmer and Ms. Wilson:	What happened?
Mr. Smith:	Well, they came to see me after Johnny missed an A by two points on one of my weekly math tests. It was the first time that he had missed an A the entire semester.
Ms. Wilson:	Were they mad?
Mr. Smith:	They were at first. But I stayed calm and explained very carefully why two points on the test really should make a difference between an A and a B.
Ms. Wilson:	What kinds of things did you tell them?
Mr. Smith:	Well, luckily I keep student data from past years for all my tests. This allows me to calculate reliability and validity coefficients for my tests using one of the PCs in the math lab. I simply explained to Johnny's parents, in everyday commonsense language, what reliability and validity of a test meant and then gave them some statistical data to support my case. I also explained the care and deliberation I put into the construction of my tests—you know, all the steps you go through in writing test items and then checking their content validity and doing qualitative and quantitative item analyses. I think they got the idea of just how much work it takes to construct a good test.
Ms. Wilson:	And?
Mr. Smith:	And after that they calmed down and were very responsive to my explanation. They even commented that they hadn't realized the science of statistics could be so helpful in determining the reliability and validity of a test. They even commended me for being so systematic and careful. Can you believe that?
Ms. Wilson:	Umm. . . reliability and validity? Do you mean we have to know the reliability and validity for every test we use?
Mr. Smith:	Ever since that lawsuit by the parents of some kid over at Central for unfair testing, the school board has made every teacher individually responsible for using reliable and valid tests. [Looking surprised, Ms. Wilson turns to Ms. Palmer and Ms. Palmer slowly and painfully nods to indicate her agreement with what Mr. Smith has been saying.]
Ms. Wilson:	Boy! I don't think I could explain reliability and validity that well—at least not to parents—and I know I wouldn't have the slightest idea of how to calculate them.

Mr. Smith: Well, I guess we won't have any preparations to worry about this weekend. Nothing but review and testing next week. You have a nice weekend.

Ms. Palmer: Well, it may not be all that bad. You've got that tests and measurements text at home, and next quarter, who knows? You may have time to plan for all this ahead of time.

Ms. Wilson: [being purposely negative] That's if I don't have to explain reliability and validity to some irate kid's parents, construct a test blueprint, learn the difference between norm-referenced and criterion-referenced tests, make a scoring key for an essay test, and of course compute some test item statistics I probably can't even pronounce!

Source: Both dialogues are from Kubiszyn, T., & Borich, G. (2007). *Educational testing and measurement: Classroom application and practice* (8th ed.). Reprinted with permission of John Wiley & Sons, Inc.

Discussion of Dialogues 1 and 2

The teacher in the first dialogue obviously did not understand how to interpret test scores and therefore made an inappropriate decision about the reading group in which she placed Jeff. What's the problem? By placing Jeff in a lower level reading group, the teacher was not challenging Jeff appropriately.

Ms. Wilson, in the second dialogue, did not know very much at all about psychological testing. Perhaps most important, she did not know that a test should be constructed or selected based on the objectives of a specific unit of instruction. Without this knowledge, we can guarantee that Ms. Wilson's tests would not have evidence of validity based on content and thus may not measure how well her students learned the material she taught. How would you feel if your classroom grade were based on your performance on tests that did not measure what you had been learning in class?

Although all test users in educational settings should be sufficiently trained on the proper use of psychological tests, following all professional practice standards, such as conducting formal validation studies, is not always a reasonable expectation for teacher-made classroom tests. Schools and teachers often use tests in their own classrooms to inform learning and instruction—they don't often select or develop standardized tests for broader use by others. Furthermore, sometimes schools and teachers do not have the resources needed to document the characteristics of their tests. For this reason, some professional practice guidelines, such as the *Standards for Educational and Psychological Testing* (American Educational Research Association [AERA], American Psychological Association [APA], & National Council on Measurement in Education [NCME], 2014) apply primarily to more formal, standardized tests—such as benchmark tests used outside of the classroom to monitor student progress—and to standardized tests that educational professionals used across multiple classrooms and whose developers have provided evidence of validity for intended uses. Nonetheless, as reinforced by the *Standards* (AERA et al., 2014), all test users in educational settings should consider whether the tests they select or use have evidence of validity and reliability/precision and are fair.

STANDARDS SPECIFIC TO EDUCATIONAL PROFESSIONALS AS TEST USERS

Given the widespread use of tests, it is not surprising that specific professional practice standards exist for using tests in educational settings. Some of the most relevant standards specific to testing in educational settings are contained in the *Standards for Educational and Psychological Testing* (AERA et al., 2014) and published in the *Professional Standards* of the National Association of School Psychologists (NASP) (2010/2017). The *Standards for Educational and Psychological Testing* (AERA et al., 2014) includes two chapters particularly relevant to those who use tests in educational settings. Chapter 12 of the *Standards* includes standards for (a) those who design and develop educational assessments, (b) those who use and interpret educational assessments, and (c) those who administer, score, and report educational assessment results. Some of these testing standards are summarized in Figure 12.1 (AERA et al., 2014). A complete list and description of the standards specific to educational settings can be found in the *Standards* book, available at the AERA website for purchase (http://www.aera.net/Standards14).

FIGURE 12.1 ■ Testing Standards Specific to Educational Testing and Assessment

Sample Summarized Standards for Educational Testing and Assessment

- Design and development of educational assessments
  - States, districts, or schools that mandate testing programs should include very clear information on how the test results are to be used, and should monitor the impact and consequences (good and bad) of mandated tests.
  - When using tests designed for multiple purposes (e.g., to monitor student growth and to evaluate schools), evidence of validity, reliability/precision, and fairness is needed for each purpose.
  - Tests developed to measure student achievement of material should have documented evidence available so users can understand the extent to which the test samples the knowledge assessed.
  - To faciliate more informative interpretation of tests, local norms should be developed and used along with published norms, especially when the local population of students differs from the population of the published norm group.
  - Computer and multi-media based tests should include evidence that the test format is feasible for measuring the assessed construct and that the test is accessible to all students.

- Use and interpretation of educational assessments
  - Test users should avoid providing test preparation activities and materials to students that may affect the validity of the test score inferences.
  - Test users should provide evidence that students have had an opportunity to learn the knowledge and skills assessed when test results can signficantly affect decisions about student promotion or graduation.
  - Test users should provide students a reasonable number of opportunities to demonstrate knowledge or skill mastery, using alternate forms of a test or sound alternatives, when promotion or diploma receipt depend on the test score.
  - Test users should consider more than just a single test score when making a decision that will significantly impact a student.
  - Those who supervise other test users should be familiar with, and be able to articulate and train others to articulate evidence for reliability/precision, validity of intended interpretations, and fairness of scores.
  - Educational testing program administrators should ensure that individuals who interpret and use test results to make decisions are qualified or have help from those who are qualified.

- Administration, scoring, and reporting educational assessment results
  - Testing program administrators should provide individuals who administer and score tests the needed documentation, training, and oversight to ensure they understand the importance of adhering to the test developer directions test and are proficient in test administration and scoring procedures.
  - Score reports provided to individuals should clearly present, or include the supplementary information necessary for individuals to interpret the scores (e.g., the measurement error associated with each sore, norming study results).
  - Score reports that include recommendations for instructional interventions or materials should include rationale for and evidence supporting the recommendations.

Source: Adapted from *Standards for Educational and Psychological Testing* (AERA, APA, NCME, 2014).

Chapter 13 of the *Standards* (AERA et al., 2014) also includes standards for those involved in designing, developing, and using information from tests used in program evaluation, policy studies, and accountability systems. In educational settings, test results are often used to inform public policy and to evaluate programs—test results are used to substantiate initiating, continuing, modifying, terminating, or expanding programs and policies. Test results are often also used for accountability—to determine positive or negative consequences for individuals (such as students and teachers) and institutions (such as schools and school districts). In program evaluation, in policy studies, and for test-based accountability systems, groups of people take a test and key stakeholders use the aggregated scores to make inferences about performance and use these inferences to make important decisions. Often the testing is high stakes—the testing has serious consequences—as decision makers use test scores from a sample or an entire population to draw conclusions (e.g., about the effectiveness or quality of a program, or about teacher performance) and make important decisions (e.g., eliminating a program or determining teacher pay). Given the important decisions made using test scores and the consequences of the decisions, those who mandate, design, implement, or who make decisions based on program evaluations, policy studies, and accountability systems should abide by the standards in Chapter 13 of the *Standards* (AERA et al., 2014). The standards are organized into two clusters:

- Cluster 1: Design and Development of Testing Programs and Indices for Program Evaluation, Policy Studies, and Accountability Systems

- Cluster 2: Interpretations and Uses of Information From Tests Used in Program Evaluation, Policy Studies, and Accountability Systems

NASP (2017a) also has professional standards to guide the work of those who use tests in educational settings—specifically, school psychologists. Anticipated to be updated in the year 2020, the 2010 *NASP Professional Standards* consists of four documents that communicate NASP's position on the qualifications and expected practices of school psychologists who provide services in the educational setting to help children succeed academically, as well as behaviorally, emotionally, and socially.

1. Standards for Graduate Preparation of School Psychologists

2. Standards for the Credentialing of School Psychologists

3. Principles for Professional Ethics

4. Model for Comprehensive and Integrated School Psychological Services

Perhaps the document with the standards most relevant to test use is NASP's (2017b) *Principles for Professional Ethics*. The *Principles* are organized into four sections. Each section has multiple principles with associated standards. While a complete copy of the *Principles* is available on the NASP website (https://www.nasponline.org/standards-and-certification/professional-ethics), Figure 12.2 includes six examples of the standards school psychologists are expected to abide by when using tests.

FIGURE 12.2 ■ Six Examples of Standards for School Psychologists

Standard II.3.2 (p.7).

- School psychologists use assessment techniques and practices that the profession considers to be responsible, research-based practice
- School psychologists select assessment instruments and strategies that are reliable and valid for the child and the purpose of the assessment. When using standardized measures, school psychologists adhere to the procedures for administration of the instrument that are provided by the author or publisher or the instrument. If modifications are made in the administration procedures for standardized tests or other instruments, such modifications are identified and discussed in the interpretation of the results.
- If using norm-referenced measures, school psychologists choose instruments with up-to-date normative data.
- When using computer-administered assessments, computer-assisted scoring, and/or interpretation programs, school psychologists choose programs that meet professional standard for accuracy and validity. School psychologists use professional judgment in evaluating the accuracy of computer-assisted assessment findings for the examinee.

Standard II.3.5 (p.7).

- School psychologists conduct valid and fair assessments. They actively pursue knowledge of the student's disabilities and developmental, cultural, linguistic, and experiential background and then select, administer, and interpret assessment instruments and procedures in light of those characteristics.

Standard II.3.8 (p.8).

- School psychologists adequately interpret findings and present results in clear, understandable terms so that the recipient can make informed choices.

Standard II.4.4 (p.8).

- Parents have right to access any an all information that is used to make educational decisions about their children.
- School psychologists respect the right of parents to inspect, but not necessarily to copy, their child's answers to psychological test questions, even if those answers are recorded on a test protocol.

Standard II.5.1 (p.9).

- School psychologists maintain test security, preventing the release of underlying principles and specific content that would undermine or invalidate the use of the instrument. Unless otherwise required by law or district policy, school psychologists provide parents with the opportunity to inspect and review their child's test answers rather than providing them with copies of the their child's test protocols. However, on parent request, it is permissible to provide copies of a child's test protocols to a professional who is qualified to interpret them.

Standard II.5.3 (p.9).

- School psychologists maintain test security, preventing the release of underlying principles and specific content that would undermine or invalidate the use of the instrument. Unless otherwise required by law or district policy, school psychologists provide parents with the opportunity to inspect and review their child's test answers rather than providing them with copies of the their child's test protocols. However, on parent request, it is permissible to provide copies of a child's test protocols to a professional who is qualified to interpret them.

Source: Copyright © 2010 by the National Association of School Psychologists, Bethesda, MD. Reprinted/Adapted with permission of the publisher. www.nasponline.org

SPECIFIC USES OF PSYCHOLOGICAL TESTS IN EDUCATIONAL SETTINGS

As you are now aware, many educational professionals are test users and they make a variety of decisions based on test scores. As test users, educational professionals are ethically obligated to abide by the relevant standards for selecting, developing, administering, scoring, interpreting, and using test scores to make decisions. Now, we are going to discuss, in more detail, some specific uses of psychological tests in educational settings. We focus first on how educational professionals use tests for making decisions in the classroom—at the beginning, during, and at the end of instruction. Following a discussion of how professionals use tests to make selection and placement decisions, and counseling and guidance decisions, we discuss how tests are used for program, curriculum, and administrative policy decisions.

Tests Used for Making Decisions in the Classroom

Teachers, at the primary, secondary, and college levels, must make a variety of decisions in the classroom. Teachers must decide whether students are ready to learn new material, and if so, they must determine how much of the new material students already know. Teachers must decide what information students are learning and what information they are having difficulty learning. Teachers must also decide what grades students have earned. Teachers often use tests, combined with other assessment methods, to help them make these and other types of decisions.

Teachers make some of these decisions at the beginning of a course or unit of instruction and other decisions during or at the end of instruction. Teachers often use test results to answer questions they have—the answers to which will allow them to both evaluate and improve student learning. For example, Table 12.2 contains some questions the authors of your text might ask during different phases of the instructional process when teaching college-level courses. Teachers at primary and secondary levels might also ask such questions.

Decisions Made at the Beginning of Instruction

At the beginning of a course or before a new unit of instruction, teachers will often use psychological tests as **placement assessments**, which are used to determine the extent to which students possess the knowledge, skills, and abilities necessary to understand new material and how much of the material to be taught students already know. For example, as a teacher, one of this textbook's authors may decide to give the students in her research methods course a pretest to measure their understanding of basic statistics before proceeding to the last section

TABLE 12.2 ■ Questions Teachers Might Ask	
Question asked at the beginning of a course or before beginning instruction	• What knowledge and skills do my students already possess?
Questions asked during instruction	• What knowledge and skills are my students learning? • Where do my students need help?
Questions asked at the end of instruction	• What knowledge and skills have my students learned? • What grade have my students earned?

of the course, which covers data analysis techniques. She may use this information to determine whether she needs to begin her discussion of data analysis techniques by focusing on basic data analysis skills or whether she can go right into advanced data analysis skills. She might also use this information to break the class into two groups: those students who have basic statistical knowledge and can be taught more advanced data analysis techniques, and those who lack basic statistical knowledge and must be taught the basics. She might also administer a test to measure how much her students already know about advanced statistical techniques. If students have mastered some of the material, she may modify her teaching plans or place students into different levels of advanced instruction.

Decisions Made During Instruction

Periodically throughout the school year, teachers may administer tests as **formative assessments**. Formative assessments help teachers determine what information students are and are not learning during the instructional process so that the teachers can identify where students need help and decide whether it is appropriate to move to the next unit of instruction. Teachers do not use these test scores to assign grades; instead teachers use formative assessments to make immediate adjustments to their own curricula and teaching methods. That is, teachers can use the results of formative assessments to adjust the pace of their teaching and the material they are covering. For example, in a tests and measurements course, we may choose to administer a test at the end of every unit of instruction, or chapter, to determine what students have and have not learned. If a number of students do poorly on a particular test item or group of items, we may choose to spend more time reviewing the material. If only a few students do poorly on a test item, we may choose to work with those students individually and assign them additional reading or problems.

If a student continues to experience problems with some material, teachers may suggest evaluating the student's learning abilities using a more thorough **diagnostic assessment**—an in-depth evaluation of an individual. Diagnostic assessments often include psychological tests that consist of many very similar items. For example, a teacher may administer a diagnostic test to a student who is having difficulties adding numbers. In the test, one group of test items may require the test taker to add two numbers that do not require any carrying (e.g., 3 + 5). Another set may require the test taker to add items requiring minimal carrying (e.g., 5 + 6), and another group of test items may require more carrying (e.g., 56 + 84). These slight differences allow the teacher to determine the exact difficulty the learner is experiencing.

Often, school psychologists conduct diagnostic testing because tests designed for use by teachers might not be thorough enough to detect some learning difficulties. School psychologists are specifically trained to conduct the evaluation and diagnostic testing necessary to identify specific learning difficulties. For more information on what school psychologists do, see For Your Information Box 12.1.

To understand individual students' needs so they can design interventions to address individual needs, in addition to reviewing existing data, school psychologists conduct assessments by observing students; interviewing students, parents, and teachers; and administering psychological tests. They conduct assessments to make both low-stakes decisions (more frequent and routine reversible decisions based on less formal and less rigorous assessments) and high-stakes decisions (less frequent and routine, often irreversible decisions from more formal and rigorous assessments; NASP, 2009). According to NASP (2009), school psychologists use assessments, including psychological tests, for the some of the more common purposes summarized below.

- **Routine Classroom Decisions.** There are a variety of routine classroom decisions that are informed by less formal assessments, which have unknown or modest technical adequacy. Less formal assessments often contribute those data that are routinely recorded in grade books, teacher logs/notes, and notes between home and

FOR YOUR INFORMATION BOX 12.1

HOW SCHOOL PSYCHOLOGISTS USE PSYCHOLOGICAL TESTS

School psychologists work with a variety of individuals in the educational setting, including students, teachers, family members, school administrators, and other school-employed mental health professionals. They work with these individuals to help schools successfully accomplish six things:

1. improve academic achievement
2. create safe, positive, school climates
3. promote positive behavior and mental health

4. strengthen family–school partnerships
5. support diverse learners
6. improve schoolwide assessment and accountability

How school psychologists accomplish these is below:

Improve Academic Achievement

- Promote student motivation and engagement
- Conduct psychological and academic assessments
- Individualize instruction and interventions
- Manage student and classroom behavior
- Monitor student progress
- Collect and interpret student and classroom data
- Reduce inappropriate referrals to special education

Create Safe, Positive School Climates

- Prevent bullying and other forms of violence
- Support social–emotional learning
- Assess school climate and improve school connectedness
- Implement and promote positive discipline and restorative justice
- Implement schoolwide positive behavioral supports
- Identify at-risk students and school vulnerabilities
- Provide crisis prevention and intervention services

Promote Positive Behavior and Mental Health

- Improve students' communication and social skills
- Assess student emotional and behavioral needs
- Provide individual and group counseling
- Promote problem solving, anger management, and conflict resolution
- Reinforce positive coping skills and resilience
- Promote positive peer relationships and social problem solving
- Make referrals to and coordinate services with community based providers

Strengthen Family–School Partnerships

- Help families understand their children's learning and mental health needs
- Assist in navigating special education processes
- Connect families with community service providers when necessary
- Help effectively engage families with teachers and other school staff
- Enhance staff understanding of and responsiveness to diverse cultures and backgrounds
- Help students transition between school and community learning environments, such as residential treatment or juvenile justice programs

Support Diverse Learners	Improve Schoolwide Assessment and Accountability
• Assess diverse learning needs • Provide culturally responsive services to students and families from diverse backgrounds • Plan appropriate Individualized Education Programs for students with disabilities • Modify and adapt curricula and instruction • Adjust classroom facilities and routines to improve student engagement and learning • Monitor and effectively communicate with parents about student progress	• Monitor individual student progress in academics and behavior • Generate and interpret useful student and school outcome data • Collect and analyze data on risk and protective factors related to student outcomes • Plan services at the district, building, classroom, and individual levels

Source: Copyright © 2014 by the National Association of School Psychologists, Bethesda, MD. Reprinted/Adapted with permission of the publisher. www.nasponline.org

school. NASP recognizes that routine classroom decisions are dynamic, numerous, and of relatively low-stakes, so it is often appropriate to use less formal approaches to assessment. The quantity and accumulation of data from less formal assessments often provide adequate guidance to serve students who are typically functioning. Supplemental assessment is necessary to guide service delivery for students with atypical functioning.

- **Screening Decisions.** Routine screening is necessary to ensure that students are making adequate progress and to identify students with deficit levels and rates of achievement within critical domains of academic and mental health. Effective systems screen at least annually and often three to four times per year. Screening assessments are critical to effective service delivery at the individual, group, and systems levels; therefore, they are "moderate stakes" assessments that should be conducted using measures of appropriate technical adequacy. Screening data are used to guide resource allocation to prevent and remediate problems by allocating resources to prevent and remediate deficits.

- **Problem Definition and Certification.** Assessment guides the allocation of resources for the purpose of problem prevention and remediation. Problems should be measured and quantified whenever supplemental or intensive resources are allocated to prevent or remediate deficit levels and increase rates of development. In conjunction with other educational decisions and evaluations, it is critical that problems be well defined and certified in a manner that is meaningful, measurable and monitorable.

- **Problem Analysis for Instruction/Intervention Planning.** Assessment for the purpose of problem analysis occurs to identify the causal and maintaining variables that contribute to educational problems at the individual, group, and system levels. Problem analysis occurs to isolate intervention targets and provide recommendations for instruction and intervention. These decisions are intended to optimize the match between student needs and services that are provided.

- **Program Evaluation and Accountability.** Instruction and intervention services should be assessed using summative, interim, and formative assessment. Summative assessment data, such as end of the year assessments and statewide testing, should be used routinely to evaluate the effect of core, supplemental, and intensive services at the system, group, and individual levels respectively. Interim assessments, which occur three to four times annually, and formative assessments, which are used at least monthly, are used strategically to evaluate program effects over brief periods.

- **Diagnostic and Eligibility Decisions.** The data collected and used to guide each of the previously listed educational decisions are integrated and synthesized as part of diagnostic and eligibility decisions. These are high-stakes decisions that substantially impact the lives of students and their families. School psychologists rely on a multimethod, multisource, and, often, multisetting approach to assessment as they function within a multidisciplinary team. (NASP, 2009)

Decisions Made at the End of Instruction

At the end of the year, or at the end of a unit of instruction, teachers and administrators at the state and district levels typically use tests as **summative assessments** to help them determine what students do and do not know (to gauge student learning) and to assign earned grades. For example, a teacher may administer a final exam to students in an introductory psychology class to determine whether students learned the material the teacher intended them to learn and to determine what grades students have earned. The same teacher may administer a state- or district-required standardized test of achievement to determine how students' knowledge compares with the knowledge of students in other locations or whether students have achieved important benchmarks (such as learning targets or objectives).

Sometimes students confuse formative and summative assessment. Teachers may use the same tests as both formative and summative assessments. However, when used as a formative assessment, the test is used to direct future instruction—to provide the teacher with information about what information students have already mastered and where the teacher should spend his or her time teaching. When used as a summative assessment, the test is often used as a final evaluation—for example, to determine what grade to assign to students.

Additional Ways Assessment Can Benefit the Instructional Process

Psychological tests can benefit the instructional process in other ways. For example, tests can be used to help motivate students and help students understand their strengths and weaknesses. Tests can be used to help students retain and transfer what they have learned to new problems, issues, and situations. Tests can also be used to help teachers evaluate the effectiveness of their teaching methods. Table 12.3 includes some examples of how tests can benefit the instructional process. Tests can also help students and teachers understand learning styles. See On the Web Box 12.1 for more information on assessing learning styles.

Tests Used for Selection and Placement Decisions

Some educational institutions offer admission only to select individuals (e.g., magnet schools, some private secondary schools, colleges and universities, graduate and professional schools).

TABLE 12.3 ■ Additional Ways Tests Can Benefit the Instructional Process	
Student motivation	Tests are great tools for motivating students. Tests contain items to measure student learning. When a student takes a test, the student can see what knowledge, skills, or abilities he or she is expected to learn. After taking a test, a student typically receives the test back with test items marked correct or incorrect. A student can use what he or she is expected to learn, as well as what he or she did indeed learn, to target future study efforts.
Retention and transfer of learning	Tests can help students retain information and apply retained information to day-to-day activities. Tests expose students to information repeatedly and require students to practice demonstration of knowledge. Repeated exposure to information and practice can facilitate the retention of information. Also, often tests contain application test items—that is, they require learners to apply learned information to real-world situations. Exposure to such information can help learners understand how what they are learning can be applied to different situations.
Student self-assessment	Tests can promote self-awareness. Test results provide students with objective information about what they know (their strengths) and what they must still learn (what they do not know, or their development areas). Students can use their strengths and development areas to make decisions about themselves, such as whether to continue studying a specific content area.
Instructional effectiveness	Test results can help teachers understand the effectiveness of their teaching methods. If many students perform poorly on a test (or on a particular section of a test), this may indicate that they were not yet ready to learn the material or the teaching methods were ineffective. Although there may be other reasons for poor performance (e.g., poorly written test items), teachers may want to consider modifying learning outcomes or changing their instructional methods.

Likewise, some educational institutions offer special programs for students once they begin attending those institutions (e.g., gifted learning programs, English-as-a-second-language programs, honors degree programs). Some institutions even offer students the opportunity to enroll in different levels of a course (e.g., Math 101 instead of Math 100, German 200 instead of German 100). Administrators and testing specialists are often responsible for deciding who will be selected for admittance to educational institutions and who will be selected for and benefit from specific programs or classes within educational institutions. Teachers often create their own tests to make decisions in the classroom, and administrators and testing specialists often use standardized tests of achievement, aptitude, and intelligence to make such selection and placement decisions in educational settings.

Tests Used for Selection Decisions

Educational institutions have numerous requirements for admissions and use various criteria when reviewing applications to make admissions decisions. See On the Web Box 12.2 for a look at the role of tests in the admissions process for a highly competitive institution of higher education: the University of California, Los Angeles (UCLA).

Many educational institutions (e.g., some private secondary schools, most colleges and universities, most graduate and professional schools) require students to submit standardized test scores as a part of the application process. At the least, colleges and universities typically require undergraduate applicants to submit their scores on the SAT or the ACT. For a comparison of the SAT and ACT, see For Your Information Box 12.2. Graduate nonbusiness schools often require students to submit their scores on the Graduate Record Examination (GRE). The GRE measures verbal reasoning, quantitative reasoning, critical thinking, and analytical writing skills not directly related to any specific field of study.

ON THE WEB BOX 12.1
ASSESSING LEARNING STYLES

Your *learning style* refers to the way you learn best. Students can benefit from understanding their learning styles. Because your learning style guides the way you learn, understanding it should help you study more effectively using techniques that will improve the chances that what you study you will understand and retain. Teachers can also benefit from understanding students' learning styles. Because these guide the way students learn, teachers can adjust their teaching styles to better facilitate the learning styles of students.

Many tests are available to help students understand their learning styles. Many of the tests assess different types of learning styles. For example, some tests measure learning style as visual, auditory, kinesthetic, or tactile. Others measure learning style using the Jungian dimensions of introversion/extroversion, intuition/sensation, thinking/feeling, and judging/perceiving. Many of these tests are available free of charge online. Some of the most frequently referenced online learning style tests, and what they measure, are listed below.

Test	Description	Website
Memletics Learning Styles Inventory	Measures preferred learning styles based on seven styles: visual, aural, verbal, physical, logical, social, and solitary	www.crs.sk/storage/memletics-learning-styles-inventory.pdf
Paragon Learning Style Inventory	Measures preferred learning style and cognitive preference based on the four Jungian dimensions: introversion/extroversion, intuition/sensation, thinking/feeling, and judging/perceiving	www.calstatela.edu/faculty/jshindl/plsi/index.html
Index of Learning Styles	Measures preferred learning style based on four dimensions: active/reflective, sensing/intuitive, visual/verbal, and sequential/global	www4.ncsu.edu/unity/lockers/users/f/felder/public/ILSpage.html
Learning Styles Self-Assessment	Measures preferred learning style based on four styles: visual, auditory, kinesthetic, and tactile	www.ldpride.net/learning_style.html
Learning Style Inventory	Measures preferred learning style based on three preferences: visual, auditory, and kinesthetic	https://www.gadoe.org/Curriculum-Instruction-and-Assessment/Special-Education-Services/Documents/IDEAS%202014%20Handouts/LearningStyleInventory.pdf

Professional schools typically require students to submit their scores on the following:

- Medical College Admission Test (for application to medical school)
- Law School Admission Test (for application to law school)
- Dental Admission Test (for application to dental school)
- Graduate Management Admission Test (for application to business school)

ON THE WEB BOX 12.2
ROLE OF TESTS IN THE ADMISSION PROCESS AT THE UNIVERSITY OF CALIFORNIA, LOS ANGELES

www.admissions.ucla.edu/prospect/adm_fr/frsel.htm

Educational institutions have numerous requirements for admission, and their administrators evaluate applications and make admission decisions using various criteria. For example, UCLA—one of the most sought-after universities in the nation, with more than 102,000 applicants (not including transfer students) for the fall 2017 entering class—evaluates applicants both academically and personally using various unweighted criteria: college-preparatory academic achievement (e.g., number, rigor, and grades in courses), personal qualities (e.g., leadership, character), likely contributions to the intellectual and cultural vitality of the campus, performance on standardized tests (e.g., SAT, ACT, and Advanced Placement or International Baccalaureate HL tests), achievement in academic enrichment programs, other evidence of achievement (e.g., performing arts, athletics), the opportunities afforded to candidates, and challenges faced by the applicant (UCLA, 2018).

While UCLA uses standardized test scores as part of the selection process, it does not require a minimum test score (i.e., there is no cut score), to be considered for admission. Trained readers use test scores as one part of the admissions decision and look for a demonstrable relationship to curriculum and to Academic Senate statements of competencies expected of entering college students.

To learn more about how a variety of institutions of higher education use tests during the admission process, including military academies, visit the websites in the following table.

Institution of Higher Education	Admission Website
University of Washington	admit.washington.edu/Admission/Freshmen/Review
University of North Carolina at Chapel Hill	admissions.unc.edu/Apply/default.html
Rollins College	www.rollins.edu/admission/
Harvard University	https://college.harvard.edu/admissions
U.S. Military Academy	www.westpoint.edu/admissions/SitePages/Home.aspx
U.S. Naval Academy	www.usna.edu/admissions

- Optometry Admission Test (for application to optometry school)
- Pharmacy College Admission Test (for admission to pharmacy school)
- Veterinary Admission Test (for admission to veterinary medicine school)

Portfolios

Although art professionals, such as musicians, artists, photographers, writers, and models, have long used portfolios to display samples of their work, the use of portfolios in the educational setting is relatively new. It was not until the 1990s that portfolios became popular assessment tools in education. Today, many educators use **portfolios**, or collections of an individual's work, to highlight and assess that part of student learning and performance, which may be difficult to assess with standardized testing.

More detail about the GRE can be found in **Test Spotlight 12.1** in Appendix A.

FOR YOUR INFORMATION BOX 12.2

DIFFERENCES BETWEEN THE SAT AND THE ACT

Sample SAT Item	Sample ACT Item
A special lottery is to be held to select the student who will live in the only deluxe room in a dormitory. There are 100 seniors, 150 juniors, and 200 sophomores who applied. Each senior's name is placed in the lottery 3 times; each junior's name, 2 times; and each sophomore's name, 1 time. What is the probability that a senior's name will be chosen? A. 1/8 B. 2/9 C. 3/7 D. 3/8* E. ½	A rock group gets 30% of the money from sales of its newest compact disc. That 30% is split equally among the 5 group members. If the disc generates $1,000,000 in sales, how much does one group member receive? A. $30,000 B. $50,000 C. $60,000* D. $200,000 E. $300,000

In the past, colleges and universities stipulated which college admissions test they would accept (usually the SAT or the ACT). Colleges and universities on the West Coast and East Coast, including those in the Northeast, typically required the SAT. Colleges and universities in the Midwest typically required the ACT. Today, most colleges and universities will accept either test. Given this information, it makes sense that college-bound high school students take both the SAT and ACT and submit the test on which they scored best. However, for various reasons, it is not always possible for all college-bound students to take both tests. At a minimum, college-bound students should realize that although these tests measure some of the same skills (see the similar sample questions above), they also measure different skills. Therefore, the test they choose can dramatically affect their chances for admission to a college or university. Depending on their skills, students may perform better on the SAT than on the ACT or vice versa.

The SAT	The ACT
• Aptitude test that measures skills students have learned in school • Consists of four sections: evidence-based reading, writing and language, math, and an optional essay • Math makes up 50% of score • Math section includes geometry, trigonometry, and data analysis • Measures more vocabulary • Does not test English grammar • Is not entirely multiple choice • Points are deducted for wrong answers (has a guessing penalty) • Policy is to send all scores to universities and colleges	• Content-based achievement test that measures what students have learned in school • Consists of five sections: English, mathematics, reading, science, and an optional writing test • Math makes up 25% of score • Math section does not include data analysis • Tests less vocabulary • Tests English grammar • Is entirely multiple choice • Scored based on number of questions correctly answered (does not have a guessing penalty) • Students can decide what scores to send to universities and colleges

Source: Adapted from ACT (2015) and TPR Education IP Holdings, LLC (2018).

Because a portfolio includes a collection of work, it can tell a story about a student. Portfolios may include observations of a student's behavior (e.g., observing a student forming a sculpture), the results of specific projects (e.g., research reports, scrapbooks), other items selected by an individual that reflect what he or she has learned (e.g., photographs, sculptures, videotapes, reports, models, narratives, musical scores), as well as other information.

Because a growing number of educators believe a single test is not a good measure of an individual's ability or knowledge, admissions offices are now assessing portfolios for information on making admissions decisions. The use of portfolios in college admissions is reforming how admissions offices evaluate candidates. For example, in 2007, Rollins College administrators announced that students applying for admission beginning in the fall of 2008 did not have to submit ACT or SAT scores. According to David Erdman, dean of admissions for Rollins's College of Arts and Sciences,

> it is too easy to be distracted by low test scores that are not accurate predictors of a student's college academic potential. . . . We want to take a more holistic approach and believe that a candidate's academic record, level of challenge in course work, talents, interests, and potential to contribute to the Rollins and local community should be as important, if not more important, than test scores. (PR Newswire Association, 2008, para. 2)

Rollins College administrators recognized that not all students perform well on standardized tests and that students have other intelligences besides those assessed on standardized tests of aptitude and achievement. Therefore, instead of standardized test scores, with the new policy, Rollins applicants could submit supplemental materials: (a) a graded paper from a core academic course in the senior year and (b) a portfolio showcasing their strengths, talents, or interests. Sometimes these portfolios consist of theatrical performances and musical scores, sometimes they consist of slides of photography and sculptures, and sometimes they consist of scrapbooks of community service involvement. However, although Rollins allows students to submit portfolios instead of standardized test scores for admissions consideration, applicants who submit only portfolios and writing samples are not yet eligible for academic merit scholarships.

According to the National Center for Fair and Open Testing (2018), over 1,000 4-year colleges do not use ACT or SAT scores of students graduating from U.S. high schools to make admission decisions for a large numbers of students. Schools on the list include smaller private colleges such as Hamilton College and state universities such as Washington State University. Some of the 1,000-plus schools are allowing students with minimum grade point averages [GPA] or specific class ranks to not submit test scores, while other schools ask for test scores but do not use them for admission purposes. Instead, they use the scores to help place students in courses or programs and/or for research purposes only.

Despite their increasing popularity and numerous advantages, portfolios are subjective assessment tools, making them time-consuming to design, implement, maintain, and evaluate. As with any evaluation (e.g., a teacher-made test, a standardized test, an essay), portfolios must be constructed using test specifications and standards (AERA et al., 2014). If they are constructed using test specifications and standards, educators will have more confidence that the portfolios measure what they are intended to measure and will be better able to compare portfolio scores.

Established, objective criteria for portfolio evaluation also must exist. The criteria should address what type of performances educators are willing to accept as evidence that a student displays the intended learning outcomes and that the student displays work that truly shows his or her ability. Educators can use the criteria to prepare rating scales or scoring rules for evaluating the portfolio. Without written guidelines and evaluator training, the portfolio will likely lack evidence of reliability and validity. Portfolios are subject to the same standards of technical quality as other forms of tests (AERA et al., 2014).

Tests Used for Placement Decisions

To qualify for placement in a program (e.g., a gifted program, an honors program, a remedial program, an English-as-a-second-language program), many primary, secondary, and postsecondary educational institutions require students to take standardized tests. In many cases, the results of an achievement, aptitude, or intelligence test are used, along with other evaluative information, to determine whether an individual would benefit from the program. For example, educators may use the results of an achievement test, along with general classroom performance, to place a student in a gifted or honors program.

Some educational institutions also require students to take placement tests before enrolling in certain courses. For example, college educators may use the results of a standardized test of math achievement, along with a student's performance in high school math courses, to place the student in the appropriate college-level math course.

Many tests used to make placement decisions are what we call **high-stakes tests**. When students' test performance significantly affects educational paths or choices, a test is said to have high stakes (AERA et al., 2014). High-stakes testing also involves test scores' being used to determine whether a student is retained in a grade level, is promoted to the next grade level, or graduates.

Tests Used for Counseling and Guidance Decisions

Have you ever asked yourself one or more of the following questions: Should I go to college? What should I major in? What career should I pursue? Psychological tests can play a major role in helping answer these questions. Along with other evaluative information, career counselors use the results of psychological tests to make counseling and guidance decisions. They use test results to help individuals understand their interests, strengths, abilities, and preferences and to translate this information into career guidance decisions. One commonly used test is the Self-Directed Search (SDS). Developed by John Holland, the SDS measures interests and abilities, which are matched to the interests and abilities of individuals who are both satisfied and successful in their careers. See On the Web Box 12.3 for a list of tests commonly used to provide career counseling and guidance to individuals.

See **Test Spotlight 12.2** in Appendix A for more detail about the SDS.

Tests Used for Program, Curriculum, and Administrative Policy Decisions

Educational administrators are responsible for maintaining and improving the quality of our educational system. Of course, administrators must have a way of assessing the quality of the educational system and a way of assessing what would improve the quality of the system. As you would expect, educational administrators use the results of psychological tests, along with other evaluative information, to make administrative policy decisions. For example, two schools may use two different math curricula, and district administrators might want to know which curriculum fosters greater student learning. At the end of the school year, district administrators may decide to administer math achievement tests to the students in each curriculum to determine which curriculum is benefiting students the most. Administrators may use the results of the test, along with other information, to determine which curriculum should be implemented or dropped. Likewise, district, state, and national educational administrators may use the results of psychological tests and other information to determine where money should be spent (e.g., they may decide to give money to a school to buy more books because its students' reading scores are low) or what program should be implemented

ON THE WEB BOX 12.3
TESTS USED FOR COUNSELING AND GUIDANCE DECISIONS

For many years, people have been using psychological tests to understand vocational interests and make career guidance decisions. The use of tests for this purpose probably began in 1915, when James Miner developed a questionnaire to help students make vocational choices. However, the first authentic vocational test was developed 12 years later by E. K. Strong. In 1927, Strong developed the first version of his Strong Vocational Interest Blank. After another 12 years, G. F. Kuder developed the first version of his Kuder Preference Record. Now, in the 21st century, a variety of measures of vocational interest are available. Below are some of the most popular tests, along with the publishers' websites, for measuring vocational interest.

Campbell Interest and Skill Survey	www.pearsonassessments.com/tests/ciss.htm
Career Assessment Inventory–The Enhanced Version	www.pearsonassessments.com/tests/cai_e.htm
Jackson Vocational Interest Survey	www.sigmaassessmentsystems.com/assessments/jvis.asp
Kuder assessments	https://www.kuder.com/solutions/kuder-career-planning-system/assessments/
Self-Directed Search	www.self-directed-search.com
SIGI[3]	www.valparint.com
Strong Interest Inventory	https://www.cpp.com/en-US/Products-and-Services/Strong

(e.g., they may decide to start a gifted program because a number of students scored in the 99th percentile on intelligence tests). In the News Box 12.1 describes another important way that boards of education and school superintendents use test scores.

NORM-REFERENCED, CRITERION-REFERENCED, AND AUTHENTIC ASSESSMENT OF ACHIEVEMENT

Norm-Referenced Tests

Throughout this chapter, we have discussed how tests are used in educational settings, providing you with examples of tests along the way. All of these tests can be classified as either norm-referenced or criterion-referenced tests. **Norm-referenced tests** are standardized tests in which one test taker's score is compared with the scores of a group of test takers who took the test previously. As you recall from the "How Do Test Users Interpret Test Scores?" chapter, the comparison group is called the norm group. Norm-referenced tests allow us to determine how well an individual's achievement compares with the achievement of others and to distinguish between high and low achievers. You may remember taking a test and then receiving your

IN THE NEWS BOX 12.1
PAYING TEACHERS FOR STUDENT TEST PERFORMANCE

In 2001, Congress authorized the No Child Left Behind Act to improve the proficiency of K–12 students. In 2009, President Obama and the U.S. secretary of education announced the Race to the Top plan, dedicating more than $4 billion to improve teaching and learning in our nation's schools and, in part, to encourage U.S. states to implement teacher performance-based pay systems (U.S. Department of Education, 2014). In 2010, the National Governors Association and the Council of Chief State School Officers initiated the Common Core State Standards Initiative (2014) detailing what K–12 students should know in math and English language arts at the end of each grade. And, in 2015, President Obama signed the Every Student Succeeds Act (U.S. Department of Education, 2018). Common to all these initiatives is improving student achievement in K–12, with standardized testing playing a significant role in measuring achievement. With the push for standardized testing has come a push for paying teachers based on student test performance. In all three cases, students' standardized tests scores are used to make important decisions.

Should teachers' pay be based on how students perform on standardized tests? The issue has been one of our nation's hottest over the past decade, with advocacy groups and opponents continuing the debate. While some are in favor of rewarding teachers based on student test performance—and some school districts already have teacher performance-based pay systems in place—others are adamantly opposed. Supporters report that pay for performance will improve the historically implemented pay system of teachers, which is uniform across teachers and weakly related to teacher effectiveness. They believe performance-based pay will help improve teacher quality and therefore help improve student achievement. While teacher pay-for-performance programs can vary, of primary concern to some is paying teachers based on students' standardized test scores. The critics cite serious potential pitfalls. One of the most significant pitfalls relates to the job responsibilities of teachers. For example, if teachers are measured based on student test scores, teachers are being measured only on a small part of a teacher's job responsibilities. And, how does a teacher get rewarded if he or she does not teach one of the subjects tested in standardized tests? Furthermore, many factors besides teaching quality may affect student test performance. One teacher who adamantly opposed performance-based pay based pointed to how teachers cannot control the students who are assigned to their classrooms, stating, "Your mother and father just got a divorce, your grandfather died, your boyfriend broke up with you: those kinds of life-altering events have an effect on how you do in class that day, through no fault of the teacher whatsoever" (Turner, 2010, para. 5).

A quick search of the web will reveal how widely debated the topic of teacher pay for performance is. Using just the key words "teacher pay for performance" yielded over 516 million results in 2018. To learn more about the history of and debate over teacher pay for performance, access just some of the resources at the URLs below.

- **Association for Supervision and Curriculum Development:** http://www.ascd.org/publications/educational-leadership/nov09/vol67/num03/the-problem-with-performance-pay.aspx

- **Parents Across America:** http://parentsacrossamerica.org/performancepay/

- **Public School Review:** https://www.publicschoolreview.com/blog/should-a-teachers-pay-be-influenced-by-student-test-scores

- **National Education Association:** http://www.nea.org/home/36780.htm

- **The RAND Corporation:** http://www.rand.org/content/dam/rand/pubs/reprints/2010/RAND_RP1416.pdf

- **Vanderbilt University:** https://my.vanderbilt.edu/performanceincentives/

- **MLive:** http://www.mlive.com/education/index.ssf/2012/04/survey_strong_support_for_mich.html

After reading more about teacher performance-based pay, reflect on the professional practice guidelines discussed in the "What Are the Ethical Responsibilities of Test Publishers, Test Users, and Test Takers?" chapter and earlier in this chapter.

- Does using student standardized test results to set teacher pay align with the professional practice guidelines? If it does, how? If not, why not?

- What steps should educational professionals using tests in such a manner take to ensure that all professional practice guidelines are followed?

results in terms of a percentile, such as the 85th percentile. Such score interpretations typically are provided for norm-referenced tests.

Educators use norm-referenced tests to compare students' performance with the performance of other students. With norm-referenced tests, we can compare a student's performance with the performance of his or her classmates or with the performance of students in general. We can compare the performance of students at one school with the performance of students at other schools. We can make statements such as "Zachary scored better than 60% of his third grade classmates on the math achievement test" and "Students at XYZ High School performed better than 70% of schools in the South on the SAT." One such norm-referenced test is the Stanford Achievement Test.

Some educators believe that using norm-referenced tests to measure student achievement can be harmful to the educational process. They state that because teachers and other educators know the material that norm-referenced tests measure, instead of teaching the subject matter, they do whatever it takes to improve their students' chances of scoring well—"teaching to the test" and teaching test-taking skills. For a list of some commercially available, national norm-referenced tests used by educational institutions, see On the Web Box 12.4.

Criterion-Referenced Tests

On the other hand, **criterion-referenced tests** are tests that compare a test taker's scores with an objectively stated standard of achievement such as the learning objectives for this chapter. With criterion-referenced tests, an individual's performance is based on how well he or she has learned a specific body of knowledge or skills or on how well the individual performs compared with some predetermined standard of performance.

Criterion-referenced tests allow us to make statements such as "Zachary has learned 50% of the material he needs to know to demonstrate proficiency in third grade mathematics" and "Zachary still needs to work on his multiplication." Many teacher-made classroom tests are criterion-referenced tests.

Many educators believe that criterion-referenced tests are more useful to students and teachers than are norm-referenced tests because instead of comparing a student's performance with the performance of other students, criterion-referenced tests help identify how much material a student has learned and what the student must still learn. Furthermore, using criterion-referenced tests makes it possible for every student to achieve the criteria necessary for earning an A. As you know, on norm-referenced tests, most test takers are likely to earn the "average" score—no matter how well they perform. For a comparison of the traditional differences between norm- and criterion-referenced tests, see Table 12.4.

Authentic Assessment

Although they are efficient and typically easy to score, some individuals criticize norm- and criterion-referenced tests because they measure understanding rather than application, are too structured, and often contain only true/false or multiple-choice questions. Some contend that the focus must be changed from measuring understanding to measuring application—or students' ability to apply the knowledge and skills they gain to performing real-world tasks and solving real-world problems. Authentic assessment does this. The focus of **authentic assessment** is on assessing a student's ability to perform real-world tasks by applying the knowledge and skills he or she has learned. Proponents of authentic assessment believe that students acquire their knowledge to perform a task or produce a product—and assessment should focus on evaluating students' ability to perform the task or produce the product. Authentic assessment relies on more than one measure of performance, is criterion referenced, and relies on human judgment.

ON THE WEB BOX 12.4
COMMON NATIONAL NORM-REFERENCED TESTS USED BY EDUCATIONAL INSTITUTIONS

SAT	sat.collegeboard.com
ACT	http://www.act.org/
GRE	www.ets.org/gre
Stanford Achievement Test	psychcorp.pearsonassessments.com/haiweb/cultures/en-us/productdetail.htm?pid=SAT10C
Iowa Tests of Basic Skills	https://www.hmhco.com/programs/iowa-assessments

TABLE 12.4   ■   Comparison of Norm-Referenced and Criterion-Referenced Tests

	Norm-Referenced Tests	Criterion-Referenced Tests
What is the purpose of the test?	The purpose is to determine how well an individual's achievement compares with the achievement of others and to distinguish between high and low achievers.	The purpose is to determine whether an individual has learned a specific body of knowledge or can demonstrate specific skills as identified in a predetermined standard of performance.
What does the test measure?	It measures broad knowledge and skills that come from academic textbooks and teacher syllabi and that are based on the judgments of curriculum subject matter experts.	It measures narrow knowledge and skills taught in a specific educational curriculum or unit of instruction, as defined by specific instructional objectives.
What are the characteristics of the test items?	Test items are constructed to distinguish between high and low performers. Knowledge and skills typically are tested by one to four items that vary in level of difficulty.	Test items are constructed to match the most critical learning objectives or outcomes. Knowledge and skills typically are tested by multiple items, of similar level of difficulty, to obtain an adequate sample of individual performance and to minimize the effect of guessing.
How are the scores interpreted?	An individual's raw score is calculated and then compared with the scores of others (the appropriate norm group). Raw scores are transformed and reported in more meaningful units such as percentiles or grade equivalents.	An individual's raw score is calculated and then compared with the total possible score on the test. Raw scores are then transformed and reported in more meaningful units such as percentages.

Source: Adapted from Popham (1975). *Educational evaluation.* Englewood Cliffs, NJ: Prentice Hall.

Traditional and authentic assessments are grounded in different reasoning and practice (Mueller, 2011). If you examine the mission statements of most schools, you will likely find discussion of developing students into productive citizens. While there is often significant overlap in the mission of schools, you will often find two different perspectives on assessment: traditional and authentic.

Traditional assessment includes using standardized criterion- and norm-referenced tests and teacher-created tests. With the traditional assessment model, curriculum drives assessment. Assessments to measure knowledge and skills are developed and administered to measure the extent to which students acquire the knowledge and skills of the curriculum. Here is the rationale: From the traditional assessment perspective, to be productive citizens, students must demonstrate certain knowledge and skills. Curricula are created, and teachers in schools deliver curricula to teach students the knowledge and skills. To determine whether students have gained the required knowledge and skills, schools must measure gained knowledge and skills using traditional assessment techniques—or tests.

On the other hand, with the authentic assessment model, assessment drives the curriculum. Educational administrators and classroom teachers identify the tasks students must perform to demonstrate mastery of knowledge and skills. To teach students to perform the tasks, and to ensure that students have the essential knowledge and skills to perform the task, administrators and teachers develop curricula. Here is the rationale: From the authentic assessment perspective, to be a productive citizen, students must be able to perform real-world, meaningful tasks. The objective of school is to develop students' ability to perform the tasks they will face in the real world. To determine whether students can perform the tasks, teachers must ask students to perform tasks that replicate real-world challenges.

For example, one of this textbook's authors used to teach children to do gymnastics. Instead of asking gymnasts to complete a traditional test to measure their knowledge of gymnastics and their ability to perform key skills, the author required the gymnasts to perform tasks essential to being a successful gymnast (e.g., demonstrating balance, doing forward and backward rolls). The same can be done for academic subjects. For example, we can teach students to not just understand the concepts associated with an academic subject, such as mathematics and statistics, but to *do* mathematics and statistics (Mueller, 2011). We can assess students' performance by having them perform tasks in which math and statistics are required in the real world—such as trying to predict the winner of an election and calculating the margin of error—or calculating the probability of winning the lottery, or determining where traffic lights should be installed based on the percentage of accidents at intersections.

Both traditional and authentic assessments have defining attributes. Table 12.5 includes Mueller's (2011) elaboration of these attributes. Traditional assessments tend to fall more toward the left of the continuum, while authentic assessments fall more toward the right end.

Traditional and authentic assessments also differ with respect to the acceptability of teaching to the test. By *teaching to the test*, we are typically talking about the test preparation practices of teachers and the courses students enroll in to prepare for standardized tests (e.g., the SAT). Test preparation practices include such things as drilling on test content (not on curricular content that is not assessed or covered by the test) and providing students with outdated test items from high-stakes standardized tests (Popham, 2000).

Most articles we read include discussion of how teaching to the test is bad. With the traditional assessment model, teaching to the test is indeed discouraged; however, under the authentic assessment model, teaching to the test is encouraged. As discussed in previous chapters, when designing tests, we typically representatively sample knowledge and skills in order to measure a specific content area. With traditional assessment, if teachers drill students only on the sample of knowledge and skills measured by the test, then test performance will

TABLE 12.5 ■ **Defining Attributes of Traditional and Authentic Assessment**

Traditional Assessments	Authentic Assessments
Selecting a response	Performing a task
On traditional assessments, students are typically given several choices (for example, a, b, c, or d; true or false; which of these match with those) and asked to select the right answer. In contrast, authentic assessments ask students to demonstrate understanding by performing a more complex task usually representative of more meaningful application.	
Contrived	Real-life
It is not very often in life outside of school that we are asked to select from four alternatives to indicate our proficiency at something. Tests offer these contrived means of assessment to increase the number of times you can be asked to demonstrate proficiency in a short period of time. More commonly in life, as in authentic assessments, we are asked to demonstrate proficiency by doing something.	
Recall/recognition	Construction/application
Well-designed traditional assessments (i.e., tests and quizzes) can effectively determine whether students have acquired a body of knowledge. Thus, tests can serve as a nice complement to authentic assessments in a teacher's assessment portfolio. Furthermore, we are often asked to recall or recognize facts, ideas, and propositions in life, so tests are somewhat authentic in that sense. However, the demonstration of recall and recognition on tests is typically much less revealing about what we really know and can do than when we are asked to construct a product or performance out of facts, ideas, and propositions. Authentic assessments often ask students to analyze, synthesize, and apply what they have learned in a substantial manner, and students create new meaning in the process as well.	
Teacher-structured	Student-structured
When completing a traditional assessment, what a student can and will demonstrate has been carefully structured by the person(s) who developed the test. A student's attention will understandably be focused on and limited to what is on the test. In contrast, authentic assessments allow more student choice and construction in determining what is presented as evidence of proficiency. Even when students cannot choose their own topics or formats, there are usually multiple acceptable routes toward constructing a product or performance. Obviously, assessments more carefully controlled by the teacher offer advantages and disadvantages. Similarly, more student-structured tasks have strengths and weaknesses that must be considered when choosing and designing an assessment.	
Indirect evidence	Direct evidence
Even if a multiple-choice question asks a student to analyze facts or apply them to a new situation, rather than just recall the facts, and the student selects the correct answer, what do we now know about that student? Did the student get lucky and pick the right answer? What thinking led the student to pick that answer? We really do not know. At best, we can make some inferences about what the student might know and be able to do with that knowledge. The evidence is very indirect, particularly for claims of meaningful application in complex, real-world situations. Authentic assessments, on the other hand, offer more direct evidence of application and construction of knowledge. For example, putting a golf student on the golf course to play provides much more direct evidence of proficiency than giving the student a written test. Can a student effectively critique the arguments someone else has presented (an important skill often required in the real world)? Asking a student to write a critique should provide more direct evidence of that skill than asking the student a series of multiple-choice, analytical questions about a passage, although both assessments may be useful.	

Source: Mueller, J. (2011).

likely not be reflective of student knowledge and skill in the entire content area. Therefore, teachers are discouraged to teach to the test.

However, with authentic assessment, students learn how to perform real-world tasks. From the observational learning theory literature, we know that when individuals see examples of how to perform a task well, they will more quickly and more effectively perform the task. Furthermore, if you inform students of the knowledge and skills required to effectively perform the task, this really will not affect their ability to apply the knowledge and skills in the real world. Unlike traditional assessment, with authentic assessment there is usually not a right or wrong answer; rather, we are able or not able to perform a task. Therefore, teachers are encouraged to teach to the test; they are encouraged to show learners what good performance looks like and clarify the knowledge and skills required to perform well.

For many of the reasons discussed above, during the early 1990s, authentic assessment in educational settings increased in popularity (Wiggins, 1993). Today, authentic assessment plays a significant role in assessing student performance. In the classroom, authentic assessment typically requires students to perform tasks and create portfolios. For example, to measure a student's knowledge of validity, a teacher may require the student to give an oral report on the validity of a particular test or to design some tests of validity. To measure a student's level of mathematics knowledge, a teacher may require the student to keep a notebook with the solutions to math problems or to answer open-ended math problems. To measure a student's understanding of the plot of a story, a teacher may require the student to create a diorama. In industrial-organizational psychology, we call these assessments *work samples*.

Some educators claim that authentic assessment is a more fair and accurate measure of student achievement. Other educators criticize authentic assessment because the reliability and validity of authentic assessment are unknown and because authentic assessment is impractical for school systems that need to perform large-scale testing. Obviously, more research is necessary to determine which type of testing is best for measuring student achievement and ability.

If you want to know whether a student can write, many experts would suggest that you require the student to write something. Requiring him or her to write will help you determine whether the student can perform the task. Emphasizing these types of assessments would likely improve the assessment of learning outcomes, but perhaps other types of tests should not be forgotten because they too play an important role. Knowledge is a critical component of much of what we do. To be good writers, we must have a good knowledge of vocabulary, grammar, and spelling. However, a writing sample does not always evaluate this knowledge effectively because it is easy to hide inabilities in an open-ended task. When we write, we are apt to use only words we know, to write only sentences we know how to punctuate, and to include only words we are confident we can spell.

Chapter Summary

Professionals in educational settings, including educational administrators, teachers, and other testing professionals such as school psychologists, make important decisions every day using the results of standardized and teacher-made tests. The educational professionals use test scores to make inferences to help make important decisions about teaching, learning, and outcomes. The consequences resulting from using test scores to make decisions can be significant.

As test users, educational professionals who use tests are ethically bound to follow the professional practice standards specific to using tests in educational

(Continued)

(Continued)

settings. They should be properly trained on the appropriate use of tests and should consider whether the tests they select or use have evidence of validity and reliability/precision and are fair.

During the instructional process, teachers use psychological tests as placement assessments (to determine whether students are ready to learn new material and to determine how much of the material they already know), formative assessments (to determine what information students are and are not learning), diagnostic assessments (to determine students' learning difficulties more accurately), and summative assessments (to determine what students have learned and to assign grades accordingly). In the classroom, psychological tests can also help motivate students, help students retain and transfer what they have learned, help students understand their strengths and weaknesses, and provide teachers with information regarding the effectiveness of their teaching methods. Administrators and testing specialists use psychological tests to make selection and placement decisions. Unlike those used in the classroom, selection and placement decisions are typically made using standardized tests of achievement, aptitude, and intelligence. Career counselors use the results of psychological tests, along with other information, to help individuals explore their interests, abilities, and preferences and to consider career options that align with these. Educational administrators also use psychological tests to maintain and improve the quality of educational systems. They may use the results of tests to select the best curriculum for a school and to determine where funds should be directed.

Many different types of psychological tests are used in educational settings, and each can be classified as either a norm-referenced or a criterion-referenced test. Norm-referenced tests allow us to compare an individual's performance with the performance of a previously tested group of individuals in order to determine how well the individual performed relative to a particular norm group. Criterion-referenced tests allow us to compare an individual's score with an objectively stated standard of achievement in order to determine the extent to which the individual has obtained desired knowledge and/or skills. Most teacher-made classroom tests are criterion-referenced tests. Some educators believe that norm- and criterion-referenced tests do not measure what is important in real life. Instead, they support increased use of authentic assessment. Authentic assessment involves evaluating a student's ability to apply information to real-world settings using more than one measure of performance. When teachers require students to perform tasks and create portfolios, they are using authentic assessment techniques.

Engaging in the Learning Process

Learning is the process of gaining knowledge and skills through schooling or studying. Although you can learn by reading the chapter material, attending class, and engaging in discussion with your instructor, more actively engaging in the learning process may help you better learn and retain chapter information. To help you actively engage in the learning process, we encourage you to access our new supplementary student workbook. The workbook contains critical thinking activities to help you understand and apply information, and help you make progress toward learning and retaining material. If you do not have a copy of the workbook, you can purchase a copy through sagepub.com.

Key Concepts

After completing your study of this chapter, you should be able to define each of the following terms. These terms are bolded in the text of this chapter and defined in the Glossary.

authentic assessment	formative assessments	placement assessments
criterion-referenced tests	high-stakes test	portfolio
diagnostic assessment	norm-referenced tests	summative assessments

Critical Thinking Questions

The following are some critical thinking questions to support the learning objectives for this chapter.

Learning Objectives	Critical Thinking Questions
Describe the types of decisions educational administrators, teachers, and other educational professionals make using psychological test results.	• How would you prioritize the types of decisions professionals in educational settings make using the results of psychological tests? • Which educational professional(s) makes the most important decisions using psychological tests? • What psychological tests do career counselors at your college or university use and what types of decisions do they help students make based on test results? • What program, curricular, or administrative policy decisions has you state's Department of Education made based on the results of psychological tests?
Explain why educational administrators, teachers, and other educational professionals are test users and why they need to follow professional practice standards.	• What details would you use to support that educational administrators, school psychologists, and teachers are test users? • How would convince test users in educational settings that knowing professional practice standards is critical? • How would you explain to a friend the consequences of educational professionals not following professional practice standards? Consider the consequences to test takers, educational institutions, and society as a whole.
Explain the professional practice standards specific to those who use tests in educational settings.	• What would you do to educate administrators and teachers about the professional practice guidelines specific using tests in educational settings? • Which professional practice guidelines, from the current chapter and from the *What are the Ethical Responsibilities of Test Publishers, Test Users, and Test Taker* chapter, would you recommend professionals in educational settings be familiar with and why?

(Continued)

(Continued)

Learning Objectives	Critical Thinking Questions
Describe how professionals specifically use psychological tests in educational settings.	• What are some personal examples of how test results have been used before, during, and after instruction to make important decisions about you? • What are some personal examples of how test results have been used to make selection and placement decisions, and/or counseling and guidance decisions about you?
Explain the differences between norm-referenced tests and criterion-referenced tests, as well as authentic assessment.	• What questions would you ask an expert who recently developed a standardized test for use in a high school setting to determine if the test developed was norm-referenced or criterion-referenced without using the terms "norm" or "criterion?" • What might happen if psychological tests were abolished in educational settings and 100% replaced with authentic assessment? Would the consequences differ for primary schools, secondary schools, or colleges/universities?

13

HOW ARE TESTS USED IN CLINICAL AND COUNSELING SETTINGS?

"I started working with a therapist to help me get over a problem with anxiety. She asked me to take a couple of tests at our first meeting and then asked me to repeat one of them a month later. How come?"

"I went to the counseling center at school for help with a personal problem I was having with my girlfriend. Before I even met with a counselor, they asked me to complete a long test with a lot of true and false questions. What were they looking for?"

"My friend told me that his brother was admitted to a psychiatric hospital, and while he was there, he had to take something called the inkblot test. What is that and why did he have to take it?"

Psychological tests are invaluable in clinical and counseling settings. They are used at the beginning of treatment to assess the kinds of problems a client is struggling with, as well as to assess the severity of a problem. They are used during treatment to monitor progress and at the end of treatment to assess treatment outcomes. Tests are also are used to clarify diagnoses and to assess obstacles to progress when treatment is not as effective as expected. Finally, psychological tests are an important component of a therapeutic assessment, a form of assessment, which provides insight to clients and promotes change (Finn, 2007).

Various clinicians and consultants administer psychological tests in clinical and counseling settings. Psychotherapists and others responsible for providing treatment to clients administer tests. Psychologists who serve as consultants to psychotherapists, physicians (and other medical providers), attorneys, school personnel, and hospital treatment teams administer tests. Mental health professionals, including psychologists, counselors, social workers, psychiatrists, and psychiatric nurses, administer tests to assist in diagnosis and treatment planning. Regardless of who is administering the psychological test, when properly used in clinical and counseling settings, psychological test results are always combined with information that is gathered in other ways, such as from a clinical interview; a review of school, medical, or legal records; interviews with people who know the client (such as a parent, spouse, or teacher); and/or observations of the client during an assessment session.

The tests clinicians and consultants use must be psychometrically sound; that is, they must have evidence of reliability/precision and validity for their intended use. If a test is not psychometrically sound, the test results may be inaccurate and potentially harmful. An easy way to understand this is to think about what could happen if results from a medical laboratory test were inaccurate or invalid for their intended purpose. Inaccurate test results could lead to misdiagnosis and ineffective or even harmful treatment.

In this chapter, we discuss the many ways tests are used in clinical and counseling settings, such as in psychotherapists' offices, hospitals, and counseling centers—anywhere clients are treated for mental health problems or problems in daily living. We review the kinds of tests, and the specific tests, that are used in such settings and offer case examples to demonstrate how they are used. We review in depth how psychological testing is used in the assessment of three common conditions: autism spectrum disorders, depression, and Alzheimer's disease. We also review the technical issue of incremental validity and the meaning of evidence-based assessment. Finally, we discuss the end product of test use in clinical and counseling settings—providing feedback to clients and preparing a written psychological evaluation report.

THE WORK OF CLINICAL AND COUNSELING PSYCHOLOGISTS

Clinical and counseling psychologists and other mental health professionals address concerns of clients that range from serious mental illness, such as schizophrenia and bipolar disorder, to problems in living, including relationship conflicts and career indecision. They work in a variety of settings with people of all ages, from young children to the very old. Typically, in clinical settings, clinical psychologists treat more serious problems, and in counseling settings, counseling psychologists treat more everyday problems, but there is a great deal of overlap.

Clinical and counseling psychologists usually are licensed by the same state public health or education authorities, and they work under the same licenses and regulations. Most clinical and counseling psychologists have doctoral degrees, either PhDs or doctorates in psychology (PsyD). Most, but not all, clinical and counseling psychologists are mental health professionals. Social workers, counselors, and advanced practice psychiatric nurses usually have master's degrees and are also treatment providers for people with mental health problems, as are psychiatrists who have medical degrees and complete 4-year residencies, with a minimum of 3 years working with patients with mental disorders.

Mental health professionals work with clients in private offices, agencies, public and private clinics, hospitals, and university counseling centers. These are all clinical and counseling settings. The professionals work with individuals, couples, and families, and they see clients individually and in small groups. Mental health professionals use varied approaches to treatment, depending on their training, preferences, the client populations they serve, and the settings they work in. Most use **evidence-based treatment methods**—treatment methods with documented research evidence that the methods are effective for solving the problems being addressed. However, evidence-based methods are not available for every client in every situation.

Clients have unique histories and more often than not have more than one mental health-related problem. For example, a client might have anorexia, depression, anxiety, and learning disabilities and be in the midst of a divorce or have other complicated family problems. An evidence base for treating this particular constellation of problems has not likely been developed, so the clinician must make clinical decisions based on other factors, relying on his or her experience and training, the clinical literature, and the expertise of colleagues and supervisors. See For Your Information Box 13.1 for an example of a client with more than one health-related problem. You will see that Mrs. M has unique needs, with a few different problems, and the therapist she was referred to had to use a variety of tools, including psychological tests, to assess her condition and formulate a treatment plan.

MENTAL HEALTH PRACTITIONERS' USE OF PSYCHOLOGICAL TESTS

In medical settings, physicians and other health care providers diagnose a wide range of physical ailments. They also sometimes diagnose mental health disorders. To diagnose both physical and mental health disorders, they examine patients for signs and symptoms of illness and attempt to determine the underlying cause. Symptoms are problems the patient reports and signs are indicators the physician observes during a physical exam or through laboratory or other tests.

Mental health problems, mental illness, mental disorder, behavioral health problems, and *psychiatric disorders* are different labels for the same thing, defined in the fifth edition of the *Diagnostic and Statistical Manual of Mental Disorders* (DSM) as "a clinically significant disturbance in an individual's cognition, emotion regulation, or behavior that reflects a dysfunction in the psychological, biological, or developmental processes underlying mental functioning" (American Psychiatric Association, 2013, p. 20). Some common examples of mental disorders are depression, anxiety, eating disorders, attention-deficit/hyperactivity disorder (ADHD), borderline personality disorder, learning disorders, and substance use disorders. There are hundreds of other disorders as well. See For Your Information Box 13.2 for more information about the DSM and a discussion of some of the less common and new disorders.

FOR YOUR INFORMATION BOX 13.1

THE CASE OF MRS. M

Mrs. M was 35 years old, married, and the mother of a 12-year-old son. A neurologist referred Mrs. M to a behavioral practitioner because she was experiencing frequent headaches and problems sleeping. The neurologist referred Mrs. M for behavioral therapy instead of medication because Mrs. M was 28 weeks pregnant.

The practitioner gathered information regarding Mrs. M's problem during two assessment sessions. During the first session, the practitioner interviewed Mrs. M to determine the range of her concerns. In that interview, Mrs. M reported that she and her husband were having frequent arguments, usually about disciplining their son. Mrs. M was also given a semistructured interview regarding her headaches and sleep problems. She reported that over the past 3 years, her headaches had become more frequent and more severe. At the time of her first session, every day she was experiencing severe headaches that lasted 2 to 4 hours. She also reported that her husband was more helpful and attentive when she had a headache, and she feared his helpfulness would lessen if her headaches improved. She recalled that her sleep problems started about the same time as her headaches. Her symptoms included needing roughly an hour to fall asleep, and her sleep was fragmented and shallow, with frequent awakenings.

Between the first and second assessment sessions, Mrs. M was asked to quantify her behavior problems by rating her headaches each hour on a 5-point scale (0 = *no headache*, 5 = *very severe headache*). She also kept a sleep diary in which she recorded time taken to fall asleep, number of nightly awakenings, amount of sleep lost, and time of waking in the morning. Mr. and Mrs. M also completed the Dyadic Adjustment Scale (Spanier, 1976) to assess marital adjustment, the Spouse Verbal Problem Checklist (Carter & Thomas, 1973) to assess satisfaction with communication, and a marital attitudes questionnaire.

Based on information gathered during the first assessment session, Mrs. M's marital relationship was identified as an important concern and possibly linked to her headaches and sleep problems. Therefore, both Mr. and Mrs. M completed assessments during the second session.

The data gathered by Mrs. M on her headaches and sleep agreed with what she reported in her interview. She had experienced no headache-free hours during the previous week, and her sleep was interrupted two to five times nightly. Scores on the Marital Satisfaction Questionnaire placed Mr. M within the satisfied range. Mrs. M indicated dissatisfaction with the marital relationship. Scores on the Spouse Verbal Problem Checklist indicated that both Mr. and Mrs. M perceived communication problems, although their explanations of the problems were different.

Because depression is often associated with chronic pain and sleep disturbance, Mr. and Mrs. M completed the Beck Depression Inventory (Beck, Steer, & Garbin, 1988). Mr. M's score was well within the nondepressed range. Mrs. M's score indicated mild depression, but her responses showed her depression to be related to pain rather than mood or cognitive concerns.

During this session, Mr. M was also given an unstructured interview to determine his perceptions of marital difficulties, and both Mr. and Mrs. M were given a semistructured interview regarding behaviors and methods to improve the relationship. The couple was also asked to discuss a topic that caused arguments at home for 10 minutes. This discussion was audiotaped, and two assessors independently rated the couple's interactions using the Marital Interaction Coding System (Weiss & Heyman, 1990). This behavioral assessment indicated high rates of positive and negative statements by Mrs. M, mostly negative statements by Mr. M, and low rates of problem solving by both.

Based on the data gathered during the two assessment sessions and at home by Mrs. M, the practitioner concluded that Mrs. M's headaches and sleep disturbance were probably caused by distress with her marital relationship. Furthermore, the data indicated that general communication problems, rather than child management issues, were contributing to her marital distress.

In cases like those of Mrs. M, psychological assessment in the form of interviews and objective tests provides important information such as underlying problems and contextual issues. This information allows the practitioner to design an intervention or a treatment program that addresses the root causes of behavioral problems instead of symptomatic issues.

FOR YOUR INFORMATION BOX 13.2

LESS COMMON DISORDERS IN THE *DSM*-5

The *DSM*, a handbook published by the American Psychiatric Association and now in its fifth edition, contains critical information for diagnosing over 300 mental disorders. The *DSM*-5 is the authoritative book medical and mental health professionals and all other parties involved in the diagnosis and treatment of mental health conditions use to help them diagnose mental disorders. The handbook contains not only descriptions and symptoms of mental disorders, but also criteria health care professionals can use to consistently and reliably diagnose mental disorders.

Although it is not without its critics, the *DSM*-5 has no serious competitors for the classification of mental disorders. The *DSM*-5 covers a very broad range of mental health conditions, from mild and not very disabling to severe, and includes problems that are common as well as those that are very unusual. The book organizes and classifies mental health problems, provides criteria (lists of signs and symptoms) to use as guidelines to diagnose them, and includes descriptive information about each one. The *DSM*-5 is consistent with the International Classification of Diseases (ICD), established by the World Health Organization. The 11th revision (ICD-11) is the most recent, released in June, 2018. The ICD-11 differs from the *DSM*-5 in that it does not include extensive descriptive information of disorders or criteria to use in diagnosing them.

While some of the disorders in the *DSM* may be very familiar to you, such as depression, anxiety, ADHD, posttraumatic stress disorder, and alcoholism, others you may not have associated with mental disorders, such as hoarding and cannabis withdrawal. The table below contains some mental disorders less commonly known by the public.

Regardless of what they are called, professionals diagnose mental health problems, like medical problems, by examining signs and symptoms. The clinician typically takes a history, observes the client, and asks the client questions as part of the initial evaluation. Psychological testing contributes to the diagnostic process by providing information about signs and symptoms and their underlying cause. For example, a child who becomes agitated at school when he or she has to read aloud could be anxious, but he or she could also have a reading disorder or ADHD. Psychological tests can help clarify the nature of the problem and provide data to help determine effective treatment or other kinds of interventions.

Disorder	Brief Description
Developmental coordination disorder	Delay in the development of coordinated motor skills
Narcolepsy	Recurrent periods of an irrepressible need to sleep
Pica	Persistent eating of nonnutritive, nonfood substances
Trichotillomania	Recurrent pulling out of one's hair
Intermittent explosive disorder	Recurrent behavioral outbursts representing a failure to control aggressive impulses

Note that not everyone who meets with a clinician has a diagnosable mental health disorder. A client might seek help from a clinician for a family problem or to sort out what career path to take and might not meet diagnostic criteria for any mental disorder.

Professionals use a wide variety of psychological tests in clinical and counseling settings to diagnose mental health conditions and to help plan treatment. The one or more tests they use depend on client needs and the individual preferences of clinicians and consultants. While professionals are not required to use specific tests to diagnose mental health conditions, evidence-based guidelines are emerging that may encourage using some tests and not others for diagnosing mental health conditions or planning treatment. The American

Psychological Association (APA) advocates that psychologists should use **evidence-based practice**, defined as "the integration of the best available research with clinical expertise in the context of patient characteristics, culture, and preferences" (APA, 2018c, para. 2). Evidence-based guidelines would include unbiased recommendations, based on the best clinical research findings, to help professionals choose the best tests for diagnosing mental health conditions and planning treatment.

Some of the most common types of tests professionals use in clinical and counseling settings are described in the sections that follow.

Structured Interviews

Clinicians frequently interview clients, as a part of the assessment process, to gather information they will use to help diagnose problems and plan treatment programs. The typical clinical interview does not ordinarily qualify as a psychological test. The clinical interview is not intended to measure samples of behavior in order to make inferences. The clinician merely asks unstructured, yet purposeful questions to gather information.

However, some kinds of interviews do qualify as psychological tests. Semistructured and structured clinical interviews require clinicians to ask specific questions, include a representative sample of one or more behaviors, and provide, at minimum, guidelines for interpreting results, if not a formal scoring rubric. **Structured clinical interviews** require the interviewer to follow a fixed format in asking questions, while **semistructured interviews** allow more flexibility. Some semistructured interviews, such as the Structured Clinical Interview for *DSM*-IV Axis I Disorders (SCID-I; First, Spitzer, Gibbon, & Williams, 1996), cover a wide range of mental health concerns. Other semistructured interviews are concerned with a single diagnosis, such as the Brown Attention-Deficit Disorder Scales or the Yale–Brown Obsessive Compulsive Scale, Second Edition (Y-BOCS-II; Storch et al., 2010). The Structured Clinical Interview for *DSM*-IV Axis II Personality Disorders (SCID-II; First, Gibbon, Spitzer, Williams, & Benjamin, 1997) is focused on assessing personality disorders.

The American Psychiatric Association publishes the SCID, and mental health professionals or trained interviewers administer the SCID to make diagnoses based on the *DSM*.

The SCID has been revised over the years to align with revisions to the *DSM*. The SCID includes an interview booklet and a questionnaire. The interview booklet includes specific questions clinicians should ask during an interview. When the interview is complete, clinicians follow scoring criteria for each response and complete a score sheet, which provides a score for each mental health disorder. The questions are in modules specific to diagnostic categories. The clinician can also use a questionnaire, which the patient completes, as a screening tool to help shorten the interview.

There are both research and clinician versions of the SCID. Researchers often use one of several research versions of the SCID to establish mental health diagnoses in research studies and to validate other instruments. For example, Karstoft, Andersen, Bertelsen, and Madsen (2014) conducted a study to examine the diagnostic accuracy of the Posttraumatic Stress Disorder Checklist–Civilian

Version (PCL-C), developed to diagnose posttraumatic stress disorder. To determine the diagnostic accuracy of the new instrument, the researchers gathered convergent evidence of validity by examining the relationship between Danish soldiers' scores on the PCL-C and the SCID. Because the SCID is already known to accurately diagnose posttraumatic stress disorder, this convergent evidence of validity would provide evidence for the PCL-C's diagnostic accuracy.

Another commonly used semistructured interview is the Y-BOCS. Acknowledged as the gold-standard measure of **obsessive compulsive disorder** (OCD)—a mental disorder characterized by repetitive, intrusive ideas or behavior—the Y-BOCS measures the presence and severity of symptoms. The clinician is guided to ask the client a range of detailed questions about specific obsessive thoughts and compulsive behaviors, notes the current and past presence of each, and rates the severity of the symptoms based on specific criteria. Clinicians' ratings rely on patients' reports, observations, and the reports of others. Storch et al. (2010) revised the Y-BOCS in 2010. The newer version, the Y-BOCS-II, has research supporting its reliability/precision and evidence of validity for intended use. Reliability coefficients for internal consistency, test–retest, and interrater reliability are all greater than .85 (Storch et al., 2010). Studies indicate the Y-BOCS has demonstrated convergent evidence of validity based on its relationship with other variables. Y-BOCS scores correlate strongly with clinician ratings of the severity of OCD symptoms and moderately with measures of worry and depressive symptoms.

Behavior Rating Scales

Clinicians who treat children frequently use behavior rating scales. Clinicians can use the scales early in treatment, to develop a treatment plan, or any time in treatment to clarify a diagnosis and revise a treatment plan. As the name implies, behavior rating scales typically require an informant, usually a parent or teacher, to rate a client with regard to very specific behaviors. There are also self-report versions of behavior rating scales for which clients rate their own behaviors.

The Child Behavior Checklist (CBCL; Achenbach, 1991) is a good example of a behavior rating scale. As a standard test in psychopathology that others use to gather convergent evidence of validity, the CBCL requires an adult to note if a statement about a child he or she knows well is "not true, somewhat or sometimes true, or very or often true." Statements are concerned with a range of behaviors, including aggressive behavior, rule-violating behavior, social problems, physical complaints, withdrawal, and others. There are over 100 individual items that are rated. Individual items include, for example, "bites fingernails," "gets teased a lot," and "hangs around with others who get in trouble." Specific items are grouped into clusters and scores for each cluster are reported as T scores and percentiles. There are normative data for different genders and age groups, so the client's score in each cluster can be compared with those of similar children. The CBCL is a good example of a psychological test. The CBCL is a standardized test; that is, the test items are the same for each test taker, the instrument includes a representative sample of behavior, and there are rules for scoring and interpretation.

Research indicates that the CBCL has evidence of reliability/precision, with overall coefficients for internal consistency and test–retest reliability typically at .8 or above, with modest interrater reliability coefficients of approximately .66 (Doll, 1994; Furlong, 1994). Because the test serves as a standard upon which others gather convergent evidence of validity, reviewers report that gathering evidence of validity based on relations with other variables, using traditional measures of validity, is difficult. However, a body of convergent and discriminant evidence of validity does exist.

Symptom Checklists and Symptom-Based Self-Report Tests

Clinicians also use symptom checklists and self-report tests, which clients complete themselves. These kinds of tests list feelings, thoughts, and behaviors that are related to psychiatric disorders, such as depression. Some, such as the Symptom Checklist 90–Revised (SCL-90-R; Derogatis, 1977), cover a broad range of mental health conditions, while others, such as the Beck Depression Inventory II (BDI-II), have a narrow focus. Clinicians use symptom checklists and symptom-based self-report tests in the initial stages of treatment, to evaluate a client's level of distress and for treatment planning. Clinicians also use the checklists and tests after treatment has started to monitor progress. The SCL-90-R and the BDI-II are both very well researched and have strong bodies of evidence to support reliability/precision and convergent and discriminant evidence of validity for diagnosis and monitoring of treatment progress. However, like other psychological tests, they are not intended to be used on their own, without additional data gathered by a clinician through interview and observation. Detailed information regarding reliability/precision and validity for intended use can be found in the *Ninth Mental Measurements Yearbook.*

The BDI-II has 21 items, each reflecting a client's experience of a particular depression-related symptom. Each item is rated on a four-point scale. The test yields a total score, which is interpreted as a client's overall level of depression. The score is based on self-report, and the questions are straightforward, so clients taking the test must be motivated to be honest and open about their experiences. Similarly, the SCL-90-R has 90 items covering nine clinical areas, including depression, anxiety, paranoid ideation, psychosis, and others. The client rates each item on a five-point scale.

There are numerous other symptom-based self-report tests, with varying degrees of research evidence supporting their use. For example, there are symptom-based self-report tests relevant to eating disorders, ADHD, anxiety, substance abuse, and many other clinical problems.

Comprehensive, Clinically Oriented Self-Report Tests

Comprehensive, clinically oriented self-report tests are widely used in clinical settings (Camara, Nathan, & Puente, 2000). They are powerful tools for gathering information about personality and emotional functioning, as well as about symptoms and diagnostic concerns. They are most typically used for planning treatment and for consultation and less likely to be used for monitoring progress or outcome. The Minnesota Multiphasic Personality Inventory-2 (MMPI-2), Personality Assessment Inventory (PAI), and the Millon Clinical Multiaxial Inventory-III (MCMI-III) are the most frequently administered of these kinds of tests. Each was developed for clinical purposes and normed on clinical populations.

MMPI-2

The MMPI-2 is a 1989 revision of a test that was originally published in the 1940s. It is still very widely used in clinical and other settings. Although it was initially intended for clinical purposes and related to psychiatric diagnoses, the MMPI-2 is also considered a measure of personality traits. The MMPI-2 requires the test taker to respond to over 500 true/false questions, many of which are empirically but not obviously related to a clinical diagnosis. That is, research evidence indicates that an item tends to be scored a certain way by individuals who have a particular diagnosis, even though it's not obvious that the item is related to the diagnosis. The most basic interpretation of the test yields scores on 10 clinical scales and 5 validity scales, scales that are relevant to how consistently, honestly, and openly the test taker responded to questions. (Test takers might be motivated to over-report or underreport symptoms, depending on both personality variables and the circumstances of testing.) In addition to the basic scales, numerous supplementary and content scales have been developed over the years the MMPI-2 has been in use.

A new version of the MMPI, the MMPI-2 Restructured Form (MMPI-2-RF), was introduced in 2008. It is shorter than the MMPI-2 and incorporates some other changes. The MMPI-2-RF hasn't replaced the MMPI-2, in part because so much research has been done on the MMPI-2 that doesn't automatically apply to the MMPI-2-RF.

In clinical practice, the MMPI-2 is used to understand the personality characteristics of a client and how they might influence treatment, as well as in formulating diagnostic impressions, anticipating response to treatment, and making treatment plans.

More detail about the MMPI-2 can be found in **Test Spotlight 11.1** in Appendix A.

PAI

The PAI is a newer test than the MMPI-2. The PAI was first published in 1991. As with the MMPI-2, test scores have some relevance to personality variables as well as clinical concerns, and the PAI incorporates validity scales to determine if the test taker is over- or underreporting symptoms and responding consistently. The PAI has more than 300 items (fewer than the MMPI-2), and individuals taking the test rate the items on a four-point scale (*false, not at all true*; *slightly true*; *mainly true*; and *very true*). The body of research on the PAI is not as extensive as the body of research on the MMPI-2, but it is expanding. The PAI has scales specifically relevant to treatment concerns, such as attitude toward treatment, level of stress and social support, and suicidal ideation. Clinicians can use the PAI to assist in diagnosis and for treatment planning. The assessment of personality traits is less comprehensive than that of the MMPI-2.

More detail about the PAI can be found in **Test Spotlight 5.1** in Appendix A.

MCMI-III

The MCMI-III is the 1994 revision of a test that was first developed in the late 1970s. Although like the MMPI-2 and PAI, it is a comprehensive self-report measure of personality and clinical problems, the MCMI-III focuses on personality disorders and symptoms related to personality disorders, a subset of mental disorders. A personality disorder, as defined in *DSM*-5, is

> an enduring pattern of inner experience and behavior that deviates markedly from the expectations of the individual's culture, is pervasive and inflexible, has an onset in adolescence or early adulthood, is stable over time, and leads to distress or impairment. (American Psychiatric Association, 2013, p. 645)

For example, a person with borderline personality disorder has a pattern of unstable relationships, self-image, and mood as well as high levels of impulsivity. A person who has a personality disorder may also have a clinical diagnosis such as depression or anxiety, due to chronic interpersonal and other difficulties. However, a person with depression or anxiety may or may not have a personality disorder. The MCMI-III is much shorter than the MMPI-2, with only 175 true/false questions leading to scores on clinical scales corresponding to several personality disorders and clinical syndromes. Like the MMPI-2 and PAI, the MCMI-III includes validity scales and has a large body of research supporting its reliability/precision and validity for intended use differentiating among diagnostic groups.

Performance-Based, or Projective, Clinically Oriented Personality Tests

Performance based, or projective, clinically oriented personality tests are the most controversial of the psychological tests commonly used in clinical and counseling settings. Like the other tests, qualified professionals administer these types of tests in a standardized manner and follow guidelines for scoring, although for some tests in this category, the scoring guidelines are vague and idiosyncratic, and perhaps ineffective. The controversy for tests in this category is over the lack of research supporting the reliability/precision of measurement and validity for intended use (e.g., see Jayanti, 2014). The most widely used of these controversial tests are the Rorschach psychodiagnostic technique and the Thematic Apperception Test. Kinetic family drawings, where individuals are asked to draw a person or an object, and other kinds of drawing tests are also widely used, especially with children. The Rorschach psychodiagnostic technique, also known as the Rorschach inkblot method (Rorschach, 1921), was initially developed in the 1920s and has been used more or less consistently since then, with a number of changes and adjustments, although no changes have been made to the original 10 inkblots. For this test, 10 inkblots are shown to the client, one at a time, and the client is asked what each one might be. In the more recent versions of the test, the client is also asked to elaborate on what made the inkblot look like the image he or she described so that each response can be scored.

The Exner Comprehensive System (Exner, 2003) was developed in the 1980s out of a synthesis of a number of competing scoring systems and research that collected normative data for children and adults. In the Exner system, the client's Rorschach responses are coded and tabulated, resulting in summary scores that are relevant to various aspects of personality functioning, such as self-perception, coping strategies, quality of thought processes, and emotional responsiveness. A review of the literature characterized the interpretation of the different summary scores as more well validated or less well validated by research studies (Mihura, Meyer, Dumitrascu, & Bombel, 2013), and a new approach to administering and scoring the Rorschach (called the Rorschach Performance Assessment System) has recently been developed (Meyer, Viglione, Mihura, Erard, & Erdberg, 2011). Although there remains a lot of controversy about the validity of Rorschach results for illuminating aspects of personality functioning or diagnostic concerns, there is consensus that the test has evidence of validity for assessing certain aspects of functioning, specifically, thought disorder (Mihura et al., 2013), an important issue for the diagnosis of schizophrenia and other psychotic disorders. The validity of the Rorschach test for assessing other aspects of functioning remains controversial, with psychologists having strong opinions on both sides of the question. Those who support the use of the Rorschach test in clinical settings find the test useful in clarifying diagnostic issues, treatment planning, and understanding broad and narrow aspects of personality functioning. It is typically used as part of a more comprehensive assessment, along with other kinds of psychological tests, as well as interview and other nontest approaches to understanding client functioning and needs.

On the Web Box 13.1 discusses an important and ongoing controversy about the publication of the Rorschach inkblots on Wikipedia.

The Thematic Apperception Test (TAT) is another widely used performance-based, or projective, test. The TAT was also developed many years ago, in the 1930s, and the same set of stimuli is used today. A TAT kit includes 31 black and white drawings, each one on a different card. The clinician administers a subset of the 31 cards, asking the client to make up a story for each one and to include specific details in the story. The client typically dictates the story to the clinician, who writes it down verbatim. Although scoring systems have been developed for the TAT, they are not widely used. Rather, the clinician interprets the client's responses in a qualitative fashion. In other words, although the test may be administered in a standardized manner, the scoring rules can be quite vague and idiosyncratic. Demonstrating reliability/

ON THE WEB BOX 13.1
TEST SECURITY AND THE RORSCHACH INKBLOT TEST

With the advent of wireless Internet transmission in the 21st century, secrets are hard to keep. A number of websites even make it their business to provide an opportunity for their members to provide information and tell secrets.

As you probably know, Wikipedia, a free online encyclopedia whose site members write the articles, is one such site, and that's where James Heilman, an emergency room doctor from Moose Jaw, Saskatchewan, posted the Rorschach inkblots and their most popular responses in an article about the test. Since Heilman posted all 10 inkblots in June 2009, the Rorschach test and its stimuli have become more controversial than ever, and the Wikipedia page focused on the Rorschach includes even more detailed information about the test.

Bruce L. Smith, past president of the International Society of the Rorschach and Projective Methods, has said in reference to the inkblots, "The more test materials are promulgated widely, the more possibility there

is to game it . . . [which would] . . . render the results meaningless" (as cited in N. Cohen, 2009, p. A1). Those who wish to stop Wikipedia from displaying the inkblots have several reasons:

- Tens of thousands of research studies, according to Smith, have been published that have normative results for these particular inkblots.

- The Rorschach test is still in use.

- Use of the test has even been written into assessment guidelines recognized by local courts and governments.

Yes, new inkblots could be used, these advocates concede, but those blots would not have had the research—"the normative data," in the language of researchers—that allows the answers to be put into a larger context.

---

precision and evidence for validity of test results for describing personality functioning is highly problematic, given the uniqueness of each client's responses, and the use of the test in clinical settings is controversial. Nevertheless, the TAT remains popular among clinicians who use it, along with other tests and sources of information, to gather data about personality and emotional functioning and clients' concerns (Groth-Marnat, 1997). For example, Groth-Marnat (1997) noted that clinicians may find the TAT valuable because it offers "not only highly rich, varied, and complex types of information, but also personal data that theoretically bypass a subject's conscious resistances" (p. 458).

A third type of measure, **projective drawings**, also has a place among some clinicians, especially for evaluating children. Children might be asked to draw a picture of their family doing something, in a kinetic family drawing (Burns & Kaufman, 1970), or they might be asked to draw a person or to draw a house, a tree, and a person. Scoring systems have been developed over the years, including methods of assessing cognitive maturity on the basis of drawings (e.g., see Mitchell, Trent, & McArthur, 1993). However, clinicians often use an impressionistic, global appraisal of the drawing focusing on degree of health or pathology, with some research support for the effectiveness of this approach (Groth-Marnat, 1997). Similar to the TAT, rules for scoring are vague at best, and controversies remain over the reliability and validity of projective drawings in illuminating clinical concerns. Nevertheless, projective drawings are often used by clinicians tasked with evaluating children and adolescents, alongside other sources of data.

See For Your Information Box 13.3 for a description of a projective drawing test—the Draw-A-Person test. Included is a discussion of scoring systems for interpreting the test and research examining the validity of the test in assessing a child's developmental level and social and emotional functioning.

FOR YOUR INFORMATION BOX 13.3
THE DRAW-A-PERSON PROJECTIVE TECHNIQUE

The Draw-A-Person technique is a popular choice among counselors who work with victimized children, and several authors have suggested scoring schemes that relate to emotional and sexual violence (e.g., Van Hutton, 1994; Wohl & Kaufman, 1995).

The assessor gives the test taker a blank sheet of paper, usually 8½ by 11 inches, and a soft pencil or crayon. She asks the participant, "Will you please draw a person?" In response to questions about which person or what kind of person or drawing, the assessor says, "Draw whatever you like in any way you like." The assessor also assures the participant that artistic talent is not important and is not part of the exercise. After the first drawing is completed, the assessor asks the participant to draw a person whose sex is opposite that of the first person drawn. For instance, the assessor may say, "This is a male figure [or man]; now please draw a female [or woman]." Figure 13.1 shows an example of the sorts of drawings that might be produced by the participant.

There are various methods for interpreting and scoring the resulting drawings. These scoring schemes, not the test itself, provide the quantitative data that allow researchers to look for evidence of reliability and validity. Studies appropriately assess interscorer reliability as well as evidence of construct validity.

Van Hutton (1994) reported rigorous development of her scoring system for the Draw-A-Person test that included conducting a pilot test similar to the pilot tests described in "How Do We Develop a Test?" She reported high interscorer reliability (> .90) for three scales in her scheme and .70 for the other scale. She also found discriminant evidence of validity because the scorers were able to use the scores on one scale to

FIGURE 13.1 ■ The Draw-A-Person Projective Technique

Source: From Hammer, *The Clinical Application of Projective Drawings*, 4th ed. Copyright © 1975. Courtesy of Charles C. Thomas Publisher, Ltd., Springfield, IL.

successfully separate test takers into two categories: normal children and sexually abused children. The remaining scales, however, were not predictive of any criteria (Dowd, 1998).

Cognitive and Memory Testing

Cognitive testing refers to the use of tests that measure global and narrow intellectual abilities. This information can be important for a subset of clients in clinical settings but is not routine in such settings. Rather, cognitive testing is used when there are specific questions about a client's cognitive strengths and weaknesses that have relevance to diagnostic considerations or treatment planning. This kind of testing is typically completed by a consultant rather than the clinician providing treatment, although that is not always the case. It might be needed, for example, if there are questions of low intellectual functioning, giftedness, or ADHD.

It might also be used as part of a comprehensive group of tests when there are complications in formulating a diagnosis or providing treatment.

The Wechsler Intelligence Scale for Children, Fourth Edition (WISC-IV; and the newest revision, the WISC-V), for children and adolescents, and the Wechsler Adult Intelligence Scale, Fourth Edition (WAIS-IV), for adults, are extremely popular with clinicians. They are well researched and widely used. Results of these tests are considered very reliable and valid indicators of cognitive ability. Although each of these tests results in an overall intelligence quotient (IQ) score, the tests are more useful in the clinical setting, and many other settings, when clusters, or index scores, are reviewed. Specific indexes measure verbal abilities, perceptual abilities, working memory, and quickness in completing routine information-processing tasks, or processing speed. Index scores in these four areas can be compared to determine the client's strengths and weaknesses. Index scores and the global, or full-scale, IQ are also interpreted relative to the test scores of other people of similar age, so that conclusions can be drawn about the client's strengths and weaknesses relative to other people. Test findings have relevance to academic achievement and everyday functioning.

There are other tests of cognitive abilities, such as the Stanford–Binet. It also has strong research support for reliability/precision of measurement and validity for assessing cognitive functioning (Johnson & D'Amato, 2005).

In the News Box 13.1 discusses a 2014 Supreme Court ruling, which determined that the strict use of IQ cutoff scores in Florida death penalty cases was unconstitutional. The court previously found that executing inmates with intellectual disabilities was cruel and unusual punishment and therefore not permissible under the law.

Memory testing is used in clinical settings when there are specific questions about memory functioning, for example, in an adult who expresses memory concerns. As with tests of cognitive ability, consulting psychologists or neuropsychologist (see below), rather than the treating clinician, typically administer memory tests. The Wechsler Memory Scale, Fourth Edition (Wechsler, 2009), is one example of a comprehensive test of memory functioning. Tests of memory functioning such as the Wechsler Memory Scale have strong research support for reliability/precision of measurement and validity for evaluating memory functioning.

> More detail about the Stanford–Binet Intelligence Scales, Fifth Edition, can be found in **Test Spotlight 1.2** in Appendix A.
>
> More detail about the WAIS-IV can be found in **Test Spotlight 1.1** in Appendix A.

Neuropsychological Testing

Neuropsychologists are specially trained clinicians who focus on the relationship between brain functioning and behavior. A neuropsychologist might evaluate a child with epilepsy or an adult following traumatic brain injury to determine the client's needs and to make treatment or educational recommendations or recommendations to improve functioning. Neuropsychologists also might evaluate children or adults who have learning problems or ADHD. Neuropsychologists use a very wide range of specialized tests to assess different aspects of brain functioning, such as spatial perception, motor performance, and speed of information processing. Some neuropsychologists use a standard group of tests for most patients, while others pick and choose which tests to use on the basis of the brain functions that need to be assessed. Each approach has its advantages.

Clinicians without specialized training as neuropsychologists conduct screenings for neuropsychological, or brain-based, problems in functioning, typically using a group of tests to cover a range of functions. They review test results in conjunction with data obtained through interviews, observations, and records and refer to neuropsychologists for more in-depth evaluations of brain functioning when needed.

IN THE NEWS BOX 13.1
THE SUPREME COURT, IQ CUTOFF SCORES, AND THE DEATH PENALTY

In May 2014, the U.S. Supreme Court determined that Florida's strict IQ cutoff for deciding if an inmate was intellectually disabled was unconstitutional. In a 2002 case, *Atkins v. Virginia*, the court first recognized that executing individuals with intellectual disabilities violated the constitution's prohibition against cruel and unusual punishment. In the case of *Hall v. Florida*, Florida used a fixed IQ score of 70 as a cutoff to determine if an individual had intellectual disabilities and was eligible for the death penalty. But using a fixed IQ score violates the manner in which IQ tests are intended to be used. As we discussed in the chapter, "What Is Test Reliability/Precision?" test scores are meant to be interpreted with respect to a standard error of measurement. An IQ score is most accurately expressed as a confidence interval around a true score and not as the true score itself. The standard error of measurement for the intelligence test that Hall took was 2.5 points, so the 95% confidence interval around Hall's score was from 66 to 76. Writing for the majority in the 5-to-4 decision, Justice Anthony M. Kennedy wrote, "Florida seeks to execute a man because he scored a 71 instead of 70 on an I.Q. test." The court ruled that using a fixed IQ score as the determining factor of whether a person was intellectually disabled in death penalty cases was too rigid and therefore struck down the Florida law as unconstitutional.

For Your Information Box 13.4 offers the example of Mrs. P, a woman with brain damage who benefited from neuropsychological evaluation. The testing showed areas of both strength and weakness, and her therapist was able to work with her to improve her independent living skills and quality of life.

Specialized Forensic Testing

Forensic psychologists are concerned with the intersection between mental health or neuropsychological problems and the law. They might be involved in evaluating whether an individual is competent to stand trial, determining custody of children in a contested divorce, or sorting out what kind of treatment would benefit a juvenile offender. They might also evaluate individuals who are requesting financial damages in lawsuits following accidents or for any number of other reasons. Often, their "client" is the court; that is, they are tasked with providing specific information to the court in order to address questions posed by the court. However, forensic psychologists could be hired by either side in a dispute.

Forensic psychologists sometimes use specialized psychological tests to assist in addressing referral questions. For example, the Test of Memory Malingering, developed in 1996 by Tom Tombaugh, is intended to distinguish between legitimate memory impairment and memory impairment that is being "faked" by the test taker for some kind of secondary gain.

On the Web Box 13.2 lists a number of tests and the websites of their publishers. The publishers provide a lot of detailed information about each test, including how it is used, whom it is appropriate for, how long it takes to administer, and psychometric data.

FOR YOUR INFORMATION BOX 13.4
THE CASE OF MRS. P

Mrs. P was 32 years old and hospitalized for post-partum depression following the birth of her second child. She had many fears and phobias, particularly of dirt and contamination that she could not control. She acted helpless and inadequate. For instance, she often burned food when she cooked.

Mrs. P's history revealed that she had been born prematurely and there had been a question of whether she would survive. Psychological tests at the time of her admission showed clear signs of organic brain damage that had not been detected before. During her lifetime, Mrs. P had developed an attitude of helplessness and inadequacy, and she required the support of others for most tasks.

When the test results were given to Mrs. P, she was told that she had a number of strengths as well as certain limitations. In other words, it was clear that she had the ability to do certain things she was not doing. Her therapist told her she would be expected to begin doing the things she could do.

Mrs. P resisted the therapist's interpretation and maintained that the tests were inaccurate. The therapist, however, constantly pointed out what she was doing and, using the test results, supported Mrs. P's efforts to become more self-sufficient.

A remarkable change took place. Mrs. P began to entertain friends and accept responsibilities that she would have avoided previously.

Source: Adapted from Shore (1972).

CASE EXAMPLES OF HOW TESTS ARE USED IN CLINICAL AND COUNSELING SETTINGS

The cases below are three of many possible examples of how psychological tests are used in clinical and counseling settings. None of them are based on real clients, but all are realistic. The first example, Joanne, is of a typical client in an outpatient private practice setting. Testing is used to make a diagnosis, plan treatment, and measure progress. The second example, Jesse, is of a young man who made a suicide attempt and was admitted to a psychiatric hospital. Testing is used to clarify his diagnosis and plan his treatment. The third example, Juan, is of a college student who was being seen for the first time at a university counseling center. Testing is used as part of a routine intake to help with clinical decision making and treatment planning.

Joanne

Joanne sought treatment with a psychologist at the suggestion of her physician, who suspected that she had OCD based on some of Joanne's phone calls to the office in the past year. The psychologist had a specialty practice in the treatment of OCD in children and adults. Joanne was 23 years old and had never previously seen a mental health provider. Although based on an initial interview and her conversation with Joanne's doctor the psychologist strongly suspected that Joanne was struggling with OCD, and she wanted to find out more about it

ON THE WEB BOX 13.2
PSYCHOLOGICAL TESTS USED FOR DIAGNOSIS AND INTERVENTION

Clinicians and counselors use a variety of standardized and projective personality tests for diagnosis and intervention. The table below lists the websites of the tests' publishers, where you can learn more about the tests.

Test	Website
Minnesota Multiphasic Personality Inventory	www.pearsonassessments.com
Personality Assessment Inventory	www.parinc.com/
Millon Clinical Multiaxial Inventory–III	www.millon.net
Structured Clinical Interview for *DSM* Disorders	http://www.scid5.org/
Thematic Apperception Test	www.pearsonassessments.com
Rorschach inkblot test	www.pearsonassessments.com
Draw-A-Person test	www.pearsonclinical.com

before initiating treatment. She also wanted to know more about whether Joanne was struggling with depression. She administered a structured interview for OCD, the Y-BOCS, and she asked Joanne to take the BDI-II. She planned to administer both of these instruments about once a month to monitor Joanne's progress. She also evaluated Joanne with a thorough clinical interview, and she spoke with Joanne's mother, with Joanne's permission, about her developmental history, family history, and everyday behavior.

Jesse

Jesse was admitted to an inpatient psychiatric hospital following a suicide attempt. Although he was making steady progress in treatment, he continued to be disorganized in his thought process, and the treatment team felt unsure about whether he had an underlying psychotic disorder. They requested a psychological evaluation to address this question. The hospital psychologist administered the WAIS-IV, the PAI, and a Rorschach inkblot test to gather data as part of the evaluation for a psychotic disorder.

Juan

Juan made an appointment at the counseling center at the university he attended. He had no previous treatment history. The clinician asked him to complete the MMPI-2 prior to the initial session, so he could get a sense of direction for treatment as well as information about the seriousness of Juan's difficulties.

PSYCHOLOGICAL TESTING IN DEPTH: ASSESSING AUTISM, DEPRESSION, AND ALZHEIMER'S DISEASE

Autism Spectrum Disorders

Data from the Centers for Disease Control and Prevention, from 2018, indicate that autism spectrum disorders affect 1 in 42 boys and 1 in 189 girls in the United States, or 1 in 68 children. **Autism spectrum disorders** are developmental disabilities that affect communication and social interaction and involve restricted interests and stereotyped, repetitive patterns of behavior. Autism spectrum disorders can be mild or severe with regard to degree of disability. For many, problems associated with autism are present from infancy and last a lifetime, although there can be improvement and even remission of symptoms for some children. Some children appear to develop normally through the toddler years but regress to autistic behaviors when they get a little older. They lose some capacities they had previously developed.

Autism is a serious diagnosis, and it needs to be made with care, given the implications of a missed diagnosis or an incorrect one. The earlier treatment is started, the better the outcome. The challenge in diagnosing autism spectrum disorders is to differentiate normal from abnormal development in social interaction, communication, and interests.

Autism is typically first identified through screening in routine well-child visits at a pediatrician's office, using one of several screening tools. An example of a screening tool is the Ages and Stages Questionnaire, Third Edition (Squires, 2009), which assesses development and social–emotional functioning from early infancy through age 5½ based on parents' responses to a questionnaire. If concerns about an autism spectrum disorder are identified through screening, the child is typically referred for a multidisciplinary comprehensive evaluation. The comprehensive evaluation includes hearing and vision screenings and other medical tests, as well as a thorough assessment of social and communication capacities. The Autism Diagnostic Observation Schedule, Second Edition (ADOS-2; Lord, Rutter, DiLavore, Risi, Gotham, & Bishop, 2012), is a well-researched, widely used method of assessing autism via standardized behavioral observation of child behavior and can be an important part of a comprehensive evaluation. For this test, which is used with children as young as 12 months as well as for older children and adults, a trained examiner presents activities and observes and codes the child's (or adult's) behavior. Cutoff scores provide firm diagnostic indicators. The Autism Diagnostic Interview–Revised (ADI-R; Lord, Rutter, & Le Couteur, 1994) is a structured interview for parents of children older than 18 months who are being evaluated for autism spectrum disorders. The examiner asks parents general and specific questions about their children's social and communication activities. As with the ADOS-2, responses to the ADI-R are scored, and research-based cutoff scores are available to assist in diagnosis. The ADI-R is used with an instrument like the ADOS-2, which evaluates a child directly.

For Your Information Box 13.5 describes three tests frequently used by health care providers to screen for developmental or behavior problems in early childhood.

Depression

One of the leading causes of disability in individuals between the ages of 15 and 44 is depression. In 2016, over 16.1 million American adults met the diagnostic criteria for a major depressive disorder (Anxiety and Depression Association of America, 2016). Depression is present throughout the world and afflicts people of all ages. Depression can be acute or chronic, mild

FOR YOUR INFORMATION BOX 13.5
COMMON DEVELOPMENTAL SCREENING TESTS

Gesell Developmental Schedules

The Gesell Developmental Schedules (Knobloch, Stevens, & Malone, 1980) represent a refinement of early attempts to construct a taxonomy of normal development. The first Gesell schedules, published in 1940, represented the results of longitudinal studies conducted by Arnold Gesell and his colleagues at Yale University (Ames, 1989). An assessor using the Gesell schedules observes and records a child's responses to predetermined toys and other stimuli. Information provided by a parent or caregiver then supplements the observational data to determine neurological defects or behavioral abnormalities (Anastasi & Urbina, 1997).

Bayley Scales of Infant and Toddler Development

The Bayley Scales of Infant and Toddler Development, Third Edition (Bayley, 2006), use a methodology similar to that of the Gesell schedules; however, the Bayley scales are generally considered to be better constructed and accompanied by more evidence of reliability/precision and validity. The battery is composed of five scales: Cognitive, Language, Motor (based on child interaction), Social–Emotional, and Adaptive Behavior (based on parent questionnaires). Like the Gesell schedules, the Behavior rating scale relies on information provided by the child's caregiver. Norms for the Cognitive, Language, and Motor scales are based on 1,700 children representing ages from 16 days to 43 months and representative of the U.S. population in terms of race/ethnicity, geographic regions, and parental education level. The norms for the Social–Emotional scale were based on 456 children aged 5 to 42 months. The norms for the Adaptive Behavior scale were based on 1,350 children age birth to 5 years 11 months. Nancy Bayley designed the battery to assess developmental status rather than to predict subsequent ability levels.

Denver Developmental Screening Test

The Denver Developmental Screening Test (Frankenburg, Dodds, Fandal, Kazuk, & Cohrs, 1975) is another norm-referenced battery designed specifically for early identification of developmental or behavioral problems. The target audience for this battery is children from birth to 6 years of age. Unlike the Bayley scales, the Denver Developmental Screening Test requires no special training for the administrator and takes only a short interval of time—approximately 20 minutes—to administer. This test measures four developmental areas: personal–social development, fine motor development, language development, and gross motor development. The test contains 105 items that are administered according to the child's chronological age. The authors of the test report evidence of test–retest reliability, content based evidence of validity, and construct validity.

or severe. It can be a phase of bipolar disorder or a response to high levels of stress. It can be associated with psychotic symptoms and/or suicidal behavior. It can occur by itself or along with a wide range of other mental health and medical problems. Individuals struggling with depression are often prescribed antidepressants, and they are often treated with psychotherapy by clinicians in all kinds of outpatient settings.

Depression in an adult can be assessed informally by clinicians during a traditional clinical interview. The clinician might ask about sleep and appetite, mood, suicidal feelings, and other symptoms of a depressive disorder. Self-report tests are another approach to eliciting symptoms associated with depression and can also inform the clinician about the severity of symptoms. For example, the BDI-II is a very well researched self-report test that is scored by the clinician. Scores correspond to depression severity. The BDI-II is especially useful for screening large populations for depression and for monitoring the severity of depression during treatment (Joiner, Walker, Pettit, Perez, & Cukrowicz, 2005). Joiner et al. (2005) recommended a structured interview, such as the SCID, along with some other assessment tools, to establish a diagnosis of depression and assess some of the features that are important for treatment and client safety. Joiner et al. noted that using the SCID along with self-report tests would constitute evidence-based assessment for depression. However, clinicians may feel that administering these tests is too time-consuming and not necessary.

Many other psychological tests have scales or scores relevant to the diagnosis of depression. The MMPI-2 and the PAI both have depression scales, and the Rorschach psychodiagnostic technique has a number of depression indicators, including an index of scores that is associated with depression, the Rorschach Comprehensive System Depression Index (Mihura et al., 2013). Mihura et al. (2013) found that the Depression Index has moderate evidence for validity in assessing depression.

Evaluating depression in a cooperative, articulate adult is not very complicated. However, there are many instances in which evaluating depression is complicated. For example, a clinician might need to evaluate depression in an individual who has intellectual disabilities, or a young child, or an uncooperative adolescent. Clients such as these cannot or, sometimes, will not use language to talk about their feelings, thoughts, and experiences. There are also important cultural differences in the experience and expression of depression symptoms, and these need to be taken into account. For example, suppressing the expression of emotions is associated with poorer psychological functioning for European American but not Chinese college students (Soto, Perez, Kim, Lee, & Minnick, 2011). There are also age-related differences that challenge clinicians. Depression in an elderly individual might appear to be something else. Psychological tests can be helpful in making a diagnosis in these complex situations, but the clinician must ensure that the tests have appropriate normative data and are valid for assessing depression in the population in question.

Another problem that arises in the assessment of depression is the presence of **comorbid disorders**, that is, the presence of mental health problems in addition to depression. How is depression evaluated in a client who is alcohol or drug dependent, or in a client who has anorexia? These are challenging problems, and psychological tests can be part of the clinician's toolbox for solving them. For example, a clinician might administer the BDI-II along with a comprehensive self-report personality test, such as the MMPI-2, and a specific test that measures substance abuse problems and use test results from all three measures to help clarify the diagnosis, in addition to conducting a clinical interview and perhaps a review of records and conversation (with permission of the client) with a family member.

Clients with depression are at increased risk for suicide, and suicide risk needs to be assessed initially and, sometimes, repeatedly during treatment with depressed clients. The Columbia-Suicide Severity Rating Scale (Posner et al., 2009) is a recently developed semistructured interview that can serve both purposes, using different versions. It has early research support and has been made available without charge to clinicians and others who might be in a position to assess suicide risk. There are separate scales for children and adults and an accompanying risk assessment tool to aid clinicians in judging risk. Another test, the Suicide Probability Scale, is discussed in the chapter, "How Do We Gather Evidence of Validity Based on Test–Criterion Relationships?"

Alzheimer's Disease

Alzheimer's disease is a progressive illness that causes a deterioration in cognition and memory, or dementia, due to changes in the brain. Approximately 200,000 individuals are afflicted with early-onset Alzheimer's disease (before age 50), with 5.3 million affected individuals developing the illness after age 65 (Alzheimer's Association, 2018). Individuals with Alzheimer's disease suffer a gradual loss of memory, thinking, and speaking skills and often have behavioral and emotional symptoms such as anxiety, agitation, and depression. At this point, Alzheimer's disease cannot be definitively diagnosed until after a patient dies and then only through pathology studies of the brain. However, scientists are working hard to find ways of predicting and detecting Alzheimer's disease. For example, researchers are currently investigating whether biomarkers can be used to predict Alzheimer's disease 2 to 3 years before the onset of symptoms in healthy people (Abbott, 2014). In addition, recent research using functional magnetic resonance imaging data may someday allow clinicians to detect Alzheimer's disease even at the preclinical stage. Psychological tests, however, contribute to a functional assessment of dementia, and medical tests can rule out causes of dementia other than Alzheimer's disease, such as Parkinson's disease or a stroke. Psychological tests as well as other forms of psychological assessment are also useful in the diagnosis of depression, which can cause dementia like symptoms known as pseudodementia. It is essential to rule out depression in an individual who is showing signs of dementia, because depression is treatable and pseudodementia can be reversed.

The National Institute on Aging (n.d.) notes that early diagnosis of Alzheimer's disease is important so that patients and families can plan for the future and treatment can be initiated to preserve functioning for as long as possible. There is no treatment available, however, that reverses the underlying disease. Alzheimer's disease is expected to affect more people in coming years. Alzheimer's disease also has an impact on millions of caregivers.

Psychological tests of memory, language, attention, and problem solving, among other brain functions, can be useful in diagnosing dementia. There are many tests of these functions that have strong psychometric properties, but fewer have age appropriate normative data, an important consideration for choosing which tests to administer. Other challenges in conducting a psychological assessment of individuals who are suspected to have Alzheimer's disease include ensuring that patients have sufficient cognitive ability to give informed consent for the assessment, evaluating individuals who have medical problems and take medications (either or both of which can make the interpretation of test results difficult), and accurately determining patients' premorbid levels of functioning (the levels of functioning the patients were capable of before they became ill), an important factor in determining if there have been changes in functioning reflective of dementia. Psychological tests to assess depression can also be important in the assessment of dementia, but these too must have strong psychometric support and age-appropriate normative data. The BDI-II and the Geriatric Depression Scale are two tests that meet these criteria (Beck et al., 1996; Yesavage et al., 1982–1983).

More detail about the Mini-Mental State Examination can be found in **Test Spotlight 4.1** in Appendix A.

Two other psychological tests are specifically geared toward evaluating patients suspected of having dementia. The Dementia Rating Scale–2 (Mattis, 2001) measures cognitive functioning in individuals to age 105 and older and can be used repeatedly to measure changes in cognitive functioning over time. The Mini-Mental State Examination (Folstein, Folstein, & McHugh, 1975) is a brief screening measure of cognitive impairment and can be used repeatedly with patients who are ill or impaired to estimate the severity of cognitive impairment.

Another important issue for the clinician conducting an assessment of dementia is the need to provide feedback about test results with clinical skill and sensitivity, preferably to the patient and someone who is there for support (APA, 2010). The clinician must also be prepared to offer recommendations for assistance and intervention when test results are consistent with a diagnosis of dementia. The APA has developed and updated guidelines for the assessment of dementia in older adults addressing these issues and more.

EVIDENCE-BASED ASSESSMENT

As is evident in the case examples and the examination of psychological testing in autism spectrum disorders, depression, and Alzheimer's disease, psychological tests are rarely used in isolation. Multimethod assessment, or the use of test batteries, a group of tests that work together, is typical of most assessment situations. Adding tests always increases the cost and time to conduct an assessment, but does the test add value? Does adding a test offer more information for answering referral questions and making decisions about a client? In other words, does it have incremental validity? See the chapter, "How Do We Gather Evidence of Validity Based on Test–Criterion Relationships?" for an in-depth discussion of incremental validity when multiple tests are being used to predict a criterion.

Meyer et al. (2001), in a seminal article about the value of psychological assessment, noted that assessment tools serve different functions and advocated for multimethod assessment in order to measure "the full scope of human functioning" (p. 145). Other psychologists question the value of adding more tests, because there is little evidence that adding more tests, or adding any tests to other types of assessment approaches such as a clinical interview, improves clinical decision making. The challenge for resolving these issues is that the research needed to address these questions is difficult to conduct and very difficult to apply to an individual case (Hunsley & Meyer, 2003).

The question of incremental validity is one consideration of evidence-based assessment. Another important consideration is using tests that have strong psychometric properties, that is, tests that have documented reliability/precision and that have been demonstrated to be valid for the intended purpose of the assessment. There are many psychological tests available that meet these criteria to a greater or lesser extent, and there is no reason to use a test that does not meet these criteria if a test that meets these criteria is available. However, for some assessment needs, available tests may not have strong psychometric properties, perhaps because the research needed to demonstrate validity for a certain purpose has not yet been completed or may not be possible to conduct.

Evidence-based guidelines for assessment of mental disorders require, first of all, an evidence-based understanding of the nature of the disorder in question. What exactly is depression, or schizophrenia, or ADHD? Currently, these mental health conditions and others are defined by the diagnostic criteria that describe them in the *DSM-5*. The authors of the *DSM-5* concede that the "science of mental disorders continues to evolve" (American Psychiatric Association, 2013, p. 5). It is more advanced in some areas than in others. Finally, evidence-based guidelines for assessment have to take into account the advantages and disadvantages of a range of psychological tests. Some may be briefer or more convenient; others may have stronger psychometric properties.

A recent journal article with a review of evidence-based assessment of conduct disorder (CD) provides a good example of the issues involved in establishing an evidence base for the assessment of a mental disorder. Barry, Golmaryami, Rivera-Hudson, and Frick (2013) defined CD based on the *DSM*-IV and noted that the "behaviors that constitute CD are varied" and that "youth with CD can differ greatly on the course of the disorder and in the potential causal processes leading to the disorder" (p. 57). They also noted that revisions to the *DSM* have implications for evidence-based assessment of the disorder. (Diagnostic criteria are a kind of moving target, evolving with advances in the scientific understanding of the disorder.) Specifically, the authors pointed out that research indicates that the age of onset of CD has implications for what needs to be assessed. For example, it is important to assess for neuropsychological deficits for those individuals who have an earlier age of onset of CD and not important to assess for neuropsychological deficits in most instances when there is a later age of onset. Another issue that has relevance for assessment of CD is the presence of "callous-unemotional (CU)" traits. Youth with CU traits show a lack of empathy and guilt and respond to different kinds of treatment than other youth. Thus, as the authors stated, "evidence-based assessment of conduct problems requires combining knowledge of this research and causal theories on the etiology, development, and phenomenology of CD with the selection of assessment methods that have evidence supporting their reliability, validity, and utility" (Barry et al., 2013, p. 59). They concluded that a clinical interview for contextual information, behavior ratings from multiple informants, a narrow measure of CU traits using multiple informants, and direct assessment of the child would constitute evidence-based assessment of CD at this time.

THE PSYCHOLOGICAL TESTING REPORT AND CLIENT FEEDBACK

There are two final products of psychological testing in most clinical and counseling contexts—a meeting with the client to go over results and a written psychological evaluation report. Providing feedback to the client is an ethical obligation per the Standards for Educational and Psychological Testing (American Educational Research Association [AERA], APA, & National Council on Measurement in Education [NCME], 2014). Feedback can be very therapeutic and a powerful experience for both the client and the clinician. The purpose of the feedback session is to provide the client with information about test findings and, more important, conclusions about the findings and recommendations for treatment or intervention, assuming treatment is needed. The feedback session is a good opportunity to explain the nature of a client's problems to the client and often to his or her spouse or parent. For example, if a client is found to have a reading disability, the feedback session is an opportunity to discuss what that means and how to manage it.

A written report is prepared when the testing is completed in response to a referral, not when testing is done in a treatment context. The report is usually prepared for the person who made the referral, but it is often provided to the client as well. The report also might become part of a legal, educational, or medical record. The report needs to be prepared with a great deal of care, keeping in mind the needs of the audience for the report. It should be easy to read, answer referral questions, include recommendations, and be free of jargon.

Chapter Summary

Clinical and counseling settings are offices, hospitals, agencies, clinics, and other environments staffed by professionals with expertise in helping people with mental health problems or problems in everyday life. Psychologists and other mental health professionals administer psychological tests in clinical and counseling settings for a variety of reasons. They use tests to make diagnoses, plan treatment, monitor treatment progress, and assess treatment outcomes. They also use tests to answer questions posed by others about a client's problems and strengths, or posed by clients themselves. Tests are available in a variety of formats, including structured interviews, behavior rating scales, self-report personality tests, projective tests, cognitive

and memory tests, and specialized neuropsychological and forensic tests. The test used depends on a client's needs and on the preference of the clinical or counseling professional. Psychological tests can be useful when diagnosing autism spectrum disorders, depression, and Alzheimer's disease. Psychologists and other mental health professionals use tests in conjunction with information they gather in other ways, such as clinical interview, reviews of records, interviews with informants, and observing behavior.

Regardless of how information is gathered, the final product of psychological testing in most clinical and counseling contexts is a meeting with the client to go over results and a written psychological evaluation report.

Engaging in the Learning Process

Learning is the process of gaining knowledge and skills through schooling or studying. Although you can learn by reading the chapter material, attending class, and engaging in discussion with your instructor, more actively engaging in the learning process may help you better learn and retain chapter information. To help you actively engage in the learning process, we encourage you to access our new supplementary student workbook. The workbook contains critical thinking activities to help you understand and apply information, and help you make progress toward learning and retaining material. If you do not have a copy of the workbook, you can purchase a copy through sagepub.com.

Key Concepts

After completing your study of this chapter, you should be able to define each of the following terms. These terms are bolded in the text of this chapter and defined in the Glossary.

autism spectrum disorders

comorbid disorders

evidence-based practice

evidence-based treatment methods

obsessive compulsive disorder

projective drawings

semistructured interviews

structured clinical interviews

Critical Thinking Questions

The following are some critical thinking questions to support the learning objectives for this chapter.

Learning Objectives	Critical Thinking Questions
Explain the work of clinical and counseling psychologists and other mental health counselors.	• How is the work of clinical and counseling psychologists similar and different?
Describe how mental health practitioners use psychological tests to diagnose mental health problems, plan treatment programs, monitor client progress, and assess treatment outcomes.	• How is the diagnosis process mental health practitioners use similar to and different from the diagnosis process physicians' use? • What important decisions are made using the results of psychological tests administered in clinical and counseling settings? • How would you describe the pros and cons of mental health professionals using the SCID to make diagnoses based on the DSM?
Discuss how psychological tests are used in the diagnosis of autism spectrum disorders, depression, and Alzheimer's disease.	• How has psychological testing benefited individuals with symptoms of an Autism Spectrum Disorder, Depression, and Alzheimer's Disease?

(Continued)

(Continued)

Learning Objectives	Critical Thinking Questions
Define evidence-based assessment.	• What is the value of using evidence-based guidelines for assessment of mental health problems? • Why is not always a productive practice to add additional tests to a group of tests used to diagnose a psychological disorder? When might it be useful to do so?
Explain the two final products of psychological testing in clinical and counseling settings.	• If you were a mental health practitioner, what information would you discuss when conducting a feedback session with a client after administering one or more psychological assessments? • If you were the client of a mental health practitioner, what information would you like to know after taking one or more psychological tests?

HOW ARE TESTS
USED IN ORGANIZATIONAL
SETTINGS?

LEARNING OBJECTIVES

After completing your study of this chapter, you should be able to do the following:

- Understand the different types of tests that employers routinely use for pre-employment testing.

- Describe the characteristics of a performance test, and discuss two types of performance tests used by organizations.

- Describe the five-factor model of personality, and name two tests that are based on this model.

- Discuss two types of integrity tests, and describe the criticism these tests have received.

- Describe the three ways in which validity evidence can be generalized to new situations.

- Discuss performance appraisal instruments, give examples of three types of rating scales, and describe four types of rating errors.

"When I applied for a job, the company had two people interview me. The interviewers asked very similar questions about the same topics. Isn't one interview enough?"

"The company I interviewed with also asked me to complete a written test. What was that for?"

"Where I work, they do random drug tests. One time I tested positive because I took some cough syrup the night before. I really resent being treated like a criminal."

"It's performance appraisal time again. My future depends on these ratings, and I'm not convinced they really show what a good worker I am."

Business and government have a long history of using psychological tests for hiring, performance evaluation, and research. In this chapter, we focus on how psychological tests are used in organizations. We examine various types of tests that employers use for hiring and evaluating employees, such as interviews and tests of performance, personality, and integrity. We consider legal constraints on employment testing legislated by Congress and interpreted by the executive branch and the federal court system. Finally, we describe how organizations use psychological assessment to evaluate employee performance.

Today organizations use psychological tests in a variety of areas. For example, they use the results of tests to make hiring decisions and rating scales to evaluate employees' performance. Organizational surveys are a major source of information about employee attitudes, skills, and motivation. Marketing research involves surveying consumers' attitudes and assessing their behavior. In addition, individuals often use interest inventories to choose or change their career goals.

On the Web Box 14.1 provides information about PSI Talent Management, a full service assessment provider that offers organizations and private consultants access to a wide range of commercially available online tests as well as test development and test delivery services.

PRE-EMPLOYMENT TESTING

Psychological assessment provides the basis for hiring employees in most organizations. The most popular method of assessment is the employment interview. Organizations sometimes supplement interviewing with one or more psychological tests that measure performance, skills, abilities, or personality characteristics. Drug and integrity testing—not polygraphs (lie detectors)—have also become acceptable methods for screening out candidates who may have undesirable behaviors or attitudes.

In the News Box 14.1 describes four myths that business executives cite as their reasons for not using pre-employment testing.

The Employment Interview

The employment interview is the most popular method of pre-employment assessment used by organizations. Types of interviews vary from the **traditional interview**, in which the interviewer pursues different areas of inquiry with each job candidate, to highly **structured interviews**, which are standardized, with the same questions asked of each job candidate. We focus on the ends of this continuum, keeping in mind that employers often use interviews that have varying amounts of flexibility and structure.

Traditional Interview

Few managers are willing to risk hiring an employee they have not met. The traditional, unstructured interview serves the "getting to know you" function; however, research shows that it falls far short of being a reliable or valid predictor of job performance. The unstructured interview's shortcomings were apparent in 1915 to Scott, who reported disagreement among managers interviewing potential salesmen (Cascio, 1991). Current research provides evidence that traditional, unstructured interviews can have much lower validity than the structured interviews that we discuss in the next section. For instance, a meta-analysis (i.e., a synthesis of

ON THE WEB BOX 14.1
MANY COMMERCIAL TESTS AVAILABLE ONLINE TO ORGANIZATIONS FROM PSI TALENT MANAGEMENT
https://www.psionline.com

PSI Talent Management is a full service testing/consulting company that provides a wide variety of test development, test delivery, and organizational consulting services. One of the testing services that it provides enables clients to purchase and administer online tests from many different publishers. Organizations and consultants can purchase the tests directly from PSI instead of having to contact each publisher individually.

PSI provides a uniform testing platform for all the tests that it delivers so that the test taker has a consistent testing experience even when taking tests from multiple publishers. Organizations that create their own tests can also use the well-known PAN test delivery platform to deliver their tests along with any commercially published tests they may also use.

PSI provides access to a wide range of different types of tests such as clinical assessment tools, personality assessment, pre-employment screening, and mechanical and technical skills tests. You can browse its catalog and read basic descriptions of the tests that it offers at https://www.psionline.com/assessments. Sample reports and technical manuals for the tests are also available for download.

To gain access to the tests, users must fill out a form that describes their academic and professional qualifications. Only users who in the test publisher's opinion have the necessary education, training, and experience to properly use and interpret tests are granted access. This is the same type of process that individual test publishers use to qualify prospective purchasers.

While the service PSI provides can be very convenient, there may be some downsides to providing easy access to such a wide range of tests. What do you think those downsides might be?

---

research results from different yet similar studies) of unstructured interviews used to predict supervisory ratings for entry-level jobs yielded a validity coefficient of only .20 (Huffcutt & Arthur, 1994). By comparison, the same study demonstrated that strongly structured interviews in which each candidate was asked the same questions and a formal scoring system was used had a validity coefficient of .57. This meta-analysis combined the data from more than 32,000 subjects across 425 different studies of interview validity.

Structured Interview

Many shortcomings of the traditional interview, including its low reliability/precision and validity, can be overcome by structuring the interview and the interviewing procedure. In a fully structured interview, the interviewer has a preplanned interview and a quantitative scoring scheme. Each candidate receives the same questions in the same order. The interviewer then rates the candidate's answers on an anchored rating scale. Interviewers undergo training on question delivery, note taking, and rating. Such training standardizes the treatment candidates receive as well as the ratings and resulting interview scores. Such standardization increases interrater reliability, internal consistency, and validity.

Structured **behavioral interviews**, which focus on past behaviors rather than attitudes or opinions, also provide better predictions of job performance. Questions that ask candidates to provide

© Sharon Dominick/iStockphoto

IN THE NEWS BOX 14.1
FOUR MYTHS ABOUT PRE-EMPLOYMENT TESTING

Unfortunately, some organizations, both large and small, avoid using reliable and valid tests for hiring. Here are four myths they often cite as their reasons for relying on unstructured interviews and tests that have not been validated.

Myth 1: The Organization Will Be Sued

Organizations are always at risk for being sued; however, using reliable and valid selection tools can increase productivity and retention. In the event that a suit is brought against an employer, the first line of defense is to demonstrate that the test was a valid predictor of job performance and consistent with business necessity. There are also many types of employment tests that research has shown do not discriminate against people who belong to a protected class (such as race, gender, and age).

Myth 2: Pre-Employment Tests Cost Too Much

Published employment tests with documentation of reliability and validity can be expensive to purchase and administer. Purchase costs may range from $25 to $200 per individual. However, most researchers and human resources professionals agree that the cost of a bad hiring decision is much greater. Hiring an unsuitable person results in lower productivity, lost opportunities, an unfilled position, coaching or training costs, and possibly the cost of hiring a replacement. Every dollar an employer invests in testing has a substantial return on investment in reduced absenteeism, improved productivity, lower turnover, safer working environments, reduced insurance premiums, and decreased employer liability.

Myth 3: Pre-Employment Testing Is Too Time-Consuming

Some tests, such as structured interviews, do indeed take time from several people in the organization as well as the time of the applicant. However, new tests and testing formats are now available that can be administered efficiently and accurately and can be scored in as little as 30 minutes. Some are administered using a computer, and applicants can even take some tests prior to applying for a job.

Testing systems that provide interpretive reports that can be shared with supervisors and others in the organization save time in the decision-making process. Employers might find that a reliable and valid testing system actually expedites the hiring process.

Of course, the more important the job, the more important it is to choose the right candidate. For executive positions, some organizations use a 1- or 2-day assessment center process. Given the costs of making bad hiring decisions, these organizations still find this process beneficial and time saving.

Myth 4: Pre-Employment Testing Does Not Work

Despite some 100 years of scientific research on selection tests, some executives may still find the process of testing to be counterintuitive. These executives often believe that they can spot a good or unsuitable job candidate in a brief interview. Fortunately, both the research literature and professional publications report on the benefits of using a reliable and valid testing system for screening job applicants. In addition, most test publishers and human resources consultants will conduct a validity study within the organization that can provide quantitative evidence that the test works and that the benefits of using the test outweigh the costs.

Source: This article was first published on IRMI.com and is reproduced with permission. Copyright 2015, International Risk Management Institute, Inc.

specific accounts of the behaviors they have used in the past (e.g., planning a project, accomplishing a goal) offer information that is more relevant for interviewers to rate. Some behavioral interviews ask candidates to describe past performance, and others ask candidates to describe how they would go about doing something in the organization, such as developing a marketing plan or training course. Behavioral interviews usually require the interviewer to rate the quality of the interviewee's answer using some type of behaviorally anchored rating scale.

Table 14.1 provides a sample of a structured behavioral interview question intended to assess an applicant's ability to create innovative solutions to business challenges, probing questions that the interviewer may choose to ask to elicit more information, and behavioral standards that provide benchmarks for rating each interviewee's answers.

Evidence of validity based on content for the structured interview is established by developing questions using competency modeling (which is covered in "How Do We Gather Evidence of Validity Based on the Content of a Test?"), creating a detailed job description, or conducting a formal job analysis. In Greater Depth Box 14.1 describes the process of job analysis in more detail.

Using a content-based strategy, the interview is valid to the extent that it covers important job functions and duties without including information about individual characteristics that are unrelated to job performance. As we discuss later in this chapter, evidence that the interview is job related is especially important in the event that an employer is sued because of claims that the selection system disadvantaged one group of applicants over another. As we discussed earlier in the text, the validity of constructs measured by a behavioral interview can be investigated using both exploratory and confirmatory factor analysis.

Research suggests that the interview will continue as a primary method of assessing job candidates. Unfortunately, many companies continue to use traditional interviews instead of structured interviews. Di Milia (2004) reported that human resources professionals in Australia strongly support using structured interviews conducted by two or three interviewers, although there is research evidence to suggest that individual interviews may be more valid than group interviews (McDaniel, Whetzel, Schmidt, & Maurer, 1994).

TABLE 14.1 ■ Sample Question From a Behavioral Interview

Question: One of the most common management tasks is creating innovative solutions to business problems. Please tell me about a time when you were responsible for developing an innovative solution to a specific business problem.

Probing Questions	Behavioral Standards
• In what way was the solution you developed innovative?	**Poor Response:** Suggests standard conventional solutions and does not pursue innovative opportunities **Good Response:** Suggests solutions that are non-obvious, but also practical and achievable
• What alternative approaches did you consider, if any?	**Poor Response:** Did not consider alternative approaches and assumed the first approach suggested would be useable **Good Response:** Considered multiple alternative approaches and could identify the pros and cons of each one
• What were the relative benefits and risks of your approach compared with those of the other approaches?	**Poor Response:** Did not consider risks as well as benefits to the solutions proposed **Good Response:** Could articulate the risks and benefits of solutions proposed and could order them in terms of amount of risk and/or benefit that might be realized

IN GREATER DEPTH BOX 14.1
JOB ANALYSIS

"What do you do?" is a common question asked at parties or social gatherings. For organizations, it is an important question that has many implications for managing people. Even if you know a person well, you may have only a general idea of what his or her job requires. Organizations require specific information about the activities of employees so as to make important decisions about hiring, training, and evaluating employees.

Job analysis is a systematic assessment method for answering the question "What do you do?" in organizations. There are a number of ways to conduct job analysis, all of which provide a systematic and detailed procedure for documenting the activities of the job. A typical job analysis provides information on the following job factors:

- *Functions:* A group of activities that allow the job incumbent to accomplish one of the primary objectives of the job. Examples include analyzing financial data, coordinating interdepartmental communications, and supervising employees.

- *Tasks:* Actions taken by the job incumbent that accomplish a job function. Examples include estimating sales revenue to prepare a budget and monitoring customer service representatives to ensure high standards of courtesy.

- *Knowledge:* A body of related information that the worker needs to know to perform job tasks. Examples include knowledge of company policies regarding budget procedures and knowledge of the company's products and services.

- *Skills:* A group of observable and measurable behaviors acquired through training that the worker needs to perform a variety of job tasks. Examples include skill in planning and prioritizing work activities and skill in listening to others.

- *Abilities:* A physical or mental competency based on innate characteristics (generally not trained) that the worker needs to perform job tasks. Examples include the ability to stand for extended periods and the ability to lift up to 50 pounds.

- *Other characteristics:* Interests or personality traits that the worker needs to perform in or cope with the job environment. Examples include the willingness to work night shifts, conscientiousness, and honesty.

Most job analysis methods involve interviewing incumbents (persons currently in the job) and their supervisors and verifying that information by administering a job analysis questionnaire. The questionnaire asks incumbents and supervisors to rate job tasks on their importance and how often they are performed. Tasks that are identified as important and frequently performed become *critical tasks*. The critical tasks are then analyzed to determine the knowledge, skills, abilities, and other characteristics that the job incumbent needs to be successful in performing them.

Job analysis is an important prerequisite to employment testing because psychologists and the court system recognize it as a method for providing evidence of validity based on content. For example, a job analysis for "real estate salesperson" may specify a need for knowledge of local zoning laws, interpersonal skills, an ability to climb several flights of stairs, and a willingness to work on Sundays. Therefore, when assessing job applicants for real estate salesperson, the organization should choose assessment methods that yield information on those factors. Other factors, such as a college degree, might seem appealing, but unless they are specified in the job analysis, they would not be appropriate job requirements.

Source: Adapted from McIntire, Bucklan, and Scott (1995).

Interviews do serve useful purposes other than prediction of job performance. For instance, interviewers can provide candidates with useful information regarding the organization and can set expectations about what the job will entail. When candidates have realistic expectations, they are likely to remain on the job longer than will candidates who did not receive legitimate information about the job (Jones & Youngblood, 1993; Meglino, DeNisi, Youngblood, & Williams, 1988). In addition, the interview provides an opportunity to begin building positive relationships that will help new employees adjust and will prevent negative perceptions among those who are not selected for hire.

Performance Tests

This category of tests includes a broad range of assessments that require the test taker to perform one or more job tasks. For instance, **assessment centers** are large-scale simulations of the job that require candidates to solve typical job problems by role-playing or by demonstrating proficiency at job functions such as making presentations and fulfilling administrative duties. (See In Greater Depth Box 14.2 for more information about the assessment center method.) A **work sample** is a smaller scale assessment in which candidates complete a job-related task such as building a sawhorse or designing a doghouse. A driving test is a performance test that organizations often use to assess people applying for jobs as heavy equipment operators or bus drivers.

Psychologists often categorize performance tests as either high or low fidelity. **High-fidelity tests** replicate job settings as realistically as possible. In a high-fidelity assessment, test takers use the same equipment that is used on the job and complete actual job tasks. For instance, pilots are often trained and assessed on sophisticated flight simulators that not only simulate flight but also re-create typical emergencies. Such high-fidelity tests allow job candidates to perform in realistic situations; however, they remove the risk for unsafe or poor performance. In other words, if the job applicant does not fly the plane well, the resulting crash is simulated, not real! Assessment centers are also generally considered to be high-fidelity tests.

Low-fidelity tests, on the other hand, simulate the task using a written, verbal, or visual description. The test taker may respond by answering an open-ended or multiple-choice question. Some interview questions serve as low-fidelity performance tests. For example, behavioral interview questions ask respondents to describe a situation and give detailed information about how they performed in that situation.

In the News Box 14.2 contains a job posting for the position of firefighter in central Florida. The posting describes the kinds of tests that the applicants will be required to take. Based on the description, do you think that the required physical agility test would be a work sample? Would you classify it as a high-fidelity simulation? Why or why not?

Situational Judgment Tests

Another type of low-fidelity simulation that has become increasingly popular for use in personnel selection over the past 20 years is a **situational judgment test** (Whetzel & McDaniel, 2009). This type of test presents job candidates with written or video-based scenarios that pose work-related dilemmas along with four or five possible courses of action that the candidates might take in response. The task is to identify the most effective action in each situation. Some tests ask the test taker to identify both the most and the least effective actions. There are a number of different methods that can be used to score these types of tests. One common scoring procedure is to develop an answer key based on the opinions of a group of subject matter experts regarding how effective each available choice is. The closer the correspondence between the test takers' responses and the subject matter experts' opinions, the higher the score. For Your Information Box 14.1 contains two examples of situational judgment test questions. One of the questions might be used in a situational judgment test for leadership, while the other might be used in a situational judgment test for sales.

IN GREATER DEPTH BOX 14.2
THE ASSESSMENT CENTER METHOD

An assessment center is a method—not a place—that organizations use for assessing the extent to which individuals demonstrate skills critical to success in a job. Depending on the job, these skills might include leadership, problem solving, teamwork, decision making, planning, and organizing. Organizations use the results of assessment centers to make decisions regarding hiring, promoting, and training individuals.

A typical assessment center contains several job simulations that engage the test taker in role-play activities. Some common simulations, known as exercises, include the following:

- The in-basket exercise, in which the test taker is provided with several days' worth of hypothetical incoming mail, phone messages, and memos likely to be received on the job. Directions instruct the test taker to take appropriate action on each memo and piece of mail.

- Role-play, in which the test taker interacts with one or more persons (trained assessment center role-players) to solve problems encountered on the job. The test taker is typically provided some background information prior to the role-play. A typical theme might be handling a difficult employee or customer.

- Leaderless discussion group, in which the test taker is placed in a small group with the goal of discussing or solving a job-related issue.

In all of these exercises, trained assessors observe and document test takers' behaviors during the simulations and make judgments regarding the test takers' demonstration of expertise on well-defined dimensions of job performance.

Although psychologists had been combining assessment methods for a number of years, a selection program used by the U.S. Office of Strategic Services (OSS) during World War II is credited with marking the beginning of the assessment center movement (Smither, 1994). The OSS, a forerunner to the Central Intelligence Agency, developed a 3-day psychological screening program for potential agents that was used to predict how an individual would perform (and succeed) as a spy. What was different and remarkable about this screening program was that candidates for the job of spy were observed and evaluated on a number of behavioral simulations.

One role-play required the candidate to devise a cover story in 12 minutes that would explain why he was carrying secret government files. Three examiners then questioned the candidate relentlessly in a manner that became progressively more hostile and abusive. After the questioning ended, all candidates were told they had failed the exercise and then were directed to another office, where a friendly colleague encouraged them to discuss the exercise. When the candidates relaxed and openly discussed their interrogations, they found that they had made a fateful misjudgment: They had just confided important information—not to a friend but rather to another examiner (Smither, 1994).

After World War II, large industrial organizations began to use the assessment center method to hire managers. Gatewood and Feild (1997) cited the Management Progress Study of AT&T, begun in 1956, as the first industrial application of the method. Other early users included Michigan Bell, Sears Roebuck, and General Electric. Such programs provided information that was used for hiring and promotion decisions based on managers' performance and personality.

During the next two decades, assessment centers continued to achieve growing acceptance. One expert (S. Cohen, 1978) estimated that during the early 1970s, the number of organizations using assessment centers had grown from 100 to 1,000. Assessment centers also took on importance in the public sector as state and local governments discovered that this method was fair and accurate for hiring police officers and firefighters.

Today, assessment centers are still utilized for hiring, developing, and promoting employees. Many Fortune 500 and smaller emerging companies use assessment centers, primarily for management jobs, although a number of companies discontinued or streamlined their programs as part of the austerity movement of the 1980s. A major barrier to the use of assessment centers during the 1990s was the labor cost. Assessment centers require a number of professionally trained assessors and role-players. Because untrained assessors are not likely to provide accurate judgments or ratings, assessors must be professionally trained on observing, documenting, and rating behaviors.

Most assessment centers rely on a strategy of developing evidence of validity based on content. The *Uniform Guidelines on Employee Selection Procedures* (1978) require organizations to link tests that are used for selection with a thorough job analysis to provide evidence of the test's validity based on its content.

Research suggests that assessment centers provide one of the best predictors of job performance. A meta-analysis of validation studies estimates the criterion-related validity for assessment centers to be .53 for job potential and .36 for job performance (Gaugler, Rosenthal, Thornton, & Bentson, 1987).

A related advantage for the assessment center method is its relative lack of sex and race bias.

The results of a validation study (Knowles & Bean, 1981) for an assessment center that the City of St. Louis used to select captains in its fire department are typical. This examination contained a written test and an assessment center. On the written test, the average score for Blacks was more than 8 points lower (statistically different at $p < .05$) than the average score for Whites; however, on the assessment center, the average score for Blacks was less than 1 point different from that of Whites (not statistically different). This study suggests that assessment centers produced lower instances of race bias, a finding that was confirmed in later studies. Likewise, assessment center scores do not show differences in the average ratings for men and women.

It is important to recognize that a situational judgment test is a measurement method, not a construct. Although the name "situational judgment" seems to imply that we are measuring some type of capacity to make sound judgments in work-related situations, the actual constructs being measured in any situational judgment test will depend on what the questions have been designed to measure. You probably can see that the two questions presented in For Your Information Box 14.1 are measuring different constructs, one related to leadership and the other related to sales. As a result, knowing whether a person responded correctly on one of the questions would not provide you with much information regarding whether he or she would be likely to answer the other question correctly. This is because while both questions are using the same method (a situational judgment test), they are measuring different constructs (leadership vs. sales). Interestingly, both questions might appear on the same test if the test were a situational judgment test of sales leadership.

Situational judgment tests are often designed to measure multiple constructs (sometimes even within a single question). Because of this, internal consistency reliability/precision estimates such as coefficient alpha are typically much lower than those that are found on other types of tests. Therefore, for situational judgment tests, it is more appropriate to use test–retest reliability coefficients.

You might imagine that performance on low-fidelity tests would provide less valid and useful information than performance on high-fidelity tests. Recent research indicates that this may not always be the case. Lievens and Patterson (2011) conducted a study to examine the validity of a knowledge test, a low-fidelity simulation (a situational judgment test), and a high-fidelity simulation (an assessment center) that were used as part of a selection system for physicians in the United Kingdom. The physicians were competing for entry into a specialty training program to become general practitioners. The criterion measures used for the study were the performance ratings made by the physicians' supervisors on six different dimensions of professional practice during the training program (which lasted 3 years).

The researchers were interested in evaluating the validity of each of the three measures of job performance as well as whether any of the tests had incremental validity over the others for predicting performance. In other words, if we evaluated the amount of variance the assessment center accounted for in job performance, would adding a situational judgment test to

IN THE NEWS BOX 14.2
AD TO SOLICIT APPLICANTS FOR JOB OF FIREFIGHTER

Employment Testing at Lake Tech Fire Academy, 1565 Lane Park Cut Off, Tavares, FL 32778

For projected job openings in Mt. Dora, Tavares, Mascotte, The Villages, and Clermont Fire Departments for 2012

Requirements: FF2/EMT/PM State of Florida certification and a valid Florida Drivers License

Test Overview: The test comprises two parts, a written test and physical agility test (PAT). The 100-question written test consists of 50 firefighter questions in reference to the IFSTA Essentials of Firefighting and Fire Department Operations 5th edition and 50 EMT questions in reference to Emergency Pre Hospital Emergency Care 9th edition. The written test is limited to the first 200 paid applicants, and the top 50 scoring applicants will qualify to take the PAT. The PAT is timed, and you will be ranked according to the time it takes you to complete the test as well as your written score. The PAT is conducted in full bunker gear, breathing air, and consists of

© Stockbyte/Thinkstock

1. Hammer slide

2. Carrying a high-rise pack (100 ft. of 1¾) to the 5th floor of the tower and down

3. Hoist a roll of 2½ inch hose to the 5th floor of the tower on a rope

4. Drag a 185 lb. rescue dummy 120 ft.

5. Pull a charged, 1¾ inch hose line 75 ft.

Lake Tech will provide Scott SCBAs, if needed. There will also be a limited number of bunker coats and pants available. Lake Tech encourages you bring your own NFPA approved bunker gear. Applicants will have to provide their own gloves, hood, and boots.

Scores will be given to the participating departments for consideration when hiring new firefighters. The test scores will be good for one year.

Testing Fees/Dates:

- Written test $25, deadline for payment and registration October 7, 2011. Test date October 12, 2011, at 6:00 pm.

- PAT $75, deadline for payment and registration October 19, 2011. Test dates October 22 and 23 starting at 8:00 am. You will be assigned a specific time slot when you register for the PAT.

The employment ad above shows the selection process for the job of firefighter in central Florida. Persons who apply for this job will be informed ahead of time of the processes and requirements related to the job. Not only are a State of Florida certification and valid Florida driver's license required, but applicants must also bring specialized equipment for the work-sample part of the test, the PAT. In addition, applicants are required to pay for taking the tests.

The advertisement contains acronyms familiar to those who are interested in firefighting. How many of the acronyms do you understand? Might the familiarity with the acronyms be a predictor of who will be the best candidates for the job?

As you can see, firefighting is a career. Those who aspire to this career will be challenged intellectually as well as physically. Those who aspire to be industrial and organizational psychologists may well find themselves developing training and testing instruments for this essential and respected occupation.

Source: Printed with permission from the Lake Tech Fire Academy.

FOR YOUR INFORMATION BOX 14.1
EXAMPLES OF SITUATIONAL JUDGMENT TEST QUESTIONS

Here are examples of two different situational judgment test questions. The first might be used in a test for supervisory judgment, and the second might be used for sales.

1. Joan has been working for your company for 3 years. In the past, she has always been a reliable employee who has rarely been late to work. Over the past 4 weeks, you have noticed that she has been 15 minutes late to work on two occasions without an explanation. Other employees on your team have noticed it as well. Today, you noticed that she was late to work again, this time by 5 minutes. Which of the following actions would be most effective to take?

   a. Do nothing. Joan has been a reliable employee for several years, and you do not want to damage her motivation.

   b. Call her into your office immediately to ask for an explanation for why she was late today, but do not bring up the fact that she was late a number of other times.

   c. Walk past her desk and give her a knowing smile to indicate to her by your body language that you are aware that she was late again so that you don't have to run the risk of talking to her about something that might be a personal problem.

   d. Make note of the number of times that she has been late so you can bring it up at her next performance review as the performance issue is really too small to discuss now.

2. A customer has called you to let you know that a competitor is offering a promotional rebate for a top-selling product or service that you also sell. You have the option of offering a comparable program, but it will impact both your profit and compensation. Which of the following actions would be most effective to take?

   a. Offer your rebate program only to the customer who gave you the information regarding the competitor's program.

   b. Offer a matching rebate program plus additional incentives to all customers who currently buy this product to ensure that you do not lose their business.

   c. Create an email announcement to efficiently communicate your rebate program to all of your customers whether or not they currently buy the product.

   d. Call all of your customers that currently buy this product to offer them your rebate program.

Source: Wilson Learning Corporation.

the mix enable us to make more accurate predictions over and above that of the assessment center alone? Likewise, if we used just the situational judgment test to predict performance, would adding the assessment center enable us to make a more accurate prediction of job performance over and above that of the situational judgment test alone?

The results were very interesting. After correcting for range restriction (necessary because only the highest scoring candidates were admitted to the training program), all of the tests were found to be valid predictors of job performance. The knowledge test's validity coefficient for predicting overall job performance was .54, the assessment center's was .50, and the situational judgment test's was highest of all at .56! The tests for incremental validity showed that the situational judgment test predicted a statistically significant amount of additional variance (5.9%) in job performance over the knowledge test alone. But one of the most interesting results was found when looking only at the incremental validity of the assessment center over and above the combination of the knowledge and situational judgment tests. The knowledge and situational judgment tests together accounted for a total of 35.3% of the variance in job performance. When the assessment center was added, a total of 37.4% of the variance in job performance was accounted for. This means that the addition of the assessment center accounted for only an additional 2.1% of variance in job performance. This highlights an important question one needs to ask when developing any selection system: At what point does the expense of adding additional tests to a selection system, especially expensive-to-develop tests like assessment centers, exceed the practical value that will be provided by adding them? This is not always an easy question to answer.

So you can see that it is not always true that a low-fidelity simulation will have less predictive power than a high-fidelity simulation. As we have observed, this has important practical implications for the development of a selection system. However, one thing to keep in mind is that there are constructs important for job performance that may not be easily measurable via low-fidelity simulations. For instance, verbal and nonverbal communication skills or composure under pressure would be difficult to measure using a situational judgment test. So it is always important to ensure that the selection tools you design are capable of measuring all the constructs that are important for job performance. Even though you may be explaining only a small amount of additional variance in job performance by adding another test, if you are able to measure a different construct important for job success that none of your other tests are measuring, it may be worth the cost.

Personality Inventories

Personality inventories measure enduring constructs usually referred to as **personality traits**. Traits such as conscientiousness, extraversion, and agreeableness are seen by personality theorists as constructs that predispose persons to behave in certain ways. Personality theorists also suggest that the strength of various traits varies from person to person. Therefore, we might expect a person who has a high degree of extraversion to be more outgoing and energetic in a social situation than a person with a low degree of extraversion.

More detail about the 16PF can be found in **Test Spotlight 14.1** in Appendix A.

Cattell began conducting studies on personality assessment during the 1940s that culminated in 1949 with the publication of the 16 Personality Factor Questionnaire (16PF). Cattell's test, which stimulated the development of a number of tests and is itself in its fifth edition, defines the adult personality in terms of 16 normal personality factors. Researchers have found relationships between some factors on the 16PF and absenteeism and turnover. The 16PF has also been used to predict tenure, safety, and job performance (Krug & Johns, 1990).

More detail about the HPI can be found in **Test Spotlight 14.2** in Appendix A, including a link to a sample report that might be used when the HPI is used for employee selection.

The psychological literature contains numerous personality theories and as many or more personality tests. One widely accepted personality theory is the **five-factor model**, which proposes that there are five central personality dimensions: extroversion (also called surgency), emotional stability (also called neuroticism), agreeableness, conscientiousness, and openness to experience. For Your Information Box 14.2 provides a brief description of this theory and its five core dimensions.

The Hogan Personality Inventory (HPI; R. Hogan & Hogan, 1992) is partially derived from the five-factor model and is widely used for organizational testing and decision making.

FOR YOUR INFORMATION BOX 14.2
THE FIVE-FACTOR THEORY OF PERSONALITY

There is a long history of researchers attempting to identify the number of traits that account for the individual differences we routinely observe in people. In 1884, Francis Galton used a dictionary to attempt to identify all the English language terms that were used to describe human personality traits. In 1936, Allport and Odbert refined the list to include 4,500 descriptive terms. Raymond Cattel (1943) started with these traits and used the statistical technique of factor analysis to see if the relationships between these terms could be explained by a smaller number of descriptive terms or factors. He concluded that there were 35 complex, bipolar variables that these 4,500 traits could be reduced to. However, subsequent research was unable to replicate the complex structure that Cattel found. In 1961, two researchers working for the U.S. Air Force, Tupes and Christal (1961), reanalyzed Cattel's along with some other researcher's data and determined that it only took five factors to adequately account for the relationships among all Cattel's variables. They named the five factors: surgency, agreeableness, dependability, emotional stability, and culture. According to Digman (1990),

Tupes and Christal's work was reported in a little known Air Force technical report and remained unknown to most personality researchers of that time. However, another researcher, Warren Norman (1963) new of the research and was able to replicate the five-factor structure.

Robert McCrae and Paul Costa (1997) later made significant contributions to the five-factor theory by demonstrating a variety of applications and developing three personality inventories—the original NEO Personality Inventory (NEO PI; discussed in our first chapter), the current NEO PI-3, and the shorter NEO Five Factor Inventory—that assess personality using the five-factor model. McCrae and Costa named their factors:

- Neuroticism
- Extraversion
- Openness
- Agreeableness
- Conscientiousness

In the past, personnel psychologists discouraged using personality tests as employment tests because research seemed to show the relationship between personality and job performance to be minimal at best, and nonexistent in many cases. For instance, Hunter and Hunter's (1984) meta-analysis suggests that personality tests are among the poorest predictors of job performance. Recently, however, personnel psychologists have begun to look more favorably on personality tests that reflect the five-factor model (Gatewood & Feild, 1997; Heneman, Heneman, & Judge, 1997). One frequently cited meta-analysis, by Barrick and Mount (1991), suggests that *conscientiousness* serves as a valid predictor of job performance for all occupational groups studied using three types of criteria. *Extraversion* and *emotional stability* appear to be valid predictors of job performance for some, but not all, occupations. Gatewood and Feild (1997) posited that "specific personality dimensions appear to be related to specific jobs and criteria" (p. 601).

More recent reviews have suggested that personality measures can be quite valuable in organizational decision making. Ones, Dilchert, Viswesvaran, and Judge (2007) stated that the "Big Five personality variables as a set predict important organizational behaviors (e.g., job performance, leadership and even work attitudes and motivation)" (p. 1010). They reported moderate to strong correlations ranging from .20 to .50.

There are other tests of normal personality that have been used in organizational settings. One of the oldest is the California Psychological Inventory (CPI). Gaugh, the original developer of the CPI, studied with one of the developers of the Minnesota Multiphasic Personality

More detail about the NEO PI-3 can be found in **Test Spotlight 1.3** in Appendix A

Inventory (MMPI) at the University of Minnesota. The most current version, CPI 434, contains 434 questions that measure 18 dimensions of personality across four broad domains: social expertise and interpersonal style, maturity, normative orientation and values, achievement orientation, and personal interest styles. There are also 13 additional scales designed to measure more applied dimensions, such as managerial potential and tough-mindedness. In 2002, a shortened version of the test, the CPI 260, was developed specifically for human resources applications in organizations.

More detail about the CPI can be found in **Test Spotlight 14.3** in Appendix A.

One area of interesting ongoing research in the area of using personality tests for employee selection is the degree to which the results of the tests can be influenced when the test taker does not respond in an honest fashion, generically referred to as "faking." Faking occurs when people try to respond to the test questions in a way that presents themselves in the most positive fashion. Presenting oneself in the most positive fashion is called socially desirable responding (Edwards, 1957). When this behavior is intentional, it is also called impression management (Paulhaus, 1984). If job candidates can fake the results of a selection test, the validity of the results for predicting job performance might be compromised. There is disagreement in the literature regarding the degree to which faking on personality tests actually reduces the correlation (validity coefficients) between the test and a criterion measure. For instance, Holden (2007) instructed students to attempt to distort their scores on a test of extraversion by responding in a way would that result in the highest extraversion score regardless of how much they felt the questions actually described their personality. This was called "faking good." Another group of students was instructed to respond as honestly as possible to the test questions. The personality test scores obtained in each condition were then correlated with the roommates' ratings of the student's extraversion (the criterion). The correlation of the scores between the group instructed to respond honestly with their roommates' ratings was .54. The correlation of the scores between the group instructed to fake good with their roommates' ratings was .11. So in this study, faking reduced the relationship between the test and the criterion.

A different outcome was reported by Ones, Viswesvaran, and Reiss (1996) on the effect that socially desirable responding has on the relationship between the Big Five dimensions of personality and overall job performance. Through a large-scale meta-analysis, they found that the correlation between the Big Five personality dimensions and job performance was not reduced even when there was evidence of socially desirable responding or faking.

In an effort to shed some light on these (and other) contradictory research findings, Paunonen and LeBel (2012) conducted a statistical simulation to investigate the effect that socially desirable responding might have on the relationship between personality test scores and a criterion. They created a data set that contained simulated scores on a personality test along with simulated scores on a criterion. The data sets were constructed in such a fashion that the personality test scores and the criterion scores were correlated with one another at approximately .2, .4, and .6 to simulate different levels of validity when no social desirable responding was present. The researchers then simulated the impact of socially desirable responding by adding points to each score in the data set to represent the effect that socially desirable responding would have. The method they used to determine how many points to add to each person's simulated score was based on the idea that the higher a person's "true score" on a trait, the less motivated he or she would be to respond in an untruthful (more socially desirable) fashion. On the other hand, people who have low true scores on a trait that may be associated with a desired outcome (such as being hired for a job) would have more incentive to distort their responses. So the researchers added more points to the lower simulated personality test scores than they did to the higher ones to model this assumption. Once these modifications to the simulated data were made, the personality test scores were again correlated with the criteria to evaluate the impact that social desirability bias made to the original validity coefficients.

The results were that adding social desirability bias to the simulated test scores only made a minor difference in the resulting validity coefficients. For instance, when the true correlation between the test scores and the criterion was .40, adding a moderate amount of socially desirability bias only reduced the correlation to .397. Even adding a large amount of social desirability bias to the same test score data only reduced the correlation to .345. The authors concluded that their study was consistent with other studies showing that socially desirable responding (faking good) on personality tests has only a minor effect on empirical validity coefficients. However, the definitive answer to why some studies find that faking on personality tests does affect the validity coefficient while others don't is still to be determined.

Finally, J. Hogan, Barrett, and Hogan (2007) conducted a study on faking on a personality test actually used to make employment decisions. They collected data on 5,266 people who had reapplied for jobs in the transportation industry for which they had previously been rejected. The applicants had taken the HPI when they first applied (but were rejected) for the jobs and then again when they reapplied for the jobs a minimum of 6 months later. The assumption was that applicants who were rejected for a job based in part on the personality test that they took would have a strong motivation to change (fake) their responses when they took the test the second time. However, the results were that only 5.2% of the applicants improved their score on any of the scales on the personality test. Also, scale scores were just as likely to change in the negative direction as the positive one. Only 3 applicants of the 5,266 who reapplied for the jobs changed scores to a greater degree than one would expect by chance (outside the 95% confidence interval) on all five of the scales on the test. The authors concluded that "faking on personality measures is not a significant problem in real-world selection settings" (J. Hogan et al., 2007, p. 1270).

Even though there are questions to be answered regarding the impact that faking has on personality tests, research does continue on methods to reduce faking. For Your Information Box 14.3 includes a discussion of an interesting study conducted in China on a new method to reduce faking in employee selection contexts.

Another interesting area of current research on the relationship between personality tests and job performance is the question of whether a person can actually possess too much of an otherwise desirable personality trait. As we mentioned earlier in this chapter, the Big Five trait of conscientiousness has consistently been shown to be an effective predictor of job performance (Barrick & Mount, 1991). But there is a question as to whether more is always better. Current research suggests that it may not be.

N. Carter and colleagues (2014) investigated the nature of the relationship between conscientiousness and job performance. They proposed that the usual linear relationship found between conscientiousness and job performance might be an unintentional result of the method that is commonly used to score personality tests. In most personality tests, test takers indicate the degree to which the statements on the test describe them, often a five-point scale with anchors that range from *strongly disagree* to *strongly agree*. The score on the trait is the simple sum of the responses to the individual questions. The researchers proposed that this simple sum is not the best estimate of the amount of the trait the person actually possesses. They argued that people evaluate how much a personality test item is like them by estimating how closely the item fits how they really see themselves. If the fit is especially good, they will strongly agree with the item, if it is especially bad, they will strongly disagree. This might seem obvious enough, but N. Carter and his colleagues (2014) suggested that simply summing the responses to arrive at a total score can cause an error in the estimation of the true amount of the trait that someone actually possesses. For example, consider the statement "I pay attention to details." It is presumed that someone high on conscientiousness would very strongly agree with this statement. However, N. Carter and his colleagues (2014) believed that a person who is extremely high in conscientiousness might not "very strongly agree" with this statement and instead only "agree" with it. This is because the statement is not extreme enough to capture

FOR YOUR INFORMATION BOX 14.3
A NEW PROCEDURE FOR REDUCING FAKING ON PERSONALITY TESTS

In 2012, Jinyan Fan and his colleagues designed a procedure and conducted a study intended to reduce faking on a personality test that was being used to select staff positions at a large university in the People's Republic of China (Fan et al., 2012). They referred to the procedure as a "test-warning-retest procedure" (p. 867). There were two phases to the process, both of which required computer administration to implement. In the first phase, the test taker completed three short "tests." The first was called a bogus statement (BS) scale. The BS scale asked test takers how familiar they were with nonexistent concepts or whether they had ever performed "nonexistent" tasks (e.g., "I am familiar with the Automatic Textbook Citation Creation System"; Anderson, Warner & Spencer, 1984). These types of scales are designed to detect extreme faking (Dwight & Donovan, 2003). If a test taker claims knowledge of experience with too many of these bogus statements, it is treated as an indication that he or she is faking. The second test was Paulhaus's (1998) IM scale, which is a measure of subtler impression management or socially desirable responding tendencies. The third test given in Phase 1 included 3 of the 16 scales on the Chinese version of the 16PF (Emotional Stability, Rule-Conscientiousness, and Privateness). As we discussed earlier in this chapter, the 16PF is a well-known test designed to measure personality traits in normal adults.

If a test taker's score was too high on either the BS or the IM test based on a normative cutoff score, he or she was identified as a possible faker and received a polite warning message via the computer. The warning message informed the test taker that he or she had responded to two scales that were designed to detect socially desirable responding and that the computer had detected "some unusual response patterns in the answers" (Fan et al., 2012, p. 869). The message went on to say that the test taker's response patterns were consistent with someone who was answering the questions in a socially desirable manner, which might be different from how the person might truly describe himself or herself. The message concluded by telling the test taker that individuals who repeatedly distorted their responses were easily identified and eliminated from consideration for a position. As an experimental control, test takers who were identified as nonfakers were also presented with a message that simply

told them that the system was working well and that the same questions they had already answered might be presented more than once. (This was because the faking scales were to be presented again in Phase 2.) After the messages were displayed, the testing continued into Phase 2. In this phase, the test takers completed the BS and IM scale a second time, as well as 15 of the 16 scales of the 16PF personality inventory. (One of the scales on the 16PF was not included because it was considered to be more a measure of cognitive ability than personality.) In addition to high scores on both the BS and IM tests, test takers who were faking also were expected to have elevated scores on those 16PF scales that were most easily identifiable as being job related, such as the Rule-Conscientiousness and the Emotional Stability scales.

The results indicated that those subjects who were warned about their response patterns in Phase 1 showed a different pattern of responding in Phase 2. There were significant decreases for both the IM score and the BS score for those test takers who were warned in Phase 1. In comparison, there was no significant change in either the IM or BS score in Phase 2 for those test takers who were not warned in Phase 1. The scores on the personality scales showed a similar pattern of results. The mean scores on both the Rule-Conscientiousness scale and the Emotional Stability scale decreased significantly in Phase 2 for the test takers who were warned but remained unchanged for those who were not.

There was one other interesting finding in the study. While the scores of test takers who were warned declined in Phase 2 on both the Rule-Conscientiousness scale and the Emotional Stability scale, their scores on the Privateness scale did not decrease by nearly as much. The authors suggested that this indicates that job applicants don't fake equally across all scales on personality tests. Scales that are believed to be most job related are more subject to faking than those scales that are believed to be irrelevant to the job.

What do you think of this approach to reduce faking? Can you think of some drawbacks that this approach might have? What are some of the other possible reasons that might account for the reduction on the scores of the personality test in Phase 2 of the study?

the person's image of himself or herself. If the statement said something like "I invariably pay attention to details without exception," then a test taker who is exceptionally high in conscientiousness would be more likely to "very strongly agree" with it. As a consequence, people who are most extreme on a trait might not strongly endorse the items on the test that one would expect. Therefore, the true trait score of a person who is very extreme on a trait could be underestimated by his or her test score.

There are alternative scoring methods we can use to deal with this issue. The methods involve using a particular type of item-response theory (IRT) to score the test instead of the usual method, which simply sums the test takers' ratings on the questions within a scale. N. Carter et al. (2014) found that when these methods (called ideal point models) were used to score personality tests, the usual linear relationship found between conscientiousness and job performance changed. Instead, the relationship became curvilinear, meaning that job performance improved as conscientiousness scores increased, but only to a certain point. Once that point was reached, job performance began to decrease. They reported that this occurred 100% of the time in their research. Perhaps this result should not be surprising. Intuitively, one could envision how very extreme conscientious could also be associated with rigidity and lack of flexibility that could negatively affect job performance. This is sometimes colloquially referred to as analysis paralysis and can negatively affect good decision making. Clearly more research will be necessary to replicate these findings, but it seems that where the relationship between conscientious and job performance is concerned, more is not always better.

In closing this section on personality tests, we want to show how combination of psychological testing with social media can create some unintended, and many people would say, negative consequences. In the News Box 14.3 is an example of how a personality test based on the five-factor model came together with Facebook to advance a political agenda in the 2016 United States presidential election.

Integrity Testing

Economic pressures for businesses to become more efficient and competitive have contributed to a growing concern with employee theft and other issues related to the honesty and integrity of workers. According to the 2002 Retail Security Survey conducted by the University of Florida, employees are responsible for 48.5% of retail theft, costing retailers $15 billion annually (J. Horan, 2003). Fitzgerald (2003) called dishonest employees "the enemy within" (p. G7), and she noted that in Canada, retail employees are responsible for 33% of theft, just short of the 38% by customers, according to the Retail Council of Canada. Writing in *Forbes*, Schoenberger (2004) had this to say about data theft by employees: "Integrity, not ability or the fear of getting caught, is all that separates a conscientious employee from a thief" (p. 82).

J. Horan (2003), writing in *Chain Store Age*, suggested that employers customize alarm systems to catch employees leaving the store with store merchandise. However, according to Fitzgerald (2003), the first line of defense is prevention, and employers need to "hire smart" by asking the right questions of applicants. Assessments for integrity fall into two general categories: physiological measures and paper-and-pencil tests.

Polygraph Testing

The **polygraph**, or lie detector test, is the best-known physiological measure associated with evaluating how truthfully an individual responds to questioning. The process was invented by William Marston, who created Wonder Woman, an early comic book character who elicited the truth from criminals with her magic lasso (Lilienfeld, 1993). The character was further popularized in 2017 in a very successful movie! A trained polygraph administrator interprets

IN THE NEWS BOX 14.3
USING A FIVE-FACTOR MODEL PERSONALITY TEST FOR POLITICAL PURPOSES

In the 2016 U.S. presidential election, social media was extensively used (and some say abused) for political purposes. A company named Cambridge Analytica contracted an application developer to write a "personality quiz" that could be distributed via Facebook. It was named "thisismydigitallife." This so called quiz was actually a personality test based on the Five Factor Model of personality, and was taken by 320,000 Facebook users. But because Facebook allowed certain companies (such as Cambridge Analytica) access to their database for "research purposes," the company was also able to gather personal data on all the Facebook friends of anyone who took the quiz without their explicit consent—a total of over 50 million people. Because Cambridge Analytica was hired by the campaign of presidential candidate Donald Trump, it enabled them to create targeted ads directed at certain U.S. voters that could directly address their personal interests, biases, fears or other personal characteristics.

The way this was accomplished was to build a computer algorithm that could find links between the personality characteristics of individuals uncovered via the "quiz" with other information that was discoverable from their Facebook profiles such as their age, gender, religion, political views and a host of other variables. Ultimately, this resulted in the generation of over 4000 data points on each U.S. voter according to Alexander Nix who was the chief executive of Cambridge Analytica. In a 2016 presentation Nix said, "If you know the personality of the people you are targeting, you can nuance your messaging to resonate more effectively with those key audience groups."

What lessons do you think can be learned from this? How might you change your behavior regarding taking on line "quizzes" from unknown sources?

Source: http://www.thehindu.com/news/international/how-a-personality-quiz-on-facebook-helped-donald-trump-find-his-voters/article23310128.ece

---

physiological data recorded by a polygraph machine. The machine generates a number of graphs of physiological responses such as skin resistance, pulse or heart rate, and respiration.

The theory behind the use of the polygraph suggests that when an individual gives an untruthful response, he or she exhibits increases in skin resistance, pulse or heart rate, and respiration. To evaluate honesty, the administrator asks a set of predetermined questions that establishes a physiological baseline for truthful responses. Then the administrator asks other questions regarding topics such as employee theft. When an individual's physiological response increases above the baseline, the administrator may judge that the test taker did not answer the questions truthfully.

There are two problems with this theory. First, an individual's physiological responses may increase for a number of reasons, such as general discomfort and nervousness. Second, some individuals can control their physiological responses better than other individuals can. Lilienfeld (1993) concluded that there is no scientific evidence that a specific "lie response" exists and suggested that polygraph users are making the "Othello error"—taking signs of distress as proof of unfaithfulness or dishonesty.

Gatewood and Feild (1997) stated that the major drawback to using polygraphs for selection is that they generate a high rate of **false positives**—mistakenly classifying innocent test takers as guilty. In addition, polygraphs may also misclassify a large number of guilty individuals as innocent (Lilienfeld, 1993). Ruscio (2005) pointed out two myths regarding polygraph testing. The first is that the polygraph process is a scientific and objective way to learn whether a person is lying or telling the truth. The second is that polygraph testing is infallible and contains no error. Ruscio concluded that organizations need to find other processes to replace or supplement polygraph testing.

The Employee Polygraph Protection Act of 1988, which forbids the use of the polygraph as an employment test, was passed by Congress in recognition of the stigma associated with incorrectly labeling applicants as untruthful and causing them to be rejected for employment. Although some employers (e.g., those that provide security services, government agencies) are exempted from the 1988 federal law, the poor predictive validity of polygraphs makes their usefulness for any situation highly suspect. For Your Information Box 14.4 describes the ambivalent attitude the U.S. Congress and the executive branch have demonstrated regarding scientific studies of the polygraph.

Paper-and-Pencil Integrity Tests

As an alternative to physiological tests for screening applicants, a number of publishers now offer paper-and-pencil tests. These fall into two categories: overt tests and personality-oriented tests. Overt tests ask test takers to provide information about their past behavior (e.g., "How many times have you borrowed cash from an employer without permission?") or to respond to hypothetical situations (e.g., "Is it okay to make personal phone calls from work?"). Personality-oriented tests purport to measure characteristics that are predictive of honest behavior and positive organizational citizenship using items that relate to the Big Five personality factors. Although both types yield similar results, the differences between overt and personality-oriented tests relate to the underlying constructs measured by the tests. Overt tests correlate with honesty and supervision attitudes, and personality-oriented tests correlate with self/impulse control, home life/upbringing, risk taking/thrill seeking, diligence, and emotional stability (Wanek, Sackett, & Ones, 2003).

Paper-and-pencil integrity tests have been the subject of much research and debate among psychologists. A meta-analysis of validation studies of integrity tests yielded encouraging results (Ones, Viswesvaran, & Schmidt, 1993). First, although prediction of documented thefts was low (.13), integrity tests predicted counterproductive behaviors much better (.29 vs. .39). Second, there was evidence that these validities generalized across situations. Finally, in addition to predicting counterproductive behaviors, the meta-analysis showed that integrity tests correlated with supervisory ratings of job performance at .41.

Critics point out, however, that studies available for Ones and colleagues' (1993) meta-analysis were conducted by the test publishers themselves, not by independent researchers, and that such studies often contained serious methodological flaws (Camara & Schneider, 1994, 1995; Lilienfeld, 1993). Other researchers have expressed concerns that integrity tests may systematically misclassify some honest individuals as dishonest and that most paper-and-pencil integrity tests are highly susceptible to faking (Lilienfeld, Alliger, & Mitchell, 1995).

An interesting study reported by Lilienfeld (1993) tested 41 monks and nuns—assumed to excel in the trait of honesty—using a well-known honesty test. The monks and nuns scored lower (more dishonest) than did a group of college students and a group of incarcerated criminals! Lilienfeld concluded that honesty tests, designed as an alternative to the polygraph, suffer from the same deficiencies as does the lie detector.

In 2012, Van Iddekinge and his colleagues conducted a more recent meta-analysis of 104 studies that investigated the evidence of validity of integrity tests based on their relationship with external criteria (Van Iddekinge, Roth, Raymark, & Olde-Dusseau, 2012). The criteria included job performance, training performance, counterproductive work behavior, and turnover. The meta-analysis included a similar proportion of studies from test publishers and non–test publishers. The results confirmed some the concerns expressed by earlier researchers

FOR YOUR INFORMATION BOX 14.4
SCIENCE OR VOODOO?

In 1988, when the Employee Polygraph Protection Act became law, Peter Persaud was pleased with its constraints on polygraph testing for selection. Earlier that year, Persaud had been denied a job as vice president at a bank in Miami because he had failed two polygraph tests. Furthermore, Persaud stated he was angered by the examiner, who persistently asked questions about stealing and kickbacks and who expressed disbelief when Persaud told her that he had no credit card debt and that he owned two houses without mortgages (Karr, 1988). At the time, many in science and government believed that the ban on polygraph testing, which did not apply to federal agencies, did not go far enough.

In March 2001, after the arrest of Russian spy Robert Hanssen, Federal Bureau of Investigation (FBI) director Louis Freeh decided to increase polygraph testing of bureau workers with access to intelligence information ("FBI Director Freeh Orders Stepped-Up Polygraph Tests," 2001). Despite scientific studies that pointed out problems with the validity of polygraph testing, the FBI was using polygraphs to screen FBI agents for hiring. Aldrich Ames, arrested 2 years later and convicted of spying while working for the Central Intelligence Agency (CIA), might have been apprehended sooner if the agency had not relied on polygraph testing to clear Ames from suspicion. The arrests of Hanssen and Ames humiliated and discredited the FBI, the CIA, and the broader intelligence community.

In August 2001, the senators from New Mexico introduced a bill to limit polygraph testing of personnel at the U.S. Department of Energy (DOE) nuclear weapons facilities. The bill directed the DOE to exempt more employees from polygraph testing and to consult the National Academy of Sciences (NAS) research on polygraph testing at the DOE in order to establish a permanent testing program. The reason for the bill was the imposition by Congress of polygraph testing at Los Alamos National Laboratory and other sites as an extra security measure. Scientists and other personnel at the facilities blamed the polygraph for a decline in morale and difficulty in recruiting and retaining qualified employees ("Sen. Pete Domenici Introduced a Bill," 2001).

Two years later, after the completion of the NAS report, the DOE ignored the academy's research that recommended against using polygraphs for security screening. Instead, the DOE issued a statement maintaining that it did not believe the polygraph accuracy issues raised by the NAS warranted abandoning use of the polygraph as a screening tool (Frazier, 2003). Donald Kennedy (2003), writing in *Science*, stated that the DOE has otherwise relied on scientific knowledge and principles to carry out its responsibilities. For instance, the agency started the Human Genome Project, supports alternative energy research, and administers programs in biomedical research, science, and technology. Finally, the department continually pledged to use the best science when carrying out its responsibilities. Kennedy believed that the polygraph ruling reflected bad science.

By the end of the year, the DOE changed its earlier stance and recommended a decrease in testing of approximately 75%. One scientist at Lawrence Livermore National Laboratory stated the polygraph was still a *voodoo test* (Frazier, 2003).

about the quality of previous validity studies. When the researchers looked specifically at the results of studies that met what they termed generally accepted professional standards for validity research, they found that the validity coefficients to be modest. Most of the estimates were below .2, and many approached .1, even when corrected for unreliability in the criterion. However, the authors did find higher validity coefficients when the tests were used to predict self-reported counterproductive work behavior (.26 uncorrected and .32 corrected for unreliability). Like previous researchers, they also found that the validity coefficients from studies conducted by the test publishers were higher (.27) than the coefficients from studies that were not conducted by the test publishers (.12).

As you might imagine, the publishers of personality tests did not agree with these results (Harris et al., 2012). The publishers criticized the research on a number of grounds. Some of the criticisms were focused on the choice of studies that Van Iddekinge et al. (2012) included in their meta-analysis, the types of statistical corrections that were used, omitting data that showed that applicants have positive responses to integrity tests, and the lack of emphasis placed on the ability of integrity tests to predict counterproductive work behavior. The publishers also disagreed with the implication that the test results of studies conducted by the publishers themselves were biased.

Cognitive Tests

Cognitive tests are assessments that measure the test taker's mental capabilities, such as general mental ability tests, intelligence tests, and academic skills tests. Most cognitive tests have been developed for use in educational or clinical settings. When a job analysis indicates that cognitive skills are important for high performance, cognitive tests are useful for inclusion in a pre-employment assessment. Hunter and Hunter (1984) found that the validity of cognitive tests for pre-employment screening were the most accurate for "thinking" jobs ($r = .53$) such as manager and salesperson.

> **Test Spotlight 14.4** in Appendix A describes the Wonderlic Basic Skills Test, a cognitive test used by organizations.

Barrett, Polomsky, and McDaniel (1999) conducted a meta-analysis of the validity of written tests used in the selection and training of firefighters. Cognitive tests showed high validity (.42) with job performance criteria and even higher validity for predicting training criteria.

Legal Constraints

When Congress passed the Civil Rights Act of 1964, one of the specific areas addressed was hiring by organizations. As discussed in the chapter, "Why Is Psychological Testing Important?" Title VII of the Civil Rights Act covered employment practices, including psychological testing that resulted in discrimination against minorities and women. Following passage of the Civil Rights Act, various federal agencies in the executive branch as well as the federal courts began to issue guidelines and case law that sought to define the steps organizations should take to comply with the requirements of Title VII. The proliferation of guidelines and case law resulted in the federal government's publication of the *Uniform Guidelines on Employee Selection Procedures* (1978). Note that Congress did not pass the *Uniform Guidelines*, and therefore they are not federal law. However, they do suggest procedures for organizations to follow that enhance the fairness and legal defensibility of their employment practices. The *Uniform Guidelines* were compiled with the help of psychologists and present what can be referred to as "best practices" when using psychological tests in organizations. While the Civil Rights Act is usually viewed as one legal mechanism for protected groups such as women and minorities to challenge a selection procedure, it also has been used to challenge "reverse discrimination," a situation in which a majority group feels that it has been harmed because of an allegation that less qualified minority candidates were chosen for jobs. In the News Box 14.4 describes an unusual case of reverse discrimination that the Supreme Court recently decided. You can find the *Uniform Guidelines* at www.uniformguidelines.com/uniformguidelines.html.

Generalizing Validity Evidence

According to federal case law, any process that is used to make a hiring decision is defined as a test. Therefore, the *Uniform Guidelines* apply to all employment screening devices—including application blanks (forms), reference checks, letters of reference, and even employment interviews. The *Uniform Guidelines* and federal case law suggest that all employment tests should

IN THE NEWS BOX 14.4
THE SUPREME COURT DECIDES A REVERSE DISCRIMINATION CASE—*RICCI v. DeSTEFANO*

On July 1, 2009, the Supreme Court handed down a decision in a case brought by a group of firefighters, 18 White and 1 Hispanic, that centered around the examination that the City of New Haven, Connecticut, used for making promotional decisions to the rank of lieutenant and captain. In 2003, the city had used a professionally designed multiple-choice test along with an oral examination to make promotional decisions. The multiple-choice exam constituted 60% of the final score, while the oral examination constituted 40%. After receiving the test scores, the city realized that no African American firefighters and only one Hispanic firefighter would be promoted if the city used the test scores to make the promotion decisions. Because the results disproportionately favored the White candidates, the city feared that it would face an adverse-impact lawsuit from the minority candidates if it went forward with the promotions. As a result, the city decided to discard the test scores and not promote anyone. The White firefighters who had passed the test, and would have been eligible for promotion had the test been used, filed a suit of their own against the city. They claimed they had been intentionally discriminated against based on their race because they had been denied promotion even though they scored higher on the test.

The Supreme Court, in a 5-to-4 decision, ruled that the City of New Haven had wrongly denied the White firefighters their promotions. The lead opinion, written by Justice Anthony Kennedy, said that the city's fear of an adverse-impact lawsuit was not a sufficient reason to discard the results of a test unless there was a "strong basis in evidence" that the city would suffer liability as a result of such a lawsuit, and that no such basis was warranted in this case.

You may be wondering why there would be any question of the city's potential liability had the minority firefighters brought an adverse-impact claim given the results of the test. The answer lies in an amendment to

Title VII of the 1964 Civil Rights Act passed by Congress in 1991. The law provides that when a test disproportionately disadvantages one group over another, a defense against this claim is to demonstrate that the test was job related (valid), that it was consistent with business necessity, and that there was no equally valid but less discriminatory alternative available. However, during the litigation, the City of New Haven did not claim or provide evidence that it believed that the results should be discarded because of flaws in the design of the test or that the test was not a valid predictor of on-the-job performance.

On the other hand, the justices who dissented from the majority were concerned with the fact that nearly 60% of the population of New Haven belonged to a racial minority. If the city used test scores to make promotional decisions, minorities in the future would not be properly represented in the leadership of the fire department, just as they were not represented in the past when there was intentional discrimination.

This case underlines two different views on what is important when tests are used for individual decision making. One view focuses on the validity of the tests—are they job related and equally predictive of future performance for all demographic groups who take the test? The other view focuses on a social policy issue of fairness, concerned with whether there is equality for all groups regarding the outcomes of testing. Clearly, it is important to remember the differences in the two views expressed by the Supreme Court. A test that demonstrates evidence of validity may not be considered fair by everyone, and a test that is considered fair by some may not necessarily be valid. The concepts associated with test validity are centered around scientific issues; the concepts associated with fairness are centered around issues of social policy. What do you think the court should have decided in this case?

be job related and based on a job analysis. Employers should use only tests for which there is evidence of validity for the scores. Organizations should maintain records regarding the race, sex, and ethnic group membership of the applicant pool and the final group of persons hired for the job. When a test results in adverse impact—exclusion of a disproportionate number of persons in a group protected by federal law, referred to as a **protected class**—the employer should find an alternative method for assessing job candidates. Since the publication of the *Uniform Guidelines*, industrial and organizational psychologists have been conducting research to find testing instruments that not only have significant evidence of validity but also yield results that do not discriminate against a protected class.

One issue that frequently arises in organizations that wish to use a pre-employment test for selecting employees is demonstrating that the test is valid for use in that organization. You may remember the important concept that validity is not a function of the test itself, but rather whether there is evidence to support the interpretation of the test scores. Also, you will remember that one piece of evidence of validity for a pre-employment test would be data showing that people who score higher on the test do better on the job. You have learned that there are a couple of ways in which this evidence can be gathered (the predictive method and the concurrent method). In practice, however, data gathering and validation studies may be seen as too expensive and time-consuming for an organization to undertake. For example, hiring new employees is often an immediate business need, and conducting validity research can be time-consuming. Second, to develop some types of validity evidence, such as evidence based on relationships with criteria, a large number of participants (more than 30) must be available for testing in order to be confident of the results. For an employer who has only a few employees in a particular job, it may be impossible to conduct that type of study.

One of the ways that organizations can deal with this issue is via something referred to as the generalization of validity evidence. There are three strategies that can be useful when it becomes necessary to make a case that evidence of validity will generalize from one situation to another. The strategies are meta-analysis, synthetic validity, and transportability (Society for Industrial and Organizational Psychology, 2003). While we will talk about all three strategies in this section, we will present more detail on transportability, as it is the technique that is most commonly used in organizational settings.

Meta-analysis is a statistical technique that accumulates the results of multiple studies on comparable or similar constructs into a single result. The goal is to provide a better estimate of the true population value of a predictor–criterion relationship than that provided by any one individual study. In effect, meta-analysis is an analysis of analyses (Glass, 1976; Hunter & Hunter, 1984). The idea is that by combining the results of multiple studies into a single, larger analysis, one can reduce the impact that statistical artifacts have on the results. These artifacts (such as small sample sizes, range restriction, or low criteria reliability) can sometimes cause different studies of the same phenomena to reach different and sometimes contradictory conclusions about the strength of the relationship between their predictors and criteria. This can happen when artifacts lower a study's statistical power. When this occurs, the study will be less able to detect a significant relationship between the predictor and criterion even if one is actually present.

In the organizational psychology literature, meta-analysis has been generically referred to as validity generalization. This is because the procedure is often used to address the question of why a certain construct (like personality test scores) seem to be valid for predicting criteria (like job performance) in one study but not in another. In other words, the relationship between the predictor and criteria did not generalize across the different study populations. The question that needs to be answered is whether the different results across the studies is due to statistical artifacts or to true differences in the relationship between the predictors and criteria in the population. If the results can be shown to be largely attributable to statistical artifacts, then one might be able to conclude that the validity of the test scores really does generalize across the populations. Meta-analysis is the statistical technique that is used to address these kinds of questions. However, it can be conducted only when the validity studies that are to be analyzed are based on the relationship between a test and external criteria (i.e., criterion-related evidence of validity). Validity studies based on content- or construct-based evidence cannot be combined via meta-analysis.

An interesting example of the use of meta-analysis comes from the medical literature. Between 1959 and 1988, 33 clinical trials had been done to evaluate the efficacy of a clot-dissolving agent (streptokinase) in patients hospitalized with heart attacks. Twenty-seven of the 33 trials showed that there were no statistically significant effects on mortality for those patients who received the drug versus no treatment or placebo. In 1992, Lau and his colleagues performed a meta-analysis on all the clinical trials that had been done on streptokinase. When the results of all the studies were combined via meta-analysis, they showed that streptokinase actually did significantly reduce the odds of dying by 20%. The results of the studies were generalizable across many different patients, physicians, hospitals, and times. The statistical artifacts present in many of the previous studies prevented researchers from obtaining statistically significant results.

A second strategy for generalizing validity evidence is called **synthetic validity**, or job component validity (Lawshe, 1952; Society for Industrial and Organizational Psychology, 2003). In this approach, existing evidence of validity is generalized from one group of jobs to another if it can be shown that the same job components are present in both. Job components are defined as clusters of work behaviors that are similar across multiple jobs or job families, such as problem-solving skills, mechanical aptitude skills, clerical skills, and the like (J. W. Johnson & Carter, 2010). Synthetic validity is based on the idea that when jobs or job families share the same components, the personal characteristics that predict performance in one job would also predict performance in the other. Therefore, a test that validly measures an attribute important for job success in one job or job family should be equally valid for any job for which the same attribute (job component) is also required. Once the job components for a job or job family are identified along with the tests that have been previously been validated to measure these components, a synthetic validity coefficient can be computed. This is accomplished by statistically combining the already known test–job component correlations across all the job components necessary to perform the new job. This is different from the traditional criterion-related approach to calculating validity coefficients because the calculations don't rely directly on the correlations between individuals' scores on the tests with their performance criteria scores in the actual job being validated. This makes it possible to estimate the validity of a selection battery in cases in which it would not be possible or practical to conduct a local validity study. This approach has been shown to produce validity coefficients very close to those produced using traditional validity calculation procedures (Hoffmann, Holden, & Gail, 2000; Hoffman & McPhail, 1998; J. W. Johnson & Carter, 2010). However, detailed knowledge of the actual work performed is necessary to use this approach to ensure that the job components (and tests to measure them) that are chosen for inclusion are important predictors of successful job performance.

A third, and more common, strategy used to generalize validity evidence is **transportability**. Transportability occurs when a case is made that because a test has been shown to be valid for a particular use, it can be presumed to also be valid for another, similar use (Society for Industrial and Organizational Psychology, 2003). The need for this strategy can occur when a test that has been validated for selection of employees into one job is proposed to select employees into a different but similar job.

For instance, suppose a test developer has created a test to hire retail salespeople. While the test was being developed, it was shown to be a valid predictor of sales performance of retail clothing salespeople, household goods salespeople, and giftware salespeople. Now, suppose the owner of a small number of flower shops is looking for a test to help him or her select salespeople. It is not likely that he or she would be in a position to conduct his or her own local validity study for the reasons cited above. However, the test he or she is interested in was validated on a group of jobs very similar to the one for which he or she is hiring. He or she may be able to presume that the test would be valid for him or her use as well without actually conducting his or her own study.

Whether it is appropriate to rely on the concept of transportability when deciding whether to use a test in a different setting or for a different job is a subjective judgment. There are at least two criteria that should be present before deciding that the validity evidence for a test will generalize. First, test users need a study that demonstrates evidence of validity for the original use of the test. Second, there must be evidence that there is a strong similarity between the content and requirements of the job for which the test was originally validated and the new job. For instance, if the test in our example was proposed for selection of business-to-business telephone equipment salespeople, the transportability argument would be much less compelling because of the large differences between the necessary skill sets of retail salespeople and business-to-business salespeople. Therefore, even if prior research has shown that the test is a valid predictor of success in a retail sales job, it may not be an accurate predictor of success in a business-to-business sales position. The test should be used only after a local validation study is conducted.

Here is an example of how one of the authors of this book used a transportability strategy to generalize the validity of an assessment center for use with a different company than the one for which it was originally developed. This assessment center was originally developed and validated for the selection of sales managers for a large telecommunications company. The psychologists who designed the assessment center gathered evidence of its validity by first performing a job analysis of the sales manager's job to identify the knowledge, skills, and abilities (KSAs) necessary to successfully perform the job in this company. Then the psychologists designed assessment center simulations so sales managers would be able to demonstrate those KSAs by performing tasks that were similar to those they would actually perform on the job. You may recognize this to be a content-based approach to establishing evidence of validity.

After this assessment center was developed and validated, a different telecommunications organization wanted to use the same assessment center to select its sales managers. Because the business need was immediate and the company was filling only a small number of positions, it was not practical to conduct a full validity study to establish evidence of validity specifically for this company. Therefore, the psychologists decided to use a transportability strategy to provide the necessary evidence of validity. To accomplish this, they asked a group of subject matter experts from this company who were very familiar with the requirements of the job to evaluate how closely the KSAs measured in the assessment center matched the KSAs necessary to perform the duties required of their sales managers. Then these experts were asked to determine how closely the simulated tasks contained in the assessment center matched the types of tasks that their sales managers actually performed on the job. The ratings provided by these experts were analyzed to ensure that all the KSAs and tasks contained in the assessment center were relevant to the job performance of the sales managers. The experts' ratings indicated that there was a strong relationship between what was measured in the assessment center and the requirements of their sales managers' job. Therefore, the psychologists concluded there was sufficient evidence that the validity of the assessment center could be transported or generalized for the selection of sales managers in the new company.

PERFORMANCE APPRAISAL

Most organizations carry out formal evaluations of employees' job performance, called **performance appraisal**. Usually, each employee's supervisor or manager completes a performance appraisal form that requires assigning numerical values to employees' performance. These performance appraisals qualify legally as tests. Performance appraisals should be a part of an organization's overall business strategy. As such, they often act as organizational interventions and information-gathering procedures.

Addressing the various types of performance appraisal systems is beyond the scope of this textbook; however, in this section we do discuss several psychometric methods that underlie the performance appraisal process.

Ranking Employees

One in five Fortune 500 companies uses **forced ranking** as a method of performance appraisal (G. Johnson, 2004). As you may recall, when managers rank people, they compare the performance of one employee with that of other employees. To rank employees, the supervisor must decide who is the "best" employee, the "next best" employee, and so on based on predetermined dimensions or criteria.

Another method for performance appraisal is **forced distribution**, which requires the supervisor to assign a certain number of employees to each performance category, such as "poor," "below average," "average," "above average," and "outstanding," so that the appraisals are distributed in a way that resembles a normal curve. Using this method, no matter how well each person performs, some employees will always be ranked as "outstanding" and some will always be ranked as "poor."

The idea that a company must identify and reward top performers with bonuses and development opportunities and must train or dismiss its lowest performers leads to the use of forced ranking and forced distribution. Ranking individuals does prevent a manager from assigning all people to one category—for example, assigning all individuals to the "exceeds expectations" category. On the other hand, ranking employees may result in identifying workers who are performing satisfactorily as "poor" when compared with their peers. Forced ranking and forced distribution are controversial methods of assessing employee performance. Many management consultants advise against them because they may force the supervisor to place an employee into a category that does not accurately describe his or her performance.

Rating Employees

For annual or semiannual performance assessment, most organizations prefer to rate employee performance using a scale that specifies job dimensions or job behaviors. The traditional method for assessing employees is to ask supervisors or managers to rate employee performance. The rating scales are similar to those used in surveys.

As you can see, Figure 14.1 shows **graphic rating scales** that provide visual indicators to help the manager rate employees. Guided by the numbers or words, called **anchors**, the rater chooses the category that best represents the employee's performance on the specified dimension. Any type of rating format can be used with any rating dimension.

A **behaviorally anchored rating scale (BARS)** is another rating method that uses on-the-job behaviors as anchors for rating scales that represent job dimensions. Using BARS, such as the sample item in Figure 14.2, the rater chooses the rating category by reading the behaviors and placing a mark on the scale that is most representative of the employee's performance on that dimension. Research on the BARS method suggests that these scales provide more

FIGURE 14.1 ■ **Examples of Graphic Rating Scales**

EXAMPLE A: Check the box that describes the employee on each dimension.

		1	2	3	4	5	
Performance	Low				✓		High
Efficiency	Low			✓			High

EXAMPLE B: Rate the employee's performance.

	Outstanding	Above Average	Average	Below Average	Poor
Performance		✓			
Efficiency			✓		

EXAMPLE C: Choose the example that is most descriptive of the employee.

	Consistently error free	Usually error free	Requires follow-up to correct errors	Frequent errors with time-consuming corrections
Accuracy		✓		

	Submissions are always on time	Submissions are most often on time	Submissions are sometimes on time	Submissions are rarely on time
Timeliness of submissions				

EXAMPLE D: Choose the face that reminds you of the employee.

				✓

EXAMPLE E: Check all items that apply to the employee.

Courteous	✓
Attentive	✓
Uninterested	
Inquiring	

Hard Worker	✓
Unorganized	
Creative	✓
Shy	

FIGURE 14.2 ■ Example of a Behaviorally Anchored Rating Scale

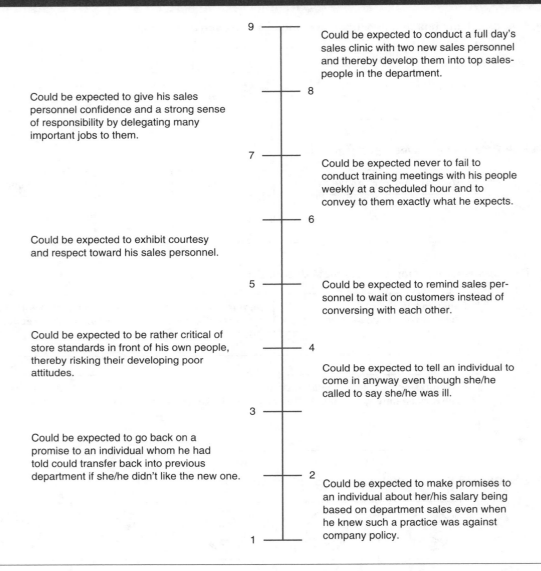

Source: Copyright © 1973 by the American Psychological Association. Reproduced [or Adapted] with permission. Campbell, J. P., Dunnette, M. D., Arvey, R. D., & Hellervik, L. V. (1973). The development and evaluation of behaviorally based rating scales. *Journal of Applied Psychology, 57*(1), 15–22. http://dx.doi.org/10.1037/h0034185. No further reproduction or distribution is permitted without written permission from the American Psychological Association.

accurate ratings of employee behavior than do traditionally anchored rating scales. However, they are difficult and time-consuming to develop and require concentrated rater training because of their complexity.

Raters can also evaluate performance by rating how frequently the employee performs important behaviors on the job. This method, known as the **behavioral checklist**, is illustrated in Figure 14.3. The checklist can be developed directly from the frequency ratings of the job analysis survey.

FIGURE 14.3 ■ Two Dimensions From a Behavioral Checklist

TOPIC (APPROPRIATE, INFORMATIVE)

Behavior Shown	Almost Never	A Few Times	Some-times	Many Times	Almost Always
Gave examples from organizations					
Referred to sources when making assertions					
Wandered from the topic					
Demonstrated enthusiasm for topic					
Provided information in a clear and logical order					
Demonstrated knowledge and understanding of the topic					
Defined terms and jargon					

PUBLIC SPEAKING SKILLS

Behavior Shown	Almost Never	A Few Times	Some-times	Many Times	Almost Always
Spoke clearly and audibly					
Connected sentences with "uh," "um," etc.					
Spoke too rapidly for audience understanding					
Spoke in a monotone voice					
Read from notes					
Used distracting gestures					
Used vulgar or politically incorrect language or phrases					

Rating Errors

Ratings of job performance involve making subjective decisions about how to quantify job performance. As you recall, measurement that involves making subjective judgments often contains error. Industrial psychologists have identified a number of systematic rating errors that occur when raters judge employee performance.

- **Leniency errors** result when raters give all employees better ratings than they deserve, and **severity errors** result when raters give all employees worse ratings than they deserve.

- **Central tendency errors** result when raters use only the middle of the rating scale and ignore the highest and lowest scale categories.

- A **halo effect** occurs when raters let their judgment on one dimension influence judgments on other dimensions. For instance, an employee who receives a low rating on "quality of work" may also be rated low on "quantity of work" even though the employee actually meets the performance standards for quantity output.

To avoid inaccurate ratings, organizations should provide rater training for all persons conducting performance appraisals. Because research on rater training (Fay & Latham, 1982) suggests that such training programs usually have only short-term effects, it is a good idea for organizations to provide "brush-up" courses for training raters. Training objectives should include mastering observing behavior, avoiding making rating errors, and maintaining consistent standards across employees (intrarater reliability).

Who Should Rate?

Traditionally, organizations have given the job of rating employee performance to the employees' supervisors or managers. During recent years, however, companies have begun to use a method of performance appraisal and developmental feedback called **360° feedback**. In this method, employees receive ratings from those they work with on a day-to-day basis, such as their managers, peers, direct reports, and customers. In addition, employees rate themselves. These ratings are aggregated, except for the self-ratings and supervisor ratings, to provide employees with information on every dimension by every rater. This method provides rich feedback for the person being rated and may be perceived by some as fairer because misperceptions or rating errors by one person can be balanced by the opinions of others. Again, careful attention should be paid to training everyone to rate the performance of others honestly.

Chapter Summary

The employment interview is the most widely used method for pre-employment testing. Most companies use the traditional interview, although structured interviews have been shown to have greater reliability and validity. Organizations also use performance tests, such as assessment centers and work samples, to assess how well job candidates can perform job tasks. High-fidelity performance tests replicate the job setting in detail. Low-fidelity performance tests such as situational judgment tests simulate job tasks using written, verbal, or visual descriptions.

Personality inventories measure stable and enduring constructs usually referred to as *personality traits*, such as conscientiousness, extraversion, and agreeableness, that predispose people to perform certain behaviors. The most popular theory among personality theorists today is the five-factor model. In the past, personnel psychologists discouraged the use of personality tests as employment tests because researchers had shown little relation between personality and job performance. Recently, because of research that has demonstrated that personality measures can be predictive of job performance, personnel psychologists have begun to look much more favorably on personality tests that reflect the five-factor model. However, there is concern regarding the degree to which faking affects the validity of personality tests when used for employee selection.

Organizations interested in assessing job candidates' integrity may use paper-and-pencil tests; however, Congress has forbidden most organizations from using the polygraph, or lie detector, for employment testing. When a job analysis indicates that cognitive skills are important for high performance, cognitive tests are useful for inclusion in a pre-employment assessment.

When Congress passed the Civil Rights Act of 1964, one of the specific areas addressed was hiring by organizations. The *Uniform Guidelines on Employee Selection Procedures* (1978) and federal case law suggest that all employment tests should be job related and have evidence of validity. Organizations should maintain records regarding protected classes applying for jobs. If a test results in adverse impact, an employer can be required to show evidence of the test's validity and that there was no other equally valid test that would have had less adverse impact. If it is not practical to conduct a local validity study, organizations sometimes rely on a validity generalization strategy to justify the use of the test.

Most employers conduct performance appraisals to evaluate the performance of their employees. Most organizations ask supervisors to evaluate employee performance by either ranking or rating employees on a number of predetermined dimensions, traits, and/or behaviors. The most popular method of rating employee performance uses a graphic rating scale. Two other scales based on observing and rating behaviors are BARSs and the behavioral checklist. Persons who rate performance should be trained to avoid ratings errors such as leniency, severity, central tendency, and the halo effect. During recent years, many companies have starting using 360° feedback, in which employees compare self-ratings with ratings received from their supervisors, peers, subordinates, and customers.

Engaging in the Learning Process

Learning is the process of gaining knowledge and skills through schooling or studying. Although you can learn by reading the chapter material, attending class, and engaging in discussion with your instructor, more actively engaging in the learning process may help you better learn and retain chapter information. To help you actively engage in

the learning process, we encourage you to access our new supplementary student workbook. The workbook contains critical thinking activities to help you understand and apply information and help you make progress toward learning and retaining material. If you do not have a copy of the workbook, you can purchase a copy through sagepub.com.

Key Concepts

After completing your study of this chapter, you should be able to define each of the following terms. These terms are bolded in the text of this chapter and defined in the Glossary.

anchors
assessment center
behavioral checklist
behavioral interviews
behaviorally anchored rating
    scale (BARS)
central tendency errors
cognitive tests
false positive
five-factor model
forced distribution

forced ranking
graphic rating scale
halo effect
high-fidelity test
job analysis
leniency errors
low-fidelity tests
meta-analysis
performance appraisal
personality traits
polygraph

protected class
severity errors
situational judgment test
structured interview
synthetic validity
360° feedback
traditional interview
transportability
work sample

Critical Thinking Questions

The following are some critical thinking questions to support the learning objectives for this chapter.

Learning Objectives	Critical Thinking Questions
Understand the different types of tests that employers routinely use for pre-employment testing.	• What are some of the issues that employers might have to consider when selecting a test for pre-employment use? • What are the similarities and differences between a traditional interview and a structured interview? Why might you prefer one over the other? • How would you design a structured *and* traditional interview question for a customer service representative role? • What would be a good example of a behavioral interview question for a customer service representative position?
Describe the characteristics of a performance test, and discuss two types of performance tests used by organizations.	• What examples of high fidelity and low fidelity performance tests have you taken in the past? What made each a high- or low-fidelity test? • Can you think of any classes that a college student might take that would include a performance test? Would it be a high fidelity or low fidelity test? • Describe how you might construct a performance test for the job of college professor. Would it be a high fidelity or low fidelity test?
Describe the five-factor model of personality, and name two tests that are based on this model.	• Based on what you have learned in previous chapters, what are some concerns you might have for using personality tests for selection purposes? • What personality tests, if any, have you taken that were developed based on the five-factor model? • Do you think that there would be any way to "cheat" on a personality test? If so, how might one do it?

Discuss two types of integrity tests, and describe the criticism these tests have received.	• How would you explain the following two seemingly contradictory set of facts?
	   ○ Polygraph tests are generally not allowed for employee selection purposes and they are also not generally admissible as evidence in court.
	   ○ None the less, polygraph tests are routinely used in high stakes situations such as screening personnel involved in security related professions.
	• What facts would you use to support the use of polygraph tests in your organization?

Describe the three ways in which validity evidence can be generalized to new situations.	• In what situations would generalizing validity evidence might not be appropriate? • What are some reasons why the validity of tests of cognitive ability might generalize more easily to different circumstances than personality tests?
Discuss performance appraisal instruments, give examples of three types of rating scales, and describe four types of rating errors.	• Based on what you've learned in the current and previous chapters, how might rater errors in performance appraisal affect the statistical properties of a test? • Why would your textbook authors include performance appraisal in a textbook on psychological testing?

APPENDIX A

Test Spotlights

TEST SPOTLIGHT 1.1
WECHSLER ADULT INTELLIGENCE SCALE, FOURTH EDITION (WAIS-IV)

Title	Wechsler Adult Intelligence Scale, Fourth Edition (WAIS-IV)
Author	David Wechsler
Publisher	Pearson Assessments 19500 Bulverde Road San Antonio, TX 78259-3710 www.pearsonassessments.com
Purpose	The WAIS-IV is designed to assess the intellectual ability of adults. The test measures both verbal and nonverbal skills using a battery of 10 core subtests and 5 supplementary subtests. The subtests are based on four domains of intelligence: Verbal Comprehension, Perceptual Reasoning, Working Memory, and Processing Speed. The WAIS-IV is designed for use in educational settings for the purpose of planning and placement for older adolescents and adults. It can also be used to diagnose the extent to which neurological and psychiatric disorders may affect mental functioning. The test is individually administered. It takes approximately 59 to 100 minutes to administer the test for the Full Scale IQ (FSIQ) and four index scores. Test materials include two stimulus books, two response booklets, a record form, and the administration manual. The test can be scored by hand or by using the WAIS-IV Scoring Assistant software.
Versions	The original version of the WAIS was published in 1939. At that time, it was known as the Wechsler–Bellevue Intelligence Scale. The test was designed to incorporate verbal and performance scores into a composite intelligence scale. The WAIS-IV is available in 16 languages. The revisions to the WAIS-IV include updated norms, an extended age range (16–90 years), an expanded FSIQ range, improved floors and ceilings to obtain a more accurate measure at each extreme, improved subtest and composite reliability/precision, shortened testing time, and revised instructions.

(Continued)

(Continued)

	The WAIS–IV also removed four subtests (Object Assembly, Picture Arrangement, Digit Symbol-Incidental Learning, and Digit Symbol-Copy) from the previous version (WAIS-III). Three new subtests (Visual Puzzles, Figure Weights, and Cancellations) were added. Twelve subtests (Similarities, Vocabulary, Information, Comprehension, Block Design, Matrix Reasoning, Picture Completion, Digit Span, Arithmetic, Letter-Number Sequencing, Symbol Search, and Coding) were revised with new items and revised scoring.
Scales	The WAIS-IV has four main scales that make up the FSIQ, and each main scale has several subtests, including supplemental subtests that can be used to replace one of the core subtests when necessary:
	The Verbal Comprehension Index (VCI) scale contains four subtests: Similarities, Vocabulary, and Information are core subtests, and Comprehension is supplementary.
	The Perceptual Reasoning Index (PRI) scale contains five subtests: Block Design, Matrix Reasoning, and Visual Puzzles are core subtests, and Picture Completion and Figure Weights are supplementary.
	The Working Memory Index (WMI) scale contains three subtests: Digit Span and Arithmetic are core subtests, and Letter-Number Sequencing is supplementary.
	The Processing Speed Index (PSI) scale contains three subtests: Symbol Search and Coding are core subtests, and Cancellation is supplementary.
	When FSIQ is significantly influenced by the WMI and PSI, a General Ability Index can be calculated from the VCI and PCI.
Report	Multiple sample reports are available at https://images.pearsonclinical.com/images/Products/WAIS-IV/WAISIV_WMSIV_Writer_Report_21yrMale.pdf
	http://images.pearsonclinical.com/images/products/wais-iv/wais-iv_wiat-ii_sample_report.pdf
Reliability/ Precision and Validity	Both the individual scale reliability estimates and the full test reliability estimates are quite high, ranging from .90 for the PSI scale and .96 for the VCI scale. The reliability estimate for the FSIQ is .98. These reliability estimates are the same as or higher than the WAIS-III.
	Evidence of construct validity was provided by the correlations between the WAIS-IV and the WAIS-III, on both the individual scales and the full test. The correlations were quite high in all cases. For the VCI scale it is .89, for the PRI scale .83, for the WMI scale .89, and for the PSI scale and FSIQ .94.
Sources	Spies, R. A., Carlson, J. F., & Geisinger, K. F. (Eds.). (2010). *The eighteenth mental measurements yearbook*. Lincoln, NE: Buros Institute of Mental Measurements.
	Pearson Education. (2012d). *Wechsler Adult Intelligence Scale–Fourth Edition* (WAIS-IV). Retrieved from http://www.pearsonclinical.com/psychology/products/100000392/wechsler-adult-intelligence-scalefourth-edition-wais-iv.html?Pid=015-8980-808&Mode=summary#tab-scoring

TEST SPOTLIGHT 1.2
STANFORD-BINET INTELLIGENCE,
SCALES–FIFTH EDITION (SB5)

Gale H. Roid

Title	Stanford–Binet Intelligence Scales–Fifth Edition (SB5)
Author	Gale H. Roid
Publisher	PRO-ED 8700 Shoal Creek Boulevard Austin, TX 78757-6897 www.proedinc.com
Purpose	The SB5 was designed to assess intelligence and cognitive abilities in children and adults ages 2 to 89 and older. The SB5 is most commonly used to diagnosis learning disabilities and exceptionalities in children, adolescents, and adults. The test measures five factors of cognitive ability: fluid reasoning, knowledge, quantitative reasoning, visual–spatial processing, and working memory.
	The Full Scale IQ is individually administered through 10 subtests, five nonverbal (Nonverbal Knowledge, Nonverbal Quantitative Reasoning, Nonverbal Visual Spatial Processing, Nonverbal Working Memory, and Nonverbal Fluid Reasoning) and five verbal (Verbal Fluid Reasoning, Verbal Quantitative Reasoning, Verbal Visual Spatial Reasoning, Verbal Working Memory, and Verbal Knowledge).
	At the start of the test, the administrator gives two routing subtests (Nonverbal Fluid Reasoning and Verbal Knowledge). These identify the starting level (from 1 to 6) for the remaining subtests.
	The scales have varying administration times that range from 15 to 75 minutes. Individual items on the scale are generally not timed. The Full Scale IQ takes 45 to 75 minutes to administer. The Verbal and Nonverbal IQ scales can be administered in 30 minutes each. There is also an Abbreviated Battery IQ consisting only of the two routing subtests that takes 15 to 20 minutes to administer.
	Numerous scores can be produced from the test data, including composite scores, subtest scaled scores, percentile ranking, confidence intervals, age equivalents, and change-sensitive scores. The tests can be scored by hand or by computer using the SB5 Scoring Pro program.
Versions	The original version of the test was published in 1916. Since then, it has gone through five revisions. The most recent version, SB5, was published in 2003 and is an update to the fourth edition, published in 1986. The SB5 updates included adding a new factor of cognitive ability, Visual Spatial Processing, and reducing the number of subtests from 15 to 10. Additional toys and objects to manipulate for young children, additional nonverbal content, and new items that distinguish between high and low extremes of functioning were added. Last, record forms and books were updated to enhance ease of use, and norms were expanded to include elderly abilities.
Scales	The scales include the Full Scale IQ, two domain scores (Nonverbal IQ and Verbal IQ), and five Factor Indexes (Fluid Reasoning, Knowledge, Quantitative Reasoning, Visual Spatial Processing, and Working Memory).
Report	There is an extended score report and a shorter, narrative summary report. Sample reports are available at http://guardianadlitem.org/wp-content/uploads/2015/08/Sample-Educational-Evaluation_Redacted.pdf And http://www.tnspdg.com/pdf/Andrew%20Smith%20Master.pdf

(Continued)

Reliability/ Precision and Validity	Reliability/precision was calculated through various methods such as test–retest reliability, interscorer agreement, and the split-half method. Mean reliability coefficients for Nonverbal subtests are between .85 and .89. Mean reliability coefficients for Verbal subtests are between .84 and .89. Mean reliability coefficients for the Full Scale IQ is .98, for Nonverbal IQ .95, for Verbal IQ .96, and for the Abbreviated Battery IQ .91.
	Average reliability coefficients for the Factor Index scores were as follows: Fluid Reasoning .90, Knowledge .92, Quantitative Reasoning .92, Visual Spatial Processing .92, and Working Memory .91.
	The SB5 technical manual (cited in the *Mental Measurements Yearbook*) presents a study comparing the SB5 to the SB4. The study found that the correlation between the Full Scale scores was .90. Construct validity was also examined through comparison of the SB5 and the Wechsler Adult Intelligence Scales III, and the correlation found was .82.
Sources	Kush, J. C. (2005). Review of the Stanford–Binet Intelligence Scales: Fifth Edition. In R. S. Spies & B. S. Plake (Eds.), *The sixteenth mental measurements yearbook*. Lincoln, NE: Buros Institute of Mental Measurements.
	PRO-ED, Inc. (2012). *Stanford–Binet Intelligence Scales–Fifth Edition (SB-5)*. Retrieved from https://www .proedinc.com/Downloads/14462%20SB-5_OSRS_UserGuide.pdf

TEST SPOTLIGHT 1.3
NEO PERSONALITY INVENTORY–3 (NEO-PI-3)

Psychological Assessment Resources, Inc P.O. Box 998 Odessa, FL 33556-0978 www. parinc.com

Robert R. McCrae

Title	NEO Personality Inventory–3 (NEO-PI-3)
Author	Paul T. Costa Jr. and Robert R. McCrae
Publisher	PAR 16204 North Florida Avenue Lutz, FL 33549 www.parinc.com
Purpose	The NEO-PI-3 is used to assess normal personality in children and adults ages 12 and up. It measures the Big Five factors of personality (referred to as *domains*): Extraversion, Agreeableness, Conscientiousness, Neuroticism, and Openness to Experience. The NEO-PI-3 provides a summary of an individual's emotional, interpersonal, experiential, attitudinal, and motivational styles. The NEO-PI-3 is used in a variety of fields, including clinical psychology, psychiatry, behavioral medicine, counseling, industrial/organizational psychology, and education and personality research. The NEO-PI-3 can be group or individually administered and takes approximately 30 to 40 minutes to complete. It contains 240 items and three validity-check items designed to identify whether a respondent is honestly and accurately completing the inventory. Each item is rated on a five-point scale. The NEO-PI-3 can be administered via pencil and paper, or it can be administered and scored electronically with the NEO Software System. The NEO-PI-3 contains two parallel versions. There is a self-report (Form S) and an observer report (Form R), which is written in the third person and can be used as a supplement to the self-report.
Versions	In addition to the NEO-PI-3, there is a shortened form of the NEO Personality Inventory, the NEO Five-Factor Inventory–3, which has 60 items and provides scores on the five domain scales only. There is also a previous version of the inventory, the NEO PI-R, as well as a version that eliminates the Neuroticism scale, the NEO-4, designed to be used in career and personnel counseling, in which differences in an individual's anxiety and depression are generally less relevant. As part of the update from the NEO PI-R to the NEO-PI-3, 38 items were replaced, and the new assessment is now suitable for middle school–age children and adolescents. In addition, separate norms are now available for adolescent (12-20 years) and adult (21 years and older) test takers. Clinicians can continue using the NEO PI-R.
Scales	The scales include the following five domains and six traits that define each domain: • Neuroticism (Anxiety, Angry Hostility, Depression, Self-Consciousness, Impulsiveness, Vulnerability) • Extraversion (Warmth, Gregariousness, Assertiveness, Activity, Excitement-Seeking, Positive Emotions) • Openness (Fantasy, Aesthetics, Feelings, Actions, Ideas, Values) • Agreeableness (Trust, Straight-Forwardness, Altruism, Compliance, Modesty, Tender-Mindedness) • Conscientiousness (Competence, Order, Dutifulness, Achievement Striving, Self-Discipline, Deliberation)

(Continued)

(Continued)

Report	A sample report can be found at https://www.parinc.com/Products/Pkey/275#resources https://www.parinc.com/Products/Pkey/274
Reliability/ Precision and Validity	In terms of reliability/precision, internal consistency coefficients range from .89 to .93 for the domain scales on both Form R and Form S. Internal consistency coefficients for the facet scales range from .54 to .83 for both Form R and Form S. In terms of validity, evidence exists that groups of individuals who differ on test construct also differ in group mean scores in theoretically predictable ways. For example, psychotherapy patients tend to score high on Neuroticism and drug abusers tend to score low on Agreeableness and Conscientiousness. Further evidence of validity comes from comparing NEO-PI-3 scores to scores on other personality inventories. According to Costa and McCrae (2008), there have been over 2,000 published articles and books attesting to the validity of the NEO. Construct validity has been demonstrated by the observation that the scales on the NEO have been shown to correlate in predictable fashion with many other well-researched tests of personality including the MMPI, the PAI, and the Millon Clinical Multiaxial Inventory. The scales have also shown to have predictive evidence of validity in a wide range of applications including vocational interests, ego development and diagnoses of personality disorders. Studies on the Revised NEO Personality Inventory also show convergent and discriminant evidence of (construct) validity with other personality tests such as the Self Directed Search, Meyers-Briggs Type Indicator, and the Personality Research Form.
Sources	Benson, N., & Kluck, A. S. (1995). Review of the NEO Personality Inventory–3. In J. C. Conoley & J. C. Impara (Eds.), *The twelfth mental measurements yearbook*. Lincoln, NE: Buros Institute of Mental Measurements. Botwin, M. D. (1995). Review of the Minnesota Multiphasic Personality Inventory–A. In J. J. Kramer & J. C. Conoley (Eds.), *The twelfth mental measurements yearbook*. Lincoln, NE: Buros Institute of Mental Measurements. Carlson, J. F., Geisinger, K. F., & Jonson, J. L. (2014). *The nineteenth mental measurements yearbook*. Lincoln, NE: Buros Center for Testing. Costa, P. T., & McCrae, R. R. (2008). The revised NEO personality inventory (NEO-PI-R). *The SAGE Handbook of Personality Theory and Assessment, 2.* 179-198. doi:10.4135/9781849200479.n9 PAR. (2018a). *NEO Personality Inventory–3 (NEO-PI-3)*. Retrieved from https://www.parinc.com/Products/Pkey/275

TEST SPOTLIGHT 1.4
MYERS–BRIGGS TYPE INDICATOR (MBTI)

Reprinted by permission of CAPT Archives.

Reprinted by permission of CAPT Archives.

Katherine Cook Briggs   Isabel Briggs Myers

Title	Myers–Briggs Type Indicator (MBTI)
Author	Katherine Cook Briggs and Isabel Briggs Myers
Publisher	CPP 1055 Joaquin Road, 2nd Floor Mountain View, CA 94043 www.cpp.com
Purpose	The MBTI is a personality test that helps individuals understand their personality preferences. The MBTI was developed in 1943 by Katherine Briggs and her daughter, Isabel Briggs Myers, and was based on the psychological-type framework of Carl Jung and on their belief that understanding differences in personality preferences can help individuals interact with others more effectively. After extensive reading of Jung's theories and an intense study of people, Briggs and Briggs Myers determined that people differ in four primary ways. They referred to these differences as preferences and likened them to how we favor one of our hands over the other. Although every individual uses both hands, most individuals have a preference for, or favor, using one hand over the other. The results of the MBTI provide individuals with insights into their own personality preferences and can serve as a catalyst for improving relationships with others. The MBTI is often used for team development, conflict management, leadership and coaching, and career exploration. The MBTI is most appropriate for adults and students ages 14 years or older. Caution should be taken when using the MBTI with younger children because research suggests that types are less developed with younger children and individuals who are less mature. Available in paper-and-pencil format and online, the self-administered MBTI requires individuals to respond to forced-choice questions. It is available in approximately 30 languages and takes 15 to 25 minutes to complete.
Versions	Various versions of the MBTI are available. • Form M, referred to as the standard form since 1998, is written at the 7th-grade reading level and consists of 93 items. Developed for individuals age 14 years or older, Form M includes one booklet containing the 93 items, an answer sheet, and interpretive information. Simple scoring instructions are also included. In addition, there is a self-scorable version that is ideal for use in workshop settings where there is limited time available for scoring. • Form Q consists of 144 items (93 items from Form M plus 51 additional items). This version extends the personality preferences to include explanations of why individuals of similar type may behave differently. Each preference is further expanded. • The Murphy–Meisgeier Type Indicator for Children consists of 43 items and is specially designed for use with children ages 8 to 18 years. This form can be scored by computer. • MBTI Step III instrument consists of 222 forced choice items written at the 9th-grade reading level for ages 18 and older. This form is designed to assess current use of perception and judgment with three Sufficiency scales (confidence, stamina, and compensatory strain) and 26 developmental scales.

(Continued)

(Continued)

Scales	The MBTI provides data on four sets of preferences:

Where you focus your energy—Extroversion (E) or Introversion (I)

How you take in information—Sensing (S) or Intuition (N)

How you make decisions—Thinking (T) or Feeling (F)

How you deal with the outer world—Judging (J) or Perceiving (P)

When these four sets of preferences are combined, they result in 16 different personality types:

ISTJ	ISFJ	INFJ	INTJ
ISTP	ISFP	INFP	INTP
ESTP	ESFP	ENFP	ENTP
ESTJ	ESFJ	ENFJ	ENTJ

Report	The typical MBTI report includes (a) a description of where personality types come from, (b) an explanation of how the individual's responses were used to determine his or her expressed personality preference, (c) a description of the individual's personality type, and (d) the clarity of the individual's preferences (how strong each preference was). A sample report can be found at https://www.cpp.com/en-US/Products-and-Services/Sample-Reports

Reliability/ Precision and Validity	Reliability/precision studies indicate that the MBTI has good test–retest reliability, with the reliability/ precision of the S–N, E–I, and J–P scales being higher than that of the T–F scale. In test–retest studies, individuals tend to be typed with three of the four type preferences 75% to 90% of the time (the preference on which they vary is typically one where the preference was relatively weak). Test–retest reliability coefficients tend to range between .73 and .83 (E–I), .69 and .87 (S–N), .56 and .82 (T–F), and .60 and .87 (J–P). Estimates of internal consistency range between .55 and .65 (E–I), .64 and .73 (S–N), .43 and .75 (T–F), and .58 and .84 (J–P). Although the reliabilities are good across age and ethnic groups, reliabilities with some groups on some scales may be somewhat lower. For children, the reliabilities of the scales are extremely low; therefore, the MBTI should be used with caution with children.
	A number of validity studies indicate good relationships, in expected directions, providing evidence of construct validity. For example, the MBTI test user's manual includes correlations of the four preference scales with a variety of scales from other personality and interest instruments, including the 16 Personality Factors, Million Index of Personality Styles, California Psychological Inventory, NEO Personality Inventory, Fundamental Interpersonal Relations Orientation–Behavior, Adjective Checklist, Strong Interest Inventory, Skills Factors Inventory, Skills Confidence Inventory, Salience Inventory, Values Scale, Work Environment Scale, Maslach Burnout Inventory, Coping Resources Inventory, and State–Trait Anxiety Inventory. Although numerous validity coefficients are reported in the manual, correlation coefficients for the four scales range between .66 and .76 (E–I), .34 and .71 (S–N), .23 and .78 (T–F), and .39 and .73 (J–P). No evidence exists in the literature that the MBTI correlates with measures of job performance; therefore, the MBTI is not appropriate for job screening, placement, or selection without an independent criterion-related validation study using a large sample of applicants or employees.

Sources	Carlson, J. F., Geisinger, K. F., & Jonson, J. L. (2017). *The twentieth mental measurements yearbook*. Lincoln, NE: Buros Center for Testing.
	Center for Applications of Psychological Type. (2012). *The forms of the MBTI instrument*. Retrieved from http://www.capt.org/mbti-assessment/mbti-forms.htm
	Consulting Psychologists Press. (2009). *Myers–Briggs Type Indicator interpretive report: Report prepared for Jane Sample*. Retrieved from https://www.capt.org/mbti-assessment/mbti-forms.htm
	Martin, C. (2012). *The sixteen types at a glance*. Retrieved from http://www.capt.org/the_mbti_instrument/type_descriptions.cfm
	Myers, I. B. (1998). *Introduction to type* (6th ed.). Palo Alto, CA: Consulting Psychologists Press.
	Myers, I. B., McCaulley, M. H., Quenk, N. L., & Hammer, A. L. (1998). *MBTI manual: A guide to the development and use of the Myers–Briggs Type Indicator* (3rd ed.). Palo Alto, CA: Consulting Psychologists Press.

TEST SPOTLIGHT 2.1
SAT

Title	SAT
Author	College Board
Publisher	Educational Testing Service
	660 Rosedale Road
	Princeton, NJ 08541
	www.ets.org
Purpose	Taken by more than 2 million high school juniors and seniors a year and used by most American colleges as a part of the admissions process, the SAT is a college entrance exam believed by many to be the most independent, objective, and standardized measure available for predicting success in college—more specifically, for predicting 1st-year college grades. The SAT, which previously was referred to as the Scholastic Aptitude Test, was developed in 1926 by Carl Campbell Brigham for the College Entrance Examination Board. At that time, people believed that the test measured an individual's aptitude or innate intelligence. Over time, primarily in response to awareness that individuals can improve SAT scores through preparation (an unlikely outcome if the test truly measured aptitude), the board revised the Scholastic Aptitude Test, added a writing sample, and called it the Scholastic Assessment Test. Today the College Board states that "SAT" no longer stands for anything; the SAT is just the SAT. It is administered in the United States, Puerto Rico, and the U.S. territories seven times a year, and six times a year overseas. Students can register online to take the SAT and receive their reports online.
Versions	In 2005, the College Board introduced a revised SAT, which not only includes an additional section in writing, but reflected minor changes in content to the verbal and mathematics section. The verbal section was renamed as the critical reading section. The mathematics section was updated to include more advanced mathematics and quantitative comparison items were removed.

- The SAT consists of the SAT Reasoning Test and the SAT Subject Tests.

- The SAT Reasoning Test measures the critical thinking skills students need for academic success in college. The Reasoning Test is a timed test (3 hours 45 minutes) that measures the critical thinking, reasoning, and writing knowledge and skills that students have developed over time.

- The SAT Subject Tests, formerly called Achievement Tests, measure mastery of content in different subject areas. The SAT Subject Tests fall into five general categories: English (Literature), history (U.S. History and World History), mathematics (Mathematics Level 1 and Mathematics Level 2), science (Biology, Chemistry, and Physics), and languages (Chinese With Listening, French, French With Listening, German, German With Listening, Spanish, Spanish With Listening, Modern Hebrew, Italian, Latin, Japanese With Listening, and Korean With Listening). Each SAT Subject Test is a timed (1-hour) multiple-choice test. (Although some of the tests have unique formats. For example, for some of the language tests, students must bring CD players with them to the testing center.)

(Continued)

(Continued)

- The PSAT/NMSQT and PSAT10 (preliminary) for high school juniors and seniors measures evidence-based reading, writing and language, and math tests based on knowledge gained from high school and information necessary for college success. The tests take 2 hours and 5 minutes to complete and a scale range of 40-1440. The key content features included in the test require the test taker to figure out the meaning of words (those typically used in college and the workplace). The reading test is a compilation of multiple choice questions based on one or multiple passages, graphs, tables, and charts. The writing and language portion contains questions that require proofing and fixing mistakes by reading passages and answering multiple-choice questions. The math portion has questions on math, science, and history and the questions provide problems the test taker must solve and answer multiple-choice questions or grid-ins (a calculator is used for half the test).

- In March 2016, a new version of the SAT was released and includes three tests: reading, writing and language, and math. The content of the reading test involves reading a passage and answering multiple-choice questions on how a person receives, thinks, and uses information with textual evidence and no prior knowledge is required. The writing and language test requires the test taker to read a passage and answer multiple-choice questions based on the information presented and no prior knowledge is required. The math test contains problem-solving questions where the test taker will answer multiple choice, grid-in, or bubble choice questions. Colleges and universities may require the essay portion for admittance, which is available as an option. The first task to write the essay is to read a passage and then explain the author's argument with evidence. The math test contains questions that the test taker must solve followed by answering the question with multiple choice, grid-in, and bubble choices

Scales	The SAT Reasoning Test consists of three sections: critical reading, mathematics, and writing. Each section is scored on a scale of 200 to 800 (with two writing subscores for multiple-choice questions and the essay).
Report	The SAT Reasoning Test score report includes (a) the individual's raw score and a 200- to 800-point scaled score for the critical reading, math, and writing sections; (b) a 0- to 12-point essay subscore; (c) information about the individual's responses, such as questions they answered correctly and incorrectly; (d) a percentile rank representing how the individual scored in comparison with other test takers at the state and national levels; and (e) a copy of the individual's essay. The report also includes detailed information about the characteristics of the colleges to which the test taker requested that score reports be sent (e.g., type of school, size of school, diversity of freshman class, high school preparation requirements, freshman admission statistics and admission criteria, admissions and financial aid application deadlines). Although all students who take the SAT will receive their SAT score reports in the mail, score reports are also available online and are free to every student who takes the SAT. The online service contains a number of features to help students interpret their SAT scores.
Reliability/ Precision and Validity	Most reliability/precision studies show that the SAT is a reliable test. Internal consistency studies show reliability coefficients exceeding .90, suggesting that items measure a similar content area. Test–retest studies generally show reliability coefficients ranging between .87 and .93, suggesting that individuals tend to earn similar scores on repeated occasions.
	Researchers have conducted many studies on the validity of the SAT. In terms of content validity, over the years careful attention has been paid to reviewing SAT content to ensure that it does not become out of date, reflects appropriate and up-to-date subject matter, and contains vocabulary consistent with that used in college-level study. High school and college administrators have also spent considerable time in reviewing and modifying or removing SAT items that may be viewed as offensive because of cultural bias, sexist language, and so on.
	For decades, the College Board and other researchers have been examining the relationship among SAT scores, college grades, and other measures of success (e.g., grade point average [GPA], attrition, teacher ratings, awards and honors).

Although research suggests that the SAT does not equally predict the college success of male and female students, traditional students and nontraditional students, or racial and cultural subgroups, many criterion-related validity studies indicate that SAT scores correlate with college grades and other tests used in the admissions process. One of the strongest correlations of the SAT with high school grades and freshman-year college grades exists for traditional White students (vs. nontraditional students who return to school later in life). SAT scores also show an acceptable correlation with a combination of high school grades. SAT scores are also the strongest predictor of freshman-year grades. Most validity studies suggest that SAT scores, when combined with high school records, are predictive of college freshman-year grades, with uncorrected validity coefficients ranging between .35 and .42 (and with corrected validity coefficients somewhat higher).

In 2008, the College Board released new information regarding evidence of validity for the 2005 updated version of the SAT. Since the SAT is intended to measure student potential for success in college, many consider the most critical form of validity to be evidence of the test's predictive validity, that is, the extent to which the SAT is a good predictor of college performance.

Across the United States, 726 colleges and universities provided 1st-year performance data from the fall 2006 entering class. The results show that the changes made to the SAT did not substantially change how predictive the test is of 1st-year college performance. SAT scores were correlated at .35 (.53 adjusted) with 1st-year GPA (FYGPA). SAT writing scores were most highly correlated, at .33 (.51 adjusted), with FYGPA.

Data for the new version of the SAT is not available at this time. The questions on the new version differ from the old version and data from both tests will not be compared. Data collection will begin in 2018 and end in 2019, with information based on 2017 high school graduates who took the new SAT.

To read more about the validity of the SAT, go to https://research.collegeboard.org/sites/default/files/publications/2012/7/researchreport-2008-5-validity-sat-predicting-first-year-college-grade-point-average.pdf

Sources

Carlson, J. F., Geisinger, K. F., & Jonson, J. L. (2017). *The twentieth mental measurements yearbook*. Lincoln, NE: Buros Center for Testing.

Elert, G. (1992). *The SAT: Aptitude or demographics?* Retrieved from http://hypertextbook.com/eworld/sat.shtml

Kobrin, J. L., Patterson, B. F., Shaw, E. J., Mattern, K. D., & Barbuti, S. M. (2008). *Validity of the SAT for predicting first-year college grade point average*. Retrieved from https://research.collegeboard.org/sites/default/files/publications/2012/7/researchreport-2008-5-validity-sat-predicting-first-year-college-grade-point-average.pdf

National Center for Fair and Open Testing. (2007). *The SAT: Questions and answers*. Retrieved from http://www.fairtest.org/facts/satfact.htm

TEST SPOTLIGHT 4.1
MINI-MENTAL STATE EXAMINATION, SECOND EDITION (MMSE-2)

Title	Mini-Mental State Examination, Second Edition (MMSE-2)
Author	Marshal Folstein, Susan Folstein, Travis White, and Melissa Messer
Publisher	PAR 16204 North Florida Avenue Lutz, FL 33549 www.parinc.com
Purpose	Originally developed in 1975, the MMSE is a cognitive ability test used by many clinicians to systematically and quickly assess cognitive status. Clinicians use the MMSE to screen for cognitive impairment, determine the severity of cognitive impairment, monitor changes in impairment over time, and document response to treatment. The MMSE is one of the most commonly used tests for complaints of memory problems or when there is reason to believe that an individual has a cognitive impairment such as dementia. The MMSE, for ages 18 and older, is most effectively used with older, community-dwelling, hospitalized, and institutionalized adults and takes approximately 5 to 10 minutes to administer.
Versions and Scales	The MMSE-2 improves on the original by standardizing its administration and altering some of the original MMSE items. The MMSE-2 demonstrates high equivalency with the original MMSE, allowing test users to switch from the original MMSE to the MMSE-2: Short Version without compromising longitudinal data and without any change in the normal range of scores. An even briefer version, the new MMSE-2: Brief Version, is designed for rapid assessment in a variety of settings. The MMSE-2: Expanded Version, a slightly longer version, is more sensitive to subcortical dementia and to changes associated with aging. It is sufficiently difficult that it does not have a ceiling effect. Equivalent, alternate forms (Blue and Red) of each MMSE-2 version have been developed to decrease the possibility of practice effects that can occur over serial examinations. The Pocket Norms Guide provides norms for all versions of the MMSE-2.
Report	The publisher offers Mental Status Reporting Software that provides qualified professionals with the ability to organize information related to an individual's mental status and to generate a mental status report. Following are a few samples from the report. A complete sample report can be found at http://www4.parinc.com/WebUploads/samplerpts/MSRS.pdf

Sample A. Client   Page 2

1234-5678   07/15/2002

MMSE Results

The patient's score on the MMSE is below the cutoff score (23) that has been found to be most effective in identifying dementia in research studies. The possibility of cognitive impairment characteristic of dementia is further supported when her performance is compared to the performance of individuals of similar age and education level from the MMSE normative sample (Folstein, Folstein, & Fanjiaug, 2001).

The patient had difficulty on the MMSE in the following area(s):

Orientation to Time

Orientation to Place

Comprehension

Reading

Writing

Drawing

Sample A. Client   Page 3

1234-5678   07/15/2002

MSRS Checklist Results

The patient is right-handed. The patient was alert and responsive. Her orientation, attention, and concentration were impaired. Appearance was consistent with her stated age. Eye contact during the evaluation was good. The patient was dressed appropriately and her grooming appeared to be adequate. Regarding her motor functioning, no apparent abnormalities were observed. No gait disturbances were noted. Some evidence of impaired vision was noted.

Some word finding difficulties in her speech were observed. Prosody was normal. No auditory comprehension difficulties were apparent. No apparent disturbances in remote memory were noted, but some impairment in both immediate and recent memory was evident. The patient's intellectual ability was estimated to be average. Executive functioning problems were evidenced by planning and organization deficits. Affect was flat. Her mood was anxious. Information about the patient's interpersonal behavior was not recorded. The patient denied having suicidal or homicidal ideation. Her thought content was appropriate for the situation. Thought processes were disconnected and/or incoherent. No delusions were conveyed by the patient. She denied experiencing hallucinations. Judgment, reasoning, and insight were poor.

The patient was referred by family/friend. Status is voluntary, outpatient. Patient completed intake form with assistance

Comments

Additional information observed about this patient during the evaluation includes the following:

None

(Continued)

(Continued)

	07/15/2002		Page 4
Sample A. Client			
1234-5678			07/15/2002
Longitudinal Profile Record			
	07/15/2002		
	07/30/2001	07/15/2002	
MMSE (Raw)	23	21	
MMSE (T)	27	9	
Consciousness	Alert	Alert	
Orientation	x3	Impaired	
Attention/Concentration	n.a.d.	Impaired	
Appearance	Consistent with stated age	Consistent with stated age	
Eye Contact	Good	Good	
Dress	Appropriate	Appropriate	
Grooming	Adequate	Adequate	
Motor Functioning	n.a.d.	n.a.d.	
Gait	n.a.d.	n.a.d.	
Visual Perception	Impaired vision	Impaired vision	
Speech	n.a.d.	Word finding difficulties	
Prosody	n.a.d.	n.a.d.	
Auditory Comprehension	Other	n.a.d.	
Immediate Memory	n.a.d.	Impaired	
Recent Memory	n.a.d.	Impaired	
Remote Memory	n.a.d.	n.a.d.	
Estimated Intellectual Ability	Average	Average	

Note: n.a.d. = No apparent disturbances; x3 = oriented to person, place, & time.

Sample A. Client				Page 7
1234-5678				07/15/2002
Item Responses				

MMSE Responses

1. 1	7. 1	13. 1	19. 3	25. ?
2. 1	8. 0	14. ?	20. 1	26. 0
3. 1	9. 1	15. ?	21. 1	27. 1
4. 1	10. 1	16. ?	22. 1	28. 1
5. 0	11. 1	17. ?	23. 1	29. 0
6. 1	12. 1	18. ?	24. 1	30. 0
				31. 0

Conc 0

MSRS Responses

1. 1	7. 1	13. 1	19. 2	25. 1
2. 1	8. 1	14. 1	20. 5	26. 7
3. 2	9. 1	15. 2	21. 5	27. 1
4. 2	10. 1	16. 2	22. 0	28. 1
5. 1	11. 6	17. 1	23. 2	29. 3
6. 1	12. 3	18. 2	24. 2	30. 3

Hx Left Hand 0

Reliability/ Precision and Validity

Most research studies regarding the MMSE indicate a relatively high reliability/precision of test scores. Many studies have gathered evidence of test–retest reliability and have documented that test–retest reliability may decline over time. Test–retest reliabilities for psychiatric and neurologic patients range from .38 to .92 with a time lapse of 24 hours to 2 years Test–retest reliabilities using the Pearson correlation range from .86 to .92 with time lapses of less than 1 year. The test-retest reliability for MMSE- 2 BV was .44 and .80 for forms SV and BV. Many studies have also gathered evidence of interrater reliability. Interrater reliability estimates range from .69 to 1.00 depending on the sample population. Few studies examine and report internal consistency reliability estimates. One study reports an internal consistency reliability coefficient of .764.

(Continued)

(Continued)

Research reveals evidence of validity based on content. For example, a study by R. Jones and Gallo (2000) came close to replicating the original structure of the MMSE, identifying five factors subsequently replicated by Baños and Franklin (2002). Predictive validity studies appear to provide conflicting results; some suggest that individuals whose test scores indicate cognitive impairment are later diagnosed with cognitive impairment at least 79% of the time, whereas others suggest a high false-positive rate of up to 86%.

Reviewers of the instrument remind users that the MMSE relies heavily on verbal response and reading and writing. Therefore, clinicians should be cautious about interpreting MMSE results for patients with hearing and visual impairments and patients who have low English literacy or communication disorders. Patients with these characteristics may perform poorly due to factors other than cognitive ability.

Sources	Albanese, M. A. (2001). Review of the Mini Mental State Examination. In B. S. Plake, J. C. Impara, & R. A. Spies (Eds.), *The fifteenth mental measurements yearbook*. Lincoln, NE: Buros Institute of Mental Measurements.
	Baños, J. H., & Franklin, L. M. (2002). Factor structure of the Mini-Mental State Examination in adult psychiatric patients. *Psychological Assessment*, 14, 397–400.
	Jones, R. N., & Gallo, J. J. (2000). Dimensions of the Mini-Mental State Examination among community dwelling older adults. *Psychological Medicine*, *30*, 605–618.
	Kluck, A. S., & Zhuzha, K. (2017). Test review of Mini-Mental State Examination, 2nd Edition. In J F. Carlson, K. F Geisinger, & J. L. Jonson, *The twentieth mental measurements yearbook*. Lincoln, NE: Buros Center for Testing.
	Lopez, M. N., Charter, R. A., Mostafavi, B., Nibut, L. P., & Smith, W. E. (2005). Psychometric properties of the Folstein Mini-Mental State Examination. *Assessment, 12*, 137–144.
	PAR. (n.d.). *MMSE-2: Mini-Mental State Examination* (2nd ed.). Retrieved from http://www.minimental.com
	Ward, S. (2001). Review of the Mini Mental State Examination. In B. S. Plake, J. C. Impara, & R. A. Spies (Eds.), *The fifteenth mental measurements yearbook*. Lincoln, NE: Buros Institute of Mental Measurements.

TEST SPOTLIGHT 5.1
PERSONALITY ASSESSMENT INVENTORY (PAI)

Leslie C. Morey

Title	Personality Assessment Inventory (PAI)
Author	Leslie C. Morey
Publisher	PAR 16204 North Florida Avenue Lutz, FL 33549 www.parinc.com
Purpose	Leslie C. Morey developed the PAI as an objective alternative to the Minnesota Multiphasic Personality Inventory (MMPI). The PAI is an objective personality test designed to identify a number of psychological disorders in adults (ages 18 years and older) relevant to clinical diagnosis, treatment planning, and screening for psychopathology. The test takes approximately 50 to 60 minutes to administer, 15-20 minutes to score the test, and requires a 4th grade education. The PAI contains 344 statements for which the test taker must choose one of four responses: *false, not at all true*; *slightly true*; *mainly true*; and *very true*. Sample statements on the PAI resemble the following: My friends are available if I need them. Much of the time I'm sad for no real reason. My relationships have been stormy. I have many brilliant ideas.
Versions	The original version (Morey, 1991) is available in paper-and-pencil format in English and Spanish. Another version, PAI Software Portfolio Version 2.2, is available on CD-ROM. A separate test, the PAI-A, is available for assessment of children and adolescents 12 to 18 years of age.
Scales	The PAI has 11 clinical scales (Somatic Complaints, Anxiety, Anxiety-Related Disorders, Depression, Mania, Paranoia, Schizophrenia, Borderline Features, Antisocial Features, Alcohol Problems, and Drug Problems), 5 treatment scales (Aggression, Suicidal Ideation, Stress, Nonsupport, and Treatment Rejection) that measure characteristics that affect treatment, and 2 interpersonal scales (Dominance and Warmth) that provide information about the test taker's relationships with others. In addition, the PAI has 4 validity scales (Inconsistency, Infrequency, Negative Impression, and Positive Impression) that are used to determine whether the test taker answered the questions consistently and in good faith.
Reliability/ Precision and Validity	The reliability/precision of the PAI has been estimated using internal consistency estimates. The median reliability estimate ranged from .81 to .82 to .86 for the general community sample, college student sample, and clinical sample, respectively. Test–retest reliability estimates for the clinical scales taken at either 24 or 28 days ranged from .79 to .92.

(Continued)

(Continued)

	The test manual for an earlier edition (Morey, 1991) contains a number of validity studies for the clinical and validity scales. For example, the validity scales were correlated with the L, F, and K scales of the MMPI and with the Marlowe–Crowne Social Desirability Scale to determine discriminant and convergent evidence of validity. Also, PAI scales (validity, clinical, treatment, and interpersonal) were correlated with the MMPI, the Beck Depression Inventory, the Wahler Physical Symptoms Inventory, and the Fear Survey Schedule, yielding moderate validity coefficients. The new manual contains 133 pages of validity studies, including correlations between certain PAI scales and the NEO Personality Inventory in a general community sample. Correlations were in the direction expected (e.g., the PAI Anxiety scale correlated at .75 with the NEO Neuroticism scale, the PAI Paranoia scale correlated at −.54 with the NEO Agreeableness scale).
Report	The publisher offers a Clinical Interpretive Report that provides qualified professionals with the ability to organize information related to an individual's personality. A complete sample report can be found at https://www.parinc.com/Products/Pkey/287 or https://www.parinc.com/WebUploads/samplerpts/PAI_Correctional_PiC2.pdf
Sources	Cox, A., Thorpe, G., & Dawson, R. (2010). Review of the Personality Assessment Inventory. In R. A. Spies, J. F. Carlson, & K. F. Geisinger (Eds.), *The eighteenth mental measurements yearbook*. Lincoln, NE: Buros Institute of Mental Measurements. Morey, L. C. (1991). *Personality Assessment Inventory*. Odessa, FL: Psychological Assessment Resources. PAR. (2018b). *Personality Assessment Inventory*. Retrieved from https://www.parinc.com/Products/Pkey/299

TEST SPOTLIGHT 5.2
TEST OF NONVERBAL INTELLIGENCE, FOURTH EDITION (TONI-4)

Rita J. Sherbenou   Susan K. Johnsen

Title	Test of Nonverbal Intelligence, Fourth Edition (TONI-4)
Author	Linda Brown, Rita J. Sherbenou, and Susan K. Johnsen
Publisher	PRO-ED 8700 Shoal Creek Boulevard Austin, TX 78757-6897 www.proedinc.com
Purpose	The TONI-4 is a nonverbal intelligence test that does not require the use of language, written or verbal, for administration. The TONI-4 is designed to measure intelligence, aptitude, abstract reasoning, and problem solving. The test takers indicate their answers in any means at their disposal, such as pointing, nodding, or making any other gesture that can be properly interpreted by the test administrator. The TONI-4 is designed for individuals that have or are suspected to have communication disorders such as dyslexia, aphasia, or other learning or speech difficulties. It can also be used in populations that do not speak English and is designed so that no knowledge of U.S. culture is required. It is appropriate for a wide range of ages (6 years to 89 years 11 months). The test taker is asked to respond to abstract figures that present a problem along with four to six possible responses. The test items do not use words, numbers, or pictures. Unlike previous versions, with the TONI-4, the examiner may give oral instructions to the test taker. The test is made up of 6 practice items and 60 scored items presented in order of increasing difficulty. The test continues until three of five items are answered incorrectly. Test administration takes approximately 15 to 20 minutes.
Versions	The TONI-4 is the fourth revision of the test, with two equivalent forms (A and B), which enable the test to be used in situations in which pre- and posttesting are needed. The revision included adding 15 new items to improve ceiling and floor effects. This test can be useful to evaluate student progress or treatment effectiveness.
Scales	Results are reported in a standard score format scaled to have a mean of 100 and a standard deviation of 15. Percentile ranks are also reported based on a normative sample of 2,272 participants from 31 U.S. states. The demographic characteristics of the sample are balanced in terms of age, gender, ethnicity, and other factors.
Report	This test does not generate a report because the test administrator records the participant's responses in an answer booklet. Then the administrator scores and interprets the responses by referencing the test norms.
Reliability/ Precision and Validity	The average internal consistency reliability using coefficient alpha is .96. Test–retest reliability is estimated to be between .88 and .93 for school-age participants and between .82 and .84 for adults. However, the participants in the study were not representative of the target population. The average alternate form reliability across all age groups based on an immediate test–retest design ranged between .67 and .89 across different age groups and standardization samples. With a delayed design, the reliability was estimated to be .83 with school-age participants and .86 with adults. Interscorer agreement was calculated to be .99. Evidence of construct validity is provided via correlations with other versions of the TONI as well as with other tests measuring similar constructs. The correlation of the TONI-4 with the TONI-3 was .74. The TONI-4 also correlated with three school achievement tests with coefficients ranging from .55 to .78.

(Continued)

(Continued)

Sources	Carlson, J. F., Geisinger, K. F., & Jonson, J. L. (2014). *The nineteenth mental measurements yearbook*. Lincoln, NE: Buros Center for Testing.
	Ritter, N., Kilinc, E., Navruz, B., & Bae, Y. (2011). Test review. *Journal of Psychoeducational Assessment, 29*, 484–488.
	Strauss, E., Sherman, E. M., & Spreen, O. (2006). *A compendium of neuropsychological tests: Administration, norms and commentary* (3rd ed.). New York: Oxford University Press.

TEST SPOTLIGHT 5.3
WISCONSIN CARD SORTING TEST (WCST)

Title	Wisconsin Card Sorting Test (WCST)
Author	Originally developed by David A. Grant and Esta A. Berg Revised and updated by Robert K. Heaton, Gordon J. Chelune, Jack L. Talley, Gary G. Kay, and Glenn Curtiss
Publisher	PAR 16204 North Florida Avenue Lutz, FL 33549 www.parinc.com
Purpose	Originally designed to assess perseveration and abstract thinking, the WCST is increasingly being used by clinicians and neurologists as a neuropsychological instrument to measure executive functions performed by the frontal lobe of the brain (strategic planning, organized searching, using environmental feedback to shift cognitive sets, directing behavior toward achieving a goal, and modulating impulsive responding). The test is appropriate for a wide range of ages (6.5–89 years). The test administrator places four stimulus cards in front of the test taker in a specific order. The administrator then gives the test taker a deck of 64 response cards. The cards include a picture of various shapes (circles, crosses, triangles, and stars), numbers (1, 2, 3, and 4), and colors (red, yellow, blue, and green). The administrator asks the test taker to match each of the cards with one of the four stimulus cards that the test taker thinks it matches. The administrator tells the test taker whether his or her response is correct or incorrect, and the test taker proceeds through the various sorting possibilities. After 10 consecutive correct answers to one card, such as color, the sorting shifts to the next card, such as number. Once done with the first deck of response cards, the examinee is given the second deck of 64 cards to continue sorting. The administrator records the responses in a test booklet. The responses are then scored on three dimensions (correct/incorrect, ambiguous/unambiguous, and perseverative/nonperseverative). The test has no time limit, and the test taker can take as much time as is needed with the sort. The test typically takes about 20 to 30 minutes to complete.
Versions	The original version was published in 1981. A revised version with updated norms was published in 1993. In addition to the paper-and-pencil version, a computer-based version of the WCST is also available. A shortened version of the test, WCST-64, using only one deck of 64 cards, is available as well.
Scales	The WCST allows clinicians and neuropsychologists to assess frontal lobe functions using five scales: strategic planning, organized searching, using environmental feedback to shift cognitive sets, directing behavior toward achieving a goal, and modulating impulsive responding.

(Continued)

(Continued)

Report	A sample report can be found at http://www4.parinc.com/WebUploads/samplerpts/WCSTCV4_Report.pdf

Pages 1 and 2 from the Wisconsin Card Sorting Test Computer Version 4 Research Edition Sample Score Report are reproduced below.

Wisconsin Card Sorting Test: Computer Version 4 Research

Edition by Robert K. Heaton, PhD, and PAR Staff

Client Information

Last Name: Examinee	Test Date: 09/18/2009
First Name: John	Test Description: (no description)
Client ID: 25641	
Birth Date: 07/26/1956	Rapport: Good
Age: 53 years, 1 month	Cooperation: Adequate
Gender: Male	Effort: Adequate
Ethnicity: Caucasian (not of Hispanic origin)	On Medication: No
Education: 8 years	Description of Medication:
Handedness: Right	
Occupation: U	

Caveats

Use of this report requires a thorough understanding of the Wisconsin Card Sorting Test (WCST; Berg, 1948; Grant & Berg, 1948), its interpretation, and clinical applications as presented in the WCST Manual (Heaton, Chelune, Talley, Kay, & Curtiss, 1993). This report is intended for use by qualified professionals.

This report reflects an administration using the standard 128-card paper-and-pencil version of the WCST. The normative scores used in this program were developed by Heaton et al. (1993), using the standard WCST version. Users should refer to the WCST Manual (Heaton et al., 1993) for the clinical interpretation of this score report. Clinical interpretation of the WCST requires professional training and expertise in clinical psychology and/or neuropsychology. The utility and validity of the WCST as a clinical measure of cognitive ability are directly related to the professional's background and knowledge and, in particular, familiarity with the information contained in the WCST Manual.

WCST results should be interpreted within the context of a larger clinical assessment battery and relevant clinical and historical information about this client. Additionally, use of WCST scores for clinical or diagnostic decisions should not be attempted without a good understanding of brain-behavior relationships and the medical and psychological factors that affect them.

Version: 1.04 (4.51.029)

Client: John Q. Examinee

Client ID: 123456789

Test Date: 05/14/2003

Page 2 of 4

Test Results

WCST scores	Raw scores	Age and Education Demographically Corrected			U.S. Census Age-Matched		
		Standard scores	*T* scores	Percentile scores	Standard scores	*T* scores	Percentile scores
Trials Administered	113						
Total Correct	92						
Total Errors	21	114	59	82%	97	48	42%
% Errors	19%	118	62	88%	100	50	50%
Perseverative Responses	5	145	80	99%	110	57	75%
% Perseverative Responses	4%	145	80	99%	125	67	95%
Perseverative Responses	5	145	80	99%	110	57	75%
% Perseverative Responses	4%	145	80	99%	126	67	96%
Nonperseverative Errors	16	96	47	39%	90	43	25%
% Nonperseverative Errors	14%	97	48	42%	90	43	25%
Conceptual Level Responses	87						
% Conceptual Level Responses	77%	117	61	87%	100	50	50%
Categories Completed	6			> 16%			> 16%
Trials to Complete 1st Category	15			11–16%			11–16%
Failure to Maintain Set	3			6–10%			6–10%
Learning to Learn	-2.67			11–16%			> 16%

(Continued)

(Continued)

Reliability/ Precision and Validity	The reliability/precision of the WCST has been estimated using the interscorer reliability method (Clark, 2001; Trevisan, 2003). Experienced clinicians showed a range of interscorer reliability between .88 and .93 and a range of intrascorer coefficients between .91 and .96. Coefficients found for novice examiners were also adequate—between .75 and .97 for both inter- and intrascorer data. Reliability/precision has also been estimated using the internal consistency method. Internal consistency reliability using volunteers from the University of Colorado Health Sciences Center resulted in acceptable reliability scores ranging from .60 to .85.
	Numerous validity studies have demonstrated the construct validity of the WCST by comparing individual performance on the WCST with performance on other measures. Studies of adults with closed head injuries, demyelinating diseases, seizure disorders, and schizophrenia, as well as studies of children with traumatic brain injuries, seizures, learning disabilities, and attention deficit hyperactivity disorders, suggest that the WCST provides a valid method of assessing executive function in these individuals. Studies also suggest that the WCST is sensitive to frontal lesions as well as to dysfunction in other areas of the brain.
Source	Clark, E. (2001). Review of the Wisconsin Card Sorting Test, revised and expanded. In B. S. Plake & J. C. Impara (Eds.), *The fourteenth mental measurements yearbook*. Lincoln, NE: Buros Institute of Mental Measurements.
	Strauss, E., Sherman, E. M., & Spreen, O. (2006). *A compendium of neuropsychological tests: Administration, norms and commentary* (3rd ed.). New York: Oxford University Press.
	Trevisan, M. S. (2003). Review of the Wisconsin Card Sorting Test–64 Card Version. In B. S. Plake, J. C. Impara, & R. A. Spies (Eds.), *The fifteenth mental measurements yearbook*. Lincoln, NE: Buros Institute of Mental Measurements.

TEST SPOTLIGHT 5.4

BAYLEY SCALES OF INFANT AND TODDLER DEVELOPMENT, THIRD EDITION (BAYLEY-III)

Nancy Bayley

Title	Bayley Scales of Infant and Toddler Development, Third Edition (BAYLEY-III)
Author	Nancy Bayley
Publisher	Pearson Assessments
	19500 Bulverde Road
	San Antonio, TX 78259-3710
	www.pearsonassessments.com
Purpose	The BAYLEY-III was designed to assess the developmental level of children aged 1–42 months and to assess children who are developing slowly and who might benefit from cognitive intervention.
	The BAYLEY-III is administered to one child at a time and takes approximately 30 to 60 minutes. The child is given a variety of age-specific objects or toys, and the psychologist observes how the child uses the objects and then assigns a score based on a detailed scoring scheme provided by the test publisher. The child's score is then compared with the norms for that age group to determine developmental progress. Caregivers complete the Adaptive Behavior Assessment System, Second Edition, which assesses the child's ability to demonstrate adaptive skills when needed.
Versions	The original version of the Bayley Scales was published in 1969. The second edition became available in 1993. The third edition was published in 2006 and includes updated materials, revised instructions, and improved involvement of caregivers.
Scales	The BAYLEY-III consists of five scales
	1. The Cognitive scale assesses how the child thinks, learns, and reacts to the world.
	2. The Language scale measures how well the child recognizes sounds, understands spoken words, and communicates using sounds, gestures, or words.
	3. The Motor scale assesses how well the child can move his or her hands, fingers, and whole body to make things happen.
	4. The Social-Emotional scale assesses development by identifying the social-emotional milestones that are usually achieved by certain ages.
	5. The Adaptive Behavior scale asks caregivers to evaluate how well the child can adapt to the demands of everyday life and demonstrate those skills when needed.
Report	A Bayley Scales report is long and technical. A sample caregiver's report (the report given to the parents, guardian, or physician) can be found at http://images.pearsonclinical.com/images/dotcom/Bayley-III/ParentSASampleReport.pdf

(Continued)

(Continued)

Reliability/ Precision and Validity	Coefficient alpha estimates of individual scales ranged from .86 for Fine Motor to .91 for Cognitive, Expressive Communication, and Gross Motor. The reliabilities for the Social-Emotional scales ranged from .83 to .94, while the reliabilities of the Adaptive Behavior scales ranged from .79 to .98. Test–retest reliability estimates ranged from .77 to .94, with the higher reliability estimates not unexpectedly found for the older children.
	The BAYLEY-III manual provides evidence of validity based on content and relationship with other variables (both criteria and constructs). Confirmatory factor analysis was also performed, demonstrating that a three-factor solution (Cognitive, Language, and Motor) fit the data in the standardization sample well except in the youngest sample, in which a two-factor solution was also supported. Correlations with the Wechsler Preschool and Primary Scale of Intelligence, Third Edition, and the Bayley Cognitive scale were reported to range from .72 to .79.
Sources	Albers, C. A., & Grieve, A. J. (2007). Test review: Bayley N. (2006). Bayley Scales of Infant and Toddler Development—Third Edition. *Journal of Psychoeducational Assessment, 25,* 180–198.
	Bayley, N. (1993). *Bayley Scales of Infant Development* (2nd ed.). San Antonio, TX: Psychological Corporation.
	Harcourt Assessment. (2006). *Bayley III Scales of Infant Development caregiver report*. Retrieved from http://images.pearsonclinical.com/images/dotcom/Bayley-III/ParentSASampleReport.pdf
	Tobin, M., & Hoff, K. (2007). Review of the Bayley Scales of Infant and Toddler Development (3rd ed.). In K. F. Geisinger, R. A. Spies, J. F. Carlson, & B. S. Plake (Eds.), *The seventeenth mental measurements yearbook*. Lincoln, NE: Buros Institute of Mental Measurements.

TEST SPOTLIGHT 6.1
FUNDAMENTAL INTERPERSONAL RELATIONS ORIENTATION–BEHAVIOR (FIRO-B)

Will Schutz

Title	Fundamental Interpersonal Relations Orientation–Behavior (FIRO-B)
Author	Will Schutz
Publisher	CPP Inc.
	1055 Joaquin Road, 2nd Floor
	Mountain View, CA 94043
	www.cpp.com
Purpose	The FIRO-B is a personality instrument that measures an individual's interpersonal needs—more specifically, how an individual typically behaves with other people and how the individual expects others to act toward him or her. Developed during the late 1950s, the FIRO-B is based on the theory that beyond our needs for survival, food, shelter, and warmth, we all have unique interpersonal needs that strongly motivate us. These needs relate to three fundamental dimensions of interpersonal relationships: inclusion, control, and affection. The FIRO-B provides valuable insights into how an individual's need for inclusion, control, and affection can shape his or her interactions with others. The test is appropriate for ages 13 and over and takes approximately 10 to 15 minutes to complete.
	The FIRO-B is used in one-on-one coaching sessions, small groups, or teams and is well suited for team building and development, individual development, management training programs (leadership), communication workshops, organizational development, and relationship counseling.
	The results of the FIRO-B profile provide further insights into areas such as the following:
	• How individuals "come across" to or are perceived by others and whether this is the impression they intend to create
	• How and why conflict develops between people
	• How people can manage their own needs as they interact with others
	The FIRO-B consists of 54 items that the individual is asked to respond to in the following two formats:
	1. A frequency rating scale identifying how often the individual engages in the behavior described in the item: *never, rarely, occasionally, often, usually*
	2. A selectivity rating scale eliciting how many people the individual engages in the behavior described in the item: *nobody, one or two people, a few people, some people, many people, most people*
Scoring/ Theory	The FIRO-B is available in various formats, including self-scorable booklet, hand-scorable format using scoring keys, computer-scorable mail-in answer sheets used for interpretive reports, CPP software system, and Intranet and Internet online administration and scoring. More information is available at https://www.skillsone.com/en/index.aspx

(Continued)

(Continued)

	In the early 1980s, Will Schutz expanded the underlying theory and updated the FIRO-B to Element B. Element B was published by the Schutz Company and now serves as the foundation for a comprehensive methodology for organizational transformation. For more information about Element B, go to https://thehumanelement.com/pages/methodology/
Versions	Only one version has been successfully administered to individuals ages 14 to 90 years. This version can be self-scored or scored by a professional. There is no particular education level recommended so long as the examinee has vocabulary sufficient to understand the items and instructions as well as the cognitive level of functioning sufficient to understand a verbal or written interpretation of results. It is the responsibility of the user to ensure that the individual taking the test can understand and answer the items and, if the self-scorable format is used, to calculate the scores accurately.
Scales	The FIRO-B consists of six scales representing combinations of the three need areas (Inclusion, Control, and Affection) with the two behavior dimensions (Expressed and Wanted):
	Inclusion: This need indicates how much an individual generally includes other people in his or her life and how much attention, contact, and recognition the individual wants from others.
	Control: This need indicates how much influence and responsibility an individual wants and how much the individual wants others to lead and influence him or her.
	Affection: This need indicates how close and warm an individual is with others and how close and warm the individual wants others to be with him or her.
	Expressed: This dimension indicates how much an individual prefers to initiate behavior, what the individual actually does, and what is actually observed by others.
	Wanted: This dimension indicates how much an individual prefers others to initiate behavior toward him or her and whether the individual shows it openly or not.
	FIRO-B results are displayed in a 2 × 3 grid that includes the following six scales:
	1. Expressed Inclusion: How often do you act in ways that encourage your participation in situations?
	2. Expressed Control: How often do you act in ways that help you direct or influence situations?
	3. Expressed Affection: How often do you act in ways that encourage warmth and closeness in relationships?
	4. Wanted Inclusion: How much do you want to be part of others' activities?
	5. Wanted Control: How much leadership and influence do you want others to assume?
	6. Wanted Affection: How much warmth and closeness do you want from others?
Report	Several reports are available, including the FIRO–Business Profile, the FIRO–Business Leadership Report, the FIRO-B Profile, the FIRO-B Interpretive Report for Organizations, and the Leadership Report Using the FIRO-B and MBTI.
	To view the sample reports, go to https://www.cpp.com/en-US/Products-and-Services/Sample-Reports
Reliability/ Precision and Validity	Reliability/precision studies indicate that the FIRO-B has good test–retest reliability over short periods of time, with correlations on the three need areas and two behavior dimensions between the two testing sessions ranging between .72 and .85 for junior high school students, between .73 and .82 for college students, and between .71 and .82 for adults. Reliability/precision studies also indicate that the FIRO-B has acceptable ranges of internal consistency, with alpha coefficients for the six scales ranging between .85 (Wanted Affection) and .96 (Wanted Inclusion).

Construct validity studies demonstrate convergent evidence and divergent evidence of validity with expected scales on the Myers–Briggs Type Indicator assessment, the California Psychological Inventory, and the Adjective Checklist. Evidence of validity based on relationships with external criteria suggest that individuals with different FIRO-B scores clearly self-select into different occupations in ways that suggest they are doing so, at least in part, because they perceive opportunities to satisfy some of their interpersonal needs in these occupations. You can find more information from the technical guide at shop.cpp.com/pdfs/2225.pdf.

Sources	Hammer, A. L., & Schnell, E. R. (2000). *FIRO-B: Technical guide*. Mountain View, CA: CPP.
	Waterman, J. A., & Rogers, J. (1996). *Introduction to the FIRO-B*. Mountain View, CA: CPP.

TEST SPOTLIGHT 8.1
MATHEMATICS SELF-EFFICACY SCALE (MSES)

Courtesy of Nancy Betz

Nancy Betz

Title	Mathematics Self-Efficacy Scale (MSES)
Author	Nancy Betz and Gail Hackett
Publisher	Mind Garden 707 Menlo Avenue, Suite 120 Menlo Park, CA 94025 www.mindgarden.com
Purpose	The MSES was developed to assess a person's beliefs that he or she is capable of performing math-related tasks and behaviors. The current (1993) version of the MSES contains 34 items divided into two parts: Everyday Math Tasks (18 items) and Math-Related Courses (16 items). The test is meant for use with college freshmen and takes approximately 15 minutes to administer. The test taker rates each item in the test on a 10-point scale that describes his or her confidence in completing the task indicated by the question. The section on Math-Related Courses asks how confident the test taker is about being able to complete the course listed with a grade of A or B. Sample Questions: | 0	1	2	3	4	5	6	7	8	9
---	---	---	---	---	---	---	---	---	---

No confidence at all		Very little confidence		Some confidence		Much confidence		Complete confidence		
										
										Confidence Scale
										
										• How much confidence do you have that you could successfully:
										
										   o Determine the amount of sales tax on a clothing purchase?
										   o Calculate recipe quantities for a dinner for 3 when the original recipe is for 12 people?
										
										• Please rate the following college courses according to how much confidence you have that you could complete the course with a final grade of A or B:
										
										   o Economics
										   o Calculus
										   o Accounting
										   o Biochemistry

Versions	The original version was published in 1983. Since then, the authors have made considerable changes twice, most recently in 1993. The 1993 version changed from a three-part instrument to a two part instrument. Math Problems (18 items) was dropped from the new version.

Reliability/ Precision and Validity	For the 1983 version, internal constancy reliability estimates were given as .96 for the total scale, .92 for the Math Tasks subscale, and .92 for the Math-Related Courses subscale. Two-week test–retest reliability estimates were given as .94. No reliability estimates are provided for the 1993 version.
	Evidence of validity was provided for the 1983 version based on the test's relationship with other variables. Total MSES scores were correlated with math anxiety ($r = .56$) and confidence in doing math ($r = .66$). No validity estimates are provided for the 1993 version.
Sources	Ciechalski, J. C. (2001). Review of the Mathematics Self-Efficacy Scale. In B. S. Plake & J. C. Impara (Eds.), *The fourteenth mental measurements yearbook*. Lincoln, NE: Buros Institute of Mental Measurements.
	Mindgarden. (2005–2009). *Mathematics Self-Efficacy Scale*. Retrieved from http://www.mindgarden.com/products/maths.htm
	Smith, E. V., Jr. (2001). Mathematics Self-Efficacy Scale. In B. S. Plake & J. C. Impara (Eds.), *The fourteenth mental measurements yearbook*. Lincoln, NE: Buros Institute of Mental Measurements.

TEST SPOTLIGHT 8.2
STATE–TRAIT ANGER EXPRESSION INVENTORY–2 (STAXI-2)

Title	State–Trait Anger Expression Inventory–2 (STAXI-2)
Author	Charles D. Spielberger
Publisher	PAR 16204 North Florida Avenue Lutz, FL 33549 www.parinc.com
Purpose	The STAXI was originally published in 1988 to measure the intensity of anger in adolescents) and adults (ages 16 – 63). Revised in 1999, the STAXI-2 measures the intensity of anger (State Anger) and one's disposition to experience angry feelings as a personality trait (Trait Anger). The inventory is a self-report, 57-item test. Using a four-point scale, test takers rate themselves in terms of intensity of anger at a particular point in time and how often the anger is experienced, expressed, and controlled. The STAXI-2 is typically used for anger research and for screening and measuring outcomes of anger management programs. The test takes approximately 12 to 15 minutes to administer.
Versions	The STAXI-2 was expanded from 44 to 57 items and now has a companion test for children and adolescents ages 9 to 18 (STAXI-2 C/A).
Scales	The inventory consists of six scales measuring the intensity of anger and the disposition to experience angry feelings. • State Anger: the current intensity of angry feelings (has three subscales) • Trait Anger: general and ongoing expressions of anger (has two subscales) • Anger Expression–In: how often anger is suppressed • Anger Expression–Out: how often anger is expressed • Anger Control–In: how often the person tries to control anger within by calming down • Anger Control–Out: how often the person visibly seeks to control anger There are also five subscales (State Anger–Feeling, State Anger–Verbal, State Anger–Physical, Trait Anger–Temperament, and Trait Anger–Reaction) and an Anger Expression Index, an overall measure of expression and control of anger.
Report	Results are often reported in the Interpretive Report, which includes summary scores for the scales and subscales, general interpretive information for the test taker's scale and subscales, and an overview of any health or medical risks the test taker may face based on his or her inventory scores.

Section I from the State–Trait Anger Expression Inventory-2 (STAXI-2) Sample Interpretive Report is printed below.

Section I

This Score Summary Table presents the raw scores, percentiles, *T* scores, and score levels (low, moderate, high, very high) for each valid STAXI-2 scale and subscale. The percentile results are shown graphically on a following page; the raw scores for each of the 57 items are reported in the Item Response Summary Table.

STAXI-2 Score Summary Table

Scale/subscale	Raw score	Percentile	*T* score	Score level
State Anger				
S-Ang	22	85	58	high
S-Ang/F	7	60	48	low-moderate
S-Ang/V	10	90	66	high
S-Ang/P	5	50	40	low-moderate
Trait Anger				
T-Ang	19	65	52	moderate
T-Ang/T	5	30	42	moderate
T-Ang/R	11	80	56	high
Anger Expression and Anger Control				
AX-O	12	20	42	low
AX-I	16	55	50	moderate
AC-O	28	80	58	high
AC-I	24	50	50	moderate
AX Index	24	30	44	moderate

Note: "---" indicates a scale that is invalid due to an excessive number of missing items.

STAXI-2 Item Response Summary Table

State Anger		Trait Anger		Anger Expression and Anger Control			
Item	Response	Item	Response	Item	Response	Item	Response
1.	1	16.	2	26.	4	42.	3
2.	1	17.	1	27.	2	43.	1
3.	2	18.	1	28.	3	44.	3
4.	1	19.	3	29.	2	45.	2
5.	1	20.	3	30.	3	46.	3
6.	1	21.	1	31.	2	47.	2
7.	1	22.	2	32.	3	48.	3
8.	1	23.	2	33.	2	49.	2
9.	2	24.	1	34.	4	50.	4
10.	2	25.	3	35.	1	51.	1
11.	1			36.	3	52.	3
12.	2			37.	1	53.	2
13.	3			38.	4	54.	3
14.	1			39.	2	55.	1
15.	2			40.	3	56.	3
				41.	3	57.	2

To view a complete sample report, go to https://www.parinc.com/Products/Pkey/429

(Continued)

(Continued)

Section III

Medical Health Issues

Several of the STAXI-2 scales have been linked to health problems, particularly coronary heart disease (CHD), including hypertension, blood pressure problems, and cardiovascular reactivity. Several studies have investigated the relationship between anger, lipid levels, platelet aggregation, and other indicators of CHD to determine whether a person's level or type of anger increases the risk of CHD when overwhelmed by anger and other emotions. The STAXI-2 scales that have been found to be most closely associated with cardiovascular and other medical or health problems are presented below together with a brief evaluation of the respondent's scores. Please note that not all of the problems are likely for all members of the same STAXI-2 groups; many studies are correlational and thus do not have clear causal links. Furthermore, many of the studies have been carried out with Caucasian males, further limiting the applicability of the results.

State Anger (*S-Ang*)

This person scored in the high or very high range on *S-Ang*. Her *S-Ang* score is more like people with hypertension than normotensives. However, it should be noted that males with addiction problems also show higher *S-Ang* scores than males without addiction problems. For both males and females, higher preoperative *S-Ang* scores have been associated with poorer postoperative outcome, and higher *S-Ang* scores before exercise are related to higher systolic blood pressure (SBP) after exercise. If any of these factors are relevant to this individual, a referral for cognitively based anger management training needs to be seriously considered before surgery or extensive exercise. No research findings are yet available for the *S-Ang* subscales.

Trait Anger (*T-Ang*)

This respondent's *T-Ang* score is in the low or moderate range. Thus, there is little chance that she will experience elevations in blood pressure, hypertension, or coronary heart disease problems as a result of being chronically angry.

However, some preliminary data on elevated *T-Ang/R* scores suggest that this person may be more prone to experience elevations in either diastolic blood pressure (DBP) or systolic blood pressure (SBP) as a function of her high anger reactivity.

Anger Expression-Out (*AX-O*)

This person's *AX-O* score is in the low or moderate range. This suggests she has no increased risk of developing hypertension or CHD problems related to the expression of anger outwardly toward other people or objects.

Anger Expression-In (*AX-I*)

AX-I is the single best predictor of blood pressure among the STAXI-2 scales and tends to be most closely associated with hypertension. There are suggestions of relationships to other CHD variables as well.

Reliability/ Precision and Validity	The reliability/precision of the STAXI-2 has been established by calculating internal consistency. Alpha coefficients ranging between .73 and .95 provide evidence of internal consistency for the scales and subscales. Lindqvist, Daderman, and Hellstrom (2003) found coefficient alpha values for the scales that ranged between .64 (Anger Expression–Out) and .89 (Anger Control–In). The test manual does not provide evidence of test–retest reliability.
	The author reports evidence of construct validity for the scales and subscales on the STAXI-2. However, most evidence of validity for this test relies on studies conducted with the original version, even though the STAXI-2 is quite different from the original version. Extensive evidence exists for the validity for the original versions of inventory based on concurrent validation studies. Scores on the original inventory tend to correlate with scores on other assessment instruments, including the Multiphasic Inventory, Buss-Durkee Hostility Inventory, and the Eysenck Questionnaire.
Sources	Freeman, S. J. (2003). Review of the State–Trait Anger Expression Inventory–2. In B. S. Plake, J. C. Impara, & R. A. Spies (Eds.), *The fifteenth mental measurements yearbook*. Lincoln, NE: Buros Institute for Mental Measurements.
	Klecker, B. M. (2003). Review of the State–Trait Anger Expression Inventory–2. In B. S. Plake, J. C. Impara, & R. A. Spies (Eds.), *The fifteenth mental measurements yearbook*. Lincoln, NE: Buros Institute for Mental Measurements.
	Lindqvist, J. K., Daderman, A. M., & Hellstrom, A. (2003). Swedish adaptations of the Novaco Anger Scale 1998, the Provocation Inventory, and the State–Trait Anger Expression Inventory–2. *Social Behavior and Personality, 31*, 773–788.
	PAR. (2012). *State–Trait Anger Expression Inventory–2 (STAXI-2)*. Retrieved from http://www4.parinc.com/products/product.aspx?Productid=STAXI-2

TEST SPOTLIGHT 11.1

MINNESOTA MULTIPHASIC PERSONALITY INVENTORY–2 (MMPI-2)

Starke R. Hathaway   James N. Butcher   J. C. McKinley

Title	Minnesota Multiphasic Personality Inventory–2 (MMPI-2)
Author	Starke R. Hathaway, J. C. McKinley, and James N. Butcher
Publisher	University of Minnesota Press, Test Division
	Mill Place, Suite 290
	111 Third Avenue South
	Minneapolis, MN 55401
	www.upress.umn.edu/test-division
	The University of Minnesota Press, representing the Regents of the University of Minnesota, published the MMPI-2.
	As publisher, the University of Minnesota Press, working with its consulting board, is responsible for the substantive development of the tests, including any revisions to them. The university exclusively licenses Pearson Assessments to produce, market, and sell the MMPI test products and to offer scoring and interpretive services.
Purpose	The original MMPI—the most widely used personality test in the world—was developed during the late 1930s and published in 1943 as a tool for routine clinical assessment. Its purpose was to help clinicians assign appropriate diagnoses to persons who showed signs of mental disorders. The developers gathered a large number of questions from textbooks, personality inventories, and clinicians. They administered the questions to patients for whom diagnoses were available in hospitals and clinics in Minnesota. Then they analyzed the responses by grouping them by diagnostic category. They put in the MMPI only those questions that were answered differently by a diagnostic group (e.g., schizophrenic patients). They also added three "validity" scales to detect respondents who answered questions dishonestly. When revising the MMPI, the authors added three more validity scales. (Note that validity scales do not assess the validity of a test's scores.) The test is appropriate for ages 18 and older and takes approximately 60 to 90 minutes to administer.
Versions	During the 1980s, a restandardization committee studied and revised the MMPI. The MMPI-2, published in 1989, was developed using a sample of persons (1,138 men and 1,461 women) randomly chosen from seven regions of the United States. The sample was designed to resemble the 1980 U.S. census in age, gender, minority status, social class, and education. (As you recall, "How Do Test Users Interpret Test Scores?" discusses the process and implications of developing norms for tests.)
	The MMPI–Adolescent, a parallel inventory to the MMPI-2, is available for adolescents aged 14 to 18. The MMPI-2-RF (restructured form) contains 338 items to streamline the test as well as the MMPI-A-RF.
Scales	The MMPI-2 includes 567 items and is composed of more than 120 scales within the following 8 categories: Validity Indicators, Superlative Self-Presentation Subscales, Clinical Scales, Restructured Clinical Scales, Content Scales, Content Component Scales, Supplementary Scales, and Clinical Subscales).
	The MMPI-2 has 10 clinical scales:

    1. Hypochondriasis: excessive or exaggerated concerns about physical health

    2. Depression: issues of discouragement, pessimism, and hopelessness as well as excessive responsibility

3. Conversion Hysteria: sensory or motor disorders that have no organic basis, denial, and lack of social anxiety

4. Psychopathic Deviation: degree to which relatively normal individuals have a willingness to acknowledge problems, including a lack of concern for social or moral standards with a tendency for "acting out"

5. Masculinity/Femininity: attitudes and feelings in which men and women are thought to differ (originally a measure of homoerotic feelings)

6. Paranoia: interpersonal sensitivities and tendencies to misinterpret the motives and intentions of others, including self-centeredness and insecurity

7. Psychastenia: excessive worries, compulsive behaviors, exaggerated fears, generalized anxiety, and distress, including declarations of high moral standards, self-blame, and rigid efforts to control impulses

8. Schizophrenia: strange beliefs, unusual experiences, and special sensitivities related to schizophrenia

9. Hypomania: excessive ambition, elevated energy, extraversion, high aspirations, grandiosity, and impulsive decision making

10. Social Introversion: social shyness, preference for solitary pursuits, and lack of social assertiveness

The MMPI-2 contains nine validity scales, each of which contains a group of questions that provide information on the test taker's level of honesty and motivation during test administration. On the original MMPI, the Lie scale, the Infrequency scale, and the Correction scale were designed to indicate whether the respondent lied, minimized, or exaggerated difficulties; responded randomly; or demonstrated an unwillingness to cooperate. Three new validity scales were added during the test's revision. The Back-Page Infrequency scale provides a score for a test taker's diligence in completing the test, the True Response Inconsistency scale is designed to measure lack of cooperation, and the Variable Response Inconsistency scale provides a measure of the test taker's inconsistency. These scales are important for interpreting test results because, as you recall from "What is Test Reliability/Precision?" error can be added to the test score when the test taker does not answer questions truthfully or honestly.

To review a breakdown of the other scales included in the MMPI-2, go to https://www.upress.umn.edu/test-division/mtdda/webdocs/mmpi-2-training-slides/interpretation-of-mmpi-2-clinical-scales

Report	To learn more about available MMPI-2 reports, and to view sample reports, access the URLs below: • http://www.pearsonclinical.co.uk/Psychology/AdultMentalHealth/AdultForensic/MinnesotaMultiphasicPersonalityInventory-2(MMPI-2)/ForThisProduct/Sample-Reports.aspx
Reliability/ Precision and Validity	Because the developers of the MMPI and MMPI-2 placed questions on scales based on their ability to distinguish groups with specific diagnoses (rather than grouping questions according to how well they measured the same construct), the internal consistency of the MMPI-2 is low. Test–retest reliability is higher, indicating that scores remain somewhat consistent over time (Rojdev, Nelson, Hart, & Fercho, 1994). Because empirically based tests are developed without regard to validity evidence based on content, no link can be made between a domain of mental disorders and the MMPI-2. The increasing use of the MMPI stimulated a large body of research regarding its validity in various situations. Much of the research was critical, including charges regarding low validity. For example, critics noted that the norming sample for the MMPI was drawn from one region and contained mostly people of one race and ethnic background (Colligan, Osborne, Swenson, & Offord, 1983). Definitions of neurotic and psychotic conditions also changed after the MMPI was developed. For instance, in 1994, the latest revision of the *Diagnostic and Statistical Manual of Mental Disorders* discarded homosexuality, a disorder the original MMPI purportedly identified as a mental disorder. The norm group for the MMPI-2 contained 2,600 individuals, ages 18 years and older, who were selected as a representative sample of the U.S. population.

(Continued)

(Continued)

	The MMPI-2, although significantly improved over the original version, still is presented as valid based on evidence of the original version. Some researchers, such as Rojdev and colleagues (1994), have reported evidence of validity. Rossi, Van den Brande, Tobac, Sloore, and Hauben (2003) have also reported convergent evidence of validity for the MMPI-2 with the Millon Clinical Multiaxial Inventory–III, a personality test designed to provide diagnostic and treatment information to clinicians in the areas of personality disorders and clinical syndromes.
Sources	Acheson, S. K. (2017). Test review of the Minnesota Multiphasic Personality Invventory-2-Restructured form. In J. F. Carlson, K. F. Geisinger, & J. L. Jonson, J. L. (Eds.), *The twentieth mental measurements yearbook*. Lincoln, NE: Buros Center for Testing.
	Archer, R. P. (1992). Review of the Minnesota Multiphasic Personality Inventory–2. In J. J. Kramer & J. C. Conoley (Eds.), *The eleventh mental measurements yearbook*. Lincoln, NE: Buros Institute of Mental Measurements.
	Claiborn, C. D., & Lanyon, R. (1995). Review of the Minnesota Multiphasic Personality Inventory–A. In J. J. Kramer & J. C. Conoley (Eds.), *The twelfth mental measurements yearbook*. Lincoln, NE: Buros Institute of Mental Measurements.
	Colligan, R. C., Osborne, D., Swenson, W. M., & Offord, K. P. (1983). *The MMPI: A contemporary normative study*. New York: Praeger.
	Pearson Education. (2018a). *MMPI-2 (Minnesota Multiphasic Personality Inventory–2)*. Retrieved from http://www.pearsonassessments.com/tests/mmpi_2.htm
	Rojdev, R., Nelson, W. M., III, Hart, K. J., & Fercho, M. C. (1994). Criterion-related validity and stability: Equivalence of the MMPI and the MMPI-2. *Journal of Clinical Psychology, 50*, 361–367.
	Rossi, R., Van den Brande, I., Tobac, A., Sloore, H., & Hauben, C. (2003). Convergent validity of the MCMI-III personality disorder scales and the MMPI-2 scales. *Journal of Personality Disorders, 17*, 330–340.

TEST SPOTLIGHT 12.1
GRADUATE RECORD EXAMINATION (GRE)

Title	Graduate Record Examination (GRE)
Author	Educational Testing Service (ETS)
Publisher	Educational Testing Service Rosedale Road Princeton, NJ 08541 www.ets.org
Purpose	The GRE consists of the GRE General Test and eight GRE Subject Tests that gauge undergraduate achievement in eight fields of study. The GRE General Test and Subject Tests are entrance exams many graduate, professional, and business programs use to aid in the admissions process. Developed more than 60 years ago, the GRE General Test measures some of the reasoning skills that develop over time and that graduate school administrators believe are essential to success in graduate school. The GRE General Test measures verbal reasoning, quantitative reasoning, critical thinking, and analytical writing skills. The GRE Subject Tests measure some subject matter content knowledge often emphasized in undergraduate education. The GRE General Test is offered online, year round, at computer-based testing centers worldwide. It is offered at paper-based test centers where computer-based testing centers are not available. It takes approximately 3 to 3.75 hours to respond to the writing prompts and answer the 28 to 38 questions in each section. The GRE Subject Tests are offered three times a year at paper-based testing centers worldwide. The number of questions on each subject test varies from approximately 68 to more than 200, and most are multiple choice. ETS offers practice books for each of the Subject Tests.
Versions and Scales	The GRE General Test consists of seven sections that are used to calculate the following three scores: • Verbal Reasoning: tests the ability to analyze and assess written material and synthesize information obtained from the material, to analyze relationships among parts of sentences, and to recognize the relationships between words and concepts (includes two 30-minute sections) • Quantitative Reasoning: tests the understanding of simple math concepts, knowledge of fundamental mathematical skills, and the ability to reason quantitatively and solve problems in a quantitative setting (includes two 3-minute sections) • Analytical Writing: tests critical thinking and analytical writing skills by assessing the ability to express and support complex ideas, evaluate an argument, and maintain a focused and logical discussion (includes two 30-minute sections) • A final 30-minute section is used for pretesting new items and is not scored.

(Continued)

(Continued)

The GRE Subject Tests measure undergraduate achievement in eight disciplines:

- Biochemistry, Cell and Molecular Biology
- Biology
- Chemistry
- Computer Science
- Literature in English
- Mathematics
- Physics
- Psychology

Prior to the fall of 2006, the GRE General Test was administered year round in the United States, Canada, and various other countries. Although usually computer based, it was still offered in paper-and-pencil format, typically three times a year, in places where computer-based testing was not available. The sections of the computer-based version of the GRE (Verbal Reasoning and Quantitative Reasoning) were adaptive. That is, test takers received questions that were based on the level of ability displayed in early questions by the test takers. The adaptive versions used fewer questions than the paper-and-pencil version. With one question presented at a time, and beginning with a question of moderate difficulty, subsequent questions were based on whether test takers answered the previous question correctly or incorrectly. The test continued until test takers had received and answered the required mix of question types and question content.

In the fall of 2006, ETS introduced a significantly revised GRE General Test. Some general changes include the following:

- The time for the test increased from 2.5 hours to slightly more than 4 hours, with new content, a new structure, and different types of questions.
- The test is now administered 29 times a year, instead of continuously, through the ETS global network of Internet-based centers and through Prometric, the world's largest computer-based testing network.
- The test is no longer offered in a computer adaptive format; rather, each student who takes the test on a given day sees the same questions in the same order. Furthermore, no student sees the same questions on different dates.
- There are experimental questions that do not count toward the final score (but will be used to select questions for future versions of the test).
- The traditional 200- to 800-point scales for the Verbal Reasoning and Quantitative Reasoning sections were replaced with a scale that is approximately 120 to 170 points. The Analytical Writing section continues to be scored on a scale from 0 to 6.

Some of the major changes to each section include the following:

- Analytical Writing: although 15 minutes shorter, includes more focused questions to ensure original analytical writing
- Verbal Reasoning: places a greater emphasis on higher cognitive skills, less dependence on vocabulary, and more reading passages
- Quantitative Reasoning: provides more real-life scenarios and data interpretation questions, fewer geometry questions, and an on-screen four-function calculator that allows test takers to calculate square roots

According to ETS, the new version was designed to increase the validity of the test scores; that is, to provide a more accurate measure of how qualified applicants are to do graduate-level work. The new design leverages advances in psychometric design, technology, and security measures, and it provides test score users with better information on graduate school applicants' performance.

Report	Reports are generated and sent to students who take the computerized version of the GRE approximately 10 to 15 days after test administration. Reports are generated and sent to students who take the paper-and-pencil version approximately 4 to 6 weeks after test administration. If students take the GRE more than once, their GRE score reports will show the scores they have earned on each administration over the past 5 years.
	Although the GRE score report was likely to change with the introduction of the revised test in October 2006, the 2005–2006 GRE General Test score report includes (a) a single score for the test taker's performance on the Analytical Writing section, ranging from 0 to 6, with the score typically being the average of scores from two trained readers (if the two scores differ by more than 1 point, a third reader determines the scores), and (b) a raw score (the number of questions the test taker answered correctly) and a 200- to 800-point scaled score (a score that reflects differences in difficulty between test editions) for both the Verbal Reasoning and Quantitative Reasoning sections. The GRE Subject Test score report includes an individual's raw score and a 200- to 990-point scaled score as well as subscores on a 20- to 99-point scale for the Biochemistry, Cell and Molecular Biology; Biology; and Psychology Subject Tests.
	To learn more about how the GRE General Test and GRE Subject Tests are scored and reported, go to www.ets.org/gre.
	The GRE test changed again in August 2011. To find out more about the changes in the test and how to prepare to take the new GRE test, go to www.ets.org/gre/revised_general/know.
Reliability/ Precision and Validity	Many reliability/precision studies show that GRE General Test and GRE Subject Test scores are reliable. For example, ETS reports the reliability coefficients for the three sections of the GRE General Test (Analytical Writing, Verbal Reasoning, and Quantitative Reasoning) to be .72, .92, and .91, respectively. The reliability coefficients for the Subject Tests range between .90 and .95, with subtest reliability coefficients ranging between .85 and .91.
	Similarly, research studies indicate that GRE General Test scores are valid predictors of success during the 1st year of graduate school; however, available samples of minority students have been very small. Correlations between GRE General Test scores and graduate 1st-year GPA range between .24 and .29 for Analytical Writing, .22 and .33 for Quantitative Reasoning, and .28 and .33 for Verbal Reasoning. However, when combined with undergraduate GPA, correlation coefficients across all sections range between .44 and .48, suggesting that the combination of General Test scores and undergraduate GPA is a better predictor of graduate 1st-year GPA.
	Studies of validity using the predictive method suggest that the GRE Subject Tests predict graduate 1st-year GPA moderately, with correlation coefficients ranging between .27 and .51. However, the combination of Subject Test scores and undergraduate GPA shows much more predictive ability, with correlation coefficients ranging between .43 and .58.
Sources	Educational Testing Service. (2012a). *Frequently asked questions about the GRE® revised General Test*. Retrieved from http://ets.org/gre/general/about/faq/
	Educational Testing Service. (2012b). GRE® *guide to the use of scores*. Retrieved from http://www.ets.org/s/gre/pdf/gre_guide.pdf

TEST SPOTLIGHT 12.2
SELF-DIRECTED SEARCH (SDS)

John L. Holland

Title	Self-Directed Search (SDS)
Author	John L. Holland
Publisher	PAR 16204 North Florida Avenue Lutz, FL 33549 www4.parinc.com
Purpose	The SDS is a career interest inventory. It can be extremely useful to adolescents and adults (ages 11-70) who might wonder what career path to follow, who want to support a tentative choice, or who want to make sure they have not overlooked obvious alternatives. The SDS can also be useful to individuals seeking a second career, returning to school, or questioning the suitability of their current jobs. The results of the SDS provide individuals with insights into the personality types that they are most like and occupations from the *Dictionary of Occupational Titles* (Coutsoukis & Information Technology Associates, 1995–2011) that map careers that reflect individuals' interests and abilities. Available online and in paper-and-pencil format in more than 25 languages, the SDS is a self-administered test that takes approximately 15 to 20 minutes to complete. It measures six personality types:

1. Realistic (R): Realistic people like jobs such as automobile mechanic, air traffic controller, surveyor, farmer, and electrician. They have mechanical and athletic abilities and like to work more with things than with people. They are described as asocial, conforming, frank, genuine, hardheaded, inflexible, materialistic, natural, normal, persistent, practical, self-effacing, thrifty, uninsightful, and uninvolved.

2. Investigative (I): Investigative people like jobs such as biologist, chemist, physicist, anthropologist, geologist, and medical technologist. They have mathematical and scientific ability and prefer to work alone and to solve problems. They are described as analytical, cautious, complex, critical, curious, independent, intellectual, introspective, pessimistic, precise, rational, reserved, retiring, unassuming, and unpopular.

3. Artistic (A): Artistic people like jobs such as composer, musician, stage director, writer, interior decorator, and actor or actress. They have artistic abilities, enjoy creating work, and have good imaginations. They are described as complicated, disorderly, emotional, expressive, idealistic, imaginative, impractical, impulsive, independent, introspective, intuitive, nonconforming, open, original, and sensitive.

4. Social (S): Social people like jobs such as teacher, religious worker, counselor, clinical psychologist, psychiatric caseworker, and speech therapist. They like to work with others and like to help people with their problems. They are described as ascendant, cooperative, empathic, friendly, generous, helpful, idealistic, kind, patient, persuasive, responsible, sociable, tactful, understanding, and warm.

5. Enterprising (E): Enterprising people like jobs such as salesperson, manager, business executive, television producer, sports promoter, and buyer or purchasing agent. They have leadership and speaking abilities, like to influence people, and are interested in politics and money. They are described as acquisitive, adventurous, agreeable, ambitious, domineering, energetic, excitement seeking, exhibitionistic, extraverted, flirtatious, optimistic, self-confident, sociable, and talkative.

6. Conventional (C): Conventional people like jobs such as bookkeeper, stenographer, financial analyst, banker, cost estimator, and tax expert. They have clerical and arithmetic ability, like to organize things, and prefer to work indoors. They are described as careful, conforming, conscientious, defensive, efficient, inflexible, inhibited, methodical, obedient, orderly, persistent, practical, prudish, thrifty, and unimaginative.

Versions	There are multiple versions of the SDS available.

- The SDS Form E, known as Form "Easy," consists of 198 items and was developed for adults and high school students with limited education or reading skills. With directions written at the sixth-grade reading level, Form E contains three booklets: an Assessment Booklet, the Job Finder/Occupational Classification Booklet, and the interpretative booklet titled You and Your Job. The Job Finder for this form includes 800 job titles that focus exclusively on occupations at lower levels of educational preparation. Most jobs require a high school education or less and reflect a wide variety of industries and occupational groups.

- The SDS Form R, known as Form "Regular" and the most widely used career interest inventory in the world, consists of 118 items and was designed primarily for use with high school students, college students, and adults. Form R contains seven components: an Assessment Booklet, the Occupations Finder and Alphabetized Occupations Finder, the You and Your Career Booklet, the Leisure Activities Finder Booklet, the Educational Opportunities Finder Booklet, the SDS Technical Manual, and the SDS Professional User Guide. In 2013, the fifth edition SDS Form R was redesigned without item changes and in 2017 was named the StandardSDS. The SDS CE: Career Explorer was designed for use with middle and junior high school students and is written at a level more appropriate for this younger group.

- The SDS Form CP: Career Planning was designed for individuals who are looking for greater levels of professional responsibility and would like to explore higher-level careers.

Report	The typical SDS report includes (a) a description of the six personality types; (b) a two- or three-letter code representing a combination of the personality types that matches the individual's interests most closely (depending on the form used); (c) an explanation of how to use the code during the career planning process; (d) a listing of occupations, fields of study, and leisure activities that are consistent with the individual's two- or three-letter code; and (e) additional information on following through on the career planning process.

A sample report is available at https://www.parinc.com/WebUploads/samplerpts/SDS%20Sample%20Professional%20Report%20new%202016.pdf

Reliability/ Precision and Validity	Many studies assess the reliability/precision of the SDS scores. In general, these studies indicate that the SDS scores have good test–retest reliability. For example, Form R has demonstrated test–retest correlations for summary codes ranging between .76 and .89 over intervals from 4 to 12 weeks. Reliability/precision studies on Form R also indicate that the SDS has acceptable ranges of internal consistency, with coefficients ranging between .72 and .92 for the various scales and between .90 and .94 for the summary scale. Form E also has demonstrated acceptable levels of internal consistency, with coefficients ranging between .94 and .96 for the summary scale and between .81 and .92 for the other scales.

A significant number of studies have explored evidence of validity of the SDS using the concurrent method, and in general all of these have been supportive, with most validity coefficients at or above .65. According to the *Mental Measurements Yearbook*, one drawback of the SDS is that it does not provide predictive evidence of validity. To gather this evidence, researchers would need to follow up with individuals who took the SDS to determine how well the results of the test matched the individuals' ultimate occupational choices and job satisfaction.

(Continued)

(Continued)

Sources	Brown, M. B. (2004). Review of the Self-Directed Search (4th ed.). In J. J. Kramer & J. C. Conoley (Eds.), *The eleventh mental measurements yearbook*. Lincoln, NE: Buros Institute of Mental Measurements.
	Carlson, J. F., Geisinger, K. F., & Jonson, J. L. (2017). The twentieth mental measurements yearbook. Lincoln, NE: Buros Center for Testing.
	Coutsoukis, P., & Information Technology Associates. (1995–2011). *Dictionary of occupational titles*. Retrieved from http://www.occupationalinfo.org
	Holland, J. L., Fritzsche, B. A., & Powell, A. B. (1996). *SDS: Technical manual*. Odessa, FL: Psychological Assessment Resources.
	Holland, J. L., Powell, A. B., & Fritzsche, B. A. (1994). *SDS: Professional user's guide*. Odessa, FL: Psychological Assessment Resources.
	Holmberg, K., Rosen, D., & Holland, J. L. (1997). *SDS: The leisure activities finder*. Odessa, FL: Psychological Assessment Resources.

TEST SPOTLIGHT 14.1
16 PERSONALITY FACTOR
QUESTIONNAIRE, FIFTH EDITION (16PF)

Raymond B. Cattell

Title	16 Personality Factor Questionnaire, Fifth Edition (16PF, 16PFQ)
Author	Raymond B. Cattell, Karen Cattell, Heather Cattell, Mary Russell, and Darcie Karol
Publisher	PSI Talent Measurement 11590 North Meridian Street, Suite 200 Camel, IN 46032 https://www.psionline.com/
Purpose	The 16PF is a self-report personality test designed to measure normal personality traits in people 16 years or older. Originally published in 1949, the fifth edition was published in 1993. The 16PF is based on 16 scales identified using factor analysis that are grouped into five global factors. Professionals use the 16PF in various settings, including business, clinical, and school settings, to help make employee selection decisions, promote employee development, and understand client problems in the context of one's personality. The fifth edition includes 185 simple questions about daily behavior, interests, and opinions. It takes approximately 35 to 50 minutes to complete the assessment by hand and 25 to 35 minutes on a computer. The following are two sample true/false questions: When I find myself in a boring situation, I usually "tune out" and daydream about other things. When a bit of tact and convincing is needed to get people moving, I'm usually the one who does it.
Versions	The 16PF is available in a number of versions, including 16PF Fifth Edition Questionnaire, 16PF Adolescent Personality Questionnaire, and 16PF Couples Counseling Questionnaire. The test may be administered individually or in groups. The test is available in paper-and-pencil format and online, with a number of user guides and manuals available to assist with administration and interpretation. The test may be scored by hand or by computer.
Scales	The 16PF has 16 scales, each of which measures one of the following:

Warmth	Social Boldness	Openness to Change
Reasoning	Sensitivity	Self-Reliance
Emotional Stability	Vigilance	Perfectionism
Dominance	Abstractedness	Tension
Liveliness	Privateness	
Rule-Consciousness	Apprehensiveness	

The 16 scales are grouped into five global factors:

Extraversion

Anxiety

Tough-Mindedness

(Continued)

(Continued)

	Independence
	Self-Control
	The 16PF also includes three response style indices: Impression Management, Infrequency, and Acquiescence. High scores on any of these scales may serve as red flags that the test taker is not answering honestly and instead is answering in a more socially desirable way, faking, or randomly responding. This information helps those who interpret the test come to accurate conclusions.
Report	There are more than 20 different reports available for the 16PF, including a Profile Report, Competency Report, Interpretive Report, Management Potential Report, Practitioner Report, Career Development Report, and Couple's Counseling Report. One of the more popular is the Basic Interpretive Report, which includes an individual's scores on each of the 16 primary scales, the five global factors, and the three response-style indexes. This report also includes (a) a narrative report for the 16 primary factors and five global factors; (b) predicted scores on performance, potential, and behavioral indexes; (c) vocational interests along Holland's occupational interest themes; and (d) individual item responses and raw scores. A sample report is available at
	https://www.16pf.com/wp-content/uploads/Competency-Report-Ella-Explorer.pdf
	https://www.psionline.com/assessments/16-personality-factors-16pf/
Reliability/ Precision and Validity	In terms of reliability/precision, the test–retest reliability coefficients of the 16PF, Fifth Edition, for a 2-week period for the global factors range between .84 and .91. For the primary factors, test–retest reliability coefficients range between .69 and .87, and coefficient alpha values range between .64 and .85, with a mean of .74.
	Over 60 published studies provide evidence for the validity of the 16 personality traits measured on the 16PF. The test manual provides evidence of construct validity and validity using the concurrent method as well as the rationale for the 16PF structure. The administrator's manual cautions test users about making prognostic or predictive decisions from the results of the 16PF.
Sources	McLellan, M. J. (1995). Review of the Sixteen Personality Factor Questionnaire, Fifth Edition. In J. Conoley & J. C. Impara (Eds.), *The twelfth mental measurements yearbook*. Lincoln, NE: Buros Institute of Mental Measurements.
	PSI Services LLC. (2017). *16PF*. Retrieved from https://www.16pf.com/en_US/16pf-overview/key-benefits/
	Rotto, P. C. (1995). Review of the Sixteen Personality Factor Questionnaire, Fifth Edition. In J. Conoley & J. C. Impara (Eds.), *The twelfth mental measurements yearbook*. Lincoln, NE: Buros Institute of Mental Measurements.

TEST SPOTLIGHT 14.2
HOGAN PERSONALITY INVENTORY (HPI)

Joyce and Robert Hogan

Title	Hogan Personality Inventory (HPI)
Author	Robert Hogan and Joyce Hogan
Publisher	Hogan Assessment Systems
	2622 East 21st Street
	Tulsa, OK 74114
	www.hoganassessments.com
Purpose/ Versions	Since its inception, the HPI has been a measure of normal personality designed specifically to predict employment success. The Hogans began developing the HPI during the late 1970s using the California Psychological Inventory as their original model and the five-factor theory of personality as a theoretical basis for construct validity. After developing 420 questions, they tested more than 1,700 people, including students, hospital workers, U.S. Navy enlisted personnel, clerical workers, truck drivers, sales representatives, and school administrators. Analyses of these data led to a shortened inventory of 310 questions that made up the original HPI.
	Between 1985 and 1994, the HPI was administered to more than 11,000 people, most of whom were employed by organizations in the United States. The Hogans and others conducted more than 50 validity studies to assess criterion-related and construct validity. Based on these studies and factor analyses of the database of tests administered, the Hogans made revisions that yielded the revised edition currently in use. The HPI takes approximately 15 to 20 minutes to administer and is available for use in 30 languages.
Scales	The HPI contains 206 true/false statements (written at a fourth-grade reading level). The HPI has seven primary scales, six occupational scales, and a validity scale. The scale structure is supported by factor analytic research and generalizes across modes of testing, respondent cultures, and languages of translation.
	The primary scales and construct definitions are as follows:
	• Adjustment: confidence, self-esteem, and composure under pressure
	• Ambition: initiative, competitiveness, and leadership potential
	• Sociability: extraversion, gregariousness, and a need for social interaction
	• Interpersonal Sensitivity: warmth, charm, and ability to maintain relationships
	• Prudence: responsibility, self-control, and conscientiousness
	• Inquisitiveness: imagination, curiosity, and creative potential
	• Learning Approach: enjoying learning and staying current on business and technical matters

(Continued)

(Continued)

	The occupational scales and construct definitions are as follows: • Service Orientation: being attentive, pleasant, and courteous to clients and customers • Stress Tolerance: being able to handle stress, being even-tempered, and staying calm • Reliability: honesty, integrity, and positive organizational citizenship • Clerical Potential: following directions, attending to detail, and communicating clearly • Sales Potential: energy, social skill, and the ability to solve problems for clients • Managerial Potential: leadership ability, planning, and decision-making skills The HPI validity scale detects careless or random responding by the test taker. The validity referred to in the scale name is that of the test taker's response and does not provide information about the validity of the HPI itself.
Report	Reports are available in various formats that differ in content, scope, and complexity. All the most up-to-date reports for the HPI can be found at www.hoganassessments.com/reports.
Reliability/ Precision and Validity	The test manual for the HPI reports internal consistencies for the seven primary scales and subscales, obtained by testing 960 employed adults, ranging between .29 and .89. According to Joyce Hogan (personal communication, November 21, 2005), test–retest reliability coefficients range between .74 and .86. In general, subscale reliabilities are within the acceptable range and indicate substantial stability over time. Meta-analyses of HPI scales (published in peer-reviewed journals) indicate that the estimated true validities for the scales for predicting job performance are as follows: Adjustment, .43; Ambition, .35; Interpersonal Sensitivity, .34; Prudence, .36; Inquisitiveness, .34; and Learning Approach, .25 (Hogan & Holland, 2003). Early research indicated no adverse impact by race/ethnicity or gender. The HPI has been used in more than 200 validation studies to predict occupational performance across a range of jobs and industries. Jobs studied represent 95% of the industry coverage of the *Dictionary of Occupational Titles* (Coutsoukis & Information Technology Associates, 1995–2011). Since 1995, Hogan Assessment Systems has provided an Internet assessment platform to support the administration, scoring, and reporting functions of the inventory. Validation evidence continues to be collected from working adults in organizations around the world. Current norms are based on hundreds of thousands of adults who are representative of the occupational distribution in the U.S. workforce.
Sources	Coutsoukis, P., & Information Technology Associates. (1995–2003). *Dictionary of occupational titles*. Retrieved from http://www.occupationalinfo.org Hogan, J., & Holland, B. (2003). Using theory to evaluate personality and job-performance relations: A socioanalytic perspective. *Journal of Applied Psychology, 88*, 100–112. Hogan, R., & Hogan, J. (1992). *Hogan Personality Inventory manual*. Tulsa, OK: Hogan Assessment Systems.

TEST SPOTLIGHT 14.3
CALIFORNIA PSYCHOLOGICAL INVENTORY, THIRD EDITION (CPI)

Title	California Psychological Inventory, Third Edition (CPI)
Author	Harrison G. Gough and Pamela Bradley
Publisher	Consulting Psychologists Press 185 North Wolfe Road, Sunnyvale, CA 94086 www.cpp.com
Purpose	The CPI is a personality inventory first designed in 1956. The third edition, CPI 434, was published in 1996. The CPI was designed for test takers, ages 13 years and older, to measure their social and interpersonal behaviors and to predict what they will say and do in specific contexts. The CPI 434 is a self-report test that contains 434 true/false items, nearly 40% of which were taken from the Minnesota Multiphasic Personality Inventory. The CPI 434 takes about 45 to 60 minutes to complete.
Versions	There are online and paper-and-pencil versions of the CPI 434. (A modified and updated version of the test, the CPI 260, is often used for leadership selection and development.) There are four CPI types: • Alphas: externally oriented, norm-favoring • Betas: internally oriented, norm-favoring • Gammas: externally oriented, norm-questioning • Deltas: internally oriented, norm-questioning The CPI 434 contains 18 of the original 20 Folk Concept Scales (Dominance, Capacity for Status, Sociability, Social Presence, Self-Acceptance, Independence, Empathy, Responsibility, Socialization, Self-Control, Good Impression, Communality, Well-Being, Tolerance, Achievement via Conformance, Achievement via Independence, Intellectual Efficiency, Psychological-Mindedness, Flexibility, and Femininity/Masculinity). The Folk Scales are designed to capture cross-cultural personality themes that should be easily understood worldwide. The scales are grouped into four classes to measure (a) social expertise and interpersonal style; (b) maturity, normative orientation, and values; (c) achievement orientation; and (d) personal interest styles. There are 13 special purpose scales used to report on creative temperament, managerial potential, tough-mindedness, and a number of practical dimensions of operating style and behavior.
Report	CPI 434 results are displayed in three reports: • CPI 434 Profile • CPI 434 Narrative Report • CPI 434 Configural Analysis Report

(Continued)

(Continued)

The Profile Report includes a clear and organized basic interpretation of a test taker's CPI 434 results. The report includes a gender-specific profile and a combined profile based on male/female norms. These norms can be used for employment situations when gender-neutral reporting is required. The report also includes the test taker's scores on seven special purpose scales: Creative Temperament, Managerial Potential, Work Orientation, Leadership Potential, Amicability, Tough-Mindedness, and Law Enforcement Orientation.

The Narrative Report includes a well-organized comprehensive interpretation of a test taker's CPI 434 results. It includes a profile of the test taker's CPI type, level, and Folk Scale results and then elaborates on that information. The report includes predictive statements about the test taker's behavior to aid in interpretation, helping the test taker and administrator understand the test taker in a knowledgeable and objective manner. The report includes two scale profiles, one for the gender-specific norm group and one with combined male/female norms. These norms can be used in employment situations when gender-neutral norms are needed. The report also includes the test taker's results on several special purpose scales, including Creative Temperament, Managerial Potential, and Tough-Mindedness.

The Configural Analysis Report builds on the information in the Narrative Report with a more complete interpretation, including two different types of interpretations (empirical analyses derived from research and speculative analyses derived from interpretations by the test author and colleagues), which are based on combinations of scales. The report is based on the author's book *A Practical Guide to CPI Interpretation*.

To see a sample Profile Report, Narrative Report, or Configural Analysis Report, go to https://www.cpp .com/en-US/Products-and-Services/Sample-Reports

For more information on the CPI, see https://shop.cpp.com/en/cpiproducts.aspx?pc=113

Reliability/ Precision and Validity	Extensive data are provided in the CPI test manual, and reliability/validity coefficients vary. The internal consistency estimates (coefficient alpha) on the 18 Folk Scales range from .43 to .85 (median =.76), with four scales having coefficients less than .70. The Cronbach's alpha values for the 13 Specialty Scales range between .45 and .88, again with four scales having coefficients less than .70. The majority of test–retest reliability estimates among high school students are high (between .60 and .80 for a 1-year period). Among adults, the estimates for 1 year range between .51 and .80. The test's literature includes empirical evidence for the validity of the Folk Scales and the Specialty Scales. The evidence of construct validity for the Folk Scales shows moderate to strong correlations (.40 to .80) between CPI scales and measures of similar constructs from well-known and well-validated personality instruments. The power of these scales to predict individual behavior in any particular situational or observational context is consistent but relatively weak.
Sources	CPP. (2009). *The CPI Assessments*. Retrieved from https://www.cpp.com/products/cpi/index.aspx CPP. (n.d.). *California Psychological Inventory: Talent*. Retrieved from https://www.cpp.com/products/catalog/CPI434_2008.pdf Gough, H. G. (1987). *California Psychological Inventory administrator's guide*. Palo Alto, CA: Consulting Psychologists Press. Hattrup, K. (2003). Review of the California Psychological Inventory, Third Edition. In B. S. Plake, J. C. Impara, & R. A. Spies (Eds.), *The fifteenth mental measurements yearbook*. Lincoln, NE: Buros Institute of Mental Measurements.

TEST SPOTLIGHT 14.4
WONDERLIC BASIC SKILLS TEST (WBST)

E. F. Wonderlic

Title	Wonderlic Basic Skills Test (WBST)
Author	Eliot Long, Victor Artese, and Winifred Clonts
Publisher	Wonderlic Inc. 400 Lakeview Parkway, Suite 200 Vernon Hills, IL 60061 www.wonderlic.com
Purpose	The WBST provides a short measure of adult language and math skills designed to measure the job readiness of teenagers and adults. Job readiness is defined as having sufficient language and math skills to successfully carry out the written and computational requirements of the job. It is often used as part of a career school's admission testing program.
Versions	There are four equivalent forms for each subtest. Two forms must be administered in a proctored setting and two may be administered from any location with a high-speed Internet connection.

Scales	The WBST contains 50 items on each verbal skills form and 45 items on each quantitative skills form that provide measurements on Verbal, Quantitative, and Composite scales. The Verbal Scale has three subscales: Word Knowledge, Sentence Construction, and Information Retrieval. The Quantitative Scale has three subscales: Explicit Problem Solving, Applied Problem Solving, and Interpretive Problem Solving. In addition, the test estimates GED subscale scores. ("GED levels" refers to the U.S. Department of Labor system for describing job requirements in terms of six levels of ability, covering all ability levels through the completion of college, and on three dimensions: Reasoning, Mathematics, and Language.)
	
	You may find these sample questions and others on the Wonderlic website (www.wonderlic.com):
	
	Sample Question 1
	
	Choose the verb that correctly completes the sentence.
	
	Saundra _____ yesterday.
	
	    A. exercise
	    B. exercises
	    C. exercised
	    D. exercising
	
	Sample Question 2
	
	Choose the answer that most nearly means the same as the underlined word.
	
	<u>Cautious</u> means
	
	    A. thrifty
	    B. careful
	    C. boring
	    D. strong

(Continued)

(Continued)

Sample Question 3

$56 \div 4 =$

    A. 16

    B. 9

    C. 14

    D. 23

Source: Wonderlic. (2014b). *WBST sample questions.* Retrieved October 29, 2014, from http://www.wonderlic.com/assessments/skills/basic-skills-test

Report	The computer-generated Individual Score Report compares the examinee's scores with the skill level requirements of the designated job. It also reports grade-equivalent scores, and GED skill levels achieved. See below for sample report.

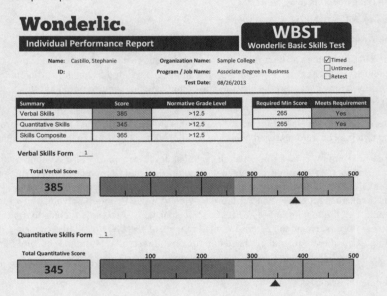

Source: Copyright © 2013 Wonderlic, Inc. A sample personnel report is available at https://www.wonderlic.com/wp-content/uploads/2017/05/BasicSkillsNonProctoredSampleIndividualScoreReport-1.pdf

Reliability/ Precision and Validity	Test–retest alternate-form correlations in the proctored setting for the Verbal Scale were .86 (n = 46) and .79 (n = 64). Test–retest alternate form correlations for the Quantitative Scale were .90 (n = 38) and .84 (n = 58). Internal consistency reliabilities (Cronbach's alpha) for the Verbal and Quantitative tests averaged approximately .92.
	The developmental history of the WBST, particularly its linkage to the job and skill descriptions in the *Dictionary of Occupational Titles*, suggests strong evidence of validity based on test content. The test content focuses on skills identified as job requirements rather than on curriculum taught. Used in the performance report format, it provides content information on specific skill areas that need review relative to overall performance and suggests the next content for study.
Sources	Donlon, T. (2001). Wonderlic Personnel Test. In B. S. Plake & J. C. Impara (Eds.), *The fourteenth mental measurements yearbook*. Lincoln, NE: Buros Institute of Mental Measurements.
	Hanna, G. S. (1998). Wonderlic Basic Skills Test. In J. C. Impara & B. S. Plake (Eds.), *The thirteenth mental measurements yearbook*. Lincoln, NE: Buros Institute of Mental Measurements.

APPENDIX B

Guidelines for Critiquing a Psychological Test

To make informed decisions about tests, you need to know how to critique a test properly. A critique of a test is an analysis of the test. A good critique answers many of the following questions. Your instructor may have additional ideas about what constitutes a good critique.

General Descriptive Information

- What is the title of the test?

- Who is the author of the test?

- Who publishes the test, and when was it published? (Include dates of manuals, norms, and supplementary materials.)

- How long does it take to administer the test?

- How much does it cost to purchase the test? (Include the cost of the test, answer sheets, manual, scoring services, and so on.)

- Is the test proprietary or nonproprietary?

Purpose and Nature of the Test

- What does the test measure? (Include scales.)

- What does the test predict?

- What behavior does the test require the test taker to perform?

- What population was the test designed for (for example, age, type of person)?

- What is the nature of the test (for example, maximal performance, behavior observation, self-report, standardized or nonstandardized, objective or subjective)?

- What is the format of the test (for example, paper-and-pencil or computerized, multiple choice or true/false)?

Practical Evaluation

- Is the test manual comprehensive? (Does it include information on how the test was constructed, its reliability and validity, composition of norm groups, and is it easy to read?)

- Is the test easy or difficult to administer?

- How clear are the administration directions?

- How clear are the scoring procedures?
- What qualifications and training does a test administrator need to have?
- Does the test have face validity?

Technical Evaluation

- Is there a norm group?
- Who comprises the norm group?
- What types of norms are there (for example, percentiles, standard scores)?
- How was the norm group selected?
- Are there subgroup norms (for example, by age, gender, region, occupation, and so on)?
- What is the estimate of the test's reliability?
- How was reliability determined?
- What is the evidence for the validity of the test?
- How was the evidence for validity gathered?
- What is the standard error of measurement?
- What are the confidence intervals?

Test Reviews

- What do reviewers say are the strengths and weaknesses of the test?
- What studies that used the test as a measurement instrument have been published in peer-reviewed journals?
- How did the test perform when researchers or test users, other than the test developer or publisher, used it?

Summary

- Overall, what do you see as being the strengths and weaknesses of the test?

APPENDIX C

Code of Fair Testing Practices in Education

CONTENTS

The Code of Fair Testing Practices in Education (*Code*) is a guide for professionals in fulfilling their obligation to provide and use tests that are fair to all test takers regardless of age, gender, disability, race, ethnicity, national origin, religion, sexual orientation, linguistic background, or other personal characteristics. Fairness is a primary consideration in all aspects of testing. Careful standardization of tests and administration conditions helps to ensure that all test takers are given a comparable opportunity to demonstrate what they know and how they can perform in the area being tested. Fairness implies that every test taker has the opportunity to prepare for the test and is informed about the general nature and content of the test, as appropriate to the purpose of the test. Fairness also extends to the accurate reporting of individual and group test results. Fairness is not an isolated concept, but must be considered in all aspects of the testing process.

The *Code* applies broadly to testing in education (admissions, educational assessment, educational diagnosis, and student placement) regardless of the mode of presentation, so it is relevant to conventional paper-and-pencil tests, computer-based tests, and performance tests. It is not designed to cover employment testing, licensure or certification testing, or other types of testing outside the field of education. The *Code* is directed primarily at professionally developed tests used in formally administered testing programs. Although the *Code* is not intended to cover tests prepared by teachers for use in their own classrooms, teachers are encouraged to use the guidelines to help improve their testing practices.

Source: Reprinted with permission. *Code of Fair Testing Practices in Education.* (Copyright 2004). Washington, DC: Joint Committee on Testing Practices. (Mailing Address: Joint Committee on Testing Practices, Science Directorate, American Psychological Association [APA], 750 First Street, NE, Washington, DC 20002-4242; http://www.apa.org/science/jctpweb .html.) Contact APA for additional copies.

Note: The *Code* has been prepared by the Joint Committee on Testing Practices, a cooperative effort among several professional organizations. The aim of the Joint Committee is to act in the public interest to advance the quality of testing practices. Members of the Joint Committee include the American Counseling Association (ACA), the American Educational Research Association (AERA), the American Psychological Association (APA), the American Speech-Language-Hearing Association (ASHA), the National Association of School Psychologists (NASP), the National Association of Test Directors (NATD), and the National Council on Measurement in Education (NCME).

The *Code* addresses the roles of test developers and test users separately. Test developers are people and organizations that construct tests, as well as those that set policies for testing programs. Test users are people and agencies that select tests, administer tests, commission test development services, or make decisions on the basis of test scores. Test developer and test user roles may overlap, for example, when a state or local education agency commissions test development services, sets policies that control the test development process, and makes decisions on the basis of the test scores.

Many of the statements in the *Code* refer to the selection and use of existing tests. When a new test is developed, when an existing test is modified, or when the administration of a test is modified, the *Code* is intended to provide guidance for this process.[1]

The *Code* provides guidance separately for test developers and test users in four critical areas:

A. Developing and Selecting Appropriate Tests

B. Administering and Scoring Tests

C. Reporting and Interpreting Test Results

D. Informing Test Takers

The *Code* is intended to be consistent with the relevant parts of the Standards for Educational and Psychological Testing (American Educational Research Association [AERA], American Psychological Association [APA], and National Council on Measurement in Education [NCME], 1999). The *Code* is not meant to add new principles over and above those in the Standards or to change their meaning. Rather, the *Code* is intended to represent the spirit of selected portions of the Standards in a way that is relevant and meaningful to developers and users of tests, as well as to test takers and/or their parents or guardians. States, districts, schools, organizations, and individual professionals are encouraged to commit themselves to fairness in testing and safeguarding the rights of test takers. The *Code* is intended to assist in carrying out such commitments.

A. DEVELOPING AND SELECTING APPROPRIATE TESTS

Test Developers

Test developers should provide the information and supporting evidence that test users need to select appropriate tests.

1. Provide evidence of what the test measures, the recommended uses, the intended test takers, and the strengths and limitations of the test, including the level of precision of the test scores.

2. Describe how the content and skills to be tested were selected and how the tests were developed.

---

[1]The *Code* is not intended to be mandatory, exhaustive, or definitive, and may not be applicable to every situation. Instead, the *Code* is intended to be aspirational, and is not intended to take precedence over the judgment of those who have competence in the subjects addressed.

3. Communicate information about a test's characteristics at a level of detail appropriate to the intended test users.

4. Provide guidance on the levels of skills, knowledge, and training necessary for appropriate review, selection, and administration of tests.

5. Provide evidence that the technical quality, including reliability and validity, of the test meets its intended purposes.

6. Provide to qualified test users representative samples of test questions or practice tests, directions, answer sheets, manuals, and score reports.

7. Avoid potentially offensive content or language when developing test questions and related materials.

8. Make appropriately modified forms of tests or administration procedures available for test takers with disabilities who need special accommodations.

9. Obtain and provide evidence on the performance of test takers of diverse subgroups, making significant efforts to obtain sample sizes that are adequate for subgroup analyses. Evaluate the evidence to ensure that differences in performance are related to the skills being assessed.

Test Users

Test users should select tests that meet the intended purpose and that are appropriate for the intended test takers.

1. Define the purpose for testing, the content and skills to be tested, and the intended test takers. Select and use the most appropriate test based on a thorough review of available information.

2. Review and select tests based on the appropriateness of test content, skills tested, and content coverage for the intended purpose of testing.

3. Review materials provided by test developers and select tests for which clear, accurate, and complete information is provided.

4. Select tests through a process that includes persons with appropriate knowledge, skills, and training.

5. Evaluate evidence of the technical quality of the test provided by the test developer and any independent reviewers.

6. Evaluate representative samples of test questions or practice tests, directions, answer sheets, manuals, and score reports before selecting a test.

7. Evaluate procedures and materials used by test developers, as well as the resulting test, to ensure that potentially offensive content or language is avoided.

8. Select tests with appropriately modified forms or administration procedures for test takers with disabilities who need special accommodations.

9. Evaluate the available evidence on the performance of test takers of diverse subgroups. Determine to the extent feasible which performance differences may have been caused by factors unrelated to the skills being assessed.

B. ADMINISTERING AND SCORING TESTS

Test Developers

Test developers should explain how to administer and score tests correctly and fairly.

1. Provide clear descriptions of detailed procedures for administering tests in a standardized manner.

2. Provide guidelines on reasonable procedures for assessing persons with disabilities who need special accommodations or those with diverse linguistic backgrounds.

3. Provide information to test takers or test users on test question formats and procedures for answering test questions, including information on the use of any needed materials and equipment.

4. Establish and implement procedures to ensure the security of testing materials during all phases of test development, administration, scoring, and reporting.

5. Provide procedures, materials, and guidelines for scoring the tests and for monitoring the accuracy of the scoring process. If scoring the test is the responsibility of the test developer, provide adequate training for scorers.

6. Correct errors that affect the interpretation of the scores and communicate the corrected results promptly.

7. Develop and implement procedures for ensuring the confidentiality of scores.

Test Users

Test users should administer and score tests correctly and fairly.

1. Follow established procedures for administering tests in a standardized manner.

2. Provide and document appropriate procedures for test takers with disabilities who need special accommodations or those with diverse linguistic backgrounds. Some accommodations may be required by law or regulation.

3. Provide test takers with an opportunity to become familiar with test question formats and any materials or equipment that may be used during testing.

4. Protect the security of test materials, including respecting copyrights and eliminating opportunities for test takers to obtain scores by fraudulent means.

5. If test scoring is the responsibility of the test user, provide adequate training to scorers and ensure and monitor the accuracy of the scoring process.

6. Correct errors that affect the interpretation of the scores and communicate the corrected results promptly.

7. Develop and implement procedures for ensuring the confidentiality of scores.

C. REPORTING AND INTERPRETING TEST RESULTS

Test Developers

Test developers should report test results accurately and provide information to help test users interpret test results correctly.

1. Provide information to support recommended interpretations of the results, including the nature of the content, norms or comparison groups, and other technical evidence. Advise test users of the benefits and limitations of test results and their interpretation. Warn against assigning greater precision than is warranted.

2. Provide guidance regarding the interpretations of results for tests administered with modifications. Inform test users of potential problems in interpreting test results when tests or test administration procedures are modified.

3. Specify appropriate uses of test results and warn test users of potential misuses.

4. When test developers set standards, provide the rationale, procedures, and evidence for setting performance standards or passing scores. Avoid using stigmatizing labels.

5. Encourage test users to base decisions about test takers on multiple sources of appropriate information, not on a single test score.

6. Provide information to enable test users to accurately interpret and report test results for groups of test takers, including information about who were and who were not included in the different groups being compared and information about factors that might influence the interpretation of results.

7. Provide test results in a timely fashion and in a manner that is understood by the test taker.

8. Provide guidance to test users about how to monitor the extent to which the test is fulfilling its intended purposes.

Test Users

Test users should report and interpret test results accurately and clearly.

1. Interpret the meaning of the test results, taking into account the nature of the content, norms or comparison groups, other technical evidence, and benefits and limitations of test results.

2. Interpret test results from modified test or test administration procedures in view of the impact those modifications may have had on test results.

3. Avoid using tests for purposes other than those recommended by the test developer unless there is evidence to support the intended use or interpretation.

4. Review the procedures for setting performance standards or passing scores. Avoid using stigmatizing labels.

5. Avoid using a single test score as the sole determinant of decisions about test takers. Interpret test scores in conjunction with other information about individuals.

6. State the intended interpretation and use of test results for groups of test takers. Avoid grouping test results for purposes not specifically recommended by the test developer unless evidence is obtained to support the intended use. Report procedures that were followed in determining who were and who were not included in the groups being compared and describe factors that might influence the interpretation of results.

7. Communicate test results in a timely fashion and in a manner that is understood by the test taker.

8. Develop and implement procedures for monitoring test use, including consistency with the intended purposes of the test.

D. INFORMING TEST TAKERS

Under some circumstances, test developers have direct communication with the test takers and/or control of the tests, testing process, and test results. In other circumstances the test users have these responsibilities.

Test developers or test users should inform test takers about the nature of the test, test taker rights and responsibilities, the appropriate use of scores, and procedures for resolving challenges to scores.

1. Inform test takers in advance of the test administration about the coverage of the test, the types of question formats, the directions, and appropriate test-taking strategies. Make such information available to all test takers.

2. When a test is optional, provide test takers or their parents/guardians with information to help them judge whether a test should be taken—including indications of any consequences that may result from not taking the test (e.g., not being eligible to compete for a particular scholarship)—and whether there is an available alternative to the test.

3. Provide test takers or their parents/guardians with information about rights test takers may have to obtain copies of tests and completed answer sheets, to retake tests, to have tests rescored, or to have scores declared invalid.

4. Provide test takers or their parents/guardians with information about responsibilities test takers have, such as being aware of the intended purpose and uses of the test, performing at capacity, following directions, and not disclosing test items or interfering with other test takers.

5. Inform test takers or their parents/guardians how long scores will be kept on file and indicate to whom, under what circumstances, and in what manner test scores and related information will or will not be released. Protect test scores from unauthorized release and access.

6. Describe procedures for investigating and resolving circumstances that might result in canceling or withholding scores, such as failure to adhere to specified testing procedures.

7. Describe procedures that test takers, parents/guardians, and other interested parties may use to obtain more information about the test, register complaints, and have problems resolved.

WORKING GROUP

Note: The membership of the working group that developed the *Code of Fair Testing Practices in Education* and of the Joint Committee on Testing Practices that guided the working group is as follows:

Peter Behuniak, PhD

Lloyd Bond, PhD

Gwyneth M. Boodoo, PhD

Wayne Camara, PhD

Ray Fenton, PhD

John J. Fremer, PhD (Cochair)

Sharon M. Goldsmith, PhD

Bert F. Green, PhD

William G. Harris, PhD

Janet E. Helms, PhD

Stephanie H. McConaughy, PhD

Julie P. Noble, PhD

Wayne M. Patience, PhD

Carole L. Perlman, PhD

Douglas K. Smith, PhD

Janet E. Wall, EdD (Cochair)

Pat Nellor Wickwire, PhD

Mary Yakimowski, PhD

Lara Frumkin, PhD, of the APA, served as staff liaison.

The Joint Committee intends that the *Code* be consistent with and supportive of existing codes of conduct and standards of other professional groups who use tests in educational contexts. Of particular note are the Responsibilities of Users of Standardized Tests (Association for Assessment in Counseling and Education, 2003), APA Test User Qualifications (2000), ASHA Code of Ethics (2001), Ethical Principles of Psychologists and Code of Conduct (1992), NASP Professional Conduct Manual (2000), NCME Code of Professional Responsibility (1995), and Rights and Responsibilities of Test Takers: Guidelines and Expectations (Joint Committee on Testing Practices, 2000).

APPENDIX D

Ethical Principles of Psychologists and Code of Conduct

PREAMBLE

Psychologists are committed to increasing scientific and professional knowledge of behavior and people's understanding of themselves and others and to the use of such knowledge to improve the condition of individuals, organizations, and society. Psychologists respect and protect civil and human rights and the central importance of freedom of inquiry and expression in research, teaching, and publication. They strive to help the public in developing informed judgments and choices concerning human behavior. In doing so, they perform many roles, such as researcher, educator, diagnostician, therapist, supervisor, consultant, administrator, social interventionist, and expert witness. This Ethics Code provides a common set of principles and standards upon which psychologists build their professional and scientific work.

This Ethics Code is intended to provide specific standards to cover most situations encountered by psychologists. It has as its goals the welfare and protection of the individuals and groups with whom psychologists work and the education of members, students, and the public regarding ethical standards of the discipline.

The development of a dynamic set of ethical standards for psychologists' work-related conduct requires a personal commitment and lifelong effort to act ethically; to encourage ethical behavior by students, supervisees, employees, and colleagues; and to consult with others concerning ethical problems.

GENERAL PRINCIPLES

This section consists of General Principles. General Principles, as opposed to Ethical Standards, are aspirational in nature. Their intent is to guide and inspire psychologists toward the very highest ethical ideals of the profession. General Principles, in contrast to Ethical Standards, do not represent obligations and should not form the basis for imposing sanctions. Relying upon General Principles for either of these reasons distorts both their meaning and purpose.

Principle A: Beneficence and Nonmaleficence

Psychologists strive to benefit those with whom they work and take care to do no harm. In their professional actions, psychologists seek to safeguard the welfare and rights of those with whom they interact professionally and other affected persons, and the welfare of animal subjects of research. When conflicts occur among psychologists' obligations or concerns, they attempt to resolve these conflicts in a responsible fashion that avoids or minimizes harm. Because psychologists' scientific and professional judgments and actions may affect the lives of others, they are alert to and guard against personal, financial, social, organizational, or political factors that might lead to misuse of their influence. Psychologists strive to be aware of the possible effect of their own physical and mental health on their ability to help those with whom they work.

Principle B: Fidelity and Responsibility

Psychologists establish relationships of trust with those with whom they work. They are aware of their professional and scientific responsibilities to society and to the specific communities in which they work. Psychologists uphold professional standards of conduct, clarify their professional roles and obligations, accept appropriate responsibility for their behavior, and seek to manage conflicts of interest that could lead to exploitation or harm. Psychologists consult with, refer to, or cooperate with other professionals and institutions to the extent needed to serve the best interests of those with whom they work. They are concerned about the ethical compliance of their colleagues' scientific and professional conduct. Psychologists strive to contribute a portion of their professional time for little or no compensation or personal advantage.

Principle C: Integrity

Psychologists seek to promote accuracy, honesty, and truthfulness in the science, teaching, and practice of psychology. In these activities psychologists do not steal, cheat, or engage in fraud, subterfuge, or intentional misrepresentation of fact. Psychologists strive to keep their promises and to avoid unwise or unclear commitments. In situations in which deception may be ethically justifiable to maximize benefits and minimize harm, psychologists have a serious obligation to consider the need for, the possible consequences of, and their responsibility to correct any resulting mistrust or other harmful effects that arise from the use of such techniques.

Principle D: Justice

Psychologists recognize that fairness and justice entitle all persons to access to and benefit from the contributions of psychology and to equal quality in the processes, procedures, and services being conducted by psychologists. Psychologists exercise reasonable judgment and take precautions to ensure that their potential biases, the boundaries of their competence, and the limitations of their expertise do not lead to or condone unjust practices.

Principle E: Respect for People's Rights and Dignity

Psychologists respect the dignity and worth of all people, and the rights of individuals to privacy, confidentiality, and self-determination. Psychologists are aware that special safeguards may be necessary to protect the rights and welfare of persons or communities whose vulnerabilities impair autonomous decision making. Psychologists are aware of and respect cultural, individual, and role differences, including those based on age, gender, gender identity, race, ethnicity, culture, national origin, religion, sexual orientation, disability, language, and socioeconomic status, and consider these factors when working with members of such groups. Psychologists try to eliminate the effect on their work of biases based on those factors, and they do not knowingly participate in or condone activities of others based upon such prejudices.

APPENDIX E

Table of Critical Values for Pearson Product–Moment Correlation Coefficients

	Level of Significance for a Two-Tailed Test				
df	.10	.05	.02	.01	.001
	Level of Significance for a One-Tailed Test				
(df = N − 2)	.05	.025	.01	.005	.0005
1	.98769	.99692	.999507	.999877	.9999988
2	.900000	.95000	.98000	.990000	.99900
3	.8054	.8783	.93433	.95873	.99116
4	.7293	.8114	.8822	.91720	.97406
5	.6694	.7545	.8329	.8745	.95074
6	.6215	.7067	.7887	.8343	.92493
7	.5822	.6664	.7498	.7977	.8982
8	.5494	.6319	.7155	.7646	.8721
9	.5214	.6021	.6851	.7348	.8371
10	.4973	.5760	.6581	.7079	.8233
11	.4762	.5529	.6339	.6835	.8010
12	.4575	.5324	.6120	.6614	.7800
13	.4409	.5139	.5923	.6411	.7603
14	.4259	.4973	.5742	.6226	.7420
15	.4124	.4821	.5577	.6055	.7246
16	.4000	.4683	.5425	.5897	.7084
17	.3887	.4555	.5285	.5751	.6932
18	.3783	.4438	.5155	.5614	.6787
19	.3687	.4329	.5034	.5487	.6652
20	.3598	.4227	.4921	.5368	.6524

	Level of Significance for a Two-Tailed Test				
df	.10	.05	.02	.01	.001
	Level of Significance for a One-Tailed Test				
(df = N − 2)	.05	.025	.01	.005	.0005
25	.3233	.3809	.4451	.4869	.5974
30	.2960	.3494	.4093	.4487	.5541
35	.2746	.3246	.3810	.4182	.5189
40	.2573	.3044	.3578	.3932	.4896
45	.2428	.2875	.3384	.3721	.4648
50	.2306	.2732	.3218	.3541	.4433
60	.2108	.2500	.2948	.3248	.4078
70	.1954	.2319	.2737	.3017	.3799
80	.1829	.2172	.2565	.2830	.3568
90	.1726	.2050	.2422	.2673	.3375
100	.1638	.1946	.2301	.2540	.3211

Source: Data from Fisher, R. A., & Yates, F. (1963). *Statistical tables for biological, agricultural, and medical research.* Edinburgh, UK: Oliver & Boyd. Copyright © 1963 by Addison Wesley Longman Ltd., Pearson Education Limited, Edinburgh Gate, Harlow Essex CM20.

Note: To be significant, the *r* obtained from the data must be equal to or larger than the value shown in the table.

GLOSSARY

absolute decisions: Decisions that are made by seeing who has the minimum score needed to qualify.

abstract attributes: Attributes that are more difficult to describe using behaviors because people disagree on which behaviors represent the attribute; examples include personality, intelligence, creativity, and aggressiveness.

accessibility: The degree to which a test allows test takers to demonstrate their standing on the construct the test was designed to measure without being disadvantaged by other individual characteristics such as age, race, gender, or native language.

acculturation: The degree to which an immigrant or a minority member has adapted to a country's mainstream culture.

achievement tests: Tests that are designed to measure a person's previous learning in a specific academic area.

acquiescence: The tendency of some test takers to agree with any ideas or behaviors presented.

adaptive testing: Using tests developed from a large test bank in which the test questions are chosen to match the skill and ability level of the test taker.

age norms: Norms that allow test users to compare an individual's test score with scores of people in the same age group.

alternate forms: Two forms of a test that are alike in every way except for the questions; used to overcome problems such as practice effects; also referred to as parallel forms.

anchors: Numbers or words on a rating scale that the rater chooses to indicate the category that best represents the employee's performance on the specified dimension.

anonymity: The practice of administering tests or obtaining information without obtaining the identity of the participant.

aptitude tests: Tests that are designed to assess the test taker's potential for learning or the individual's ability to perform in an area in which he or she has not been specifically trained.

area transformations: A method for changing scores for interpretation purposes that changes the unit of measurement and the unit of reference, such as percentile ranks.

assessment center: A large-scale replication of a job that requires test takers to solve typical job problems by role-playing or to demonstrate proficiency at job functions such as making presentations and fulfilling administrative duties; used for assessing job-related dimensions such as leadership, decision making, planning, and organizing.

attenuation due to unreliability: The reduction in an observed validity coefficient due to unreliability of either the test or the criterion measure

authentic assessment: Assessment that measures a student's ability to apply in real-world settings the knowledge and skills he or she has learned.

autism spectrum disorders: Developmental disabilities that affect communication and social interaction and involve restricted interests and stereotyped, repetitive patterns of behavior.

b weight: In regression, the slope of the regression line, or the expected change in the criterion (Y) for a one unit change in the predictor (X).

behavior: An observable and measurable action.

behavior observation tests: Tests that involve observing people's behavior to learn how they typically respond in a particular context.

behavioral checklist: When a rater evaluates performance by rating the frequency of important behaviors required for the job.

behavioral interviews: Interviews that focus on behaviors rather than on attitudes or opinions.

behaviorally anchored rating scale (BARS): A type of performance appraisal that uses behaviors as anchors; the rater rates by choosing the behavior that is most representative of the employee's performance.

bivariate analyses: Analyses that provide information on two variables or groups.

categorical data: Data grouped according to a common property.

categorical model of scoring: A test scoring model that places test takers in a particular group or class.

central tendency errors: Rating errors that result when raters use only the middle of the rating scale and ignore the highest and lowest scale categories.

certification: A professional credential individuals earn by demonstrating that they have met predetermined qualifications (e.g., that they have specific knowledge, skills, and/or experience).

class intervals: A way of grouping adjacent scores to display them in a table or graph.

cluster sampling: A type of sampling that involves selecting clusters of respondents and then selecting respondents from each cluster.

coefficient of determination: The amount of variance shared by two variables being correlated, such as a test and a criterion, obtained by squaring the validity coefficient.

coefficient of multiple determination: A statistic that is obtained through multiple regression analysis, which is interpreted as the total proportion of variance in the criterion variable that is accounted for by all the predictors in the multiple regression equation. It is the square of the multiple correlation coefficient, R.

cognitive impairments: Mental disorders that include mental retardation, learning disabilities, and traumatic brain injuries.

cognitive tests: Assessments that measure the test taker's mental capabilities, such as general mental ability tests, intelligence tests, and academic skills tests.

Cohen's kappa: An index of agreement for two sets of scores or ratings.

comorbid disorders: The presence of mental health problems in addition to depression.

comparative decisions: Decisions that are made by comparing test scores to see who has the best score.

competency modeling: A procedure that identifies the knowledge, skills, abilities, and other characteristics most critical for success for some or all the jobs in an organization.

computerized adaptive rating scales (CARS): Testing in which the computer software, as in computerized adaptive testing, selects behavioral statements for rating based on the rater's previous responses.

computerized adaptive testing (CAT): Testing in which the computer software chooses and presents the test taker with harder or easier questions as the test progresses, depending on how well the test taker answered previous questions.

concrete attributes: Attributes that can be described in terms of specific behaviors, such as the ability to play the piano.

concurrent evidence of validity: A method for establishing evidence of validity based on a test's relationships with other variables in which test administration and criterion measurement happen at roughly the same time.

confidence interval: A range of scores that the test user can feel confident includes the true score.

confidentiality: The assurance that all personal information will be kept private and not be disclosed without explicit permission.

confirmatory factor analysis: A procedure in which researchers, using factor analysis, consider the theory associated with a test and propose a set of underlying factors that they expect the test to contain; they then conduct a factor analysis to see whether the factors they proposed do indeed exist.

construct: An attribute, trait, or characteristic that is abstracted from observable behaviors.

construct explication: Three steps for defining or explaining a psychological construct.

construct validity: An accumulation of evidence that a test is based on sound psychological theory and therefore measures what it is supposed to measure; evidence that a test relates to other tests and behaviors as predicted by a theory.

content areas: The knowledge, skills, and/or attributes that a test assesses.

content validity: The extent to which the questions on a test are representative of the material that should be covered by the test.

content validity ratio: An index that describes how essential each test item is to measuring the attribute or construct that the item is supposed to measure.

convenience sampling: A type of sampling in which an available group of participants is used to represent the population.

convergent evidence of validity: One of two strategies for demonstrating construct validity showing that constructs that theoretically should be related are indeed related; evidence that the scores on a test correlate strongly with scores on other tests that measure the same construct.

correction for attenuation: A statistical adjustment made to a correlation coefficient (usually the validity coefficient of a test), to estimate what it would be if the reliability of the test could be measured without random measurement error.

correlation: A statistical procedure that provides an index of the strength and direction of the linear relationship between two variables.

correlation coefficient: A statistic that provides an index of the strength and relationship between two sets of scores; a statistic that describes the relationship between two distributions of scores.

criterion: The measure of performance that we expect to correlate with test scores.

criterion contamination: When the criterion in a validation study measures more dimensions than those measured by the test.

criterion-referenced tests: Tests that involve comparing an individual's test score with an objectively stated standard of achievement, such as being able to multiply numbers.

criterion-related validity: Evidence that test scores correlate with or predict independent behaviors, attitudes, or events; the extent to which the scores on a test correlate with scores on a measure of performance or behavior.

cross-validation: Administering a test another time following a validation study to confirm the results of the validation study; because of chance factors that contribute to random error, this second administration can be expected to yield lower correlations with criterion measures.

cumulative model of scoring: A test scoring model that assumes that the more the test taker responds in a particular fashion, the more the test taker exhibits the attribute being measured; the test taker receives 1 point for each "correct" answer, and the total number of correct answers becomes the raw score.

cut scores: Decision points for dividing test scores into pass/fail groupings.

database: A matrix in the form of a spreadsheet that shows the responses given by each participant (row) for each question (column) in the survey.

decennial census survey: A survey that is administered by the U.S. Census Bureau every 10 years, primarily to determine the population of the United States.

descriptive research techniques: Techniques that help us describe a situation or phenomenon.

descriptive statistics: Numbers calculated from a distribution that describe or summarize the properties of the distribution of test scores, such as the mean, median, mode, and standard deviation.

diagnostic assessment: Assessment that involves an in-depth evaluation of an individual to identify characteristics for treatment or enhancement.

differential validity: When a test yields significantly different validity coefficients for subgroups.

discriminant evidence of validity: One of two strategies for demonstrating construct validity showing that constructs that theoretically should be related are indeed related; evidence that test scores are not correlated with unrelated constructs.

discrimination index: A statistic that compares the performance of those who made very high test scores with the performance of those who made very low test scores on each item.

distractors: The incorrect responses to a multiple-choice question.

double-barreled question: A question that is actually asking two or more questions in one.

emotional intelligence: "Type of intelligence defined as the abilities to perceive, appraise, and express emotions accurately and appropriately, to use emotions to facilitate thinking, to understand and analyze emotions, to use emotional knowledge effectively, and to regulate one's emotions to promote both emotional and intellectual growth" (American Psychological Association [APA], 2018b, para. 10).

empirically based tests: Tests in which the decision to place an individual in a category is based solely on the quantitative relationship between the predictor and the criterion.

essay questions: Popular subjective test items in educational settings that are usually general in scope and require lengthy written responses by test takers.

ethical standards: Statements by professionals (not laws established by governmental bodies) regarding what they believe are appropriate and inappropriate behaviors when practicing their profession.

ethics: Issues or practices that influence the decision-making process in terms of "doing the right thing."

evidence-based practice: "The integration of the best available research with clinical expertise in the context of patient characteristics, culture, and preferences" (APA, 2014, para. 2).

evidence-based treatment method: Treatment methods with documented research evidence that the methods are effective for solving the problems being addressed.

experimental research techniques: Research designs that provide evidence for cause and effect.

experts: Individuals who are knowledgeable about a topic or who will be affected by the outcome of something.

exploratory factor analysis: A method of factor analysis in which researchers do not propose a formal hypothesis but instead use the procedure to broadly identify underlying components.

face validity: The perception of the test taker that the test measures what it is supposed to measure.

face-to-face surveys: Surveys in which an interviewer asks a series of questions in a respondent's home, a public place, or the researcher's office.

factor analysis: An advanced statistical procedure based on the concept of correlation that helps investigators identify the underlying constructs or factors being measured.

factors: The underlying commonalities of tests or test questions that measure a construct.

faking: The inclination of some test takers to try to answer items in a way that will cause a desired outcome or diagnosis.

false positive: When an innocent test taker mistakenly is classified as guilty.

field test: An administration of a survey or test to a large representative group of individuals to identify problems with administration, item interpretation, and so on.

five-factor model: A widely accepted personality theory that proposes there are five central personality dimensions: extraversion, emotional stability, agreeableness, conscientiousness, and intellect or openness to experience.

focus group: A method that involves bringing together people who are similar to the target respondents in order to discuss issues related to the survey.

forced choice: A test item format that requires the test taker to choose one of two or more words or phrases that appear to be unrelated but are equally acceptable.

forced distribution: A method of ranking employees that requires the supervisor to assign a certain number of employees to each performance category.

forced ranking: A method of performance appraisal in which managers rank employees in terms of predetermined dimensions or criteria.

formative assessments: Assessments that help teachers determine what information students are and are not learning during the instructional process.

frequency distribution: An orderly arrangement of a group of numbers (or test scores) showing the number of times each score occurred in a distribution.

generalizability theory: A proposed method for systematically analyzing the many causes of inconsistency or random error in test scores, seeking to find systematic error that can then be eliminated.

generalizable: When a test can be expected to produce similar results even though it has been administered in different locations.

grade norms: Norms that allow test users to compare a student's test score with scores of other students in the same grade.

graphic rating scale: A graph for rating employees' performance that represents a dimension, such as quality or quantity of work, divided into categories defined by numbers, words, or both.

halo effect: A rating error that occurs when raters let their judgment on one dimension influence judgments on other dimensions.

heterogeneous test: A test that measures more than one trait or characteristic.

high-fidelity test: A test that is designed to replicate the job tasks and settings as realistically as possible.

high-stakes test: A test on which student performance significantly affects educational paths or choices.

histogram: A bar graph used to represent frequency data in statistics.

homogeneity of the population: How similar the people in a population are to one another.

homogeneous test: A test that measures only one trait or characteristic.

hypotheses: Educated guesses or predictions based on a theory.

incremental validity: The amount of additional variance in a test battery that can be accounted for in the criterion measure by the addition of one or more additional tests to the test battery.

individual decisions: Decisions that are made by the person who takes the test using the test results.

individually administered surveys: Surveys administered by a facilitator in person for respondents to complete in the presence of the facilitator.

inference: Using evidence to reach a conclusion.

informed consent: Individuals' right of self-determination; means that individuals are entitled to full explanations of why they are being tested, how the test data will be used, and what the test results mean.

institutional decisions: Decisions that are made by an institution based on the results of a particular test or tests.

instructional objectives: A list of what individuals should be able to do as a result of taking a course of instruction.

integrity tests: Tests that measure individual attitudes and experiences toward honesty, dependability, trustworthiness, reliability, and prosocial behavior.

intelligence tests: Tests that assess the test taker's ability to cope with the environment but at a broader level than do aptitude tests.

intercept: The place where the regression line crosses the y-axis.

intercept bias: A type of measurement bias in which the intercept of the regression line that is used to predict a criterion of interest is not the same for all demographic groups used in the regression (e.g., men and women).

interest inventories: Tests that are designed to assess a person's interests in educational programs for job settings and thereby to provide information for making career decisions.

interitem correlation matrix: A matrix that displays the correlation of each item with every other item.

internal consistency: The internal reliability of a measurement instrument; the extent to which each test question has the same value of the attribute that the test measures.

interrater agreement: The consistency with which scorers rate or make yes/no decisions.

interscorer agreement: The consistency with which scorers rate or make decisions.

interval scales: Level of measurement in which numbers are assigned with the assumption that each number represents a point that is an equal distance from the points adjacent to it.

interview questions: The traditional subjective test questions in an organizational setting that make up the employment interview.

intrarater agreement: How well a scorer makes consistent judgments across all tests.

intrascorer reliability: Whether each scorer was consistent in the way he or she assigned scores from test to test.

ipsative model of scoring: A test scoring model that compares the test taker's scores on various scales within the inventory to yield a profile.

item analysis: The process of evaluating the performance of each item on a test.

item bias: Differences in responses to test questions that are related to differences in culture, gender, or experiences of the test takers.

item characteristic curve (ICC): The line that results when we graph the probability of answering an item correctly with the level of ability on the construct being measured; the resulting graph provides a picture of both the item's difficulty and discrimination.

item difficulty: The percentage of test takers who answer a question correctly.

item nonresponse rate: How often an item or question was not answered.

item response theory (IRT): A theory that relates the performance of each item to a statistical estimate of the test taker's ability on the construct being measured.

Item-total correlation: A measure of the strength and direction of the relationship (the correlation) between the way test takers responded to one particular test item and their total score on the test.

job analysis: A systematic assessment method for identifying the knowledge, skills, abilities, and other characteristics required to perform a job.

learning disability: A hidden handicap that hinders learning and does not have visible signs.

leniency errors: Systematic rating errors that occur when raters give all employees better ratings than they deserve.

level of measurement: The relationship among the numbers we have assigned to the information—nominal, ordinal, equal interval, or ratio.

licensure: A mandatory credential individuals must obtain to practice within their professions.

linear regression: The statistical process used to predict one set of test scores from one set of criterion scores.

linear transformations: A method for changing raw scores for interpretation purposes that does not change the characteristics of the raw data in any way, such as z scores and T scores.

literature reviews: Systematic examinations of published and unpublished reports on a topic.

low-fidelity tests: Tests that simulate the job and its tasks using a written, verbal, or visual description.

mail surveys: Surveys that are mailed to respondents with instructions for completing and returning them.

mean: The arithmetic average of a group of test scores in a distribution.

measurement: The process of assessing the size, the amount, or the degree of an attribute using specific rules for transforming the attribute into numbers.

measurement bias: When the scores on a test taken by different subgroups in the population (e.g., men, women) need to be interpreted differently because of some characteristic of the test not related to the construct being measured.

measurement error: Variations or inconsistencies in the measurements yielded by a test or survey.

measurement instrument: A tool or technique for assessing the size, amount, or degree of an attribute.

measure of central tendency: A value that helps us understand the middle of a distribution or set of scores.

measures of relationship: Statistics that describe the relationship between two sets of scores, such as the correlation coefficient.

measures of variability: Numbers that represent the spread of the scores in the distribution, such as range, variance, and standard deviation.

median: The middle score in a distribution.

meta-analysis: A statistical technique that accumulates the results of multiple studies on comparable constructs into a single result in an attempt to get the best possible estimate of the relationship between a predictor and a criterion.

mode: The most frequently occurring score in a distribution.

motor impairments: Disabilities that hinder physical movement, such as paralysis and missing limbs.

multicultural backgrounds: Experiences of those who belong to various minority groups based on race, cultural or ethnic origin, sexual orientation, family unit, primary language, and so on.

multiple choice: An objective test format that consists of a question or partial sentence, called a stem, followed by a number of responses, only one of which is correct.

multiple regression: The process whereby more than one set of test scores is used to predict one set of criterion scores.

multitrait–multimethod correlation matrix: A type of correlation matrix used in studies of construct validity that presents all the correlations between a group of different traits, attributes, or constructs, each measured by two or more different measurement methods or tests.

multitrait–multimethod (MTMM) design: A design for test validation that gathers evidence of reliability, convergent evidence of validity, and discriminant evidence of validity into one study.

multivariate analyses: Analyses that provide information on three or more variables or groups.

nature-versus-nurture controversy: A debate that focuses on whether intelligence is determined by heredity or develops after birth based on environmental factors.

nominal scale: The most basic level of measurement, in which numbers are assigned to groups or categories of information.

nomological network: A method for defining a construct by illustrating its relation to as many other constructs and behaviors as possible.

nonprobability sampling: A type of sampling in which not everyone has an equal chance of being selected from the population.

nonsampling measurement errors: Errors associated with the design and administration of a survey.

nonstandardized tests: Tests that do not have standardization samples; more common than standardized tests. Standardized tests are those designed to measure a specific construct, and after development, are administered to a large group of individuals who are similar to the group for whom the test has been designed. To interpret test scores, an individual's test score is compared to others similar to the individual.

norm group: A previously tested group of individuals whose scores are used for comparison purposes.

norm-based interpretation: The process of comparing an individual's score with the scores of another group of people who took the same test.

norm-referenced tests: Tests that determine how well an individual's achievement compares with the achievement of others and that distinguish between high and low achievers; standardized tests that have been given to a large representative group of test takers from which scores have been used to create norms.

normal curve: A symmetrical distribution of scores that, when graphed, is bell shaped.

normal probability distribution: A theoretical distribution that exists in our imagination as a perfect and symmetrical distribution; also referred to as the normal curve.

norms: A group of scores that indicate the average performance of a group and the distribution of scores above and below this average.

obsessive compulsive disorder: A mental disorder characterized by repetitive, intrusive ideas or behavior.

objective criterion: A measurement that is observable and measurable, such as the number of accidents on the job.

objective test format: A test format that has one response that is designated as "correct" or that provides evidence of a specific construct, such as multiple-choice questions.

objective tests: Tests on which test takers choose a response or provide a response and there are predetermined correct answers, requiring little subjective judgment of the person scoring the test.

operational definitions: Specific behaviors that define or represent a construct.

operational validity: Also called "true validity," it is the estimated correlation between an observed predictor measure and a criterion if the criterion were measured without error.

order effects: Changes in test scores resulting from the order in which tests or questions on tests were administered.

ordinal scales: The second level of measurement, in which numbers are assigned to order or rank individuals or objects from greatest to least (or vice versa) on the attribute being measured.

outliers: Scores that are exceptionally higher or lower than other scores in a distribution.

parallel forms: Two forms of a test that are alike in every way except questions; used to overcome problems such as practice effects; also referred to as alternate forms.

Pearson product–moment correlation coefficient: Represented by r, a correlation coefficient that measures the linear association between two variables, or sets of test scores, that have been measured on interval or ratio scales.

peers: An individual's colleagues or equals, such as other employees in a workplace or other students in a class or school.

percentage: A linear transformation of raw scores obtained by dividing the number of correctly answered items by the total number of items.

percentile rank: An area transformation that indicates the percentage of people who scored at or below a particular raw score.

performance appraisal: A formal evaluation of an employee's job performance.

performance assessments: A complex item format requiring test takers to demonstrate their skills and abilities to perform a complex task in a setting as similar as possible to the conditions that will be found when the tasks are actually performed.

personal interviews: Surveys that involve direct contact with the respondents in person or by phone.

personality tests: Tests that are designed to measure human character or disposition.

personality traits: Characteristics or qualities of a person (e.g., kind, optimistic); ongoing cognitive constructs.

phi coefficient: A statistic that describes the relationship between two dichotomous variables.

pilot test: A scientific investigation of a new test's reliability and validity for its specified purpose.

placement assessments: Assessments that are used to determine whether students have the skills or knowledge necessary to understand new material and to determine how much information students already know about the new material.

polygraph: A physiological measure associated with evaluating how truthfully an individual responds to questioning; also known as a lie detector test.

population: All members of the target audience.

portfolio: A collection of an individual's work products that a person gathers over time to demonstrate his or her skills and abilities in a particular area.

practical test: A test in which a test taker must actively demonstrate skills in specific situations.

practice effects: When test takers benefit from taking a test the first time (practice) because they are able to solve problems more quickly and correctly the second time they take the same test.

predictive evidence of validity: A method for establishing evidence of validity based on a test's relationships with other variables that shows a relationship between test scores obtained at one point in time and a criterion measured at a later point in time.

pretesting: A method for identifying sources of nonsampling measurement errors and examining the effectiveness of revisions to a question(s) or to an entire survey or test.

probability sampling: A type of sampling that uses a statistical procedure to ensure that a sample is representative of its population.

projective drawings: A psychological test in which the assessor directs the test takers to draw their own pictures.

projective technique: A type of psychological test in which the response requirements are unclear so as to encourage test takers to create responses that describe the thoughts and emotions they are experiencing; three projective techniques are projective storytelling, projective drawing, and sentence completion.

projective tests: Tests that are unstructured and require test takers to respond to ambiguous stimuli.

protected class: Persons in a group, such as ethnic class or gender, who are protected from discrimination by federal law.

psychological assessments: Tools for understanding and predicting behavior that involve multiple methods, such as personal history interviews, behavioral observations, and psychological tests, for gathering information about an individual.

psychological construct: An underlying, unobservable personal attribute, trait, or characteristic of an individual that is thought to be important in describing or understanding human behavior

psychological test: A measurement tool or technique that requires a person to perform one or more behaviors in order to make inferences about human attributes, traits, or characteristics or predict future outcomes.

psychometrics: The quantitative and technical aspects of psychological measurement.

qualitative analysis: When test developers ask test takers to complete a questionnaire about how they viewed the test and how they answered the questions.

quantitative item analysis: A statistical analysis of the responses that test takers gave to individual test questions.

random error: The unexplained difference between a test taker's true score and the obtained score; error that is non-systematic and unpredictable, resulting from an unknown cause.

random responding: Responding to items in a random fashion by marking answers without reading or considering the items.

range: A measure of variability calculated by subtracting the lowest number in a distribution from the highest number in the distribution.

ratio scales: The level of measurement in which numbers are assigned to points with the assumption that each point is an equal distance from the numbers adjacent to it and there is a point that represents an absolute absence of the property being measured, called zero (0).

raw score: The basic score calculated when an individual completes a psychological test.

reliability coefficient: The correlation between the two sets of scores on tests that are, or are expected to be, parallel; the proportion of the observed score variance on a test accounted for by the true score.

reliability/precision: The consistency with which an instrument yields measurements.

reliable test: A test that consistently yields the same measurements for the same phenomena.

replication: Administration of a test to a second, different, sample of test takers representative of the target audience as part of the test validation process.

response rate: The number of individuals who responded to a survey divided by the total number of individuals who received the survey.

response sets: Patterns of responding to a test or survey that result in false or misleading information.

restriction of range: The reduction in the range of scores that results when some people are dropped from a validity study, such as when low performers are not hired, causing the validity coefficient to be lower than it would be if all persons were included in the study.

sample: A subset of a population used to represent the entire population.

sample size: The number of people in a sample.

sampling error: A statistic that reflects how much error can be attributed to the lack of representation of the target population due to the characteristics of the sample of respondents.

scientific method: A process for generating a body of knowledge that involves testing ideas and beliefs according to a specific testing procedure that can be observed objectively.

scorer reliability: The degree of agreement between or among persons scoring a test or rating an individual; also known as interrater reliability.

self-administered surveys: Surveys that individuals complete themselves without the presence of an administrator.

semistructured interview: An interview that contains predetermined questions, but the format also allows the assessor to ask some open-ended questions and follow-up questions to clarify the interviewee's responses.

sensory impairments: Disabilities that hinder the function of the five senses, such as deafness and blindness.

sentence completion: Psychological test item format in which the assessor administers partial sentences, verbally or on paper, and asks the test taker to respond by completing each sentence.

severity errors: Systematic rating errors that occur when raters give all employees worse ratings than they deserve.

simple random sampling: A type of sampling in which every member of a population has an equal chance of being chosen as a member of the sample.

simulation: A complex item format requiring test takers to demonstrate their skills and abilities to perform a complex task in a setting as similar as possible to the conditions that will be found when the tasks are actually performed.

single-group validity: When a test is valid for one group but not for another group, such as valid for Whites but not for Blacks.

situational judgment test: A type of low-fidelity simulation that presents test takers with short scenarios that pose dilemmas along with a number of possible courses of action that could be taken in response. The task is to choose the most (or sometimes least) effective course of action from the choices provided.

slope: The expected change in Y for every one unit change in X on the regression line.

slope bias: A type of measurement bias in which the slope of the regression line used to predict a criterion is not the same for all demographic groups used in the regression (e.g., men and women).

social desirability: The tendency of some test takers to provide or choose answers that are socially acceptable or that present them in a favorable light.

Spearman–Brown formula: The formula used to estimate what the reliability of the full length test would be after the test was split into two parts to use the split half method of estimating reliability.

split-half method: A method for estimating the internal consistency or reliability of a test by giving the test once to one group of people, making a comparison of scores, dividing the test into halves, and correlating the set of scores on the first half with the set of scores on the second half.

standard deviation: A measure of variability that represents the degree to which scores vary from the mean.

standard deviation unit: A number that represents how many standard deviations an individual score is located away from the mean.

standard error of measurement (SEM): An index of the amount of inconsistency or error expected in an individual's test score.

standard scores: A widely understood transformation of raw test scores in testing, such as z scores and T scores, that allow the test user to more easily evaluate a person's performance in comparison with other persons who took the same test or a similar test.

standardization sample: People who are tested to obtain data to establish a frame of reference for interpreting individual test scores.

standardized tests: Tests that have been administered to a large group of individuals who are similar to the group for whom the test has been designed so as to develop norms; also implies a standardized procedure for administration.

stanines: Standard score scales with nine points that allow us to describe a distribution in words instead of numbers (from 1 = *very poor* to 9 = *very superior*).

state: A temporary condition, often associated with anxiety, perhaps brought on by situational circumstances.

stem: A statement, question, or partial sentence that is the stimulus in a multiple-choice question.

stratified random sampling: A type of sampling in which a population is divided into subgroups or strata.

structured clinical interview: An interview that has a predetermined set of questions in which the assessor assigns numbers or scores to the answers based on their content.

structured interview: A predetermined set of questions that the assessor asks the respondent; the assessor then scores the answers based on their content to arrive at a diagnosis or a hiring decision.

structured observations: Observations that are guided by forms or instructions that instruct an observer in collecting behavioral information, such as using a form to document the play behaviors of children on a playground.

structured record reviews: Forms that guide data collection from existing records, such as using a form to collect information from personnel files.

subgroup norms: Statistics that describe subgroups of the target audience, such as race, sex, and age.

subjective criterion: A measurement that is based on judgment, such as supervisor or peer ratings.

subjective test format: A test format that does not have a response that is designated as "correct"; interpretation of the response as correct or providing evidence of a specific construct is left to the judgment of the person who administers, scores, or interprets the test taker's response.

subtle questions: Questions that have no apparent relation to the test purpose or criterion.

summative assessment: Assessment that involves determining what students do and do not know; these are typically used to assign earned grades.

survey objectives: The purpose of a survey, including a definition of what it will measure.

survey research firms: Companies that specialize in the construction and administration of surveys and analysis of survey data for purposes such as marketing, political opinion assessment, and employee organizational satisfaction.

survey researchers: People who design and conduct surveys and analyze the results.

surveys: Instruments used for gathering information from a sample of the individuals of interest.

synthetic validity: A method used to generalize evidence of validity by combining validity coefficients on a group of tests that have each been shown to be valid predictors of a component of a job. By combining multiple tests, all the important job components can be represented, and an estimate of the overall validity of the group can be computed without having to conduct local validity studies on each test. Also referred to as job component validity.

systematic error: When a single source of error can be identified as constant across all measurements.

systematic sampling: A type of sampling in which every *n*th (for example, every fifth) person in a population is chosen as a member of the sample.

T **scores:** Standard scores, which have a mean of 50 and a standard deviation of 10, that are used to compare test scores from two tests that have different characteristics.

telephone surveys: Surveys in which an interviewer calls respondents and asks questions over the phone.

test format: The type of questions on a test.

test items: Stimuli or test questions.

test of significance: The process of determining what the probability is that a study would have yielded the observed results simply by chance.

test plan: A plan for developing a new test that specifies the characteristics of the test, including a definition of the construct and the content to be measured (the testing universe), the format for the questions, and how the test will be administered and scored.

test security: Steps taken to ensure that the content of a psychological test does not become public knowledge.

test specifications: The plan prepared before test development that documents the written test or practical exam.

test taker: The person who responds to test questions or whose behavior is measured.

test user: A person who participates in purchasing, administering, interpreting, or using the results of a psychological test.

testing environment: The circumstances under which a test is administered.

testing universe: The body of knowledge or behaviors that a test represents.

test–retest method: A method for estimating test reliability in which a test developer gives the same test to the same group of test takers on two different occasions and correlates the scores from the first and second administrations.

tests of maximal performance: Tests that require test takers to perform a particular task on which their performance is measured.

360° feedback: A method of performance appraisal in which employees receive ratings from their supervisors, peers, subordinates, and customers as well as from themselves.

traditional interview: A pre-employment interview in which the interviewer pursues different areas of inquiry with each job.

trait: A long-standing individual quality that has become an enduring part of a person's personality.

transportability: One strategy used for test validity generalization in which a case is made that a test that has been shown to be valid for one job is also valid for a different job based on evidence that the jobs are substantially similar in their requirements.

true/false: A test item that asks, "Is this statement true or false?"

true score: The score that would be obtained if an individual took a test an infinite number of times and then the average score across all the testings were computed.

univariate analyses: The computation of statistics that summarize individual question responses.

universal design: Development of a test in such a way that accessibility is maximized for all individuals for whom the test was designed.

user qualifications: The background, training, and/or certifications the test purchaser must meet.

validity: Evidence that the interpretations that are being made from the scores on a test are appropriate for their intended purpose.

validity coefficient: The correlation coefficient obtained when test scores are correlated with a performance criterion representing the amount or strength of the evidence of validity for the test.

variance: A measure of variability that indicates whether individual scores in a distribution tend to be similar to or substantially different from the mean of the distribution.

vocational tests: Tests that help predict how successful a person would be at an occupation before training or entering the occupation.

within-group norming: The practice of administering the same test to every test taker but scoring the test differently according to the race of the test taker.

work sample: A small-scale assessment in which test takers complete a job-related task such as building a sawhorse or designing a doghouse.

written test: A paper-and-pencil test in which a test taker must answer a series of questions.

z score: Standard scores, which have a mean of zero (0) and a standard deviation of 1, that are used to compare test scores from two tests that have different characteristics.

REFERENCES

Abbott, A. (2014, March 9). Biomarkers could predict Alzheimer's before it starts. *Nature*. Retrieved from http://www.nature.com/news/biomarkers-could-predict-alzheimer-s-before-it-starts-1.14834

Achenbach, T. M. (1991). *Manual for the Child Behavior Checklist/4-18 and 1991 Profile*. Burlington: University of Vermont, Department of Psychiatry.

Acheson, S. K. (2017). Test review of the Minnesota Multiphasic Personality Invventory-2-Restructured form. In J. F. Carlson, K. F. Geisinger, & J. L. Jonson, J. L. (Eds.), *The twentieth mental measurements yearbook*. Lincoln, NE: Buros Center for Testing.

ACT. (2015). *What is the difference between the SAT and the ACT?* Retrieved from http://www.actstudent.org/faq/actsat.html

Aguinis, H., Culpepper, S. A., & Pierce C. A. (2010). Revival of test bias research in preemployment testing. *Journal of Applied Psychology*, *95*, 648–680.

Aguinis, H., & Smith, M. A. (2007). Understanding the impact of test validity and bias on selection errors and adverse impact in human resource selection. *Personnel Psychology*, *60*, 165–199.

Albanese, M. A. (2001). Review of the Mini-Mental State Examination. In B. S. Plake, J. C. Impara, & R. A. Spies (Eds.), *The fifteenth mental measurements yearbook*. Lincoln, NE: Buros Institute of Mental Measurements.

Albers, C. A., & Grieve, A. J. (2007). Test review: Bayley N. (2006). Bayley Scales of Infant and Toddler Development—Third Edition. *Journal of Psycho-educational Assessment*, *25*, 180–198.

Aleccia, J. (2018, April 15). Trump's Perfect Score On Brain Test Spawns DIY Cognitive Exam. *Kaiser Health News*. Retrieved July 17, 2018, from https://khn.org/news/trumps-perfect-score-on-brain-test-spawns-diy-cognitive-exam/

Allan, J. M., Bulla, N., & Goodman, S. A. (2003). *Test access: Guidelines for computer-administered testing*. Louisville, KY: American Printing House for the Blind. Retrieved from http://www.aph.org/tests/access/index.html

Alzheimer's Association. (2018). 2017 Alzheimer's disease facts and figures. Retrieved from https://www.alz.org/facts/

American Educational Research Association, American Psychological Association, & National Council on Measurement in Education. (1999). *Standards for educational and psychological testing*. Washington, DC: American Psychological Association.

American Educational Research Association, American Psychological Association, & National Council on Measurement in Education. (2014). *Standards for educational and psychological testing*. Washington, DC: American Educational Research Association.

American Psychiatric Association. (2013). *Diagnostic and statistical manual of mental disorders* (5th ed.). Washington, DC: Author.

American Psychological Association. (1953). *Ethical standards of psychologists*. Washington, DC: Author.

American Psychological Association. (1954). Technical recommendations for psychological tests and diagnostic techniques. Washington, DC: Author.

American Psychological Association. (2000). *Report of the Task Force on Test User Qualifications*. Washington, DC: Author.

American Psychological Association. (2010). *Ethical principles of psychologists and code of conduct: Including 2010 amendments*. Washington, DC: Author. Retrieved from http://www.apa.org/ethics/code/index.aspx

American Psychological Association. (2017). *Appropriate use of high-stakes testing in our nation's schools*. Retrieved from http://www.apa.org/pubs/info/brochures/testing.aspx

American Psychological Association. (2018a). *Ethics*. Retrieved from http://apa.org/topics/ethics/index.aspx

American Psychological Association. (2018b). *Glossary of psychological terms*. Retrieved from http://www.apa.org/research/action/glossary.aspx?tab=5

American Psychological Association. (2018c). *Policy statement on evidence-based practice in psychology*. Retrieved from http://www.apa.org/practice/guidelines/evidence-based-statement.aspx

American Psychological Association. (2018d). *Rights and responsibilities of test takers: Guidelines and expectations*.

Retrieved from http://www.apa.org/science/programs/testing/rights.aspx

American Psychological Association. (2018e). Testing and Assessment. Retrieved from http://www.apa.org/science/programs/testing/index.aspx

American Psychological Association Science Directorate. (1991). *Questionnaires used in the prediction of trustworthiness in pre-employment selection decisions.* Washington, DC: American Psychological Association.

Ames, L. B. (1989). *Arnold Gesell: Themes of his work.* New York: Human Sciences Press.

Anastasi, A., & Urbina, S. (1997). *Psychological testing* (7th ed.). Upper Saddle River, NJ: Prentice Hall.

Anderson, C. D., Warner, J. L., & Spencer, C. C. (1984). Inflation bias in self-assessment examinations: Implications for valid employee selection. *Journal of Applied Psychology, 69,* 574–580.

Anton, W. D., & Reed, J. R. (1991). *CAS: College Adjustment Scales professional manual.* Odessa, FL: Psychological Assessment Resources.

Anxiety and Depression Association of America. (2016). Facts and statistics. Retrieved from https://adaa.org/about-adaa/press-room/facts-statistics

Archer, R. P. (1992). Review of the Minnesota Multi-phasic Personality Inventory–2. In J. J. Kramer & J. C. Conoley (Eds.), *The eleventh mental measurements yearbook.* Lincoln, NE: Buros Institute of Mental Measurements.

Associated Press. (2009, June 29). *Supreme Court rules for White firefighters.* Retrieved from http://www.msnbc.msn.com/id/31609275/ns/politics-sup reme_court/t/supreme-court-rules-white-firefig hters/#.TwMia5h8xCg

Association of American Publishers. (2002). *Industry statistics.* Retrieved from http://archive.today/RaG63

Association of Test Publishers. (2017). General FAQs: About tests. Retrieved from http://www.testpublishers.org/general

Axelrod, B. N., Goldman, B. S., & Woodard, J. L. (1992). Interrater reliability in scoring the Wisconsin Card Sorting Test. *Clinical Neuropsychologist, 6,* 143–155.

Bandura, A. (1977). Self-efficacy: Toward a unifying theory of behavioral change. *Psychological Review, 84,* 191–215.

Bandura, A., Barbaranelli, C., Caprara, G. V., & Pastorelli, C. (1996). Multifaceted impact of self-efficacy beliefs on academic functioning. *Child Development, 67,* 1206–1222.

Baños, J. H., & Franklin, L. M. (2000). Factor structure of the Mini-Mental State Examination in adult psychiatric patients. *Psychological Assessment, 14,* 397–400.

Barrett, G. V., Phillips, J. S., & Alexander, R. A. (1981). Concurrent and predictive validity designs: A critical reanalysis. *Journal of Applied Psychology, 66,* 1–6.

Barrett, G. V., Polomsky, M. D., & McDaniel, M. A. (1999). Selection tests for firefighters: A comprehensive review and meta-analysis. *Journal of Business and Psychology, 13,* 507–513.

Barrick, M. R., & Mount, M. K. (1991). The Big Five personality dimensions and job performance: A meta-analysis. *Personnel Psychology, 44,* 1–26.

Barry, C. T., Golmaryami, F. N., Rivera-Hudson, N., & Frick, P. J. (2013). Evidence-based assessment of conduct disorder: Current considerations and preparation for *DSM*-5. *Professional Psychology: Research and Practice, 44*(1), 56–63.

Bartlett, C. J., Bobko, P., Mosier, S. B., & Hannan, R. (1978). Testing for fairness with a moderated multiple regression strategy: An alternative to differential analysis. *Personnel Psychology, 31,* 233–241.

Bayley, N. (1993). *Bayley Scales of Infant Development* (2nd ed.). San Antonio, TX: Psychological Corporation.

Bayley, N. (2006). *Bayley Scales of Infant and Toddler Development* (3rd ed.). San Antonio, TX: Pearson.

BBC News Services. (2017). Terrorists' moral judgment probed in psychology test. Retrieved from http://www.bbc.com/news/science-environment-40047033

Beck, A. T., Steer, R. A., & Garbin, M. G. (1988). Psychometric properties of the Beck Depression Inventory: Twenty-five years of evaluation. *Clinical Psychology Review, 8,* 77–100.

Benson, N., & Kluck, A. S. (1995). Review of the NEO Personality Inventory–3. In J. C. Conoley & J. C. Impara (Eds.), *The twelfth mental measurements yearbook.* Lincoln, NE: Buros Institute of Mental Measurements.

Berg, E. A. (1948). A simple objective technique for measuring flexibility in thinking. *J. Gen. Psychol. 39,* 15–22.

Berkshire, J. R., & Highland, R. W. (1953). Forced-choice performance rating: A methodological study. *Personnel Psychology, 6,* 355–378.

Berliner, D. C., & Biddle, B. J. (1995). *The manufactured crisis: Myths, fraud, and the attack on America's public schools.* Reading, MA: Addison-Wesley.

Berry, C. M., Clark, M. A., & McClure, T. K. (2011). Racial/ethnic differences in the criterion related validity of cognitive ability tests: A qualitative and quantitative review. *Journal of Applied Psychology, 96,* 881–906.

Berry, C. M., Cullen, M. J., & Meyer, J. M. (2014). Racial/ethnic subgroup differences in cognitive ability testing: Implications for differential validity. *Journal of Applied Psychology, 99,* 21–37.

Berry, C. M., Sackett, P. R., & Sund, A. (2013). The role of range restriction and criteria contamination in assessing differential validity by race/ethnicity. *Journal of Business Psychology, 28,* 345–359.

Betz, N. E., & Hackett, G. (1986). Applications of self-efficacy theory to understanding career choice behavior. *Journal of Social and Clinical Psychology, 4,* 279–289.

Binet, A., & Simon, T. (1905). Methodes nouvelles pour le diagnostic du niveau intellectuel des anormaux [New methods for the diagnosis of the intellectual level of subnormals]. *L'Année Psychologique, 12,* 191–244.

Bond, L. (1987). The Golden Rule settlement: A minority perspective. *Educational Measurement: Issues & Practice, 6,* 18–20.

Booth, A., Johnson, D., & Edwards, J. N. (1983). Measuring marital instability. *Journal of Marriage and the Family, 44,* 387–393.

Borman, W. C., Buck, D. E., Hanson, M. A., Motowidlo, S. J., Stark, S., & Drasgow, F. (2001). An examination of the comparative reliability, validity, and accuracy of performance ratings made using computerized adaptive rating scales. *Journal of Applied Psychology, 86,* 965–973.

Botwin, M. D. (1995). Review of the Minnesota Multiphasic Personality Inventory–A. In J. J. Kramer & J. C. Conoley (Eds.), *The twelfth mental measurements yearbook.* Lincoln, NE: Buros Institute of Mental Measurements.

Brennan, R. L., & Lee, W.C. (1999). Conditional scale-score standard errors of measurement under binomial and compound binomial assumptions. *Educational and Psychological Measurement, 59,* 5–24.

Brown, A., & Maydeu-Olivares, A. (2013). How IRT can solve problems of ipsative data in forced-choice questionnaires. *Psychological Methods, 18,* 36–52.

Brown, M. B. (2004). Review of the Self-Directed Search (4th ed.). In J. J. Kramer & J. C. Conoley (Eds.), *The eleventh mental measurements yearbook.* Lincoln, NE: Buros Institute of Mental Measurements.

Burns, R. C., & Kaufamn, H. S. (1970). *Kinetic family drawings (KFD): An introduction to understanding children through kinetic drawings.* New York: Brunner/Mazel.

Butcher, J. N., Graham, J. R., Williams, C. L., & Ben-Porath, Y. S. (1990). *Development and use of the MMPI-2 content scales.* Minneapolis: University of Minnesota Press.

Camara, W. J., Nathan, J. S., & Puente, A. E. (2000). Psychological test usage: Implications in professional psychology. *Professional Psychology: Research and Practice, 31*(2), 141–154.

Camara, W. J., & Schneider, D. L. (1994). Integrity tests: Facts and unresolved issues. *American Psychologist, 49,* 112–119.

Camara, W. J., & Schneider, D. L. (1995). Questions of construct breadth and openness of research in integrity testing. *American Psychologist, 50,* 459–460.

Campbell, D. T., & Fiske, D. W. (1959). Convergent and discriminant validation by the multitrait–multimethod matrix. *Psychological Bulletin, 56,* 81–105.

Campbell, J. P., Dunnette, M. D., Arvey, R. D., & Hellervik, L. V. (1973). The development and evaluation of behaviorally based rating scales. *Journal of Applied Psychology, 57,* 15–22.

Campion, M. A., Fink, A. A., Ruggeberg, B. J., Carr, L., Phillips, G. M., & Oldman, R. B. (2011). Doing competencies well: Best practices in competency modeling. *Personnel Psychology, 64,* 225–262.

Cannell, C. F., Miller, L., & Oksenberg, L. (1981). *Research on interviewing techniques.* Ann Arbor: University of Michigan, Institute for Social Research.

Carlson, J. F., Geisinger, K. F., & Jonson, J. L. (2014). *The nineteenth mental measurements yearbook.* Lincoln, NE: Buros Center for Testing.

Carlson, J. F., Geisinger, K. F., & Jonson, J. L. (2017). *Twentieth mental measurements yearbook.* Lincoln: University of Nebraska Press.

Carpenter, D. M., Knepper, L., Erickson, A. C., & Ross, J. K. (2012). *License to work: A national study of burdens from occupational licensing.* Arlington, VA: Institute for Justice.

Carter, N. T., Dalal, D. K., Boyce, A. S., O'Connell, M. S., Kung, M., & Delgado, K. M. (2014). Uncovering curvilinear relationships between conscientiousness and job performance: How theoretically appropriate measurement makes an empirical difference. *Journal of Applied Psychology, 99,* 564–586.

Carter, R. D., & Thomas, E. J. (1973). Modification of problematic marital communication using corrective feedback and instruction. *Behavior Therapy, 4,* 100–109.

Cascio, W. F. (1991). *Applied psychology in personnel management* (4th ed.). Englewood Cliffs, NJ: Prentice Hall.

Cascio, W. F., Alexander, R. A., & Barrett, G. V. (1988). Setting cutoff scores: Legal, psychometric, and professional issues and guidelines. *Personnel Psychology, 41*, 1–24.

Cattell, R. B. (1943). The description of personality. I. Foundations of trait measurement. *Psychological Review, 50*(6), 559–594.

Cattell, R. B., & Scheier, I. H. (1961). *The meaning and measurement of neuroticism and anxiety.* New York: Ronald Press.

Cattin, P. (1980). Estimation of the predictive power of a regression model. *Journal of Applied Psychology, 65*, 407–414.

Center for Applications of Psychological Type. (2012). *The forms of the MBTI instrument.* Retrieved from http://www.capt.org/mbti-assessment/mbti-forms.htm

Center on Alcoholism, Substance Abuse and Addictions. (1995). *Readiness Ruler.* Albuquerque, NM: Author.

Centers for Disease Control and Prevention. (2012). *About the National Health Interview Survey.* Retrieved from http://www.cdc.gov/nchs/nhis/about_nhis.htm

Centers for Disease Control and Prevention. (2018). *Autism spectrum disorders (ASD): Data and statistics.* Retrieved from https://www.cdc.gov/ncbddd/autism/data.html

Charter, R. A. (2003). A breakdown of reliability coefficients by test type and reliability method, and the clinical implications of low reliability. *Journal of General Psychology, 130*, 290–300.

Chibnall, J. T., & Detrick, P. (2003). The NEO PI-R, Inwald Personality Inventory, and MMPI-2 in the prediction of police academy performance: A case for incremental validity. *American Journal of Criminal Justice, 27*, 233–248.

Chingos, M. M. (2012). *Strength in numbers: State spending on K–12 assessment systems.* Washington, DC: Brookings Institute.

Christiansen, N., Burns, G., & Montgomery, G. (2005). Reconsidering the use of forced-choice formats for applicant personality assessments. *Human Performance, 18*, 267–307.

Chun, K. T., Cobb, S., & French, J.R.P. (1975). *Measures for psychological assessment: A guide to 3,000 original sources and their applications.* Ann Arbor, MI: Institute for Social Research.

Ciechalski, J. C. (2001). Review of the Mathematics Self-Efficacy Scale. In B. S. Plake & J. C. Impara (Eds.), *The fourteenth mental measurements yearbook.* Lincoln, NE: Buros Institute of Mental Measurements.

Civil Rights Act of 1991 § 106, 42 U.S.C. § 2000e et seq. (1991).

Civil Service Act of 1883. Retrieved from http://archive.opm.gov/BiographyofAnIdeal/PU_CSact.htm

Claiborn, C. D., & Lanyon, R. (1995). Review of the Minnesota Multiphasic Personality Inventory–A. In J. J. Kramer & J. C. Conoley (Eds.), *The twelfth mental measurements yearbook.* Lincoln, NE: Buros Institute of Mental Measurements.

Clark, E. (2001). Review of the Wisconsin Card Sorting Test, Revised and Expanded. In B. S. Plake & J. C. Impara (Eds.), *The fourteenth mental measurement yearbook.* Lincoln, NE: Buros Institute of Mental Measurements.

Cleary, T.A. (1968). Test bias: Prediction of grades of Negro and white students in integrated colleges. *Journal of Educational Measurement, 5*, 115–124.

Cleary, T., Humphreys, L., Kendrick, S., & Wesman, A. (1975). Educational use of tests with disadvantaged students. *American Psychologist, 30*, 15–41.

Cofresi, N. I., & Gorman, A. A. (2004). Testing and assessment issues with Spanish–English bilingual Latinos. *Journal of Counseling and Development, 82*, 99–106.

Cohen, J. (1960). A coefficient of agreement for nominal scales. *Educational and Psychological Measurement, 20*, 37–46.

Cohen, N. (2009, July 29). Has Wikipedia created a Rorschach cheat sheet? *The New York Times*, p. A1.

Cohen, R. J., Swerdlik, M. E., & Phillips, S. M. (1996). *Psychological testing and assessment: An introduction to tests and measurements* (3rd ed.). Mountain View, CA: Mayfield.

Cohen, S. L. (1978). Letter from the editor. *Journal of Assessment Center Technology, 1*(1), 1.

College Board. (2013). *2013 college-bound seniors: Total group profile report.* Retrieved from http://media.collegeboard.com/digitalServices/pdf/research/2013/TotalGroup-2013.pdf

College Board. (2015). *Overview: Current SAT vs. redesigned SAT.* Retrieved from https://www.college board.org/delivering-opportunity/sat/redesign/compare-tests

College Board. (2018). *Class of 2017 SAT results.* Retrieved from https://reports.collegeboard.org/sat-suite-program-results/class-2017-results

College Entrance Examination Board. (2018). *Average SAT Scores of College Bound Seniors* (1952 - Present). Retrieved from https://www.erikthered.com/tutor/historical-average-SAT-scores.pdf

Colligan, R. C., Osborne, D., Swenson, W. M., & Offord, K. P. (1983). *The MMPI: A contemporary normative study.* New York: Praeger.

Common Core State Standards Initiative. (2014). *About the standards*. Retrieved from http://www.cores tandards.org/about-the-standards/

Consulting Psychologists Press. (2009). *Myers–Briggs Type Indicator interpretive report: Report prepared for Jane Sample*. Retrieved from http://www.cpp.com/images/reports/smp 261144.pdf

Cook, T. D., & Campbell, D. T. (1979). *Quasi-experimentation: Design and analysis issues for field settings*. Chicago: Rand McNally.

Coombs, W. T., & Holladay, S. J. (2004). Understanding the aggressive workplace: Development of the Workplace Aggression Tolerance Questionnaire. *Communication Studies, 55*, 481–497.

Costa, P. T., Jr., & McCrae, R. R. (1992). *NEO Personality Inventory–Revised (NEO PI-R)*. Odessa, FL: Psychological Assessment Resources.

Costa, P.T., & McCrae, R. R. (2008). The revised NEO personality inventory (NEO-PI-R). *The SAGE Handbook of Personality Theory and Assessment, 2*. 179–198. doi:10.4135/9781849200479.n9

Coutsoukis, P., & Information Technology Associates. (1995–2011). *Dictionary of occupational titles*. Retrieved from http://www.occupationalinfo.org

Cox, A., Thorpe, G., & Dawson, R. (2010). Review of the Personality Assessment Inventory. In R. A. Spies, J. F. Carlson, & K. F. Geisinger (Eds.), *The eighteenth mental measurements yearbook*. Lincoln, NE: Buros Institute of Mental Measurements.

CPP. (n.d.). *California Psychological Inventory: Talent*. Retrieved from https://www.cpp.com/products/catalog/CPI434_2008.pdf

CPP. (2009). *The CPI Assessments*. Retrieved from https://www.cpp.com/products/cpi/index.aspx

Crandall, V. C., Crandall, V. J., & Katkovsky, W. (1965). A children's social desirability questionnaire. *Journal of Consulting Psychology, 29*, 27–36.

Crawford v. Honig, 37 F. 3d 485 (9th Cir. 1994).

Creative Research Systems. (2012). *Sample size calculator*. Retrieved from https://www.surveysystem.com/sscalc.htm

Crisp, A. (2011, April 18). Student performance key in new teacher evaluations. *Chattanooga Times Free Press*, p. 29.

Crocker, L & Algina, J. (1986). *Introduction to classical and modern test theory*. New York, NY: Holt, Rinehart and Winston.

Crocker, L., Llabre, M., & Miller, M. D. (1988). The generalizability of content validity ratings. *Journal of Educational Measurement, 25*, 287–299.

Cronbach, L. J. (1951). Coefficient alpha and the internal structure of tests. *Psychometrika, 16*, 197–334.

Cronbach, L. J. (1988). Five perspectives on the validity argument. In H. Wainer & H. Brown (Eds.), *Test validity* (pp. 3–17). Hillsdale, NJ: Lawrence Erlbaum.

Cronbach, L. J. (1989). Construct validation after thirty years. In R. Linn (Ed.), *Intelligence: Measurement, theory, and public policy* (pp. 147–171). Urbana: University of Illinois Press.

Cronbach, L. J., Gleser, G. C., Nanda, H., & Rajaratnam, N. (1972). *The dependability of behavioral measurements: Theory of generalizability scores and profiles*. New York: John Wiley.

Cronbach, L. J., & Meehl, P. E. (1955). Construct validity in psychological tests. *Psychological Bulletin, 52*, 281–302.

Crowne, D. P., & Marlowe, D. (1960). A new scale of social desirability independent of psychopathology. *Journal of Consulting Psychology, 24*, 349–354.

Crowne, D. P., & Marlowe, D. (1964). *The approval motive: Studies in evaluative dependence*. New York: John Wiley.

Crum, R. M., Anthony, J. J., Bassett, S. S., & Folstein, M. F. (1993). Population-based norms for the Mini-Mental State Examination by age and educational level. *JAMA, 18*, 2386–2391.

Darwin, C. (1936). *On the origin of species by means of natural selection*. New York: Modern Library. (Original work published 1859)

de Graaf, J., & Musikanski, L. (2011). The pursuit of happiness. *Earth Island Journal, 26*(3), 56–59.

Derogatis, L. R. (1977). *The SCL-90-R Manual I: Scoring, administration and procedures for the SCL-90-R*. Baltimore, MD: Clinical Psychometric Research.

Digman, J. M. 1990. Personality structure: Emergence of the five-factor model. *Annual Review of Psychology 41.1*: 417–440.

Dillman, D. A. (1978). *Mail and telephone surveys: The total design method*. New York: John Wiley.

Di Milia, L. (2004). Australian management selection practices: Closing the gap between research findings. *Asia Pacific Journal of Human Resources, 42*, 214–228.

Distefano, M. K., Pryer, M. W., & Erffmeyer, R. C. (1983). Application of content validity methods to the development of a job-related performance rating criterion. *Personnel Psychology, 36,* 621–631.

Doak, C. C., Doak, L. G., & Root, J. H. (1996). *Teaching patients with low literacy skills.* Philadelphia, PA: J. B. Lippincott.

Doll, B. (1994). [Review of the Child Behavior Checklist]. In B. S. Plake & J. C. Impara (Eds.), *The thirteenth mental measurements yearbook.* Lincoln, NE: Buros Institute of Mental Measurements.

Donlon, T. (2001). Wonderlic Personnel Test. In B. S. Plake & J. C. Impara (Eds.), *The fourteenth mental measurements yearbook.* Lincoln, NE: Buros Institute of Mental Measurements.

Dowd, T. E. (1998). Review of the House–Tree–Person and Draw-A-Person as measures of abuse in children: A quantitative scoring system. In J. C. Impara & B. S. Plake (Eds.), *Thirteenth mental measurements yearbook.* Lincoln, NE: Buros Institute of Mental Measurements.

DuBois, P. H. (1970). *The history of psychological testing.* Boston: Allyn & Bacon.

Dunst, C. J. (1998). Review of the Bayley Scales of Infant Development: Second edition. In J. C. Impara & B. S. Plake (Eds.), *Thirteenth mental measurements yearbook.* Lincoln, NE: Buros Institute of Mental Measurement.

Dvorak, B. J. (1956). The General Aptitude Test Battery. *Personnel and Guidance Journal, 35*(3), 145–152.

Dwight, S. A., & Donovan, J. J. (2003). Do warnings not to fake actually reduce faking? *Human Performance, 16,* 1–23.

Eberhard, W. (1977). *A history of China.* Berkeley: University of California Press.

Educational Testing Service. (2012a). *Frequently asked questions about the* GRE® *General Test.* Retrieved from http://ets .org/gre/general/about/faq/

Educational Testing Service. (2012b). GRE® *guide to the use of scores.* Retrieved from http://www.ets.org/s/gre/pdf/gre_guide.pdf

Educational Testing Service. (2018). Test content and structure. Retrieved from https://www.ets.org/gre/revised _general/about/content/

Edwards, A. L. (1957). *The social desirability variable in personality assessment research.* New York: Dryden.

Edwards, J. E., & Thomas, M. D. (1993). The organizational survey process: General steps and practical considerations. In P. Rosenfeld, J. E. Edwards, & M. D. Thomas (Eds.), *Improving organizational surveys* (pp. 3–28). Newbury Park, CA: Sage.

Eells, K., Davis, A., Havighurst, R. J., Herrick, V. E., & Tyler, R. (1951). *Intelligence and cultural differences: A study of cultural learning and problem-solving.* Chicago: University of Chicago Press.

Elert, G. (1992). *The SAT: Aptitude or demographics?* Retrieved from http://hypertextbook.com/eworld/sat.shtml

Elmore, C. (1988, April). An IQ test almost ruined my son's life. *Redbook,* pp. 50–52.

Embretson, S. E. (1996). The new rules of measurement. *Psychological Assessment, 8,* 341–349.

Exner, J. E. (2003). *Rorschach: A comprehensive system, Vol. 1: Basic foundations* (4th ed.). New York: John Wiley.

Eyde, L. D., Moreland, K. L., Robertson, G. J., Primoff, E. S., & Most, R. B. (1988). *Test user qualifications: A data-based approach to promoting good test use.* Washington, DC: American Psychological Association.

Faggen, J. (1987). Golden Rule revisited: Introduction. *Educational Measurement: Issues and Practice, 6,* 5–8.

Fan, J., Gao, D, Carroll, S., Lopez, F. J., Tian, T. S., & Meng, H. (2012). Testing the efficacy of a new procedure for reducing faking on personality test within selection contexts. *Journal of Applied Psychology, 97,* 866–880.

Fay, C. H., & Latham, G. P. (1982). Effects of training and rating scales on rating errors. *Personnel Psychology, 35,* 105–116.

FBI Director Freeh orders stepped-up polygraph tests. (2001, March 1). *The Wall Street Journal,* p. A12.

Fed: Many Australians enjoying GFC, says happiness survey. (2009, September 24). Sydney, Australia: AAP General News Wire.

Fink, A. (2002). *The survey kit* (2nd ed.). Thousand Oaks, CA: Sage.

Fink, A. (2003). *The survey handbook* (2nd ed.). Thousand Oaks, CA: Sage.

Finn, S. E. (2007). *In our client's shoes: Theory and techniques of therapeutic assessment.* Mahwah, NJ: Lawrence Erlbaum.

First, M. B., Gibbon, M., Spitzer, R. L., Williams, J. B. W., & Benjamin, L. S. (1997). *Structured Clinical Interview for DSM-IV Axis II Personality Disorders (SCID-II).* Washington, DC: American Psychiatric Press.

First, M. B., Spitzer, R. L., Gibbon, M., & Williams, J. B. (1996). *Structured Clinical Interview for DSM-IV Axis I Disorders, Clinician Version (SCID-CV).* Washington, DC: American Psychiatric Press.

Fisher, M. (2014, April 12). *Inside NFL's Wonderlic Test—and why it matters.* Retrieved from http://www.foxsports.com/southwest/story/inside-nfl-s-wonderlic-test-and-why-it-matters-041214

Fisher, R. A., & Yates, F. (1963). *Statistical tables for biological, agricultural, and medical research* (6th ed.). Edinburgh, UK: Oliver & Boyd.

Fitzgerald, S. (2003, March). Stolen profits: Customer and employee theft contribute to shrink, resulting in huge losses to retailers already operating on tight margins—Clearly, the problem isn't going to go away, so what's a retailer to do? *Canadian Grocer*, p. G7.

Flynn, J. (2013). James Flynn: Why our IQ levels are higher than our grandparents' [Video]. Retrieved from http://www.youtube.com/watch?v=9vpqilhW9ul

Folstein, M. F., Folstein, S. E., & McHugh, P. R. (1975). Mini-Mental State: A practical method for grading the cognitive state of patients for the clinician. *Journal of Psychiatric Research, 12*, 189–198.

Ford, J. K., & Wroten, S. P. (1984). Introducing new methods for conducting training evaluation and for linking training evaluation to program design. *Personnel Psychology, 37*, 651–665.

Forsyth, J. (2010, December 18). How the pursuit of happiness could lead Britain to the right. *The Spectator*. Retrieved from http://images.spectator.co.uk/columnists/politics/6543408/how-the-pursuit-of-happiness-could-lead-britain-to-the-right/

Fowler, F. J., Jr. (1988). *Survey research methods*. Newbury Park, CA: Sage.

Franke, W. (1960). *The reform and abolition of the traditional Chinese examination system.* Cambridge, MA: Harvard Center for East Asian Studies.

Frankenburg, W. K., Dodds, J., Fandal, A., Kazuk, E., & Cohrs, M. (1975). *Denver Developmental Screening Test, reference manual, revised 1975 edition.* Denver, CO: LA–DOCA Project and Publishing Foundation.

Frazier, K. (2003, November/December). Polygraph testing to be scaled back at national labs. *The Skeptical Inquirer*, pp. 6, 8.

Freeman, S. J. (2003). Review of the State–Trait Anger Expression Inventory–2. In B. S. Plake, J. C. Impara, & R. A. Spies (Eds.), *The fifteenth mental measurements yearbook.* Lincoln, NE: Buros Institute for Mental Measurements.

Fritzsche, B. A., & McIntire, S. A. (1997, January). *Constructing a psychological test as an undergraduate class project: Yes, it can be done!* Poster presented at the annual meeting of the National Institute on the Teaching of Psychology, St. Petersburg, FL.

Furlong, M. J. (1994). [Review of the Child Behavior Checklist]. In B. S. Plake & J. C. Impara (Eds.), *The fourteenth mental measurements yearbook.* Lincoln, NE: Buros Institute of Mental Measurements.

Gael, S., Grant, D., & Richie, R. (1975). Employment test validation for minority and nonminority clerks and work sample criteria. *Journal of Applied Psychology, 60*, 420–426.

Galton, F. (1884). Measurement of character. *Fortnightly Review, 36*, 179–185.

Galton, F. (2000). *Hereditary genius* (1st elec. ed.). Retrieved from http://galton.org/books/hereditary-genius/text/pdf/galton-1869-genius-v3.pdf. (Original work published 1869)

Gatewood, R. D., & Feild, H. S. (1997). *Human resource selection* (4th ed.). Fort Worth, TX: Dryden.

Gaugler, B. B., Rosenthal, D. B., Thornton, G. C., III, & Bentson, C. (1987). Meta-analysis of assessment center validity. *Journal of Applied Psychology, 72*, 493–511.

Glass, G. V. (1976). Primary, secondary, and meta-analysis of research. *Educational Researcher, 5*, 3–8.

Goldman, B. A., & Mitchell, D. F. (Eds.). (2007). *Directory of unpublished experimental mental measures* (Vol. 9). Washington, DC: American Psychological Association.

Gorsuch, R. L. (1983). *Factor analysis.* Hillsdale, NJ: Lawrence Erlbaum.

Gottfredson, L. S. (1991). When job-testing "fairness" is nothing but a quota. *Industrial–Organizational Psychologist, 28*(3), 65–67.

Gottfredson, M. R., & Hirschi, T. (1990). *A general theory of crime.* Stanford, CA: Stanford University Press.

Gough, H. G. (1987). *California Psychological Inventory administrator's guide.* Palo Alto, CA: Consulting Psychologists Press.

Gould, S. J. (1982). *A nation of morons.* Retrieved from http://www.holah.karoo.net/gouldstudy.htm

Graduate Management Admission Council. (2014). *Profile of Graduate Management Admission Test.* Retrieved July, 28, 2014, from file:///Users/drlesliemiller/Downloads/2013-gmat-profile-exec-summary.pdf

Grant, D. A., & Berg, E. (1948). A behavioral analysis of degree of reinforcement and ease of shifting to new responses in a Weigl-type card-sorting problem. *Journal of Experimental Psychology, 38*(4), 404–411. http://dx.doi.org/10.1037/h0059831

Grasmick, H. G., Tittle, C. R., Bursik, R. J., & Arneklev, B. J. (1993). Testing the core empirical implications of Gottfredson and Hirschi's general theory of crime. *Journal of Research in Crime and Delinquency, 30,* 5–29.

Gregory, R. J. (2010). *Psychological testing: History, principles, and applications* (6th ed.). Boston: Pearson.

Gribbons, B. C., Tobey, P. E., & Michael, W. B. (1995). Internal-consistency reliability and construct and criterion-related validity of an academic self-concept scale. *Educational and Psychological Measurement, 55,* 858–867.

Groth-Marnat, G. (1997). *Handbook of psychological assessment* (3rd ed.). New York: John Wiley.

Groves, R. M. (1989). *Survey errors and survey costs.* New York: John Wiley.

Guernsey, L. (2000, August 6). An ever changing course: Taking admissions tests on computers. *The New York Times,* p. A32.

Guion, R. M. (1966). Employment tests and discriminatory hiring. *Industrial Relations, 5,* 20–37.

Haladyna, T. (2015). *Developing and validating multiple choice test items* (3rd ed.). New York: Routledge.

Halpern, D. (2000). Validity, fairness and group differences: Tough questions for selection testing. *Psychology, Public Policy and Law, 6,* 56–62.

Hammer, A. L., & Schnell, E. R. (2000). *FIRO-B: Technical guide.* Mountain View, CA: CPP.

Hammer, E. F. (1975). *The clinical application of projective drawings* (4th ed.). Springfield, IL: Charles C Thomas.

Haney, W. (1981). Validity, vaudeville, and values. *American Psychologist, 36,* 1021–1034.

Hanna, G. S. (1998). Wonderlic Basic Skills Test. In J. C. Impara & B. S. Plake (Eds.), *The thirteenth mental measurements yearbook.* Lincoln, NE: Buros Institute of Mental Measurements.

Harcourt Assessment. (2006). *Bayley III Scales of Infant Development caregiver report.* Retrieved from http://www.pearsonassessments.com/NR/rdon lyres/5A0CB9A1-81E5-4EA8-8962-B51AC6BD 849C/0/ParentSASampleReport.pdf

Harrington, G. M. (1975). Intelligence tests may favour the majority groups in a population. *Nature, 258,* 708–709.

Harris, W. G., Jones, J. W., Klion, R., Arnold, D. W., Camara, W., & Cinningham, M. R. (2012). Test publishers' perspective on "An updated meta-analysis": Comment on Van Iddekinge, Roth, Raymark and Odle-Dusseau. *Journal of Applied Psychology, 97,* 531–536.

Hartigan, J. A., & Wigdor, A. K. (1989). *Fairness in employment testing: Validity generalization, minority issues, and the General Aptitude Test Battery.* Washington, DC: National Academy Press.

Harvill, L. M. (1991, Summer). An NCME instruction module on standard error of measurement. *ITEMS,* pp. 33–41.

Hattrup, K. (2003). Review of the California Psychological Inventory, Third Edition. In B. S. Plake, J. C. Impara, & R. A. Spies (Eds.), *The fifteenth mental measurements yearbook.* Lincoln, NE: Buros Institute of Mental Measurements.

Haynes, S. N., Richard, D.C.S., & Kubany, E. S. (1995). Content validity in psychological assessment: A functional approach to concepts and methods. *Psychological Assessment, 7,* 238–247.

Heaton, R. K. (1981). *A manual for the Wisconsin Card Sorting Test.* Odessa, FL: Psychological Assessment Resources.

Heaton, R. K., Chelune, G. J., Talley, J. L., Kay, G. G., & Curtiss, G. (1993). *Wisconsin Card Sorting Test manual: Revised and expanded.* Odessa, FL: Psychological Assessment Resources.

Helmstadter, G. C. (1970). *Research concepts in human behavior.* New York: Appleton-Century-Crofts.

Heneman, H. G., III, Heneman, R. L., & Judge, T. A. (1997). *Staffing organizations.* Middleton, WI: Mendota House.

Herrnstein, R. J., & Murray, C. (1994). *The bell curve: Intelligence and class structure in American life.* New York: Free Press.

Hess, A. K. (2001). Review of Wechsler Adult Intelligence Scale, Third Edition (WAIS-III). In S. Plake & J. C. Impara (Eds.), *Fourteenth mental measurements yearbook.* Lincoln: University of Nebraska, Buros Institute of Mental Measurements.

Hilliard, A. (1984). *Historical perspectives on Black families.* Paper presented at the National Urban League/National Association for the Advancement of Colored People Summit Conference on the Black Family, Nashville, TN.

Hiscox. (2017). The 2017 HISCOX embezzlement study. Retrieved from https://www.hiscox.com/documents/2017-Hiscox-Embezzlement-Study.pdf

Ho, Ping-ti. (1962). *The ladder of success in imperial China.* New York: John Wiley.

Hoerger, M., Quirk, S., & Weed, N. (2011). Development and validation of the Delaying Gratification Inventory. *Psychological Assessment, 23,* 725–738.

Hoffmann, C. C., Holden, L. M., & Gale, K. (2000). So many jobs, so little "N": Applying expanded validation models to support generalization of cognitive test validity. *Personnel Psychology, 53,* 955–991.

Hoffmann, C. C., & McPhail, S. M. (1998). Exploring options for supporting test use in situations precluding local validation. *Personnel Psychology, 51,* 987–1003.

Hogan Assessment Systems. (2018). *Hogan Development Survey: The dark side of personality.* Retrieved from https://www.hoganassessments.com/assessment/hogan-development-survey/

Hogan, J., Barrett, P., & Hogan, R. (2007). Personality measurement, faking, and employment. *Journal of Applied Psychology, 92,* 1270–1285.

Hogan, J., & Holland, B. (2003). Using theory to evaluate personality and job-performance relations: A socioanalytic perspective. *Journal of Applied Psychology, 88,* 100–112.

Hogan, R., & Hogan, J. (1992). *Hogan Personality Inventory manual.* Tulsa, OK: Hogan Assessment Systems.

Holden, R. R. (2007). Socially desirable responding does moderate personality scale validity both in experimental and nonexperimental contexts. *Canadian Journal of Behavioral Science/Revue Candadienne des Sciences du Comportment, 39,* 184–201.

Holland, J. L., Fritzsche, B. A., & Powell, A. B. (1996). *SDS: Technical manual.* Odessa, FL: Psychological Assessment Resources.

Holland, J. L., Powell, A. B., & Fritzsche, B. A. (1994). *SDS: Professional user's guide.* Odessa, FL: Psychological Assessment Resources.

Holman, T. B., Busby, D. M., & Larson, J. H. (1989). *PREParation for Marriage (PREP-M).* Provo, UT: Marriage Study Consortium.

Holman, T. B., Larson, J. H., & Harmer, S. L. (1994). The development of predictive validity of a new premarital assessment instrument: The PREParation for Marriage Questionnaire. *Family Relations, 43*(1), 46–52.

Holmberg, K., Rosen, D., & Holland, J. L. (1997). *SDS: The leisure activities finder.* Odessa, FL: Psychological Assessment Resources.

Hopkins, C. D., & Antes, R. L. (1979). *Classroom testing: Construction.* Itasca, IL: F. E. Peacock.

Horan, D. J. (2003, December). Controlling theft by key holders. *Chain Store Age,* p. 166.

How a personality quiz on Facebook helped Donald Trump find his voters. (2018, Mar. 21). *The Hindu.* Retrieved from http://www.thehindu.com/news/international/how-a-personality-quiz-on-facebook-helped-donald-trump-find-his-voters/article23310128.ece

HR Certification Institute. (n.d.). *Code of ethical and professional responsibility.* Retrieved from https://www.hrci.org/docs/default-source/web-files/code-of-ethical-and-professional-responsibility(1)-pdf.pdf

HR Certification Institute. (2018). *Our HR certifications.* Retrieved from http://www.hrci.org/our-programs/our-hr-certifications

Hucker, C. O. (1978). *China to 1850: A short history.* Stanford, CA: Stanford University Press.

Huebner, E. S. (1991). Initial development of the Student Life Satisfaction Scale. *School Psychology International, 12,* 231–240.

Huffcutt, A. I., & Arthur, W. (1994). Hunter and Hunter (1984) revisited: Interview validity for entry level jobs. *Journal of Applied Psychology, 79,* 184–190.

Hunsley, J., & Meyer, G. J. (2003). The incremental validity of psychological testing and assessment: Conceptual, methodological, and statistical issues. *Psychological Assessment, 15*(4), 446–455.

Hunt, M. (1993). *The story of psychology.* New York: Doubleday.

Hunter, J. E., & Hunter, R. F. (1984). Validity and utility of alternative predictors of job performance. *Psychological Bulletin, 96,* 72–98.

Hunter, J. E., & Schmidt, F. L. (1976). A critical analysis of the statistical and ethical implications of various definitions of "test bias." *Psychological Bulletin, 83,* 1053–1071.

Hunter, J. E., Schmidt, F. L., & Hunter, R. (1979). Differential validity of employment tests by race: A comprehensive review and analysis. *Psychological Bulletin, 86,* 721–735.

HyperStat Online. (n.d.). *The effect of skew on the mean and median.* Retrieved from http://davidmlane.com/hyperstat/A92403.html

International Personality Item Pool: A Scientific Collaboratory for the Development of Advanced Measures of Personality Traits and Other Individual Differences. (2015). Retrieved February 13, 2015, from http://ipip.ori.org

International Test Commission. (2005). *International guidelines on computer-based and internet delivered testing: Version 2005.* Retrieved from http://www.intestcom.org/Downloads/ITC%20Guidelines%20on%20Computer%20-%20version%202005%20approved.pdf

International Test Commission. (2013, October 8). *ITC guidelines on test use: Version 1.2.* Retrieved from http://www.intestcom.org/Guidelines/Test+Use.php

IPAT. (2014). *The 16PF Questionnaire.* Retrieved from http://www.ipat.com/16PFQuestionnaire/Pages/default.aspx

Jack L. Hayes International, Inc. (2014, June). *Shoplifters and dishonest employees are apprehended in record numbers by U.S. retailers according to 26th annual Retail Theft Survey by Jack L. Hayes International*. Retrieved from http://hayesinternational.com/wp-content/uploads/2014/06/26th-Annual-Retail-Theft-Survey-Hayes-International-Thoughts-Behind-Numbers.pdf

Javeline, D. (1999). Response effects in polite cultures. *Public Opinion Quarterly, 63*, 1–28.

Jayanti, B. (2014). Psychologists' ambivalence toward ambiguity: Relocating the projective test debate for multiple interpretative hypotheses. *SIS Journal of Projective Psychology & Mental Health, 21*(1), 25–36.

Jenckes, T. A. (1868). *The civil service report*. Washington, DC: U.S. Government Printing Office.

Jensen, A. R. (1969). How much can we boost IQ and scholastic achievement? *Harvard Educational Review, 39*, 1–123.

John Wiley & Sons. (2000–2018). *The Leaderships Challenge: Ourapproach*. Retrieved from http://www.leadershipchallenge.com/WileyCDA/Section/id-131055.html

Johnson, G. (2004, May). The good, the bad, and the alternative. *Training*, pp. 24–30.

Johnson, J. A., & D'Amato, R. C. (2005). Review of the Stanford–Binet Intelligence Scales Fifth Edition. In R. S. Spies & B. S. Plake (Eds.), *The sixteenth mental measurement yearbook*. Lincoln, NE: Buros Institute of Mental Measurements.

Johnson. J. W., & Carter, G. W. (2010). Validating synthetic validation: Comparing traditional and synthetic validity coefficients. *Personnel Psychology, 63*, 755–796.

Joiner, T. E., Jr., Walker, R. L., Pettit, J. W., Perez, M., & Cukrowicz, K. C. (2005). Evidence-based assessment of depression in adults. *Psychological Assessment, 17*(3), 267–277.

Joint Committee on Testing Practices. (2004). *Code of fair testing practices in education*. Washington, DC: Author. Retrieved from http://www.apa.org/science/programs/testing/fair-testing.pdf

Jones, J. W., & Youngblood, K. L. (1993, May). *Effect of a video-based test on the performance and retention of bank employees*. Paper presented at the annual meeting of the Society for Industrial and Organizational Psychology, San Francisco, CA.

Jones, R. N., & Gallo, J. J. (2000). Dimensions of the Mini-Mental State Examination among community dwelling older adults. *Psychological Medicine, 30*, 605–618.

Kahn, R. L., & Cannell, C. F. (1957). *The dynamics of interviewing*. New York: John Wiley.

Kamin, L. J. (1995, February). Behind the curve. *Scientific American*, pp. 99–103.

Kantrowitz, T. M. (2014). *Global assessment trends 2014*. Alpharetta, GA: SHL Americas. Retrieved from https://www.cebglobal.com/content/dam/cebglobal/us/EN/regions/uk/tm/pdfs/Report/gatr-2014.pdf

Kaplan, R. M., & Saccuzzo, D. P. (2013). *Psychological testing: Principles, applications, and issues* (8th ed.). Belmont, CA: Wadsworth.

Karr, A. R. (1988, July 1). Law limiting use of lie detectors is seen having widespread effect. *The Wall Street Journal*, p. A1.

Karstoft, K. I., Andersen, S. B., Bertelsen, M., & Madsen, T. (2014). Diagnostic accuracy of the Posttraumatic Stress Disorder Checklist–Civilian Version in a representative military sample. *Psychological Assessment, 26*(1), 321–325.

Kennedy, D. (2003). Committed to the best science? *Science, 300*, 1201.

Klecker, B. M. (2003). Review of the State–Trait Anger Expression Inventory–2. In B. S. Plake, J. C. Impara, & R. A. Spies (Eds.), *The fifteenth mental measurements yearbook*. Lincoln, NE: Buros Institute for Mental Measurements.

Kluck, A. S., & Zhuzha, K. (2017). Test review of Mini-Mental State Examination (2nd Ed.). In J F. Carlson, K. F Geisinger, & J. L. Jonson, *The twentieth mental measurements yearbook*. Lincoln, NE: Buros Center for Testing.

Knobloch, H., Stevens, F., & Malone, A. F. (1980). *Manual of developmental diagnosis: The administration and interpretation of revised Gesell and Amatruda Developmental and Neurologic Examination*. New York: Harper & Row.

Knowles, E. F., & Bean, D. (1981). St. Louis fire captain selection: Litigation and defense of the selection procedures. *Journal of Assessment Center Technology, 4*(1), 9–22.

Kobrin, J. L., Patterson, B. F., Shaw, E. J., Mattern, K. D., & Barbuti, S. M. (2008). *Validity of the SAT for predicting first-year college grade point average*. Retrieved from https://research.collegeboard.org/sites/default/files/publications/2012/7/researchreport-2008-5-validity-sat-predicting-first-year-college-grade-point-average.pdf

Kracke, E. A. (1963). Region, family, and individual in the examination system. In J. M. Menzel (Ed.), *The Chinese civil service: Career open to talent?* (pp. 67–75). Boston: D. S. Heath.

Krall, V. (1986). Projective play techniques. In A. I. Rabin (Ed.), *Projective techniques for adolescents and children* (pp. 264–278). New York: Springer.

Krug, S. E., & Johns, E. F. (Eds.). (1990). *Testing in counseling practice.* Hillsdale, NJ: Lawrence Erlbaum.

Kryspin, W. J., & Feldhusen, J. F. (1974). *Developing classroom tests: A guide for writing and evaluating test items.* Minneapolis, MN: Burgess.

Kubiszyn, T., & Borich, G. (2007). *Educational testing and measurement: Classroom application and practice* (8th ed.). New York: HarperCollins.

Kuder, G. F., & Richardson, M. W. (1937). The theory of estimation of test reliability. *Psychometrika, 2,* 151–160.

Kuder, G. F., & Richardson, M. W. (1939). The calculation of test reliability coefficients based on the method of rational equivalence. *Journal of Educational Psychology, 30,* 681–687.

Kuncel, N. R., & Sackett, P. R. (2007). Selective citation mars conclusions about test validity and predictive bias. *American Psychologist, 62,* 145–146.

Kush, J. C. (2005). Review of the Stanford–Binet Intelligence Scales: Fifth Edition. In R. S. Spies & B. S. Plake (Eds.), *The sixteenth mental measurements yearbook.* Lincoln, NE: Buros Institute of Mental Measurements.

Larzelere, R. E., Smith, G. L., Batenhorst, L. M., & Kelly, D. B. (1996). Predictive validity of the Suicide Probability Scale among adolescents in group home treatment. *Journal of American Academy of Child and Adolescent Psychiatry, 35,* 166–172.

Lau, J., Antman, E. M., Jimenez-Silva, J., Kupelnick, B., Mosteller, F., & Chalmers, T. C. (1992). Cumulative meta-analysis of therapeutic trials for myocardial infarction. *New England Journal of Medicine, 327,* 248–254.

Laurent, J., Catanzaro, S., Joiner, T. E., Jr., Rudolph, K., Potter, K., Lambert, S., . . . Gathright, T. (1999). A measure of positive and negative affect for children: Scale development and preliminary validation. *Psychological Assessment, 11,* 326–338.

Lawshe, C. H. (1952). Employee selection. *Personnel Psychology, 6,* 31–34.

Lawshe, C. H. (1975). A quantitative approach to content validity. *Personnel Psychology, 28,* 563–575.

LeBreton, J. M., Scherer, K. T., & James, L. R. (2014). Corrections in criteria reliability in validity generalization: A false prophet in a land of suspended judgement. *Industrial and Organizational Psychology: Perspectives on Science and Practice, 7*(4), 478–500.

Lee, C., & Bobko, P. (1994). Self-efficacy beliefs: Comparison of five measures. *Journal of Applied Psychology, 79,* 364–369.

Lemann, N. (1999). *The big test: The secret history of the American meritocracy.* New York: Farrar, Straus & Giroux.

Lewis v. City of Chicago, 98 C. 5596 (2005).

Lievens, F., & Patterson, F. (2011). The validity and incremental validity of knowledge tests, low-fidelity simulations, and high fidelity simulations for predicting job performance in advanced-level high stakes selection. *Journal of Applied Psychology, 96,* 927–940.

Lievens, F., & Sanchez, J. (2007). Can training improve the quality of inferences made by raters in competency modeling? A quasi experiment. *Journal of Applied Psychology, 92,* 812–819.

Lilienfeld, S. O. (1993, Fall). Do "honesty" tests really measure honesty? *Skeptical Inquirer,* pp. 32–41.

Lilienfeld, S. O., Alliger, G., & Mitchell, K. (1995). Why integrity testing remains controversial. *American Psychologist, 50,* 457–458.

Lim, R. G., & Drasgow, F. (1990). Evaluation of two methods for estimating item response theory parameters when assessing differential item functioning. *Journal of Applied Psychology, 75,* 164–174.

Lindqvist, J. K., Daderman, A. M., & Hellstrom, A. (2003). Swedish adaptations of the Novaco Anger Scale 1998, the Provocation Inventory, and the State–Trait Anger Expression Inventory–2. *Social Behavior and Personality, 31,* 773–788.

Linn, R. (1982). Ability testing: Individual differences, prediction, and differential prediction. In A. Wigdor & W. Garner (Eds.), *Ability testing: Uses, consequences, and controversies* (pp. 335–388). Washington, DC: National Academy Press.

Linn, R. L., & Drasgow, F. (1987). Implications of the Golden Rule settlement for test construction. *Educational Measurement: Issues & Practice, 6*(2), 13–17.

Lippmann, W. (1922a). A future for tests. *New Republic, 33,* 9–11.

Lippmann, W. (1922b). The mental age of Americans. *New Republic, 32,* 213–215.

Lippmann, W. (1922c). The mystery of the "A" men. *New Republic, 32,* 246–248.

Lippmann, W. (1922d). The reliability of intelligence tests. *New Republic, 32,* 275–277.

Lippmann, W. (1922e). Tests of hereditary intelligence. *New Republic, 32,* 328–330.

Longshore, D., Turner, S., & Stein, J. A. (1996). Self-control in a criminal sample: An examination of construct validity. *Criminology, 34,* 209–228.

Lopez, M. N., Charter, R. A., Mostafavi, B., Nibut, L. P., & Smith, W. E. (2005). Psychometric properties of the Folstein Mini-Mental State Examination. *Assessment, 12,* 137–144.

Lord, C., Rutter, M., DiLavore, P. C., Risi, S., Gotham, K., & Bishop, S. (2012). *Autism Diagnostic Observation Schedule, 2nd Edition (ADOS-2).* Torrance, CA: Western Psychological Services.

Lord, C., Rutter, M., & Le Couteur, A. (1994). Autism Diagnostic Interview–Revised: A revised version of a diagnostic interview for caregivers of individuals with possible pervasive developmental disorders. *Journal of Autism and Developmental Disorders, 24*(5), 659–685.

Lyman, H. B. (1998). *Test scores and what they mean* (6th ed.). Boston: Allyn & Bacon.

Lyons, B. D., Hoffman, B. J., & Michel, J. W. (2009). Not much more than *g?* An examination of the impact of intelligence on NFL performance. *Human Performance, 22,* 225–245.

Maisto, S. A., Chung, T. A., Cornelius, J. R., & Martin, C. S. (2003). Factor structure of the SOCRATES in a clinical sample of adolescents. *Psychology of Addictive Behavior, 17,* 98–107.

Maisto, S., Krenek, M., Chung, T., Martin, C., Clark, D., & Cornelius, J. (2011). A comparison of the concurrent and predictive validity of three measures of readiness to change alcohol use in a clinical sample of adolescents. *Psychological Assessment, 24,* 983–994.

Marsden, P. V., & Wright, J. D. (2010). *Handbook of survey research* (2nd ed.). West Yorkshire, England: Emerald Group Publishing.

Martin, C. (2012). *The sixteen types at a glance.* Retrieved from http://www.capt.org/the_mbti_instrument/type_descriptions.cfm

Martin, W.A.P. (1870). Competitive examinations in China. *North Atlantic Review, 111,* 62–77.

Mattis, S. (2001). *Dementia Rating Scale-2 (DRS-2).* Odessa, FL: Psychological Assessment Resources.

McCrae, R. R., & Costa, P. T., Jr. (1997). Personality trait structure as a human universal. *American Psychologist, 52,* 509–516.

McDaniel, M. A., Whetzel, D. L., Schmidt, F. L., & Maurer, S. D. (1994). The validity of employment interviews: A comprehensive review and meta-analysis. *Journal of Applied Psychology, 79,* 599–616.

McGraw-Hill. (1970). *Examiner's manual for the California Achievement Tests, Complete Battery, Level 2, Form A.* New York: Author.

McIntire, S. A., Bucklan, M. A., & Scott, D. R. (1995). *The job analysis kit.* Odessa, FL: Psychological Assessment Resources.

McLellan, M. J. (1995). Review of the Sixteen Personality Factor Questionnaire, Fifth Edition. In J. Conoley & J. C. Impara (Eds.), *The twelfth mental measurements yearbook.* Lincoln, NE: Buros Institute of Mental Measurements.

Meade, A. W. (2004). Psychometric problems and issues involved with creating and using ipsative measures for selection. *Journal of Occupational and Organizational Psychology, 77,* 531–552.

Meade, A. W., & Fetzer, M. (2008, April). *A new approach to assessing test bias.* Paper presented at the 23trd Annual Conference of the Society for Industrial and Organizational Psychology, San Francisco, CA.

Meglino, B. M., DeNisi, A. S., Youngblood, S. A., & Williams, K. J. (1988). Effects of realistic job previews: A comparison using an enhancement and a reduction preview. *Journal of Applied Psychology, 72,* 259–266.

Melchert, T. P., Hays, V. A., Wiljanen, L. M., & Kolocek, A. K. (1996). Testing models of counselor development with a measure of counseling self- efficacy. *Journal of Counseling & Development, 74,* 640–644.

Meyer, G. J., Finn, S. E., Eyde, L. D., Kay, G. G., Moreland, K. L., Dies, R. R., . . . Reed, G. M. (2001). Psychological testing and psychological assessment: A review of evidence and issues. *American Psychologist, 56*(2), 128–165.

Meyer, G. J., Viglione, D. J., Mihura, J. L., Erard, R. E., & Erdberg, P. (2011). *Rorschach Performance Assessment System: Administration, coding interpretation, and technical manual.* Toledo, OH: Rorschach Performance Assessment System.

Michael, W. B., & Smith, R. A. (1976). The development and preliminary validation of three forms of a self-concept measure emphasizing school-related activities. *Educational and Psychological Measurement, 38,* 527–535.

Michael, W. B., Smith, R. A., & Michael, J. J. (1989). *Dimensions of Self-Concept (DOSC): A technical manual* (Rev. ed.). San Diego, CA: EdITS.

Mihura, J. L., Meyer, G. J., Dumitrascu, N., & Bombel, G. (2013). The validity of individual Rorschach variables: Systematic reviews and meta-analyses of the comprehensive system. *Psychological Bulletin, 139*(3), 548–605.

Military Advantage. (2014). *About the ASVAB*. Retrieved from http://www.military.com/join-armed-forces/asvab

Miller, L. A., Mullin, P. A., & Herrmann, D. J. (1990). *Memory processes in answering retrospective survey questions*. Paper presented at MNEMO '90, the International Symposium on Human Memory Modelling and Simulation, Varna, Bulgaria.

Miller, L., Stimely, M., Matheny, P., Pope, M., McAtee, R., & Miller, K. (2014). Novice nurse preparedness to effectively use electronic health records in acute care settings: Critical informatics knowledge and skill gaps. *Online Journal of Nursing Informatics (OJNI)*, *18*(2). Retrieved from http://www.himss.org/ResourceLibrary/GenResourceDetail.aspx?ItemNumber=30527

Millon, T. (1994). *Manual for the MCMI-III*. Minneapolis, MN: National Computer Systems.

Mindgarden. (2005–2009). *Mathematics Self-Efficacy Scale*. Retrieved from http://www.mindgarden.com/products/maths.htm

Mitchell, J., Trent, R., & McArthur, R. (1993). *Human Figure Drawing Test (HFDT): An illustrated handbook for clinical interpretation and standardized assessment of cognitive impairment*. Los Angeles: Western Psychological Services.

Miyazaki, I. (1981). *China's examination hell*. New Haven, CT: Yale University Press.

Morey, L. C. (1991). *Personality Assessment Inventory*. Odessa, FL: Psychological Assessment Resources.

Morgan, D. L., & Michaelides, M. P. (2005). *Setting cut scores for college placement* (Research Report No. 2005-9). New York: College Board.

Mueller, J. (2011). *What is authentic assessment?* Retrieved from http://jfmueller.faculty.noctrl.edu/toolbox/whatisit.htm

Murphy, C. A., Coover, D., & Owen, S. V. (1989). Development and validation of the Computer Self-Efficacy Scale. *Educational and Psychological Measurement*, *49*, 893–899.

Murphy, K. R., & Davidshofer, C. O. (1994). *Psychological testing: Principles and applications* (3rd ed.). Englewood Cliffs, NJ: Prentice Hall.

Murphy, K. R., & Davidshofer, C. O. (2005). *Psychological testing: Principles and applications* (6th ed.). Upper Saddle River, NJ: Pearson/Prentice Hall.

Myers, I. B. (1998). *Introduction to type* (6th ed.). Palo Alto, CA: Consulting Psychologists Press.

Myers, I. B., McCaulley, M. H., Quenk, N. L., & Hammer, A. L. (1998). *MBTI manual: A guide to the development and use of the Myers–Briggs Type Indicator* (3rd ed.). Palo Alto, CA: Consulting Psychologists Press.

National Association of School Psychologists. (2009). *Position statement: School psychologists' involvement in assessment*. Retrieved from https://www.nasponline.org/research-and-policy/professional-positions/position-statements

National Association of School Psychologists. (2017a). *NASP professional standards (adopted in 2010)*. Bethesda, MD: Author. (Original work published 2010)

National Association of School Psychologists. (2017b). *Principles for professional ethics*. Retrieved from https://www.nasponline.org/standards-and-certification/professional-ethics

National Association of School Psychologists. (2017c). *What are school psychologists?* Retrieved from https://www.nasponline.org/about-school-psychology/who-are-school-psychologists

National Board for Certified Counselors. (2012). *Code of ethics*. Retrieved from http://www.nbcc.org/Assets/Ethics/nbcc-codeofethics.pdf

National Center for Fair and Open Testing. (2007). *The SAT: Questions and answers*. Retrieved from http://www.fairtest.org/facts/satfact.htm

National Center for Fair and Open Testing. (2018). *More than 1000 accredited colleges and universities that do not use ACT/SAT scores to admit substantial numbers of students into bachelor-degree programs*. Retrieved from https://www.fairtest.org/university/optional

National Center for O*NET Development. (2014). *Frequently asked questions: Should states continue to use the GATB?* Retrieved from http://www.onet center.org/questions/30.html

National Institute on Aging. (n.d.). *About Alzheimer's disease: Diagnosis*. Retrieved from http://www.nia.nih.gov/alzheimers/topics/diagnosis

National Institute of Child Health and Human Development. (2018). *Learning disabilities: Overview*. Retrieved from https://www.nichd.nih.gov/health/topics/learningdisabilities

National Institute of Neurological Disorders and Stroke. (2011). *NINDS learning disabilities information page*. Retrieved from http://www.ninds.nih.gov/disorders/learningdisabilities/learningdisabilities.htm

National Retail Federation. (2018). *National retail security survey 2015*. Retrieved from https://nrf.com/resources/retail-library/national-retail-security-survey-2015

National White Collar Crime Center. (2009, October). *Embezzlement/employee theft.* Retrieved from http://www .nw3c.org/docs/research/embezzlement-employee-theft .pdf?sfvrsn=10

Neisser, U., Boodoo, G., Bouchard, T. J., Jr., Boykin, A. W., Brody, N., Ceci, S. J., . . . Urbina, S. (1996). Intelligence: Knowns and unknowns. *American Psychologist, 51,* 77–101.

Nisbett, R. E., Aronson, J., Blair, C., Dickens, W., Flynn, J., Halpern, D. F., & Turkheimer, E. (2012). Intelligence: New findings and theoretical developments. *American Psychologist, 67,* 130–159.

Norman, W. T. (1963). Toward an adequate taxonomy of personality attributes: Replicated factor structure in peer nomination personality ratings. *The Journal of Abnormal and Social Psychology, 66*(6), 574–583.

Nunnally, J. C. (1978). *Psychometric theory* (2nd ed.). New York: McGraw-Hill.

Nunnally, J. C., & Bernstein, I. H. (1994). *Psychometric theory* (3rd ed.). New York: McGraw-Hill.

O'Connor, R. (1997–2014). *Teen suicide—Risk factors and warning signs.* Retrieved from http://www.focusas.com/Suicide .html

Ones, D. S., Dilchert, S., Viswesvaran, C., & Judge, T. (2007). In support of personality assessment in organizational settings. *Personnel Psychology, 60,* 995–1027.

Ones, D. S., Viswesvaran, C., & Reiss, A. D. (1996). Role of social desirability in personality testing for personnel selection: The red herring. *Journal of Applied Psychology, 81,* 660–679.

Ones, D. S., Viswesvaran, C., & Schmidt, F. L. (1993). Comprehensive meta-analysis of integrity test validities: Findings and implications for personnel selection and theories of job performance. *Journal of Applied Psychology, 78,* 679–703.

Ortner, T. M., Weisskopf, E., & Koch, T. (2014). I will probably fail: Higher ability students' motivational experiences during adaptive achievement testing. *European Journal of Psychological Assessment, 30,* 45–56.

Pajares, F., & Miller, M. D. (1995). Mathematics self-efficacy and mathematics performances: The need for specificity of assessment. *Journal of Counseling Psychology, 42,* 190–198.

PAR. (n.d.). *MMSE-2: Mini-Mental State Examination.* 2nd ed. Retrieved from http://www.minimental.com

PAR. (2012). *State–Trait Anger Expression Inventory–2 (STAXI-2).* Retrieved from http://www4.parinc.com/products/product .aspx?Productid=STAXI-2

PAR. (2018a). *NEO™ Personality Inventory-3 (NEO™-PI-3).* Retrieved from https://www.parinc.com/Products/Pkey/275

PAR. (2018b). *Personality Assessment Inventory.* Retrieved from https://www.parinc.com/Products/Pkey/299

Paulhaus, D. L. (1984). Two component model of socially desirable responding. *Journal of Personality and Social Psychology, 88,* 348–355.

Paulhaus, D. L. (1998). *Paulhaus Deception Scales: The Balanced Inventory of Desirable Responding–7 user's manual.* North Tonawanda, NY: Multi-Health System.

Paunonen, S. V., & LeBel, E. P. (2012). Socially desirable responding and its elusive effects of the validity of personality assessments. *Journal of Personality and Social Psychology, 103,* 158–175.

Pearson Education. (2018a). *MMPI-2 (Minnesota Multiphasic Personality Inventory–2).* Retrieved from http://www.pearson assessments.com/tests/mmpi_2.htm

Pearson Education. (2018b). *Qualification levels.* Retrieved from https://www.pearsonclinical.com/psychology/qualifications.html

Pearson Education. (2018c). *Thematic Apperception Test (TAT).* Retrieved from http://www.pearsonassess ments.com/ HAIWEB/Cultures/en-us/Productdetail.htm?Pid=015-4019-046&Mode=summary

Pearson Education. (2018d). *Wechsler Adult Intelligence Scale–Fourth Edition (WAIS-IV).* Retrieved from http://www .pearsonclinical.com/psychology/products/100000392/ wechsler-adult-intelligence-scalefourth-edition-wais-iv .html?Pid= 015-8980-808

Pinker, S. (2011). *The better angels of our nature: Why violence has declined.* New York: Viking.

Pirazzoli-t'Serstevens, M. (1982). *The Han civilization of China.* Oxford, UK: Phaidon.

Popham, W. J. (1975). *Educational evaluation.* Englewood Cliffs, NJ: Prentice Hall.

Popham, W. J. (2000). The mismeasurement of educational quality. *School Administrator, 57*(11), 12–15.

Poskey, M. (2005). *Myths of behavioral preemployment testing.* Retrieved from http://www.zeroriskhr.com/pdfs/support/ hidden/clients/articles/myths-of-behavioral-preemploy-ment-testing-0113.pdf

Posner, K., Brent, D., Lucas, C., Gould, M., Stanley, B., Brown, G., . . . Mann, J. (2009). *Columbia-Suicide Severity Rating Scale (C-SSRS): Lifetime/Recent Version* (Version 1/14/09). Retrieved from http://cssrs.columbia.edu/docs/C-SSRS_1_14_09_Lifetime_ Recent.pdf

PR Newswire Association. (2008). *Rollins College announces SAT and ACT test scores optional*. Retrieved from http://www.prnewswire.com/news-releases/rollins-college-announces-sat-and-act-test-scores-optional-58363987.html

Prochaska, J. O., DiClemente, C. C., & Norcross, J. C. (1992). In search of how people change: Applications to addictive behaviors. *American Psychologist, 47,* 1102–1114.

PRO-ED. (n.d.). *TONI-4: Test of Nonverbal Intelligence – Fourth Edition*. Retrieved from http://www.proedinc.com/customer/productview.aspx?id=4787

PRO-ED, Inc. (2012). *Stanford–Binet Intelligence Scales–Fifth Edition (SB-5)*. Retrieved from https://www.proedinc.com/Downloads/14462%20SB-5_OSRS_UserGuide.pdf

PSI Services LLC. (2017). *16PF*. Retrieved from https://www.16pf.com/en_US/16pf-overview/key-benefits/

Ritter, N., Kilinc, E., Navruz, B., & Bae, Y. (2011). Test review. *Journal of Psychoeducational Assessment, 29,* 484–488.

Rodzinski, W. (1979). *A history of China*. Oxford, UK: Pergamon.

Rogers, B. G. (2001). Review of the Wechsler Adult Intelligence Scale–Third Edition. In S. Plake & J. C. Impara (Eds.), *Fourteenth mental measurements yearbook*. Lincoln: University of Nebraska, Buros Institute of Mental Measurements.

Rogers, T. B. (1995). *The psychological testing enterprise: An introduction*. Pacific Grove, CA: Brooks/Cole.

Rojdev, R., Nelson, W. M., III, Hart, K. J., & Fercho, M. C. (1994). Criterion-related validity and stability: Equivalence of the MMPI and the MMPI-2. *Journal of Clinical Psychology, 50,* 361–367.

Rorschach, H. (1921). *Psychodiagnostik*. Bern, Switzerland: Bircher.

Rossi, R., Van den Brande, I., Tobac, A., Sloore, H., & Hauben, C. (2003). Convergent validity of the MCMI-III personality disorder scales and the MMPI-2 scales. *Journal of Personality Disorders, 17,* 330–340.

Roth, P. L., Bevier, C. A., Bobko, P., Switzer, F. S., & Tyler, P. (2001). Ethnic group differences in cognitive ability in employment and educational settings: A meta-analysis. *Personnel Psychology, 54,* 297–330.

Roth, P. L., Bobko, P., & Mabon, H. (2001). Utility analysis: A review and analysis at the end of the century. In N. Anderson, D. S. Ones, H. K. Sinangil, & C. Viswesveran (Eds.), *Handbook of industrial, work and organizational psychology* (pp. 363–384). London: Sage Ltd.

Roth, P. L., Le, H., Oh, I., Van Iddekinge, C. H., Buster, M. A., Robbins, S. B., & Campion, M. A. (2013). Differential validity for cognitive ability tests in employment: Not much more than range restriction? *Journal of Applied Psychology, 99,* 1–20.

Roth, P. L., Le, H., Oh, I., Van Iddekinge, & Robins, S. B., (2017). Who r u?: On the (In) accuracy of incumbent-based estimates of range restriction in criterion-related and differential validity research. *Journal of Applied Psychology, 102,* 802–828.

Rotto, P. C. (1995). Review of the Sixteen Personality Factor Questionnaire, Fifth Edition. In J. Conoley & J. C. Impara (Eds.), *The twelfth mental measurements yearbook*. Lincoln, NE: Buros Institute of Mental Measurements.

Ruscio, J. (2005, January/February). Exploring controversies in the art and science of polygraph testing. *The Skeptical Inquirer*, pp. 34–39.

Sabatelli, R. M. (1984). The Marital Comparison Level Index: A measure for assessing outcomes relative to expectations. *Journal of Marriage and the Family, 46,* 651–662.

Salkind, N. J. (2013). *Tests & measurement for people who (think they) hate tests & measurements* (2nd ed.). Thousand Oaks, CA: Sage.

Schmidt, F. L. (1988). The problem of group differences in ability test scores in employment selection. *Journal of Vocational Behavior, 33,* 272–292.

Schmidt, F. L., & Hunter, J. E. (1981). Employment testing: Old theories and new research findings. *American Psychologist, 36,* 1128–1137.

Schmitt, N. (1996). Uses and abuses of coefficient alpha. *Psychological Assessment, 8,* 350–353.

Schoenberger, C. R. (2004, May 10). The insider. *Forbes*, p. 82.

Segal, D. L., & Coolidge, F. L. (2004). Objective assessment of personality and psychopathology: An overview. In M. J. Hilsenroth & D. L. Segal (Eds.), *Comprehensive handbook of psychological assessment, Vol. 2: Personality assessment* (pp. 3–13). Hoboken, NJ: John Wiley. Retrieved from http://media.wiley.com/product_data/excerpt/26/04714161/0471416126.pdf

Seligson, J. L., Huebner, S., & Valois, R. F. (2003). Preliminary validation of the Brief Multi-dimensional Students' Life Satisfaction Scale (BMSLSS). *Social Indicators Research, 61,* 121–145.

Sen. Pete Domenici introduced a bill to limit polygraph testing of personnel at DOE nuclear weapons facilities. (2001, August 6). *Inside Energy*, p. 11.

Sharecare, Inc. (2018). *2011 Well-Being Index findings*. Retrieved from http://www.well-beingindex.com/

Sharpley, C. F., & Ridgway, I. R. (1993). An evaluation of the effectiveness of self-efficacy as a predictor of trainees' counseling skills performance. *British Journal of Guidance and Counseling, 21,* 73–81.

Sherer, M., Maddux, J. E., Mercandante, B., Prentice-Dunn, S., Jacobs, B., & Rogers, R. W. (1982). The Self-Efficacy Scale: Construction and validation. *Psychological Reports, 51*, 663–671.

Shipley, A. (2011, October 26). Smart guy. *The Washington Post*, Met 2 Edition, p. D03.

Shippmann, J. S., Ash, R. A., Batjista, M., Carr, L., Eyde, L. D., Hesketh, B., . . . Sanchez, J. I. (2000). The practice of competency modeling. *Personnel Psychology, 53*, 703–740.

Shore, M. F. (1972). Psychological testing. In R. H. Woody & J. D. Woody (Eds.), *Clinical assessment in counseling and psychotherapy* (pp. 1–29). Englewood Cliffs, NJ: Prentice Hall.

Shrout, P. E., & Fleiss, J. L. (1979). Intraclass correlation coefficients: Uses in assessing rater reliability. *Psychological Bulletin, 86*(2), 420–428.

Silva, D. (2013). *Education experts debate high-stakes testing in public schools.* Retrieved from http://www.nbcnews.com/news/other/education-experts-debate-high-stakes-testing-public-schools-f8C11349956

Smith, E. V., Jr. (2001). Mathematics Self-Efficacy Scale. In B. S. Plake & J. C. Impara (Eds.), *The fourteenth mental measurements yearbook*. Lincoln, NE: Buros Institute of Mental Measurements.

Smith, J. E., & Merchant, S. (1990). Using competency exams for evaluating training. *Training & Development Journal, 44*, 65–71.

Smither, R. D. (1994). *The psychology of work and human performance* (2nd ed.). New York: HarperCollins.

Society for Human Resource Management. (2015). *SHRM testing center: Online testing solutions.* Retrieved from http://www.shrm.org/Templates

Society for Human Resource Management. (2018). *About the Society for Human Resource Management.* Retrieved from http://www.shrm.org/about/pages/default.aspx

Society for Industrial and Organizational Psychology. (2003). *Principles for the validation and use of personnel selection procedures* (4th ed.). Bowling Green, OH: Author. Retrieved from http://www.siop.org/_Principles/principles.pdf

Society for Industrial and Organizational Psychology. (2014). *What do integrity tests measure?* Retrieved from http://www.siop.org/Media/News/integrity.aspx

Soto, J. A., Perez, C. R., Kim, Y.-H., Lee, E. A., & Minnick, M. R. (2011). Is expressive suppression always associated with poorer psychological functioning? A cross-cultural comparison between European Americans and Hong Kong Chinese. *Emotion, 11*(6), 1450–1455.

Spanier, G. (1976). Measuring dyadic adjustment: New scales for assessing the quality of marriage and similar dyads. *Journal of Marriage and the Family, 38*, 15–28.

Speilman, F. (2013, October 23). City to borrow $78.4 million to pay for firefighter settlement. *The Chicago Sun-Times.* Retrieved from http://www.suntimes.com/news/metro/15922145-418/city-to-borrow-784-million-to-pay-for-firefighter-dis crimination-settlement.html

Spielberger, C. D. (1966). Theory and research on anxiety. In C. D. Spielberger (Ed.), *Anxiety and behavior* (pp. 3–20). New York: Academic Press.

Squires, J. (2009). *ASQ-3 user's guide* (3rd ed.). Baltimore, MD: Brookes.

Steinmann, J. (2011). Nothing inevitable about discriminatory hiring: *Lewis v. City of Chicago* and a return to the text of Title VII. *Loyola of Los Angeles Law Review, 44*, 1307–1321.

Stevens, J. (2002). *Applied multivariate statistics* (4th ed.). Mahwah, NJ: Lawrence Erlbaum.

Stevens, S. S. (1946). On the theory of scales of measurement. *Science, 103*, 677–680.

Stevens, S. S. (1951). Mathematics, measurement, and psychophysics. In S. S. Stevens (Ed.), *Handbook of experimental psychology* (pp. 1–49). New York: John Wiley.

Stevens, S. S. (1961). The psychophysics of sensory function. In W. A. Rosenblith (Ed.), *Sensory communication* (pp. 1–33). New York: John Wiley.

Storch, E. A., Rasmussen, S. A., Price, L. H., Larson, M. J., Murphy, T. K., & Goodman, W. K. (2010). Development and psychometric evaluation of the Yale–Brown Obsessive-Compulsive Scale—Second Edition. *Psychological Assessment, 22*(2), 223–232.

Strauss, E., Sherman, E. M., & Spreen, O. (2006). *A compendium of neuropsychological tests: Administration, norms and commentary* (3rd ed.). New York: Oxford University Press.

SurveyMonkey. (2018a). *Downgrading to a free plan.* Retrieved from http://help.surveymonkey.com/articles/en_US/kb/Limitations-of-the-BASIC-Free-Plan

SurveyMonkey. (2018b). *Plans & pricing.* Retrieved from https://www.surveymonkey.com/pricing/details/

Tam, S. (1996). Self-efficacy as a predictor of computer skills learning outcomes of individuals with physical disabilities. *Journal of Psychology, 130*, 51–58.

Terman, L. M. (1916). *The measurement of intelligence*. Boston: Houghton Mifflin.

Thorndike, R. M., Cunningham, G., Thorndike, R. L., & Hagen, E. (1991). *Measurement and evaluation in psychology and education*. New York: Macmillan.

Thorne, B. M., & Henley, T. B. (2001). *Connections in the history and systems of psychology* (2nd ed.). Boston: Houghton Mifflin.

Tierney, J. (2011, May 1). How happy are you? A census wants to know. *The New York Times*, p. A1.

Tipton, R. M., & Worthington, E. L., Jr. (1984). The measurement of generalized self-efficacy: A study of construct validity. *Journal of Personality Assessment, 48*, 545–548.

Tobin, M., & Hoff, K. (2007). *Review of the Bayley Scales of Infant and Toddler Development* (3rd ed.). In K. F. Geisinger, R. A. Spies, J. F. Carlson, & B. S. Plake (Eds.), *The seventeenth mental measurements yearbook*. Lincoln, NE: Buros Institute of Mental Measurements.

Tourangeau, R. (1984). Cognitive science and survey methods. In T. Jabine, M. Straf, J. Tanur, & R. Tourangeau (Eds.), *Cognitive aspects of survey methodology: Building a bridge between disciplines* (pp. 73–199). Washington, DC: National Academy Press.

TPR Education IP Holdings, LLC. (2018). SAT vs ACT. *Princeton Review*. Retrieved from https://www.princetonreview.com/college/sat-act

Tree Foundation. (2012). *CAT: Computer adaptive tests*. Retrieved from http://www.ilion-center.gr/courses/cat/

Trevisan, M. S. (2003). Review of the Wisconsin Card Sorting Test–64 Card Version. In B. S. Plake, J. C. Impara, & R. A. Spies (Eds.), *The fifteenth mental measurements yearbook*. Lincoln, NE: Buros Institute of Mental Measurements.

Trochim, W.M.K. (2006). *General issues in scaling*. Retrieved from http://www.socialresearchmethods.net/kb/scalgen.php

Tupes, E. C., & Christal, R. E., (1961). Recurrent personality factors based on trait ratings. *USAF ASD Tech Rep., 61*–97.

Turnball, W. W. (1985). *Student change, program change: Why the SAT® scores kept falling* (College Board Report No. 85-2). Retrieved from https://research.collegeboard.org/sites/default/files/pub lications/2012/7/researchreport-1985-2-student-program-change-sat-scores-failing.pdf

Turner, D. (2010, April 8). States push to pay teachers based on performance. *USA Today*. Retrieved from http://usatoday30.usatoday.com/news/edu cation/2010-04-08-teachers-pay_N.htm

Uniform guidelines on employee selection procedures, 41 C.F.R. § 603 (1978).

University of California, Los Angeles. (2018). *Freshman selection overview*. Retrieved from http://www.admission.ucla.edu/prospect/adm_fr/FrSel.pdf

U.S. Bureau of Labor Statistics. (2018a). *Consumer Expenditure Survey*. Retrieved from http://www.bls.gov/cex/

U.S. Bureau of Labor Statistics. (2018b). *Labor force statistics from the Current Population Survey*. Retrieved from http://www.bls.gov/cps/tables.htm

U.S. Bureau of Labor Statistics. (n.d.-a). *Databases, tables, & calculators by subject*. Retrieved from http://data.bls.gov/pdq/SurveyOutputServlet

U.S. Bureau of Labor Statistics. (n.d.-b). *Frequently asked questions (FAQs): Question: How are the labor force components (i.e., civilian noninstitutional population, civilian labor force, employed, unemployed, and unemployment rate) defined?* Retrieved from http://www.bls.gov/dolfaq/bls_ques23.htm

U.S. Census Bureau. (2018). QuickFacts: United States. Retrieved from https://www.census.gov/quickfacts/fact/table/US/PST045217

U.S. Congress, Office of Technology Assessment. (1990). *The use of integrity tests for pre-employment screening* (OTA-SET-442). Washington, DC: U.S. Government Printing Office.

U.S. Department of Education. (2004). *Four pillars of NCLB*. Retrieved from http://ed.gov/nclb/overview/intro/4pillars.html

U.S. Department of Education. (2014, March). *Setting the pace: Expanding opportunity for America's students under Race to the Top*. Retrieved from http://www.whitehouse.gov/sites/default/files/docs/settingthepacerttreport_3-2414_b.pdf

U.S. Department of Education. (2018). Every Student Succeeds Act (ESSA). Retrieved from https://www.ed.gov/essa?src=ft

U.S. Equal Employment Opportunity Commission. (2014). *EEOC regulations*. Retrieved from http://www.eeoc.gov/laws/regulations/

U.S. General Accounting Office. (1993, October). *Developing and using questionnaires*. Washington, DC: Author. Retrieved from http://archive.gao.gov/t2pbat4/150366.pdf

U.S. News & World Report. (2018). *Best colleges rankings*. Retrieved from http://colleges.usnews.ranking sandreviews.com/best-colleges

Van de Vijver, F.J.R., & Phalet, K. (2004). Assessment in multicultural groups: The role of acculturation. *Applied Psychology: An International Review, 53*, 215–236.

Van Hutton, V. (1994). *House–Tree–Person and Draw-A-Person as measures of abuse in children: A quantitative scoring system*. Odessa, FL: Psychological Assessment Resources.

Van Iddekiinge, C., & Polyhart, (2008). Developments in the criterion related validation of selection procedures: A critical review and recommendations for practice. *Personnel Psychology, 61*, 871–925.

Van Iddekinge, C., Roth, P., Raymark, P., & Olde-Dusseau, H. (2012). The criterion-related validity of integrity tests: An updated meta-analysis. *Journal of Applied Psychology, 97*, 499–530.

Viswesvaran, C., Ones, D. S., & Schmidt, F. L. (1996). Comparative analysis of the reliability of job performance ratings. *Journal of Applied Psychology, 81*, 557–574.

Viswesvaran, C., Ones, D. S., Schmidt, F. L., Huy, L., Oh, I. (2014). Measurement error obfuscates scientific knowledge: Path to cumulative knowledge requires corrections for unreliability and psychometric meta- analysis *Industrial and Organizational Psychology: Perspectives on Science and Practice, 7*(4), 507–518.

Wainer, H., Dorans, N. J., Green, B. F., Mislevy, R. J., Steinberg, L., & Thissen, D. (2000). Future challenges. In H. Wainer (Ed.), *Computerized adaptive testing*. Mahwah, NJ: Lawrence Erlbaum.

Wan Chai the "happiest" district in Hong Kong, first 2011 "ING LIFE Happiness Survey" finds. (2011). Retrieved from http://www.ln.edu.hk/news/2011 0802/happinessindex2011

Wanek, J. E, Sackett, P. R., & Ones, D. S. (2003). Towards an understanding of integrity test similarities and differences: An item-level analysis of seven tests. *Personnel Psychology, 56*, 873–894.

Ward, S. (2001). Review of the Mini-Mental State Examination. In B. S. Plake, J. C. Impara, & R. A. Spies (Eds.), *Fifteenth mental measurements yearbook*. Lincoln, NE: Buros Institute of Mental Measurements.

Waterman, J. A., & Rogers, J. (1996). *Introduction to the FIRO-B*. Mountain View, CA: CPP.

Wechsler, D. (2009). *Wechsler Memory Scale, Fourth Edition*. San Antonio, TX: Pearson.

Weinberg, R. S., Gould, D., & Jackson, A. (1979). Expectations and performance: An empirical test of Bandura's self-efficacy theory. *Journal of Sport Psychology, 1*, 320–331.

Weiss, D. J. (2004). Computerized adaptive testing for effective and efficient measurement in counseling and education. *Measurement and Evaluation in Counseling and Development, 37*, 70–84.

Weiss, D. J. (2011). Better data from better measurements using computerized adaptive testing. *Journal of Methods and Measurement in the Social Sciences, 2*, 1–27.

Weiss, R.I.L., & Heyman, R. E. (1990). Observation of marital interaction. In F. D. Fincham & T. N. Bradbury (Eds.), *The psychology of marriage: Basic issues and applications* (pp. 87–117). New York: Guilford.

Wheeler, V. A., & Ladd, G. W. (1982). Assessment of children's self-efficacy for social interactions with peers. *Developmental Psychology, 18*, 795–805.

Wherry, R. J. (1931). A new formula for predicting shrinkage of the coefficient of multiple correlation. *Annals of Mathematical Statistics, 2*, 440–457.

Whetzel, D. L., & McDaniel, M. A. (2009). Situational judgment tests: An overview of current research. *Human Resource Management Review, 19*, 188–202.

Wigdor, A. K. (1990, Spring). Fairness in employment testing. *Issues in Science and Technology*, pp. 27–28.

Wiggins, G. P. (1993). *Assessing student performance: Exploring the purpose and limits of testing*. San Francisco, CA: Jossey-Bass.

Winerip, M. (2011, November 6). In Tennessee, following the rules for evaluations off a cliff. *The New York Times*, p. A18.

Wohl, A., & Kaufman, B. (1995). *Silent screams and hidden cries: A compilation and interpretation of artwork by children from violent homes*. London: Taylor & Francis.

Wonderlic. (2014a). *WBST individual score report*. Retrieved October 29, 2014, from http://www.wonderlic.com/sites/default/files/u7/Basic SkillsSampleIndividualScoreReport_1.pdf

Wonderlic. (2014b). *WBST sample questions*. Retrieved October 29, 2014, from http://www.wonderlic.com/assessments/skills/basic-skills-test

Wood, J. M., Nezworski, M. T., Lilienfeld, S. O., & Garb, H. N. (2003). The Rorschach inkblot test, fortune tellers, and cold reading. *The Skeptical Inquirer, 27*(4), 29–33.

Woodworth, R. (1920). *Personal data sheet*. Chicago: Stoelting.

WorldWideLearn. (1999–2015). *Benefits of e-learning*. Retrieved from http://www.worldwidelearn.com/elearning-essentials/index.html

Yam, P. (1998, Winter). Intelligence considered. *Scientific American*, pp. 4, 6–11.

Yerkes, R. M. (1921). Psychological examining in the United States Army. In *Memoirs of the National Academy of Sciences* (Vol. *15*). Washington, DC: U.S. Government Printing Office.

Yesavage J. A., Brink, T. L., Rose, T. L., Lum, O., Huang, V., Adey, M., & Leirer, V. O. (1982–1983). Development and validation of a geriatric depression screening scale: A preliminary report. *Journal of Psychiatric Research, 17*(1), 37–49.

Zehr, M. (2011, April 6). Draft rules point way to consistency in ELL policies. *Education Week*, p. 10.

Zulig, K. J., Huebner, E. S., Gilman, R., Patton, J. M., & Murray, K. A. (1994). Validation of the Brief Multidimensional Students' Life Satisfaction Scale among college students. *American Journal of Health Behavior, 29*, 206–215.

AUTHOR INDEX

SUBJECT INDEX